BALANCHINE'S FESTIVAL OF BALLET

VOLUME TWO N-Z
INCLUDING THE INDEX

BALANCHINE'S FESTIVAL OF BALLET

SCENE-BY-SCENE STORIES OF 404 CLASSICAL
& CONTEMPORARY BALLETS
GEORGE BALANCHINE & FRANCIS MASON

VOLUME TWO N-Z
INCLUDING THE INDEX

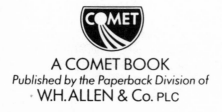

A COMET BOOK
Published by the Paperback Division of
W.H. ALLEN & Co. PLC

A Comet Book
Published in 1984
by the Paperback Division of
W.H. Allen & Co. PLC
44 Hill Street, London W1X 8LB

First published in Great Britain by
W.H. Allen & Co, 1978

Printed and bound in Great Britain by
Mackays of Chatham Ltd, Kent

ISBN 0 86379 067 4

To the Subscribers,
those who come to the ballet today, know it
and like it so much they will come also tomorrow

CONTENTS

ILLUSTRATIONS

Anna Pavlova in *La Fille Mal Gardée*

Tamara Karsavina and Vaslav Nijinsky in *Le Spectre de la Rose*

Tanaquil LeClercq and Francisco Moncion in *Afternoon of a Faun*

Cynthia Gregory and Ivan Nagy in *Giselle*

Fernando Bujones in *Le Corsaire*

Mikhail Baryshnikov, Leningrad, 1968

Lynn Seymour in *Homage to Isadora*

Maria Tallchief in *Firebird*

Suzanne Farrell and Jacques d'Amboise in *Apollo*

Suzanne Farrell and Arthur Mitchell in *Agon*

Lydia Abarca and Derek Williams in *Agon*

Lawrence Rhodes in *At Midnight*

Marcia Haydée and Richard Cragun in *Daphnis and Chloë*

Paul Russell in *Le Corsaire*

Violette Verdy in *Liebeslieder Walzer*

Edward Villella in *Brahms-Schoenberg Quartet*

Margot Fonteyn in *Homage to the Queen*

BALANCHINE'S FESTIVAL OF BALLET

VOLUME TWO N-Z
INCLUDING THE INDEX

NAPOLI

Romantic ballet in three acts. Music by E. Helsted, Gade, and Paulli. Chore-
ography and book by Auguste Bournonville. Scenery by Christensen. First
presented by the Royal Danish Ballet at the Theatre Royal, Copenhagen,
March 29, 1842.

Napoli is the great ballet by Auguste Bournonville, the dancer, choreographer,
and ballet master of the Royal Danish Ballet for many years and the founder
of its famous continuous tradition of training and performance. Since 1829,
when Bournonville mounted his first ballet in Copenhagen, ballets by him have
been danced by the Royal Danish Ballet more than four thousand times.
Napoli, the finest of them, is but a year younger than *Giselle;* but unlike
Giselle, Napoli has not been changed by succeeding generations of choreographers, dancers, and musicians: it is still danced in Copenhagen today as it
was more than one hundred and twenty-five years ago.

ACT ONE: NAPLES, BY THE BAY OF SANTA LUCIA; EVENING   Three boys are in
love with the beautiful Teresina, the daughter of a watchful widow. Teresina
loves only one, a fisherman, Gennaro. Her two suitors—Giacomo, who sells
macaroni in the town, and Peppo, who sells lemonade—try to persuade her
mother that Teresina will be better off married to one of them. Teresina, the
mother indicates, will make up her own mind. Teresina ignores her suitors as
she waits for Gennaro, who is returning to port with all the other fishermen of
the town.
    Soon the fishermen return. Gennaro embraces Teresina, and her mother re-
luctantly consents to their marriage. A monk, Fra Ambrosio, enters and asks
the fishermen and the assembled townsfolk for alms. Gennaro and Teresina
both contribute. Teresina's suitors, Giacomo and Peppo, still persist in bothering her and her mother; they try to make the girl jealous as Gennaro jokes
with a girl who has come to buy fish from him. But when Gennaro places an
engagement ring on her finger, Teresina is convinced that her happiness lies
only with him.
    The two lovers go out into the bay in order to be alone. After they have
been gone for some time, thunder and lightning fill the air. A violent storm
breaks over the Bay of Santa Lucia. Gennaro, out in the bay, rows frantically,
trying to reach shore. His fellow fishermen go to help him, and he is rescued.
But Teresina has been swept overboard by the giant waves, and no one can
find her. Gennaro curses his destiny. The girl's mother accuses him of drown-
ing Teresina, and all the people of the town abandon him.
    Gennaro is alone. He is about to despair, but then he prays beneath a like-
ness of the Madonna. Fra Ambrosio comes to him and, giving him an image of
the Madonna to carry with him for protection from harm, tells Gennaro not to
give up hope: he must take a boat and go out to sea and there find his love.
Gennaro goes to find a boat. Fra Ambrosio kneels in prayer.

ACT TWO: CAPRI; A BLUE GROTTO   In Act Two, the scene changes to an entirely different world. Here, in a blue grotto, we are in the abode of Golfo, a powerful sea sprite who rules over the sea around and about him. Two of Golfo's naiads approach the grotto in the great sea shell they use for a boat. They bring to their master Teresina, whom they have rescued. Teresina still holds the guitar she was playing to Gennaro in the fishing boat before the storm broke over Naples.

Teresina asks Golfo to return her to her home, but the sea sprite is fascinated by the girl's beauty and wishes to keep her by him. Over her head he pours the magical water of the grotto, and the girl becomes a naiad; she forgets entirely that she was ever a mortal.

All of Golfo's naiads and Tritons forgather and celebrate the initiation of the newcomer. Golfo himself makes love to her, but Teresina repulses his advances.

Gennaro's boat enters the grotto. Golfo signals his slaves to disappear: he, alone, will deal with the intruder. Gennaro beaches the boat and looks about him. He sees Teresina's guitar. He knows now that she is alive! Golfo tries to induce him to leave the grotto by causing fire to engulf the grotto, but Gennaro refuses to go. He asks for Teresina, and finally the other naiads bring the girl to him.

Of course, since she is no longer a human being, the girl does not recognize her lover. Gennaro tries to bring back her memory by speaking of their life together in Naples and by playing upon her guitar, but still the girl is unmoved. Gennaro is about to give up, when he remembers the image of the Virgin which Fra Ambrosio gave him. He beseeches the Madonna that Teresina's memory may be restored. Slowly Teresina recognizes him. She remembers their love, and the two lovers embrace.

Golfo, enraged at the reconciliation of the lovers, contrives to kidnap Teresina. But the girl will not leave Gennaro. The Tritons and naiads cannot separate them. Teresina realizes though, that they will never be able to return home unless Golfo's rage is calmed. She holds up the image of the Madonna and commands Golfo and his sea creatures to bow to the Queen of Heaven. Golfo and his Tritons and naiads submit, and the two lovers set sail for Naples in a boat weighed down with gifts.

ACT THREE: MONTE VIRGINES, NEAR NAPLES   The people of the city are gathered together on a religious pilgrimage outside Naples, when Teresina appears with her mother. The people are astonished. Gennaro arrives, and Teresina informs her friends that her lover rescued her. But her friends, who believed her dead, find that such a claim is too mysterious: perhaps witches are at work. Teresina's mother separates her from Gennaro.

Gennaro rails at Teresina's mother for believing such nonsense. The people flee in fear of witchcraft. Only Fra Ambrosio can set them right. He is sent for, blesses Gennaro, and tells the crowd how Teresina was rescued through the power of the Virgin.

Everyone believes the monk instantly, and all gather about Teresina and Gennaro. They dance to celebrate the reunion of the lovers, and Teresina and

Gennaro are lifted into a cart, in which their friends draw them toward their home, marriage, and a happy life together.

NOTES The critic Kitty Cunningham, who attended the Royal Danish Ballet festival in 1973, has written an interesting essay, "Watching Bournonville," in *Ballet Review* (Vol. 4, No. 6), in which the Bournonville ballet technique is discussed historically and also from the point of view of present dance practice. Commenting on that technique in the essay, the dancer Ellen Everett, who has danced in American Ballet Theatre's arrangement of *Divertissements from "Napoli"* (staged by Hans Brenaa), said: "Bournonville is a different language. Using the floor is stressed. This kind of dancing helps you jump and it helps you use your feet better. The way you carry yourself and the weight of the body falling helps you to do the movement. The *epaulement* is different too—especially the way you tilt from the waist and look under your arm. Every movement finishes and then melts into a *port de bras* for the real finish. But the phrasing and rhythms are the main difference. Everything feels up even when it is down."

For further reading on Bournonville technique, the volume by Lillian Moore and Erik Bruhn, *Bournonville and Ballet Technique* (London, 1961), is recommended. The writer Walter Terry is preparing a complete syllabus of the Bournonville classes and technique.

N.Y. EXPORT, OP. JAZZ

Music by Robert Prince. Choreography by Jerome Robbins. Decor by Ben Shahn. Costumes by Florence Klotz. First presented by Jerome Robbins's Ballets: U.S.A. at the Festival of Two Worlds, Spoleto, Italy, June 8, 1958. First presented in the United States by Ballets: U.S.A. at the Alvin Theatre, New York, September 4, 1958.

When *N.Y. Export, Op. Jazz* was first performed in England, the critic Richard Buckle called it "an epic of our time." He wrote that the ballet is about young people of today "and addresses these mistrustful creatures in their own language." Describing the work in a program note, the choreographer wrote: "There has always been a tremendous amount of popular dancing in America. At this time its vitality has reached a new high, developing and expanding in form and style from the basic and major contributions of the Negro and the Latin American. Because of a strong unconscious emotional kinship with those minority roots, the teenagers particularly have popularized these dances. Feeling very much like a minority group in this threatening and explosive world into which they have been born, the young have so identified with the dynamics, kinetic impetus, the drives and 'coolness' of today's jazz steps, that these dances have become an expression of our youths' outlook and their attitudes toward the contemporary world around them, just as each era's dances have significantly reflected the character of our changing world and a manner of dealing with it. *N.Y. Export, Op. Jazz* is a formal, abstract ballet based on the kinds of movements, complexities of rhythms, expressions of relationships, and qualities of atmosphere found in today's dances."

The dance action is divided into five parts. There is first of all a drop curtain proclaiming the title in bold colors and design. When this rises, we watch a group of young dancers performing against a backdrop of television aerials. They are cool, detached, staring at the audience as if we should quietly drop dead. They then ignore us and dance in their own way of forgetting. But they cannot ignore a warning in the sky which threatens to envelop them. They fall flat on their faces. The next dance, "Statics," takes place on a rooftop, where five boys have a good time with one girl. When they are through with her, they throw her out before they have to look at her. In "Improvisations," we are in a playground or a dance hall where everyone can relax and show off without adult interference. "Passage for Two," the fourth sequence, is a blues *pas de deux* for two young lovers who meet casually, become interested in each other, embrace but then separate as if nothing at all had happened. The final section, "Theme, Variations, and Fugue," is a celebration of contemporary dance rhythms and styles, beginning with formal dignity and quickening into variations and a fugue of final hopefulness and defiance.

NOTES Reviewing the London performances of *N.Y. Export, Op. Jazz*, Mary Clarke wrote in *The Dancing Times:* "It is a stunning work; it lifts you in your seat with excitement and admiration for the way it is danced and leaves you breathless with wonder about a choreographer who can orchestrate group movement so brilliantly . . . There is a kind of poetry, too, particularly in the Passage for Two when two solitary creatures make love without, you feel, even knowing each other's names . . . There is a lively sense of sympathy yet rivalry between the choreographer and the composer, Robert Prince, and a nice sense of fitness about the backcloths by Ben Shahn." In his collaboration with Robert Prince, from whom he commissioned the score, Jerome Robbins worked first with music that had been composed, secondarily with music written to conform to specific dance ideas he had in mind and—at the beginning of the last section—with no music at all. In that last section the composer wrote the theme and the first three or four variations after the dances had been set. After that, according to Robbins, the composer took over and the choreographer followed.

At the invitation of the President and Mrs. Kennedy, *N.Y. Export, Op. Jazz* was performed by Ballets: U.S.A. at the White House, April 11, 1962, in honor of the Shah and Empress of Iran.

NIGHT SHADOW (La Sonnambula)

Ballet in one act. Music by Vittorio Rieti, after Bellini. Choreography by George Balanchine. Book by Vittorio Rieti. Scenery and costumes by Dorothea Tanning. First presented by the Ballet Russe de Monte Carlo at the City Center, New York, February 27, 1946, with Alexandra Danilova as the

Sleepwalker, *Nicholas Magallanes as the* Poet, *Maria Tallchief as the* Coquette, *and Michel Katcharoff as the* Host.

This dramatic ballet was suggested by the opera *La Sonnambula* (*The Sleepwalker*) by Vincenzo Bellini. *Night Shadow* has a dark, romantic mood appropriate to the suppressed and clandestine loves that dominate the story. The time is long ago, a time of rigid conventions that the romantic spirit aimed to destroy.

The ballet begins with a masked ball in the garden of a great house. The host, an elderly man, welcomes his guests, who bow to him deferentially. Near the host stands the coquette, a beautiful young girl, who tosses her head quickly and seems to have a decided hold on his affections. Her controlled vivacity appears slightly out of place in this gathering. All join in a general dance led by the host and his partner.

The poet enters. He is a handsome young man, renowned for his work, and all the guests turn to look at him. There is a pause in all movement, and the atmosphere is expectant. Finally, reluctantly and carefully, the host introduces the poet to his mistress.

All the guests have arrived, and the host orders the entertainment to begin. The couples stand aside and watch two peasant couples in a pastoral dance, a Moorish dance by two blackamoors, followed by a harlequin, who performs an amusing, grotesque solo. The guests applaud the entertainers and gradually move out of the garden to go to supper.

The coquette and the poet watch as the others depart. Both remain on the scene. They approach each other and dance a *pas de deux* that shows us the mutual attraction they feel. The poet is somewhat passive as the willful coquette claims him. Their love duet is cut short by the return of the party. The host goes immediately to the coquette and claims her attention. He is angry. The guests sense an embarrassing tension and turn away. The coquette smiles at the host, reassures him, and takes his arm. They follow the guests and leave the poet alone.

As he is bemoaning his misfortune, he sees what appears to be a ghost coming toward him slowly. The figure is all in white and carries a tall lighted candle in one hand. As it comes closer, the poet sees before him a beautiful woman walking in her sleep. Her long black hair hangs about her shoulders, her face is composed in sleep, and she moves as in a dream, rapidly but softly, dancing across the garden on point, never descending to the ground.

The poet is instantly enamored of this strange, lovely creature, who seems to be a part of his own dream, and he approaches her. But the woman does not waken. The poet dances around her, lies before her on the ground, encircles her, begging her to waken and respond to his love. The woman does not notice him and walks alone in her own dream, stepping over his recumbent body as if he were merely a stone. She begins to drift away, out of the garden. The poet, now desperate, follows.

The coquette returns at this point for a quick rendezvous and sees her lover following the woman in white. She is furious. The host returns to the garden with his guests. The coquette takes him aside and whispers to him. The host

looks up, startled and enraged. The coquette leaves him and joins the other
guests in a formal ensemble dance. During the dance, we watch the host,
dagger in hand, leave the garden unobserved.

When the guests have applauded a final *divertissement,* the poet runs into
the garden. He staggers in pain and clutches at his heart. Blood streams
through his fingers. The couples stand back, horrified. The coquette watches
him and does not move. The poet falls to the ground and dies. The guests
stare at the beautiful woman in white, who moves, still in her sleep, across the
garden. They follow her. She is the wife of the host.

NOTES   Bellini's *La Sonnambula* (1831) merely provided the subject matter
for the ballet *Night Shadow* and not its plot. The opera tells the story of a romance between a farmer and a miller's daughter who is addicted to walking in
her sleep. The score for the ballet is an arrangement of music from *La Sonnambula* and *I Puritani,* by the same composer.

La Sonnambula—as it is now usually called—is danced by the New York City
Ballet, the Washington National Ballet, the Royal Danish Ballet, the Ballet
Rambert in London, and by a number of other companies for which John
Taras has staged the production. The New York City Ballet *La Sonnambula,* in
a setting by Esteban Francés, was first presented January 6, 1960, with Erik
Bruhn, Allegra Kent, Jillana, Edward Villella, Suki Schorer, and William
Weslow. The costumes were by André Levasseur, obtained from the Marquis
de Cuevas production in which Marjorie Tallchief and George Skibine ap-
peared for some years.

Soon after the ballet was first presented, the American critic Edwin Denby
wrote, in *Looking at the Dance:* "Mysterious in the interaction of its elements;
the vapid ballroom dances; the winsome exhibition numbers that have a perverse and cruel undertone; the elaborate, encircling artifices of the coquette's
pas de deux; the directness and space of the sleepwalking scene . . . The
progress of the piece is 'romantic'—it is disconcerting, absurd and dispropor-
tionate; but its effect when it is over is powerful and exact. It gives you a
sense—as Poe does—of losing your bearings, the feeling of an elastic sort of
time and a heaving floor. As a friend of mine remarked, 'When it's over, you
don't know what hit you.'"

NIGHTWINGS

*Music by John La Montaine. Choreography by Gerald Arpino. Decor by
Ming Cho Lee; Associate Designer, Holly Haas. Costumes by Wilma Kim.
First presented by the City Center Joffrey Ballet, September 7, 1966, with
Lisa Bradley, Michael Uthoff, and Nels Jorgensen in principal roles.*

Nightwings is set to music from *Birds of Paradise,* a score by the American
composer John La Montaine. The repeated yet varied incantations of the birdcalls are suggestive of the timelessness in nature. The composer has said that
the musical ideas on which the score is based "are taken from sounds of nature

heard in remote places: in woods and forests, at the ocean shore, in the mountains. That other world of strange sounds, not man-made, the true primeval music, is both the subject matter and the poetical idea of the piece: the rustlings, the murmurings, the sudden silences, the sustained shrill excitement of vociferous birdcalls, their merriment, and their mourning; the simplicity and the purity of the single voice, and the incalculable random complexity, the cacophony of the total aural impression, a veritable 'caldron of sound.' In the runic repetitious incantations of birds, seemingly always the same, but in fact always different, some sense of the meaning of timelessness can be felt."

In the ballet a young man sleeps on a cot in a poor room in the city on a hot summer's night. The window curtain blows in a slight breeze. A bird cage stands on the floor. He dreams. The electric signs and water towers of the surrounding cityscape rise into the heavens and the boy seems to fly too, with them. A girl-like flying creature is brought to him. He watches her carefully, then seizes her to dance. Although she, frantic and frightened at being caught, at first seems to yield to the boy's fascination, her creatures do not permit such independence. They hold her above the boy and do not permit him to come closer. Then, in a quick shift from passion to unfulfilled action, she falls on the boy and chokes him to death. He is carried beneath her back to his cot and set to rest as she hovers over him full-length, bidding him farewell. The night-winged bird is then lifted off high to disappear as the boy writhes in his sleep and the cityscape returns. The light bulb above him flickers and his dream is over. Golden clouds descend.

NIJINSKY—CLOWN OF GOD

Ballet by Maurice Béjart. Music by Pierre Henry. Costumes by Joelle Roustan and Roger Bernard. Lighting by Roger Bernard. Sound direction by Pierre Henry. First presented by the Ballet of the Twentieth Century at the Forest National Auditorium, Brussels, October 8, 1971, with Jorge Donn as The Clown of God, Paolo Bartoluzzi as the Rose, Daniel Lommel as the Golden Slave, Jorg Lanner as the Faun, Micha Van Hoecke as Petrouchka, Suzanne Farrell as the Girl in Pink, Angele Albrecht as the Nymph, Jaleh Kerendi as the Woman of the World, Cathérine Verneuil as the Ballerina, Hitomi Asakawa as the Doll, and Pierre Dobrievich as Diaghilev in the principal roles. First presented in the United States by the Ballet of the Twentieth Century at the Felt Forum, Madison Square Garden, New York, October 24, 1972.

The ballet is given in two parts, the whole consisting of eleven scenes. During the work, extracts from *The Diary of Vaslav Nijinsky* are read over the loudspeaker. It is largely upon this book, which Maurice Béjart reread in 1971, that his ballet on the life of the most renowned of all dancers is based. Béjart has said: "Of all the famous names connected with that rich and strange era of Diaghilev and the Russian Ballet, the person of Nijinsky is perhaps the most perplexing and fascinating. Even to those not particularly interested in ballet, the name and the phenomenon of this great dancer must be familiar. It is generally known that he was one of the most spectacular dancers the world has ever seen, that he was especially renowned for his sensational leap, and that his career was tragically curtailed by madness. Yet Nijinsky's personality and the forces that led to his madness are widely unknown.

"In one of his works Henry Miller, alone on an island, talks about the books he could not live without; among the two or three great titles which he cites appears *The Diary of Nijinsky*. He adds: 'I never grow tired of reading it.' The key to Nijinsky is in that *Diary*—a disturbing document about an exceptional human being.

"The *Diary* was written as his total madness was approaching and records his most inward feelings, emotions, and fantasies. In life, Nijinsky was described by his contemporaries as quiet, slow, and rather awkward, yet when he emerged upon the stage his personality was transformed and his body expressed grace, poetry, and dynamic energy. In the *Diary* yet another side of his personality is revealed—a quick, restless, and highly cultured mind reacting with intensity to the events and people around him. The *Diary* is a frightening yet uplifting book, for we watch Nijinsky's mind gradually giving way under the pressure of its own sensitivity to the horrors of the First World War, to Diaghilev's cruel treatment of him after his marriage, and to the artistic pressures of creativity. Yet beyond all this we feel his burning conviction in his role as 'Clown of God' and in his need to preach the gospel of universal love.

"This ballet does not attempt to be a biographical reconstruction of Nijinsky's life, but, taking its inspiration from the *Diary*, it tries to create a marginal note, a secret path where the heart, ideas, emotions, memories, and fantasies can live and dance an imaginary ballet on lines similar, perhaps, to those of his own thoughts during the last conscious moments of his life. Imaginative and allegorical figures come alive and enact the conflicts in Nijinsky's mind—representations of characters from his ballets and from his life. Most important among these are the three principal characters in the action: NIJINSKY HIMSELF —the artist and poet in search of Truth, who sees himself as the apostle of universal love, a mystic messenger of God; WOMAN—not just Nijinsky's own wife, but a symbol of love and poetry, a vision and a creature of the spirit; DIAGHILEV—Nijinsky's master, father, creator. In short, his God, at once feared and adored."

The setting of the ballet is a large open stage dominated by a large black cross. From left and right, high ramps descend to the open area. Everything is dark. A voice sounds: "The world was made by God, Man was made by God. It is impossible for man to understand God, but God understands God."

Béjart's "Clown of God" theme for this work is also taken from Nijinsky's *Diary:* "I will pretend to be a clown, because then they will understand me better. I love Shakespeare's clowns—they have a lot of humor, but nevertheless they express hate, they are not from God. I am a clown of God, and therefore like joking. I mean that a clown is all right when he expresses love. A clown without love is not from God."

A synopsis of the ballet follows.

PART ONE: THE NIJINSKY OF THE RUSSIAN BALLET 1. *The Creation of the World:* Inert, naked, and faceless bodies cover the stage. Under God's eyes they become animated, organized, breathing. The circle is formed. Life!

A being detaches itself from the anonymous mass and places itself in the center of the Circle. God gives him a face. It is man: The Clown of God. Slowly the Creator forms him, teaches him to live, to walk, to jump, to *Dance.*

2. *Earthly Paradise:* God creates Earthly Paradise for his most favored creature. . . . It is the age of the Russian Ballet, that torrent of images of Paradise, that revelation of color, sound, and light which, in five years, was to conquer the world. As a companion, God gives him *Dance,* personified by the Ballerina and, for friends, four guardian angels, four fantastic creatures: a Rose, a Faun, Petrouchka, and a Golden Slave, symbols of the four elements: Air, Earth, Water, and Fire.

3. *The Woman:* But his craving for a great and constant love, and his tenderness force him to create a new image of love. A woman, unreal at first, grows in his soul. Little by little she takes a tangible shape and he seeks in her the support of a creature of flesh and blood. The face of his dreams suddenly becomes the face of one woman—his WIFE.

4. *The Fall:* Nijinsky is tempted during the absence of God. He marries suddenly in South America and incurs the wrath of Diaghilev, who, when informed of the event, banishes him from the Russian Ballet. Earthly paradise crumbles. It is 1914—the end of an era.

PART TWO: THE NIJINSKY OF GOD   The search for love, for true love, is long. Diaghilev is no longer God. A god who rejects his own creation, a god who will not pardon is not a god of love, not a true god.

His companion is by his side, but she cannot follow him in his search for the Divine, in his love of Humanity. He is alone, and alone he has to suffer a long Calvary at this time, troubled as it is by the horror of war; it is this that will lead to the famous day which he called his "Marriage with God," the day of his last dance recital on January 19, 1919, when in a series of sublime improvisations, he portrayed in mime the horrors of war, the absurd, senseless, and grotesque features of his times, and his love of God and Humanity. Vaslav Nijinsky no longer exists, but may this ballet help the world to love and know this unique, angelic being, in whom physical grace reflected spiritual grace, and whose technique and genius were immense because they serve God and brotherly love.

NOTES   Writing of the ballet *Nijinsky* in the *Wall Street Journal,* Peter J. Rosenwald said: "'People want to have sports and mystery,' says Maurice Béjart, an innovative Belgian whose Ballet of the Twentieth Century comes to New York tomorrow. Mr. Béjart's company will be performing a controversial work called *Nijinsky, Clown of God,* but not at Lincoln Center or some other chaste establishment of the dance.

"Rather, *Nijinsky, Clown of God,* will get its first New York viewing at that midtown palace of cheers, boos, sweat, and liniment, Madison Square Garden's Felt Forum. As in Europe, where this ambitious work also has played in large sports arenas—such as the 5,000-seat Palais des Sports in Paris—Mr. Béjart hopes to attract some new converts to the dance from among people who might know more about Nijinsky, the race horse, than Nijinsky, the dancer. The ballet has drawn enthusiastic, animated crowds in Europe, even though it has been alternately praised and damned by European critics.

"In a masterpiece of dance theater, Mr. Béjart has fashioned a work which perfectly uses the many talents of his versatile company to tell factually and metaphorically the story of the great Ukrainian dancer, Vaslav Nijinsky, from his discovery by choreographer Serge Diaghilev of the Ballet Russe to his agonizing death in 1950, insane and lonely, believing himself to be incarnate God. Using extracts from Nijinsky's diary, the work concentrates on Nijinsky the man, Nijinsky the dancer, and Nijinsky's deeply religious yearnings. Said Nijinsky in his diary, 'I appear as a clown to make myself better understood. . . . I think that a clown is only perfect when he expresses love, otherwise he is no longer a clown of God.'

"What gives the work its vitality (and what seems to offend most academic critics) is the fusion of Nijinsky the man and the four most famous roles he portrayed: The Rose in *Spectre de la Rose*, the Golden Slave in *Scheherazade*, the Faun in *L'Après-Midi d'un Faun* and Petrouchka, the puppet with a soul, in the ballet of the same name. Not only has Mr. Béjart created five Nijinskys who often appear on the stage at the same time but he has given each of them a clown whose purpose is to symbolize their inner souls.

"From the moment when a giant papier-maché figure of Impresario Diaghilev points its finger at a mass of dancers and chooses Nijinsky, the stage is a whirl of action. Giant crosses rise from it, whole ballets within the ballet seem to take the focus of activity. The music varies from the familiar strains of Tchaikovsky's *Pathétique* Symphony to contemporary Pierre Henry's electronic score.

"There is a brilliant madness in Mr. Béjart's superimpositions of sight and sound, past and present, real and imagined, to produce a surprisingly integrated and intimate picture of Nijinsky's strange genius, his search for the relationship between art, love, and religion and an ultimate sense that the world which rejects his gifts of love is to blame for his madness and his death. Perhaps it is.

"If Mr. Béjart is sometimes excessive in his symbolism and uneven in his choreography, his dancers more than make up for these failings with stunning performances which give life to the characters and credibility to their actions. Jorge Donn's Nijinsky, Clown of God, and Suzanne Farrell as the Girl in Pink, who becomes Nijinsky's wife, are memorable and unique expressions of dance theater at its best.

"If *Nijinsky, Clown of God* has a major flaw, it is in proving that nothing exceeds like excess. It is so rich that it sometimes overwhelms itself and the spectacle overcomes its meaning. But it is never dull, never intellectual for its own sake, and never uninteresting."

LES NOCES (The Wedding)

Cantata with dances. Music and words by Igor Stravinsky. Choreography by Bronislava Nijinska. Scenery and costumes by Nathalie Gontcharova. First presented by Diaghilev's Ballets Russes at the Théâtre Gaîté-Lyrique, Paris, June 14, 1923, with Felia Dubrovska as the Bride and Leon Woizikowski as the Bridegroom. First presented in the United States by the League of American Composers at the Metropolitan Opera House, New York, April 25, 1929, with scenery and costumes by Serge Soudeikine and choreography by Elizaveta Anderson-Ivantzova.

Stravinsky's dramatic cantata *Les Noces* depicts the ancient Russian peasant marriage ritual. Singers on the stage sing words which the dancers accompany with meaningful movement.

SCENE ONE: BENEDICTION OF THE BRIDE; THE TRESSES The voice of the bride is heard chanting before the rise of the curtain. The scene is the interior of a peasant home in old Russia. The bride stands in the center of the stage, surrounded by her mother and her friends. Her friends help to calm the grief she feels at leaving her home, her fear of life with a man who seems to her now a stranger, and her hatred of the person who has arranged the match. The women tell her that her husband's father will accept her in their home and that her life will be much as it has been, that she must go through with everything for her own parents. At the bride's request, the women comb and bind her hair. They tell her that the birds outside the house are singing happily. Can't she be happy too? They ask God to bless her marriage.

SCENE TWO: BENEDICTION OF THE BRIDEGROOM; THE BRIDEGROOM'S HOUSE The bridegroom's father and friends help him to prepare for his wedding. His hair, too, is combed and anointed. All wish him good luck. The parents of both the bride and the bridegroom lament the loss of their children, who are no longer children. The friends of the families congratulate the parents.

SCENE THREE: THE BRIDE'S DEPARTURE; THE WEDDING The bride is prepared to go forth from her house to meet the bridegroom at the church. Her friends tell her she is a princess this day. At the church, the bridegroom kisses the cross. The best man declares his friend is present to greet his bride. The guests pay tribute to the bridegroom's love for his parents. The bride enters, and the wedding ceremony takes place. As the couple leaves, all congratulate them. Their parents lament.

SCENE FOUR: THE WEDDING FEAST At the wedding feast, the father of the bride presents her to the assembled guests. Men in the company inform her of the household duties she must perform. The bridegroom is informed of his responsibilities to his wife. Everyone drinks and is joyous.

An older married couple is selected, from among the guests, to warm the marriage bed. There is a toast to the young couple, after which they are conducted to the door of their room. The older couple returns to the feast.

The guests gather about the parents of the bride and the bridegroom as they sit beside the door to their children's room. The bridegroom sings of his love for his wife.

NOTES *Les Noces* was first performed in the United States in concert form, at Aeolian Hall, New York, in February 1926, under the auspices of the International Composers Guild.

Leopold Stokowski conducted the first United States performance of the complete cantata with dances. Marc Blitzstein, Aaron Copland, Louis Gruenberg, and Frederick Jacobi were the four pianists on this occasion.

Bronislava Nijinska's staging of *Les Noces* was first presented in the United States by the Ballet Russe de Monte Carlo in 1936, with Irina Baronova and Yurek Shabelevsky in the principal roles.

Nijinska's ballet was revived by the Royal Ballet in London March 23, 1966, with Svetlana Beriosova and Robert Mead in the principal roles. This production was first presented in the United States at the new Metropolitan Opera House, New York, May 2, 1967. After the London première, Mary Clarke reported in *Dance News* that the London press "has never acclaimed a ballet so unanimously." Alexander Bland wrote in *The Observer:* "The curtain rises on the Bride flanked by her companions holding her long ritual pigtails. 'Oh fair tress of my hair' sings the soprano—and this could be the motif of the whole ballet. The score weaves a crisp embroidery of words and music, poetry and slang. On the stage, in place of delicate classical curlecues and filigrees, Nijinska plaits her dancers together, kneads them into knotted mounds, tugs them backwards and forwards like lengths of thick hemp.

"The patterns are stiff and new as linen. The steps are complicated but rough, repeating like a sampler pattern. The groups are blunt and tight and rounded. Without a hint of rural charm, she evokes a peasant world where a wedding means . . . a vow, a bed, having children, dying and leaving them money and a cow. *Les Noces* is a superb example of the Diaghilev ideal—contributions of individual, almost independent merit, bound together into a single perfect skein."

A dance cantata. Music by Igor Stravinsky. Choreography by Jerome Robbins. Set by Oliver Smith. Costumes by Patricia Zipprodt. Lighting by Jean Rosenthal. First presented by the American Ballet Theatre at the State Theatre, New York, March 30, 1965, with Erin Martin as the Bride and William Glassman as the Bridegroom.

Preparing program notes for *Les Noces*, Jerome Robbins wrote: "Stravinsky used as material for *Les Noces* the ritualistic elements found in the ancient customs and traditions of Russian peasant weddings, but reserved the right to use them with absolute freedom, paying little heed to ethnolographical considerations. His purpose was not to reproduce the wedding or show a stage dramatization with descriptive music, but rather to present a ritualized abstraction of its essences, customs, and tempers.

"The text is adapted from folk songs and popular verse, typical wedding remarks, clichés of conversations, but again they are not used realistically but rather as a collage of the words spoken or sung during these traditional rites. The first half of the 'scenic ceremony' deals with the preparations, and revolves around religious elements. Alternating with these intense invocations and blessings are continual lamentations by the parents for the loss of their children, and by the bride against the matchmaker, on leaving home, and on losing her virginity.

"In the second half (the wedding feast) the grief and religious elements are forgotten in robust celebrations with food, drink, songs, toasts, boasts, bawdiness, rough jokes, etc. A married couple is selected to warm the bed and finally the marriage is allowed to be consummated while all sit outside the nuptial chamber."

The composition is divided into four tableaux which run without interruption:

TABLEAU I: PREPARATION OF THE BRIDE   Before a backdrop with two huge ironlike figures of saints, the musicians, four pianists, and a chorus file on stage. Then from both sides of the stage come the dancers in rough brown and white peasant dress. They bow to each other, to the musicians, and begin to dance. The bride flings out her two long braids on both sides and the women take up the strands and begin to plait her hair. The bride weeps and laments, her father and mother are entangled in the strands. Her tresses sing: "In the evening my mother braided you with care, she combed you with a silver comb, she combed you, she braided you. Ah, poor me, poor me. Alas, poor me." Then she is picked up like a child and taken out.

TABLEAU II: PREPARATION OF THE GROOM   The bridegroom is pushed out before the guests by his friends. As his mother berates him, we see that he is indeed her child as he crouches while his friends dance. Then one of them insists that he join them. There is a dance with his parents. Two bass voices sing: "Bless me, my father, my mother, bless your child who proudly goes against the wall of stone to break it."

TABLEAU III: DEPARTURE OF BRIDE; CODA: LAMENTATION OF MOTHERS   The bride enters in a white dress trimmed with orange and with an orange bow. She crouches in plié, then as her friends dance about her, she is lifted up and carried off in triumph. The lights dim and the two mothers lament: "My own dear one, child of mine, do not leave me, little one."

TABLEAU IV: WEDDING FEAST   When the lights come up, the bride and bridegroom are seen in the center. During a ritual dance both are raised high and then set down. The chorus sings realistic advice: "Love your wife, cherish her like your soul, shake her like a plum tree." The girl then dances to her friends and the boy to his. Then, after their bed has been warmed, they are placed together on a platform like two lost children and the marriage is consummated in quick trembling. The pianos and a bell strike a bell chord fortissimo and a solo bass sings, as a bridegroom would sing to his bride: "Dear heart, my own little wife, let us live in happiness so that all men may envy us." The bell chord tolls throughout his song, he finishes, the pianos alone take the chord, we hear it on every eighth beat, then there is no more singing, the pianos stop and we have only the persistent bell chord. The time between its sounding measures an infinity of happiness.

NOTES   Jerome Robbins's ballet was acclaimed by all the critics after its first performance. Allen Hughes in the New York *Times* called it "an overwhelming fusion of animal energy, ritualistic ardor, and rhythmic attack." Doris Hering in *Dance Magazine* said that the dancers in performance were in "what might be called a state of rhythmic grace . . . The dancers bowed . . . and then the surge began! They were drawn into a relentless sea of stamping, jumping, and somersaults. Sometimes there were brief allusions to national style in the use of squared arms or the digging of one heel into the ground and curving the feet outward. Always they seemed to be caught in something jubilant and ominous at the same time."

NOMOS ALPHA

Music by Iannis Xenakis. Choreography by Maurice Béjart. First presented by the Ballet of the Twentieth Century, at Royan, April 2, 1969, with Paolo Bortoluzzi. First presented in the United States by the same ensemble at the Brooklyn Academy of Music, New York, January 26, 1971.

This dance for the *premier danseur* of Béjart's Ballet of the Twentieth Century was designed to exploit fully the capacities of two instruments, cello and dancer, within two structures, one musical, the other choreographic, "both extending to the utmost the potentials of the two."

A boy dressed in a bright red costume stands in a cone of brilliant light. He quivers in response to the music, and moving in and out of the light, alternates styles of dance, shifting from "classical" to "demi-caractère," taking up suggestions by the cello and sometimes making fun of them. When the cello sounds like a cat meowing, the dancer makes like a cat. But there appears to be a seriousness, too, about the piece as the dancer and music interact.

Writing about *Nomos Alpha* in *Dance and Dancers* magazine, the critic John Percival said: "The solo Béjart has made by Bortoluzzi is entirely unexpected. The music, for solo cello, is supposed to drive the player to the furthest extremes of his instrument's range, and Béjart does the same for the dancer . . . There is a fantastic variety here: walking, stretching, signalling in semaphore, now fast, now slow, now smooth, now jerky, nothing repeated, all done with marvelous clarity and beautiful plastique, and nothing ever repeated although the solo lasts, I think, the best part of twenty minutes."

THE NUTCRACKER

Classic Ballet in two acts. Music by Tchaikovsky. Choreography by Lev Ivanov. Book by Lev Ivanov. Scenery by M. I. Botcharov. First presented at the Maryinsky Theatre, St. Petersburg, December 17, 1892, with Antoinetta Dell-Era and Paul Gerdt as the Sugarplum Fairy and the Prince. *First presented in Western Europe by the Sadler's Wells Ballet at the Sadler's Wells Theatre, London, January 30, 1934, with Alicia Markova and Harold Turner. This version was staged by Nicholas Sergeyev, after Ivanov. First presented in the United States in an abbreviated form by the Ballet Russe de Monte Carlo at the Fifty-first Street Theatre, New York, October 17, 1940, with Alicia Markova and André Eglevsky. Scenery and costumes by Alexandre Benois. Presented in the United States in complete form by the San Francisco Ballet, 1944, with choreography by William Christensen. Presented by the New York City Ballet, with choreography by George Balanchine, February 2, 1954, with Alberta Grant as* Clara, Susan Kaufman *as* Fritz, Michael Arshansky *as* Herr Drosselmeyer, Paul Nickel *as the* Nutcracker *and Maria Tallchief and Nicholas Magallanes as the* Sugarplum Fairy *and her* Cavalier. Scenery by Horace Armistead. Costumes by Karinska. Masks by Vlady. Revived in a new production by the New York City Ballet with scenery by Rouben Ter-Arutunian and costumes by Karinska at the New York State Theatre, December 11, 1964.

It is another sign of how popular ballet has become that today many companies perform *The Nutcracker*. It has almost become a kind of annual Christmas ritual in many American and Canadian cities. Of course this was not always so. We used to rely on a touring company to give us a truncated version of this full-length work, a ballet people used to call *Nutcracker Suite* because they knew the music better than the ballet. Now that is all different. I have heard that more than fifty groups do this ballet. The one we do in New York every Christmas was first presented in 1954 and we have been doing it every year since. There have been changes in the production (I am always making them) but in its main outlines the story and the action are about the same.

I have liked this ballet from the first time I danced in it as a boy, when I did small roles in the Maryinsky Theatre production. When I was fifteen, I danced the Nutcracker Prince. Years later in New York, when our company decided to do an evening-long ballet, I preferred to turn to *The Nutcracker*, with which American audiences were not sufficiently familiar. I accordingly went back to the original score, restored cuts that had been made, and in the development of the story chose to use the original story by E. T. A. Hoffmann, although keeping to the outlines of the dances as given at the Maryinsky. A prologue was added and the dances restaged.

The three scenes of the ballet are arranged in two acts. In the first act, we are in the real world but begin a journey to the magical kingdom of the second.

The overture to the ballet is bright and delicate. Pizzicato strings and tin-kling triangles create a light, intimate atmosphere that sets the stage for the action.

ACT ONE   When the curtain goes up, we are in a hallway of a large house looking at the door to the living room. This is the home of Dr. Stahlbaum, a city official, and his wife. It is Christmas Eve. Their children, Marie and Fritz, have fallen asleep by the door as their parents decorate the Christmas tree. Behind the keyhole, the parents and the maid are putting the finishing touches to the tree and arranging presents underneath. The children awaken and eagerly await the arrival of the guests. For there is to be a Christmas party, a family affair for relatives and close friends, but most of all a party for children.

Soon the other children arrive with their parents, and the doors are opened. All rejoice in the large, lighted tree. The grown-ups greet each other and there is much speculation among the children about what is in the packages. Now the parents organize things. Dr. Stahlbaum divides the children for games and dances. The boys do a brisk march and then there is a polite formal quadrille for the girls and the boys. Some of the grown-ups join in. Soon grandparents come to join the party, refreshments are served, and, most important of all, presents are given out.

The children are sitting quietly looking at their presents when suddenly ev-eryone looks up. Something seems to have gone wrong. The lights flicker and over the huge grandfather clock a terrifying old owl flaps his wings as the hour is sounded. Then at the door an old gentleman looking very much like the owl comes in. This is Herr Drosselmeyer, an old family friend who is also Marie's godfather. He wears a black patch over one eye. He is a mysterious man, a marvelous inventor of moving toys, and he has brought with him three large boxes and also his handsome young nephew. Drosselmeyer kisses Marie and introduces her to his nephew, whom she likes at once. The gifts in the huge boxes delight everyone—a Harlequin and Columbine and a Toy Soldier who dance to jolly tunes. Then Drosselmeyer brings out a large Nutcracker, a sol-dier, for Marie. He shows everybody how it works and Marie is clearly delighted with it. She is so pleased with it that Fritz is furious. He grabs the Nutcracker and stamps on it. The nephew chases him away as Marie weeps. Drosselmeyer plays doctor and ties a handkerchief around the Nutcracker's head.

Marie and her friends sit and rock their dolls to sleep, only to be interrupted by the rowdy boys, who disturb them with drums and bugles. The nephew brings Marie a toy bed for the Nutcracker and he is tucked in and put under the tree. All the children are tired and upset and clearly in need of sleep. Dr. Stahlbaum and his wife now lead all the guests in a final dance, Marie dancing with the nephew. At the end, they shake hands solemnly, reluctant to say good night to each other, hoping that they will meet again soon. Everyone goes off to bed, the room darkens, and only by the lights of the Christmas tree can we make out the empty space.

It is midnight. Marie enters in a white nightgown. She comes slowly into the room, being careful not to make any noise. She goes directly to the Nutcracker, takes him up and cradles him in her arms. Then she goes to her bed and sleeps. Drosselmeyer enters, takes the Nutcracker from her, and fixes his jaw with a screwdriver. He restores the Nutcracker to her. There is a rustle, the Christmas tree lights flash on and off. Marie wakes. She puts the Nutcracker back in his bed and just then old Drosselmeyer from on top of the clock flaps his arms like the owl and Marie is thoroughly terrified. What is he doing in the house, anyhow, at this time of night? Marie just manages to hide behind a curtain when a big fat rat comes in. She dashes to the couch and huddles there. Suddenly the Christmas tree and everything under it seem to be growing—even the toy soldiers. The walls of the room grow. The tree grows taller and taller, to a huge height. The mice are big too, and it is good that the soldiers are there to protect her. They battle the mice, but the mice, led by their fierce king, seem to be winning. Then the Nutcracker, grown to life size, rises from his bed and leads the soldiers.

The Nutcracker orders cannon brought and candy is fired at the mice. Marie throws her slipper, which hits the king of the mice by surprise. The Nutcracker runs him through with his sword, and the battle is won.

Marie falls onto the bed, which begins mysteriously to glide out of the room into the snowy evening. She arrives at the Kingdom of Snow and is met by the Nutcracker, who before her very eyes suddenly turns into a handsome young prince. He bows to Marie, gives her the crown taken from the king of the mice and leads her away on a magic journey. In a snowy forest, snowflakes dance.

ACT TWO: KONFITUERENBURG (THE LAND OF SWEETS) When the curtain rises, we are in the inside of a huge box of candy. Twelve angels enclose the stage, each dressed in white and gold. The Sugarplum Fairy, who rules over this Kingdom of Sweets, makes a regal entry. She dances a charming variation to the tinkling celesta. The angels enclose her in a semicircle of love. Then leading the angels off, the Sugarplum Fairy welcomes the full candy box: Chocolates and Coffee and Tea sweets, Candy Canes, Marzipan, Polichinelles, and lovely Dew Drops. At this point, to majestic heralding music, a walnut boat arrives bringing the Nutcracker Prince and Marie. The prince escorts Marie to the shore and introduces her to the Sugarplum Fairy. The fairy then asks the prince what happened. The prince then relates in pantomime how they came from far away, how the Mouse King and his men attacked Marie and the toy soldiers, how the mice were defeated finally when Marie at just the right moment threw her slipper and the King of Mice had his crown cut off, which was given as a present to Marie. The Sugarplum Fairy congratulates the prince warmly on his victory and escorts him and Marie to a candy throne high on a dais. Before the pair are placed numerous sweets and creams to eat as they watch the entertainment that has been arranged for their pleasure.

We now watch a series of dances by the creatures of the candy kingdom. When they are finished, the Sugarplum Fairy and her cavalier perform the grandest dance of all, a *pas de deux* to climax the occasion. This is exactly the kind of dance that Marie would like to do, too, one day, and she and the prince rejoice in the splendid tenderness of the royal couple. All of the candies then come back in as the Sugarplum Fairy and her cavalier bid the young couple farewell. Marie and her prince step into a royal sleigh drawn by reindeer and before our very eyes the sleigh rises right into the sky and away.

Ballet in two acts after the story "The Nutcracker and the Rat King" by E. T. A. Hoffmann. Music by Tchaikovsky. Choreography and production by Rudolf Nureyev (the Prince's variation in Act Two by Vassily Vainonen). Scenery and costumes by Nicholas Georgiadis. First presented by the Royal Swedish Ballet at the Royal Swedish Opera House, Stockholm, November 17, 1967. Presented by the Royal Ballet at the Royal Opera House, Covent Garden, London, February 29, 1968, and introduced by that ensemble to the United States at the Metropolitan Opera House, New York, May 10, 1968.

ACT ONE   It is Christmas Eve early in the nineteenth century. The wealthy mayor, Dr. Stahlbaum, is giving a party for his friends and their children. The children are dancing and playing in excited anticipation of the approaching Christmas festivities and of their presents. Herr Drosselmeyer, an old friend of the family, arrives bringing the children gifts and amuses them by his conjuring tricks. He gives Clara, his favorite, a Nutcracker, which delights her. Her brother Fritz spitefully breaks it but Herr Drosselmeyer mends it for her. After the grandparents arrive and join in the dancing Clara becomes very tired and falling asleep in her chair, has a vivid dream. The room and the Christmas tree seem to grow . . . from the wainscot a swarm of rats appears trying to capture the Nutcracker, but Clara rushes to his rescue, throwing them her favorite dolls in an effort to distract them from him. From their toy fort an army of soldiers led by the Nutcracker (who suddenly springs to life) comes to help the fight against the rats and their leader, the Rat King. A company of Hussars and another of marines fight the rat army but are overwhelmed. The Nutcracker and the Rat King are left on the battlefield. Desperately Clara flings her shoe at the Rat King. As it strikes him he falls dead and a sudden transformation takes place revealing the Nutcracker as a young, handsome prince.

ACT TWO   Together the Nutcracker Prince and Clara are carried away to an enchanted grotto. There Clara becomes frightened by bats but when the prince comes to protect her she realizes that they are actually her family and friends transformed by her nightmare.

The grotto mysteriously changes into Clara's own toy theater where she finds many of her favorite dolls brought to life. The mood changes to one of happiness and everyone dances. As Clara's dream closes she is found still sleeping in her chair. Her mother and father waken her and, as the guests take their leave, the party comes to an end. Clara is left alone, enthralled by memories of her adventures.

NOTES   Rudolf Nureyev's version of *The Nutcracker* for the Royal Swedish

Ballet was reviewed for *Dance News* by Anna Greta Stahle: "The Christmas party takes place in a palace—suggesting old St. Petersburg. The parents and children are dressed in directoire style, and the old people, like Drosselmeyer, keep to the fashion of their youth and are in rococo. The acting and miming is staged with imagination and humor; it is indeed an elegant and lively party.

"Clara is a girl of an age between child and woman, and consequently her dreams are both childish and tinged with an erotic element. Nureyev has omitted the visit to the Kingdom of Sweets and has built the *divertissement* entirely on dreams in which Clara's family and Drosselmeyer appear in different shapes. The same dancer is seen as Drosselmeyer, the Rat King, and the Prince. Clara is herself all through the ballet, dancing the usual Sugarplum Fairy *pas de deux* with the Prince as though it were a dream of herself as a princess."

Ballet in two acts. Music by Tchaikovsky. Production conceived, directed and choreographed by Mikhail Baryshnikov. Choreography for "Snowflake" dance by Vasily Vainonen. Decors by Boris Aronson. Costumes by Frank Thompson. Lighting by Jennifer Tipton. First presented by American Ballet Theatre at the Kennedy Center for the Performing Arts, Washington, December 21, 1976, with Marianna Tcherkassky as Clara, Alexander Minz as Drosselmeyer and Mikhail Baryshnikov as the Nutcracker-Prince.

This *Nutcracker* is not child's play, though it is about a young girl growing up. It is different from other productions of this ballet in its focus on the two men who are central to the life of young Clara—Drosselmeyer, her godfather in real life, and the Nutcracker-Prince, the dream figure who is created by Drosselmeyer's magic. Here the child Clara is on the point of growing up. Aided by her godfather, a dream of love materializes only to cause later doubts. This psychological drama is set within the conventional frame of *The Nutcracker:* the names are the same but the action of the ballet varies dramatically.

In the Prologue, it is Christmas Eve, a time when dreams may become reality. Drosselmeyer, godfather to Clara Stahlbaum, prepares gifts and magic dolls for the annual Christmas party at the home of her parents. Clara is to be the ballet's heroine.

ACT ONE, SCENE ONE The Stahlbaum household prepares for Christmas. Clara, her brother Fritz, their parents and grandmother are all much involved in entertaining guests while at the same time enjoying the festivities themselves. Suddenly, Drosselmeyer appears and produces a magic puppet show. The puppets act out the fairy tale of the beautiful young Princess and two suitors—the handsome Prince and the wicked Mouse King. To everyone's delight, the Prince wins the Princess. Then Drosselmeyer produces three magic life-size dolls, plus his very special gift for Clara, a small Nutcracker doll. Nobody but Clara likes this rather strange toy but she is so delighted with it that she begs her godfather Drosselmeyer to make him life-size as he did with the other big dolls. A tipsy guest accidentally breaks the little toy Nutcracker and Clara binds his broken jaw with her handkerchief. As the guests finally depart, Clara asks to be allowed to take the toy to bed with her, but her father makes her leave it underneath the Christmas tree.

SCENE TWO   It is the middle of the night. Clara steals down to see her Nutcracker and is frightened by the bat-like shadow of Drosselmeyer, who is still there in hiding. Suddenly she sees some odd creatures around the tree. They seem to be like the guests in her parents' Christmas party who have turned into giant mice, the subjects of the Mouse King. She confronts them bravely. Suddenly Drosselmeyer causes the Christmas tree to grow to an immense height and then, before her very eyes, the Nutcracker doll grows to life size and begins to move. The Nutcracker is immediately pitched into battle with the Mouse King and his army. Another army of toy soldiers appears, who also remind Clara of her little friends from that evening's festivities, and the battle is on. Clara saves the day by hurling her candle at the Mouse King. He is distracted and the Nutcracker defeats him. Drosselmeyer appears as if to remind Clara, "You wanted him to grow up. Look, I am going to give you what you begged for (what you wanted) as a reward for your kindness and love for the Nutcracker." Drosselmeyer transforms the Nutcracker into the handsome young Prince, who beckons Clara to follow him to a land of magical dreams. Once again, Drosselmeyer waves his hands and the beautiful Christmas forest appears. The dancing Snowflakes guide the Prince and Clara to the Prince's castle.

ACT TWO   The Prince takes Clara to his kingdom. When they are met at the gates by his subjects, the Prince relates the story of his victory over the Mouse King. Soon they enter the Prince's court, which is filled with beautiful puppets that spring to life at the Prince's command and dance for him and Clara. Both the Prince and Clara join in when the entire court dances the Rose Waltz. Then, mysteriously, a strange atmosphere is sensed; the happiness of the scene seems to vanish. Everything in the court begins to disappear, as if an invisible hand were destroying an illusion. Clara is disturbed and confused and even more so when Drosselmeyer appears and tells her that this "dream" is over and she must go home. Clara does everything to keep her handsome Prince and his magic kingdom. To the music generally known as the Grand Pas de Deux from the ballet, she and the Prince resist Drosselmeyer's attempt to withdraw her from her dream in a dramatic *pas de trois*. Victorious, the two young people dance happily. But as the glorious procession of the Prince's subjects concludes, Clara is unaware that she must wake up anyhow. Little by little her dream world fades away and she finds herself in the streaming sunlight of early morning.

Alan M. Kriegsman, dance critic for the Washington *Post*, called the Baryshnikov production "not only a commercial triumph but an artistic coup as well." He observed that while a child's Christmas dream is the basis for this version of the ballet, here "the child is older—a girl on the verge of adolescence—and the dream branches out to become, not just the wish-fulfillment of a candy kingdom, but an envisagement of mature love, incarnate in the Nutcracker-Prince."

When Baryshnikov's *Nutcracker* was first performed, in Washington, the critic of the Washington *Star*, Anne Marie Welsh, interviewed the dancer and choreographer and appraised his achievement: "*The Nutcracker* of Mikhail Baryshnikov is a strange and wonderful ballet.

"The ballet is all sweetness and modesty, a sensitive and serious look at the 1892 Tchaikovsky classic which, for nearly 30 years, has been a Christmas entertainment for American children.

"This version is different, and although at first it may appear less appealing to children, in the long run it deserves to be considered. For Baryshnikov—and the production—have the real dreams of children at heart.

"In his debut as a choreographer, Baryshnikov has given American Ballet Theatre more than a mere innovation. He has given them a lasting work, and a production on a scale so appropriate to ABT's younger dancers that they have seldom looked better. He has given them choreography that is consistently pure and open. All the characters of *The Nutcracker*—partygoers and children and mice and dolls and flowers—seem in touch with the ballet's essential mystery, and become essential to a single imagined vision.

"And he has given Marianna Tcherkassky, his opening night Clara, a role so lovely and so right that she has triumphed.

"The 15-minute ovation that thundered after the poignant close of last night's premiere may have been partly sentimental, but Baryshnikov—as choreographer, producer and dancer—richly deserved it.

"There are no children in this production, no tinsel-wrapped gifts, no red, white and green. In fact, there is little of the Christmas Eve realism we've come to expect from *The Nutcracker*.

"The first act of the production is focused upon what Clara, a 10- or 12-year-old, sees: Drosselmeyer, her mysterious godfather; the nutcracker he gives to her, and the cruel adult who breaks this toy she loves. The dream that soon unfolds for her is truly a child's—scary at first, then heroic, and, finally, if only for the visionary moment, fulfilled.

"Baryshnikov's most significant and stunning departure from productions which have become standard is to turn the second act *pas de deux* into a *pas de trois* for Clara, the Prince and Drosselmeyer. The melody is one of Tchaikovsky's simplest and most haunting—just the G major scale played top to bottom—and the new dance for three is perfectly attuned to its musical impulse.

"Two kindred spirits hover about American Ballet Theatre's new *Nutcracker*. E.T.A. Hoffmann, the German romantic whose fairy tale of 1816 is the basis for the ballet, wears the face of Drosselmeyer, godfather to the story's heroine. Mikhail Baryshnikov, the gifted dancer who choreographed and produced the ballet, wears the face of a prince, the object of the heroine's affection.

"When he discusses the production which had its world premiere here last night, Baryshnikov says, 'This is Drosselmeyer's evening. It is his ballet. He makes this experience of the dream for Clara because he likes her. He wants to help her grow up, but he also wants to protect her from tragedy.'

"Baryshnikov sees Hoffmann as a benevolent story teller, a giver of dreams like the Drosselmeyer this *Nutcracker* celebrates. 'His tales,' says Baryshnikov, 'are full of his own cartoons and full of his own incredible feeling about being an artist.' In fact, Hoffmann was a frustrated artist, misunderstood by his public and unhappy in his personal life.

"His stories are riddled with the grotesque and the violent, and they end, more often than not, in merciless imaginative revenges upon fictionalized enemies. The benevolence of *Nutcracker* comes partly from the lyric strain in Hoffmann, partly from Alexandre Dumas, who rewrote the original tale and changed its ending, and partly, of course, from Baryshnikov's own fertile imagination.

"The revenge motif remains, giving this *Nutcracker* its most significant difference from all previous American productions, and bringing it a step closer to Hoffmann. Clara does dream of getting back at the adults who have hurt and frustrated her. Also, the psychoanalytic meaning of the work's title has been clarified by the changes Baryshnikov has made. But the grand difference is that for Clara, unlike Hoffmann, living well, or at least dreaming of living well, is the best revenge.

"Most versions of the ballet allow Clara to fade into the background after the first act party and her subsequent dream of the nutcracker vanquishing mice. She usually becomes a passive spectator in a series of *divertissements* that satisfy her child's desire for sweet dreams; in psychological terms, for oral gratification.

"'I wanted to find a way to connect the two acts of the ballet,' says Baryshnikov, and since he envisions Clara as a 10- or 12-year-old, he solved the artistic problem by having her dream of and dance with her nutcracker-turned-prince. Hers is now a vision of adult sexual satisfaction.

"Hence, Clara dances to the *grand pas de deux* music usually reserved for the Sugar Plum Fairy. Baryshnikov makes the dance a *pas de trois* with Drosselmeyer lending moral support to the girl, who isn't quite old enough to live happily ever after with her prince.

"'Clara is just on the line of growing up,' says Baryshnikov. 'This is the first move of her child's soul. The most important moment for her is when she saves her nutcracker. It is a little miracle, and, because she is good, Drosselmeyer can give her her dream of fulfillment.'

"All the other changes Baryshnikov has made move the ballet in this same direction—towards greater psychological explicitness and coherence. He discussed those changes the other day this way:

"Drosselmeyer gives a puppet show in the first act that shows a prince rescuing a princess from the clutches of a mouse king. 'I want Clara's dream to be a collage of impressions from the party,' says Baryshnikov, 'and one of those ideas in her excited imagination comes from Drosselmeyer's little entertainment.'

"A drunken adult rather than her mischievous brother breaks Clara's nutcracker. 'Yes,' said Baryshnikov, 'this fellow is an adult, so she can have the dream about adults. I can't say the idea is particularly mine, but it is part of my experience and makes the dream more real.'

"The men at the opening party are transformed into the truly scary mice of her dream. Gone are the funny, domestic rodents of most versions. 'Again, I can't say this is my idea independently,' says Baryshnikov, 'but I want the scene to be quite frightening and terrible. I remember my own dreams as a child, my own nightmares. This is a way to connect all her impressions after the party. She is very excited by the party, and the music here is very unusual and strange.'

"The Arabian variation, 'Coffee,' is deleted from the second act *divertissements*. 'I was trying to think what I wanted to do here, and though it is a beautiful piece of music, it slows things down. I want to keep things moving. Four little dances are enough, and this way the focus can stay on Clara.'

"The ending includes Drosselmeyer in the background and Clara looking quite bereft rather than joyous. 'She is involved very much with her nutcracker,' says Baryshnikov. 'But Drosselmeyer knows she is not ready and wants to protect her from any tragedy. He is explaining the dream to her. She wants to be with her nutcracker, but she has lost him. She is in that moment between reality and sleeping and it is all fading away. "That's it," Drosselmeyer is telling her; "it's morning, it's time to come back to the world." Yellow morning light is coming through the window. It is over for her, this vision that Drosselmeyer has given to her. He's mysterious, but he is warm and loving just as the Tchaikovsky score is. He has made this experience for her because he loves her and now he will help her to understand it.'

"Given this pattern of dramatic details, it's impossible to resist the obvious question. Baryshnikov has no hesitancy in answering it. 'Yes, I am a Freudian,' he says, laughing. 'But not in my everyday life.' "*

OCTUOR

Music by Igor Stravinsky. Choreography by Richard Tanner. First presented at the New York City Ballet's Stravinsky Festival at the New York State Theatre, Lincoln Center, June 21, 1972, with Elise Flagg, Delia Peters, Lisa de Ribera, Deborah Flomine, Tracy Bennett, James Bogan, Daniel Duell, and Jean-Pierre Frohlich. Conducted by Robert Irving.

Stravinsky's famous *Octet for Wind Instruments* was first performed in Paris, October 18, 1923, at one of the Concerts Koussevitsky, the composer conducting. The following year, in an article about the piece, Stravinsky said that "form, in my music, derived from counterpoint. I consider counterpoint as the only means through which the attention of the composer is concentrated on purely musical questions. Its elements also lend themselves perfectly to an architectural construction."

Four couples are featured in Richard Tanner's ballet to the *Octuor*. There are three movements to the work, *Sinfonia, Tema con variazioni,* and *Finale.*

* Reprinted by permission of the Washington *Star.*

NOTES   Writing after the premiere in the *Daily News*, the critic Sam Norkin said: "The four skilled couples in simple summary costumes bounded through this jazzy, bustling and contrapuntal piece in a carefree manner, keenly aware of its structure. Elise Flagg was outstanding in this highly enjoyable new ballet."

ODE

> *Music by Igor Stravinsky. Choreography by Lorca Massine. First presented at the New York City Ballet's Stravinsky Festival, June 23, 1972, at the New York State Theatre, Lincoln Center, with Christine Redpath, Colleen Neary, Robert Maiorano, Earle Sieveling, and ensemble. Conducted by Robert Craft.*

Stravinsky's *Ode*, written in 1943 in elegaic commemoration of the death of Natalia Koussevitsky, is a lovely score too little known. The young choreographer Lorca Massine happily arranged dances to it for the New York City Ballet's Stravinsky Festival in 1972. After the premiere, Clive Barnes wrote in the New York *Times* that *Ode* "has its statuesque moments of sculptural identity, moments out of time when, Béjart-like, the choreographer ignores the music and creates a certain dramatic effect. This is perhaps the best thing we have seen in New York from Mr. Massine."

OFFENBACH IN THE UNDERWORLD

> *Music by Jacques Offenbach, arranged and orchestrated by George Crum. Choreography by Antony Tudor. Decor and costumes by Kay Ambrose. Lighting by Jennifer Tipton. First presented by the National Ballet of Canada in Toronto, Canada, February 1, 1955. First presented in the United States by the City Center Joffrey Ballet in Lewiston, New York, August 14, 1975.*

The action of this diverting ballet takes place in the 1870s in a fashionable cafe at an international capital. Visiting celebrities come to see, to be seen, and to amuse themselves. Among them are a famous operetta star and one of her admirers, a grand duke. A debutante of good family, accompanied by three friends, arrives veiled in order not to be recognized in a place that is "out of bounds." There is, too, a young painter, a regular patron, had he the money, who haunts the place night and day; he tries to earn a meager living by drawing sketches of the cafe's patrons. There is no story to the ballet, for the flirtations that arise at such a place at such a time are most often half forgotten by the next morning. There is neither a sad ending nor a happy ending, but only a closing time.

When the ballet was revived for New York, Celia Franca staged it. The decor was re-created by Edward Burbridge and the costumes re-created by

Ray Diffen. The City Center Joffrey Ballet production was dedicated to the memory of Kay Ambrose.

OLYMPICS

Music by Toshiro Mayuzumi. Choreography by Gerald Arpino. Setting by Ming Cho Lee. First presented by the Robert Joffrey Ballet at the City Center, New York, March 31, 1966, with Luis Fuente as the Torch Bearer, and Jon Cristofori, Richard Gain, Ian Horvath, John Jones, and Michael Uthoff as the Athletes.

Olympics is the choreographer's tribute to the Greek ideal of the athlete as "the complete man," proud of his prowess, openly competitive in games but also dedicated to the gods and a human ideal. It is an all-male work, dominated by the runner who carries the torch from Olympus to signal the beginning of the ritual games. The dancers compete, running, wrestling, executing gymnastic feats in a series of swift displays to the gods.

ONCE MORE, FRANK

Music by Carson C. Parks, Harold Arlen and Johnny Mercer, Dean Kay and Kelly Gordon. Choreography by Twyla Tharp. Costumes by Santo Loquasto. First presented by American Ballet Theatre at the New York State Theatre, Lincoln Center, July 12, 1976, with Twyla Tharp and Mikhail Baryshnikov.

Named for Frank Sinatra, whose recordings of three songs are played for the ballet, the ballet was a special piece for a gala performance. It is a dance for a boy and a girl who are both lost in the songs and coolly detached from them in bemused recollection of another time when they loved them first. The songs are "Something Stupid," "One for My Baby" and "That's Life." In his book *Baryshnikov at Work*, Mikhail Baryshnikov suggests that the dance was about the particular dancers involved, each with different backgrounds and styles, trying to find with Sinatra's help the ideal middle ground.

ONDINE

Music by Hans Werner Henze. Scenario freely adapted by Frederick Ashton from the story by Friedrich de la Motte Fouqué. Choreography by Frederick Ashton. Scenery and costumes by Lila de Nobili. First presented by the Royal Ballet at the Royal Opera House, Covent Garden, London, October 27, 1958, with Margot Fonteyn, Michael Somes, Julia Farron, and Alexander Grant in the principal roles. First presented in the United States by the Royal Ballet at the Metropolitan Opera House, New York, September 21, 1960.

"This is the story of Palemon and Ondine telling how Palemon wedded with a water sprite and what chanced therefrom and how Ondine returned to her element beneath the Mediterranean Sea."

ACT ONE, SCENE ONE: OUTSIDE BERTA'S CASTLE   Berta, returning from a hunt, is courted by Palemon, who offers her an amulet, which she scorns. She rejoins her friends, and Palemon is left alone in meditation. Suddenly, out of a fountain in the garden of the palace, a strange being, Ondine, appears, a mortal girl for the first time. She sees her shadow and, enchanted, dances. Palemon is captivated but the water sprite is alarmed at his interest and flees to the forest. Palemon follows her.

ACT ONE, SCENE TWO: A MYSTERIOUS FOREST   Tirrenio, lord of the Mediterranean, and wood sprites lie in wait for the lovers. Tirrenio tries to separate them. He warns Palemon that should he be unfaithful to Ondine, he must forfeit his life. Ondine defies Tirrenio and the lovers seek out a hermit who marries them. She gains her soul and is no longer a mere water sprite. The scene ends with Berta distraught at the acts of Tirrenio, who tries to impede her pursuit of the lovers.

ACT TWO: A PORT   After their marriage, Palemon and Ondine come to a port where they decide to embark on a ship. Berta, following, sees the lovers and bribes the captain to take her unseen on board. Not knowing of their marriage, Berta is moved by jealousy when she sees Palemon, in a transport of love, offer Ondine the amulet he once offered to her. She reproaches Palemon. Ondine at once gives the jewel to Berta. Suddenly the outraged Tirrenio rises out of the sea and snatches the amulet from Berta. Ondine runs to the side of the ship, dips her hands into water and produces an exquisite necklace which she presents to Berta. Horrified at the supernatural gift, Berta throws it at Ondine's feet. The sailors who have witnessed this magic regard Ondine with doubt and awe; they threaten her. Tirrenio, again rising from the sea to protect Ondine, beckons to her. He creates a storm and, rising on the crest of a wave, seizes her and drags her to the bottom of the sea. The storm increases.

ACT THREE: PALEMON'S CASTLE   Saved from the shipwreck, Palemon and Berta arrive from their wedding. Berta gives Palemon a present, a portrait of herself, and leaves to prepare for their guests. Palemon, in a reverie, has a vision of Ondine. Berta returns and disturbs his dream. The guests arrive and the festivities begin, but at their height strange and sinister things happen. Tirrenio, true to his warning, appears seeking vengeance. Berta is dragged out by a swarm of water sprites. Ondine appears at Tirrenio's command. Palemon now realizes that she is his only love. Ondine warns him that owing to his lack of faith, her kiss can only mean his death. Finally, sadly, she kisses him and he falls dead. She takes his body back to the sea, there to hold him in an eternal embrace.

NOTES   *Ondine* has been a favorite theme of ballet since Fouqué wrote the original story in German in 1811. The theme, like that of *La Sylphide, Swan*

Lake, Giselle, and other romantic stories, tells the story of a magic being from another world who comes to earth and loves a mortal, with dire consequences to them both. The part of Ondine was associated for many years with Fanny Cerrito, just as today it has become famous through the interpretation of Margot Fonteyn. Cerrito first danced the role in Jules Perrot's ballet to the story on June 22, 1843, in London. For her shadow dance in the first act theatrical lighting was used for one of the first times. Other dancers who have appeared in the role are Carlotta Grisi (in Russia in 1851, in Perrot's ballet with music by Pugni) and Anna Pavlova.

ONTOGENY

Music by Karel Husa. Choreography by Dennis Nahat. Setting and costumes by Willa Kim. Lighting by Nananne Porcher. First presented by American Ballet Theatre at the City Center, New York, January 6, 1971.

One dictionary defines the word "ontogeny" as "the development of the course of an individual organism." Not so much human as protozoic, the ballet begins by showing us, in fact, how chromosomes combine to make a man. He appears, pursued by his mother. He gradually acquires knowledge in his childhood, matures, and begins to understand himself. The life cycle continues. The music for the ballet is the *Third String Quartet* by Husa.

OPUS LEMAITRE

Music by Bach. Choreography by Hans van Manen. Sets and costumes by Jean-Paul Vroom. First presented by the Netherlands Dance Theatre, with Gérard Lemaitre. First presented in the United States by the Pennsylvania Ballet at the Academy of Music, Philadelphia, February 1974, with Lawrence Rhodes in the principal role.

A major work for the *premier danseur,* named for and dedicated to the choreographer's colleague Gérard Lemaitre, *Opus Lemaitre* provides the male dancer with abundant opportunity to display balance, stillness, and a personal declarative style to match the grandeur of Bach's *Toccata and Fugue in D Minor.* The leading dancer is accompanied by five couples. He stands motionless among them for the entire length of the toccata, beginning to dance at the commencement of the fugue.

OPUS ONE

Music by Anton von Webern. Choreography by John Cranko. Lighting by Gilbert V. Hemsley, Jr. First presented by the Stuttgart Ballet at the Württemberg State Theatre, Stuttgart, November 7, 1965. First presented in the

United States by the same ensemble at the Metropolitan Opera House, New York, April 30, 1969, with Birgit Keil and Richard Cragun in the principal roles.

A program note by Franz Willnauer reminds us that "genuine ballet art—like all genuine art—is ambiguous. It can be interpreted in many ways—from the stylized order of movements to the code of an incarnate calligraphy, to the symbolic dance drama of the human couple whose love and life are destroyed by the angel of death."

Set to Webern's *Passacaglia,* Op. 1, the ballet shows a life cycle in dance. A man is born. Curled up at first, he extends, is released, dances, finds a girl who comes down from above. They dance an impassioned *pas de deux* and then they are surrounded by a threatening group. Though they rejoin briefly, the girl is soon carried aloft. He reaches up for her but cannot reach her and, in despair, curls up on the ground, as at his beginning.

ORPHEUS

Ballet in three scenes. Music by Igor Stravinsky. Choreography by George Balanchine. Scenery and costumes by Isamu Noguchi. Lighting by Jean Rosenthal. First presented by Ballet Society at the New York City Center, New York, April 28, 1948, with Nicholas Magallanes as Orpheus, Maria Tallchief as Eurydice, Francisco Moncion as the Dark Angel, Beatrice Tompkins as the Leader of the Furies, Tanaquil LeClercq as the Leader of the Bacchantes, and Herbert Bliss as Apollo.

This ballet is a contemporary treatment of the ancient myth of Orpheus, the Greek musician who descended into Hades in search of his dead wife, Eurydice. With his music, Orpheus charms the God of the Dead into returning Eurydice to him. He promises not to look at her until they have reached the earth again. Eurydice, unknowing, persuades Orpheus to break this promise, thereby bringing about her irrevocable death. The ballet tells this story and its aftermath as simply as possible with its music, its dramatic action, and its dancing.

SCENE ONE: THE GRAVE OF EURYDICE   The first notes of the orchestra remind us that Orpheus's instrument was the lyre. A harp sounds descending scales in a slow, mournful rhythm accompanied by quiet strings. Eurydice is dead, and Orpheus cannot console himself with his own song. The curtain rises. Orpheus stands alone beside Eurydice's grave with his back turned. His arms hang limp, his lyre is discarded at his feet, and his head is bowed to the intensely blue sky that would pierce his sorrow with brightness. Three friends enter on the left, cross over to the grave, and place upon it relics of Eurydice. Orpheus does not notice them; he remains motionless when they place their hands on his shoulder to console him. He ignores their departure. The music ceases its slow lamentation, and Orpheus wakens from his grief. He takes up his lyre and begins a dance that expresses physical grief as well as mental anguish. He raises the lyre high above him in supplication, then holds the instrument in one hand as he dances. The song of the lyre is inadequate to his bereavement; yet the lyre is the only possession Orpheus has left, and in his dance he tries to make the instrument a partner to his woe. This effort fails, and Orpheus places the harp on Eurydice's grave, where he beseeches it to speak for her. Then he falls in despair at the grave and reaches out to pluck the lyre's strings. At this sound, a satyr and four wood sprites leap out from behind rocks in the background and attempt to distract Orpheus. Orpheus rises to meet these creatures who have been moved by his song and he darts in and out among them for a moment, but soon leaves them, to dance alone with his lyre. His misery is unabated and his pathetic figure seems to demand the sympathy of the gods he invokes to aid him. Again he stands beside Eurydice's grave with downcast eyes.

Now the prayers of Orpheus are answered. In the back, against the vivid blue sky, appears a strange, dark figure whose body is enveloped in black coils. The Angel of Death poses briefly, then moves forward toward the grieving poet. He approaches softly, so as not to disturb Orpheus in his reverie, and touches him. Orpheus stands immobile. The Angel of Death frees himself of the black coil that represents his power in Hades, raises Orpheus's arms high, and entwines the coil between his outstretched hands. As he wraps the coil about the silent musician, the Angel of Death by his intimate presence endows Orpheus with the power to accompany him on the long journey across the River Styx to Eurydice. The angel stands away from Orpheus and dances triumphantly for a moment, then prepares for the trip into Hades. He frees Orpheus of the bonds of death, then places over the minstrel's eyes a golden mask which must not be removed until the journey is over. Then he picks up the lyre, slips his arm through it, and beckons to Orpheus. Orpheus moves toward him hesitatingly; pliantly he stretches out his hand to grasp the angel's upturned palm. The open, widespread fingers of the angel close about his hand with the strength of steel. A trumpet sounds. The angel moves the lyre down his arm to rest on their clasped hands and begins to lead Orpheus on the downward journey. The music is slow and spacious as the two figures move toward the front of the stage. From above, a flowing white gauze falls in slow motion, and in front of this curtain the Angel of Death leads the blinded Orpheus on the tortuous journey. The progress in their descent into Hades is marked by bright objects that can be seen moving upward in back of the transparent curtain. The passage becomes difficult as the two figures cross the stage toward the left, and as they disappear, the angel, exhausted, pulls Orpheus over the ground. When they have gone, mysterious figures in back of the gauze push the curtain forward with a movement similar to the helpless beating of wings against a cage.

SCENE TWO: HADES   The gauze curtain rises swiftly, and crouched about the stage in fearful attitudes are the Furies, creatures of Hell who would destroy those who enter the Land of the Dead unlawfully. Bright cones of light from above illuminate their hideous and fantastic attire. The leader of the Furies proceeds to direct them harshly in a rapid, rhythmic dance. Orpheus and the angel enter on the left. The leader of the Furies turns and points at them menacingly, followed by her weird creatures. But the angel and Orpheus stand motionless. The Furies finish their dance, and their leader directs them to gather in a group. Tortured souls who have remained in the background now stir with great effort. They carry heavy burdens of rock on their shoulders and bend painfully under the strain. They set boulders down behind the group of Furies, as if to protect themselves, and all turn toward the two interlopers.

The Angel of Death moves away from Orpheus, slips the lyre from his arm, and, standing in back of the minstrel, places the lyre for Orpheus to play. But Orpheus does not understand—he cannot see—and the angel moves his hands so that they touch the strings of the harp. The angel plucks the strings, and now Orpheus comprehends and begins to play. His music is accompanied closely by two oboes and the orchestra. The lovely, soft melody of his lyre enchants the Furies, who are lulled to silence and rest. Yet Orpheus is still reluctant to play the harp as he once did, before Eurydice died, and the angel continues to exact the music from him. He knows that only by his great music will Orpheus persuade the ruler of Hades to release Eurydice. The two figures dance to the beautiful song, the angel constantly encouraging Orpheus to prolong the melody. The burdened, tortured souls move closer to hear more perfectly, and the music reflects their agony, which Orpheus's song has temporarily relieved.

But now the song is over. Orpheus bows stiffly in obeisance toward the back. In the dark recesses of the stage a strange shape begins to turn toward him. This is Pluto, God of the Underworld. Standing before him, her hands resting on his shoulders, is Eurydice. Orpheus does not move. Although he cannot see, he senses her presence and waits for Pluto's answer to his prayer. Eurydice moves forward, haltingly at first, with a slight limping motion, then more freely as her dance becomes syncopated. She turns to Pluto and beseeches him to come forward. Eurydice's arms move constantly to express her desire for freedom, and Pluto moves toward her. The Furies take Orpheus by the hand and bring him to Eurydice. Pluto joins their hands, and for a moment the two stand motionless before the god as Orpheus pledges not to look at his wife until they have ascended to earth. A blue stalactite descends from on high to symbolize the reunion, and the Dark Angel comes forward to lead Orpheus and Eurydice back to earth. He takes Orpheus by the hand, and all the inhabitants of the underworld circle the three figures, who move with hands joined to the front of the stage. The gauze curtain falls behind them, and the Dark Angel proceeds ahead, holding out Orpheus's lyre as a guide to the couple.

Orpheus and Eurydice dance together to a sumptuous melody as their journey begins. At first Eurydice merely follows Orpheus, imitating his steps as he leads the way. But the ascent is difficult, and their dance becomes for a short time a kind of portrayal of the hardships they undergo in passing unseen obstacles. Orpheus is blind, and when Eurydice is not holding him by the hand, she is lost to him. Eurydice puts herself in his way constantly: she longs increasingly for Orpheus to see her. Her longing is infinitely tender and appealing because of the warmth of the love in her own eyes; she therefore seems to tempt Orpheus to tear the mask from his face not so that he can see her, but so that she can see him as she remembers him. She wishes to help him as they proceed along the way, but the one way in which she cannot help him is by showing her love for him. Eurydice is tormented momentarily by the fact that, although they are really together once again, they are actually remote to each other: Orpheus, because he cannot see; Eurydice, because she cannot be seen by the man she loves.

The tempo and the theme of the dance change briefly as Eurydice moves away and dances before the blind Orpheus a gay and pleasant measure. She holds in her hands an invisible pipe, and plays upon it in celebration of their reunion. Orpheus catches the mood of her dance and joins her in it. Both are attempting to suppress the impassioned longings they feel so deeply. But Orpheus becomes even more intently aware of his lack of sight as Eurydice beguilingly dances out of his reach, and the principal theme of their *pas de deux* returns, this time prefaced with a short musical warning from the harp. On the extreme left, the arm of the Dark Angel still holds out the guiding lyre, and the two lovers turn to follow it. They start out as before, Orpheus leading and Eurydice duplicating his movements, but now Eurydice moves close to him in intimate contact. Orpheus tries to hold her, but she slides down to the floor, where his arms reach out desperately to find her. The melody mounts to a brief crescendo. Now that he cannot touch Eurydice, Orpheus abandons all patience and takes his head in his hands. Eurydice stands beside him, her face close to his, and he tears the mask from his eyes. There is absolute silence. Instantly she falls against him and dies. At first too stunned to move, Orpheus stretches out his arms, eager to touch her and to feel her touch. Invisible creatures of Hades push forward the gauze curtain to make good their promise and slip Eurydice away. Orpheus kneels alone, his open arms clasping the empty air.

Now that he has lost Eurydice until he himself shall die, Orpheus is afraid. Horns sound in terrifying judgment upon his fatal error. He remembers that the Angel of Death is still with him, just ahead, and he turns, half crawling, half running, to grasp his lyre. But just before his fingers reach the lyre, it disappears. Powerless now in the Land of the Dead, Orpheus knows that he is powerless, too, on earth; he crawls off in search of his lyre.

The gauze curtain rises rapidly when Orpheus has left the stage. Here again on earth the sky is still blue, but now it is bathed also in blood-colored lights. There is a small hillock in the background. At the crash of a drum, there comes in from the left a tall Thracian woman with long red hair. This is the leader of the bacchantes, pleasure-seeking women who have not known love. She stalks the scene as if seeking desirable prey, moving with quick thrusts of legs and arms, looking to the right and left. She is soon followed by eight bacchantes, all with brilliant yellow hair. Orpheus enters carrying his mask. Immediately the bacchantes surround him. Their leader seems to demand his favor. Orpheus repulses her, indignant that she should try to sully his grief. The woman smiles her contempt and tries to take the mask from him. He runs, but the bacchantes are all around him. The leader embraces Orpheus savagely with her long arms, and the two fall to the ground. They roll over and over, and Orpheus frees himself, but the bacchante rises in triumph, holding his mask. Her face contorted with demoniac delight, she throws the mask out of sight. Orpheus cannot escape. The entire orchestra imitates his terror and the ferocity of the bacchantes with frenzied, rhythmic fortissimos. The bacchantes move in for the final attack. They push Orpheus back toward the hillock. He does not resist. They push him again. His head is bowed, his body listless. The bacchantes raise his arms, and for a brief moment they seem open in supplication. The leader stalks in on Orpheus and cuts off his right arm, then his left. He raises his head; she decapitates him. The body of Orpheus lies behind the hillock, torn to pieces. The bacchantes exit, strutting proudly, unregretfully.

SCENE THREE: APOTHEOSIS   The stage is empty. Gradually the red disappears from the blue sky and the earth is bright once more. Again we hear the harp play the theme that opened the ballet, but now the accompaniment is different: this seems but a mere imitation of Orpheus's music. Apollo comes in slowly and approaches the grave of Orpheus. He kneels beside it and takes from behind the hillock a golden mask of the minstrel's face. Apollo holds the mask high, invoking the spirit of Orpheus as the God of Song, then holds it gently with his arm, as Orpheus held his lyre. The harp sounds as Apollo plucks the air before the mask, but the music—accompanied as it is by two horns—makes us all the more aware of the death of Orpheus and of Apollo's inability to call forth his music alone. Finally Apollo sets down the mask and stands poised over the grave of Orpheus. Slowly he moves his arm upward, and from the grave rises the lyre of Orpheus entwined in a long garland of flowers. The lyre rises higher and higher, carrying with it for the ages the tenderness and power of his song.

OTHER DANCES

Music by Frédéric Chopin. Choreography by Jerome Robbins. Costumes by Santa Loquasto. Lighting by Gilbert V. Hemsley, Jr. First presented at a Gala for the benefit for the Library of the Performing Arts at Lincoln Center at the Metropolitan Opera House, New York, May 9, 1976, with Natalia Makarova and Mikhail Baryshnikov. Pianist: Jerry Zimmerman.

Created for a special occasion, this dance for two has become a part of the permanent repertory. Jerome Robbins, in *Dances at a Gathering* and *In the Night,* had made enduring ballets based on Chopin's piano music. This work is an extension of his interest in that music, as reflected in an admiration for the two principal dancers. The music is four mazurkas and a waltz—the same waltz used years ago by Michel Fokine for the first solo in *Les Sylphides.*

PAGANINI

Ballet in seven scenes. Music by Sergei Rachmaninoff. Libretto and chore-
ography by Leonid Lavrovsky. Scenery by Vadim Rindin. First presented
by the Bolshoi Ballet at the Bolshoi Theatre, Moscow, April 7, 1960. First
presented in the United States by the Bolshoi Ballet at the Metropolitan
Opera House, New York, September 17, 1962, with Garosin Sekh in the
title role.

The choreographer has written: "For many years I dreamed of making a ballet
about Paganini. Perhaps this wish derived from the impressions I formed in
my youth from reading the memoirs of Paganini's contemporaries and biographers, who described his uncanny expressiveness and the remarkable plastic
quality of his body, hands, and face. In the summer of 1959 I obtained a
recording of Rachmaninoff's *Rhapsody on a Theme of Paganini.* I was deeply
moved. The beautiful and convincing treatment of the musical work dedicated
to Paganini insistently called me, a choreographer, to respond in my own professional language."

The ballet depicts Paganini's recollections of his life, from which the violinist emerges as an inspired artist wrestling with evil forces. What are described
in the seven scenes are not actual facts of his life, but Paganini's meditations
on them. The scenes are marked: "First Improvisations," "Enemies," "A Meeting," "Loneliness and Despair," "Love and Consolation," "The Joy of Creative
Work and Death," "Finale—Stronger than Death."

In portraying Paganini, the choreographer was largely governed by Rachmaninoff's own wishes expressed in a letter written to Fokine. He wanted to
see Paganini with a violin, not a real one but a fantastic one that could be
impressed on the imagination. "Thus I felt that to bring Paganini to the stage,"
noted Lavrovsky, "the dancer performing his part must have his body and
movements tuned like a perfect instrument, thus symbolizing the beauty and
power of music itself. In this way the dancer's body, arms, fingers, his 'singing'
face, could help to create on the stage a vision of the fantastic violin Rachmaninoff so longed to see."

PAQUITA

Music by Léon Minkus, orchestrated by John Lanchbery. Choreography by
Rudolf Nureyev "after the original by Marius Petipa." Staged by Marika
Besobrasova. Costumes by Freddy Wittop. Lighting by Nananne Porcher.
First presented at the Theatre Royal, Drury Lane, London, November 1965,
with students of the Royal Ballet School. First presented in the United
States by American Ballet Theatre at the New York State Theatre, Lincoln
Center, July 6, 1971, with Cynthia Gregory and Michael Denard as the
principals.

This entertaining dance ballet is all we now see of an original story ballet of two acts that enjoyed success for many years in France and Russia (*Paquita* is still in the Soviet repertory). First danced in Paris at the Opéra on April 1, 1846, by Carlotta Grisi, five years after her historic success in *Giselle*, the original choreography was by Mazilier and the music by Deldevez. The story tells of a Spanish gypsy Paquita who loves Lucien, a French nobleman. Their marriage appears to be impossible because of the difference in their social positions but all turns out well when Paquita discovers that she is, in fact, the daughter of a nobleman. The first Lucien was Lucien Petipa, brother of the great choreographer and ballet master Marius Petipa.

There have been a number of *divertissements* made from either the choreography or music of the Russian version of the French original, which had revised dances by Marius Petipa and music by Léon Minkus. Alexandra Danilova staged a one-act *Paquita* for the Ballet Russe de Monte Carlo, September 20, 1949, at the Metropolitan Opera House, New York, with Danilova and Oleg Tupine in the principal roles. The Grand Ballet of the Marquis de Cuevas from 1948 and, from 1951, the New York City Ballet for some years danced a *pas de trois* arranged to some of Minkus' music to *Paquita*. The latter, with Maria Tallchief, Nora Kaye, and André Eglevsky, was first presented at the City Center, New York, February 18, 1951, with costumes by Barbara Karinska.

The *divertissement* as arranged by Nureyev, exuberantly Spanish in character, has as its principal feature six variations for soloists, ballerina, and *premier danseur*. Enclosing these solos are group ensembles. The first introduces all the girls, who herald the arrival of the ballerina. Next, as the lights go down and the girls arrange themselves in a long diagonal across the stage, her partner enters to lead her in a dance. An interesting aspect of this *pas de deux* is that the girls who accompany the leading dancers reflect in their movements the steps and gestures of the ballerina. Eight girls and the soloists dance now to the playful rhythms of castanets. The harp now introduces the first of the six variations and it is always very interesting to see these Petipa dances. Like the variations in another of his masterworks, *The Sleeping Beauty*, they remind us of his great achievement in the classic ballet. We do not make dances like this now, perhaps, but we could make nothing if we had not had dances like these by Petipa to teach us.

After variations by two of the soloists, the *danseur* and the ballerina perform their individual dances. The circle is closed by brilliant dances for two more girls. The ballet ends in a joyous finale, the ballerina performing a dazzling variation.

NOTES   Reviewing *Paquita* in the Washington *Post*, the critic Jean Battey Lewis wrote that Cynthia Gregory, in the ballerina's role, "used her extraordinary technique to dance with a wonderful freedom. Balances were held with elegant aplomb, phrases were finished with a triumphant flourish, and she tossed off 32 fouettés, punctuated by double fouettés, with breezy precision." (October 30, 1972)

Writing of the first *Paquita* and its great ballerina Carlotta Grisi, Théophile

Gautier wrote in *La Presse*, Paris, on April 6, 1846: "This ballet, where the action is perhaps a little too melodramatic, is a complete success. The richness and strangeness of the Empire costumes, the beauty of the decor, above all the perfection of Carlotta's dancing, are responsible for this success. Her final steps in the piece are of unimaginable daring and difficulty: these are a kind of hopping on the very tip of the toe with a sudden turn made with a dazzling quickness which inspires a mixture of pleasure and fear, for its execution appears impossible, although she repeats it some eight to ten times. Thunderous applause greeted the ballerina, who was called on to perform the dance twice again after the fall of the curtain."

Readers who wish to know more about Carlotta Grisi, the first Giselle, and other great ballerinas, should read *The Ballerinas* by Parmenia Miguel.

PARADE

Music by Erik Satie. Book by Jean Cocteau. Choreography by Leonide Massine. Scenery and costumes by Pablo Picasso. First presented by Diaghilev's Ballets Russes at the Théâtre du Châtelet, Paris, May 18, 1917, with Leonide Massine, Lydia Lopokova, Nicholas Zverev, Maria Chabelska, and Leon Woizikowski in leading roles. First presented in the United States by the City Center Joffrey Ballet at the City Center, New York, March 22, 1973, with Gary Chryst, Eileen Brady, Gregory Huffman, Donna Cowen, and Robert Talmage in leading roles.

Renowned collaboration of the Diaghilev era, unique combination of the gifts of Satie, Cocteau, Massine, and Picasso, *Parade* proves yet again in the 1970s the genius of the Diaghilev Ballets Russes in generating artistic collaboration of the highest order. When relatively few of the ballets created under Diaghilev's direction can be seen in our theaters (only *Petrouchka, Firebird*—in another version, *Spectre de la Rose, Apollo,* and *Prodigal Son*), in a recent season, it is refreshing to have the impresario's incomparable gifts demonstrated again for a new generation. Until its American revival, *Parade* had not been seen for forty-seven years.

Parade has long been considered a landmark for its introduction of cubism into the theater. The idea of the ballet was Jean Cocteau's. It was he who persuaded Satie and Picasso, who had never worked with the Ballets Russes, to collaborate on this undertaking in the midst of World War I. Subtitled a "Realistic Ballet," the work was intended to heighten realism; Guillaume Apollinaire, writing in the program, put the word *surrealism* onto the printed page for the first time to describe *Parade*. This would seem to point to a contrast the ballet makes visible on the stage—a contrast between performers in a traveling circus, the real people, and their managers or impresarios—public relations men who attempt to persuade the public to enjoy their arts.

Street circuses used to be common in Paris, and it is one of these that is the subject of the ballet, where the huckstering managers parade their talent to passers-by before the start of the show, with the hope that they will pay to come inside.

Massine, *Parade*'s choreographer, has said, in describing his method of making ballets, that it is sometimes the music, sometimes the theme, or the period and atmosphere of the action. With *Parade*, "the music was supreme, although the theme, too, interested me." Satie's score, like Picasso's settings and costumes visually, radically reflected new directions in sound and sense, mixing everyday noises, the real, with the imaginative expectation.

The action of the ballet is direct and straightforward, with none of the mystery associated so often with the avant-garde. After a series of almost solemn, quasi-religious chords in a brief musical prelude, there is a brief quiet that reveals a drop curtain of "early Picasso" portraying a rustic backstage scene of players relaxing before a performance. This inner curtain rises to show a scene by the same artist that is clearly different: a curtained booth, askew but making sense at once as a stage for the public to view a performance. Here parades an odd creature, the like of which has never been seen walking—a huge, pipe-smoking man made up of angles and planes and no softness. This is the French Manager, who introduces the Chinese Conjuror, who emerges from the curtained booth to amuse us with tricks—sword swallowing, etc.—to simulated oriental music. In a splendid multicolored costume he fairly dazzles us with his entertainment and then disappears behind the curtain.

There is a flourish and another huckster comes out, this the Manager from New York, his costume an amalgam of skyscrapers and curious angles. He carries a megaphone and a sign reading PARADE. He consults and commiserates with his French colleague, then introduces his specialty, a Little American Girl, a perpetual child in white middy blouse with a bow in her hair. To the menacing sound of multiple typewriters and gun shots, she dances a machine-age number, all winsomeness and cute charm. But her dance is more than that—it epitomizes, in small compass, the European image of America as heard by an acute ear and reflected by an acute eye in 1917. The imagery is almost totally derived from popular songs and movies. As the music imitates American dance rhythms, the little girl runs the gamut of stock U.S. melodrama—cops and robbers, rescue from a storm at sea, etc., at the end of which she bounces off as cheerily as she entered. At the end, her Manager is just as disappointed as his predecessor: no audience responds enough to come into their theater. He and the French Manager cannot understand this indifference.

Now in silence comes a brown-and-white Horse, grinning from ear to ear. Somewhat bashfully he entertains us, too, and prances out. The curtains close behind him. When they part again, we see two Acrobats, a girl and a boy, who dance a circuslike *pas de deux*, simulating tricks of the ring and high wire.

After the Acrobats finish, to the sound of a screaming siren the two Managers and the American Girl return. Next, the Horse and the Conjuror, finally the Acrobats, all in a reprise of their acts. In unison, they urge us, the audience, to come into their theater to see more. When we do not, they form a kind of cortege and the Horse lies down. The curtain falls as the music of the beginning is heard again.

NOTES   There are many accounts of the origins of *Parade* but none more complete than those in *Cocteau,* Francis Steegmuller's biography of the librettist, in Leonide Massine's autobiography, and in Douglas Cooper's book, *Picasso Theatre*. Cooper, Picasso's collaborator, assisted the revival by the City Center Joffrey Ballet, and also wrote about it at length in *Dance and Dancers* magazine. He said of the presentation, which had been re-created by Leonide Massine himself:

"The famous drop curtain, revealed during the opening section of the music, showed one of the most romantically evocative and tender of all Picasso's circus compositions. But behind it lay a surprising and colorful contemporary reality. A proscenium opening, decorated with scrolls and a lyre, was painted red and yellow, and set among whitish buildings, with dark windows, and some dark-green foliage. The Chinese Conjuror had a scarlet tunic, strikingly patterned in yellow and grey, over black trousers with a yellow pattern. The two Acrobats had sky-blue tights with bold ornamental motifs in white, while the Little American Girl had a dark-blue middy jacket over a white skirt.

"Each of these turns was presented successively by one of the two so-called Managers, dancers raised to eleven-foot-high figures by an elaborately carpentered, descriptively symbolic superstructure rising from their shoulders. Both wore a sort of formal evening dress and a top hat, but were equipped with buildings and other attributes to establish their national character: thus the American had the Woolworth building, a megaphone and some flags, while the French Manager had houses, trees, a staff and a long-stemmed pipe.

"Massine cleverly characterized each role in his choreography, which made much use of mime. The subtly emphasized rhythms beaten out by the four legs of the Horse, in an enchantingly comic, acrobatic dance without music, was a triumph of his invention. While the Managers were made to convey the force of their huckstering and despair by ungainly movements, by demonstrative and angry steps and by towering over all around them.

"Massine had the good fortune to find in the Joffrey Ballet a marvelous group of young dancers who worked with him brilliantly in this recreation of *Parade*. For it is a ballet which requires the performers to show style, precision of movement, perfect timing, athletic prowess, great powers of mime and especially a sense of enjoying what they are doing. Gary Chryst, assuming Massine's original role (the Chinese Conjuror), displayed that nervous intensity, speed, suavity, and air of mystery which is required for the character. His flickering hands, his shuffle, his leaps and especially his elevation were superbly timed and amazing to watch, as were the mimed passages of his dance where he finds an egg in his pigtail, digests it and recovers it from the toe of his shoe, or swallows a sword or eats fire.

"Donna Cowen, the first native-born American ever to dance the role of the Little American Girl, showed a marvelous sense of ragtime and was by turns pert, droll and captivating as she danced and mimed her way through the episodes of the ungainly typewriter, of the encounter with Indians, of the wreck of the *Titanic* or of the rosy dawning. The graceful and wistful *pas de deux* for the two Acrobats, who tumble, climb ropes, perform trapeze and walk a tightrope, was danced with great feeling and dexterity by Brady and Huffman. The Managers and the Horse gave their numbers with great distinction and all the fun and noise of the fair. The music was rendered in strict accordance with Satie's published score so that the incidental sound effects were confined to a typewriter, a ship's siren and some revolver shots at the appropriate times."

Cooper recalls that in staging the ballet, Massine was able to consult with dancers living in New York who had once appeared in various roles, notably Maria Chabelska, Vera Nemtchinova, Lydia Sokolova, and Michel Pavloff, while Boris Kochno also made a contribution from Paris. Lydia Sokolova in her memoirs had written prophetically: "*Parade* was so delightful that I am sure it would be a favorite if it could be done today."

PARADISE LOST

Music by Marius Constant. Choreography by Roland Petit. Libretto by Jean Cau. Scenery by Martial Raysse. First presented by the Royal Ballet at the Royal Opera House, Covent Garden, London, February 23, 1967, with Margot Fonteyn and Rudolf Nureyev. First presented in the United States by the Royal Ballet at the New Metropolitan Opera House, New York, May 10, 1967, with the same cast.

This ballet is based not on John Milton but on a poem by Jean Cau: "Every paradise is found in order to be lost." What happens is that we first see a huge egg, outlined in neon, then in lights a countdown that flashes 5 . . . 4 . . . 3 . . . 2 . . . 1 . . . and then the birth of Man who turns out to be Adam. He walks down a ramp and the dancing begins.

In the words of Alexander Bland of *The Observer*, the action "is traced in a long series of solos and duets which make the first half of the ballet one of the most stimulating dance experiences in a long time—Adam exploring his nature and powers; his first intimation of pain and the birth of Eve; their mutual suspicion thawing into complete harmony; the change wrought by the Serpent, Eve twisting into seduction and Adam into aggressive sexuality, ending in a denouement as theatrically breath-taking as Nijinsky's leap in *Spectre de la Rose*." The hero runs and jumps headfirst into a huge mouth of Eve.

Innocence is further destroyed by an attacking crowd and God's wrath finally descends. Peter Williams wrote in the *Sunday Times* of London: "The fall is frozen in yet another sublime 'fallen-angel' composition—Man crashed to earth with his body curved across the neck of the sorrowing Woman."

PAS DES DÉESSES

Music by John Field. Choreography by Robert Joffrey. First presented by the Robert Joffrey Ballet Concert at the Kaufmann Auditorium, Y.M.H.A., New York, May 29, 1954, with Lillian Wellein (Taglioni), Barbara Gray (Grahn), Jacquetta Kieth (Cerrito), and Michael Lland (Saint-Léon).

Inspired by a romantic lithograph of 1846 by Bouvier, *Pas des Déesses* re-creates the ballet style of that day. At the start, four dancers are seen in the pose of this famous print. Each represents a famous dancer of the romantic era in ballet and each of the dances that follow displays the qualities made famous by the quartet—the languorous Danish ballerina Lucile Grahn, the darting Italian, Fanny Cerrito, and the floating Marie Taglioni, all strongly supported by the gallant Arthur Saint-Léon. The air of competition among the three ballerinas echoes the delicate rivalry which existed among these celebrated dancers.

The music for the ballet is by the Irish piano virtuoso John Field (1782–1837), who originated the name and style of the Nocturne. The ballet uses selected nocturnes, rondos, and waltzes.

The first *Pas des Déesses* was performed at His Majesty's Theatre, London, during the 1846 season by Taglioni, Cerrito, Grahn, and Saint-Léon. Choreography was by Jules Perrot.

PAS DE DIX

Classic ballet. Music by Alexander Glazunov. Choreography by George Balanchine. Costumes by Esteban Francés. Lighting by Jean Rosenthal. First presented by the New York City Ballet at the City Center, New York, November 9, 1955, with Maria Tallchief and André Eglevsky; Barbara Fallis, Constance Garfield, Jane Mason, Barbara Walczak, Shaun O'Brien, Roy Tobias, Roland Vasquez, and Jonathan Watts.

The music for this dance for ten (two principals plus four girls and four boys) is taken from a ballet score I have always liked since my student days in Russia, Glazunov's *Raymonda*. I danced in Petipa's original production of this ballet at the Maryinsky Theatre when I was studying at the Imperial Ballet School. Some years ago, for the Ballet Russe de Monte Carlo, Alexandra Danilova and I put together our version of Petipa's last act—the nuptial festivities of the Hungarian lady Raymonda and the Count Jean de Brienna—a dance ballet that follows the narrative.

Except for one brief variation, all the music for the *Pas de Dix* is taken from this same act, but there is no attempt here to approximate Petipa's original, which no one remembers accurately, anyway. What I have done instead is to try to make an entertaining spectacle with no story, simply a series of dances for a ballerina, her partner, and a small ensemble. The music will be familiar, I think, to those who know the Russian repertory.

PAS DE DUKE

Music by Duke Ellington. Choreography by Alvin Ailey. Scenery and costumes by Rouben Ter-Arutunian. First presented by the Alvin Ailey City

Center Dance Theatre at the City Center, New York, May 11, 1976, with Judith Jamison and Mikhail Baryshnikov.

Created for a special gala occasion and to honor the late Duke Ellington, this ballet was a *pas de deux* for two performers with radically different preparations—one a star of a modern dance company, the other a star of classic ballet. The choreographer brought the two together for a jazz ballet and made for the classic dancer a modern role he had not thought possible. The result was a memorable duet.

Clive Barnes recalled afterward in the New York *Times* that "it was remarkable how well Mr. Baryshnikov had absorbed the Ailey technique, and how well the two of them went together. It was sheer fun and Mr. Ailey was at his most persuasively inventive. It is always a delight to see Mr. Baryshnikov doing jazz movements—he performs a little naughtily, like a bright child talking faultlessly in a foreign language with a charming and slightly accentuated accent."

PAS DE QUATRE

Divertissement. *Music by Cesare Pugni. Choreography by Jules Perrot. First presented at His Majesty's Theatre, London, July 12, 1845, with Marie Taglioni, Carlotta Grisi, Fanny Cerrito, and Lucile Grahn.*

This short ballet is probably the most famous *divertissement* in the history of dance. It displayed in one work four of the greatest ballerinas of its time, bringing these talents together for several memorable performances that have excited the curiosity of dance lovers for more than a hundred years. At this distance, it is impossible for us to tell exactly what *Pas de Quatre* looked like as a ballet, but information about what it resembled, and the unprecedented occasion it undoubtedly was, has come down to us in lithographs and reviews. If the greatest ballerinas of the United States, France, England, and the U.S.S.R. were to appear together in a ballet today, we should have some approximation of the excitement caused by the original *Pas de Quatre*. If such a *Pas de Quatre* seems impossible today, we must remember that it also seemed impossible in 1845.

Among all artists there is bound to be competition, and in the 1840s it seemed unlikely that any four of the great ballerinas would consent to dance on the same stage. Marie Taglioni had been acknowledged the finest dancer in the world when she created the title role in *La Sylphide* in 1832, and even thirteen years after her first famous role, she was still considered supreme in the realm of the romantic ballet that she had helped to create. But with the coming of the romantic era, there were also other ballerinas who danced in similar ballets: exceptional among these dancers were Fanny Cerrito, who was acclaimed in the early 1840s, Carlotta Grisi, who danced in 1841 the first performance of *Giselle*, and the Danish ballerina Lucile Grahn, who had successfully danced Taglioni's role in *La Sylphide*. The fact that each ballerina had danced *Giselle* (Taglioni, Cerrito, and Grahn undertook Grisi's original role in 1843) gives us an indication of their rivalry. There was, in short, so much natural jealousy between these four—and each faction of the public showed so great an amount of enthusiasm for its chosen goddess among them—that it appeared unlikely that the ballerinas would expose themselves to any common venture.

The man who thought otherwise and acted with persistence until he achieved his goal was the enterprising manager of His Majesty's Theatre in London, Benjamin Lumley. "The government of a great state was but a trifle compared to the government of such subjects as those whom I was *supposed* to be able to command," he recollected almost twenty years after the event. "These were subjects who considered themselves far above mortal control, or, more properly speaking, each was a queen in her own right—alone, absolute, supreme."

Lumley was encouraged to assemble the four ballerinas by a success he had brought off in 1843, when Fanny Cerrito danced at his theatre in a *pas de deux* with Fanny Elssler, the fifth great ballerina of this period. Why Elssler was not invited to participate in Lumley's assembly of ballerinas in 1845 is perhaps partially explained by this earlier triumph, but not altogether so. For Elssler's fame equaled, if it did not actually exceed, Taglioni's. No doubt that is exactly the point. Taglioni's superiority was unquestioned throughout Europe until Elssler made her début at the Paris Opéra in 1834. From this point on, the rivalry between the two was bitter. Elssler taunted Taglioni and her admirers by threatening to dance *La Sylphide*, which no other dancer yet dared to do. When Elssler essayed Taglioni's famous role in this ballet in 1838, open war broke out, and seven years later it must have been clear even to Benjamin Lumley that between these rivals there could never be peace. Théophile Gautier, who was to become the originator of *Giselle*, the friend and critical sponsor of Carlotta Grisi, wrote in 1837 that Fanny Elssler's dancing had a special quality that distinguished her from all other dancers and proceeded to make his point clear in a fashion that must have made the rivalry between the newcomer and the "Sylphide" intense: ". . . it is not the aerial and virginal grace of Taglioni, it is something more human, more appealing to the senses. Mademoiselle Taglioni is a Christian dancer, if one may make use of such an expression in regard to an art proscribed by the Catholic faith; she flies like a spirit in the midst of transparent clouds of white muslin with which she loves to surround herself, she resembles a happy angel who scarcely bends the petals of celestial flowers with the tips of her pink toes. Fanny is a quite pagan dancer; she reminds one of the muse Terpsichore, tambourine in hand, her tunic, exposing her thigh, caught up with a golden clasp; when she bends freely from the hips, throwing back her swooning, voluptuous arms, we seem to see one of those beautiful figures from Herculaneum or Pompeii which stand out in white relief against a black background . . ."

And Elssler was not praised only in Europe. She came to the United States in 1840 for a three-month tour and did not return to Europe for two years— two years during which she became the toast of the nation. She was welcomed by President Martin Van Buren, escorted by his son, entertained by Congress, carried on the shoulders of adoring crowds, and so universally acclaimed that she could declare, with accuracy, that "never was an artiste more completely seated in public sympathy." In nineteenth-century America she anticipated the exclusive success enjoyed by Anna Pavlova seventy years later.

But Benjamin Lumley also had grounds for being discouraged. His predecessor at His Majesty's Theatre had announced, but had been unable to present, Taglioni, Cerrito, and Elssler in a special performance. Circumstances, too, contrived against him. He had chosen Jules Perrot, the former partner of Taglioni and the choreographer who had collaborated on *Giselle,* to arrange the dances for the *Pas de Quatre,* and everyone was ready to begin—except one of the ballerinas. Carlotta Grisi, Perrot's wife, seemed unable to fulfill her engagement on time. She was dancing in Paris; how was she to get to London for rehearsals? Lumley tells us how: "A vessel was chartered . . . to waft the sylph at a moment's notice across the Channel; a special train was engaged and ready at Dover; relays of horses were in waiting to aid the flight of the *danseuse,* all the way from Paris to Calais."

When Grisi arrived, Perrot began to work on the most difficult assignment a ballet master ever had. He had not only to invent an ensemble that the four ballerinas would perform together, he had also to devise individual dances that would display ideally the particular artistry of each performer without distracting from the excellence of her sisters. In Lumley's words, "no one was to outshine the others—unless in their own individual belief." Perrot had worked closely on other projects with each of the four dancers previously and knew their temperaments; as the finest *danseur* of his time and a choreographer of equal fame, he also knew his job.

He seemed to succeed. The ballerinas were content with what they were to dance together and pleased with their variations; the costumes were ready, the theater sold out. And then came the problem of who was to dance first—or, rather, last, for the final variation in every ballet, as in regal processions, according to Lumley, is performed by the superior artist. Cerrito, Grisi, and Grahn agreed that Taglioni, because of her unprecedented fame, should occupy this place of honor. But as to the penultimate variation, the ladies disagreed: who was to be closest to Taglioni? Cerrito and Grisi vied for the position and quarreled on stage. Finally Grisi lost her temper, called Cerrito "a little chit," and the two ballerinas vowed they would never appear together.

Perrot, in despair, told the bad news to the manager. Lumley recalled what the choreographer said: "*Mon Dieu!* Cerrito won't begin before Carlotta, nor Carlotta before Cerrito, and there isn't anything that will make them change their minds: we're finished!" And Lumley also recalled what he replied: "The solution is easy . . . In this dilemma there is one point on which I am sure the ladies will be frank. Let the oldest take her unquestionable right to the envied position."

Perrot returned to the stage to try this ruse. When he told the two ballerinas the manager's decision, everything suddenly changed: they "tittered, laughed, drew back, and were now as much disinclined to accept the right of position as they had been eager to claim it." The trick worked! Taglioni was at this time forty-one, Cerrito was twenty-eight, and Grisi twenty-six: the reverse order was thus established, with Grahn, who was twenty-four, leading with the first variation. Lumley says that "the *grand pas de quatre* was finally performed on the same night before a delighted audience, who little knew how nearly they had been deprived of their expected treat."

What this audience saw was recorded by several critics, and approximations of the performance have been given us in modern representations of this *divertissement*. When the curtain went up, the four ballerinas appeared before a romantic background. They entered in a line, holding hands; each was dressed in billowing muslin and each wore in her hair a crown of white flowers, except Cerrito, who wore flowers in the knot at the back of her head. The ballerinas smiled, walked to the footlights, and bowed. The audience could not believe it. One member of the audience did not want to believe it and threw down from the gallery a shower of placards that declared Cerrito the peer of all dancers in the world. The audience was embarrassed and frightened of the possible consequences, but then someone laughed, the dancers smiled, and the music began.

The *Pas de Quatre* commenced in soft stillness as the four ballerinas moved toward the backdrop and arranged themselves in charming tableau about Taglioni, who looked down upon her sisters with an expression of sincere sweetness. Even the slightest display of jealousy was impossible now, for each artist was thoroughly aware that the ballet would surely fail if any of them failed to be as perfect as Perrot imagined they were and that they would be responsible. And so they knelt about Taglioni, opened their arms to her in a gesture of affection and respect, and smiled as innocently as she did. They changed their position, and the graceful Taglioni seemed to fall back in their welcoming arms.

The actual dancing began with a short variation by Grahn to quick, lively music. This was followed by a *pas de deux* by Cerrito and Grisi, which came to an end as Taglioni crossed the stage in high, light leaps that seemed to make her a part of the air. This introduction was merely a hint as to what was to follow in the four virtuoso variations. Grahn came first, dancing quickly, lightly, turning and hopping on point, moving about the stage with the controlled vigor of shining youth. Next, as the music changed, Carlotta Grisi stepped forward and danced with a sharp but airy vibrancy, a solo that summed up in a few short minutes her great fame.

Taglioni and Grahn, the oldest and the youngest, now danced together to a brief romantic measure. Cerrito was posed gracefully on stage with them, apparently waiting for them to finish their duet. Suddenly she cut this dainty and quiet sequence short, darting forward like an arrow released from the taut bow and describing a long, swift diagonal of accelerated turns. She finished her variation in a display of still, balanced poses contrasted with unparalleled verve and speed.

Taglioni, as the last of these great dancers, had the most difficult variation of all: she had to show the audience that what they had rejoiced in so far could be climaxed. And this she did, not by dancing in any fashion novel to her, but in a manner that epitomized her reputation: she moved with supreme lightness and she moved effortlessly, dazzling the audience with controlled poses even in midflight. And she moved with unquestioned authority, with the highest knowledge of her great gift and of her own faithful obedience to it, pausing in perfect balance with the grace and refinement of the mature artist.

Now, at the end, the three other ballerinas joined her. They all danced together, each trying to outdo the others in a final display of virtuosity. Then, as if they all understood that competition was in vain, they arranged themselves again in the tender tableau with which they had begun. Taglioni raised her arms over her head and looked down upon the other three, who gathered about her quietly and looked toward the audience with pensive, beguiling smiles, as if they had never moved.

NOTES And what was the critical opinion of this *Pas de Quatre?* The *Times* of London called it "the greatest Terpsichorean exhibition that ever was known in Europe . . . Never was such a *pas* before. The excitement which a competition so extraordinary produced in the artists roused them to a pitch of energy which would have been impossible under other circumstances, and hence everyone did her utmost, the whole performance being a complete inspiration . . . The whole long *pas* was danced to a running sound of applause, which, after each variation, swelled to a perfect hurricane . . . Bouquets flew from every point, an immense profusion, as each *danseuse* came forward, so that they had to curtsy literally in the midst of a shower of floral gifts. Cerrito's wreaths and nosegays were more than she could hold in both her arms . . . The front of the stage was almost covered with flower leaves."

The critic of the *Illustrated London News* reported: "No description can render the exquisite, the almost ethereal, grace of movement and attitude of these great dancers, and those who have witnessed the scene may boast of having once, at least, seen the perfection of the art of dancing. . . ."

The best accounts of three of the four ballerinas are given by their contemporary Théophile Gautier. Gautier did not review the *Pas de Quatre*, but he speaks here of Taglioni the year before the London *divertissement:* "Mademoiselle Taglioni is not a dancer, she is the embodiment of dancing . . . Fortunate woman. Always the same elegant and slender form, the same calm, intelligent and modest features; not a single feather has fallen from her wing; not a hair has silvered beneath her chaplet of flowers! As the curtain rose, she was greeted with thunders of applause. What airiness! What rhythmic movements! What noble gestures! What poetic attitudes and, above all, what a sweet melancholy! What lack of restraint, yet how chaste!"

Gautier speaks of Cerrito two years after the *Pas de Quatre:* "Fanny Cerrito's principal qualities are grace of pose, unusual attitudes, quickness of movement, and the rapidity with which she covers ground; she bounds and rebounds with an admirable ease and elasticity; there is a charming grace about her whole body. . . . She radiates a sense of happiness, brilliance, and smiling ease which know neither labor nor weariness. . . ."

Of Carlotta Grisi, Gautier had this to say at the time of her début at the Paris Opéra (1841): "She is possessed of a strength, lightness, suppleness and originality which at once place her between Elssler and Taglioni." Two years later he was to write that "Grisi's dancing has a quite special style; it does not resemble the dancing of either Taglioni or Elssler; each one of her poses, each one of her movements, is stamped with the seal of originality."

Pas de Quatre with its original cast was performed only four times (July 12, 15, 17, and 19, 1845). Queen Victoria and the Prince Consort attended the third performance. Three of the original cast—Taglioni, Cerrito, and Grisi—danced in a revival of the *divertissement* that was performed twice in Lumley's theater: on July 17 and 19, 1847. Carolina Rosati replaced Lucile Grahn in these performances. Rosati at this time was only twenty years old; fifteen years later, in Russia, she was to dance the leading role in *The Daughter of Pharaoh* (Pugni), the first great success of the ballet master Marius Petipa.

A year after the first performance of the original *Pas de Quatre*, Taglioni, Grahn, and Cerrito danced together at Lumley's theater in a ballet called *The Judgment of Paris* (Pugni-Perrot). The ballerinas danced the parts of three goddesses in this *divertissement*, which was hailed almost as loudly as *Pas de Quartre*. *The Judgment of Paris* was Marie Taglioni's last new ballet.

Marie Taglioni retired soon after she danced the revival of *Pas de Quatre* and died impoverished in Marseille, France, in 1884, at the age of eighty. Fanny Cerrito, at the time of her appearance in London, had yet to achieve her fullest fame and in the 1840s and 1850s secured for herself additional triumphs. She died in 1909 at the age of ninety-two. Carlotta Grisi had new successes after the famous *divertissement*, creating the title role in *Paquita* (Mazilier-Deldevez) in 1846 and dancing at the Imperial Theatre in St. Petersburg. She was seventy-eight when she died in 1899. Lucile Grahn, the youngest of the *Pas de Quatre* ballerinas, had danced in Russia before she came to London for Lumley's *divertissement*. Trained in her native Denmark by the great Danish ballet master Auguste Bournonville, Grahn made her début at the Royal Theatre, Copenhagen, in 1835. In this theater Grahn danced a version of *La Sylphide* created for her by Bournonville (1836). This production of the famous ballet has been in the repertory of the Royal Danish Ballet ever since it was first performed. Grahn died in 1907 at the age of eighty-six.

Another historic presentation of *Pas de Quatre* took place January 24, 1972, at the City Center, New York, at the Gala Performance for the Dance Collection of the New York Public Library. Anton Dolin, who had reconstructed the ballet for American Ballet Theatre in 1941, did so again, this time bringing together Carla Fracci as Taglioni, Violette Verdy as Grisi, Patricia McBride as Cerrito, and Eleanor D'Antuono as Grahn.

LES PATINEURS (The Skaters)

Ballet in one act. Music by Giacomo Meyerbeer. Choreography by Frederick Ashton. Scenery and costumes by William Chappell. First presented by the Vic-Wells Ballet at the Sadler's Wells Theatre, London, February 16, 1937, with a cast headed by Margot Fonteyn, Robert Helpmann, and Harold Turner. First presented in the United States by Ballet Theatre at the Broad-

way Theatre, New York, October 2, 1946. Scenery and costumes by Cecil Beaton. Nora Kaye, Hugh Laing, and John Kriza danced the leading roles.

Some people watch ice skating and say how like dancing it is. *Les Patineurs* shows us how dancing, among other things, can imitate ice skating. The ballet has no story; it simply organizes what any of us might see at a skating rink into a series of nine *divertissements*. The music, arranged by Constant Lambert, is based on selections from Meyerbeer's operas *L'Étoile du Nord* and *Le Prophète*. The Ballet Theatre production is described here.

The music is whistling, thumping holiday fare. The scene is any secluded skating pond, the time, night. Snowy branches of barren trees hang over the pond; brightly colored paper lanterns light up the forest. Four couples skate across the scene. Two pretty girls follow them, slipping and turning on the ice. One of the boys in the skating party falls; his girl brushes him off, and they exit. A boy in bright green rushes in and treats us to a quick, dazzling display of virtuosity and skates off as though he'd done nothing at all.

The harp signals a romantic melody, and two lovers enter. The boy carries the girl high on his shoulder, sets her down, and she turns close to the ground. The couple are dressed in white and seem at home in the snow-laden scene. They circle the stage, the boy lifting the girl softly to the right and left. For a moment they separate; then they rejoin, and the boy spins the girl around and around. They skate away, hand in hand.

Eight couples—the girls in bright red and the boys in yellow and blue—fill the skating area. Two girls take over the pond and dance brightly to a tinkling tune. The lovers join the eight couples and dance with them a gay ensemble. The boy in green circles the stage, then leaves. Now the ensemble moves with a slower grace. The boy in green now shows off among them, and all watch him. When he is finished, they turn to watch four girls who are skating apart from the crowd; then all skate off in a circling line.

The boy in green and the two girls who danced the first *divertissement* perform a *pas de trois*. Soon they are followed by two other girls, who do an incredible number of fast, accelerated *fouettés*. The boy in green hails the others in the party to come back, and everyone promenades. Snow begins to fall. The girls resume their *fouettés*, whirling away faster than ever as the exhilarating music comes to a climax. The boy in green is challenged by their skill to turn faster than ever and he is spinning like a top when the curtain falls.

PAVANE

Music by Maurice Ravel. Choreography by George Balanchine. Lighting by Ronald Bates. First presented by the New York City Ballet at the Hommage à Ravel at the New York State Theatre, Lincoln Center, May 29, 1975, with Patricia McBride. Conducted by Robert Irving.

This work of Ravel's, the *Pavane pour une Infante Défunte*, or *Pavane for a Dead Child*, is perhaps the best-known of his compositions after the ever pop-

ular *Boléro*. This popularity is perhaps due to the name of the piece; everyone
feels sentimental about the mere idea of it. Yet Ravel himself felt that the
work owed its success to its "remarkable interpretations." He wrote: "Do not
attach to the title any more importance than it has. It is not a pavane for a
dead child but, rather, an evocation of the pavanes that could have been
danced by such a little princess as painted by Velásquez at the Spanish court."

The dance to this music is arranged for a girl who responds to a ghostly idea
among the living. The dictionary defines a pavane as a slow, stately dance. So
does this girl perform it, in a flowing white gown, gossamer and a preparation
for the shroud.

As the curtain rises, the girl, veiled, stands at the back of the stage. She
shields her eyes in grief, then begins to dance. Cradling her hands as if to hold
a child, the girl moves like the wind, yet royally, in a processional manner. In
control of her long train, she lets it swirl about her, then covers her face with it
and stands alone, grieving.

NOTES   The critic Byron Belt wrote after the premiere, in the *Long Island
Press*: "*Pavane* is an undulating treatment of mourning, at once poignant and
sensuous. Patricia McBride, swathed in white, uses a long scarf in the manner
of an Art Nouveau Isadora Duncan, but it is carried off with such fragile
beauty that the work seems astonishingly fresh and strong . . . *Pavane* . . .
was created for a dancer magnificently able to dominate the stage completely
with her virtuosity."

PELLÉAS AND MÉLISANDE

*Music by Arnold Schoenberg. Choreography by Roland Petit. Scenery and
costumes by Jacques Dupont. First presented by the Royal Ballet, March
26, 1969, at the Royal Opera House, Covent Garden, London, with Margot
Fonteyn, Rudolf Nureyev, and Keith Rosson in the principal roles. First
presented in the United States by the same ensemble at the Metropolitan
Opera House, Lincoln Center, New York, May 5, 1969. Conducted by John
Lanchbery.*

The choreographer of this ballet, Roland Petit, has written his own synopsis of
the action and a comment:

"Mélisande is lost in the forest. Golaud finds her and falls in love. She
senses that another destiny awaits her and when Pelléas, Golaud's brother, arrives, he and Mélisande instantly recognize that it has come.

"Golaud leads her away, but she returns to Pelléas with her long hair
streaming round her. Golaud becomes tormented by jealousy and, seeing the
lovers together, he stabs Pelléas. Mélisande dies of a broken heart. Reunited in
death, the lovers are resurrected for Eternity from their forest grave.

"Pelléas and Mélisande like Romeo and Juliet are part of a legend which
has through the centuries taught subsequent generations about love. The

forces that unite or divide, that kill or revive them still constitute the very substance of love.

"Today love does not have to come under the same judgment as of old, nor to surmount the same obstacles, but love itself is the same, with fewer frills and furbelows, even, perhaps, stripped naked. This is why I have chosen to play down the circumstances that we connect with Pelléas and Mélisande. Instead, I have attempted to portray them as they appear in us. Hounded by an identical destiny, we see in them what we feel happening in ourselves."

The ballet is arranged to the tone poem of the same name by Arnold Schoenberg, who wrote that "inspired entirely by Maeterlinck's wonderful drama, I have tried to mirror every detail of it."

Reviewing *Pelléas and Mélisande* after its first performance, in *The Observer* of London, the critic Alexander Bland noted that the ballet was featured at a gala to celebrate Margot Fonteyn's thirty-fifth year with the Royal Ballet: "It has been an incredible career which has seen her steadily progress to that peak of artistry where, like a mature draughtsman, she can express everything with almost nothing. She packs richness into simplicity, conceals technique under nonchalance and melts emotion into classical economy and integrity . . . There is one effective moment when Mélisande dominates the stage with a tent of gauzy tresses . . . in which Pelléas becomes voluptuously entangled."

LA PÉRI

Music by Norbert Burgmüller. Choreography by Jean Coralli. Book by Théophile Gautier and Jean Coralli. First presented at the Théâtre de l'Académie Royal de Musique, Paris, July 17, 1843, with Carlotta Grisi and Lucien Petipa. Presented in a new version by Frederick Ashton, by the Royal Ballet at the Royal Opera House, Covent Garden, February 15, 1956, with Margot Fonteyn and Michael Somes. Music by Paul Dukas. Scenery by Ivor Hitchens. Costumes by André Levasseur. First presented in the United States by the Royal Ballet, September 26, 1957, at the Metropolitan Opera House. Presented in a new version by George Skibine to the Dukas score at the Opéra, Paris, December 1966, with Calire Motte and Jean-Pierre Bonnefous. Setting by Robert D. Mitchell. Costumes and lighting by Nicholas Cernovich. First presented in the United States by the National Ballet of Washington, with Andrea Vodehnal and Steven Grebel, at the Lisner Auditorium, Washington, February 26, 1967.

According to Persian mythology, *péris* are fallen angels who assume the form of elfin sprites. There have been many ballets created around the story of Iskender and his search for the lotus, the flower of immortality, and his encounter with a *péri*. Iskender wanders far and wide searching for the flower, which he finds at last in the hand of a lovely sleeping *péri*. He steals the flower but cannot leave, for he adores the girl he sees lying before him. When she wakens, the *péri* senses his want, and dances to play upon his desire so that she may regain the flower. Iskender is bewitched and in exchange for a kiss would give her the world. He returns the flower. "Then the lotus seemed like snow and gold like the summit of Elbourz in the evening sun. The form of the *péri* appeared to melt into the light emanating from the calyx. Iskender saw her disappear. And realizing that this signified his approaching end, he felt the shadow encircling him."

This story and its heroine have fascinated choreographers and dancers for more than a hundred years. There have been many dances based on the original two-act ballet with Théophile Gautier's scenario. Grisi, Pavlova (in a version by Clustine, 1921), Spessivtzeva (in the ballet by Leo Staats, 1921), Markova (in Frederick Ashton's first version, 1931, for the Ballet Club, London), Yvette Chauvire (in the version by Serge Lifar, 1948), and others. The Dukas score was commissioned by the Russian ballerina Natalia Trouhanova and first performed by her in Paris, April 22, 1912.

PERSEPHONE

Melodrama in three scenes. Music by Igor Stravinsky. French text by André Gide. Choreography by Kurt Jooss. Scenery and costumes by André Barsacq. First presented by Ballets Ida Rubinstein at the Opéra, Paris, April 30, 1934, with Ida Rubinstein in the title role. Revived in a new version by the Royal Ballet, with choreography by Frederick Ashton at the Royal Opera House, Covent Garden, London, December 12, 1961. Scenery and costumes by Nico Ghika. Svetlana Beriosova appeared in the title role.

The ballet tells the story of Persephone, daughter of Zeus and Demeter, goddess of fertility, who was taken away to the Underworld by Pluto, its king. In the first scene, "The Abduction of Persephone," Persephone on "the world's first morning" is warned not to pick the narcissus, for whoever breathes its fragrance must come to see a vision of Hades. But Persephone admires the flower and as she smells it she glimpses the sorrowful Shades of the Underworld, who must endlessly wander until the end of time. She has pity on them. Eumolpus, the high priest, tells Persephone that if she will go to the Underworld the lot of the Shades will be happier. Pluto claims Persephone, who descends to the Underworld.

In the second scene, "Persephone in the Underworld," she has become Queen of the Shades. With her descent, Pluto has banished spring from the earth. Biting a pomegranate presented to her by Mercury, she recalls the earth above, her mother, and her earthly husband, Demaphoon. Eumolpus relates that the earthly winter will not last forever and that it is Demeter's plan to cause Demaphoon to teach men to till the soil, thereby bringing them salvation. Through his intercession, Persephone is reborn and goes to rejoin her earthly husband.

"Persephone Reborn," the final scene, shows the goddess reunited with her mother and husband; spring returns to the earth. Having restored the seasons, Persephone realizes that her destiny lies with the Shades and that she must again return to rule over them at Pluto's side. Taking a torch offered her by Mercury to light her way back into the darkness, Persephone makes her farewell.

PETROUCHKA

Ballet burlesque in one act, four scenes. Music by Igor Stravinsky. Choreography by Michel Fokine. Book by Stravinsky and Alexandre Benois. Scenery and costumes by Benois. First presented by Diaghilev's Ballets Russes at the Théâtre du Châtelet, Paris, June 13, 1911, with Vaslav Nijinsky as Petrouchka, Tamara Karsavina as the Ballerina, Alexandre Orlov as the Moor, *and Enrico Cecchetti as the* Charlatan. *First presented in the United States by Diaghilev's Ballets Russes at the Century Theatre, New York, January 25, 1916, with Leonide Massine, Lydia Lopokova, and Adolph Bolm in the principal roles.*

Petrouchka tells the story of a puppet with a human heart, a creature of straw who comes to life only to be disbelieved. Characters similar to Petrouchka, half comic, half tragic, have been common to popular theatrical tradition in Europe for hundreds of years—characters such as Pierrot and Puck, clowns no one will ever take seriously, funny men who are always unlucky but who somehow manage to have in the end more wisdom than anybody else; funny men such as Charlie Chaplin's tramp. *Petrouchka* is ballet's representation of this universal character, of what the creators of the ballet knew in their youth as the "Russian Punch and Judy Show." At first the puppet is happy to be a mere automaton. Then he falls in love with a beautiful dancer and tries to win her, though all the world seems against him. He loses her, dies, and everyone laughs. He wins by returning for the last laugh himself.

SCENE ONE: THE SHROVETIDE FAIR   The first scene of the ballet is set in a great public square in old St. Petersburg. The year is 1830; the season, winter —the last week before Lent, when all the populace gather together for final feasting and celebration. Even before the curtain rises, the orchestra tells us it is carnival time, as the cheerful blatancy of the music swells and varies to bring up images of a surging festival, where everyone is determined to have a good time in his own way. Peasants, gypsies, soldiers, and well-dressed folk, all in holiday attire, mingle in the snow-covered square. Fair booths decorated with bright bunting and flags surround an open area, and in the back stands the largest booth of all. It has blue curtains drawn across it like a stage. Above the booth, in Russian, are the words "Living Theater." Behind it are the spires of government buildings topped with flags. The crowd tries to keep warm by moving constantly; its members stamp and throw their arms around their chests as they talk to each other; some buy hot tea at a booth with a large, steaming samovar. But the cold weather serves only to intensify their good spirits. Everyone seems to be happy and carefree in the pursuit of a traditional pleasure all can share. The open, undisguised merriment of the music whirls with the circling crowd and its quick-changing rhythms accentuate the variety of noises that refuse to blend into one tune—the loud, comradely greetings, the laughter, the shrieking of persistent barkers, the vigorous dancing of three enthusiastic peasants.

The crowd hears a barrel organ grinding away in the distance, but its small sound is almost immediately drowned out by the hubbub in the square. The organ-grinder enters, playing a street song, and the people stand aside to watch his approach. With him comes a girl who carries a little rug under her arm and a triangle. She spreads the rug over the snow, strikes the triangle in a steady beat to secure everyone's attention, and begins to dance to a gay tune. Her dance is clearly designed to show the crowd how rapidly she can turn on one point without stopping; and as people begin to be impressed by her virtuosity, the organist shows off too, by grinding out the song with one hand and duplicating it on a cornet he holds with the other. When he finishes, he begins to play again his rather mournful street song, while on the other side of the stage a rival team of entertainers has appeared to attract the crowd away. There another dancer begins to turn to the tune of a hurdy-gurdy, and a new group forms about the girl and her accompanist. The organist and his partner glance over at the newcomers and speed up the tempo of their act. The two dancers and the two instruments compete openly: each of the girls imitates the other's movements, and the crowd watches first one and then the other as if they were looking at a tennis match. Finally the girls have spent all their energy and the contest is over. Both end their dances in identical positions; the spectators applaud, reward both couples, and everyone is delighted.

The square is now packed with people, who mill about greeting one another and conversing as the orchestra renews the raucous overture. Rowdy peasants come in and dance an animated Russian folk dance to the amusement of some of the crowd. The scene is now feverish with liveliness and hearty good spirits, and the music reaches a high volume to duplicate this enthusiasm. Two drummers step out from behind the blue-curtained stage at the rear and walk forward. The crowd stands back. The drums roll commandingly; everyone looks toward the stage; a loud chord from the orchestra is cut off sharply. A man with a high-peaked hat pokes his head through the curtains. This is the Charlatan, the showman in charge of the "Living Theater." Everyone is silent as they watch him. He is a showman who entertains by magic, and when he steps out from behind the curtains, no one is quite certain what he will do. His long black robe decorated with mysterious signs, his white face, and his menacing gestures attract the crowd strangely. He takes out a flute. The orchestra sounds a few weird bars suggestive of incipient evil. Then the Charlatan surprises us by playing on his instrument not an Oriental incantation, but a pleasant melody, beseeching in its repetitions. This is his magic song, the music that will bring to life the unseen show behind the closed curtains. The crowd waits, fascinated. The Charlatan gives a sudden imperious signal. The curtains fly back. We see a stage separated into three small compartments. In each compartment rests a motionless puppet, staring out at the audience with blank expression. The three figures are supported by high armrests. In the center is the prima Ballerina, with perfect, Dresden-china features and pink cheeks. She poses rigidly, waiting to be wound up. On the left is the Moor, with white eyes and a white mouth set in a coal-black face. He wears a turban, a bright blouse with a sash about his waist, and trousers of gold brocade. On the right, completely relaxed, is Petrouchka. His face is a white mask, his body is limp, like that of a rag doll. His costume has no conventional design: the loose-fitting trousers that hang down over black boots, the blouse ruffled at the neck, the haphazard cap—all make his figure absurd. While the ballerina and the Moor hold themselves erect, Petrouchka's head lolls to the side. Of the three, he is the least eager to move or to be moved. Lifeless as he is, Petrouchka therefore seems to be more natural. The ballerina and the Moor are posed tensely, ready to spring into activity, but Petrouchka's attitude suggests that perhaps he is tired of being a puppet.

The three puppets remain still as the Charlatan finishes his invocation to his magical gods. The ensuing music is low and mysterious. The Charlatan cuts it short by sounding his flute three times, whereupon Petrouchka, the ballerina, and the Moor instantly wake up and move their feet to the sharp and lively rhythms of a Russian dance. The puppets still stand, and their feet move so fast on and off the floor that their bodies seem suspended. They have come to life so spontaneously, and their feet mark each accent of the dance with such energetic unison, that it is difficult to believe they were inert but a moment before. The music becomes more demanding in its tempo, but the puppets follow the dance perfectly, as if they were toy soldiers obeying the beat of a snare drum. Now they abandon their armrests and step down. The crowd gives them room, and, to the great pleasure of the spectators, the puppets act out a dumb show almost as mechanically as they danced. Both the Moor and Petrouchka are enamored of the ballerina. The Moor flirts with her, and the ballerina seems to favor him, upon which Petrouchka, in a jealous rage, attacks his rival. The Charlatan signals for the drama to stop, and the three puppets involuntarily return to their dance routine. The stage grows darker, and the crowd begins to wander off. The Charlatan makes another signal, and the puppets immediately cease all movement and become rigid and still. The curtain falls.

SCENE TWO: PETROUCHKA'S ROOM   Now we are taken behind the scenes, into the private lives of the puppets. Petrouchka's room is a barren cell. The peaks of icy high mountains are painted all along the walls, near to the floor, while up above, near the ceiling, is a border of puffy white clouds. The room has been decorated, the set implies, for a character not altogether of this world. On the right wall hangs a large portrait of the Charlatan. A door on the left is embellished with satanic figures carrying pitchforks. Petrouchka is suddenly tossed into the room through this door by the Charlatan. The door slams shut. Petrouchka makes a feeble effort to pick himself up, but wonders whether it is worth it. His wooden gestures indicate that everything is hopeless. Here he is in prison again, with nothing to look at but a picture of his master. A piano takes up a despondent theme that embodies Petrouchka's despair, while the rest of the orchestra tries to drown it out. He moves about the room helplessly, he tries to open the door, he pounds on the walls, hoping that someone will release him. Then, all alone, he rages against the world that ignores him. As

trumpets blare a loud fanfare, Petrouchka turns to the portrait of the Charlatan and shakes his fists in challenge to the evil magician who limits his life to
public performances.

As if to prove that he is worthy of a better fate, Petrouchka then does a little dance in which he imitates human expression of feeling. The piano accompanies him. His arms are stiff, but when he holds them close to his heart and
then opens them in a gesture of hope, we see that the puppet understands
more than the dumb-show version of love. He is a marionette who might become human, but cannot because of the Charlatan who made him. His hatred
of the Charlatan is his hatred of his inarticulate self, that part of his dual nature that can but pathetically copy the human gestures for the human emotion
his other nature feels so intensely. He arouses our pity because we see that his
rage against the world is also his rage at himself. His clumsy wooden limbs try
in vain to express their freedom, and his white face is a mask of sorrow.

But Petrouchka's whole attitude changes when he turns to see that the
ballerina has entered his prison. Now the music is gay and lighthearted and
Petrouchka jumps about joyfully. The ballerina, who stands motionless on
point, registers shock at this inelegant expression of pleasure. She makes the appropriate formal gestures of delicate disapproval and turns to go. Petrouchka is
beside himself with anxiety and proceeds to increase the ballerina's distaste by
leaping higher to attract her attention. Clearly, the ballerina has had enough of
the uncontrollable puppet. She turns and leaves.

Once again Petrouchka is in despair and again, to the accompaniment of the
piano and the overpowering orchestra that represents the world he fights
against, he gives himself up to his grief. The Charlatan will always think him a
mere puppet; the ballerina will never regard him as anything but an idiotic
buffoon. He flings his exhausted body about the room, bangs against the walls,
finally succeeds in tearing open a large hole in the right wall, and collapses
when he sees that it leads nowhere.

SCENE THREE: THE MOOR'S ROOM   The Moor, too, has been imprisoned by
the showman, but his abode is ornately decorated and sumptuously furnished.
Everything is splashed with color. A large couch, covered with the skin of a
tiger and backed with cushions, is on the left. Tall, bushy palm trees are
painted on the walls. Serpents and ferocious beasts depicted in bright colors
peer out into the room through thick jungle foliage. On the right is a door or-
namented with a snake rampant. On the couch lies the Moor. He is playing
idly with a coconut. The music is slow, almost lazy, as the Moor amuses his indolence by tossing the coconut and catching it. Unlike Petrouchka, the Moor is
satisfied with his abode and appears happy whiling away the time of day like
the caged beast contentedly resigned to an imitation jungle. He is also unlike
the clown in his inhumanity: he is all puppet. He is soon bored with his simple
pastime and tries to vary it with complications: by grasping his toy with his
feet and letting it fall, by catching it in many ways. But this is not sufficient
for the Moor's entertainment. He grows angry with the coconut. He shakes it,
as an animal would shake the head of a helpless victim. He hears something
inside, but he cannot break the coconut. He pulls out his scimitar, places the

coconut on the floor at his feet. The music crashes with his effort to break the coconut in two, but it is hard as a rock. The Moor is astonished. He stares at the mysterious object that can withstand his mighty blow and decides that it must be magical. He kneels then, bows and worships his plaything as he would worship a god.

The door moves aside, and a roll on a drum signals the entrance of the ballerina. She dances in, horn held to her lips, and steps gaily about the room, the beat of the drum accompanying the tune she plays. The Moor forgets his fetish and watches her with great pleasure, a pleasure which the music expresses with brief cries. The ballerina is charmed by this simple response, so different from the open approval of Petrouchka, and obliges the Moor by danc- ing a waltz. He is delighted beyond mere approval by this performance and insists upon dancing too. His motions are primitive alongside her elegant steps, but he nevertheless tries to make his crude dance fit the rhythm of the ballerina's waltz. He fails miserably and persists in his own private rhythm as the orchestra imitates the chaos of their duet by opposing different melodies. The Moor is now infatuated with the dainty ballerina and demonstrates his affection by pulling her toward the couch. The ballerina pretends to be aghast at this behavior, but secretly she is charmed also and scarcely resists when the Moor holds her on his lap. Their amorous dalliance is interrupted, however, by strange noises from outside. One of Petrouchka's melodies is proclaimed on the trumpet, and the clown thrusts his arm in at the door in an effort to wedge himself into the room. He has imagined the plight of the ballerina and has come to her aid! The couple jump guiltily as he forces his way in; they spring apart. The jealous Petrouchka berates the Moor for his behavior and ap- proaches him menacingly as the music resounds his rage. The Moor recovers from the surprise of Petrouchka's sudden appearance and replies with animal grunts. Then he draws his scimitar and begins to chase the clown around the room. The ballerina faints on the couch, the Moor closes in on Petrouchka, whose end seems certain until he makes a quick dash for the door and escapes. The Moor is about to pursue the interloper, when he remembers the ballerina. He drops his sword, goes back over to the couch, and pulls the ballerina back onto his lap. The curtain falls as his head bobs up and down in savage satis- faction. The private lives of the three puppets have turned out to be almost identical to the dumb show they acted before the public: Petrouchka always loses.

SCENE FOUR: GRAND CARNIVAL   The Shrovetide Fair, the outside world, has gone on while we watched the inner drama backstage, and the music now takes us back to the festivities. Very little time has elapsed, for the stage is not yet dark and the celebrating crowd is by no means ready to go home. The puppet theater in the back is dark and silent. Stimulated by their continuous refreshment, the peasants are all laughing and whipping themselves up to a final high pitch of excitement. A group of nursemaids emerge from the multi- tude, line up, and start a traditional dance to a Russian folk song that is exhila- rating in its open melody; the crowd sways to the rhythm of the dance. The nursemaids' round is interrupted by deep, plodding notes from the orchestra, which herald the arrival of a trained bear. The bear swaggers clumsily onto the scene, led by his trainer, who laughs at the fears of the spectators and directs the bear in a few simple tricks. Then follows the dance of the coachmen, whose performance outrivals all the others in color and vigor. The theme to which the nursemaids danced is heard again, and the nurses join the coachmen. The couples seem to exhaust themselves in joyous abandon, but gain fresh strength with each step. Garishly dressed masqueraders—a demon, various animals—scurry about in the square trying to frighten people, but almost everyone is involved in the dance, in watching it at first, then imitating it while standing still, then participating fully, so that the stage gradually becomes a mass of whirling color. The frenzied beat of the music, and its increasingly raucous volume, intoxicates the dancers, and—as night descends on the scene and snow begins to fall—their movements in this picture frame of old Russia surge with a final expression of carnival fervor.

The enthusiasm of the revelers has not allowed them to notice that in the back, within the puppet theater, there are signs of activity behind the drawn curtains. They all turn, as they hear strange noises inside the theater, and wait expectantly. Petrouchka comes running out, the music sounds his fanfare, and we see that he is trying to escape from the Moor, who dashes out after him. The crowd is struck dumb by this apparently spontaneous life in the puppets and looks on, fascinated, as the clown tries to avoid the blows of the Moor's scimitar. The Moor's animal strength overpowers Petrouchka. The clown is cornered. He covers his head with his arms, shaking with fright. The Moor, with one blow of his sword, strikes him down. Petrouchka doubles up in pain. The music reflects his agony and his great effort to remain alive, but his legs stretch out, his whole body quivers spasmodically, and he is dead.

His death has been so realistic that the people who surround his body cannot believe that he is a mere puppet; a crime seems to have been committed. Someone calls a policeman, who observes the dead clown and hauls out the Charlatan to give an account of the strange goings on. The Charlatan is much amused at his suspicions and picks up the body to show everyone they are mistaken. Petrouchka is now a limp rag doll, a creature who could never have been anything but lifeless. The policeman is satisfied, people shake their heads, the crowd begins to leave slowly. The Charlatan remains alone, holding the puppet, and the stage is almost completely dark. He turns to re-enter the theater—perhaps to put the errant clown back in his cell—when Petrouchka's fanfare blares out loudly to stop him in his tracks. He looks up: on the top of the theater the ghost of Petrouchka shakes his fist at the Charlatan—and at everyone else who will not believe he is real.

NOTES   The idea of *Petrouchka* was first of all a musical idea. Stravinsky had finished *Firebird* and was about to begin work on his next project for Diaghilev—*The Rite of Spring*—when he interrupted his plans to compose a purely nonballetic piece. He wanted to write a piece for piano and orchestra in which the piano would seem to be attacked by the mass of instruments. It would fight back, flourish a bit, but then the large orchestra would win out.

Stravinsky began to think of this composition as a contest between a puppet, represented by the piano, and the orchestra. After he had finished it, he tried to find an idea that would express the image that had been in his mind as he composed. He found it in a word, *Petrouchka*, "the immortal and unhappy hero of every fair."

He conveyed his idea to Diaghilev, who, upon hearing the music, decided to produce a ballet on this theme as soon as possible. The painter and designer Alexandre Benois collaborated with the musician and the impresario on the story, which Michel Fokine choreographed for Nijinsky, Karsavina, Orlov, and Cecchetti.

Although it is perhaps the most famous ballet in the modern repertory, *Petrouchka* has but recently been revived with sufficient competence to remind us that its first production was a very great one indeed. Stravinsky has written in his *Autobiography* (1936): "I should like . . . to pay heartfelt homage to Vaslav Nijinsky's unsurpassed rendering of the role of Petrouchka. The perfection with which he became the very incarnation of this character was all the more remarkable because the purely saltatory work in which he excelled was in this case dominated by dramatic action, music and gesture. The beauty of the ballet was greatly enhanced by the richness of the artistic setting which Benois had created for it. My faithful interpreter Karsavina swore to me that she would never relinquish her part as the dancer, which she adored. But it was a pity that the movements of the crowd had been neglected. I mean that they were left to the arbitrary improvisation of the performers instead of being choreographically regulated in accordance with the clearly defined exigencies of the music. I regret it all the more because the *danses d'ensemble* of the coachmen, nurses and mummers, and the solo dances, must be regarded as Fokine's finest creations.

Carl Van Vechten describes Nijinsky's Petrouchka in this way: "He is a puppet and—remarkable touch—a puppet with a soul. His performance in this ballet is, perhaps, his most wonderful achievement. He suggests only the puppet in action; his facial expression never changes; yet the pathos is greater, more keenly carried over the footlights, than one would imagine possible under any conditions. I have seen Fokine in the same role, and although he gives you all the gestures the result is not the same. It is genius that Nijinsky puts into his interpretation of the part. Who can ever forget Nijinsky as Petrouchka when thrown by his master into his queer black box, mad with love for the dancer, who, in turn, prefers the Moor puppet, rushing about waving his pathetically stiff arms in the air, and finally beating his way with his clenched fists through the paper window to curse the stars? It is a more poignant expression of grief than most Romeos can give us."

Many famous dancers have since appeared in the role—Massine, Woizikowski, Jerome Robbins, Michael Kidd, Børge Ralov. Fokine revived the ballet for the Royal Danish Ballet in 1925, and for Ballet Theatre, October 8, 1942.

Petrouchka was revived by the Royal Ballet on March 26, 1957, with Alexander Grant, Margot Fonteyn, and Peter Clegg in the principal roles. Rudolf Nureyev danced the role for the first time with this company on October 24, 1963. Nadia Nerina was the doll and Keith Rosson the blackamoor. Mary Clarke wrote in the *Dancing Times:* "Let it be said at once that Nureyev captures to perfection the sawdust quality of the part. His first fall in the opening scene is just a crumble of a puppet body and all the way through one feels that the gloves contain no hands, just useless stuffing. This, of course, heightens the pathos of the character, the little pigmy soul that aspires to human loves and fears without a human body to support them. The scene in Petrouchka's cell is, as yet, only sketched; it will develop with more performances . . . but the final moment on the top of the booth, when the immortal soul asserts itself for the last time, is marvelously done. Everybody's heart must have trembled just a little bit when watching this."

Petrouchka is a ballet for which I have some sentimental recollection. In the Diaghilev production, whenever anyone was sick or unable to dance I took his part in the ballet. At one time I thought I had danced almost every male part in the ballet!

Petrouchka was revived in New York, March 13, 1970, by the City Center Joffrey Ballet under the supervision of Leonide Massine, assisted by Yurek Lazowski and Tania Massine. The principal roles were taken by Edward Verso, Erika Goodman, Christian Holder, Yurek Lazowski, and Zelma Bustilio. Noting that the ballet had not been seen in New York for twelve years, the critic Anna Kisselgoff wrote in the New York *Times* that "the spell of the decor, based on the original designs of Alexandre Benois, the magic of Igor Stravinsky's miraculous score and the radically expressive choreography of Michel Fokine are as strong as ever."

American Ballet Theatre revived *Petrouchka* June 19, 1970, at the New York State Theatre, with Ted Kivitt, Eleanor D'Antuono, and Bruce Marks in the principal roles. Clive Barnes in the New York *Times* called this production, staged by Dimitri Romanoff and Yurek Lazowski, "A sumptuous and authentic new staging that is part homage to the past and part reaffirmation of Ballet Theatre's historically classic role in American dance's future."

PICNIC AT TINTAGEL

Dramatic ballet in three scenes. Music by Arnold Bax. Choreography by Frederick Ashton. Scenery and costumes by Cecil Beaton. Costumes executed by Helene Pons. Lighting by Jean Rosenthal. First presented by the New York City Ballet at the City Center, New York, February 28, 1952, with Francisco Moncion as the Husband (King Mark), Diana Adams as the Wife (Iseult), Jacques d'Amboise as her Lover (Tristram), and Robert Barnett as the Caretaker (Merlin).

Today, on the west coast of England, stands "wild Tintagel by the Cornish seas," a rocky promontory reaching out into the water. Here we find the ruins of an ancient castle celebrated by poets and chroniclers for centuries as the stronghold of King Arthur and his Knights of the Round Table. One of King Arthur's trusted knights was Tristram, who brought the beautiful Irish maid Iseult to Cornwall to be the wife of his uncle, King Mark. The love story of Tristram and Iseult has inspired writers from the time of Geoffrey of Monmouth to the times of Tennyson, Swinburne, Wagner, Hardy, Edwin Arlington Robinson, and Jean Cocteau.

This modern ballet recalls the story of Tristram and Iseult in a setting that is centuries later. The time is 1916, the year Sir Arnold Bax composed *The Garden of Fand,* the ballet's score. The place is Tintagel.

SCENE ONE The curtain rises as the music begins. The melody is soft and magical, weaving in sound a mysterious spell. The scene is dominated by arches of gray, slatelike stone, the ruins of the castle where the romance of Tristram and Iseult took place almost a thousand years ago. A man is on stage. He is the caretaker. Dressed in green tweeds with a cap, he moves about the scene as if only he understood it, as if he shared some secret with the ancient castle that tourists could not understand.

Tourists enter on the right. They are a motoring party, dressed in the long dusters of the time. We see a man, his wife, and another man. Two other men follow behind. The husband looks about and goes over to the caretaker. As soon as he turns his back, the second man goes to the wife and takes her hand in his. She glances nervously at the other two men in their party, who are watching them, and cautions him to be discreet. The husband comes to take his wife on a tour of the castle, and they exit. As they leave, the wife waves to the second man, who walks off in the opposite direction.

The woman's maid enters, followed by her master's chauffeur and footman, who carry picnic baskets. A cloth is laid on the ground, the baskets are opened, goblets and a bottle of wine are set out, and the servants leave. The second man enters and asks the caretaker if he has seen the woman. He leaves. Now the woman inquires after the man and goes off in search of him.

The caretaker, alone, looks about quickly and takes up the bottle of wine. He opens the bottle, reaches into his pocket, gestures magically over the bottle, and then replaces it on the picnic cloth. All the picnickers return. The maid pours wine for her mistress and the second man, who stand together as the others sit on the ground. The two lovers look in each other's eyes, make a toast, and drink. As the glasses touch their lips, a trumpet is heard and the music bursts into thunderous sound. The party is alarmed, and all leave the stage.

SCENE TWO The chauffeur and footman, magically transformed into two heralds, rush in bearing the flag of King Mark. The caretaker turns around and around in the center of the stage as the scene, almost at his command, is magically transformed. The ruins disappear, and in their place, rising from the ground, stands a colonnade that graced a room in King Mark's castle. The caretaker's wish has come true: the man and the woman have drunk the magic potion, to become Tristram and Iseult, and again he is Merlin, the magician, who can stand aside and watch the workings of his mysterious art.

Merlin leaves the scene, and King Mark enters with Iseult and Tristram. Except for their costumes, they are the same as before: two men in love with the same woman. King Mark knights Tristram with his sword, and Tristram kisses the hand of his king. Then, for a brief moment, Tristram is alone with Iseult.

The lovers snatch at the opportunity to be together. They are unaware that one of King Mark's knights watches them from the colonnade in the rear. Tristram lifts Iseult lovingly in his arms. Brangaene, Iseult's maid, rushes in and separates the lovers. She warns them to be careful, that the king approaches.

King Mark enters, and Brangaene dances with Tristram so that the king will suspect nothing. Two knights propose a hunt to the king. Mark assents and asks Tristram if he will join them. Tristram, anxious to be alone with Iseult, pleads some excuse. The two knights watch this and whisper together. Iseult observes their suspicions and separates the two talkers. Now Iseult herself whispers to Brangaene how delighted she is that she and Tristram can be alone at last.

King Mark thinks it strange that Tristram will not accompany them, but leaves the scene for the hunt. His knights and heralds follow. Iseult, alone, seeks Tristram, running in and out among the arches of the colonnade. She is unaware that one of the king's knights has entered surreptitiously and concealed himself behind one of the columns to watch her. The music is quiet, expectant.

Tristram enters, and the two lovers run together from opposite sides of the stage. The orchestra commences a restrained, almost suppressed, romantic melody that gains gradually in intensity. Tristram kneels, and Iseult falls back over his shoulder. They kneel together. The spying knight moves to watch them more closely. As the melody gathers to a soaring crescendo, Tristram lifts Iseult straight into the air.

The lights dim and the music quietens. The lovers are almost motionless, content merely to be alone together, but their passion returns. To the call of a flute, Iseult entwines her body about Tristram, and the two fall to the ground in a close embrace.

The quiet of the music is broken by a sudden, shocking fortissimo. The false knight rushes out. Tristram attacks him. Brangaene, much alarmed, goes to her mistress. A herald enters with two crossed swords, and the flags of King Mark return. Mark, who has been forewarned, enters and points accusingly to Tristram. Iseult goes to her husband to plead with him, but he brushes her aside. The two knights suggest to the king that he engage Tristram in a duel. Tristram accepts the challenge, and the two men take swords from the herald and begin to fight. As she tries frantically to separate the duelers, Iseult is stabbed. The heralds holding the flags of the king let them fall to the ground. King Mark renews his attack upon Tristram and wounds him fatally. As he falls, Tristram grasps the arm of the king and sinks slowly down. King Mark moves over to stand over Iseult's body.

SCENE THREE The lights dim. Merlin returns, and the principals in the ancient tragedy disappear. Darkness envelops the scene briefly. When light returns, the castle has vanished and in its place we see again the ruins—dark fingers of stone against the sky. The wife and her lover stand together in their motoring coats, as we left them, about to drink the magic wine. They still look into each other's eyes, and for an instant we feel that they will never cease being Tristram and Iseult. But the husband steps in. He pushes his friend away. His wife's lover stands there, not understanding, holding out his glass: what has he done, he wonders?

The caretaker comes forward, and the stage darkens about him. Alone now in the castle, he holds up the crossed, gleaming swords of Tristram's mortal combat for Iseult. The curtain falls as the music that began the ballet returns us to the twentieth century, suggesting also that, at Merlin's command, the cycle might begin all over again.

NOTES   Frederick Ashton's first ballet for the New York City Ballet, *Illuminations,* had been such a success in 1950 that the American company immediately asked the distinguished English choreographer to return to the United States and mount a second work. Ashton's obligations as principal choreographer of the Sadler's Wells Ballet made it impossible for him to do this until two years later. In the meantime, however, he had agreed with the directors of the New York City Ballet on a subject: a modern treatment of the legend of Tristram and Iseult. Ashton and Cecil Beaton, who was to design the work, traveled to Tintagel, in Cornwall, England, where they observed the ruins of the ancient castle associated for centuries with the love story of Tristram and Iseult.

Ashton wished to use as a score for his new ballet *Iseult at Tintagel* (1915), by Sir Arnold Bax, Master of the Queen's Musick. The score, however, was found to be too short for his needs, and consultation with the composer suggested alternative music—Bax's *The Garden of Fand* (1916), which had had its first performance in the United States, by the Chicago Symphony Orchestra under Frederick Stock. Ashton adopted this score, cast the ballet, and in a very short space of time staged his new work.

Walter Terry reported in the New York *Herald Tribune* that "*Picnic at Tintagel*—musically, pictorially, choreographically, dramatically," was a "theatre piece of which the New York City Ballet may be justly proud . . . Not only has Mr. Ashton used well the dramatic urgency of time but he has also choreographed with craftsmanlike shrewdness and considerable artistry . . . The love duet itself is a work of great beauty . . ." On the occasion of the New York City Ballet's first presentation of *Picnic at Tintagel* in Europe, at the Edinburgh Festival in August 1952, the New York *Times* reported that the ballet "was swift, exciting and dramatic, and is likely to occupy a permanent place in British ballet."

THE PIED PIPER

Ballet in two parts. Music by Aaron Copland. Choreography by Jerome Robbins. Lighting by Jean Rosenthal. First presented by the New York City Ballet at the City Center, New York, December 4, 1951, with a cast headed by Diana Adams and Nicholas Magallanes, Jillana, Roy Tobias, Janet Reed and Todd Bolender, Melissa Hayden and Herbert Bliss, and Tanaquil LeClercq and Jerome Robbins.

The Pied Piper is a dance ballet set to Copland's *Concerto for Clarinet and String Orchestra;* its title has nothing to do with the famous Pied Piper of Hamlin and refers instead to the clarinet soloist. Copland's score (1948) was not written with a ballet in mind, but *The Pied Piper* derives its inspiration directly from the music, so that we are always being reminded visually of what we are listening to.

Many people imagine that ballets without stories, ballets that are based simply on music—and music which was not composed for ballet in the first place—are a dull prospect. Of course, it is natural for all of us to like stories; but with a little careful listening and watching, it is just as natural for us to be entertained by a visual spectacle based on a musical narrative. After all, we begin to like stories first because we hear them, listen to them, before we learn how to read. If we listen to music in the same way, we find ourselves just as entertained: we don't have to know how to read it. *The Pied Piper* is another ballet that proves how much fun we can have if we recognize this.

Before the music begins, the curtain rises. The stage is dark, and as our eyes try to see what is there, we can barely discern a man walking out from the side toward the center. He is wearing a plain business suit and carrying a clarinet. He looks around him at the bare stage, where there is no scenery—only ladders left propped up against the back wall by stagehands, and a few idle, unpainted flats standing at the left. He looks up, where a little light filters down to illuminate the plain back wall and the radiators that cling to it. He plays a few testing scales on the clarinet and ambles across the stage to the right-hand corner. There he finds a music stand, a lamp, and a high stool. He turns the music stand so that it faces the stage, adjusts the lamp, opens the music, and sits down. Harp strings are plucked softly. Low strings reflect their chords, and the piper begins to play.

The clarinet melody is slow, quiet, sounding lonely and lyrical on the empty stage. Slowly two great doors in the back wall begin to open, and a bright slash of light widens and fans out from the doorway, making an aisle of light across the stage. Two dancers, a girl and a boy, stand silhouetted in the doorway. They are listening to the mysterious music, which seems to come from nowhere. Attracted by its sweet melancholy, they walk forward, holding hands. Both of them wear rehearsal clothes. The door closes behind them. They bow their heads as they stand facing the soloist, then their bodies fall back into a dance that responds irresistibly to the plaintive romance of the music.

The boy supports the girl in low turns and high, soft lifts. The *pas de deux* is tender and yearning, the pace slow, the steps wide, open, and reaching. The dancers pause as a spotlight at the front of the stage throws their shadows against the back wall, then move over to the right, seeking refuge at the source of the music. Another girl enters on the left with a boy. They watch their shadows on the wall. The first couple cross the stage and the boy lifts the girl high over his head as the strings piercingly sound the climax of the melody. Now they join the other two for a moment. All bow low to their shadows on the back wall. A group of dancers wander in and, with the intruding couple, watch as the lovers finish their dance. In the slow rhythm of the dance and the

music, lights come up and fade one by one to make the whole stage picture
balance in the romantic mood. Lights at the back, against the wall, and on the
sides shine directly onto the stage, making a carpet of yellow light. The scene
grows dark again, and the boy lifts the girl off into the wings toward the disappearing yellow light.

The dancers who have been standing quietly, watching the love duet, look
at the soloist. The stage is now lighted, and we see that all the dancers wear
rehearsal clothes—shirts and sweaters and tights of varied colors. The piper begins a cadenza as the romantic music fades behind, and gradually the dancers
gather together to listen. Others straggle on, see the group, and listen too. This
is music that seems to be asking a question, in quick, lively, darting phrases.
The atmosphere is expectant. Instinctively the boys and girls are attracted by
the piper's song, and their bodies, almost uncontrollably, begin to answer its
phrases. A blond girl's hand shakes to the music, and she holds it out at the
end of her arm as if it didn't belong to her. The hand creeps around to the
back of her neck, and soon her whole body is miming the music.

The solo ends after a swift climbing scale; the music is curtly and demand-
ingly rhythmic. A redhead seems to go crazy with the insistence of the piper's
call. Mysteriously she finds herself climbing on a boy's shoulders. Another boy
begins to chase her. Other boys crowd in, there is a scuffle—the boys fighting,
but not touching, pointing their fingers like guns.

Drawn to the scene by the light, driving melody, another couple enter. They
join the redhead and her partner. The boys and girls separate into two groups
and follow their leaders. When a final lead couple is seen to emerge, the boy
chases the girl in mock seriousness, turns, and she chases him. Now the whole
group is dancing, responding to the music with spontaneous and spasmodic
jerkings and jivings as it becomes brisker and hysterically carefree. In different
groups, they run back and forth, crisscrossing the stage. Then, suddenly, all
the dancers are flat on the floor. Their bodies remain quiet for a minute, but
then the music drives at them again with sharp, shrieking calls and they
bounce on the floor. Their arms reach up into the air, then their legs. The
redhead tries to control her dancing legs by pressing down on the top of her
head, as if to put a lid on the vitality created by the music, but her whole
body begins to vibrate. The others rise automatically to the music's call, and
the stage is a mass of hurried, comic twitchings to the loud beat of the music.

Now the song of the clarinet above the music attracts the dancers like a
magnet, and they gather round the piper. But his music drives them back
across the stage. Grouped closely together on the side, they reach up their
hands to the clarinet's high, piercing song and bow down low when the piper
sounds a low note. This low note begins a fast ascending scale and propels
them again into motion, and in one movement all the dancers dash across the
stage toward the piper. They fall at his feet in a wave, and the music explodes
on a final high note.

PIÈGE DE LUMIÈRE (Trap of Light)

Ballet by Philippe Hériat. Music by Jean-Michel Damase. Choreography by John Taras. Scenery by Félix Labisse. Costumes by André Levasseur. First presented by the Grand Ballet du Marquis de Cuevas at the Théâtre de l'Empire, Paris, December 23, 1952, with Rosella Hightower, Vladimir Skouratoff, and Serge Golovine in leading roles. First presented in the United States by the New York City Ballet at the City Center, New York, October 1, 1964, with Maria Tallchief, André Prokovsky, and Arthur Mitchell in leading roles. Supervision and lighting by David Hays.

The creator of the idea for this ballet, Philippe Hériat of the Academy Goncourt, has described the background and action:

"From time to time, escaping convicts reach the heart of the virgin forest. Forever lost to a civilization whose stern laws alone await them, they form their own communities, living on the spoils of the hunt—the skins of wild beasts, serpents, exotic birds, and giant butterflies. This existence, cut off from the world, furnishes the ballet's theme: the scene is set in such an encampment.

"A young convict joins the band of runaways. They welcome him to their midst and, as night falls, they build a fire to lure from hiding those butterflies who appear at twilight. Species of every kind swarm through the forest. The most agile, the Iphias, and the most beautiful, the Morphide, linger a while together; but even love cannot distract them from the fatal flames. Before this trap of light the massacre begins. The young convict snares the Morphide, and the Iphias sacrifices himself to save her. She escapes, leaving with her captor the glittering traces of their encounter—gold pollen from her wings. Now, like his insect prey, he, too, becomes a hunted creature."

PILLAR OF FIRE

Ballet in one act. Music by Arnold Schoenberg. Choreography and book by Antony Tudor. Scenery and costumes by Jo Mielziner. First presented by Ballet Theatre at the Metropolitan Opera House, New York, April 8, 1942, with Nora Kaye as Hagar, *Hugh Laing as the* Young Man from the House Opposite, *Lucia Chase as the* Eldest Sister, *Annabelle Lyon as the* Youngest Sister, *and Antony Tudor as the* Friend.

This ballet tells a story to a piece of music that was inspired by a story. Schoenberg's *Verklärte Nacht (Transfigured Night)* is based on a nineteenth-century German poem called *Weib und die Welt (Woman and the World)*, which had a theme daring for its time. In the poem there are two characters, a man and a woman who walk together in a cold, moonlit wood. They are lovers. First the woman addresses the man. She tells him that she has sinned, that she is going to have a child that is not his. All this happened, she tells her lover, before she was sure of his affection, at a time when she was desperate for any kind of security. She has learned since that sensuality is no security at all and that her new love for him is the blessing she really sought. The man replies that she must not feel guilty, that their mutual love is so great that even her child will be unblemished, that it will be in reality his child. He says that, as the light of the moon embraces the dark night, her love for him will transfigure the child, just as his love for her has transformed him. There is no need for forgiveness: they have love.

Such is the story of *Pillar of Fire;* but because it is a ballet, it takes this story and presents it dramatically, introducing additional characters, giving us a picture of the community in which such an event can take place, motivating the principal characters and their actions as completely as possible. The time is about 1900. The place is any town. The curtain rises to a low throbbing of strings. We see a wide street, lined with houses, under a darkening sky. The street narrows and vanishes in the distance. In the foreground, on the right, stands a high, narrow house, its woodwork embellished with Victorian scrolls. On the front steps a girl sits, brooding. She is plainly, almost severely, dressed; her long dark hair is braided about her head. She sits absolutely erect, her whole body seeming to delight in an intense placidity that is belied only by the clenched fists in her lap. This is Hagar, who lives in this house with two sisters.

The music is dark, heavy, oppressive; yet within this gloom, the principal melody cries out yearningly. Hagar watches the townspeople pass by in the twilight. Young people walk in the street, young people in love, and we sense immediately that Hagar has never been like them. Spinsters walk down the street with exaggerated daintiness, and Hagar turns away in disgust. She herself is not a young girl, but already she is frightened: she cannot be like the beautiful young girls in love, and the spinsters suggest the only alternative. She smooths back her hair, and we see that she is not unattractive.

Her two sisters emerge from the house. One is older, prim, and straitlaced; the other is young, a blond girl with long curls, soon to become a woman. The contrast between these two is apparently the same as the difference Hagar has noted in the passers-by. The younger sister is obviously spoiled, and when the older sister seems to reprimand Hagar for sitting apart from them, the young girl pokes fun at her. A young man comes across the street to their door. Hagar is delighted to see him. He is her only friend, and she is in love with him. Now she is no longer moody, but she hesitates to display her true feelings before her family. She knows them too well. The friend observes this and, being a very polite, conventional young man, is pleasant to her sisters.

The sisters, in turn, are more than civil to him. They are thoroughly aware that he has come to the house mainly to see Hagar, but the one—older, strong, possessive—and the other—young, demanding, accustomed to having anything she wants—soon draw his attention to themselves while Hagar watches. The young sister sidles up to him, flirting with cunning innocence. The friend observes her manner, is charmed by her blind youth, and ignores Hagar. The spinster is delighted at this sudden success of her favorite and asks the friend into the house. He goes in, and Hagar again is alone. It occurs to no one that she would enjoy going with them.

Hagar's despair turns to anger and hatred. It is not enough that her sister has dominated her family; she must also dominate all those who come in contact with it. The girl sees her last hope of freedom gone: her friend is hopelessly ensnared. And so she tries to forget her hope that he will respond to her love. The house across the street aids her forgetfulness. Lights come up inside the house, and Hagar sees through the walls all she has imagined must take place within it. For this is a place where love is celebrated all night long, where bold, unpolite men come to meet their women.

Shadows of lovers embracing are thrown against the walls of the house, and Hagar reaches out in open longing. She is taken aback when a man comes out of the house and glares at her. He walks jauntily, confidently, putting himself on display a little. She pretends to be embarrassed when he looks at her boldly and openly. Under any other circumstances this man would seem absurd to her, but now he embodies all the longings that Hagar cannot satisfy in a normal way, and she is attracted to him and the mysterious life in the house across the street. The man gives her a final look and goes back inside.

Now Hagar's young sister returns with the friend. The friend observes Hagar and has no understanding of her dilemma. Instead of questioning her, instead of helping her, it is much easier for him to succumb to the designs of the younger girl. Now more a woman than a child, the girl curls herself around his affections with the sinuousness of a cat. Hagar sees that her older sister has succeeded in making of the younger a frightening, pretty projection of her own willful selfishness and turns away in horror at the contrast between the girl's innocent beauty and inner evil. Should she warn the friend? How can she? He would laugh and not believe her. And so she watches as the girl takes her friend's arm and goes off with him for a stroll in the moonlight.

As they disappear, Hagar is frantic. She despises not only her sisters, but the man who will be duped by them. She contorts her body obscenely to express the depth of her disgust. Feeling now completely severed from all she might hold dear, she turns instinctively toward the mysterious house. The man who watched her in the street sees that she is still alone and leaves the house to join her.

Hagar welcomes him, and the two dance together. The girl loses all sense of modesty and decorum and for the first time in her life gives open expression of her feelings. The man encourages her passion. When Hagar leaps across the stage, he seizes her in mid-air, cutting short her flight of freedom, directing her warmth only to himself. He takes her by the hand and leads her to the house. Now eager to learn its secrets, Hagar enters ecstatically.

When she leaves the house a little later, she is alone. The conventions she renounced to discover love renew their hold on her to expose her act as sin, and she is filled with remorse. Now she has nothing, for she has rapidly learned the inadequacy of the kind of life led by the bold young man.

Her older sister enters and sees the guilt on Hagar's face. Neighbors passing by seem to know of her guilt, and Hagar, bitterly ashamed, seeks some friendly response from the crowd. She is shunned by everyone, even by the

sordid people who frequent the house she has just left. These lovers-in-ex-
perience look at her in contempt while the youthful lovers-in-innocence
scarcely see her.

The younger sister and the friend return from their walk. While the older
sister mingles with a group of spinsters, confirming the shame Hagar has
brought on the family, the young girl cavorts with new playmates from the
house across the street. She is delighted to discover how nice they are.

The tormented Hagar can turn to no one. Obediently, like a child, she goes
with her sisters toward the house. The two women say good night to her
friend, as if to apologize for her behavior. The scene blacks out.

The street and the houses have vanished when the scene is lit again. The
three sisters find themselves outcasts from society because of Hagar's indiscretion. Secretly her two sisters are delighted at her defection; but they are
angry at what it has cost them and they repudiate her. The friend comes to
her with his sympathy and help, but Hagar cannot bear to confront him with
her evil. She seeks recognition instead from the townspeople, from the loose
women, from men like her seducer. All are aghast at her downfall and will not
help. Finally, in desperation, she reaches out pathetically to the seducer himself. He looks at her as if he'd never seen her.

Seeing her final despair, the friend returns. Hagar twists away to flee, but
now the young man will not let her go. He holds her strongly, yet tenderly,
tells her that she has forgotten his love and that he is there to stand by her and
welcome her as his own. The girl is overwhelmed with his loving kindness and
dances with him a *pas de deux* that is not only passionate, but tender. Hagar
now possesses the permanent love that she despaired of finding. The lovers
disappear for a moment, then we see them again, walking away in the distance, their hands clasped, their shoulders touching. They move slowly away
out of sight in a deep green forest to the singing romantic music.

NOTES   In 1973 American Ballet Theatre filmed for television the full-
length *Pillar of Fire* under the supervision of Antony Tudor. Sallie Wilson,
Gayle Young, Marcos Paredes, Bonnie Mathis, and Ellen Everett were the principal dancers.

The ballerina Sallie Wilson, who has excelled in the title role of this ballet,
had a number of interesting things to say about working with the choreographer Antony Tudor in an interview with the writer John Gruen, first published in *Dance Magazine*, March 1975. Excerpt: "Tudor makes you aware of
the fact that when you are stepping on the stage, you're not coming in from
the wings, but from where you are . . ."

PINEAPPLE POLL

*Comic ballet in three scenes. Music by Sir Arthur Sullivan, arranged by
Charles Mackerras. Choreography by John Cranko. Scenery and costumes
by Osbert Lancaster. First presented by the Sadler's Wells Theatre Ballet
at the Sadler's Wells Theatre, London, March 13, 1951, with Elaine Fifield*

as Pineapple Poll, *David Blair as* Captain Belaye, *and David Poole as* Jasper. *First presented in the United States by the Sadler's Wells Theatre Ballet at the Buffalo Theatre, Buffalo, New York, October 23, 1951, with Maryon Lane as* Pineapple Poll *and David Blair and David Poole in their original roles.*

Pineapple Poll is a Gilbert and Sullivan ballet, based on one of the *Bab Ballads* of Gilbert and on a selection of Sullivan's music from the famous operettas that he wrote with Gilbert's collaboration. Like *H.M.S. Pinafore* and *The Pirates of Penzance, Pineapple Poll* is typically and charmingly British. It is the first ballet to exploit the universal fame of the Royal Navy and, like our own native ballets *Rodeo* and *Fancy Free,* gives us a story that is both happy and sentimental.

The story of the ballet takes its cue from Gilbert's ballad the *Bumboat Woman's Story.* (A bumboat is a boat carrying provisions, vegetables, trinkets, and so forth, to ships at anchor.) This ballad tells the history of the bumboat woman, Pineapple Poll, who joyfully recalls her past by saying:

My cheeks were mellow and soft, and my eyes were large and sweet,
Poll Pineapple's eyes were the standing toast of the Royal fleet!

A bumboat woman was I, and I faithfully served the ships
With apples and cakes, and fowls and beer, and half-penny dips,
And beef for the general mess, where the officers dine at nights,
And fine fresh peppermint drops for the rollicking midshipmites.

SCENE ONE: PORTSMOUTH; A PUBLIC SQUARE   Poll's history in the ballet begins one day in spring in a public square at Portsmouth, the great port in South England. Painted statues of the god and goddess of the sea stand on either side of the stage, framing the scene. The buildings—shops and naval supply stores—are clean and brightly painted. In the distance, over the shoulder of the statue of an admiral that stands in the background, we see the pointed roofs of warehouses and masts of anchored ships. On the right stands a pub, the Steam Packet. Jasper, potboy at the pub, is busy polishing the window that advertises wines and spirits.

Jasper turns and watches longingly as two pretty girls come into the square, dancing with a sailor. The sailor is dressed in a typical British seaman's uniform of the late nineteenth century; the girls wear colorful summer dresses. Two other tars enter the Steam Packet; a crowd of girls come in with a group of sailors, take partners, and dance. Two girls who are left without partners go to the door of the pub and knock. Two sailors come out to join them, and the waltzing couples pause for refreshment. The sailors call Jasper to bring them pots of beer, and the potboy runs frantically back and forth from the pub to the street with tankard after tankard. Finally he, too, is in need of refreshment and downs two mugs of beer before he reaches the sailors. The hearty tars toss him about, and he retreats to the door of the Steam Packet to watch them renew their dance. The vigorous dance ends with all the girls sitting on their partners' knees.

The music is bright and merry, a triangle tinkles, and Pineapple Poll dances into the square. She is dressed in a candy-striped dress and wears green ribbons in her red hair. She carries on her head a basket filled with flowers and trinkets, and soon all the sailors are surrounding her. Poll sells most of her wares and begins to dance. From the door of the pub, Jasper waves to her. She does not acknowledge his greeting, and he places his hand over his heart, signifying his love for her. He, too, would like to buy a trinket from Pineapple Poll and goes through all his pockets, one by one, searching for the one coin he knows he possesses. He finds a piece of silver and approaches Poll hopefully, but she treats him like any other customer and when he gives her the flower he has purchased, she throws it on the ground. Poll, however, consents to dance with him briefly, and Jasper holds her in his arms until he sees that his love is not requited; he returns to the pub.

The girls and the sailors promenade about the square, and Poll, without a partner, picks up the flower Jasper gave her and for a moment reconsiders. Then she tosses it away again and circles the stage. She and all the girls stop their dancing at this point and watch breathlessly the entrance of Captain Belaye:

> Of all the kind commanders who anchor in Portsmouth Bay,
> By far the sweetest of all was kind Lieutenant Belaye.
> Lieutenant Belaye commanded the gunboat, *Hot Cross Bun,*
> She was seven and seventy feet in length, and she carried a gun.

The tars salute their captain while the girls begin to swoon. Captain Belaye, dark and handsome, wears a blue jacket, white duck trousers, and an officer's cap at a natty angle. Belaye jauntily inspects his crew, who automatically line up before him. He straightens one of the sailor's neckerchiefs and tries to act as if he were oblivious to the admiring glances of the girls. Casually he touches Poll's cheek, and she steps back in a romantic daze.

The orchestra sounds a drum roll, and Belaye begins to dance. His merry, rapid dance depicts the routine of life at sea: he peers through an imaginary long glass, climbs imaginary ropes, and orders his crew about. The crew, who stand in back of him during this solo, throw their hats in the air at a final dazzling display of virtuosity by their commander. The girls rush to surround him. The tars take their swooning partners out of the square, lest they begin to devote all of their time to the side-whiskered captain. Poll is the last reluctant girl to leave the scene and whirls out of sight, dizzy with love for the captain.

Belaye is alone for a moment, but soon he is joined by a pretty overdressed young lady and her chaperone. This is Blanche, the girl he wants to marry, accompanied by her aunt, Mrs. Dimple. Blanche is all decked out in red, white, and blue and clearly is in love with her fiancé's navy. Mrs. Dimple, in black, wears a high feathered hat and brandishes an umbrella, which gets in the way every time the captain tries to speak to her or to Blanche. He and Blanche snatch a few moments together; he embraces her, and the music is romantic. But Mrs. Dimple is on the job again; the music mimics her busybody authority as she scolds the two lovers. They begin to dance together, but Mrs. Dimple good-humoredly interferes again and in the process drops her umbrella and shawl over and over again. When she turns away to look about the square, Belaye kisses Blanche; upon the return of the crowd, he escorts her and Mrs. Dimple to another part of the town.

Poll observes his departure disconsolately, and all the girls follow her example in a slow ensemble dance that is listless and despondent. The sailors try to cheer the girls up, but the girls will have none of them. The tars are a little angry now and play tug of war with their sometime sweethearts. When they end up flat on their backs, they vow vengeance on their handsome captain.

Good Captain Belaye dances back in at this point, and again the girls are in a daze. The sailors rage as the girls reach out to touch him and blow him kisses frantically. Belaye reprimands them as if they, too, were members of his crew, but the sailors are still jealous and threaten him. He dances in their midst and is tossed about by the men, as the girls continue flirting. Belaye dances gaily down through a line of adoring girls, who kneel and try to touch him as he passes, and the curtain falls.

SCENE TWO: THE QUAYSIDE   Night has fallen. A drop curtain places us on a dock that stretches out into Portsmouth Harbor. *H.M.S. Hot Cross Bun* is seen at the right. Above the ship's anchor chain a nude figurehead winks amusingly. Across the water a lighthouse stands at the end of a long seaside quay, where the Lord Nelson Tavern and the customhouse face us. Captain Belaye strides across the scene and mounts the gangway, shaking his head at the impertinent lasses of Portsmouth town.

Pineapple Poll follows him. She knows that the *Hot Cross Bun* has been ordered back to sea and is sad that she will not see Belaye for some time. Then, on the right, at the foot of the gangway, she discovers a discarded sailor's uniform. Suddenly her face brightens and she rushes off into the wings.

Liberty has expired for the crew of the *Hot Cross Bun,* and in slow single file the sailors make their way across the dock to their ship. When they have disappeared up the gangway, Poll returns. She now wears white sailor's pants and her mood has changed completely:

> And I went to Lieutenant Belaye (and he never suspected me!)
> And I entered myself as a chap as wanted to go to sea.

Poll is delighted at the ruse, whirls happily, puts on the blue jacket, takes the ribbons out of her hair, and adjusts the sailor hat at a jaunty angle. Now she is ready for sea. She steps up the gangway with salty determination.

The music now sounds a pathetic strain, and Jasper arrives on the scene. He is looking for Poll and has come to the dock as a last resort. He cannot find her and, as he looks down at the water, he fears the worst. Suppose she has thrown herself into the sea, all for the love of Captain Belaye! Jasper doesn't quite believe it, but soon he finds it impossible to believe anything else: there on the dock is Poll's hair ribbon and there are her discarded clothes. Jasper shakes his fist at the *Hot Cross Bun* and weeps for his lost love. He knows she is dead. He holds Poll's dress against his shoulder, as if she were still dancing with him, and caresses the dress. Slowly he walks away.

SCENE THREE: ON BOARD H.M.S. HOT CROSS BUN   The curtain rises, the music brightens, and we find ourselves on the afterdeck of Captain Belaye's ship. In the back, under the poop deck, is the captain's cabin. The white ensign of the Royal Navy flies free in the wind. Belaye is at the helm. The crew lines up at quarters on deck, and Captain Belaye leaves the helm to put them through their paces. He dances before them, long glass in hand. The crew watch respectfully, all that is except the sailor Pineapple Poll, who adores her captain so much that she can barely keep in line. At Belaye's command, Poll spreads her arms wide and the rest of the crew, in a close line, turn around her, like an anchor chain winding around a capstan.

Although the crew seem to be exhausted and Poll is plainly seasick, Belaye has other tasks for them to do and orders them to aim one of the ship's guns at a target he spies in the distance. The crew haul out a cannon, set it in place, load it, and stand ready. Belaye walks over to fire the gun and is astonished to see his crew hold their hands to their ears and run to the starboard side. The cannon is delayed in firing, and when it finally explodes, Pineapple Poll falls back in a dead faint. The other sailors don't know what to do, and Belaye tries to revive this supersensitive member of his crew. He is holding Poll in his arms when she recovers, and this is sufficient to send her into another swoon.

At this point Belaye sees that the *Hot Cross Bun* has reached its destination: Portsmouth àgain! He takes a ring out of his pocket and smiles. He all but drops Poll, runs across the deck, and leaps over the side to the dock. Poll is left alone for a moment and assumes that all the crew will go ashore. But then she observes that the men are behaving in a curious fashion, very unlike the seafaring type, and a number of curious incidents come back to her:

> We sailed that afternoon at the mystic hour of one,—
> Remarkably nice young men were the crew of the *Hot Cross Bun*.
> I'm sorry to say that I've heard that sailors sometimes swear,
> But I never yet heard a Bun say anything wrong, I declare.
>
> When Jack Tars meet, they meet with a "Messmate, ho! What Cheer?"
> But here, on the *Hot Cross Bun*, it was "How do you do, my dear?"
> When Jack Tars growl, I believe they growl with a big big D—
> But the strongest oath on the *Hot Cross Bun* was a mild "Dear me!"

One sailor, striding across the deck with affected saltiness, stops to primp girlishly at the porthole of the captain's cabin. No wonder, Poll says to herself, that:

> Belaye would admit that his men were no great use to him,
> "But then," we would say, "there is little to do on a gunboat trim.
> I can hand, and reef, and steer, and fire my big gun too—
> And it is such a treat to sail with a gentle well-bred crew."

Poll begins to wonder where Captain Belaye has gone and picks up his long glass to train it on the town. One of the crew points out that she's looking through the wrong end and grabs the instrument to have a look himself. Captain Belaye leaps back aboard, and they are delighted at his return until they see that he is not alone. He lifts over the side his new bride, Blanche, and Mrs. Dimple.

When the sailors see Blanche in her wedding dress, they fall over in a mass faint. All but Poll, that is, who is so angry that she goes to the captain and claims him for her own. Blanche will not believe her, and Poll takes off her hat and jacket to prove that she has been intimate with Belaye on the ship. Belaye cannot believe his eyes. No one can believe their eyes when all the sailors tear off their false beards and turn out to be girls too!

Blanche now hates her new husband and will not listen when he tries to explain that he is surprised by all this. She is threatening to leave him when the real "Jack Tars," the real crew of the *Hot Cross Bun*, climb over the bulwarks to berate their captain for sailing away with their girls. Attacked from all sides, Belaye can do nothing. Some of the girls swoon and fall over the helm. But the sailors will have no more nonsense. They grab the girls, throw them on the deck, and stand over them triumphantly. Belaye leaves with his Blanche and her aunt.

The girls seem delighted at this reconciliation and rock contentedly back and forth in their sailors' arms. Now Jasper enters with Poll and they dance together happily. Poll is joyful that at least one man can be constant in his affections! Captain Belaye and his new wife have now settled their argument and they enter with Mrs. Dimple. Belaye is in full-dress uniform—gold epaulets and cocked hat. Mrs. Dimple carries his regular jacket and cap; she goes and presents them to Jasper. The potboy puts both of them on. Poll kisses him, admires his appearance, and they leave the scene to the sailors.

The crew of the *Hot Cross Bun* dance a vigorous, rowdy number and then hail the return of Jasper. Poll joins Jasper; he lifts her high in his arms, then releases her, and Poll dazzles the assembled crowd with rapid, whipping turns on point. Belaye and Blanche return; Poll circles the stage swiftly and then rejoins Jasper. The crew and their girls stand aside as Jasper and Belaye, arm in arm, lead the procession of principals. When these two come to the front of the stage, they separate and stretch between them a large Union Jack, which they drape about Mrs. Dimple's shoulders. She kneels between the two happy couples, umbrella in one hand, trident in the other. Some of the sailors move forward and lift her high over the deck. They begin to turn her as the other sailors and their girls circle them, and the curtain falls as Mrs. Dimple, ruling Britannia with all her might, smiles down upon all the happy lovers.

A POEM FORGOTTEN

Music by Wallingford Riegger. Choreography by Eliot Feld. Scenery and costumes by José-Luis Cuevas. Lighting by Jules Fisher. First presented by the American Ballet Company at the Brooklyn Academy of Music, New York, October 22, 1970, with Daniel Levans, Edward Henkel, Christine

Kono, Cristina Stirling, Elizabeth Lee, Larry Grenier, James Lewis, and Richard Munro. Conductor: Isaiah Jackson.

A recollection of childhood, boyhood, and youth, *A Poem Forgotten* is a narrative work to the *Concerto for Piano and Wind Quintet* of Wallingford Riegger. The curtain rises, and we see on stage, his back to us at first, a boy, naked to the waist, going through the ritual of being born. He falls back, sucking his thumb, his father helps him, and gradually he learns to crawl, jump, and walk. No sooner does he do so, however, than his mother emerges with a little sister for him. The two children play as the parents make love. Against a backdrop of boyhood images, the father carries the mother away and the children are alone.

A red beanie on the back of his head, the boy now jumps down from a bench and tests his adolescent strength. His sister, fascinated also by her growing attractions, sits on the bench while the boy enjoys seduction by a girl in purple. When she goes, however, the boy hides his face in shame and wants to cry out. He joins his sister on the bench and wiggles his thumb.

After an interval, he and the sister sit rocking as three rowdy boys play roughly. He joins them: there is some trouble, but the girl in purple breaks it up. This scene is caught in a frozen tableau, with the boy stretched out on the floor. The three hoodlums now attack the girl in purple as the sister, watching, lifts her dress above her waist, wishing it were her. The boy goes to lie at his sister's feet as his father re-enters, carrying the boy's mother.

NOTES   Anna Kisselgoff in the New York *Times* called *A Poem Forgotten* "a brilliant, personally phrased essay on a young man's memories of his adolescence. Its idiom . . . is really expressive, not expressionist, and this is not a minor ballet . . . Daniel Levans, so obviously slated to become an exceptional dancer, was outstanding."

POÈME DE L'EXTASE (Poem of Ecstasy)

Music by Alexander Scriabin. Choreography by John Cranko. Designed by Jürgen Rose. First presented by the Stuttgart Ballet at the Württemberg State Theatre, Stuttgart, March 24, 1970, with Margot Fonteyn, Jan Stripling, Bernd Berg, Heinz Clauss, Richard Cragun, and Egon Madsen in principal roles. First presented in the United States by the same ensemble at the Metropolitan Opera House, New York, July 21, 1971.

The choreographer John Cranko expressed the essence of his ballet, derived from a story by Colette, in his own words: "At a party given by a great diva, there appears among the guests a young man who falls in love with her. At first she is flattered, then she remembers, more and more vividly, her former lovers, realizes that her life is already fulfilled and finally sends him away."

The ballet is set to the *Poème de l'Extase* of Scriabin and also to that composer's *Sonata No. 9*, orchestrated by Wolfgang Fortner.

The American critic Hubert Saal wrote in *Newsweek* (August 2, 1971):
"Fonteyn is wonderful. In that frenetic atmosphere, she stands out as the one
distinct figure, delicate but strong, nobly resigned to age. 'What I like about
the ballet,' she says, 'is that it's all one piece—the decor, the music, the choreography. It all goes together in a special period style and requires its own posing and line and fresh possibilities for *arabesques*. It's remarkable the number
of different things you can do with *arabesques*. I suppose it's really the most
important movement in ballet . . . Few ballerinas are lucky enough to get a
new ballet, much less a role tailor-made for my personality. I can act my age.
It's about someone looking back on her memories rather than forward to them.
It's something I can put myself into easily, like a nice coat.'"

The British critic John Percival wrote at great length about *Poème de l'Extase* in *Dance and Dancers* magazine:

"Cranko's intention was to get away from the little-girl image to which
ballerinas are mostly confined. They spend most of their lives playing sixteen-
year-old princesses, adolescent peasant girls, neglected younger daughters, and
other similar characters, with a whole host of our feathered friends (swans,
firebirds, bluebirds) for light relief. As Cranko remarked, an actress as she
grows up graduates to new and often more interesting roles, a dancer is stuck
with much the same kind of role all her life. His first idea was to make a ballet
based on *Medea* but he decided the story could not be made clear enough in
dancing. So after various possibilities had been discussed, he announced that
he had settled on a plot based on Colette's novel *Break of Day*. At the premiere, one disgruntled colleague complained of having read the book in preparation and found it completely irrelevant. I could not agree: the novel to my
mind provides both the situation and the motivation—but the story has under-
gone a complete change of setting and therefore of emphasis and development
in Cranko's treatment.

"The idea is, briefly, that a mature woman (not old, but past her youth) has
a young man fall in love with her. After some hesitation, she rejects him because she has built a contented life for herself and carries with her the memory of her former lovers; she prefers to keep all that as something already
achieved, and concentrate on her life now rather than risk a new adventure
that might be disappointing. Don't run off to read the novel for an idea of
what the ballet looks like—Colette's heroine lives in a cottage near the sea and
works in her garden; Cranko's heroine is a fine lady with a salon, clearly in a
fashionable town where there is lots of society. In a brief program note he
describes her as a great stage star, but I don't think there is any real indication
of this in the ballet—only that she is clearly much admired and respected by
the guests who throng the room where the first scene takes place.

"I don't know whether the ballet's chosen style dictated the choice of music
or vice versa, but they go marvelously together. A program note acknowledges
that choreography and production draw their inspiration from the work of the
painter Gustav Klimt (1862–1918), who was one of the practitioners of the
style known variously as *Jugendstil* (so called after the Munich magazine
which served as a rallying point for the movement) or Art Nouveau. Richly or-
namented, sensuous, full of natural-looking forms organized in a very artificial

way, it is a style well suited both to ballet and to today's taste, besides providing an apt parallel to the swirling, swooning, orgiastic music of Scriabin's *Poem
of Ecstasy*.

"Cranko's designer, as on several earlier occasions, is Jürgen Rose, who has
made the ballet as stunning visually as in every other respect. The settings
have a remarkable amount of detail in them and much rich coloring, so that
you might expect the dancers to be lost in the confusion, but in practice it is
all so meticulously worked out that every detail remains clear. And the work
evokes its chosen model without in any way losing its own individuality.

"The first scene—perhaps prologue would be more accurate—is set in an
elaborately furnished period drawing room. The walls are champagne colored,
with decorations in red and blue. Above a large round seat rises an ornate wire
structure supporting a huge pale orange bowl from which curls a faint whiff of
smoke suggesting incense; above this is a multi-colored hanging bowl lamp
that mirrors its shape. At the side and in a recess at the back are smart black
and white upright chairs.

"The people who enter are dressed in smart frocks with big hats, or in formal jackets with ties; the atmosphere is one of studied ease, very formal infor-
mality. Their movements are very artificial too, with particularly elaborate
ways of holding or moving their hands. They move about like people at a
party waiting for the real point of the party to arrive. A young man enters at
the back, at first unnoticed by the others: more eager, more earnest and less
affected than the rest, he seems slightly out of place, and clearly he feels a certain coolness on their part towards him, for he goes to sit alone in an alcove.

"Suddenly a woman enters quietly from the opposite corner. She has her
back to us but at once we know that she is the one who has been awaited.
Graciously and with studied charm she acknowledges the greetings of the assembled company. But now the youngster, too, comes to her, a little too
warmly for a stranger, and she turns away from him, but he persists in paying
attention to her. For a moment she seems rather annoyed, but her carefully
held poise continues, and when he returns after everyone else has gone,
she dismisses him with a single gesture of one arm. Alone, she lies on her
couch . . .

"The lights dim; when they come up once more the walls of the room and
all furniture except the couch have disappeared (and the couch vanishes, too,
once she has got up from it). At the back of the stage, a vast curtain tumbles
billowing from above, followed by another: they are painted with multicolored swirling patterns of great beauty. The boy has returned; like the
woman he is now dressed in a simpler, more stylized version of the realistic
clothes they wore before. We have left reality for the world of her imagination,
and now the visions of her past lovers come to her, wrapped in great cloaks of
red, blue, black and white or white and gold. First all of them together; then
they go and return one by one, this time appearing in turn from behind those
great curtains. Without their cloaks they look almost naked, but their flesh-
colored tights are embroidered each with a different jewel-like pattern. Each
dances with her in turn, and each time the boy tries to intervene and take the

place of this rival from the past, so that this part of the ballet (the greater part, in fact) becomes a tumultuous series of solos, duets and trios.

"Jan Stripling is the first to appear: tall, slim but strong, mature and quietly forceful in appearance and manner. Next Bernd Berg: smaller, more impetuous, in some respects a little like Egon Madsen, who plays the youngster; and this similarity is emphasized by giving them a kind of danced duel in which they echo each other's leaps and turns. Now Heinz Clauss, a little older than the others in appearance, and very gentle but with the air of a hard core of strength in reserve. Finally Richard Cragun, almost Bacchic in appearance and overwhelming in the youthful virility with which he hurtles round the stage.

"Now the boy is again alone with the woman and for a moment his hopes rise as she caresses his head while he kneels before her. But even while she pulls his head against her body, she is gazing across to where the four lovers have again returned, this time all together. They seize her and run with her held between them in a great circle round the stage; they lift her high above them, wrapped in their cloaks like a statue of winged victory. Then, two by two, they take the corners of those great curtains at the back and, as the music reaches its last orgasmic climax, run with them diagonally right across the stage. The curtains fall from where they hung, billowing behind the running men, right across the stage and out of sight. The light begins to dim. Realizing his fate, the boy backs away out of sight and out of the woman's life. She stands alone, looking after her visions and again raising one arm, this time to reach after them. But it is not a sad longing she feels, rather a sense of fulfillment. She raises both arms and curls them round her head, smoothing her face with a caressing movement, then her hands drop, first to her breasts and then to hang by her side. And as she stands there, a smile, a look of ineffable joy comes over her face.

"It is a marvelous role for Fonteyn. She has caught exactly the visual style of the ballet—that first entrance, her hands held at a slight angle, her arms curving gently down, her hip thrust a little to one side so that her dress also flows curvingly, her head alertly poised: you know at once that she is going to be exactly right. The personality too: even though she comes on with her back to you, there is not for a moment any doubt (and would not be, even if you did not recognize her) that here is the star—both in real life and in the character she is playing. But more than this: there is depth and warmth too, there is a living person there, not just a dancer, but a woman, not a conventional ballerina but a great dance-actress. And the best thing about this performance is that the humanity of it is achieved through the deliberately artificial style. It is not a question of two different aspects, a mannered exterior and a natural interior, nor a question of achieving humanity in spite of the artificiality, but actually through the elaborate artifice. The poses and movements, any one of which could have come from a painting of this period, are necessarily contrived, stylized, yet at the same time they express the emotions in a natural way. See how she stands with the back of one hand against her lips, her body and arms a carefully contrived pattern of curves and angles—it could look simperingly shallow, but it does not, it conveys the feelings of a woman who has accepted a certain way of life but can look within herself with truth and understanding.

"Fonteyn's dancing in *Poème* (and I must stress that it is a real dancing role, not just an acting part) is mainly in duets, trios or larger ensembles with her five partners. And what partners they are. All four of the visions are so strong, they look so handsome and manly, they dance with such fire and strength, they support her with such tenderness and firmness too; and each emerges also as a real individual. Cragun has the role needing most virtuosity (some of the leaps in which he swirls in the air are fantastically unexpected and yet done with such apparent ease)—but all of them have to dance hard, and they all do it well. You would be hard put to it to find another company which could cast these four roles successfully—and that is without mentioning Madsen in the lead, who has to keep up with all four of them right through the ballet, dancing like a dream—yet what you notice more than his dancing is the way he brings the boy to life, the eagerness of his admiration for the woman at the beginning, contrasted with the artificiality of the rest of the assembled company; his engaging mixture of diffidence and assertiveness; the way he responds to the challenge of each remembered rival; and the look of absolute brokenheartedness on his face at the end when he realizes he is defeated."

PRESENCE

Music by Bernd Alois Zimmermann. Choreography by John Cranko. Scenery and costumes by Jürgen Schmidt-Oehm. First presented by the Stuttgart Ballet at the Württemberg State Theatre, Stuttgart, May 16, 1968. First presented in the United States by the same ensemble at the Metropolitan Opera House, New York, June 20, 1969, with Marcia Haydée, Richard Cragun, and Heinz Clauss in the principal roles.

A ballet for the well-read, *Presence* has as its main characters Don Quixote, Ubu Roi, and Molly Bloom. The choreographer has said that the characters are in no way intended as literal copies after Cervantes, Jarry, and Joyce, but are rather the omnipresent reflections of certain of their aspects common to us all.

Presence, said Cranko, "is a series of portrait-dialogues revealing the protagonists: Don Quixote, the Dreamer, who hardly knows whether he is a part of a dream or reality, whether he himself is the dream or is conceived by the dream of another; Roi (King) Ubu, the Mighty, a remorseful and naïve Cain who seeks to destroy everything that stands in his way; and with them, Molly, the Woman—Goddess, Prostitute, Virgin in one—the Mother of us all, and the Creation of us all." The ballet is in five episodes, each in the form of a pantomime.

In an interview in *Opera News* (October 11, 1969), in which he discussed much of his work in detail, John Cranko recalled that originally *Presence* "was an idea that came from the composer . . . It has no rhythm at all, just structures and textures; this bit's spiky and that bit's oily, this bit's flat and that bit's high. Zimmermann chose the three characters—Ubu, Molly Bloom and Don Quixote—and I used them in alternating sequences of pantomime and dance."

PRINCE IGOR

Ballet in one act. Music by Alexander Borodin. Choreography by Michel Fokine. Scenery and costumes by Nicholas Roerich. First presented by Diaghilev's Ballets Russes at the Théâtre du Châtelet, Paris, May 18, 1909, with Adolph Bolm, Sophie Fedorova, and Helen Smirnova in the principal parts. First presented in the United States by Diaghilev at the Century Theatre, New York, January 18, 1916, with Bolm, Lubov Tchernicheva, and Sophie Pfanz.

Set to the music of the "Polovtsian Dances" from the second act of Borodin's opera *Prince Igor*, this is purely a dance ballet, without any connection with the plot of the opera. When it was first performed with full chorus and orchestra, the ballet served to introduce to Western Europe the unimagined color of Russian music and dancing combined in a striking single work.

The scene, when the curtain rises, is suffused in the violet light of the approaching dawn. The light of two campfires is thrown against two great tents made of animal skins. Gathered about the fires, the men and women of the Polovtsy tribe sleep soundly. In the distance, around other campfires, other members of the tribe are curled in sleep. A lone warrior stands on watch.

One of the sleeping girls begins to stir. She raises her arm, rises, and stretches. As soon as she is fully awake, she goes from group to group, gradually waking the whole tribe. The somnolent music becomes expectant in its rhythm, as the drowsy villagers prepare for their daily tasks. The sun rises, and the people's dark garments take on their vivid natural colors.

The girl moves forward, turns rapidly, and begins to dance to the music. Other girls join her dance; in the back a group of youths accompany them. The young warlike villagers are unable to contain the vigor which sleep has stored up within them; they seek to release their energy. The girls sit on the ground as one of the boys comes forward and dances with keen strength, spinning swiftly to the pulsating rhythm of the music. The girls surround him, gyrating with brilliant turns. As the youth concludes his dance, the girls fall at his feet.

A great warrior, the leader of the tribe, moves forward, brandishing a brilliant sword. A dozen girls appear, as if at his silent command, and dance softly. Their primitive costumes are embellished with flowing gauze, which follows their movements in dancing waves. A girl in white, with long braided hair, is among them. The music mounts in intensity; the girls sit on the ground and a brave warrior leaps over their heads. He dances fiercely, called by some distant battle call. The girls dance in a group, as a formation of warriors circle their leader. The warrior slides forward, brandishing his weapon, and the entire ensemble forms a warlike tableau to the insistent demand of the music.

The men gather in the center of the stage and dance around and around to the demanding tempo. The girls enclose them in a wide circle of whirling movement. Suddenly the music hesitates. The two groups cross the scene quietly, then the men move up behind the girls and lift them high. The youths slap their thighs in their enthusiasm for battle and they race back and forth across the stage.

Six of the Polovtsy girls come to the front and dance with an energy that emulates the warriors' strength. They are joined by the girls dressed in gauze, who reassert the femininity of their sex. But the warlike dancers take over again, stomping the ground with their feet and clapping their hands to the beat of the music. The finest warrior of them all comes forward and, as the entire tribe beats out the rhythm of his dance, the brave Polovtsian dances a whirling climax to the ballet. He comes forward to the footlights and continues his dance, turning like a persistent top. The whole tribe gathers behind him and turns with him. The scene is alive with whirling movement as the curtain falls.

PRINTEMPS

Music by Claude Debussy. Choreography by Lorca Massine. Costumes designed by Irene Sharaff. First presented by the New York City Ballet at the New York State Theatre, January 13, 1972, with Violette Verdy in the principal role.

Describing *Printemps* in her review of the premiere in the New York *Post*, Frances Herridge said the ballet "was a picture of Spring, come gently to life— all innocence and sweet frolic, full of freshness and grace, and utterly feminine in the romantic spirit of time past. It was as though Isadora Duncan, inspired by Botticelli's *Primavera,* had gamboled with her girls to the lyrical music of Claude Debussy."

The dance indicates the years' remaking and shows how a new spring spirit can take over from the old.

THE PRIVATE LESSON

Music by Georges Delerue. Choreography by Flemming Flindt. Decor and costumes by Bernard Daydé. First presented at the Opéra Comique. Paris, April 6, 1964. First presented in the United States by the Royal Danish Ballet at the New York State Theatre, New York, December 17, 1965, with Mette Hønningen, Henning Kronstam, and Mona Kiil.

Based on a play by Eugène Ionesco, *The Private Lesson* tells of a lesson given by a psychopathic ballet master.

The scene is the ballet master's classroom. His pianist is preparing for the day's lesson when the bell rings and a young girl arrives. She is shown to the dressing room. When she returns ready for her practice the ballet master enters. The lesson at first goes well, but with complicated exercises on *pointe*, the pupil has difficulties and complains. The pianist is sent away. The ballet master insists that the girl continue, becoming more and more incensed. The dancer is almost hypnotized by him. In the end, the ballet master loses his temper and strangles her.

The pianist returns and the ballet master behaves like a little boy who is sorry and asks for help. She reproaches him indulgently and together they carry the girl's body away. Again the pianist prepares for a lesson. She picks up some overturned chairs when suddenly the bell rings . . .

PRODIGAL SON

Ballet in three scenes. Music by Sergi Prokofiev. Choreography by George Balanchine. Scenery and costumes by Georges Rouault. First presented by Diaghilev's Ballets Russes at the Théâtre Sarah Bernhardt, Paris, May 21, 1929, with Serge Lifar in the title role, Felia Dubrovska as the Siren, Michael Fedorov as the Father, and Leon Woizikowski and Anton Dolin as Servants to the Prodigal Son. Revived by the New York City Ballet at the City Center, New York, February 23, 1950, with Jerome Robbins as the Prodigal Son, Maria Tallchief as the Siren, Michael Arshansky as the Father, and Herbert Bliss and Frank Hobi as Servants to the Prodigal Son. Lighting by Jean Rosenthal.

The story of the prodigal son is told first in the Bible: ". . . A certain man had two sons. And the younger of them said to his father, Father give me the portion of goods that falleth to me. And he divided unto them his living. And not many days after the younger son gathered all together, and took his journey into a far country, and there wasted his substance with riotous living. And when he had spent all, there arose a mighty famine in that land; and he began to be in want . . . And he would fain have filled his belly with the husks that the swine did eat: and no man gave unto him. And when he came to himself he said, How many hired servants of my father's have bread enough to spare, and I perish with hunger! I will arise and go to my father, and will say unto him, Father, I have sinned against heaven and before thee, and am no more worthy to be called thy son: make me as one of thy servants. And he arose and came unto his father. But when he was yet a great way off, his father saw him, and had compassion, and ran, and fell on his neck, and kissed him. And the son said unto him, Father I have sinned against heaven, and in thy sight, and am no more worthy to be called thy son. But the father said to his servants, Bring forth the best robe, and put it on him; and put a ring on his hand, and shoes on his feet: And bring hither the fatted calf, and kill it; and let us eat, and be merry: For this my son was dead, and is alive again; he was lost, and is found . . ." (St. Luke, 15:11–24)

This ballet tells the parable dramatically, with certain necessary omissions from and additions to the original story, but with the central theme preserved.

SCENE ONE: HOME   The curtain rises almost immediately after the orchestra has played the first few bars of a strong, high-spirited theme. The scene is opulently colored. A painted backdrop depicts the distant view and imaginative sky line of the ancient Near East. A bright yellow sun hangs in a rich blue sky over a port with a lighthouse watching over the sea. At the right, in the back, is the opening to a tent; on the left, toward the front, stands a low picket fence with a small gate. Two boys, friends to the prodigal son, are busy about the scene, hurriedly arranging a store of large wine jugs as if they are preparing for a long journey. The prodigal son emerges from the tent, followed by two sisters. He is dressed in a short blue tunic and an open vest. His sisters, dressed in long, flowing garments, try to engage his attention, but the carefree youth ignores them to greet his friends. He picks up one of the wine jugs and throws it to one of them playfully. The music becomes terse in tempo, and the prodigal son dances vigorously in response to its pounding rhythm. With robust gaiety he seems to act out for his friends the adventures in store for them away from home and to reveal, at the same time, an innocent, headstrong spirit that urges him to seek those adventures. His sisters are frightened at his strong determination to leave home so selfishly and watch apprehensively. The prodigal son leaps about the stage with boundless energy, oblivious to their care. His dance stops in an open gesture when he looks up, to find himself face to face with his father, who has come out of the tent. He is embarrassed for an instant and steps back.

As a new, poignant melody begins, the father beckons to his children. They come and sit before him, the son unwillingly, but obediently. The son's attention wanders, and the father patiently turns his head back to the family circle. He holds up his arms over his children and looks upward in humble prayer. He touches their heads softly. The son turns away in protest at the ritual, but his father persists gently. When the son twists his body away, the father takes the boy's hand and places it on his sisters' hands.

The tension between the son and the father increases; the son turns away in disgust, leaps up, and flaunts his indifference in his father's face. The father rises and stands motionless and unprotesting in his grief, as his son dances in defiance before him. The son's temper is so high and his eagerness to leave home so intense that his sisters watch in terror and sadness. His dance is closely similar to his first dance, but here he is emboldened by anger. He ignores his family, beckons to his two friends, and points toward the open highway. They gather together their gear and run off through the gate, closing it hastily behind them. In a final gesture of rebellion, the son turns rapidly in the air before his father, dashes across the stage, and jumps high over the fence after his companions. The sisters stand close to their father in sympathy, but the old man walks forward slowly, raises his hand in unacknowledged farewell, and stands for a moment watching. Then he motions his daughters to the tent and follows them into their home. The scene blacks out.

SCENE TWO: IN A FAR COUNTRY   The backdrop has been changed when the lights come up again. Still heavily colored, it now depicts an open tent furnished with a festive table. The small, symbolic fence that figured in the

first scene stands as it was, on the left. A loud, crashing march heralds the arrival of a group of revelers, who enter on the left in a close line. They wear
short tunics and white tights. All of them are bald. The manner in which they
cross the stage to the raucous music is grotesque. As they separate, the beautiful, jubilant melody that will dominate the scene receives its first statement
from the orchestra. They go over to the fence, turn it upside down, and we see
that the prop is also a long black table. The table is moved back. The revelers
form in short lines before it and hop across invisible lines toward each other,
playing some fantastic game. Four of them lie down on the stage and spread
their legs to form a star. One of the revelers lies across the middle of the star
as the others move forward and rotate the pattern their companions have
made. Their frolic is renewed until the prodigal son enters on the right with
his two friends.

The revelers cease their play and gather in a close group on the other side
of the stage; they are just as frightened as the intruders. The prodigal son
doesn't see them at first. Then he approaches carefully, urging his friends to
follow. They refuse, and he abandons his fears, to greet the strangers with
open cordiality. He tries to shake hands with one of them, then with another,
but all the revelers pull their hands back. He doesn't understand. They touch
his rich clothes covetously and come closer. He hesitates and moves away apprehensively, but his friends force him back and he remembers the wine they
have brought with them. He tells his companions to give the revelers drink,
and immediately the situation changes. The revelers form a parade behind
him, and the prodigal son is carried on the shoulders of his two friends. Everyone is now his friend. He is lifted up and, from above, shakes hands with all of
his new companions. They throw him side to side in jovial welcome. Then he
dances between his two fellows as everyone watches admiringly. He grasps
their hands elatedly, and all the revelers rush to shake his hand. The whole
group dances boldly and vigorously with the prodigal son. He jumps over the
table as the dance ends, and all gather about him.

The siren comes in, dancing on point slowly and seductively to a tune of
Oriental character. She wears a tight red tunic about her slim body, a high
headdress, and from her shoulders there trails a crimson cape of velvet. The
men watch her intently; the prodigal son is dazzled by her strange beauty and
the confidence with which she fascinates. She turns slowly, wrapping the cape
around the upper part of her body, then unwinds the garment. She handles the
cape as if it were a part of her own body—an animate object obedient to her
will. When the cape is fully extended behind her, the siren steps back over it,
pulls it up between her legs, and winds it around them. Holding the cape with
one arm, she dances proudly. She seems oblivious to the fact that she is being
watched; this dance seems to please her more than it could please anyone else.
She drops the cape and falls to her knees in an attitude of conventional despair. Then she rises, proud and assertive, to turn intricately on point. She
throws the cape behind her, falls back on her arms, and, moving slowly on her
hands and points, drags it across the floor. Then she kneels low and pulls the
cape up over her head, covering her body completely.

The prodigal son, now helplessly attracted, moves from behind the table and pulls the cape away. The siren rises on point, unsurprised. He tosses the garment aside as she turns to look at him. The prodigal son becomes now as obedient to her desire as the castoff raiment. He stands transfixed as the siren dances before him. She turns with strong, sinuous grace and holds out her arms in a gesture of approval and welcome. She approaches him closely; the prodigal son places his hands on her waist; they move backward in response to her lead. The siren pushes him back against the table. The revelers gather about them, and the siren is thrown back high above the table, into the waiting arms of her accomplices. She sits in triumph over the suppliant prodigal son, who lies on the table beneath her.

The siren is lifted down and sits facing the prodigal son. His eyes look down. His two friends begin a dance to amuse the group. Relieved by this distraction, the prodigal son watches with the others, but glances at the siren when her eyes leave his face. The siren touches his hand and moves her fingers up his arm to caress the golden medallion that hangs about his throat. He looks her full in the face.

His friends finish their dance, kneel before the table, and everyone applauds. The siren and the prodigal son come forward, watching each other intimately. They stand apart. It is as if he were imitating her movements. The siren falls back in his arms. She repulses his caress and entwines her arms back around his neck, and the two dance forward. They pause, and he puts his head between her legs, rises, and the siren sits proudly on his shoulders. Then she slides down his back. She stands on point before him and coils her leg about him, holding him fast, as he turns her. She releases him, and he pulls her over his back; the siren's hands reach out for her feet so that her body forms a hoop about him. Her body snakes about him completely, and slowly she slides to the floor. He steps out of the coil, rolls the siren upright, and holds her under her arms. Her knees rest on his feet as he moves across the stage. Now the prodigal son becomes bold and caresses the siren openly. He sits at her feet, his knees drawn up. She approaches him and sits on his head while resting her feet firmly on his knees. Now she rises straight up, arrogant in her voluptuousness and power. She steps away, and the prodigal son lies supine. She lies back across his body; their legs tangle. Now powerless, the prodigal son lies entwined in the siren's grasp. She gestures in insidious exultation.

The music pounds and shrieks fircely. The prodigal's two friends pull the couple apart. Their companions are now reveling in drunkenness and force the prodigal son to join them. They drag his exhausted body about the stage while the siren watches from the table. He seeks her help, but the profligates carry her above the table and she pours wine down his throat as he slides down the table beneath her. They lift him high and carry the siren under him. Both are held by the waist as their bodies fall back hideously. They embrace frantically, are finally released, and two drunkards crawl under their legs. The prodigal staggers from group to group in his intoxication and falls against the table, where he cannot distinguish one of his companions from another. The siren watches him expectantly. He rushes up on the table, but the revelers tilt it up high under him and he slides down it, all his strength spent. The siren places her pointed toe on his chest in triumph.

The table now stands up on end. The revelers conceal themselves behind it. The prodigal is shoved back against the table, where he rests helpless. Hands reach out from either side and move down his body. The friends rush out from behind, turn him upside down, shake him, and collect his gold greedily. They stand aside as the siren is carried out. She stands upright on a man's shoulders, her arms akimbo. She gets down and gathers up all the remaining gold. Now the thieves rob the prodigal of all his outer garments, even his shoes. He is still unaware of what they have done to him, and the debauchers celebrate by crawling over and under each other, like eels. The siren yanks off the prodigal's gold medallion, kisses it, and exits. Her companions leave the scene, running across the stage, back to back, like many-legged insects.

The prodigal son wakens slowly from his stupor. He slides down the table to the ground and falls on his face. He pulls himself back up, gripping the table with agonized effort. He looks down at his hands, then at his body. He remembers and holds his head in disbelief. Stretching his hand up plaintively in despair, he acknowledges the betrayal of his friends and his own self-betrayal. He falls to the ground, sees water, crawls to it, drinks, and curls up like a child. He rises, looks behind him at the scene of his debauchery, and struggles off on his knees.

The profligates return, bringing their loot with them. The siren follows. The table is now turned upside down to form the gate and fence. The siren's companions run to the fence, arrange themselves within it, and the siren joins them. One of the men lifts high the end of her crimson cape, others begin a rowing motion, and the table becomes a ship, the siren's cape its sail, and her arched body its figurehead. Her companions blow their trumpets, and the scene blacks out.

SCENE THREE: HOME   The stage is set as it was for the first scene. The prodigal son, covered now with a thin and tattered black cloak, crawls across the stage, supporting his exhausted body with a staff. The music is dark, almost funeral-like in its persistent beat. The traveler's progress is slow and, to him, endless, for he has no idea where he is. He looks about hopelessly. Suddenly he sees the gate to his home. He staggers toward it, reaches out his hand, touches it, and collapses with the effort.

His sisters emerge from the tent. One of them sees him and calls to the other. Together they go to him and open the gate to lead him in lovingly. The piercing melody of the music reflects their great joy. They stand on either side of their kneeling brother as their father comes out. They are so happy that they do not move. The father remains near the door of his home. The son slowly and hesitatingly raises his head and looks up at his father. He beseeches him with outstretched arms. The father does not move. The son twists away toward the fence, but he has no sooner moved than his father raises his hand to keep him. He turns back toward his home, bows his head to the ground, and stretches his arms out behind in self-denial. With head still bowed, he crawls toward his father slowly, wretchedly. He falls full length just as he nears him, reaches out to drag himself forward by grasping his father's feet. He pulls himself up, clinging to his father's arms. The father reaches out to gather him close in forgiveness, love, and protection and, holding him like a child, he covers his son with his cloak.

THE PROSPECT BEFORE US

Dramatic ballet in seven scenes. Music by William Boyce. Choreography by Ninette de Valois. Scenery and costumes by Roger Furse. First presented by the Sadler's Wells Ballet at the Sadler's Wells Theatre, London, July 4, 1940, with Pamela May, Mary Honer, Margaret Dale, Frederick Ashton, Robert Helpmann, and John Hart among the principals. First presented in the United States by the Sadler's Wells Theatre Ballet at the Pabst Theatre, Milwaukee, Wisconsin, November 3, 1951, with Svetlana Beriosova, Pirmin Trecu, Stanley Holden, Pauline Harrop, and Michael Hogan among the principals.

The Prospect Before Us, or Pity the Poor Dancers, is a comedy based on eighteenth-century English art, music, and theatrical history. The art is that of the colorful caricaturist Thomas Rowlandson (1756–1827), one of whose drawings, entitled The Prospect Before Us, gives the ballet its name; the music is an arrangement by Constant Lambert of selections from the works of the English composer William Boyce (1710–79); and the history is taken from an incident related in John Eber's History of the King's Theatre.

The King's Theatre and its rival, the Pantheon, were popular London theatres of the time. Rowlandson's engraving shows us the stage of the Pantheon, where the celebrated French dancers Mademoiselle Théodore and Monsieur Didelot are dancing a ballet before an enthusiastic audience. But there were also enthusiastic audiences at the King's Theatre. The ballet The Prospect Before Us tells us the story of these two theatres—the intense rivalry of their managers, the resorting to any means to achieve success, the fierce competition for guest artists, and the pitiable condition of dancers who did not know from one day to the next on which stage they would appear.

SCENE ONE: THE STAGE OF THE KING'S THEATRE, 1789 After the orchestra has played a brief, charming overture, the curtain rises on a ballet rehearsal backstage at the King's Theatre. Five ladies of the ballet await the direction of Monsieur Noverre, the great ballet master, who stands on the right studying a choreographic chart. Madame Noverre sits in the background, knitting. Monsieur Didelot, the *premier danseur*, paces up and down, wondering when the devil Noverre will get on with the show. Mademoiselle Théodore, the *première danseuse*, wanders in. She sits down on the stage and blithely tries on one pair of dancing slippers after another while her fellow performers fret. Finally she finds a pair that suits her, and the rehearsal resumes. Monsieur Noverre pulls Monsieur Didelot into the rehearsal, and this *premier danseur* automatically supports Mademoiselle Théodore in a series of poses. He is not the least bit interested in dancing with her, and when he lifts her indifferently, the girl begins to complain. Didelot rages back at her.

Mr. Taylor, the manager of the King's Theatre, enters with a party of guests. The manager of the Pantheon Theatre, Mr. O'Reilly, wanders in to see what his chief competitor is up to. He trips over some of the dancers and watches the rehearsal with broken, humble envy. When the great Vestris is given a chance to rehearse his variation, he is so disdainful of these spectators that he merely indicates with his fingers the difficult steps he will dazzle them with in actual performance.

The visitors parade off the stage, and the rehearsal ends. When Mr. Taylor returns, Monsieur Noverre and his wife attack him with a demand for more money. As the three squabble over a contract, Mr. O'Reilly tries vainly to find out how much money Taylor is giving them. Finally Taylor accedes to Noverre's demands and he and his rival are alone.

Mr. Taylor and Mr. O'Reilly sit down on chairs at the back of the stage. Poor O'Reilly sits wrapped in thought as Taylor regales him with stories of the dancers, the unprecedented success they will have, and the money he will rake in. He brings out a bottle and offers his friend a drink. O'Reilly hardly notices his glass and drinks almost automatically as he sits sulking, thinking that all this might be his. But suddenly O'Reilly leaps up from his chair, claps his friend on the back, and is all expansive good humor. Taylor is bewildered by this change of mood, but listens patiently as O'Reilly gabbles about the beauty of the dancers and congratulates him on his good fortune. Soon O'Reilly staggers off and Mr. Taylor sits alone, wondering what on earth could have happened to change his rival's mood so quickly.

SCENE TWO: THE BURNING OF THE KING'S THEATRE   Mr. Taylor finds out the answer to his rival's strange behavior soon enough. It is June 17, 1789. A drop curtain depicting the burning of his theatre falls on the previous scene. Mr. Taylor ambles by, not noticing that anything is wrong. O'Reilly enters and calls his attention to a blazing wreckage. Taylor despairs. The dancers come into the street to watch the fire, and O'Reilly instantly directs them toward his theatre, the Pantheon, where new, profitable jobs await them. Mr. Taylor tries to get between his rival and his dancers, but O'Reilly steps over his back to welcome Monsieur Noverre and his wife and take them on to his theatre.

SCENE THREE: A LONDON STREET   Four kids in ragged clothes run into a street in the poor section of the city. A half-dressed harridan looks down from the window of a nearby house as they play aimlessly, tumbling and dancing and clapping hands. They hear a parade approaching and sit down, their backs to the footlights, as a strange procession enters. A horn player and drummer announce the arrival of a party of poor, impoverished dancers, who enter carrying a model of the Pantheon Theatre. Mr. O'Reilly is evidently not paying them very well, for written across the model of his theatre is the legend "Pray Remember the Poor Dancers."

SCENE FOUR: THE STAGE OF THE PANTHEON THEATRE   Mr. O'Reilly's opening night has come, and he sits watching the first performance of the ballet in a stage box on the left. Mr. Taylor observes his rival's success from the opposite box on the right. Dancers enter and, before a conventional pastoral backdrop, enact a *divertissement* with some semblance of plot. Mr. Taylor is anxiously looking for empty seats in the house and does not give his full attention to the ballet. Mr. O'Reilly is delighted with the dancing and when Monsieur Didelot wanders about the stage, anxiously looking for his love, does not in the least hesitate to direct him toward the right girl.

A girl in the *corps de ballet* stands in front of poor Mr. Taylor, obstructing his view of the stage. When another girl prevents Mr. O'Reilly from watching the stage, he flirts with her openly and outrageously, and all but pulls her into the box with him. Soon Mr. O'Reilly gets so carried away by the wonder and beauty of this performance in his own theatre that he, too, must become a part of the *divertissement*. He steps out of his box onto the stage and stumbles about awkwardly among the dancers. He is gradually enveloped by the *corps de ballet* and becomes, at the end of the ballet, a grotesque and embarrassed figure of the final tableau. The curtain falls as O'Reilly poses thus in triumph and Taylor, in his box, despairs at his rival's success.

SCENE FIVE: THE STAGE OF THE NEW KING'S THEATRE   Some time has passed: it is now 1790. Mr. Taylor has secured funds and has rebuilt the King's Theatre. The curtain rises on the stage of the new theatre, its equipment refurbished to duplicate the first scene of the ballet. The stage is dark. Four men stand near the footlights, disputing. Their shadows are thrown up against the back wall of the stage, making a comic enlargement of their obviously petty argument. One of the men is Mr. Taylor; the others are his lawyers, who prance about daintily examining a contract as they pursue their legal dialectic. The problem is: can Mr. Taylor, with his New King's Theatre, oblige Monsieur Noverre and his dancers to return, or has Mr. O'Reilly of the Pantheon a legal right to their continued services? O'Reilly observes the dispute.

The lawyers decide in favor of O'Reilly, who oddly enough is impatient with his advantage. He has grown tired of the whims, tempers, and persistent demands of the great choreographer and wishes to be rid of dancers forever.

SCENE SIX: THE BURNING OF THE PANTHEON   Hardly has Mr. O'Reilly had a chance to return to his theatre with his problem than the Pantheon catches on fire, and, as in Scene Two, we are treated to the pyrotechnical drop curtain. Mr. O'Reilly dances a jig of delight before his flaming theatre and sees himself happily released from the uncertainties of the world of ballet. He is so delighted with the fire that he turns around and warms his pants near its flames.

His dancers, the girls first, flee the burning wreckage. They flee with obvious pleasure: perhaps they, abetted by the dauntless Mr. O'Reilly, have had a hand in the holocaust! Mr. Taylor welcomes them with open arms. Monsieur Noverre and his wife are the last to accept their former manager's greetings and to accompany him back to the New King's Theatre. Mr. O'Reilly, his troubles now but a heap of ashes, looks upon the smoking scene with the uncontrolled relish a stepfather might feel in seeing off to school a thankless child. He will pay for it, in the end, but now he is happy.

SCENE SEVEN: THE STAGE OF THE NEW KING'S THEATRE   Back at Mr. Taylor's
new theatre, Monsieur Noverre is again rehearsing his dancers on their home
stage. Monsieur Vestris uses the back of one of the chairs for a bar and warms
up for his solo, while the ballet master and his wife hover busily over the *corps
de ballet.*

Mr. Taylor enters, followed by the inevitable parade of lawyers. Now that
the Pantheon has burned down, there is no problem: the French artistes can return to the King's Theatre without fear of suit from Mr. O'Reilly. Mr. Taylor
shakes hands with the lawyers one by one, and they dance about him joyfully.

In the midst of this celebration, Mr. O'Reilly stumbles in. He has lost his
wig and his coat, and his stockings flap about his ankles: he is very drunk.
Whether he is drunk because he is happy or drunk because he is sad, we cannot at first determine, but it soon appears that he has had second thoughts:
again he is jealous of Mr. Taylor, who always seems to have all the luck, what
with his faithful dancers, his friends to lend him money, and his brand-new
theatre.

As soon as he sees the dancers, he begins to imitate them, ruthlessly and ab-
surdly, burlesquing both the ladies and the gentlemen in their artificial poses.
When they reprimand him, he apes their movements even more outrageously.
Finally O'Reilly collapses on the floor, where he sits with affected dignity.
Monsieur Noverre cannot quite believe that he can be so intoxicated. The rank
odor of spirits that the besotted manager breathes upon him causes the dancing master almost to swoon. The dancers are aghast at this scandalous interruption to their rehearsal and exit in a huff, followed by Monsieur Noverre and
his wife. O'Reilly hoots at them, and as Madame Noverre passes, he grabs hold
of her skirt and almost pulls her to the floor.

Mr. Taylor sees nothing for it but to give his unfortunate friend more to
drink: it would be useless to *stop* him from drinking. The two sit side by side,
as they did at the end of Scene One, Mr. Taylor happy and triumphant, brag-
ging of his good fortune, whispering stories about the dancers, and clapping
poor Mr. O'Reilly on the back again and again to display his bumptious good
nature. After all, business is business, he seems to say, one must not cast out
one's rivals. And business is business, also, to Mr. O'Reilly, who all of a sudden, drunk as he is, comes to. He slaps Taylor on the back and staggers about
the stage, almost falling into the orchestra, wholly possessed with a new and
brilliant idea. He clutches his rival's bottle of whisky in his arms and, zigzag-
ging, nearly tripping, he stumbles off into the wings. Mr. Taylor, left alone, recalls that O'Reilly was similarly jubilant some while back, when, just as now,
he had no right to be. Drunk as O'Reilly is, could he be plotting another ruse?
Could he? After all, there is a limit to the number of new King's Theatres. The
curtain falls.

PULCINELLA

*Dramatic ballet in one act. Music by Igor Stravinsky, based on scores by
Giambattista Pergolesi. Choreography by Leonide Massine. Scenery and*

costumes by Pablo Picasso. First presented by Diaghilev's Ballets Russes at the Théâtre National de l'Opéra, Paris, May 15, 1920, with Leonide Massine as Pulcinella, Tamara Karsavina as Pimpinella, Vera Nemtchinova as Rosetta, Lubov Tchernicheva as Prudenza, Stanislas Idzikowski as Caviello, Nicholas Zverev as Florindo, Enrico Cecchetti as Il Dottore. First presented in the United States by the New York Music Guild in Chicago, 1933, with choreography by Laurent Novikoff.

Stravinsky's score for *Pulcinella* is based on music by the great Neapolitan, Giambattista Pergolesi. The story of the ballet is based on an early eighteenth-century Italian manuscript found in Naples, and its principal characters are taken from the *commedia dell'arte,* the popular Italian masked comedy, which, beginning in the sixteenth century, captured the imagination of all of Europe with its universal types: the pathetic Pierrot, the heartless and flirtatious Columbine, the deathless Pulcinella (Punch, to the English-speaking world), and others. The ballet tells a new variation of Pulcinella's immortality.

A narrow street in Naples is the scene. A volcano can be seen in the distance, over the bay at the end of the street. The end house to the left is that of Tartaglia, whose daughter, Rosetta, is beloved by the youth Caviello. The end house to the right is that of *Il Dottore* (the doctor), whose daughter, Prudenza, is beloved by Florindo.

At the beginning of the ballet Caviello and Florindo enter to watch the houses of their sweethearts. Soon Prudenza and Rosetta look out of their windows. They smile at their suitors, seemingly encouraging them, then pour water out over their heads. The doctor, meanwhile, has discovered the presence of the boys and drives them away.

Pulcinella enters—the familiar figure with a long, pendulous red nose. He dances in the street to the tune of a small violin he plays. His dance and his music attract the girls. Prudenza, who clearly adores him, tries to embrace him. Pulcinella chases her back into her house. Rosetta appears, properly chaperoned by her father, Tartaglia. She tells him that she is in love with Pulcinella and must marry him. Tartaglia upbraids her for loving the ugly little man, but Rosetta ignores him. She tries to interest Pulcinella, who is as indifferent to her as he was to Prudenza. She dances before him. Enchanted, Pulcinella kisses her and takes her for a partner in a dance.

Pimpinella, Pulcinella's wife, discovers the two dancing together. The husband protests that he is innocent, that he still loves only her; Pimpinella is at length convinced of it, and the couple dance.

Meanwhile the two suitors, Caviello and Florindo, have been watching the street. They have seen that Pulcinella is the favorite of both Rosetta and Prudenza, and they are furious with jealousy. Their rage is still more inflamed when it becomes obvious that Pulcinella dares to reject the advances of the girls.

They attack Pulcinella, both jumping on him at once. Pimpinella screams for help, and both Rosetta and Prudenza rush out to help. The boys flee, and poor Pulcinella, left in the hands of three women, all eager to assist him, is almost torn in two by their fierce sympathy.

Summoned by their fathers, the two girls return to their homes. Pulcinella dances with his wife.

Florindo and Caviello have been waiting for this moment. They re-enter the street, disguised in black cloaks, carrying swords. Just as they run for him, Pulcinella sees them. He crosses himself hurriedly and pushes his wife into their house. Before he can enter too, he is caught by the two boys. Florindo strikes him dead with his sword. The murderers leave. Pulcinella gets up as if nothing had happened to him. He turns down the street and disappears.

The stage is empty for a moment. Then an astonishing thing happens. Four little Pulcinellas enter, carrying on their shoulders a fifth Pulcinella, apparently dead. They lay the corpse down in the street and dance.

Tartaglia and the doctor come out with their daughters, to see what has happened. The two girls, horrified to see their Pulcinella lying thus in the street, helplessly hover over his body. The doctor examines Pulcinella and declares him dead.

A magician joins them and assures the girls that he can bring Pulcinella back to life. The four little Pulcinellas and the two girls anxiously await the result of his mysterious incantations. The two fathers stand aside, disbelieving. After pommeling Pulcinella's body thoroughly, the magician commands him to live again. Pulcinella gets up, and the onlookers rejoice. The two girls swear to him that he is their only love.

Their fathers, however, remain unconvinced, even by appearances. To prove these skeptics wrong, the magician takes off his long cloak and wig: *he* is the real Pulcinella! His friend, Fourbo, has been the body.

Fourbo and Pulcinella trick the two fathers into retreating into their homes. Pimpinella comes into the street and, seeing two Pulcinellas, runs away in horror. Fourbo, still alias Pulcinella, brings her back.

Now everyone tries to get into the act. Caviello and Florindo enter, wearing Pulcinella disguises, to renew their romances with Rosetta and Prudenza. The girls accept them. Pimpinella, Rosetta, and Prudenza are dancing with three fake Pulcinellas. The real Pulcinella intervenes and kicks each of his imitators. While his friend Fourbo seeks safety in the magician's costume, Pulcinella unmasks the other two impostors before their girls.

The doctor and Tartaglia, still astonished by the goings on, are persuaded by Fourbo, the magician, to permit their daughters to marry Florindo and Caviello. The fathers agree. Pulcinella dances joyfully with Pimpinella, and the magician declares that they and the other two couples are man and wife.

NOTES Massine's *Pulcinella* was first presented in the United States by the City Center Joffrey Ballet, in 1974. The New York première was at the City Center, October 9, 1974.

Music by Igor Stravinsky. Choreography by Jerome Robbins and George Balanchine. Scenery and costumes by Eugene Berman. Lighting by Ronald Bates. First presented by the New York City Ballet at the Stravinsky Festival, 1972, at the New York State Theatre, Lincoln Center, June 23, 1972, with a cast headed by Edward Villella and Violette Verdy. Conducted by Robert Irving.

I am proud that the painter Eugene Berman, who died December 14, 1972, soon after *Pulcinella* was completed, designed this ballet for us. His help, friendship, and collaboration were essential. I had long felt that the original idea of the ballet from the Diaghilev days was just not interesting enough for the stage any more. But Jerome Robbins and I loved the music. So did Stravinsky's friend Berman, who was of course almost an Italian, so immersed was he in Italy, living there, painting there, knowing that beautiful country, its art and its traditions and theater, too, in all its variations. Berman was a kind of specialist in the *commedia dell'arte,* the improvisational theater identified with the great natural mimicry of the clowns of Naples, what Lincoln Kirstein has called the "underground manual idiom of scurrilous tricks and gesture." It was just those tricks that inspired us to do this new ballet with Berman to Stravinsky's music and I am glad that we did it. Robbins and I enjoyed putting the piece on; we even enjoyed dancing in the first performances, and if the ballet doesn't last as we made it, both of us know that Berman's part in it ought to. Good painters go on forever.

You just have to read the story of the first *Pulcinella,* described above in the first version, to see how complicated it all was for the audience to understand. Our idea was to simplify so that everything would be clear, and we hit on a variation of not only the Pulcinella myths, but the Faust myth, too. We decided that Pulcinella, a Neapolitan scamp, would make a pact with the devil to save his skin. He would then, as would be expected, renege on his promise, but his girl would rescue him, in spite of his having given her a hard time all along. Jerome Robbins and I had worked together before on a compressed story ballet, *Tyl Ulenspiegel,* where he, as the hero, made the whole of a personal as well as political and religious plot idea wonderfully clear in a matter of minutes. (One of the reasons Robbins is such a great choreographer is his great gift as a dancer; we can't remember that too often.)

To see the ballet and enjoy it, I hope words are not really necessary. It might be good to hear the recording that Stravinsky conducted of his lovely music (Col. ML-4830) and to read Robert Craft's notes on that album. As for the action:

Berman's superb drop curtain of Pulcinella and Stravinsky's signature rises on a graveyard scene. Eight Pulcinellas as pallbearers bring to his tomb a white skeleton recumbent on a catafalque. The Pulcinellas are beside themselves with grief. They put the skeleton in the tomb, nevertheless, weeping and wailing all the time.

The Devil arrives. At the tomb, he obliges the skeleton to look over the list of sins the deceased Pulcinella has committed, etc. He then tempts the deceased to sign a pact by which he will rise from the dead if he obeys the Devil in the future. The skeleton signs and then, miraculously, comes out of the grave a full-fledged Pulcinella. His girl, who had despaired at his death, rejoices. She cannot believe that her love has been restored to her. Pulcinella, however, intent on a reunion with his fellow comics, repulses her cruelly. The Devil drags him away to meet several fascinating ladies. In a brief scene in a brothel, the ladies, at the Devil's command, respond to his desires.

Pulcinella leads on a group of his fellow clowns as the baby Pulcinellas watch. He dresses then in a woman's dress and in this disguise, suddenly becoming a beggar, is seen asking for alms at a street fair of acrobats. This is simply a disguise for thievery, of course. The police spot him. He eludes them, then just as the police think they have cornered him, all his identical Pulcinella friends turn up and they don't know *whom* they are chasing. Victorious over the law, Pulcinella passes out the loot among his friends. He gives too fast, however, and there is nothing left for himself! Alone, he laments. A skeleton appears, brought onto the scene by the Devil; Pulcinella shivers in terror at this reminder of the pickle the Devil got him out of. Now when his girl comes onto the scene, he does not dismiss her rudely. The chorus sings as the Devil gives him a scroll; this is the pact he has signed.

A funeral procession of another Pulcinella passes. The Devil reminds Pulcinella of the flames of hell that await him. Then a young boy appears, blond and attractive, especially to the Devil, who can't keep his eyes off the boy. Suddenly blind to all else, the Devil follows the boy. Pulcinella has again escaped.

He and his girl are reunited. Pulcinella indicates that for some reason he is terribly, terribly hungry; ravenous, in fact. So a long table and a huge pot are brought in. Quickly, a potful of pasta is produced out of the pot. Pulcinella and his friends eat so much they collapse. The Devil arrives with his scroll again. Before he knows what has happened to him, Pulcinella's pals put him in the pot and give the scroll to their friend.

The scene shifts now to a solo by the girl, followed by one for Pulcinella, dressed now all in a white costume festooned with black balls. The brass in the orchestra begins a richly melodic section and the *pas de deux* for the two lovers begins. A dance of celebration for all the villagers follows, after which Pulcinella and his girl come forward to the front of the stage, with all their friends, to blow kisses to the audience.

PULCINELLA VARIATIONS

Music by Igor Stravinsky. Choreography by Michael Smuin. Scenery by Jack Brown. Costumes by Stanley Simmons. First presented by American Ballet Theatre at the Metropolitan Opera House, New York, July 11, 1968.

The program note reads: "Stravinsky, feeling sympathetic affinities with the music of Pergolesi, produced in this composition what is, in effect, a portrait of Pergolesi and his time." Similarly, the ballet presents, without a plot or story, a dance impression of the world of *commedia dell'arte*, the world of Punch and Harlequin and Columbine.

NOTES Writing of this production, Walter Terry in the *Saturday · Review* said that "*Pulcinella Variations* turned out to be a delight, the best work of

choreography yet by Michael Smuin, a highly virtuosic dancer in the company
. . . What he has done is to retain the antic nature of the *commedia dell'arte*,
for he has choreographically distilled its very essence from all its many
flavors."

PUSH COMES TO SHOVE

*Music by Franz Joseph Haydn and Joseph Lamb, arranged by David E.
Bourne. Choreography by Twyla Tharp. Costumes by Santo Loquasto.
Lighting by Jennifer Tipton. First presented by American Ballet Theatre
at the Uris Theatre, New York, January 9, 1976, with Mikhail Baryshnikov,
Marianna Tcherkassky, Martine van Hamel, Clark Tippet, and Christopher
Aponte as principals. Conductor: Akira Endo.*

A mix of old and new music, time past and present, new and old dance, *Push
Comes to Shove* displays the genius of the contemporary dancer in rare and
droll combinations. Doris Hering wrote in *Dance Magazine:* "It's like a giant
Euclidean doodle with a firm undercurrent of pure ballet logic."

Push Comes to Shove introduces ballet's first modern folk hero, in a
modified Chaplin style. He appears, in practice clothes and derby hat, in front
of the curtain as the piece begins and starts to react to Joseph Lamb's *Bohemian Rag 1919.* Two girls join him and under the palsy-walsy horseplay there
is a wry suggestion of feeling. Which doesn't last long. For before we know
it the stage picture has changed to a formal area, the music is Haydn's
Symphony No. 82 in C, and the vaudeville hero is now *premier danseur* and
acting and dancing like one for real. Except maybe he is a pugilist, ready to
knock 'em all out. The fancy girl dancers who take over the stage scare him off
and then another group of girls seizes the stage, dancing to Joseph Lamb
again. The hero comes and goes, there are dance situations that make jokes.
Both sides, as epitomized in the hero, part hoofer/beatnik/street crazy, part
danseur noble, are played off against each other. The hero dances this schizo-
phrenia for all he is worth. His derby hat, which is like an ever present talisman throughout the ballet, being played with and tossed about, reminds us of
the dual nature of what is happening: a modern audience watching a new
ballet danced by remarkable classical performers trained in an old technique.
Push Comes to Shove holds the mirror up to the audience and to the dancers
and the company they keep.

Time said that *Push Comes to Shove* "just might be the most important
dance event of the year." Frances Herridge wrote soon after the premiere in
the New York *Post:* "Baryshnikov is so irresistible with his Peck's Bad Boy insouciance and his spoofing of bombast that you don't notice at first how amusing the rest of the group is . . . There are speeded-up sequences reminiscent
of Mack Sennett. There are manipulated duets that made puppets of the ladies. And there are loose nuts everywhere. In short, there's not a dull moment."

Writing about the ballet in the *Times* of London, the critic John Percival
said: "At the heart of *Push Comes to Shove* is a hilarious performance by

Mikhail Baryshnikov. In effect, he is playing the Twyla Tharp role: the little bundle of nerves and muscles, glaring out from a moplike fringe. Sheer energy is his *métier* here, manifested in sudden bursts of wild spinning or fantastic jumps. But it is put over with an absolutely cool manner and a vaudeville comic's timing.

"In fact, Baryshnikov by no means carries the work alone. Martine van Hamel, just coming into bloom as a ballerina (I saw her charming Sylphide, and heard everyone raving about her Swan Queen and her Raymonda), has an aloof allure that is irresistible. Making up a trio of contrasted personalities, appearances and manners is Marianna Tcherkassky, small and pertly pretty.

"Those three principals dance a wickedly funny *pas de quatre* with a black bowler hat in the prelude, which is set to Joseph Lamb's *Bohemian Rag*, and each of them leads one movement of the main ballet, which is danced to Haydn's 'Bear' Symphony. Yes, the two musical styles do go together, thanks to the unfailing ingenuity of Tharp's invention. The mixture of tradition and irreverence even passes into Santo Loquasto's costume designs, which make the men wear woollen leg-warmers beneath their calf-length velvet pants."

THE RAKE'S PROGRESS

Dramatic ballet in six scenes. Music by Gavin Gordon. Choreography by Ninette de Valois. Book by Gavin Gordon. Scenery and costumes by Rex Whistler. First presented by the Sadler's Wells Ballet at the Sadler's Wells Theatre, London, May 20, 1935, with Walter Gore as the Rake and Alicia Markova as the Betrayed Girl. First presented in the United States by the Sadler's Wells Ballet at the Metropolitan Opera House, New York, October 12, 1949, with Harold Turner as the Rake and Margot Fonteyn as the Betrayed Girl.

This ballet is based on the series of paintings of the same name by the great English satirist William Hogarth. Hogarth showed in this famous work the gradual corruption of an adventurous youth who suddenly found himself endowed with unlimited money. The scenery and costumes, the characters—their situation and their dancing—are a vivid reproduction of eighteenth-century London, its people, and their habits as Hogarth saw them. The music is an appropriate eighteenth-century style.

SCENE ONE   The curtain rises on a drop curtain that depicts a street in eighteenth-century London. Georgian houses, public buildings, and a church line both sides of a cobblestone street that extends into the distance. When this curtain rises, we find ourselves in the elegant apartment of the rake. There are doors left and right, and across the back there is a large window. The rake is a youth who has recently come into a fortune, and this morning all the merchants, hangers-on, and toughs who hope to profit by his good luck are paying their daily call. He is still in his night clothes, but this doesn't prevent a tailor from measuring a new coat for him. The rake seems to enjoy this attention, however, and is hardly disturbed when his jockey informs him that his horse won an important race the day before. Now a fencing master takes over and beseeches the rake to practice at his art. The rake obliges him briefly, then practices the horn under the direction of a musician.

The rake begins to dress, and all come to his assistance when needed. When he is fully dressed, he turns to his dancing master. The dancing master takes out a violin and, as he plays on the instrument, shows the rake fancy steps. The rake is not very agile, despite his youth; the truth is that he is not accustomed yet to the gestures of the youthful rich.

The dancing lesson is interrupted by an altercation at the door. There a determined old woman is arguing familiarly with the maid. She forces the maid, her daughter, into the room and follows after. The old harridan upbraids the rake for seducing her daughter and threatens blackmail. The pretty girl obviously does not approve of this procedure and is embarrassed when the rake gives her mother money. They leave the scene, and the dancing lesson continues. The drop curtain falls as the rake succeeds in affecting the manner, if not the skill, of the dance his teacher has set him.

SCENE TWO   Three ladies of the town, apparently on their way to a party, parade the street in front of the drop curtain. The rake's maid and her mother pass them. When the curtain rises, we find ourselves in a bedchamber. The room is hardly private, however, for the two women sitting at a table on the right are clearly of loose character. They are drinking and gossiping together. Three other winsome bawds are exchanging jokes in the center of the room; they guffaw lustily at the slightest innuendo. In the back, on the left, in a curtained alcove, is an unmade bed. A lush painting of Venus and Mars in a gilt frame hangs on the back wall, giving the room an air of hopeful respectability.

Soon a friend of the rake's swaggers into the room, followed by the rake himself. Rake he is determined to be: he is drunk and delighted with himself. The girls take immediate advantage of him and his friend, treating them as if they were the only attractive men in the world.

The guests are treated to *divertissements* by a professional dancer, who does an eighteenth-century version of the striptease by removing her stockings, and a female ballad singer, who creaks out a song. This song delights the drunken rake, who throws his arm about the ballad singer and insists upon joining her. The music goes to his head, unfortunately, and he begins to pass out.

He is revived, however, as the girls begin to dance. Soon everyone in the room is dancing, whirling and whirling about in a manner that reflects the rake's intoxication. The rake expresses his admiration for this display by throwing coins about the room. One of the rowdy girls scurries about trying to pick up all the money, while the others devote themselves to affected gaiety to amuse the rake. The curtain falls, leaving the rest of the bawdy scene to our imagination.

SCENE THREE   Before the drop curtain, three creditors lie in wait to accost the rake. He strolls in haughtily. They present their bills, which are long overdue, and demand payment. Evidently the rake has run through his inheritance rather rapidly, for he is not in the least condescending: he is afraid. The pretty maid whom we met in the first scene comes into the street. As we might have expected, from her annoyance with her demanding mother, she does not despise her seducer. On the contrary, she observes him with some sympathy and intercedes in his quarrel with the creditors. The poor serving maid tells the men that she will pay the bills! The rake appears to be unimpressed by this expression of love, but the creditors are pleased with her promise; they exit. The rake goes on down the street, immediately forgetting the trouble he has had. The girl does a dance that expresses her love for the rake and the impossibility of its fulfillment.

SCENE FOUR   The rake has seriously come down in the world, for this time the curtain rises on a low gambling dive. The rake, no longer dressed in finery, enters and joins three burly-looking characters in a game of cards. Cleaned out in the higher-class gaming rooms and brothels, he imagines that he can easily regain his losses among such ignorant folk. His fellow players are cleverer than he thinks, however, and luck seems to be against him. He begins to lose steadily. He clings to his few coins as if they were the last moments of a happy life. It is not difficult for us to imagine that the betrayed girl, the lovely chambermaid he has spurned, would have a great deal of pity for him. The poor devil cannot bear to lose: he loses not only his money, but his connection with reality, as he hopes that this last bet will bring back all the opulence of his former life—the tailors and jewelers and race-track touts indebted to *him* again, much wine, many women, and endless song. Simultaneously he sees that if he loses, he will enjoy none of these things: that leaves, for him, poor fellow, nothing. The last wager is made, the last card is turned up, the tables are turned; he is wiped out! Less rake than pauper, the unfortunate fellow collapses.

SCENE FIVE   Before the curtain, the betrayed girl dances alone, hoping that the rake, who has now been put in the debtor's prison, will be released and come back to her.

SCENE SIX   When the curtain comes up again the scene, like the rake's progress, has gone from bad to worse: we are in a madhouse, a dark place and damp, where therapy consists of filthy isolation. The more dangerous lunatics can be seen behind iron grilles, posing as kings and cardinals. Creatures less preoccupied sit in an open area. One of these men entertains himself and his fellow madmen by a grotesque dance with a rope, which outlines in the air the images that haunt him.

The outside door clangs open, and the rake is thrown into the cell. The men watch the new inmate while he tries, as they did, to escape. When he falls to the floor exhausted, they display their individual manias for his benefit. While the rake looks at them, we think for a moment that he is not really mad, that there has been some mistake: an eighteenth-century solution to a down-and-outer's problem, some gross misjudgment. But we are wrong. The rake rises and dances like a demon.

The girl he has betrayed comes to visit him and tries pathetically to make him remember her, but now this man's only thought is to escape from her, to escape from everyone, to get out. He attacks the door again, and again he falls to the floor. The lovely girl attempts to mend his agony by sweet and loving gestures that might give him some hope. Her thoughtfulness and devotion are contrasted vividly with the fashionable world that her lover has left, when some well-dressed ladies enter the asylum and observe the inmates for entertainment and diversion.

The rake becomes hysterical, catatonic, and thrashes about the floor uncontrollably. He dies in the midst of his paroxysms. The betrayed girl holds him close in her arms, weeping that her love might have saved him, weeping that he did not understand the path of self-destruction.

RAPSODIE ESPAGNOLE

Music by Maurice Ravel. Choreography by George Balanchine. First presented at the New York City Ballet's Hommage à Ravel at the New York State Theatre, Lincoln Center, May 29, 1975, with Karin von Aroldingen and Peter Schaufuss in leading roles.

Ravel knew Spain well. The Spanish composer Manuel de Falla has recalled that "Ravel's Spain was a Spain ideally presented by his mother, whose refined conversation, always in excellent Spanish, delighted me, particularly when she would recall her youthful years spent in Madrid."

I found the music exciting for its vigor, clarity, and wonderful flamenco from the first and tried to arrange some expressive yet simple dances for passionate young persons.

RAYMONDA

Ballet in three acts. Music by Alexander Glazunov. Choreography by Marius Petipa. First presented at the Maryinsky Theatre, St. Petersburg, January 19, 1898. First presented in the United States in abbreviated form by the Ballet Russe de Monte Carlo at the City Center, New York, March 12, 1946, with choreography by Alexandra Danilova and George Balanchine. First presented complete by the Kirov Ballet at the Metropolitan Opera House, New York, September 16, 1964, with Irina Kolpakova as Raymonda, Vladilen Semenov as Jean de Brienne, and Gennady Selutsky as Abderachman.

Glazunov's music for *Raymonda* contains some of the finest ballet music we have. And Petipa's original choreography, which I remember from student appearances at the Maryinsky Theatre, was superb. But his story was nonsense, difficult to follow, and, in the words of an old Russian balletomane Prince Lieven, "it has everything but meaning," as you will see. It takes place in medieval Hungary.

ACT ONE, SCENE ONE   Raymonda, betrothed to Jean de Brienne, who is away at war, celebrates her birthday at the home of her aunt, a countess. Jean sends his fiancée gifts, among them a tapestry portrait of himself, and announces that he will arrive the next day. But Abderachman, a Saracen chief, pays an unexpected visit to the castle. He admires Raymonda, attempts to lure her with rich gifts.

ACT ONE, SCENE TWO   Raymonda dreams that her lover descends from his portrait and leads her into the garden to dance a *pas de deux*. But this vision is dispelled and in Jean's place Raymonda finds the sinister Saracen, who renews his advances. Raymonda swoons.

ACT TWO   At a reception the countess gives in honor of the Saracen, Raymonda anxiously awaits Jean's arrival. But Abderachman approaches her passionately and insists that she dance with him. She accepts and the Saracen then commands his retinue to entertain Raymonda with jugglers and dancing. Moors and Spaniards join in a dance that becomes fierce with intensity; at its height the Saracen attempts to abduct Raymonda. At that point, who should arrive but Jean de Brienne, accompanied by his old father, King Andrew II of Hungary. Raymonda rushes to Jean's arms. He and his followers threaten Abderachman and his retinue, but the king intervenes and proposes single combat for the rivals. The ensuing duel is furious and Abderachman falls.

ACT THREE   A festival is being held at Jean de Brienne's castle to celebrate his marriage to Raymonda. The festival begins with a *grand pas hongrois* in which Raymonda dances a variation and Jean a final solo before the lovers are united forever.

NOTES   Rudolf Nureyev staged his version of the complete *Raymonda* with the Royal Ballet's touring company at the Festival of Two Worlds in Spoleto in 1964. Doreen Wells and Nureyev appeared in the principal roles. Act III of this production, with scenery and costumes by Barry Kay, was presented by the Royal Ballet at the Royal Opera House, Covent Garden, July 16, 1966, with Doreen Wells and David Wall. Alexander Bland, reviewing this and other ballets on the same program in *The Observer*, wrote that David Wall "finally and triumphantly established himself as the most promising British dancer since the war, heading for the international class. In *Les Sylphides* he gave . . . an almost faultless performance, very much in the Nureyev style; his young boy in *The Invitation* . . . was rather more than adequate: and finally he came up at the end of the evening to give his *Raymonda* solo a mixture of dash, control, musicality, and style of which any Kirov dancer could have been proud."

Nureyev staged *Raymonda* for the Australian Ballet in 1965. In 1972 he mounted it for the Zurich Ballet in a production designed by Nicholas Georgiadis, in 1975 for American Ballet Theatre. In Zurich, Nureyev and Marcia Haydée danced the first performance. Reviewing it in *Dance and Dancers* magazine, the British critic John Percival wrote:

"The Zurich Ballet is more used to appearing alone in some quite ambitious productions, but I doubt whether its dancers have tackled anything as taxing as Nureyev's *Raymonda*. This has been completely rethought and drastically changed since the two previous productions Nureyev has mounted. The good features of those productions remain: the marvelous Glazunov score, full of dreamy waltzes and exciting rhythms; some brilliant solos preserving Petipa's choreography; and the biggest of all classical roles for a ballerina (now even augmented beyond what we saw before). These virtues have been increased, too; the score is now played complete, and almost in the composer's original order, except for one change in Act Three to give the hero an extra solo; and the new choreography which Nureyev has added is well devised to show off the dancers and to make the best of the preserved Petipa.

"The trouble with *Raymonda* has always been the story . . . Nureyev has found a surprisingly simple way to make sense of the whole. He takes his cue from the fact that there was always a dream sequence, designed to allow Raymonda a duet with her admirer Jean de Brienne in the early part of the ballet, although the plot did not actually introduce him until near the end. Nureyev considerably enlarged this dream to cover not just one scene but a substantial part of Act One and almost the whole of Act Two.

"What happens now is that Raymonda is first seen playing with her friends (two girls and two troubadours) while preparations are going on all around for her marriage as soon as Jean gets back from the wars. Pretty soon he arrives with the King of Hungary (in whose forces he has been serving) and offers her a present: a tapestry banner he has brought back from the Crusades. Left alone, Raymonda imagines the dark Saracen warrior from whom Jean won this. She falls asleep, and in her dream the banner grows until it becomes the Saracen's tent. The traditional love duet with Jean remains, but in addition there are scenes alone with the Saracen, Abderachman; others in which he and Jean phantasmagorically exchange places; and others again in which both appear dancing with her and her friends. For a while Abderachman persuades Raymonda (and her girl friends) to remain with him, enjoying the divertissement of Spanish and oriental dances he provides; but at last the nobly retiring Jean is provoked into challenging his rival. They compete at archery, fight with lances on horseback, and finally engage in a duel with swords, in which Jean, with one mighty blow, shatters his enemy's helmet and wounds him, presumably fatally. Now Raymonda can unreservedly give Jean her heart and her hand—and at this point she wakes up to find him and her friends come to look for her. Thus Act Two ends happily, and Act Three is, as usual, the wedding celebration.

"This makes a more interesting story, for its own sake and also as a portrait of Raymonda's inner struggle. The presence of the troubadours, poetic exponents of the artificial conventions of courtly love, among her friends is evidence that she is not really ready, when the ballet starts, for the wedding which is imminent. Together the friends play at being in love, but Raymonda's games are still childish. Jean's devotion is at first too reticent to awaken her; only when her dreams conjure up the dark figure of her animus, and Jean proves able to defeat this imagined rival, does she come to terms with her hidden longings.

"The role of Raymonda thus becomes dramatically interesting, and Marcia Haydée (who danced the first four performances of the production) makes the most of this. But it is still, above all, an immensely demanding virtuoso role, with so many solos that I lost count, each showing off a different aspect of technique—leaps, turns, balances and so on. There is a beautiful lyric solo with a scarf; a solo in which she jumps repeatedly to land with a stabbing thrust on full point; and of course that haunting last-act solo with its hints of melancholy beneath a surface of surpassing grandeur."

Nureyev staged his production of *Raymonda* for American Ballet Theatre in New York in 1975. Cynthia Gregory and Nureyev danced the first performance. John T. Elson wrote in *Time* magazine:

"*Raymonda* is a two-hour experience in pure dance. And what dancing there is! . . . The incandescent Miss Gregory danced the role as if it had been created for her alone, carrying out variation after variation—six in all—with radiant confidence. The breathtaking pauses at the peak of her balances last only a second or so; yet they seem to embody T. S. Eliot's haunting lines in *Burnt Norton*: 'At the still point of the turning world . . . There the dance is, but neither arrest or movement.'"

Marius Petipa's original scenario for *Raymonda*, including his instructions to the composer, Glazunov, has been translated by Debra Goldman for *Ballet Review* (Vol. 5, No. 2).

RAYMONDA VARIATIONS

Music by Alexander Glazunov Choreography by George Balanchine. Scenery by Horace Armistead. Costumes by Karinska. First presented by the New York City Ballet at the City Center, New York, December 7, 1961, with Patricia Wilde and Jacques d'Amboise in the leading roles.

I have already mentioned in speaking of *Pas de Dix* how I have always liked the music Glazunov wrote for the ballet *Raymonda*. This ballet also has music taken from Glazunov's score for *Raymonda*, but it is music of an entirely different character from *Pas de Dix*. Originally called *Valse and Variations*, the ballet consists of dances for two principals, soloists, and a *corps de ballet*. There is no story, only the music to dance to.

When the curtain goes up, twelve girls stand posing in an elegant garden. They dance for us and then the principals, another girl and then a boy, join them. Next, the girl and the boy are alone for an adagio. This is followed by a series of nine variations, or solos, by five of the girls and the two principals. The ballet concludes with a coda and a finale by all the dancers.

To try to talk about these dances in any useful way outside the music is not possible; they do not have any literary content at all and of course have nothing to do with the story of the original ballet *Raymonda*. The music itself, its grand and generous manner, its joy and playfulness, was for me more than enough to carry the plot of the dances.

THE REAL McCOY

Music by George Gershwin. Choreography by Eliot Feld. Setting and costumes by Rouben Ter-Arutunian. Lighting by Thomas Skelton. First presented by the Eliot Feld Ballet at the New York Shakespeare Festival Public Theatre, December 7, 1974, with Eliot Feld in the leading role. Pianist: Gladys Celeste Mercader.

The Real McCoy recaptures the past and projects it into the present. With the authenticity of George Gershwin's music as a floor to walk on, the action has other points to make, too, about the American Dream. The hero of the piece, a bright, brash young man, a mix of James Cagney and Fred Astaire, indicates at the start that any kid can be a star, like Astaire maybe. Perhaps he is, in fact, George Gershwin? The painted backdrop of rainbows reminds us that much is being sought after, in the '30s fashion.

A guy in a top hat, with cane, and a blonde on a chaise longue turn the sofa into a canoe and go paddling. They meet curious adventures. At the end, the hero dances frantically. Seeking a cocktail feeling of joy or experiencing the Real McCoy?

REFLECTIONS

Music by Peter Ilyich Tchaikovsky. Choreography by Gerald Arpino. Lighting by Jennifer Tipton. First presented by the City Center Joffrey Ballet at the City Center, New York, February 24, 1971, with Erika Goodman, Dana Sapiro, Denise Jackson, Glenn White, and Henry Berg as the principals. Cellist: Warren Lash. Conducted by Walter Hagen.

Arranged to Tchaikovsky's *Variations on a Rococo Theme for Violoncello and Orchestra, Reflections* is a dance ballet with no plot beyond the beauties of the score. This music, not often enough heard, is of interest to those who know only Tchaikovsky's familiar works. There is, first of all, the statement of the theme, danced by a group of seven girls. Seven variations then follow, the first two danced by girls, the third a *pas de deux*, the fourth a *pas de trois* for three girls, the fifth another *pas de deux*, the sixth yet another, and the seventh an ensemble for all the dancers. There is no setting, only the dancers providing absorbing displays of reflected virtuosity to the music.

THE RELATIVITY OF ICARUS

Music by Gerhard Samuel. Text by Jack Larson. Choreography by Gerald Arpino. Set and costumes by Rouben Ter-Arutunian. Lighting by Thomas Skelton. First presented in New York City by the City Center Joffrey Ballet at the City Center, October 17, 1974, with Ann Marie DeAngelo as the Sun, Russell Sultzbach as Icarus, and Ted Nelson as Daedalus. Soprano: Joan Bell. Conducted by Seymour Lipkin.

The story of two men, father and son, who escaped from the labyrinth on self-made wings, has been told many times. This ballet is a variation on that story, based on the poem by Jack Larson and the music by Gerhard Samuel.

Daedalus was the builder of the Labyrinth on the island of Crete. He and his son Icarus were later imprisoned in the Labyrinth. To escape from it and the Minotaur, the monstrous man-bull who dwelt there, they fashioned wings of feathers and wax, which enabled them to fly. Icarus, however, flew too near the sun, the wax on his wings melted, and he fell into the sea, thenceforth called Icarian.

The text by Jack Larson for the music that accompanies the action follows:

As it was with Icarus,
Imprisoned in the labyrinth of his father's creation
Punished by the echoes of a monster's satisfaction
He wished to escape in wings from the confusion of earth.
As it was with Icarus,
Wanting to fly from memories of a Minotaur's birth
Away from mutilated bodies of handsome young men
From the echoes of rape and massacre of young women:
As it was with Icarus,
Out of the labyrinth in wings of things of feathers and wax
Straining free of gravity into air currents that relax
He took flight into the transforming softness of the clouds.
As it was with Icarus,
Even the clouds mushroom in echoes of thunderous shrouds
And though he flies straight as light, like light he'll curve near the moon
And return to the labyrinth a trillion light years too soon.
As it was with Icarus,
Soar to the sun, it's only a mass of multiplied light
Transmuting its brilliance into the curvature of night
Like his too warm wings, the escape expands as it contracts.
And disappears from space as impermanent as wax.
As it was with Icarus,
So it is with all of us.*

The action of the ballet takes place in a remarkable luminous and reflecting setting that catches light and movement, expanding and focusing, deflecting and returning, in much the same way as interpretations of myth invariably return to the primal story.

First the Sun, a lovely girl, dances around a raised area on which Daedalus lies. The Sun reveals him to us and from Daedalus springs full-armed his son Icarus. Bound to his father by cords about his wrists, Icarus is taught to fly. The cords, however, make it impossible for him to fly free of Daedalus.

Daedalus is enamored now of the Sun, and would follow her, sensing even the danger he sees in loosening the cords and abandoning his son. But the boy is more deeply tempted than the father. To free himself, he strangles Daedalus. The liberated Icarus then plunges into an endless fall. The Sun turns again about the earth.

In a long, discursive essay, "Arpino's *Icarus:* Confrontations with the Fall," in *Dance Magazine* (January 1975), Richard Philp writes: "Nobody was unmoved by *Icarus* . . . I believe that we all seem to have seen something in the ballet which is familiar; it holds a mirror up before us and reflects experience which is difficult to reject, or accept . . .

"For one of the simplest interpretations, with which the ballet's strongest supporters are content to settle, I borrow a quote from Nietzsche's *Zarathustra:* 'Many a one hath cast away final worth when he hath cast away his servitude.'

"Wherever *Icarus* is danced, the ballet will continue to evoke comment and interpretation which will have to deal to some extent with the meaning of myth and the nature of human freedom. Visually, I think of *Icarus* and remember the struggling movements outwards, away from, beyond; conversely, there is also a sense of restriction, withdrawal, retreat. To rephrase Nietzsche: When Icarus casts off his servitude [to Daedalus], he is in effect casting away himself Icarus, like many of us, cannot function without the flexing pressures of obligation."

REMEMBRANCES

Music by Richard Wagner. Choreography by Robert Joffrey. Set by Rouben Ter-Arutunian. Costumes by Willa Kim. Lighting by Jennifer Tipton. First presented by the City Center Joffrey Ballet at the City Center, New York, October 12, 1973, with Francesca Corkle and Jonathan Watts as principals. Conducted by Seymour Lipkin. Pianist: Stanley Babin. She, Who Sings: *Donna Roll.* She, Who Remembers: *Jan Hanniford.*

Remembrances is a ballet about looking back. As a woman sings her recollections of past love, a woman who remembers remains at her side to watch and reach out toward a danced re-enactment of the past.

The program recalls that Richard Wagner, in 1849, having taken an active role in the revolutionary movement in Germany, was forced to flee with his wife, Minna, and to settle in Switzerland. There, in Zurich, he met a wealthy silk merchant, Otto Wesendonck, who, at his wife Mathilde's urging, became Wagner's patron. It was not long before "something dangerously like a love affair" developed between Mathilde and Wagner.

Some of Wagner's work is inextricably linked with his relationship to Mathilde. In 1853 he wrote for her personal album a sonata that is described by one of his biographers, Paul Bekker, as "a summary of the past and a promise for the future, a delicate act of homage to the woman who had inspired the music which was now to flow from him in an almost unbroken stream." Written on the manuscript of the sonata, as a motto, is the inscription: "Do you know what will follow?"

Mathilde Wesendonck and Wagner became artistic collaborators a few years later, when in 1857–58 he set to music five of her poems. The poems are entitled *Der Engel* (*The Angel*), *Stehe Still* (*Stand Still*), *Im Treibhaus* (*In the Greenhouse*), *Schmerzen* (*Tears*), and *Träume* (*Dreams*). Wagner said that *Im Treibhaus* and *Träume* could be described as "studies" for *Tristan und Isolde*.

In 1935 Arturo Toscanini discovered a lost, unpublished piece of Wagner's known as the *Porazzi Theme*, which the composer had played on the afternoon of his death. Dating from 1859, this theme had been jotted down on the back of a sketch for *Tristan*, relating to the lovers' invocation to the night.

These musical works of Wagner's are the score for the ballet and set the scene for its backward look.

The ballet carries as its motto this quotation from Shelley:

Music, when soft voices die
Vibrates in the memory.

The pianist begins the music in the dimly lit auditorium. The house slowly darkens with the quiet music. Soon a girl in a long dress walks slowly across the stage. She reaches out in a gesture of longing and sits down. Following her now comes another girl, her double, who is to sing what the first girl feels and acts as she watches the scene that flows before her.

A girl dances with a boy, it is apparently long ago and almost lost to the memory but soon other images come back, the lovers are among friends, four other couples. The scene appears to be a clearing high above a cavernous bay, the sea shimmering in the distance; the setting resembles an oculus that is focused on a far-off place, the sea, mountains, enclosed in a curved landscape of the memory.

Two couples dance to the music of the first song. Then later, the lead girl, alone, dances and seems to suffer, but her lover rejoins her.

There is a recognition between the woman who watches her past and the girl who dances it. Others now dance to the low threnody of strings. Finally, the girl is left by herself, kneeling. She rises; her partner returns. Later among the happy couples, the lovers seem to expire. She, Who Remembers reaches out to them and gestures to She, Who Sings. But her young image only looks back at her.

NOTES Writing in *Dance and Dancers* about *Remembrances*, Patricia

Barnes referred to the ballet as "perhaps the best thing Robert Joffrey has yet achieved. . . . It is a lushly romantic work, matching the music's soul and passion. . . . Corkle has always been a brilliant young technician. In *Remembrances* Joffrey has seen another side of her. One is tempted to say that this ballet has made her a great dancer. She performed it as if her heart was on fire, with a sincerity and depth that were remarkable. In her movement there was a dramatic tension and in her musicality a wealth of understanding of what can transform a simple movement into art.

"Jonathan Watts . . . was here making his first stage appearance in nine years. . . . He is now dancing better than ever, even after such a long lay-off period. Always an immaculate stylist, in *Remembrances* he was superb, partnering with tenderness, possessing elegant *ports de bras* and unforced dignity."

LES RENDEZVOUS

Ballet divertissement in one act. Music by François Auber, arranged by Constant Lambert. Choreography by Frederick Ashton. Scenery and costumes by William Chappell. First performed by the Sadler's Wells Ballet at the Sadler's Wells Theatre, London, December 5, 1933, with a cast headed by Alicia Markova, Stanislas Idzikowski, Pearl Argyle, Ninette de Valois, and Robert Helpmann. Revived with new decor by William Chappell, November 16, 1937. First presented in the United States by the Sadler's Wells Theatre Ballet at the Northrop Auditorium, Minneapolis, Minnesota, November 7, 1951, with Elaine Fifield and Pirmin Trecu in the principal roles. First performed by the Royal Ballet at Covent Garden, London, May 7, 1959.

Les Rendezvous is a dance entertainment set to music from Auber's *L'Enfant Prodigue*. In a private park, young couples promenade and dance to give appropriate expression to youthful sentiments that take hold of their ebullient spirits. There is no plot.

The curtain rises on a bright, sunny scene. A high white fence of wrought iron stands out against a light-green back cloth. The gate to the park, in the center, is open. The orchestra plays music that is light and charming, music suggestive of the good nature we always feel when we watch boys and girls show their happiness by dancing together. Trumpets sound a fanfare and the ballet begins.

Young couples out for a stroll dance into the park one by one from the corners of the stage. They are all dressed in white; the girls wear pink ribbons in their hair and pink sashes, and the boys wear belts of light blue. The young people move back and forth across the park. Finally there are six couples. They stand on either side of the gate, and a seventh couple enters. They pass down the line formed by their friends, greet them effusively, and then, more formally, shake hands.

Now the couples divide into different groups and fill the stage with shifting, quick movement. The boys dance alone briefly, then leave the stage to a couple who dance a short *pas de deux*. The boy lifts the girl off into the wings; the music is rapid and joyful, the lift is long and slow, and there is an effect of joyfulness mixed with romance. Other boys enter and lift their partners more rapidly, more in direct imitation of the music. Six girls surround the romantic couple when they return, and the introduction to the ballet finishes as the boy again lifts the girl into the wings.

Four girls dance a bright *pas de quatre*. They are joined by their partners and leave the stage as the boy of the lead couple enters and dances a bold leaping-and-turning variation to brilliant, flourishing music. The boy gestures toward the gate, his girl rejoins him there, and they leave the stage together. The other couples have returned and form three tableaux about the stage. The boy, reaching out to his partner who kneels below, comes back, leading his girl forward, and the two of them dance a slow, romantic duet. Four of the boys lift the girl to their shoulders as the adagio ends. There she poses gracefully, as the girls gather about her raised figure, hold hands, and enclose her with a circle of arabesques.

The music becomes saucy and bouncing. A girl bounds on stage with two partners, turning from the arms of one boy into the arms of the other. The two boys lift her high into the air, release her, and their steps quicken to the hastening music. The *pas de trois* finishes as all three kneel.

Next the lead girl dances alone. She leaps onto the scene, turns dizzily, delighting us with her deft, swift movement. She is very pretty, apparently in love, and enjoys showing off a little. Boys emerge from the wings one by one and bow to the girl, in tribute to her beauty and her masterful dance. She bows gratefully in return and leaves the stage on the left.

Rhythmic handclaps are heard off-stage. Six boys run into the park to dance in unison a strong, buoyant ensemble, dazzling with its long, high leaps, multiple turns, and the quick, steady certainty with which they finish their brilliant sequence of movement. A trumpet fanfare announces the arrival of six girls, who join their partners for a brief dance before the reappearance of the ballerina, who whirls about the stage. The *corps de ballet* returns and forms a background for another virtuoso variation by the ballerina's partner, who places his hands on his shoulders and spins like a top.

Four girls approach the boy and blindfold him. He plays their game for a moment, then turns in their midst and rushes off as the ballerina enters on the right to hop backward on point in a long diagonal. All the couples are now on stage. They bow to each other and bid their partners a fond farewell. One by one, they leave the park through the gate. When the ballerina disappears into the wings, her partner leaps after her in a high trajectory. Four girls, who remain in the park, pose amusingly, as if the fun has just begun.

REQUIEM CANTICLES

Music by Igor Stravinsky. Choreography by Jerome Robbins. Lighting by Ronald Bates. First presented by the New York City Ballet at the Stravinsky Festival, June 25, 1972, at the New York State Theatre, Lincoln Center,

New York, with Merrill Ashley, Susan Hendl, Bruce Wells, and Robert Maiorano as principals. Soprano: Elaine Bonazzi. Bass: William Metcalf. Conducted by Robert Craft.

Stravinsky's *Requiem Canticles,* for contralto, soloists, and orchestra, first performed in 1966 at Princeton, New Jersey, was selected by Jerome Robbins as one of his ballets for our Stravinsky Festival in 1972. That event, which marked the composer's ninetieth birthday, also mourned his death as we hope he would have wished us to do, with celebration. *Requiem Canticles* was the final ballet of the Festival.

Stravinsky had earlier informed the New York City Ballet that he planned the *Requiem Canticles* "as an instrumental work originally, and I composed the threnody for wind instruments and muffled drums, now at the center of the work, first. Later I decided to use sentences from six texts of the traditional Requiem service, and that time I conceived the triangulate instrumental frame of the string *Prelude,* wind-instrument *Interlude,* and percussion *Postlude.* The *Requiem Canticles* are concert music, but the celebration of death is to be played in memory of a man of God, a man of the poor, a man of peace."

Robbins's *Requiem Canticles* was an appropriate finale in dance to what was, for many of us on both sides of the footlights, a memorable week.

A *Village Voice* critic said of the ballet: "Mr. Robbins's piece, conducted by Robert Craft, accentuated the energy heard in the music. Here were granite blocks of black-clothed dancers staring out at the audience in the *Prelude* and shaking in tight spasms. The choral sections followed, with the *Exaudi* bringing in slow gestures and walkings, the *Dies irae* frenzied with lifts and aimless striding, the *Tuba mirum* showing Bruce Wells as a sort of Angel Gabriel ready to call everyone to judgment, the non-vocal *Interlude* leaving the stage to four dancers full of expectation, *Rex tremendae* bringing back the corps in their block phalanxes, Merrill Ashley bursting out of a semicircle of corps in *Lacrymosa,* the *Libera me* letting the corps members converge on one another on their knees and making room for short solos by Miss Ashley and Susan Hendl before the group goes into asymmetric attitudes; and finally the drums and bells of the *Postlude* setting off a mechanism of ticking bodies, limbs, and finally just heads in open-mouthed, silent cries of fear and marvel."

REVENGE

Dramatic ballet in four scenes with prologue. Music by Giuseppe Verdi. Choreography by Ruth Page. Book by Ruth Page with the collaboration of Nicolas Remisov. Scenery and costumes by Antoine Clavé. First presented by Les Ballets des Champs-Élysées at the Théâtre de l'Empire, Paris, October 17, 1951, with Sonia Arova as Azucena, Vladimir Skouratoff as Manrico, Jacqueline Moreau as Leonora, and Gérard Ohn as the Count di Luna. First presented in the United States by Ruth Page Ballets at the Civic Opera House, Chicago, November 26, 1955, with Sonia Arova, Oleg Briansky, Alicia Markova, and Bentley Stone in the principal roles.

Like the ballet *Carmen, Revenge* is also based on a great popular opera—Verdi's *Il Trovatore*. The ballet is faithful to the opera's theme of passionate revenge and condenses into a comparatively short space of time the principal elements of the musical drama. The time is the sixteenth century. The place is Spain.

PROLOGUE: THE COURTYARD OF THE CASTLE OF THE COUNT DI LUNA The elderly Count di Luna has two infant sons, of whom he is very proud. One day an old gypsy woman is discovered hovering over the cradle of one of these boys. The child's nurse, suspecting sorcery, sounds the alarm, and the old count's servants capture the gypsy. The hag pleads that she meant no harm, that she was only interested in reading the child's fortune. She is driven out of the castle, but when the child becomes ill, she is brought back. At the count's order, she is burned at the stake for sorcery. His child recovers.

The old gypsy's young daughter, Azucena, dances in despair as the flames of her mother's burning light the distant sky. Gentlemen of the count's household stand on the steps of the courtyard watching the fire with indifference. Azucena vows to avenge her mother's horrible death. She steals the count's other son and flees into the night.

SCENE ONE: THE CASTLE Twenty years have passed. The old Count di Luna is dead. On his deathbed he urged his remaining son never to abandon search for his brother. Unknown to the new count, his brother still survives as Manrico, whom Azucena has brought up as her own son.

Both the Count di Luna and Manrico are in love with the beautiful Leonora, lady in waiting to the queen. Leonora favors Manrico, and the count, enraged that the girl should prefer a ragged gypsy to a nobleman, is determined to separate them. Leonora escapes with Manrico to a gypsy camp.

SCENE TWO: THE GYPSY MOVEMENT The Count di Luna traces the two lovers and comes in person to the gypsy camp. There he challenges Manrico to a duel. The young gypsy, warned by a premonition, reluctantly consents to this contest, and the two brothers, completely ignorant of their relationship, begin to fight. Manrico gains the upper hand and might easily slay the count. The premonition returns, and he stays his hand. Azucena regrets that her ward has not killed the count; after twenty years, she can still think only of revenge.

The count, enraged by jealousy and Manrico's contempt, is determined to force his love on Leonora. He sends her to prison with Manrico.

SCENE THREE: IN FRONT OF THE PRISON The two lovers endure torture in prison by the count's order. Leonora, in desperation, promises that she will marry the count if he will set Manrico free.

SCENE FOUR: THE BETROTHAL The marriage ceremony has been arranged. Manrico, who does not know that she has arranged for his release, accuses Leonora of faithlessness. But Leonora, unwilling to marry the count, has taken poison and urges Manrico to seek his freedom. Manrico discovers what she has done and weeps as she dies in his arms.

The Count di Luna orders Manrico's execution. The youth bids farewell to his foster mother, who despairs that her revenge means such a sacrifice. But when Manrico is dead, she weeps no more. She turns to the Count di Luna in fierce triumph. Glorying in her revenge, she holds out to him the locket that hung about the neck of his brother twenty years before. To the count's horror at this secret, Azucena responds with demoniac exultation: she has had her revenge at last.

REVERIES

Music by Peter Ilyich Tchaikovsky. Choreography by John Clifford. Costumes by Joe Eula. Lighting by Ronald Bates. First presented by the New York City Ballet at the New York State Theatre, December 4, 1969, with Conrad Ludlow, Anthony Blum, Johnna Kirkland, Gelsey Kirkland, and ensemble.

The fourth ballet by John Clifford, *Reveries* uses music from Tchaikovsky's *Suite No. 1* (the first, third, fourth, and sixth movements). The plot of the ballet is the plot of the music.

The curtain rises after a brief orchestral introduction. The first movement, marked *Introduction and Fugue*, is staged for a boy and twelve girls who, dressed in flowing pink, surround their romantic hero. He is seen in a spotlight, center. Detached at first, he kneels and watches the girls dance, then joins them under the dark, starry sky. His dance is like magic, and they all seem to respond like flowers in the wind. He leaves the girls then to commence to dance to the fugue. The boy returns to dance and fall at the feet of his Muses. They soon leave, the scene darkens and he, too, departs.

To the third movement of Tchaikovsky's Suite, *Intermezzo*, the dance begins in a diagonal of light on a dark stage. Four boys and four girls face each other. The stage brightens, a boy lifts on a girl in white, and the orchestra plays a romantic theme. The couple dances, he catching her under the arms as she leaps. As the music ends, he kneels before her, then holds her as she falls into his arms. A brilliant soloist in blue dances in dynamic contrast to the lyricism of the lovers.

The *Marche Militaire* is led by a girl who matches the brilliance of Tchaikovsky's melody with the help of a small group of four girls. The finale, *Gavotte*, brings the four principals together in a climactic ensemble of complication and exuberance.

NOTES Clive Barnes wrote in the New York *Times:* "*Reveries* is John Clifford's best piece to date, and is a lovely piece of choreography. . . . He really illuminates the music. There is a sumptuous and love-rapt *pas de deux* for Johnna Kirkland and Conrad Ludlow, and beautiful solos for Anthony Blum and Johnna's brilliant kid sister, Gelsey Kirkland. . . . The entire piece is elegant yet fun."

Arlene Croce, editor of *Ballet Review*, wrote of John Clifford in *Playbill* in 1969: "The youngest of the New York City Ballet's dancer-choreographers is twenty-one-year-old John Clifford. Clifford came to New York from Los Angeles and was awarded a scholarship to the School of American Ballet, where he entered the choreography workshop in 1966. He made his choreographic debut with *Stravinsky Symphony* in the spring of 1968 and has revised it steadily ever since. His second ballet, to Vaughan Williams' *Fantasia on a Theme of Thomas Tallis*, is a lyrical work about two real people and a dream couple whom the real people prefer to one another. Premièred early this year, *Fantasies* was a hit with both critics and audiences, and Clifford has been invited to stage his next ballet for the company's Sixth Annual Spring Benefit on May 8, on the same program with new works by George Balanchine and Jerome Robbins. Robbins, who returns this spring to choreograph for the company after more than a decade's absence, provided Clifford with his earliest inspiration. Shortly before spring rehearsals began, Clifford was to be found at the State Theatre, where Robbins was taking class.

" 'I've been watching Jerry work on his new piece,' he told an interviewer. 'I'm rehearsing it but I don't know if I'm going to be in it yet. The way he squeezes everything he can get out of you! I can't do that yet. He's a rhythm choreographer of course—he uses every last bit of rhythm. And he's so thorough. I think he thought about *The Cage* for years before he did it, thought it all out and knew exactly what he wanted to do. When I first joined the company I would watch every performance of *The Cage* and people would say, "Well, John, what did you like this time?" The first large-scale choreography I ever saw was the film of *West Side Story*. I've seen it more than twenty times. When it came out again recently, I went back. I think it affected my spatial concepts when I began to choreograph. I used to try and set bits of movement in the background that only ended up confusing the stage picture. I was choreographing selectively as if for a camera. I didn't realize that in the theater the spectator has to have a central focus because he's stationary; he can't move around like a camera picking up this and that. You know those funny, insectlike things the girls do in *The Cage?* Well, they do a lot with their arms and hands you really can't see, but only because the stage is so dark. I wish it could be brighter. I'd like to do a horror ballet like that some day. Actually, whether you do story ballets or not depends on the music. I consciously try to do something different in each piece. The Stravinsky—a neo-classical abstract work. Mr. B. thought it would be good for me to work with that score. Next, a long romantic piece with a bit of a story. Now I'm using Bernstein's *Prelude, Fugue and Riffs*. It's a jazz score from the same period as Stravinsky's *Ebony Concerto*, but it's not going to be set as a "jazz ballet" in that sense because it would look dated. I don't read music or have a record-player. I go to the library and listen to records. When I hear something I like, I file it away in the back of my mind. I hadn't heard the *Tallis* until about a year ago, on the Coast, when somebody played it for me. I didn't care for it too much then. But it came back to me for *Fantasies*. When I'm making a piece, I don't try to get the dancers to consciously project a meaning. I don't tell them what they're supposed to do except over coffee. Ideally, you just want the dancer to be. You try and get the ones you know will look right for the part in the first place, then things happen. . . . I have projects going all the time. This company is so full of terrific dancers but we have such an enormous rep they don't often have the energy to show off. Right now, in addition to the Bernstein, I'm choreographing a Bartók ballet over at the school, and a rock ballet—rock music. It's only a 7½-minute piece but it's the hardest thing I've ever done. I tried doing classical *pas de deux* movements but it didn't work, it looked too contrasty. Then I did regulation discothèque and hated it. Now, last night, I had them all just walk. It was better. I want to do all kinds of things—multimedia . . . using singers and speech . . . opera. I have this terrific idea but I won't talk about it. I think Lincoln Kirstein thinks I'm mad.'"

RITE OF SPRING (*see* LE SACRE DU PRINTEMPS)

RITUALS

Music by Béla Bartók. Choreography by Kenneth MacMillan. Designer: Yolanda Sonnasend. First presented by the Royal Ballet at the Royal Opera House, Covent Garden, London, December 11, 1975, and introduced to the United States by the same ensemble April 27, 1976, at the Metropolitan Opera House, New York.

Set to the *Sonata for Two Pianos and Percussion* of Bartók, *Rituals* is a dance ballet about Japanese formalized sport and theatre. The first scene shows the preparation for combat and self-defense for which movements have been derived from Japanese boxing, sumo wrestling, and a Japanese form of Tai-Chi. The second scene is inspired by the Bunraku Puppet Theatre and the third shows a "very emotional situation"—the birth of a child—in the impressive style of some forms of Japanese theatre.

The Royal Ballet visited Japan in 1975, which gave the choreographer Kenneth MacMillan an opportunity to watch the Kabuki theatre and Nō plays. The studied lack of emotion in the Japanese theatre inspired him to make a work of that character in ballet.

THE RIVER

Original score by Duke Ellington. Choreography by Alvin Ailey. Costumes by Frank Thompson. Lighting by Gilbert V. Hemsley, Jr. Special lighting by Nicholas Cernovitch. First presented by American Ballet Theatre at the New York State Theatre, Lincoln Center, New York, June 25, 1970, with a cast headed by John Prinz, Alexandra Radius, Hans Ebbelaar, Marcos

Paredes, Eleanor D'Antuono, Cynthia Gregory, Ivan Nagy, Dennis Nahat, Sallie Wilson, and Keith Lee. Conducted by Jaime Leon.

A quotation from the musician Duke Ellington prefaces the ballet: ". . . of birth . . . of the well-spring of life . . . of reaffirmation . . . of the heavenly anticipation of rebirth. . . ." The work itself is the result of collaboration between Duke Ellington and Alvin Ailey. In its musical entirety, the work consists of a *Prologue,* an *Epilogue,* and eleven sections. These are entitled: *Spring, Spring Run, Meander, Giggling Rapids, Falls, Vortex, Lake, Mainstream (Riba), Two Cities, The Sea (Mother),* and *Spring.*

First presented by American Ballet Theatre in an unfinished state that was later completed, on June 29, 1971, *The River* was appraised by critic Jean Battey Lewis of the Washington *Post* as a work with "an alive and joyous quality, a life force that carries along its series of solos, duets and group dances in a headlong sweep. . . . *The River* is not only a well-spring of free, unforced, imaginative movement. It is also a tribute to Ailey's gifts as a director and developer of talent that he has created passages which capture so sensitively the strengths of some of Ballet Theatre's finest dancers."

Writing of *The River* soon after its première, in *The Saturday Review,* the critic Walter Terry said: "The Ailey ballet *The River,* with an original score by Duke Ellington, was not completed by première time, so for the season it was given in part as 'six dances from a work in progress.' A full appraisal, of course, must wait, but the Ailey dance brilliance—wonderful freshets of movement designs to delight the eye—are already there. There are patterns of mass motion that are utterly beautiful, but there are also such choreographic concentrates as Eleanor D'Antuono's incredibly fast solo *Vortex;* Cynthia Gregory (with either Ivan Nagy or Gayle Young) in a cool and graceful *pas de deux,* surrounded by ensemble movements, called *Lake;* Dennis Nahat's jaunty *Mainstream;* and the curiously haunting *Two Cities,* danced by Sallie Wilson and Keith Lee, each in separate pools of light, each lonely, each reaching out across the unseen barrier of river, of distance, of divisiveness, of solitary spirit, however you care to interpret it, and, finally, bridging the abyss."

A year later, Deborah Jowitt wrote in the *Village Voice:* "Alvin Ailey has added three more sections to *The River.* One, called *Sea,* certainly rounds the whole piece out, since the sea people, Erik Bruhn and Natalia Makarova, can now open the ballet by pulling away from the 'spring' (Keith Lee) in a receding wave and return at the end in a slow, coiling floor duet that seems to spawn that wellspring again. *Meander,* for Mimi Paul, Ted Kivitt, and Ian Horvath, is a playful, jazzy, carelessly sensuous *divertissement*—very nicely danced, but not terribly compelling in its movement concept. *Giggling Rapids* features Bruhn and Makarova in a fast, almost kittenish exchange. She has a beautifully innocent body to go with her strength, and both are exuberant performers. As for the whole idea, well, the crowd loved seeing these two jazz it up (so good-sporty of them), but watching Bruhn reminded me of Cathy Berberian singing Beatles songs. Technique and persona not completely compatible with the material.

"There were other good things in *The River.* Dennis Nahat did marvelous things with the rhythmic shape and impetus of his little solo in *Falls,* and Eleanor D'Antuono has mastered *Vortex* completely, so that now her turns and swirls unleash little spurts of power without obvious effort or preparation."

RODEO

Ballet in two scenes. Music by Aaron Copland. Choreography and book by Agnes de Mille. Scenery by Oliver Smith. Costumes by Kermit Love. First presented by the Ballet Russe de Monte Carlo at the Metropolitan Opera House, New York, October 16, 1942, with a cast headed by Agnes de Mille as the Cowgirl, *Frederic Franklin as the* Champion Roper, *and Casimir Kokitch as the* Head Wrangler. *Revived by Ballet Theatre at Rhine-am-Main Air Force, Frankfurt, Germany, August 14, 1950.*

Rodeo, subtitled "The Courting at Burnt Ranch," is a love story of the American Southwest. The problem it deals with is perennial: how an American girl, with the odds seemingly all against her, sets out to get herself a man. The girl in this case is a cowgirl, a tomboy whose desperate efforts to become one of the ranch's cowhands create a problem for the cowboys and make her the laughingstock of womankind.

SCENE ONE The corral of Burnt Ranch. The ballet's brief overture begins with a crash of cymbals and continues with a rowdy, rhythmic melody reminiscent of the wild west. The music becomes quiet, and the curtain rises on the corral of Burnt Ranch. The time is Saturday afternoon, the time of the weekly rodeo, about the turn of the century. Against an orange-red sky whose intense heat seems to bear down on the scene, a high wooden fence encloses the parched, dusty ground of the corral. Half a dozen lazy cowhands stand about, idling away the time. Among them stands the cowgirl, self-assertive in a bright red shirt, brown hat tilted back over her head, and brown pants and boots. Long pigtails hang down her back. One of the cowhands holds his hand up to shield his eyes from the glaring sun and looks out into the distance. Another cowboy rides in, twirling his arm over his head in a lassoing motion. The cowgirl hitches up her pants, as if to prepare for the rodeo that is about to begin. The cowboys tell her that she can't come along and ride off rapidly. Not to be outdone so easily, the cowgirl decides to follow them and rushes off to the right, roping the air with a fast-turning arm.

Three cowhands ride on vigorously. Six of their fellows join them, and all dance wildly, imitating in their movements the jolts and tricks of the rodeo. The music is fierce and a challenge to the dancers. The cowgirl re-enters and tries to join one of the groups. The cowgirl secretly hankers after the head wrangler, and watches him anxiously. He and the others motion to her to go away—she isn't wanted. The girl is used to this kind of treatment, however, and stays put, trying to compete in the rodeo. She disgraces herself, and the head wrangler is about to lose all patience with her.

But suddenly the corral is transfigured by the arrival of girls in city clothes—

Eastern friends of the rancher's daughter, who have come out with her to get a taste of ranch life. The cowboys slap their thighs in enthusiastic welcome; the girls wave to them with their handkerchiefs and giggle among themselves in feigned bashfulness. The cowgirl is both contemptuous and envious of their finery; she is visibly disgusted by their silly flirting.

The champion roper steps out to show off his skill before the girls. When the head wrangler steps over to them politely and takes off his hat to the rancher's daughter, the cowgirl can bear it no longer and rides off in a jealous fit of petulance. Four women from the ranch come out to watch the rodeo. They are entertained until the cowgirl rides in on what appears to be a bucking bronco. All the women raise their hands in despair at this foolish show-off. The cowgirl falls. The Eastern girls rush over to her and can't control their laughter: never in *their* born days has a *girl* done anything like that. The cowgirl is furious. She gets up and thumbs her nose at the women. Soon, alone with the cowboys, the girl sees that she's made a fool of herself all around; the women may laugh at her, but the men are worse: their silence makes her despair. She tries to regain her old familiarity with them. They ignore her and stare into the distance. The head wrangler jerks his thumb toward the house, telling her to leave the corral. He is the one man in the world the girl respects: smothering her tears, she obeys him.

The rodeo is over. The girls wave at the champion roper as he leaps away. The scene darkens, the music softens, the womenfolk cross the stage, moving slowly, bravely, yet wistfully, and there is created an impression of what home is like after a tiring, busy day. The cowboys cross the stage behind the women, and when the girls step backward, hesitating in their homeward march, the men move forward to them, place their arms about their waists, and move forward again with them.

The couples disappear. The cowgirl re-enters and tries to attract the head wrangler's attention. But it's as if she weren't even there: he goes to the rancher's daughter, who stands demure in her long blue dress with ribbons in her hair, lifts her softly, and takes her off into the night.

The cowgirl dances for a moment alone, trying to shake off what she knows has happened to her. She isn't any good as a woman and she's a miserable failure as a cowhand. The head wrangler returns. He doesn't understand what's wrong with this strange girl. A cowboy calls to him, and he leaves before the girl can tell him. The womenfolk try to call the girl home; she ignores them. The champion roper crosses the back of the corral, snapping his fingers in private anticipation of the Saturday night dance at the ranch house. He disappears. The cowgirl falls to the ground, all alone now with her problem. The stage blacks out around her.

A bright blue drop curtain, decorated with galloping wild horses, falls in front of the scene. Four couples rush out and begin a square dance. A caller shouts out directions to the dancers, and the couples respond by moving quickly into more intricate patterns as he commands. Soon they are out of breath, but turning still more rapidly and now shouting as they run around and around in a circle, faster and faster. They run off into the wings.

SCENE TWO   The ranch house. The curtain rises on the ranch house. The
cowgirl is sitting alone on a bench at the left, watching three cowboys dance a
jig to a jazzy piano accompaniment. One of the cowboys is the champion
roper, dressed now in his Saturday-night best—violet shirt, a loud vest of
cowhide, and striped yellow pants. He jumps high into the air and clicks his
heels together repeatedly. The cowgirl, still dressed in the dusty clothes of the
corral, feels out of place, though she is making an obvious effort to enjoy herself. The boys finish their jig. Three couples come in and dance about the
room, oblivious to whether anyone is watching them. Two of the couples waltz
into the parlor as the remaining pair quarrel: the boy kisses the girl, and she
rushes out.

The boy despairs of women and sits down beside the cowgirl. She tries to
comfort him, man to man. But another girl has come in looking for a partner.
She sees the boy alone, lifts her dress flirtatiously, and runs out. He chases
after her. The cowgirl can see no hope for such an idiot. The champion roper
strides back in and notices the lonely girl. He doesn't know what the matter is;
but since this is Saturday night and dancing time, he can see only one cure.
He tells her to get up and dance. The cowgirl says she doesn't know how to
dance. Well, first, he tells her, you'd better look a little cleaner. He tries to fix
her face up and smacks the dust off her bottom.

Just as the girl is beginning to forget about the head wrangler, he comes in
and goes over to the rancher's daughter. The cowgirl forgets all about the
champion roper. He loses patience with her; after all, he's just as interested in
other girls as she is in the head wrangler: He was only trying to make her have
a good time. When the champion roper walks out on her, the girl begins to
cry. She looks at the romantic dancing couple and falls to the floor in tears.

Gradually the room fills with people. The bench is moved back, and everybody gets ready for a community dance. The girls line up on one side, the
boys on the other. Bravely, the girl decides to try again and hopefully stands
in line with the girls. The boys approach and take their partners; the cowgirl is
left standing alone! The music becomes sweet and lyrical; the couples form a
circle; the boys lift the girls tenderly high above them; the girl turns away.

The champion roper dances in, jumping high in the air, clicking his heels together, breaking the romantic spell. When he finishes this bit of exhibitionism,
he comes over and leans on the girl's shoulder. She stifles a sob. The other couples leave the scene. The roper puts his hand under her chin and tells her to
cheer up, to try to dance with him again. He opens his arms wide, the girl
smiles, hitches up her belt, comes close to him, and everything is all right for a
few seconds while they dance.

Everything is spoiled, however, by the head wrangler and the rancher's
daughter, who come back and remind the cowgirl of her real love. The roper
catches her watching them; before he can do anything about it, she has run
away. The roper sees a girl walking alone and pursues her into the wings.

All the cowboys and their girls dance now, filling the scene with violent
color and vigorous movement. The couples clap their hands joyously in rhythm
to the music. They stop dancing all at once and stare, as the cowgirl comes in,

dressed from head to foot in bright red. The girls are shocked by this lack of taste; the boys are eager to find out what it means.

The champion roper goes to her, hitches up his pants, and asks her to dance. Even in her new dress the girl hitches up her clothes, too. They dance. The violins saw away at a square-dance theme, and the moving couples form a circle around them.

The cowgirl finds herself standing between the head wrangler and the roper. Both want to dance with her. The wrangler has forgotten the rancher's daughter long enough to notice the cowgirl. The roper and the wrangler throw the girl back and forth between them. She tries to escape, but the wrangler grabs her and tries to kiss her. The roper steps in and says, "No! She's my girl!" He takes her face in his hands and kisses her hard. He kisses her again, harder. Both of them wake up: they've both been wrong all along and didn't know what was happening. The head wrangler rejoins the rancher's daughter, and the whole group dances happily. As the curtain falls, the girls step into stirrups formed by the boys' hands and stand poised high over their heads. The cowgirl and the roper look into each other's eyes.

NOTES *Rodeo* has been a steady favorite in the United States and on American Ballet Theatre's many tours abroad. That was proved especially true when the company revived the ballet in 1972, in New York, at their engagement at the City Center. Writing of that performance in *Dance Magazine,* the critic Nancy Mason said: "America was ripe for *Rodeo* when performed by Ballet Russe in 1942. We were at war; national feeling was running high. Although Women's Lib may now quibble about the theme—'How to get a man'— *Rodeo* isn't dated because it deals with basic emotions.

"The action's set on a ranch in the Southwest and concerns a tomboy (Christine Sarry) who prefers riding a horse to wearing a dress. She's the tagalong of the cowboys, desperately and unreciprocally in love with the Head Wrangler (Marcos Paredes). Aaron Copland's music offers rowdy and rhythmic accompaniment.

"There couldn't be better casting for the tomboy. Christine Sarry even looks the part with her cropped brown hair and stubborn expression. What's more, she's a superb actress and comedienne; a powerpacked little dynamo who can stir laughter or tears. One really feels for her plight and wishes her well. Projecting incredible energy, she'd meet any challenge by pushing back her hat, hitching up her trousers, then diving right in. Shyness underlies this gumption. Here's a girl more at home on the back of a horse than in any social situation.

"The turning point arrives at the Saturday night dance, where Chris is finally persuaded by the Champion Roper (Terry Orr, alternating with William Carter) to put on a dress and join the party. A few minutes later she dashes in and everything halts abruptly. Gone are the baggy trousers; in their place, a sensible red jumper and ankle-length boots; on her face, a triumphant, excited grin. The Head Wrangler does a double-take. Then there's a competition between him and the Champion Roper for her heart.

"In *Rodeo* virtuoso tap dancing was used for the first time in a ballet. It also focused international attention on utilizing American folk themes in ballets. It changed the course for the musical theater; the next year Agnes de Mille choreographed *Oklahoma*.

"What a happy thought that *Rodeo* is back in the active repertoire. The company performs it with infectious zeal and good feelings. It's a perfect vehicle for Christine Sarry; Terry Orr delights with his easygoing and confident Roper interpretation. And it's good to see William Carter. . . . He created an honest and charming 'big brother' feeling."

In his book *Inside American Ballet Theatre*, Clive Barnes records a long interview with Agnes de Mille on the origins of *Rodeo*.

RODIN, MIS EN VIE

Music by Michael Kamen. Choreography by Margo Sappington. Costumes by Willa Kim. First presented by the Harkness Ballet at the Harkness Theatre, April 17, 1974, with Jeanette Vondersaar, Chris Jensen, and Zane Wilson in principal roles.

Rodin's sculpture come to life is the interesting idea behind this unusual ballet, which uses a specially commissioned score by Michael Kamen. Many familiar works by the great French artist (who once sculpted Nijinsky) are seen here in varied characterizations. The ebb and flow of the movement of sculptural bodies is seen to have a different quality from usual dance action and gesture. We are reminded of what must have attracted Rodin to dance and what must have generated some of his idealized figures as well as the power of his memorable studies and groupings. The work concludes in a dramatic tableaux with all of the figures "draped like some Dantesque vision," in Patricia Barnes's phrase, "over a vast scaffolding . . . It was particularly impressive."

ROMANCE

Music by Johannes Brahms. Choreography by Eliot Feld. Costumes by Stanley Simmons. Lighting by Jennifer Tipton. First presented by the American Ballet Company at the Brooklyn Academy of Music, New York, April 20, 1971, with Anna Laerkesen, Christine Sarry, Elizabeth Lee, Cristina Stirling, John Sowinski, Richard Munro, Daniel Levans, and Kenneth Hughes. Pianist: Harry Fuchs.

A dance ballet for four girls and four boys to some of Brahms's later piano music, *Romance* has no narrative action. The drama of the piece and the atmosphere of each of the dances derive from the choreographer's response to the music and the response of his dancers to that impulse. The dances are accompanied by a pianist who sits at his instrument on the left side of the stage. There are benches on stage and the costumes and deportment of the dancers suggest a formal occasion. The four couples appear in various combinations and ensembles; at one point two boys perform a display piece. The music is drawn from nine piano works, mostly intermezzos (Opus 116, Opus 118, Opus 119, and a final *Capriccio,* Op. 76). These pieces are in many ways ideal for dances; they are brief, about three or four minutes each, and can be easily heard, and seen, as continuous, though there is no thematic connection.

A thematic connection, of course, can be given in dance form, and while romance is indeed the theme of the ballet and several couples are wrapt in it to the exclusion of everything but speed in conquest and fulfillment, the ballet plays its variations on the main subject: frustration, wrong matches, ill-fated meetings. The evocation here of different situations in love—tenderness, regret, jealousy—is what *Romance* is all about. If you do not know these piano pieces by Brahms, I commend them to you.

ROMEO AND JULIET

Shakespeare's tragedy of *Romeo and Juliet* has been turned into dance by many choreographers. The six ballets described below are the most familiar:

Ballet in three acts, based on the play by Shakespeare. Music by Sergei Prokofiev. Libretto by Leonid Lavrovsky, Sergei Prokofiev, and Sergei Radlov. Choreography by Leonid Lavrovsky. Décor by Pyotr Williams. First presented at the Kirov State Theatre of Opera and Ballet, Leningrad, January 11, 1940, with Konstantin Sergeyev and Galina Ulanova in the title roles, A. V. Lopukhov as Mercutio, and S. G. Karen as Tybalt. Revised and presented at the Bolshoi Theatre, Moscow, December 28, 1946. First presented in the United States by the Bolshoi Ballet at the Metropolitan Opera House, New York, April 16, 1959, with Galina Ulanova and Yuri Zhdanov in the title roles.

The Soviet production relates Shakespeare's story in thirteen scenes, with a prologue and epilogue.

PROLOGUE Friar Laurence, sage and philosopher, blesses the marriage of Romeo and Juliet. The three figures stand motionless in tableau in front of three arches.

ACT ONE, SCENE ONE: THE MAIN SQUARE OF VERONA As dawn breaks, Romeo, son of Montague, is seen wandering alone about the deserted streets of Verona. Three servants leave the house of Capulet and walk across the square to join some girls in the inn. They are soon embroiled in a quarrel with two servants of Montague, the sworn enemy of their house. Swords are drawn and a fight starts. More and more people, including Benvolio, nephew of Montague, and Tybalt, nephew of Lady Capulet, join in the fray. Paris, who has come to Verona to seek the hand of Capulet's daughter, Juliet, reaches the square when the fighting is at its fiercest. Montague and his hated rival,

Capulet, unsheathe their swords and attack each other. The tocsin rings; its sound, reverberating through the city, brings crowds to the square. The prince of Verona then appears. He stops the fighting and an edict, forbidding disturbances in the city streets, is proclaimed. Tybalt leaves, cursing the Montagues.

Before the curtain, in a transitional *Front Scene,* the Capulet household is preparing for a ball. Juliet's nurse, carrying a beautiful dress, stops to reprimand some servants who have stolen food from the kitchen.

ACT ONE, SCENE TWO: JULIET'S ROOM   In her room, the walls covered with tapestries, Juliet plays hide-and-seek with her nurse instead of dressing for the ball. Lady Capulet comes into the room and tells Juliet that Paris has asked for her hand in marriage. Juliet protests that she is too young, but leading her to the mirror, her mother shows her that this is not so.

Front Scene: The preparations for the ball are almost finished. The servants carry in food and wine.

ACT ONE, SCENE THREE   The guests, including Verona's most illustrious citizens, troubadours, and many friends of Juliet's, arrive for the ball; among the last to come are Paris and his page.

Front Scene: Hearing music, Romeo's friends Mercutio and Benvolio decide to disguise themselves and go to Capulet's ball. They persuade Romeo to join them. He puts on a domino mask.

ACT ONE, SCENE FOUR: THE BALLROOM OF THE CAPULETS' PALACE   Juliet with all their guests awaits the arrival of her parents, who now enter. Paris presents Juliet with a bouquet. The ball now begins with a formal dance during which the men lay cushions at the feet of the ladies, kneel and kiss the hems of their skirts. The ladies and gentlemen then dance separately, followed by a slow and stately ensemble. Now Juliet, who has been arranging flowers and watching, dances herself. The dance of the guests is resumed briefly and then Juliet dances again. Romeo and his friends enter. He is enchanted by Juliet and approaches her. Paris, however, intercedes. Mercutio dances to distract the guests. As they dance together, Romeo tells Juliet how beautiful she is. His mask falls from his face and Juliet sees him for the first time. Juliet is captivated. This man she could really love. But then Tybalt appears and thinks he recognizes Romeo, a sworn enemy of the family. He tells old Capulet. Romeo quickly puts his mask back on. Although Tybalt there and then wishes to attack Romeo, Mercutio comes between them.

Front Scene: After the guests have left, Juliet learns from her nurse that it is none other than Romeo, son of her father's enemy Montague, with whom she has fallen in love.

ACT ONE, SCENE FIVE: THE GARDEN   Juliet cannot sleep and comes out on her moonlit balcony. She can only think of Romeo, whom she suddenly sees in the garden. They confess their love for each other and dance.

ACT TWO, SCENE ONE: THE MAIN SQUARE OF VERONA   Revelers throng the square. There are dances for the crowd and waitresses at the inn. A procession enters carrying an image of the Madonna. Benvolio and Mercutio flirt with ladies at the cafe and dance with the waitresses and there is another ensemble for the revelers. The nurse pushes her way through the crowds, looking for Romeo to give him a message from Juliet. He enters the square and the nurse whispers to him.

Front Scene: Romeo reads that Juliet has consented to be his wife and rapturously presses the letter to his heart.

ACT TWO, SCENE TWO: FRIAR LAURENCE'S CELL On a simple table stand some flowers and a skull, which the friar is contemplating when Romeo enters. Romeo kneels before the friar and asks him to marry them secretly. Nervously waiting for Juliet to come, his hands play with the skull and the flowers. Juliet, wearing a black cape, rushes in. Friar Laurence marries them and hopes that their union will end the strife between the Montagues and Capulets.

Front Scene: The Montagues and Capulets are in the main square as the procession of the Madonna moves across. Mercutio buys fruit and gives it to his friends. Tybalt bursts into rage when a peddler's tray accidentally knocks into one of his companions. Both families are cruelly sensitive now to any possible offense.

ACT TWO, SCENE THREE: THE MAIN SQUARE OF VERONA Revels continue in the square with a tambourine dance. Mercutio dances with waitresses at the inn. Tybalt enters and challenges Mercutio to a duel. Romeo tries to call it off and make peace but Tybalt mocks him and goads Mercutio into fighting. Mercutio is hit, struggles bravely against death but dies. Tybalt leaves, laughing. Romeo tries to hear Mercutio's heart and mourns. The body is borne out. Just as Romeo follows after, Tybalt comes back, insolent, swaggering. Romeo draws his sword, dashes up the stairs, and kills him. Romeo flees. The Capulets rush from their palace with the nurse. Lady Capulet so laments her kinsman's death that she is carried out gesturing wildly on his bier. The prince of Verona declares Romeo an exile for life.

ACT THREE, SCENE ONE: JULIET'S ROOM At dawn the next morning, Romeo opens the curtain onto the balcony and watches the sun. Juliet pulls the curtain back and the two lovers dance an impassioned *pas de deux*. But the household is stirring and Romeo must go. He embraces Juliet for the last time. As he leaves by the balcony, Juliet's parents and Paris enter with the nurse. Paris tries to woo Juliet but is scorned. Hurt by Juliet's rebuff, Paris leaves. Juliet tells her parents that she will not marry him. They are angry and threaten to disown her. The mother and the nurse leave and the father tries to force Juliet to submit to his will. She dances in despair when he has finally left her alone. Then quickly she finds her cape and runs out.

Front Scene: Juliet rushes to Friar Laurence.

ACT THREE, SCENE TWO: FRIAR LAURENCE'S CELL Juliet prays and relates her plight. She sees a dagger on the table and seizes it. Gently taking the dagger from her, Friar Laurence gives her instead a phial of sleeping potion which she must drink. She will then fall asleep, he tells her, and her parents, thinking her dead, will bury her in the family tomb. Meanwhile, Romeo, warned by Friar Laurence, will return under cover of darkness and take her away from Verona.

ACT THREE, SCENE THREE: JULIET'S BEDCHAMBER It is evening and Juliet is with her family and Paris. She consents to marry Paris, they dance together, and her parents are jubilant. The nurse brings the wedding gown. Juliet is alone. She knows she must drink the potion but delays in a dance of indecision. She then quickly swallows the potion and falls back on the bed. Soon it is morning. Her friends come with troubadours to celebrate her engagement. Paris enters, eager to see his bride. But the wedding dress lies on a chair and Juliet still sleeps. Her mother comes and orders the nurse to waken her. She goes to the bed but starts back with a cry of terror. Juliet lies lifeless on the bed. All weep.

ACT THREE, SCENE FOUR: A STREET IN MANTUA Romeo, alone, expresses his sorrow at his separation from Juliet. Outpacing Friar Laurence's messenger, Romeo's servant Balthasar arrives from Verona with the news that Juliet is dead. Stunned by grief, Romeo does not know what to do, then decides that he must go to his beloved.

ACT THREE, SCENE FIVE: THE CAPULET TOMB Many attend Juliet's funeral and her body is placed in the family vault at the top of a flight of steps. Paris prays there and leaves. It grows dark. Romeo comes in, mounts the steps, removes her shroud and holds Juliet in his arms. He kisses her, then picks her up to carry her briefly down the steps. He ascends again, holding her high over his head, and places her on her tomb. He then drinks a phial of poison and dies, falling back down the steps. Juliet now awakes from her sleeping potion. She sees Romeo and at first thinks him perhaps asleep, as she has been, but he is dead. She takes his dagger at once and stabs herself. She falls back over his body.

EPILOGUE Over the bodies of their children, the Montagues and the Capulets, followed by the populace, take each other's hands and swear to end their feud. All kneel.

NOTES Prokofiev's score to *Romeo and Juliet* was completed September 8, 1935, soon after his return to Russia from Paris. It was first performed at a concert in Moscow in October of that year. Prokofiev's plan at that time was that the ballet should end happily, with Juliet resurrected in her tomb and a final joyous *pas de deux* for the two lovers. This idea received some criticism and the composer abandoned it. He said at the time: "I have taken special pains to achieve a simplicity that will, I hope, reach the hearts of all listeners. If people find no melody and no emotion in this work of mine, I shall be very sorry; but I feel that they will, sooner or later."

Some time elapsed before the score was first used for ballet, and this was in Brno, Czechoslovakia in 1938. Meanwhile, two suites arranged by Prokofiev were played in the U.S.S.R. and the United States.

The Soviet choreographer Leonid Lavrovsky published notes about his conception of the ballet, which was first produced in 1940: "The depths of passion and ideas, the intensity of feeling conveyed by the protagonists of Shakespeare's tragedy, demand the fusion of dance with mime. In ballet, words are absent and the effect of every phrase of mime must correspond with the spoken language of the stage characters. Mime should never descend to trivial, commonplace, imitative gestures, but become a genuine theatrical performance, in which characters, emotion, and passion are expressed by the movements of the body, instead of by the varied intonations of the voice. Ballet is a choreographic play in which the dancing must arise naturally from the mimed action, or the mimed action be the logical sequence of the dancing."

A film of Lavrovsky's *Romeo and Juliet* was produced in the U.S.S.R. in 1954, with Galina Ulanova.

When the Bolshoi's *Romeo and Juliet* was first presented in New York, Edwin Denby, writing about it for *The Hudson Review* (now included in his book *Dancers, Buildings and People in the Streets*), spoke of Ulanova's vividness:

"Bending her neck toward her partner in a lift of the Bedroom Scene, the gesture had the tragic quiet Pasternak speaks of. Or take the opposite kind of moment. Faced with marriage to County Paris, Juliet, her mantle flung round her, desperately rushes along the apron to Friar Laurence; armed by him with the sleeping potion, she flings the mantle round her again, and rushes desperately along the apron back home. The fling, the rush, the exact repeat are pure 'Perils of Pauline.' But Ulanova's art at that moment is so brilliant the audience breaks into delighted applause.

"You can find out something about Bolshoi style by trying the gymnastics of Ulanova's fling and rush yourself. Standing in the middle of the room, fling an arm across your chest, and at the same time raise the breastbone as high as it will go, bending it over at the top so it pushes the neck back. Don't let go, keep forcing the breastbone further, but in addition push the neck forward as hard as you can, and lift your head until you feel 'desperately resolved.' (It may make you cough.) And now, keeping the stance you are in unchanged, rush about the room with an incredible lightness and rapidity. If your family is watching, they will pick you off the floor, and urge you to try harder.

"The special stance of fling and rush you just tried (it involves a backbend between the shoulder-blades) is not classical. It has been called the pouter-pigeon silhouette by Walter Terry, and that is just how it looks. But when Ulanova does it, you feel it means, 'Here is my heart.'

"But if you notice that, you also notice her feet. In light runs on toe (bourrée steps) they seem to touch the floor sensitively. You see how keen the pointed foot looks in the air, during attitudes, arabesques, and passés, how clearly the leg defines and differentiates the different classic shapes. Below the waist Ulanova is a strict classicist; above the waist she alters the shape of classic motions now slightly, now quite a lot, to specify a nuance of drama (for ex-

ample, the pouter-pigeon silhouette). Neither element—the lightness below or
the weight above—is weakened for the sake of the other; the combined motion
keeps fluid. And often while one movement is ebbing to its end, another seems
already welling up in the midriff."

*Narrative ballet in one act, based on the play by Shakespeare. Music by
Frederick Delius. Choreography by Antony Tudor. Scenery and costumes
by Eugene Berman. First presented by Ballet Theatre at the Metropolitan
Opera House, New York, April 6, 1943, with Alicia Markova as Juliet, Hugh
Laing as Romeo, Nicolas Orloff as Mercutio, Antony Tudor as Tybalt, and
Jerome Robbins as Benvolio.*

This dramatic ballet compresses into one vivid act the tragic love story of
Romeo and Juliet. Within a single-unit setting representing the ordered golden
beauty of the Italy of the Renaissance, the narrative proceeds without scenic
interruption; and what might be spoken of as "scenes," in an ordinary dramatic spectacle, move together and coalesce with a flow that suggests the inevitability of the tragedy itself.

The score for the ballet is an arrangement by Antal Dorati of selected works
by Delius: *Over the Hills and Far Away, The Walk to the Paradise Garden,
Eventyr,* and *Brigg Fair.*

PROLOGUE   The curtain rises immediately on a drop curtain depicting the
entrance to a palace in Verona. There are two great arches to the left and
right, and in the center, cut out of the curtain, is a draped entry. A spotlight
centers on this doorway, and Romeo steps out cautiously. He looks behind
him, and Rosaline, a beautiful girl, follows him. Romeo takes her hand and attempts to embrace her. Rosaline warns him that he is too hasty, and Romeo
follows her impatiently within.

Now members of the opposing families of Montague and Capulet dance
onto the scene and challenge each other. The two leaders of the factions, Mercutio and Tybalt, are eager for a contest, and the two groups commence
dueling. But the heads of the two houses at variance with each other enter
with their wives and order their kinsmen to desist. The men reluctantly abandon their fighting and bow to the peers. It is apparent that their battle will be
renewed at the first opportunity. Romeo and his friend Mercutio remain
behind when the others have left. Only the entrance of the fair Rosaline persuades them that they have better business elsewhere.

BALL AT THE HOUSE OF THE CAPULETS   The drop curtain rises on a wide,
open area of red marble enclosed by a decorative colonnade. Couples in richly
embroidered costumes are dancing in elegant, courtly fashion. The music softens, and Juliet enters on the right. She lingers slightly, hesitating to step into
the ballroom, for she knows what awaits her. She greets her parents warmly,
yet formally. Capulet turns to introduce her to a young nobleman, Paris, but
Juliet seeks instead the company of her cousin Tybalt. The understanding

Tybalt consoles her, but also reminds her of her duty and leads her to Paris. The assembled company begin to dance again, and Juliet accepts Paris as her partner.

Romeo enters on the right. He looks directly at Juliet. Juliet, her back to Paris for a moment, glances back at him. As Paris bends down to kiss her hand, Juliet looks across the room toward Romeo. The dance continues, and Romeo chooses a partner to join the ball. The two couples dance on opposite sides of the room. The set pattern of the dance separates them, and Juliet and Romeo despair of meeting. Soon the entire company circles the hall and the dance ends. The guests proceed to move toward the rear for refreshment, and Romeo and Juliet are alone.

Romeo falls at her feet and declares the overpowering love he has felt since he saw her. He rises, their faces touch, and they kiss. Then, formal again, the two bow to each other and begin to dance together a delicate, flowing measure. When the dance is over, they realize that they must separate and both say their farewells. But as they turn to go, they move together again and kneel.

Mercutio and Tybalt emerge from the banquet hall. Juliet's nurse urges her away, lest there be trouble. Tybalt warns Romeo and turns to Juliet questioningly, and all depart.

ROMEO WOOS JULIET IN THE CAPULET ORCHARD   The lights dim. White drapes are drawn across the back colonnade. Four torchbearers enter on the right, followed by Romeo and Mercutio. Romeo is preoccupied and will not listen to his friend's appreciation of the beauty of the evening. Mercutio grows impatient and tells his friend that the romance he contemplates is out of the question. The music builds in intensity, and Romeo refuses to heed Mercutio's advice. Mercutio leaps to the back of one of the torchbearers and urges Romeo to follow them to a tavern. Romeo pretends to go, then conceals himself. The others return to look for him, but soon follow after Mercutio.

Two couples enter. Romeo holds his arm across his face, lest he be recognized. The couples disappear, and Romeo dances alone. Above the colonnade at the rear, Juliet looks down into the orchard and sees her lover. She is enchanted and rests her head sweetly on the balcony railing, wondering when he will look up and see her. Romeo glances up and blows kisses to her. She returns the kisses, but warns him away. Just as he hides behind a pillar on the right, Juliet's nurse comes into the garden. No sooner has she departed than Tybalt and Paris stroll by. When they are alone again, Romeo holds out his hands to Juliet and from above she gestures to him yearningly. Romeo gestures defiance of their families and proposes marriage. Juliet consents.

BETROTHAL OF ROMEO AND JULIET BY THE FRIAR   Drapes are drawn across the colonnade, and Friar Laurence stands in his cell. Romeo enters. He is impatient and afraid and paces the floor. There is a sound at the door, and Romeo rushes to see who it is. Friar Laurence pulls him back warningly Romeo's back is turned as Juliet runs into the room. He turns to her, and the two kneel before the friar, who blesses them. Juliet rises, turns rapidly, and falls low in Romeo's arms. Then she rushes off into the night, promising him that her nurse will bring him a message.

STREET SCENE   The curtains are drawn back, the friar disappears, and the open area becomes the street. It is still night. A cripple and a blind man enter, followed by the gay Mercutio and a friend. Romeo enters, followed by Juliet and her nurse. The nurse beckons Juliet away. The concern of the lovers is contrasted with the friction between their families, for Tybalt has entered and threatened Mercutio in earnest. The two fight, their kinsmen join the battle, and the music is ominous, like the sound of an approaching storm. Mercutio is stabbed by Tybalt and dies in Romeo's arms.

Romeo recovers from his grief and attacks Tybalt. He leaps to his back, forces him down, and stabs him to death. Now there is no hope of reconciling the two families. Romeo does not know what to do. Friar Laurence enters and takes the dagger from him. Finally the youth is persuaded that he must flee for his life.

Juliet and her nurse enter the square and see what has happened. Juliet weeps for Tybalt, but then, suddenly desperate, instructs the nurse to run to Romeo and reassure him.

ROMEO'S FAREWELL TO JULIET   The scene is Juliet's bedroom. Day is breaking. Juliet rises first and dances joyfully, with a sweet, youthful happiness, as Romeo watches her from the bed. She returns to him, he lifts her, and they embrace. Romeo prepares to leave. He must escape from Verona. They will meet elsewhere. Juliet weeps because of her happiness and its quick ending. They kiss. Romeo departs, and Juliet falls back on the bed, still weeping.

PREPARATIONS FOR THE WEDDING OF JULIET TO PARIS   Some time passes, and handmaidens to Juliet enter with her nurse to prepare her for the marriage her parents have insisted upon. They waken Juliet. Instantly she sits up and looks off into the direction that Romeo took when he left her. She cannot believe that this day she must marry another man. The nurse holds her in her arms and tries to comfort her. Juliet rises and protests to her father that she cannot marry Paris. Capulet refuses to listen to her or to his wife, who tries to intercede for Juliet.

Then, to the accompaniment of a melody almost unbearable in its sweetness and pathos, Juliet's four handmaidens form a tableau beside her. They hold before her a wedding dress of gold, and Juliet slips her arms into it as if the cloth were on fire.

When she is dressed, she weeps softly in her father's arms. Her father blesses her and places on her head a shining crown. She is presented with a bouquet of white flowers. Friar Laurence enters, and Juliet falls into his arms. When they are unobserved, the friar gives her a vial containing a secret drug and instructs her to drink it without delay: all may yet be well.

Juliet walks away, drinks the contents of the vial, whirls frantically, and swoons. Her family gathers about her. Six women bear slowly across the stage a great cloth trimmed in somber black.

PROCESSION TO THE TOMB   Two of Juliet's attendants head her funeral procession. Juliet lies on a bier carried high by her black-cloaked kinsmen. Her father and mother follow behind. When the procession has passed, the women holding up the cloth of mourning disappear to reveal another scene.

SCENE IN THE VAULT OF THE CAPULETS   We are in Juliet's tomb. She lies immobile on her bier, her hands pressed together at her breast. Romeo enters. He imagines that his beloved is dead and drinks a vial of poison. He falls at the foot of the bier.

Juliet gradually revives from the drug she has taken. She rises. Romeo sees her, pulls himself up with difficulty, reaches out for her, and—when Juliet comes to him—lifts her with his remaining strength. He falls. Juliet understands what has happened. She spins around and around frantically. Romeo rises again and lifts her in his arms. He holds her for a moment, then collapses across her bier. He dies. Juliet looks down upon him. She takes out his dagger, waits for a moment, and—rising suddenly on point, as if to meet the happiness only death can bring her—stabs herself in the heart. She falls across her lover's body and, with her last gesture, touches his face.

NOTES   Tudor's *Romeo and Juliet* was revived by American Ballet Theatre, July 22, 1971, at the New York State Theatre, Lincoln Center. The critic Deborah Jowitt wrote in the *Village Voice:* "What Antony Tudor did in his 1943 *Romeo and Juliet*, now revived by Ballet Theatre, makes it one of the most brilliant and interesting of recent ballets. In particular, he has worked with the structure of the play so as to situate it in the kind of Renaissance time and space with which Shakespeare's work has so many affinities.

"As Wylie Sypher pointed out in his *Four Stages of Renaissance Style*, the plot of *Romeo and Juliet* is an essay in symmetry and proportion. Capulet is weighed against Montague, Romeo's passion against Paris's suitability, love against hate, night against day, rashness against prudence, etc. Time is compressed into forty-two hours; space is defined and confined by the walls of Verona's chambers, gardens, piazzas. There is none of the depth, irregularity, or ripeness of the later *Hamlet* or *Macbeth*.

"Tudor has set his version of this sad and lyrical equation in what might be compared to a continuous Botticelli frieze. There is an emphasis on elegant, agitated, fastidiously sensual flow rather than on volume. It is as if Tudor had speeded up the heartbeat of the play, so tremulous is one's reaction to it. His space, like Botticelli's, is almost more medieval than Renaissance: depth is created by temporary hierarchies, events separated in time can coexist in space. When Romeo and Juliet wind through the pillars of the piazza in an ecstatic return from their wedding, they are small upstage figures, seen through the minor bustle of the square. When Juliet, enveloped by the nurse, weeps over Tybalt down left, their figures are balanced by those of Romeo and Friar Laurence consulting hastily down right. And the two tableaux are separated by a temporary 'wall' formed by two watching women. Tudor's use of these women is another odd detail. They witness the action from different positions, like those little faces in the corners of certain medieval paintings.

"The effect of all this compression on the spectator is fascinating. There is no blood, thunder, bombast; the action is drawn lightly over you like a veil while you sit in a state of almost febrile tension. Events, briefly sketched, flow out of each other; even what Tudor has chosen to show or not show is revealing. Nothing seems to have any preliminaries. The Montague boys' decision to attend the Capulet ball is conveyed to Mercutio's brusquely beckoning finger, while the powerful effect of the lovers' first meeting on Romeo and his friends is shown more fully. Letters are not delivered, potions are drunk, marriages are arranged at high speed and with pictorial clarity.

"Eugene Berman's marvelous pillars, archways and porticos hold and shape the action, add to the morbid delicacy of atmosphere. When a curtain is drawn to reveal the ball in progress, the dancers first appear cramped, too large for the space they inhabit—another painterly touch. Tudor's choice of excerpts from Delius is extremely unusual. The music meanders along its own path—painting a lush, summer atmosphere that is neither dramatically nor rhythmically assertive, but full of feeling. Often it creates a curious tension between its dreamy flow and the action of the play. For instance, the insistent little tappings and steppings of the court dances begin to be almost ominous against the inconclusive music.

"Since nothing in this ballet ever really stops, pauses for large scale 'dance numbers' would have been unthinkable. Tudor has built the dancing out of gesture so subtly and naturally that you are not aware of anything but the continuous unfolding of this lyrical disquisition on action. There is a ball scene, of course, quietly and slowly built up. There is no *grand pas de deux* for the balcony scene: alone on the stage floor, Romeo bursts into an exulting stammer of leaps and postures and wide-flung gestures, while Juliet on the balcony above returns his passion with slow and happy stretchings and curvings of her body and arms. Even the morning-after-the-wedding scene turns into a dance imperceptibly through a series of muted rushings, claspings, near-swoons.

"Because nothing seems calculated, no particular moments of dance can be easily isolated. Pointe work has a special expressive function. Juliet steps up onto pointe as if some delicate emotional balance were at stake, or as if she were on unfamiliar ground. In some of her steps, she might be swooning upward."

The critic Marcia Siegel wrote in the Boston *Globe:* "Antony Tudor's *Romeo and Juliet* is a beautiful ballet. An extraordinary ballet. I think it's the best new ballet I've seen this year, even though it's really a revival, originally choreographed in 1943 for the infant Ballet Theatre. Restaged July 22 by that company, with Carla Fracci and Ivan Nagy in the opening-night title roles, it's a deeply moving and interesting work. I don't know when I've seen a ballet with such clarity and distinction of detail.

"Tudor saw the perennial story in quite intimate terms, encompassed in one act with several scenes. This makes for a tighter production—the story moves quickly, building to its powerful tragic end, without the long interpolations of sword-play and ceremony that pad out more grandiose Romeo and Juliet ballets. There's considerably less display dancing, smaller crowds, and less exposition, but I think this makes sense. Tudor's ballet is about the star-crossed lovers. The John Cranko and Kenneth MacMillan versions we've seen here in recent years are about the spectacular possibilities of a full-length ballet based on Shakespeare's play—quite a different thing.

"Fracci and Nagy are splendid as the doomed couple. Fracci is one of our best actress-dancers, and Nagy, released by Tudor's unstereotyped movement from the conventional suffering nobility of his other roles, was more convincing, more alive to the dramatic situation than I've ever seen him. All their scenes together breathed wonder and changeableness, joy touched with disbelief, a sort of shining despair.

"Tudor set the ballet in the Italian Renaissance, and much of the movement looks like the paintings and court dances of the period—the men with one leg turned out and pointing a fashionable toe, the women tilting back with their weight thrust mincingly forward. At times the company looked awkward with these stylizations, but Bruce Marks as Tybalt, Rosanna Seravalli as Lady Capulet, and Bonnie Mathis as Rosaline showed me immediately what the shape of the movement is, how it works. What intelligent character dancers these three are!

"There's more in this ballet, both in its dancing and production, than I can discuss in one day, but Tudor's choice of Delius' music is indicative of his unusual concept. The elegaic, rich-textured, but not especially dancy score seems at first too impressionistic to support the tragedy. But in fact it reinforces the ballet's delicate romanticism and isn't overpowering as the more familiar Prokofiev *Romeo and Juliet* usually is.

"Eugene Berman's multilevel set suggests both the scaffolded flexibility of a Shakespearean stage and the columns and perspective of an Italian painting. . . .

"I went back to see Antony Tudor's *Romeo and Juliet*, given by American Ballet Theatre, and found it as fascinating as I had the first time. It's a ballet of ideas—not philosophical or moral preachings, but ideas about how to present a classic story.

"Ballets are produced in such quantity here, and with so little attention to durability, that they often seem to be a matter of choosing new spices to liven up the same old hamburger. Tudor's *Romeo* constitutes a rethinking of every aspect of the narrative ballet. He uses all theatrical elements to suggest the depth and universality of the theme, instead of just letting us recognize what we already know about it.

"Eugene Berman's opening drop shows a small Romanesque building, possibly a tomb, suspended against a blue sea or sky, just hanging there, a door to something insubstantial and timeless. Classical allusions keep recurring quietly. You notice during the principals' first duet that the other guests at the Capulets' ball have seated themselves beyond some pillars, at a dinner table in another room. Their backs are to the audience; they are too close to the stage for realism. They look flat, like the background of a Renaissance painting. Juliet's friends, dressed like Botticelli nymphs, lift a shroud across the stage where Juliet's drugged body lies, and stand there throughout the funeral procession, echoing the statues perched atop the colonnaded set.

"The changes of scene—there are about ten of them—are accomplished in a variety of ingenious ways, many involving characters in the ballet. In fact, two 'attendants' watch the whole ballet from a bench downstage, moving around to draw curtains and even, at one point, simulating a wall. They are spectators of the tragedy who also help present it to us, and at the same time they belong to the House of Capulet as servants. This is an Elizabethan device as well as a classical reference. Realistic theater didn't come along till the late nineteenth century, and Tudor isn't offering us a modern romance. Other critics have objected to the extremely stylized quality of this *Romeo*, as if that were a drawback, and as if *all* ballet weren't a stylization to begin with. I suggest that Tudor's concept of production has the same elevating effect on the story that Shakespeare's poetry has."*

Ballet in eleven scenes with prologue, based on Shakespeare's play. Music by Sergei Prokofiev. Choreography by Frederick Ashton. Scenery and costumes by Peter Rice. First presented by the Royal Danish Ballet at the Royal Theatre, Copenhagen, May 19, 1955, with Mona Vangsaae and Henning Kronstam in the title roles. First presented in the United States by the Royal Danish Ballet at the Metropolitan Opera House, New York, September 26, 1956.

Frederick Ashton's ballet follows this scenario:

At Verona there is constant feuding between the families of Montague and Capulet. A party of young men from Montague's household are present at an entertainment at Capulet's house. Among them is Romeo, who falls in love at first sight with Juliet, Capulet's only child. Romeo and Juliet declare their love for each other. They are secretly married by Friar Laurence. The brawls are continued. Romeo's friend Mercutio is killed by Tybalt, of the House of Capulet. Romeo kills Tybalt and is forced to flee. He takes refuge with Friar Laurence.

Meanwhile, old Capulet decides that Juliet shall marry Count Paris. The friar, hoping to bring about a reconciliation, advises Romeo to say farewell to Juliet and to hide in Mantua. When he learns of old Capulet's decision, he gives Juliet a sleeping draught which will produce a deathlike sleep. Juliet is believed dead, and is buried in the vault of her ancestors. The friar's message to Romeo miscarries. Supposing that his wife is indeed dead, Romeo hurries to the tomb, and commits suicide over her body. Juliet wakes too late, finds Romeo dead, and kills herself with his dagger.

Ballet in three acts after William Shakespeare. Music by Sergei Prokofiev. Choreography and staging by John Cranko. Décor and costumes by Jürgen Rose. In the repertory of the National Ballet of Canada. First staged by John Cranko for the ballet of La Scala, Milan, at the Teatro Verde, in Venice,

* Reprinted from Marcia B. Siegel's book, *At the Vanishing Point*, 1972.

July 26, 1958; this production was extensively revised and first presented by the Stuttgart Ballet at the Württemberg State Theatre, Stuttgart, December 2, 1962. The Stuttgart Ballet production was first presented in the United States at the Metropolitan Opera House, New York, June 18, 1969, with Marcia Haydée as Juliet, Richard Cragun as Romeo, Jan Stripling as Tybalt, and Egon Madsen as Mercutio.

The scene is Verona.

ACT ONE, SCENE ONE: THE MARKET PLACE   As day breaks, Romeo, son of Montague, is found declaring his love to the fair Rosaline. With the sunrise, the market place fills with townspeople, among whom are members of the two rival families, the Capulets and the Montagues. Tempers flare and a quarrel develops. The Duke of Verona appears and warns the two factions that death will be the ultimate punishment if the feud does not stop. Romeo and his friends Benvolio and Mercutio make reluctant peace with Tybalt, a kinsman of the Capulets.

ACT ONE, SCENE TWO: JULIET'S GARDEN IN THE CAPULETS' HOUSE   Juliet receives her first ball dress from her mother, Lady Capulet, and learns that she is to meet the noble Paris to whom she will be betrothed on the following day. Now she must bid farewell to her childhood.

ACT ONE, SCENE THREE: OUTSIDE THE CAPULETS' HOUSE   Guests appear for the Capulets' ball, among them Rosaline. Romeo and his friends, masked, follow her to the ball.

ACT ONE, SCENE FOUR: THE BALLROOM   Juliet dances with Paris but suddenly she and Romeo behold each other, and it is love at first sight. Tybalt, suspecting Romeo's identity, tries to start an argument but is prevented by Juliet's father who abides by the laws of hospitality.

ACT ONE, SCENE FIVE: JULIET'S BEDROOM   On the balcony outside her bedroom Juliet dreams of Romeo. He appears below in the garden. They declare their eternal love.

ACT TWO, SCENE ONE: THE MARKET PLACE   A carnival is in progress in the main square. Romeo, indifferent to the gaiety around him, is discovered by Juliet's nurse, who brings him a letter from her. She asks Romeo to meet her at the chapel of Friar Laurence.

ACT TWO, SCENE TWO: FRIAR LAURENCE'S CELL IN THE FOREST   In his cell, Friar Laurence joins the young lovers in marriage.

ACT TWO, SCENE THREE: THE MARKET PLACE   At the height of the carnival, Romeo returns to the square. Tybalt accosts him but Romeo declines to fight.

Mercutio, angered, engages in a duel with Tybalt, and dies at his hands. Romeo, distraught, turns on Tybalt and kills him.

ACT THREE, SCENE ONE: THE BEDROOM   In Juliet's bedroom the lovers are awakened by the sunrise, and Romeo, under sentence of exile, must leave Juliet and Verona. Lord and Lady Capulet enter with Paris, but Juliet rejects him.

ACT THREE, SCENE TWO: FRIAR LAURENCE'S CELL IN THE FOREST   Juliet, appealing for help to Friar Laurence, receives a potion from him that will place her in a deathlike sleep. He explains that Romeo will find her in the family tomb and both can escape together.

ACT THREE, SCENE THREE: THE BEDROOM   Juliet agrees to her marriage with Paris. After he leaves with her parents, she takes the sleeping draught and is thought to be dead when her family and friends discover her.

ACT THREE, SCENE FOUR: THE CAPULET FAMILY CRYPT   Romeo, who has never received Friar Laurence's message revealing the plan, believes Juliet to be dead and rushes to her tomb. There he finds the mourning Paris and kills him. Embracing Juliet for the last time, he plunges his dagger into his heart. Juliet awakens to find Romeo dead. Grief-stricken, she kills herself.

Reviewing a performance of Cranko's ballet by the Stuttgart Ballet at the Metropolitan Opera House in the spring of 1973, the critic Andrew Porter wrote in *The New Yorker:* "There can be little dispute that Prokofiev's *Romeo and Juliet* is the most successful full-length ballet score written since Tchaikovsky's. I have seen it set to movement in six different versions, and only one of them—Serge Lifar's, for the Paris Opéra—was without marked merit. John Cranko's, created for the Stuttgart Ballet in 1962, and chosen for the opening night, last week, of the company's current Metropolitan season, is a very successful dance drama that has worn well. It continues to display the special virtues and strongly individual character of the troupe for whom it was made, and provides extended, uncommonly telling roles for the major stars—Marcia Haydée, Egon Madsen, and Richard Cragun—that shine in the splendid ensemble. The Royal Ballet, they say, dances best in New York; perhaps the Stuttgarters do so, too. I was bowled over on the first night by the power and eloquence of their presentation, and certainly Jürgen Rose's *Romeo* scenery and costumes never look as handsome and striking as they do on the Metropolitan stage. Dramatic force, potent projection, is a mark of German dancing; in Stuttgart, with his international team of dancers, Mr. Cranko has combined this force with Royal Ballet 'school,' developed his artists by composing new works for and 'on' them, and created one of the world's leading companies.

"Approaches to a Shakespeare ballet are almost as diverse as those to a Shakespeare opera. Prokofiev in his *Romeo* score devised appropriate melodies and motifs for the characters and their attributes (Juliet as a girl, Juliet as a woman, Romeo's ardor, Mercutio's wit, etc.), wrote movements that mount to passionate climaxes in the right places, supplied the necessary (and some unnecessary) ensemble dances, and achieved all this with his wonted flair for theatre music. Leonid Lavrovsky did the original choreography; his version was first performed, in Leningrad, in 1940. He worked on the piece with Prokofiev (and once told me how tiresome and silly the composer had been—wanting, for a while, a happy ending, not wanting to lose a Dance of Carpet Sellers that he had somehow managed to bring in). While Prokofiev's 'libretto' was, so to speak, the plot, the characters, and their emotions, the choreographer added a more detailed attention to Shakespeare; in his version specific lines from the play seem often to ring out from the motion of the dancers: Romeo's 'O! she doth teach the torches to burn bright' when first he sees Juliet, his 'I do protest I never injur'd thee' to Tybalt, and then, after Mercutio's death, 'Fire-ey'd fury be my conduct now,' Juliet's 'My only love sprung from my only hate,' her 'Is there no pity sitting in the clouds?,' and many others. By comparison, Ashton's version for the Royal Danish Ballet, in 1955, to the same score, was a Lamb's Tale that became lyric poetry in the duets for the lovers. Kenneth MacMillan's *Romeo* for Covent Garden, ten years later, borrowed Cranko's solutions to the structural problems set by Prokofiev's ensembles, and acquired its special character from the detailed concentration on Juliet's development. In the monologues and duologues of MacMillan's version there is the same sense found in Lavrovsky's of words just below the surface of the dance. The successive quatrains and couplets of the antiphonal sonnet spoken by Romeo and Juliet when first they meet ('If I profane with my unworthiest hand') are transmuted into plastic imagery. Cranko's *Romeo* is more generalized, less intense in its close-ups. We do not follow the balcony and bedroom scenes 'line by line'; his approach, like Prokofiev's, is less literary. But the dances do not lack emotion, and they flow effectively. Cranko's presentation of the world around the tragedy—the street scenes, the assembly of Capulet's guests, the ball—is the most successful of all; a theatre flair kin to Prokofiev's is apparent in his handling. I miss Juliet's pas de deux with Paris on the wedding morning, a poignant moment in both the Lavrovsky and the MacMillan versions; the Friar Laurence scenes are rather skimpy, and Act III passes too swiftly. (Lavrovsky did well to insert a solo for Romeo in Mantua, corresponding to 'Is it even so? then I defy you, stars!') Comparisons are helpful in description; in its own right, Cranko's *Romeo* is an excellently vigorous, youthful, unrhetorical yet affecting work, couched in a fluent, eclectic choreography that I suppose could be called free-Fokine with modern ingredients, and very skillful in its theatrical shaping.

"The first night presented the nonpareil cast of Miss Haydée and Mr. Cragun in the title roles and Mr. Madsen as Mercutio. The second brought a new Juliet, the young Joyce Cuoco, touching and vulnerable, a promising actress and fleet technician—prone, in fact, to phrase some of the lyrical choreography too crisply. The Romeo and Mercutio swapped roles: Mr. Madsen now made a courteous, romantic Romeo, rather less boldly ardent than Mr. Cragun had been, while as Mercutio Mr. Cragun lacked only the twinkling beats with which Mr. Madsen had tripped through the Queen Mab solo. Jan Stripling's cold, strong Tybalt, the contrasted interpretations of Paris from Reid Anderson (a formal wooer) and Vladimir Klos (more tender), and Andrew Oxenham's bright Benvolio deserve mention; so do the unforced buoyancy, verve, and warmth with which the whole company took the stage."°

Ballet in three acts. Music by Sergei Prokofiev. Choreography by Kenneth MacMillan. Scenery and costumes by Nicholas Georgiadis. Lighting by William Bundy. First presented by the Royal Ballet at the Royal Opera House, Covent Garden, February 9, 1965, with Rudolf Nureyev and Margot Fonteyn as Romeo and Juliet. First presented in the United States by the Royal Ballet at the Metropolitan Opera House, New York, April 21, 1965.

The English critic and editor Peter Williams has said, "The game of love and death is the theater's trump card, and Shakespeare was no fool about what made good theater, the rules of which have varied little in any language from the threshing floors of Greece until the present day." Kenneth MacMillan's version of *Romeo and Juliet*, while based on the Prokofiev score used by a number of choreographers, varies substantially in treatment and detail.

ACT ONE, SCENE ONE: THE MARKET PLACE   The curtain rises on a dark stage. Then, to pizzicato strings, the stage is gradually lighted, revealing the market place. It is early morning, and the market is not yet busy. Romeo enters and tries to declare his love for the lovely Rosaline, who rejects him. Romeo joins his friends Mercutio and Benvolio, and, as day breaks and the market begins to fill up with butchers and farmers, Romeo takes off his cape and watches idly. A girl tries to entice him away. With two other harlots, she becomes involved with Romeo and his friends. A quarrel now develops between Tybalt, a nephew of Capulet, and Romeo. The Capulets and Montagues are of course sworn enemies and a fight begins. The heads of the two families join the dispute and do not assist a solution. The Prince of Verona appears and is obliged to order them to cease their feuding. All place their swords on the ground at his command, in front of the slain, but the two families stand opposite each other, obstinate in their rage.

ACT ONE, SCENE TWO: JULIET'S ANTEROOM IN THE CAPULETS' HOUSE   After a brief musical interlude, the curtain rises on a bright and cheerful room. There are large bird cages to the right and left, and Juliet's nurse sits waiting. Juliet runs in and we are reminded at once that this girl who will become a tragic figure is at heart a child of fourteen. She plays with a doll. She reacts like a spoiled child, too, when her mother and father come in with Paris, whom she does not like. But Juliet is nevertheless interested somewhat in anyone who would express interest in marrying her; she yields to her father's insistence and is nice to him. When the Capulets and Paris leave, Juliet wants to resume her play with the doll, but the nurse points out that her childhood is over, that she

° From *A Musical Season* by Andrew Porter (Viking Press); © 1973 Andrew Porter. Originally in *The New Yorker.*

is a young woman now, about to be beloved. Juliet clutches her heart. The curtain falls.

ACT ONE, SCENE THREE: OUTSIDE THE CAPULETS' HOUSE   Two huge iron gates guard the entrance to the Capulet palace, where guests are arriving for a masked ball. Romeo, Mercutio, and Benvolio, disguised in masks, enter. Romeo flirts with a lady who drops a rose for him to pick up—the fair Rosaline. Then he and his friends dance a vigorous, high-spirited *pas de trois*. They decide then to follow the lady into the ball. They are aware that they do so in some danger.

ACT ONE, SCENE FOUR: THE BALLROOM   Romeo and his friends arrive at the height of the festivities. Still infatuated with Rosaline, Romeo follows her. He comes face to face with Juliet for a moment. As Juliet dances with Paris, Romeo watches, bewitched. As Paris kneels to kiss her hand, Juliet turns, sees Romeo, and is visibly disturbed. She is given a mandolin and strums it as six of her friends dance. But their dance is interrupted by one for Romeo, as if Juliet could not get him out of her mind. He dances marvelously for her alone, and kneels at her feet, taking her mandolin. But Paris quickly intercedes and Juliet dances. Romeo, irresistibly drawn to her, comes to join Juliet, catching her about the waist. Mercutio, seeing that Romeo is entranced with Juliet, dances to distract attention from him. Later, Tybalt recognizes Romeo and orders him to leave, but Capulet intervenes and welcomes him as a guest in his house.

ACT ONE, SCENE FIVE: OUTSIDE THE CAPULETS' HOUSE   As the ball breaks up and the guests depart, Tybalt follows Romeo out. Lord Capulet intervenes and Tybalt is restrained from pursuing Romeo.

ACT ONE, SCENE SIX: JULIET'S BALCONY   Unable to sleep, Juliet comes out on her balcony, throws off her scarf and leans against a column. She thinks of Romeo. Suddenly he is there, below in the garden. She runs swiftly down the long flight of steps to him. He drops his cloak and goes to her. He puts his hand to her heart and then dances for her. Now they dance together, confess their love, and the die is cast.

ACT TWO, SCENE ONE: THE MARKET PLACE   The market bustles with activity; buyers and sellers jostle together, hooded monks mingle with the crowd. Romeo, who can think only of Juliet, watches as a wedding procession passes and dreams of the day he will marry her. Her nurse enters on the right, seeking Romeo. She gives him a letter in which he rejoices: Juliet has consented to marry him, but with their families so opposed, they must do this secretly. Thinking only of his bride, Romeo dances joyfully, then embraces the nurse and rushes out.

ACT TWO, SCENE TWO: THE CHAPEL   The music is somber as the curtain rises on Friar Laurence's cell. The monk enters and prays. First Romeo and then Juliet and the nurse come. All kneel before the monk. Friar Laurence joins the

hands of the two lovers, hoping that their union will end the strife between the
Montagues and the Capulets. The nurse weeps.

ACT TWO, SCENE THREE: THE MARKET PLACE   Meanwhile, the crowd in the
market place is still celebrating. Interrupting the revelry, Tybalt tries to pick a
fight with Romeo. At such a time, Romeo will not duel his wife's kinsman. But
Tybalt will be fought with and before anyone can intercede, Mercutio has accepted the challenge and the two enemies fight with swords. Romeo begs Mercutio to stop. Tybalt stabs Mercutio in the back. Mercutio staggers. He still
tries to fight, but dies with gaiety, his sword becoming for a moment his guitar
as he plays his own lament. As Mercutio dies, Romeo in revenge attacks
Tybalt and kills him. Romeo is exiled. Lady Capulet holds the body of her
nephew, swaying back and forth in her grief as her husband watches helplessly.

ACT THREE, SCENE ONE: JULIET'S BEDROOM   Romeo and Juliet lie together
on a canopied bed. He kisses her as the sun comes through the window. She
sleeps on for a bit but soon they rise to dance ecstatically of their mutual joy.
At the end they are sick with sadness that they must part. After a long kiss
Romeo rushes to the balcony and away, while Juliet hurries back to bed just as
the nurse enters. Her parents soon follow with Paris. Juliet, to her father's
rage, repulses Paris. The nurse begs her to bahave, but she cannot. She prays
to her father to forget this marriage. When he will not she throws herself on
the bed and cries like a child. But the family closes in on her, bearing down
and insisting. Juliet seems to reconsider but instead of going to Paris and being
nice to him she circles him on point. Capulet will tolerate this no longer; he
and his wife take Paris away. They leave Juliet lying in despair. She sits up
then at the foot of the bed, vulnerable yet sure, tormented but determined to
find a way out for herself and her lover. She takes up her cloak, gestures toward the balcony as if that would bring Romeo back, prays frantically, and
then rushes off to see Friar Laurence.

ACT THREE, SCENE TWO: THE CHAPEL   Juliet falls at the friar's feet and begs
for help. He gives her a phial of sleeping potion which will make her fall into
a deathlike sleep. The monk further undertakes to warn Romeo that Juliet has
taken the potion and is not really dead but that she must be rescued from the
family tomb.

ACT THREE, SCENE THREE: JULIET'S BEDROOM   Juliet, back in her room,
hides the phial under the pillow. When her parents come, she begs her
mother's pardon. Her father is pleased that she seems to have come to her
senses. Juliet dances for Paris but resists any real contact with him. He kisses
the hem of her dress. Her parents decide not to force matters and then Juliet is
alone. She goes to the bed for the phial, but is frightened at the possible consequences of taking it. Suppose she will really die? What if the potion does not
work at all and she is compelled to marry Paris anyway? She sits at the foot of
the bed and again she is a child, younger than we saw even at the beginning,

caught up in a fate beyond her. But she takes the phial, drinks the sleeping potion, and expires on the bed.

The next morning Juliet seems to be asleep when six friends of the bride enter with flowers. They remark how quiet she is and try to waken her. The nurse comes in with Juliet's wedding dress and then her parents arrive. The nurse falls full length beside the bed when Capulet declares that his daughter is dead. All lament.

ACT THREE, SCENE FOUR: THE CAPULET FAMILY CRYPT   The curtain rises on the grim interior of an underground cavern. Juliet lies on a bier in the center. Her family mourns and monks with candles lament her passing. Paris remains behind to bid farewell to Juliet, but Romeo, disguised as a monk, throws off his cloak and attacks him. Paris is killed. Believing Juliet to be dead (the message from Friar Laurence has miscarried), but not believing it possible, Romeo lifts her from the bier and holds her. He dances with the dead body of his beloved, trying to revive her, but she falls back always in his arms. He places her on the tomb, then drinks a phial of poison that he has brought with him. Juliet wakes, but as she moves off the tomb she sees Romeo's body. She takes his dagger, which he has dropped near Paris's body, plunges it into her breast, and embraces Romeo.

Ballet in three acts. Music by Sergei Prokofiev. Choreography by John Neumeier. Scenery and costumes by Jürgen Rose. Lighting by Jorgen Mydtskov. Produced by John Neumeier assisted by Ray Barra and Henning Kronstam for the Royal Danish Ballet at the Royal Theatre, Copenhagen, December 20, 1974. First presented in the United States by the Royal Danish Ballet at the Metropolitan Opera House, New York, May 20, 1976.

A compression of four crucial days in April of a Verona long ago, this *Romeo and Juliet*, after defining the strife between the two enemy families, shows the rise and fall of the love of the daughter of one for the son of the other. The frame of the ballet, while showing the background of the city and the carnage engendered by hatred, focuses on intimacy. The *pas de deux* govern the action.

ACT ONE: THE FIRST DAY   Crowds throng the market place of Verona in front of the house of the Capulets on the day before the Feast of San Zeno, the city's patron saint. Infatuated with Rosaline, Juliet's cousin, Romeo pays court to her. Servants of the rival houses of Capulet and Montague clash until the Prince of Verona insists upon a cessation of hostilities.

The Capulets, entertaining at a huge ball, introduce their daughter Juliet to the Count Paris, whom they have selected as her husband. Crashing the party, Romeo finds himself face to face with a creature unimaginable to him. Juliet responds in similar fashion and, after the ball, under her balcony, the two meet to declare their love under the moon.

ACT TWO: THE SECOND DAY   In the midst of celebrations in the city, Romeo proposes marriage to Juliet and they are wed in secret by Friar Laurence. Back in the center of the town, unaware of what has taken place elsewhere, cousins of the newly wed pair, Mercutio and Tybalt, fight a duel, in which Mercutio, of Romeo's family, is killed. Coming upon the action, Romeo, in horror, and unable to prevent this outcome, challenges Juliet's cousin Tybalt and kills him.

ACT THREE: THE THIRD DAY   Tybalt's funeral calls out all the Capulets. Romeo, after his wedding night with Juliet, is obliged to flee because of his part in the duel. Endeavoring to escape her marriage to Count Paris, Juliet consults Friar Laurence, who arms her with a potion that will cause her to appear dead for a day. Pretending to assent to her parents' will, Juliet takes the potion.

ACT FOUR: THE FOURTH DAY   Believing her dead, Juliet's parents mourn deeply. Her funeral is prepared. Romeo, on his way to Mantua, learns of her death and races back to Verona, seeking Friar Laurence, who might have explained the liberation he and Juliet had arranged. He fails to find him and goes to Juliet, who is laid out in her tomb. Believing her dead, he stabs himself. Awakening from her day's sleep, Juliet finds her beloved at her side. Finding him dead, she kills herself with his dagger.

The critic George Dorris has written an important essay, "Prokofiev and the Ballet," which examines in detail the scores of *Romeo and Juliet* and other ballets by that composer (*Ballet Review*, Vol. 4, No. 6).

ROOMS

Music by Kenneth Hopkins. Choreography by Anna Sokolow. First presented at the YM-YWHA, New York, February 24, 1955, with Beatrice Seckler, Eve Beck, Donald McKayle, Jeff Duncan, Jack Moore, Sandra Pine, Judith Coy, and Paul Sanasardo.

Anna Sokolow has written of this work: "I wanted to do something about people in a big city. The theme of loneliness and non-communication evolved as I worked. I like to look into windows, to catch glimpses of unfinished lives. Then I ask: 'What is there, and why?' Then I thought of using chairs as if they were rooms, each dancer on his own chair, isolated from all the others though physically so close to them."*

Rooms has been danced by the Alvin Ailey Company, by the Netherlands Dance Theatre, and by the City Center Joffrey Ballet (September 7, 1967). Reviewing the latter production, Clive Barnes wrote in the New York *Times:*

* From *The Modern Dance, Seven Statements of Belief,* edited by Selma Jeanne Cohen, Wesleyan University Press, 1966.

"The pattern of *Rooms* is the pattern of a run-down rooming house. Eight straight-backed people are found sitting on eight straight-backed kitchen chairs. The chairs are their rooms, their patch of frightening privacy in an alien world. The people in the rooms, remote, removed, separate in the way of separateness of cities, are trying vainly to connect with life. They fail.

"Miss Sokolow shows us, with a series of dance images accurate enough to be painful, the shabbiness of their aspirations. A man dreams of escape, a girl dreams of love, a boy sees a false world as a flurry of jazz. Miss Sokolow forces us to peek into the windows of an apartment house we have all, however fleetingly, visited, but would prefer to forget."

THE ROPES OF TIME

Music by Jan Boerman. Choreography by Rudi van Dantzig. Scenery and costumes by Toer van Schayk. First presented by the Royal Ballet at the Royal Opera House, Covent Garden, London, March 2, 1970, with Rudolf Nureyev, Diana Vere, and Monica Mason in the principal roles. First presented in the United States by the same ensemble at the Metropolitan Opera House, New York, May 13, 1970, with the same principals.

The ballet is prefixed by a quotation from the British writer and critic Richard Buckle: "Every journey we make is an adventure into the unknown; each arrival a birth and each departure a death." The characters in the ballet are a Traveller, Life, and Death.

The curtain rises on a dark stage. A man stands to the left, on top of a hemisphere, or egg, where he balances for a moment, then falls, to the sound of crashing glass. The pinnacle rises and out from under the Traveller is born. Dancing amidst ten boys young like himself, the Traveller becomes an individual and begins his life journey. Death enters and watches. So, too, does Life. The Traveller dances with her but Death cuts in and the Traveller is caught between. So begins the journey in which the two dominant figures accompany the venturing Traveller to the end. No sooner does he succeed in showing self-mastery than he is brought back, as it were, to earth. He returns at last to his birthplace to die.

In an interview about his ballet, Rudi van Dantzig said that the inspiration for it was a performing artist he much admires who has sustained a career well beyond the usual span, triumphing over age and adversity. The Traveller as performing artist, on trial before the public, is thus an important aspect of the ballet.

A ROSE FOR MISS EMILY

Music by Alan Hovhaness. Choreography by Agnes de Mille. Costumes and scenery by A. Christinia Giannini. Lighting by Gene Lowery. First presented at the North Carolina School of the Arts, Winston-Salem, October

24, 1970, with Gemze de Lappe and David Evans in leading roles. First presented by American Ballet Theatre at the City Center, New York, December 30, 1970, with Sallie Wilson and Bruce Marks in leading roles. Lighting by Tom Skelton.

The choreographer Agnes de Mille has said of her ballet: "It is a story of narcissism . . . self-love, possessiveness and destruction. It is a story about a woman who eats up all the things she loves and then destroys herself."

Miss de Mille's program note reads: "Preoccupation with the morbid is a marked characteristic of the American psyche. It has passed into great literature with Edgar Allen Poe, William Faulkner, Ambrose Bierce and Shirley Jackson.

"This little melodrama, suggested by the masterpiece 'A Rose for Emily' by William Faulkner, seems, because of its stark terror, to lie outside normal experience; it is, however, universal.

"In every life there is an aspect of the personality sealed off and entombed, protected from the abrasive and healing effects of reality, cherished because it is safe, and because it is comforting. This buried person, this self-haunted mourner dotes on experiences and events that are ended, living on a febrile and false world of reflections. We call this sealing off memory; it can be and often is, a form of death."

The curtain rises to the ominous sound of low drum rolls and piano chords. A group of children stand in front of a house in the Old South. There is a jalousied porch, overgrown with creeping vines. The young persons act as if something mysterious has happened within; they seem to giggle in their dread of the unknown. A girl does an imitation of the la-de-da lady of the house, who can be seen dimly behind a scrim. The scrim rises and Miss Emily is seen, in a long gray dress. She dances but hobbles in her attempt to be glamorous. She suffers as a girl comes to give her a rose. The girl drops the flower before Miss Emily can take it and, giggling, leaves. Miss Emily places the rose on a couch, where a cover seems to hide a laid-out figure.

Now, looking in a mirror, the distraught woman recalls her past. A back curtain rises and we are in a scene recollecting her youth. Five girls in red are seen dancing. As Miss Emily looks back, the girls enclose her in a semi-circle, she embraces them and becomes, too, a girl in red—one of them. She is suddenly alone. A man comes to her. They dance together passionately, suppressed feeling rising to the surface. She crawls to his feet, asking for something he seems unable to give. She is embarrassed then and gets up. The man gives her a rose, which she secures at her shoulder, and the dance is resumed. It finishes as she claims the man, holding him fiercely in her arms.

There is silence as four masked couples enter. They appear to be a bit scandalized by what they see, but the man joins them. Miss Emily watches in horror as a young girl in pink blows him a kiss. Two other girls are attracted to him, too. Miss Emily tries to take him away, clinging to his back. She begs him; he rejects her; in suppressed fury she wraps her scarf around his neck and strangles him. He falls back on the couch, and dies. Her body trembles at his death, but she covers him and poses there, fascinated by a vision of her own glamour.

In a dance of triumph and self-justification, she relives the earlier scene, seeing herself and her lover as one of six happy couples. Putting back on now her old lady's dress of gray, she writhes on the floor in despair, reaching out for her lover.

The young people of the first scene return. They observe that Miss Emily has died. Placid at that discovery, they take up the body of Miss Emily and place it on the couch, on the blanket of rotten flowers that has covered the body of her lover all these years. One of them then lifts up a corner of the cover to look underneath.

LA ROSE MALADE

Music by Gustav Mahler. Choreography by Roland Petit. First presented by Les Ballets de Marseille at Le Palais des Sports, Paris, January 10, 1973, with Maya Plisetskaya. First presented in the United States by the Bolshoi Ballet at the Metropolitan Opera House, New York, September 18, 1974.

Set to music from Mahler's *Symphonies No. 2* and *5*, this ballet is based on the poem by William Blake:

O Rose, thou art sick!
  The Invisible worm,
That flies in the night,
    In the howling storm,
  Has found out thy bed
    Of crimson joy;
And his dark secret love
  Does thy life destroy.

The complete ballet, in three long parts, expands these eight lines into a dance work that has no plot but attempts to capture certain moods, feelings, and passions reflective of the poem. Only one of these parts was danced at the American premiere, by Plisetskaya and Alexander Godunov.

Choreographed especially for the Soviet ballerina by Roland Petit, *La Rose Malade* was created during Plisetskaya's residency in Paris with Petit's company in 1972.

LE SACRE DU PRINTEMPS (The Rite of Spring)

Ballet in two parts. Music by Igor Stravinsky. Choreography by Vaslav Nijinsky. Book by Igor Stravinsky and Nicholas Roerich. Scenery and costumes by Nicholas Roerich. First presented by Diaghilev's Ballets Russes at the Théâtre des Champs-Élysées, Paris, May 29, 1913, with Marie Piltz as the Chosen One. Rechoreographed by Leonide Massine and presented by Diaghilev's Ballets Russes at the Théâtre des Champs-Élysées, 1920, with Lydia Sokolova as the Chosen One. *First presented in the United States, with new choreography by Massine, at the Academy of Music, Philadelphia, April 11, 1930, under the auspices of the League of Composers. Martha Graham danced the leading role in the first American presentation.*

Stravinsky has said that the "violent Russian spring" that seemed to begin in an hour was like the whole earth cracking. . . . It was "the most wonderful event of every year of my childhood." In 1910, when he was finishing *Firebird*, the composer had an unexpected vision: "I saw in imagination a solemn pagan rite: wise elders, seated in a circle, watching a young girl dance herself to death. They were sacrificing her to propitiate the god of spring." The ballet that resulted from this vision made musical and theatrical history. The score, long a masterpiece of the modern repertoire, has become more popular in the concert hall than in the theater, although there continue to be a number of ballet versions (one by Kenneth MacMillan for the Royal Ballet, with scenery and costumes by Sydney Noland, May 3, 1962, was introduced in North America the following year, May 8, 1963).

Subtitled "Scenes of Pagan Russia in Two Parts," the ballet returns us to a time when primitive rites dominated the lives of the Russian tribes. Every year spring was consecrated by a human sacrifice.

FIRST TABLEAU: ADORATION OF THE EARTH   A musical prelude recalls man's first relations with the world about him. The curtain rises. In a wasteland scene dominated by great masses of stone, young girls and boys sit in separate groups. They do not move, they wait and watch, as if expecting some sign from the stone shafts they revere. The girls rise, as if drawn by the abundance of Nature to which the music calls their attention. A wise man stands among the dancers; the girls rush around and around him. Now he moves toward the sacred mound of the enclosure. The girls follow and bow before him. The opening phrase of the ballet—the quiet, plaintive cry of man against all-powerful Nature—is repeated.

The strings sound strong, persistent chords that rouse the young men. To the virile beat of the music, they begin to dance, their movements accelerating at its demand, their feet stamping, stamping the earth. The girls join in the dance, the music becomes joyous, and the adolescents abandon themselves to the swift, exuberant rhythms of the orchestra.

This music changes sharply. A new, penetrating melody shrieks warningly and disturbs the young people. The happiness of the boys and girls shifts abruptly to fierce savagery. They split into different groups; the boys face the girls and move toward them. The boys seem bent on attack, but at the last minute they hesitate; they move back and forth in an almost helpless effort, ignorant of their own true intent. The rhythmic crescendos give place to the soft trilling of flutes. Now the boys break their formation, and each carries a girl away.

Four boys remain on the scene. They choose four girls, lift them up on their backs, and dance slowly, bending low under the weight of their burdens in imitation of the plodding chords of the music. This "Round Dance of Spring" gradually increases in volume, and all the adolescents participate. All the dancers step back as the trilling flutes repeat their love call.

Drums herald the beginning of a contest between two rival tribes. Groups of men from each tribe engage in vigorous games. In the midst of their activity, the wise man, represented in the orchestra by a portentous melody on the tuba, tries to interrupt the games. The stronger theme of the games at first drowns out the wise man's theme, then recedes. The men turn to the wise man. There is a brief, taut silence, then all the men fall to the ground and worship the earth.

The drum rolls loudly, and all rise to dance, as if they had felt the pulse of the earth and been renewed by its power. The dance grows frenzied in its intensity. The curtain falls.

SECOND TABLEAU: THE SACRIFICE   Night is about to fall as this second scene begins; the setting sun has turned the sky scarlet. The girls sit near the wise man at a fire. One of these girls must be chosen by the others to make the sacrifice to the earth: this girl must dance herself to death. The music is calm; the figures on stage are quiet and they are unafraid. The girls regret what they have to do, but they are resigned to it with a kind of physical tiredness that the music reflects. They do not feel that they are victimized by Nature, but rather that they must obey what they believe to be its rules.

Soon the girls rise and move in the patterns of the "Dance of the Mysterious Circles." Their movements are trancelike, as if they themselves were not to make their dreadful decision. Their inspiration arrives, and they rush to the periphery of the scene; the chosen one stands alone in the center of the stage.

Now begins the dance that glorifies the victim. The chosen one remains motionless as the girls and men of the tribe whirl around her. All are transfixed at her power. They invoke the spirit of their ancestors, terrified anew by the force of Nature. Marking the relentless, sharp rhythms of the music with their feet, their dance reaches an ultimate expression of uncontrolled glory in sacrifice.

All the tribe members retire to watch the chosen one. The orchestra sounds strong, militant chords, trumpets blare harshly, cutting the air. The dance of the chosen one begins. The brutal savagery of the demanding music compels her to imitate it. Brief moments of comparative quiet, which seem at first to be periods of rest and release, are in reality more deadly because of the thrashing force that follows them. The girl is now wholly a part of the music, part of the earth. Hypnotized by her movements, the tribe joins in the violent dance. The chosen one begins to lose her strength, but—forced on by the convulsive violence of the music—is endowed with a new, superhuman compulsion. When it seems that Nature can demand no more, the girl is pushed into a fresh frenzy. Then she falls. She is dead.

The men of the tribe catch her up in their arms and hold her high over their heads before the sacred mound. The people of the tribe rush around her, holding up their arms. At the last slapping crescendo of the music, they fall to the earth.

NOTES   The first assistant to Nijinsky in the creation of the first version of *Le Sacre du Printemps*, Dame Marie Rambert, who later founded ballet in Britain and developed the gifts of Tudor, Ashton, de Mille and many others, has written in a way no one else can match of the background of this ballet in her autobiography, *Quicksilver* (1972):

"It was the painter Roerich who first suggested the subject of *Sacre du Printemps*. He then worked on the theme with Diaghilev, Stravinsky and Nijinsky. It was to be prehistoric Russia and represent the rites of spring. Stravinsky had finished his magnificent score by 1912, and we started the rehearsals with the company that same year.

"Nijinsky again first of all established the basic position: feet very turned in, knees slightly bent, arms held in reverse of the classical position, a primitive, prehistoric posture. The steps were very simple: walking smoothly or stamping, jumps mostly off both feet, landing heavily. There was only one a little more complicated, the dance for the maidens in the first scene. It was mostly done in groups, and each group has its own precise rhythm to follow. In the dance (if one can call it that) of the Wisest Elder, he walked two steps against every three steps of the ensemble. In the second scene the dance of the sacrifice of the Chosen Virgin was powerful and deeply moving. I watched Nijinsky again and again teaching it to Maria Piltz. Her reproduction was very pale by comparison with his ecstatic performance, which was the greatest tragic dance I have ever seen.

"The first night of that ballet was the most astonishing event . . . at the first sounds of the music, shouts and hissing started in the audience, and it was very difficult for us on the stage to hear the music, the more so as part of the audience began to applaud in an attempt to drown the hissing. We all desperately tried to keep time without being able to hear the rhythm clearly. In the wings Nijinsky counted the bars to guide us. Pierre Monteux conducted undeterred, Diaghilev having told him to continue to play at all costs.

"But after the interlude things became even worse, and during the sacrificial dance real pandemonium broke out. That scene began with Maria Piltz, the Chosen Virgin, standing on the spot trembling for many bars, her folded hands under her right cheek, her feet turned in, a truly prehistoric and beautiful pose. But to the audience of the time it appeared ugly and comical.

"A shout went up in the gallery:

"'*Un docteur!*'

"Somebody else shouted louder:

"'*Un dentiste!*'

"Then someone else screamed:

"'*Deux dentistes!*'

"And so it went on. One elegant lady leaned out of her box and slapped a man who was clapping. But the performance went on to the end.

"And yet now there is no doubt that, musically and choreographically, a masterpiece had been created that night. The only ballet that could compare with it in power was Bronislava Nijinska's *Los Noces*, created in 1923. She, like her brother, produced a truly epic ballet—so far unexcelled anywhere."

Music by Igor Stravinsky. Choreography by Maurice Béjart. First presented by the Ballet of the Twentieth Century at the Théâtre Royale de La Monnaic, in December 1959. First presented in the United States by the same ensemble at the Brooklyn Academy of Music, New York, January 26, 1971, with Tania Bari and Jorge Donn in principal roles.

The choreographer of this version of *Le Sacre*, Maurice Béjart, has written: "What is Spring but an immense primordial force, which after long sleeping under the mantle of winter, suddenly bursts forth, kindling new life in all things. . . . Human love, in its physical aspects, symbolizes the act by which the divinity creates the Cosmos and the joy the divinity thereby derives. At a time when the borders that divide the human spirit are gradually crumbling, we must begin to speak in terms of the culture of all mankind. Let us avoid folklore that is not universal and only retain the essential forces of mankind which are the same the world over and throughout all periods of history.

"Let this ballet then be stripped of all the artifices of the picturesque in a Hymn to this union of Man and Woman in the innermost depths of the flesh, a union of heaven and earth, a dance of life and death, as eternal as Spring."

Rejecting, therefore, the original scenario of Stravinsky and Roerich, this *Sacre* celebrates instead the mating of a young man and woman. Writing in the New York *Times*, Anna Kisselgoff has said that Béjart's "use of group patterns and rhythmic pulse gives this *Sacre* an underivative look. . . . The chosen maiden is not sacrificed literally but thrown into a physical union with an equally virginal male. . . . The Puritans did not ban Maypole-dancing in England for nothing and Béjart has given his strikingly designed fertility ritual the primitive physical force it needs. It works."

The English critic Peter Williams has written in *Dance and Dancers* magazine: "The mass ritualistic movements leading up to the final orgasmic moment make pretty powerful theatre, in which the music plays a vital part."

Rudolf Nureyev danced Béjart's ballet on March 12, 1971, at the Palais des Sports, Brussels.

John Taras choreographed a new version of *Le Sacre* for La Scala, Milan, December 9, 1972. Natalia Makarova danced the principal role. Scenery and costumes were designed by Marino Marini.

June 21, 1976, Glen Tetley's version of *Le Sacre*, created in 1975 for the Munich Opera Ballet, was first presented in the United States by American Ballet Theatre at the Metropolitan Opera House, New York. Scenery and costumes were by Nadine Baylis, lighting by John B. Read. The cast was led by Mikhail Baryshnikov, Martine van Hamel, and Clark Tippet.

The action depicts a vernal sacrifice and renewal of the human spirit.

Bill Zakariasen wrote in the *Daily News* after the first performance in New York: "Those expecting pagan rites of ancient Russia were no doubt disappointed, yet for the first time in my experience, the choreography matched the elemental power of Stravinsky's music."

SACRED GROVE ON MOUNT TAMALPAIS

Music and lyrics by Alan Raph. Choreography by Gerald Arpino. Set designed by Robert Yodice from a concept by Ming Cho Lee. Costumes by David James. First presented by the City Center Joffrey Ballet at the City Center, New York, November 2, 1972, with Starr Danias, Russell Chambers, and Russell Sultzbach in leading roles. Conducted by Sung Kwak.

From antique times, men and women have gone to sacred groves to celebrate the earth's renewal every spring. Mount Tamalpais, in Marin County, California, overlooking San Francisco Bay and the Pacific beyond, is the scene of this extensive dance ballet that explores the drive, innocence, and sophistication of contemporary youth. There is a pastoral marriage and evidence of other commitments ". . . to build from a moment onward/to build a beginning./ Come to the wall around you/Come through the wall around you./ Come and see/look and see/follow me." The score, with lyrics, which includes the *Canon in D* by Johann Pachelbel, was commissioned by the Foundation for American Dance, Inc.

The action depicts a wedding ceremony and the attendant celebration, followed by the birth of a son who represents a kind of prophet to the young persons on Mount Tamalpais.

NOTES   Writing about the ballet in the New York *Times*, Clive Barnes said that "Mr. Arpino has conceived his ballet as an exaltation of the human spirit. Californians (perhaps) in a Greek mood are dancing out fancies of renewal. Two lovers—Starr Danias and Russell Chambers—produce, quite suddenly, a full-grown son, Russell Sultzbach. . . . Miss Danias dances like a still thought in a quick world—there is a special quietness to her lyricism, a youthful melancholy, that Mr. Arpino so instinctively picks up. He creates beautifully for her, and Mr. Chambers, ardent and provocative, makes her a nicely matched partner. The assertive radiance of Mr. Sultzbach was also used to strong effect."

In a special portfolio by Olga Maynard on Gerald Arpino's "Berkeley ballets" for *Dance Magazine* (September 1973), the choreographer is quoted as saying that *Sacred Grove on Mount Tamalpais* polarizes its audiences: "'For some (for whom the distance is too far from the real Mount Tamalpais, and the Berkeley life-style), the ballet is incomprehensible. It is not a work that should be approached intellectually, but as an experience. But people come to me, in every city that The Joffrey dances *Sacred Grove on Mount Tamalpais,* to say that it has made them feel beautiful again. I am very grateful for that. . . .

"'The choreographer cannot deliberately make a ballet to appeal to an audience; he has to start from personal inspirations. He has to trust the ballet, to let it stand on its own strengths—or fall on its weaknesses. If it reaches the audience, then he is lucky that round!

"'In *Trinity* and *Sacred Grove on Mount Tamalpais* I have been able to look at the world through the eyes of the young—to touch the heart of the matter of what it is to be young in this place and time. I could not have done this unless I had gone to Berkeley.

"'The choreographer (especially in the United States) needs Berkeley. Materialistic things, from which art cannot be separated, force us into certain perspectives, they sometimes narrow those perspectives, as tall buildings confine the sight of the sky. At Berkeley, The Joffrey had a true freedom, and our company was able to refresh and to replenish its spirit. Joffrey and I are very conscious of the free spirit that identifies this company; the dancers are very important to the company. They *are* The Joffrey.

"'As artists, they are very sensitive to an atmosphere and at Berkeley we all felt, very intensely, the free, open spirit that is the stamp of The Joffrey.'"

SALTARELLI

Music by Antonio Vivaldi. Choreography by Jacques d'Amboise. Scenery and costumes by John Braden. Lighting by Ronald Bates. Dedicated to the Drs. B. and L. Krynski. First presented by the New York City Ballet at the New York State Theatre, Lincoln Center, May 30, 1974, with Christine Redpath, Merrill Ashley, and Francis Sackett as principal dancers.

The *saltarello*, an old Italian court dance, derived from the word for "jump," also had its popular manifestation among the people. Clive Barnes has said that it might be regarded as the Roman counterpart of the southern *tarantella*. This ballet by Jacques d'Amboise, a dance occasion without narrative, is performed on a *saltarello* base to music by Vivaldi (the *Concerto in D Minor* F.XI No. 19 and the *Concerto Grosso in D Minor*, Op. 3, No. 11). *Saltarelli* is a reworking of an earlier work mounted in 1973 for the Ballet de San Juan in Puerto Rico.

Writing in *The Record*, Barbara Archer said that the ballet "reflects the ease and breeziness Jacques d'Amboise usually brings to his own dancing. As its name suggests, the ballet transmits a constant energy."

Using seven dancers, the ballet varies lively presentation with quiet *pas de deux*. "There is a certain poetic touch," wrote Clive Barnes in the New York *Times*, "that through a chain of associations, can recall the tenderness and melancholy of Picasso's blue and rose periods."

SARABANDE AND DANSE

Music by Maurice Ravel. Choreography by Jacques d'Amboise. Costumes by John Braden. Lighting by Ronald Bates. First presented at the New York City Ballet's Hommage à Ravel at the New York State Theatre, Lincoln Center, May 29, 1975, with Colleen Neary in the principal role. Conductor: Robert Irving.

Ravel wrote orchestrations of Debussy's *Sarabande* and *Danse* as a tribute to the great French composer who had died in 1918. Since the compositions are in effect dance works it was only natural that Jacques d'Amboise should have used them for our Ravel Festival in 1975. He did so for dance works expressive of the music without any specific narrative idea.

SCÈNES DE BALLET

Classic ballet in one act. Music by Igor Stravinsky. Choreography by Anton Dolin. First presented by Billy Rose at the Ziegfeld Theatre, New York, December 7, 1944, as part of the revue The Seven Lively Arts. *Alicia Markova and Anton Dolin danced the leading roles. Presented by the Sadler's Wells Ballet at the Royal Opera House, Covent Garden, London, February 11, 1948, in a new version with choreography by Frederick Ashton and scenery and costumes by André Beaurepaire. Margot Fonteyn and Michael Somes were the principal dancers.*

Stravinsky wrote the music to this ballet after the forms of the classical dance, and the work consequently has no literary meaning or plot. In the composer's words, "The parts follow each other as in a sonata or in a symphony in contrasts or similarities."

The pattern of the ballet follows the divisions of the score. *Scènes de Ballet* is danced by two soloists and a *corps de ballet* of four boys and twelve girls. Stravinsky specified different dances for the eleven parts of his score.

The brief opening fanfare heralds an introduction by the *corps de ballet*, "Moderato." Now the ballerina dances a variation to bright, quick rhythms. After a brief pantomime section, "Lento," the *pas de deux* begins. In the Sadler's Wells production, the ballerina in the adagio is supported by five men. As they support her in pirouettes at one point, she keeps turning and another partner steps in to support her. A variation for the *danseur* "Risoluto," is followed by a variation for the ballerina. During her dance, her partner kneels before her and holds his hand to his heart; the four boys recline about him. There is another brief pantomime "Andantino," a final dance by the *corps de ballet*, "Con moto," and an apotheosis. Here the music gradually mounts in grandeur; the ballerina and her partner stand together in the center of the stage, and about them the *corps de ballet* are arranged in their original tableau.

Music by Igor Stravinsky. Choreography by John Taras. First presented at the New York City Ballet's Stravinsky Festival, June 22, 1972, at the New York State Theatre, Lincoln Center, with Patricia McBride and Jean-Pierre Bonnefous in the leading roles.

Well-known in Britain in Frederick Ashton's version, *Scènes de Ballet* is not familiar enough in America and my colleague John Taras at the New York City

Ballet made a new ballet to this music for our Stravinsky Festival. The dancing celebrates the beauty of the score, which was arranged originally as a
showpiece for an eminent dancer and her partner.

Writing in the *Daily News* after the premiere, the critic Sam Norkin said:
"Taras has devised sweeping, lyrical movement for his two soloists, Patricia
McBride and Jean-Pierre Bonnefous, who danced in the lavender mood of the
decor. The trumpet solo for their pas de deux was sensitively played by
Theodore Weis."

SCHEHERAZADE

*Dramatic ballet in one act. Music by Nikolai Rimsky-Korsakov. Choreogra-
phy by Michel Fokine. Book by Alexandre Benois. Scenery and costumes
by Léon Bakst. First presented by Diaghilev's Ballets Russes at the Théâtre
National de l'Opéra, Paris, June 4, 1910, with Ida Rubinstein as Zobeide,
Vaslav Nijinsky as the Favorite Slave, and Enrico Cecchetti as the Chief
Eunuch. First presented in the United States by Gertrude Hoffman's Saison
Russe at the Winter Garden, New York, June 14, 1911.*

Color is the dominant element in this lavish ballet, color as brilliant and
resplendent as the Eastern sun—color in music and dancing, in lush decor, and
in the burning passions that consume the principal characters in the story.
Those who are familiar with Rimsky-Korsakov's music, which the ballet uses,
know that it is an orchestral suite—program music appropriate to a series of
stories told by the beautiful Scheherazade to fascinate her husband. The
makers of the ballet chose to abandon the composer's musical scheme and to
fashion a dance drama out of the first story in the *Arabian Nights,* a drama
that would embody all the mystery, passion, and violence that all these tales
contained.

The first movement of the suite, the section known as "The Sea and Sin-
bad's Ship," is played by the orchestra before the curtain rises. Its music insin-
uates an Oriental atmosphere, prognosticating the voluptuous adventure the
ballet relates and intimating the excitement and deadly risks attendant upon it.
The second movement begins; the curtain rises.

The scene is the great hall of an Oriental palace. Rich hangings of purple
and green and orange are looped from the ceiling, creating an impression of
abundant wealth that spends itself on every conceivable extravagance. On the
left a purple stairway carpeted with golden cloth leads to the upper reaches of
the palace. In the back there are three small blue doors decorated with silver
stars. The king, Shahriar, sits upon his royal cushion. He ignores the members
of his court as he turns constantly to caress Zobeide, his favorite concubine
and leader of his harem.

The scene is relaxed and luxurious, the music languid. Eight girls of the
harem recline lazily on multicolored cushions. Shahriar evidently wishes not to
be distracted from his dalliance as he rests in the cool, open room. But his
brother, Shah Zeman, who sits beside him, endeavors to engage his attention.

Shahriar's chief eunuch, an obese, conniving caricature of a man, waddles before him, unctuously suggesting entertainment. Shahriar grants him permission by his silence, and the chief eunuch claps his hands. Three girls dressed in gold run out, bow to their master, and sit down together to perform a preface to their specialty. Shahriar holds Zobeide in his arms and does not notice them. The girls rise and dance sinuously. No one is amused.

The chief eunuch and several attendants assist Shahriar to rise. He is a tall man, whose costume is covered with jewels; a high gold collar surrounds his proud bearded face. His brother looks with hatred upon Zobeide, who stands beside her lord and master, her supple, yielding body scarcely disguised in transparent gauze and myriad ropes of pearls. She pleads with Shahriar for a favor. He refuses and points off into the distance. He commands a hunt in the forest. Zobeide is enraged: she has been embarrassed before the entire harem. She stalks away and flops down on a cushion, to look on with sulking defiance.

Shah Zeman, suspicious of Zobeide's fidelity to his brother, seizes upon the sudden tension between the two lovers and whispers his fears to the king. Shahriar listens. Although he is annoyed by her behavior, he disbelieves the gossip about his favorite. Shah Zeman persists, and briefly the king is a willing listener. Zobeide turns away contemptuously. The king calls over several of his attendants and gives them secret instructions. They bow and retreat.

All the girls save Zobeide rise from their cushions to bid their lord farewell and to wish him luck on the hunt. Four of the girls circle him. He protests lightly, but when four others surround him, he bends down to kiss two of the concubines. The girls dress him for the hunt. Shahriar looks over at Zobeide, enraged by her rage and by her power over him.

The chief eunuch brings in silver halberds. The trumpeting music heralds the start of the expedition. Shahriar attempts to persuade Zobeide that she has no cause for her anger. The sullen concubine resists his explanation at first, then fondly bids him farewell. All the girls kneel and hold up their hands beseechingly as Shahriar walks past them with his entourage toward the waiting expedition. Several girls wave to him. The chief eunuch exits with his master.

Now free from care and eager to enjoy their own pleasure, the harem women gather together and whisper excitedly, like schoolgirls. The light dims. They run to the back of the room and peer through the keyholes of the locked doors. They consult again and exit, bringing with them chests of jewels. One of the girls pulls in the chief eunuch, who protests helplessly. The girls surround him and, by the movement of their bodies, try to secure a favor. The eunuch refuses. All the girls circle about him, but the adamant eunuch shoos them off. One of the girls steals the big ring of keys he carries at his waist. He chases her and takes them back. The girls kneel about him, and the eunuch's resistance begins to disappear. Shall he, or shall he not? The girls see that he requires a bribe and dangle dazzling necklaces before him. The eunuch consents.

He walks to the doors at the back and unlocks one of them. Three Negro slaves dash out, like quick stallions, to their waiting lovers and throw them down upon the cushions. The second door is unlocked; three other couples are reunited in heated, reclining embraces. It is as if the girls, each momentarily out of favor with the king, are rejoicing openly in their contempt for his fickle affection as they welcome the eager advances of their secret lovers. The slaves, who so seldom gain admittance to the harem, cover their bodies with frantic kisses.

Zobeide pleads with the chief eunuch to open the third door. He turns away. Zobeide stamps and insists. The eunuch demands payment. She takes up a necklace, throws it at his feet, and now, consumed by her desire, drags him impatiently toward the door. She stands beside it in a voluptuous pose, slithering like a cat. The door opens. The favorite slave sneaks out with wary delight. He sees Zobeide; she stands breathless, her head thrown back, as he touches her body intimately. The chief eunuch exits.

The girls of the harem and their lovers abandon themselves to riotous dancing. Servant boys enter. Zobeide and the favorite writhe together on the cushions. The favorite slave springs up, and everyone watches as he throws himself into a vigorous dance. Now the entire group moves about the stage in whirling circles. The music whips their natural excitement into a frenzy of pleasure. The favorite slave holds the group fascinated with his bold leaps and assertive passion. The room becomes a whirling mass of climactic, flashing color. Zobeide and her lover are lost to each other on the king's divan. At its height, Shahriar rushes in, his scimitar raised threateningly. The hunt was but a ruse designed by his brother to expose the unfaithfulness of Zobeide.

The group rushes away from him like a receding wave. The king's men stand poised, with their swords ready to strike them down. Zobeide and the slave are so involved in their ecstasy that at first they do not notice. The slave springs up as he sees the king; Zobeide gropes back toward the corner of the stairs and tries to press her body into the wall. The slave dashes across the stage. Shah Zeman cuts him down in mid-flight, and the slave falls. His legs rear up into the air, his body refusing to die. The shah strikes again, and the slave expires. The king's soldiers chase the slaves and the concubines, killing them mercilessly at his command. The eunuch is stabbed to death.

Zobeide pleads with the king for her life as his men close in on her with their scimitars. He orders them aside and the repentant woman kisses his hand. The king pulls his hand away. Zobeide reminds him of his devotion to her and her faithfulness to him. For a moment Shahriar believes her and is fascinated again by her loveliness. He embraces her and kisses her. As he raises his eyes, his brother kicks viciously at the body of Zobeide's secret lover and reminds him of her betrayal. He pushes her away. He hesitates. He does not wish to kill the woman he loves, despite her infidelity, for her repentance appears so genuine, but his kingly honor demands that a price be paid for his abused pride. He stands irresolute. His cohorts move toward Zobeide. Before they reach her, she pulls out a dagger and stabs herself in the belly. Her body doubles up over her arm. She is dead. The men drop their swords. Shahriar raises his arms in despair and weeps over her. His pride seems as nothing compared to his lost love.

NOTES *Scheherazade*, the work that popularly identified the "new Russian Ballet" in the early days of Diaghilev's Ballets Russes, has managed to be in the active repertory of one company or another ever since. Its initial fame is understandable when we recall that its subject matter was new to its first audiences and when we remember its principal dancers. Tamara Karsavina soon took over the role of Zobeide, while Nijinsky continued in the part of the favorite slave. Carl Van Vechten wrote that "Karsavina's *Zobeide* is a suggestive picture of languorous lust, and Nijinsky, as the principal slave, alternates between surprising leaps into the air and the most lascivious gestures; like some animal, he paws the reclining Sultana." The librettist of the ballet, Alexandre Benois, wrote that Ida Rubinstein was "absolutely inimitable . . . in her proud, cunning and unrestrained passion" and that Nijinsky as the favorite slave was "half-cat, half-snake, fiendishly agile, feminine and yet wholly terrifying."

What has happened to *Scheherazade* since, is best reflected in a review by Edwin Denby in the New York *Herald Tribune:* "Seen on a ballet program today, *Scheherazade* . . . is an illustrious warhorse foundering in dishonor. Not that there isn't some kind of life left in the old girl. The bundling and the clinches are still fine for laughs and whistles and cries of 'Take it off' . . . A great many people register sex all over the stage with an earnestness that is disarming rather than embarrassing. But one wonders what *Scheherazade* looked like when it scandalized our parents or when Parisians swooned at the lushness of it in 1910. In the 1910 photographs the slave girls look soft and abandoned. Nijinsky bounded about them like a panther in thrilling spasms that grew to a paroxysm of death at the climax. Bakst the great decorator—the Berman of his day—dazzled the public by the sensual shock of the brilliant decor. And the 'slavic harmonies' of Rimsky's score dunked the orgy on the stage in a bath of gold.

"Nowadays the small orchestra, the clumsily executed decor, the earnest but overworked dancers can't create any sense of abandon. The trouble is that there is no dance form, nothing for them to do as dancers. There is only miming and hubbub, and that doesn't keep for thirty years. A dance ballet can keep fresh because of its form, because arms and legs stay arms and legs; but when the dancers have to pretend to be something they aren't, a ballet disintegrates into a charade."

The first production of *Scheherazade* in the United States was not rehearsed by Fokine and not authorized by him. It remained for Diaghilev's Ballets Russes to present the first authentic version in this country, January 17, 1916, at the Century Theatre, New York. Nijinsky danced *Scheherazade* with Diaghilev's company for the first time in the United States on April 15, 1916, at the Metropolitan Opera House.

SCHERZO À LA RUSSE

Music by Igor Stravinsky. Choreography by George Balanchine. Costumes by Karinska. First presented by the New York City Ballet at the Stravinsky Festival, June 21, 1972, at the New York State Theatre, Lincoln Center, New York, with Karin von Aroldingen and Kay Mazzo in leading roles.

This is a lovely piece of music by Stravinsky that he originally composed for a movie in Hollywood but was never used. It lasts about five minutes but it is a charming, accurate evocation of an old Russian dance, and I liked very much arranging it for two girls and their girl friends in our Stravinsky Festival. It is certainly a Russian dance, as I recall such things from my childhood and my training in ballet there, but I do not mean the piece as any kind of sentimental gesture to the past. All of my dances to Stravinsky music are reflections of what he and I, together, might have done. My luck was that our working together lasted so long.

SCHERZO FANTASTIQUE

Music by Igor Stravinsky. Choreography by Jerome Robbins. First presented at the New York City Ballet's Stravinsky Festival, at the New York State Theatre, Lincoln Center, June 18, 1972, with Gelsey Kirkland, Bart Cook, Victor Castelli, Bryan Pitts, and Stephen Caras. Conducted by Robert Irving.

At the beginning of our Stravinsky Festival at the New York State Theatre— the festival that celebrated the ninetieth birthday of the composer, who had died the previous year—I said that without music there can be no dance and that Stravinsky, more than any other composer, created music for dancers. The *Scherzo Fantastique*, an early work, first performed in 1909, gives us an idea not only of what the young composer most admired in those days but an idea of what he was to become. It is a piece for large orchestra lasting about sixteen minutes. The impresario Diaghilev heard the first performance, and it was this piece, and *Fireworks*, that interested him in the possibility of Stravinsky's composing music for ballet.

Jerome Robbins arranged to *Scherzo Fantastique* a dance for a girl and four boys, an exuberant work with no narrative that reflected the youth and brio of the score.

Writing about it in the *Daily News*, Sam Norkin said that "the ballet is appropriately swift and buoyant. The dancers spend most of their time spinning aloft, conceding to gravity only grudgingly. Gelsey Kirkland in filmy yellow was a delightful sprite in counterpoint to the men in the cast.

SCHERZO FOR MASSAH JACK

Music by Charles Ives. Choreography by Lar Lubovitch. Costume consultant, John Dayger. Lighting consultant, Beverly Emmons. First presented by American Ballet Theatre at the City Center, New York, January 17, 1973, with Daniel Levans, Ruth Mayer, Keith Lee, Bonnie Mathis, William Carter, Christine Sarry, and Ian Horvath in the leading roles. Assistant to Mr. Lubovitch: Ernest Pagano. Violin: Alexander Horvath. Piano: Howard Baer.

An impressionistic dramatic dance about the Old South, *Scherzo for Massah Jack* presents and comments on aspects of antebellum plantation mythology and reality. The choreographer, Lar Lubovitch, describes his ballet as "a pure dance piece to illuminate the music of Charles Ives." The ballet develops its themes much as Ives developed the music for his *Trio*—by exploiting the variations possible on old American tunes and hymns. What Ives does with the song "My Old Kentucky Home" is similar to the choreographer's idea to probe and reveal new aspects of the familiar—here the pathos, absurdity, and tragedy of a familiar racist drama.

SCHUBERTIADE

Music by Franz Schubert. Choreography by Michael Smuin. First presented by American Ballet Theatre at the City Center, New York, January 1, 1971, with Paula Tracy and Vane Vest, Cynthia Gregory and Gayle Young, Sallie Wilson and Marcos Paredes, Diana Weber and John Prinz, and Eleanor D'Antuono as principal dancers.

A pianist plays Schubert waltzes and *Ländler* on stage for this dance ballet, named for what the Viennese call a Schubertiade—a civilized time at home for friends and family with fine music to play and dance to. And there is an intimate family atmosphere to the ballet, where children are present, too. Relationships between persons at the party become apparent as we go along; there is a sense of competitiveness among the boys, the girls are eager to outdress their peers, and it is clear how a number of the young couples feel about each other.

Writing in *Dance and Dancers* magazine, Patricia Barnes said that in *Schubertiade* "a mood is created and there is enough variety in the dancing to keep one's attention happily engaged. Diana Weber and John Prinz, in particular, have been given some of the most attractive choreography in the ballet. The brief, playful *pas de deux* was a delight and Prinz's virtuoso solo later on demonstrated his buoyance and excellent beats to fine effect. Weber, a meticulously precise young dancer, improves all the time . . . and it was nice to see Terry Orr, dashing and elegant, in another well-constructed male solo. Smuin, himself a brilliant dancer, really knows how to choreograph for men. Among the rest, Cynthia Gregory, Eleanor D'Antuono, Paula Tracy, Sallie Wilson and Gayle Young stood out, and at a later performance I was also impressed with the charm and delicacy of Karena Brock replacing D'Antuono."

SCHUMANN CONCERTO

Ballet in three movements. Choreographic concerto by Bronislava Nijinska. Music by Robert Schumann (Piano Concerto in A minor). Scenery and costumes by Stewart Chaney. First presented by Ballet Theatre at the Metro-

politan Opera House, New York, September 27, 1951, with a cast headed by Alicia Alonso and Igor Youskevitch.

The romantic mood of Schumann's music is the inspiration for this abstract ballet. Two central figures represent the romantic center of the ballet, and above this couple a *corps de ballet* of boys and girls dance as a background. The setting is romantic, too. Three gray stone arches draped with red cloth frame a backdrop that depicts a high, desolate cliff.

FIRST MOVEMENT: ALLEGRO AFFETTUOSO   When the curtain rises, after a long musical introduction, we see on stage the ballerina, who stands in an attitude of wistfulness. She is dressed all in white, in full romantic costume. To the right is her lover, who holds out his arms to her longingly. The couple and the small group of girls who stand to either side of them begin to dance. What they dance has no plot in any usual sense; they exit and re-enter, not continuing a pattern they have started, but simply dancing along with the dynamics of the music. The piano in the concerto represents no one in particular. When the music becomes vigorous, groups of boys cross the stage in high leaps. The *premier danseur* dances with one of these groups and exits. The ballerina now performs a variation. Her partner returns to watch as she circles the stage with rapid turns. They leave the stage to the *corps de ballet* briefly. The music becomes quiet; six of the girls form a tableau. The ballerina rejoins them, still turning, to the accompaniment of soft trills of the piano. Three of the boys lift her high, carry her around the stage and off into the wings. She and her partner return, as the last chords of the first movement begin, and join the *corps de ballet* to dance its final measures.

SECOND MOVEMENT: INTERMEZZO   The light dims. Eight girls in rust-color skirts covered with black net join other girls dressed in softly tinted dresses to form a backdrop for a *pas de deux* between the ballerina and her partner. Alternately, with the rhythm of the music, the *premier danseur* supports the ballerina in swift pirouettes that stop sharply with the music's hesitation and high lifts that end, again, with pirouettes. As the dance progresses, the ballerina turns more and more rapidly; her white dress seems to be in a perpetual whirl about her moving figure.

THIRD MOVEMENT: ALLEGRO VIVACE   The scene brightens, and a new backdrop reveals in the distance ancient ruins, overrun with moss and weeds and grass. A luminous yellow sun in a cloudless sky shines down on the nostalgic vista. The ballerina and her partner return. Three boys go to the front of the stage and recline to watch the ballerina dance. Soon they rise and, with a second group of men, stand at either side of the stage as the ballerina moves across it. She leaves the scene now to her partner, who dances brilliantly down a diagonal formed by the male *corps de ballet*. All the girls come back and reform a tableau, as the two principals dominate the scene. The ballerina encircles her lover with accelerated terms; he spins in the air, as the music reaches a crescendo of joyousness, and carries her off into the wings. The different

units of the *corps de ballet* fill the stage with movement until the principals
join in for the finale. The curtain falls as the ballerina is lifted high above the
group. Her lover stands facing us with outstretched arms.

SCOTCH SYMPHONY

*Classic ballet in three parts. Music by Felix Mendelssohn. Choreography
by George Balanchine. Scenery by Horace Armistead. Costumes by Karinska
and David Ffolkes. Lighting by Jean Rosenthal. First presented by the
New York City Ballet at the City Center, New York, November 11, 1952,
with Maria Tallchief, André Eglevsky, Patricia Wilde, Frank Hobi, and
Michael Maule in the principal roles.*

When the New York City Ballet appeared at the Edinburgh Festival in August
1952, I had my first opportunity to see the great massed demonstration of parade units from the Scottish regiments in the famous nocturnal Military Tattoo.
I greatly enjoyed this spectacle, as I also enjoyed seeing Scotland as a whole.
It occurred to me that when my company returned to New York, we might do
a Scottish ballet. Scotland, after all, was the scene of the first great romantic
ballet, *La Sylphide,* and a new ballet might well recollect this fact as it also
remounted dances in the Scottish manner. Mendelssohn, too, had written his
Scotch Symphony, and this music seemed to me appropriate for the idea I had
in mind.

Back in New York, we decided to do the ballet *Scotch Symphony* almost immediately, omitting the first movement of Mendelssohn's score, which is not
appropriate for dance.

In the first movement of the ballet there are general dances by the ensemble, all in appropriate Scottish costume: there is a *pas de trois* by a girl and
two boys, and there are solo passages for the girl.

The second movement is an adagio for a ballerina and her partner that represents, without a story, the general mood and atmosphere of the romantic
ballet as epitomized in such ballets as *La Sylphide.*

The third movement is again an ensemble, in which the ballerina and her
partner participate with *pas de deux* and variation, joining the soloists and
corps de ballet in a finale.

SEA CHANGE

*Music by Benjamin Britten. Choreography by Alvin Ailey. First presented
by American Ballet Theatre at the Opera House, Kennedy Center for the
Performing Arts, Washington, D.C., October 26, 1972, with Sallie Wilson
and Royes Fernandez as principals.*

A dramatic dance for a girl and her drowned lover, *Sea Change* is introduced with two notes in the program: "Love transcends all bounds—including death," and a lyric from *The Tempest:*

Full fathom five thy father lies;
Of his bones are coral made;
Those are pearls that were his eyes;
Nothing of him that doth fade,
But doth suffer a sea-change
Into something rich and strange . . .

The action is divided into four parts, corresponding to the music of Benjamin Britten's *Four Sea Interludes* from *Peter Grimes,* the ballet's score.

In the first part, *Dawn,* the death of a fisherman at sea is mourned by his friends. In *Sunday Morning,* a girl, the dead man's wife, remote and detached, dances midst a vigorous dance by the young men of the village. In *Moonlight,* her love for the lost mariner is recapitulated as we see them dance together. In the final *Storm,* love appears to transcend death and the lovers are reunited.

The late John Cranko also made a ballet called *Sea Change.* Set to music by Sibelius, with scenery and costumes by John Piper and presented first by the Sadler's Wells Theatre Ballet at the Gaiety Theatre, Dublin, Ireland, January 18, 1949, the ballet told the story of another village situation. A ship goes to sea, there is a storm and all but one of the men return. While the villagers rejoice in their deliverance, the wife of the lost seaman, a young bride, interrupts the scene in a wild outpouring of grief. At the end, she scans the horizon in quiet despair. The critic Clive Barnes has called *Sea Change* "John Cranko's first major ballet."

SEA SHADOW

Music by Michael Colgrass. Choreography by Gerald Arpino. Setting by Ming Cho Lee. First presented by the Robert Joffrey Ballet at the Delacorte Theatre, Central Park, New York, September 5, 1963, with Lisa Bradley and Paul Sutherland. Music for the first performance was a movement of Ravel's Concerto in G for Piano and Orchestra.

Called "a poem-in-dance," *Sea Shadow* is a dramatic *pas de deux* in which a sprite from the sea visits a dreaming boy on a beach. The ballet might be called a modern treatment of the Ondine theme, for attracted as the boy is by the sea sprite, it becomes clear that she will lead him not only to happiness but also to his death. In a mesmeric, underwater rhythm, the dance is performed to a score by the contemporary composer Michael Colgrass. The critic Walter Terry has called *Sea Shadow* "one of the most beautiful duets in all ballet."

THE SEASONS

Music by Alexander Glazunov. Choreography by Marius Petipa. First presented at the Hermitage Theatre, St. Petersburg, February 7, 1900. First presented by the Stuttgart Ballet, in a production by John Cranko, at the Württemberg State Theatre, Stuttgart, June 15, 1962. Completely revised by Mr. Cranko in a new version which was first presented in the United States at the Metropolitan Opera House, New York, April 30, 1971.

While the first ballet to Glazunov's great score (one that is more familiar, from excerpts we know, than we suspect) included four danced tableaux of the seasons and an apotheosis, John Cranko's production also makes of the work a major opportunity for a reigning ballerina. He provides her with no less than three of the seasons—Winter, Summer, and Autumn. (Spring is led by two girls.) Each of these parts of the ballet is supported by soloists and *corps de ballet,* but the emphasis is on personal virtuosity and dance display. Summer and Autumn are both *pas de deux,* the latter rivaling the former in exuberance.

When *The Seasons* was first presented in America, Clive Barnes wrote in the New York *Times* that "Cranko has never choreographed with more authority. . . . The dancing has a range, scope and sheer bigness that have to be associated with the Bolshoi Ballet and nothing else. . . . Cranko's pure dance choreography has more vigor than it ever had. . . . The dancing is the best the Stuttgart has ever given us."

SEBASTIAN

Ballet in one act and three scenes. Music and libretto by Gian-Carlo Menotti. Choreography by Edward Caton. Scenery by Oliver Smith. Costumes by Milena. First presented by Ballet International at the International Theatre, New York, October 31, 1944, with Francisco Moncion in the title role. Restaged with new choreography by Agnes de Mille for American Ballet Theatre, May 27, 1957, with Lupe Serrano and John Kriza in principal roles. Restaged with new choreography by John Butler for the Netherlands Dance Theatre, Amsterdam, Autumn 1963, and introduced to the United States in 1966 by the Harkness Ballet, with Brunilda Ruiz, Lawrence Rhodes, Roderick Drew, Hester Fitzgerald, and Sarah Thomas in principal roles. Scenery and costumes by Jacques Noel, lighting by Nicholas Cernovich.

This dramatic ballet is set in Venice at the end of the seventeenth century. The prince, in love with a notorious courtesan, has two possessive sisters who wish to break up the affair. They steal her veil, knowing that its possession will enable them to exercise black magic over her. Constructing a wax image of the courtesan, they cover it with her veil and plan to kill her by piercing the image with arrows. But the Moorish slave Sebastian, who has loved the courtesan, substitutes himself for the wax figure and takes the deadly arrows. By his self-sacrifice, he breaks the evil power, reuniting the prince with his beloved.

SECRET PLACES

Music by Wolfgang Amadeus Mozart. Choreography by Gerald Arpino. Setting by Ming Cho Lee. Lighting by Thomas Skelton. Pianist: Stanley Babin. Dedicated in living memory of Lorraine Squadron. First presented by the City Center Joffrey Ballet at the City Center, New York, February 20, 1968, with Lisa Bradley and Dermot Burke.

A dance for two young lovers, Secret Places is performed to the second movement of Mozart's *Piano Concerto No. 21 in C Major* (K. 467). The dance begins in silence. The curtain rises on a dark woodland scene where the rays of the sun barely penetrate. On the left stand three golden trees. A girl enters. She walks through the glade, touches gently one of the trees, then goes. A boy comes from the opposite direction, looks about, leaves. The girl returns but this time as she starts to go her walk speeds up and becomes almost a dance step. Similarly with the boy; and as the two go and return yet again, just missing an encounter, their steps accelerate in speed and intensity so that there is an urgency in the air. Finally, as she leaps backward into the air, the boy is there to catch her, she is safe, they are together and the dance, with the music, begins.

Thoughtful and introspective with the score, the dance mirrors quiet joy, cautious discovery, exultation, and celebration of first love. At the end, the boy holds the girl high, she descends in a graceful pose, and they walk off into the forest.

SEPHARDIC SONG

Traditional music arranged by Manuel Valls. Choreography by Eliot Feld. Setting and costumes by Santo Loquasto. Lighting by Jennifer Tipton. First presented by the Eliot Feld Ballet at the New York Shakespeare Public Theatre, May 30, 1974, with Naomi Sorkin, George Montalbana, Suzanne Erlon, Valerie Felt, and Elizabeth Lee. Flute, Paul Dunkel; guitar, Fred Hand; soprano, Meria Sargon.

This is a dance ballet performed to Iberian Jewish songs that are sung at the side of the stage. There is an atmosphere and feeling of the nearby sea in ropes or nets that are set against a sunset in the background. The persons who inhabit the ballet seem to be fisherfolk. There are different combinations. Four girls begin the piece, weaving in and out in a kind of chain to the songs that are being sung. Wives of fishermen at sea, they await their return. Later, one comes—or is he a lover?—to dance with one of the girls. The idea appears to be that everyone here is beloved—a friend, perhaps a lover—at any event all united and unafraïd.

Reviewing the ballet for *Dance News*, the critic Nancy Goldner wrote: "This is one of those deceptively simple ballets, in which dancers 'just dance' . . . Feld has really caught the essence of lament because he discovers its neutrality—neither sad nor happy, but a mixture; in short, lyrical. As such it is a profound embodiment of the music, traditional Spanish songs, with their tantalizing off-key Flamenco mode."

In 1975 a new setting by Ming Cho Lee and costumes by Stanley Simmons replaced the first designs.

SERENADE

Classic ballet in four parts. Music by Peter Ilyich Tchaikovsky. Choreography by George Balanchine. Costumes by Jean Lurçat. First presented by students of the School of American Ballet at the estate of Felix M. Warburg, White Plains, New York, June 9, 1934. Presented by the producing company of the School of American Ballet at the Avery Memorial Theatre, Hartford, Connecticut, December 6, 1934, with Kathryn Mullowney, Heidi Vossler, and Charles Laskey in the principal roles.

Named after its music—Tchaikovsky's *Serenade in C major for String Orchestra*—*Serenade* tells its story musically and choreographically, without any extraneous narrative. Because Tchaikovsky's score, though it was not composed for the ballet, has in its danceable four movements different qualities suggestive of different emotions and human situations, parts of the ballet seem to have a story: the apparently "pure" dance takes on a kind of plot. But this plot, inherent in the score, contains many stories—it is many things to many listeners to the music, and many things to many people who see the ballet.

Most people would agree that a nonprogrammatic piece of music doesn't have to have a story to be a pleasure: we enjoy symphonies by Tchaikovsky and Mozart just as much as we enjoy a symphony with a story, such as Beethoven's *Pastorale*. *Serenade* is programmatic only insofar as its music is programmatic.

To tell a story about something is simply a very human way of saying that we understand it. Making a ballet is a choreographer's way of showing how he understands a piece of music, not in words, not in narrative form (unless he has in mind a particular story), but in dancing.

The four movements of Tchaikovsky's score are danced in the following order, without interruption: (1) Piece in the Form of a Sonatina: *Andante non troppo, Allegro;* (2) Waltz; (3) Tema Russo: *Andante, Allegro con spirito;* (4) Elegy. Twenty-eight dancers in blue costumes dance the ballet before a blue background.

FIRST MOVEMENT   The orchestra plays the strong and spacious opening chords of the brief Andante section and repeats them deeply before the curtain rises. When we see the stage, a group of girls stand in a tableau of crossing lines. It is night. The shadowed light that shines upon them is soft. They are motionless at first, then respond to the music as the light brightens and the new melodious Allegro is heard.

The girls dance in small groups, forming patterns on the stage. One girl dances alone, turning, posing, leaping among the others. Others seem to imitate her originality, but then all are whirling faster and faster in a wide circle together. Suddenly, quickly, each girl stands motionless in the same tableau that opened the ballet, and the familiar chords of the introductory Andante are repeated.

One girl comes in late. She finds her place in the group and stands with the other girls. A boy enters at the back of the stage. As he walks forward toward the girl, her friends leave the stage.

SECOND MOVEMENT   A waltz begins as the boy reaches the girl. They begin to dance together, the girl moving away from him, then rejoining him. When her friends re-enter, the girl dances joyously among them; then she and her partner lead them in a dance, the boy lifting the ballerina high in front of the group. The waltz slowly and softly ends, and the group walks off to the tempo of its concluding rhythms.

THIRD MOVEMENT (the fourth movement in the original suite)   Five girls remain on stage. They sit together on the stage as the music is quiet, turning toward each other in gentle movements. They rise and, at the first sound of the brilliant Russian melody, respond immediately and dance with open gaiety. A boy rushes on and meets a girl; they dance together; and when the ensemble runs off, as the music finishes, we see that the girl has fallen to the floor, her head buried in her arms. She is alone.

FOURTH MOVEMENT   Another girl brings a boy to her. This girl walks behind the boy, guiding him forward: it is as if she moved him, as if he saw only what she wished. When they reach the fallen girl, the boy helps her to rise and now dances with the two of them. He remains with them, dancing with one of them alone, then both together, until there comes a time when he must choose. The girl who possessed him first, the girl who brought him to the other, claims him irrevocably and he leaves with her. The forsaken heroine collapses, revives briefly, and then is lost. Three boys lift her straight up above their shoulders. Her body arches back slowly as they carry her forward in a quiet procession; her arms open wide.

NOTES   Serenade was my first ballet in the United States. Soon after my arrival in America, Lincoln Kirstein, Edward M. M. Warburg, and I opened the School of American Ballet in New York. As part of the school curriculum, I started an evening ballet class in stage technique, to give students some idea of how dancing on stage differs from classwork. Serenade evolved from the lessons I gave.

It seemed to me that the best way to make students aware of stage technique was to give them something new to dance, something they had never seen before. I chose Tchaikovsky's *Serenade* to work with. The class contained, the first night, seventeen girls and no boys. The problem was, how to arrange this odd number of girls so that they would look interesting. I placed them on diagonal lines and decided that the hands should move first to give the girls practice.

That was how *Serenade* began. The next class contained only nine girls; the third, six. I choreographed to the music with the pupils I happened to have at a particular time. Boys began to attend the class and they were worked into the pattern. One day, when all the girls rushed off the floor area we were using as a stage, one of the girls fell and began to cry. I told the pianist to keep on playing and kept this bit in the dance. Another day, one of the girls was late for class, so I left that in too.

Later, when we staged *Serenade,* everything was revised. The girls who couldn't dance well were left out of the more difficult parts; I elaborated on the small accidental bits I had included in class and made the whole more dramatic, more theatrical, synchronizing it to the music with additional movement, but always using the little things that ordinarily might be overlooked.

I've gone into a little detail here about *Serenade* because many people think there is a concealed story in the ballet. There is not. There are, simply, dancers in motion to a beautiful piece of music. The only story is the music's story, a serenade, a dance, if you like, in the light of the moon.

Serenade has seen a number of different productions. It was produced by the American Ballet, the company made up of our dancers at the School of American Ballet, in its first season, at the Adelphi Theatre, New York, March 1–15, 1935. It was staged for the Ballet Russe de Monte Carlo, October 17, 1940, at the Metropolitan Opera House, with costumes by Lurçat and a cast headed by Marie-Jeanne, Igor Youskevitch, and Frederic Franklin. In 1941 *Serenade* was mounted for the South American tour of the American Ballet Caravan in a new production with costumes by Alvin Colt. In 1947 it was staged for the ballet of the Paris Opéra. On October 18, 1948, *Serenade* became part of the permanent repertory of the New York City Ballet. This production has costumes by Karinska.

The leading role in *Serenade* was first danced by a group of soloists, rather than by one principal dancer. In a number of productions, however, I arranged it for one dancer. But when the New York City Ballet was to make its first appearance in London, at the Royal Opera House, Covent Garden, in the summer of 1950, it seemed appropriate to introduce the company by introducing its principal dancers and the leading role was again divided and danced by our leading soloists.

Serenade is now danced by many ballet companies in the United States and abroad. A few years ago I finally succeeded in expanding the ballet so that it now uses all of the score of the Tchaikovsky "Serenade for Strings," something I had wanted to do for a long time. The interesting thing is that while some knowing members of the audience noticed this change and spoke to me about it, the critics didn't seem to notice at all! Perhaps they had seen the ballet too often!

Serenade was danced by students of the School of American Ballet at their annual program in 1974, at the Juilliard Theater, Lincoln Center, New York.

Don Daniels has written a long essay, "Academy: the New World of *Serenade*," in *Ballet Review* (Vol. 5, No. 1, 1975–76).

SERENADE IN A

Music by Igor Stravinsky. Choreography by Todd Bolender. Costumes by Stanley Simmons. Pianist: Madeleine Malraux. First presented at the New York City Ballet's Stravinsky Festival, June 21, 1972, at the New York State Theatre, Lincoln Center, with Susan Hendl, Robert Maiorano, Robert Weiss, and ensemble.

Stravinsky's *Sonata in A for Piano* is dated 1925 and lasts twelve minutes—just long enough for each of the four movements to fill one side of a ten-inch recording in those days. Stravinsky never resented specifics about time. When we were working on new ballets together he always wanted to know precisely how long a particular dance or *pas d'action* would last, so that his music would be a perfect fit.

Todd Bolender arranged a dance ballet to the *Sonata* for our Stravinsky Festival. There are four movements—*Hymne, Romanza, Rondoletto,* and *Cadenza Finale.*

Writing after the premiere in the New York *Post*, the critic Frances Herridge said that "the solos and duets are lovely. The movement is softly romantic and stunningly danced by the long-legged Susan Hendl in one of her most important roles to date."

The New York City Ballet was fortunate to have the French pianist Madeleine Malraux play the music on this occasion.

THE SEVEN DEADLY SINS

Music by Kurt Weill. Choreography by George Balanchine. Libretto by Bertolt Brecht. First presented by Les Ballets 1933 at the Théâtre de Champs-Élysées, Paris, June 7, 1933, with Lotte Lenya and Tilly Losch in the leading roles. First presented in the United States by the New York City Ballet at the City Center, New York, December 4, 1958, with Lotte Lenya and Allegra Kent in the leading roles. Translation by W. H. Auden and Chester Kallman. Scenery and costumes by Rouben Ter-Arutunian.

This is a ballet in song and dance about the seven deadly sins—sloth, pride, anger, gluttony, lust, avarice, and envy. The words and music were commissioned by Les Ballets 1933, for which I did the choreography. Twenty-five years later, when the New York City Ballet was about to celebrate its tenth anniversary at the City Center, Lincoln Kirstein, who had seen the original production, suggested that it might be revived.

Kurt Weill's Three-Penny Opera had been playing to full houses in New York for some years and the time seemed to be ripe for presentation of another important Weill-Brecht collaboration. When Lotte Lenya consented to participate and to sing the leading role again, I knew we would indeed have to do it.

I did not remember many details of the original production, which had been performed for only a few weeks in 1933, but working with Weill's score and the libretto, a great deal came back to me. Rouben Ter-Arutunian's setting and costumes were immensely helpful in making the work unified.

The ballet is the story of two Annies, a singing Annie who narrates the progress of a silent dancing Annie in her search for enough money to build a home for her family back in Louisiana. Annie travels to seven American cities, in each of which she encounters a sin. Annie I is the experienced alter ego of the innocent Annie II. Sings Annie I

"She's the one with the looks, I'm realistic;
She's just a little mad, my head is on straight.
You may think you can see two people,
But in fact you see only one
And both of us are Annie."

At the beginning, we see Annie's family gathered under a fringed lampshade, lamenting Annie's indolence. They call her "Lazy Bones," ask her to "think of us" and to send money for the "little home down by the Mississippi." In Scene 1, "Sloth," Annie I photographs Annie II compromising innocent passers-by for blackmail.

In Scene 2, "Pride," Annie works as a cabaret dancer in Memphis and talks about art, which Annie I deprecates. Speaking for Annie's family, she explains that

"When a man has paid for his evening,
He expects a good show in return . . .
Leave your pride to those who can well afford it . . ."

In Scene 3, "Anger," Annie is in Los Angeles working as a movie extra. While she is sickened at the cruelty she sees there, Annie I sings that "open disapproval of injustice is widely disapproved," and that "Unforgiving anger is from the Devil."

Scene 4, "Gluttony," takes place in Philadelphia, where Annie II does well as an acrobatic dancer. Because of her career, however, she must diet heavily. "Gluttons," sing the family, "never go to heaven."

Scene 5 is in Boston, where Annie is loved by a wealthy man but loves another. The singing Annie persuades her that love for love's sake is nothing but "Lust."

In Scene 6, "Envy," in San Francisco, Annie II envies others while Annie I sings:

"Don't let the flesh and its longings get you,
Remember the price a lover must pay,
And say to yourself when temptation besets you—

What is the use?
What is the use?
Beauty will perish and youth pass away."

Scene 7, "Avarice," sung by the family, shows Annie set up in Baltimore:

"She must be doing all right
And raking it in
To get in the news like that . . ."

After the seven years and the seven cities and the seven sins, the two Annies
return to the little house in Louisiana. The family sings:

"Who fights the Good Fight and all Self subdues
Wins the Palm, gains the Crown."

SHADOW OF THE WIND

*Ballet in six parts. Music by Gustav Mahler. Choreography by Antony
Tudor. Scenery and costumes by Jo Mielziner. First presented by Ballet
Theatre at the Metropolitan Opera House, New York, April 14, 1948, with
Igor Youskevitch, Hugh Laing, Dimitri Romanoff, Alicia Alonso, John Kriza,
Mary Burr, Ruth Ann Koesun, Crandall Diehl, Diana Adams, Nana Gollner,
Muriel Bentley, and Barbara Fallis in principal roles.*

Shadow of the Wind is based on Mahler's *Song of the Earth*, a symphony for
alto and tenor with orchestra. The critic Alfred Meyer has observed of this
song cycle which is based on ancient Chinese texts: "It is not the earth that
sings, and the poems deal less with the aspects of nature than with the philosophy of human existence."° The choreographer has said that his ballet symbolizes the impermanence of existence, the Chinese philosophy of accepting the
mutations of life and bowing before them. Like the seasons, human experience
is cyclical and has no sudden beginning or end.

In keeping with his interpretation of the score, the setting for Tudor's ballet
is also Chinese. To the first song for solo tenor, "The Drinking Song of Earthly
Woe," five men, one an old poet, another an old warrior, dance to the words:
"O man, what is the span of thy life?/Not a hundred years art thou permitted
to enjoy/The vanities of this earth!" The second song, for alto, about loneliness
in autumn and the passing of life, is transposed in dance terms to be a presentation of an abandoned wife: "Autumn in my heart too long is lasting. O sun
of love, never again wilt thou shine to dry my bitter tears?" The tenor's song of
youth describes a pretty Chinese landscape with a green and white porcelain
pavilion in a little pool that is reached by a bridge of jade. "My Lord Summons Me" is the name of the dance for a girl, a boy, and the ensemble. "The
Lotus Gatherers" is the title of the next section, which is performed by a girl
and the ensemble to a contralto solo about beauty, where youthful maidens

° See THE SONG OF THE EARTH, page 560.

pluck lotus flowers at the shore, where lovers play at longing. The fifth part, "Conversation with Winepot and Bird," is accompanied by the tenor lament that all life is woeful and wine the only reality. The final dance, "Poem of the Guitar," is performed to Mahler's "Farewell" for contralto: the poet waits for his friend for a last farewell but looks to the coming spring to waken the world anew.

SHADOWPLAY

Music by Charles Koechlin. Choreography by Antony Tudor. Scenery and costumes by Michael Annals. First presented by the Royal Ballet at the Royal Opera House, Covent Garden, January 25, 1967, with Anthony Dowell, Merle Park, and Derek Rencher in the principal roles. First presented in the United States by the Royal Ballet at the new Metropolitan Opera House, May 2, 1967, with the same principals.

Shadowplay is an allegory about growing up. The scene is the jungle, where a Boy with Matted Hair sits alone. Creatures from the jungle world surround him and although he would prefer to be alone, he sees that he cannot remain passive to relationships. "Arboreals and Aerials"—monkeys and bright birds—come and then a dominating male figure called "Terrestrial" confronts the boy. He will not, however, submit to his will. The boy is then drawn to a "Celestial" figure, a beautiful goddess whose remoteness enchants him, but again masters his feelings after two close encounters. He is now a different person and his air of authority as he sits alone in the jungle affects the animals, too, who ape his civilized gestures and would copy his example. Then instinctively he copies theirs and scratches himself; the end is something like the beginning.

Shadowplay is set to music by the French composer Charles Koechlin (1867–1950), who wrote seven orchestral works on themes drawn from *The Jungle Book* by Rudyard Kipling. The score of the ballet consists of the last of these, *Les Bandar-Log*, and selections from *La Course de Printemps*. The ballet uses *The Jungle Book* situation as a point of departure for larger allegory. The critic Clive Barnes wrote after its New York *première* that the ballet "has as many meanings as an onion has layers, but basically it seems to be about the realms of experience and the attainment of grace . . . Tudor has produced a strange and engrossing work, a ballet that even at first glance has the look and feel of a major work."

Shadowplay was presented by American Ballet Theatre in 1975 for Mikhail Baryshnikov.

SHÉHÉRAZADE

Music by Maurice Ravel. Choreography by George Balanchine. Lighting by Ronald Bates. First presented by the New York City Ballet at the Hommage à Ravel at the New York State Theatre, Lincoln Center, May 22,

1975, with Kay Mazzo and Edward Villella as principals. Conducted by Robert Irving.

Our plans for the Ravel Festival at the New York City Ballet were well advanced when I decided that I wished to add yet another work. *Shéhérazade* was Ravel's first piece composed for orchestra and one of his first works to be performed in public. His friend Tristan Klingsor, the painter and poet, had told Ravel tales of his travels in the East and the composer, attracted since his childhood to the exotic, the mysterious and fantastic, began work on an elaborate conception of an opera based on Galland's *A Thousand and One Nights.* He actually only finished the *Overture,* which is used for this ballet. Later, Ravel set three of Klingsor's poems as a song cycle, for yet another version of *Shéhérazade.*

The ballet's action is simple to describe—it is a dance for a girl and boy accompanied by two couples and eight girls. If it all seems to take place in another world remote from the present time, well, that is a way of thinking of Shéhérazade and the tales she told.

SINFONIETTA

Music by Malcolm Williamson. Choreography by Frederick Ashton. Costumes by Peter Rice. First presented by the Royal Ballet at the Royal Shakespeare Theater, Stratford-on-Avon, February 10, 1967, with Doreen Wells and David Wall in principal roles.

Sinfonietta is a modern ballet with new music by one of England's leading young composers and a new design idea conceived by one of Britain's art colleges. Against the backdrop on stage moving shapes and light patterns are projected to accompany the dances. There is no story.

The ballet, like the music, is in three parts: toccata, elegy, and tarantella. The first is arranged for two couples, the second for a girl and five boys. This part, the elegy, has been called by the English critic Andrew Porter a "new Rose Adagio in a marvelous modern idiom." Here the girl is held and carried so that she seems never to touch the ground. The final movement is a brisk and gay tarantella for the ensemble from which one of the boys darts in and out to perform brilliant and challenging variations.

Music by Paul Hindemith. Choreography by Jacques d'Amboise. Lighting by Ronald Bates. Dedicated to Bunny and Arthur Horowitz. First presented by the New York City Ballet at the New York State Theatre, Lincoln Center, January 9, 1975.

The late Paul Hindemith, one of the half-dozen leading composers of the present century, came from Germany to teach at Yale University in 1940; he remained there the rest of his life. Lincoln Kirstein has noted that Hindemith, an extremely prolific composer, "was particularly interested in dancing." Among his earliest compositions were the famous *Triadic Ballet; Nobilissima Visione* (St. Francis): Massine/Tchelitchew (1938); and *Herodiade* for Martha Graham (1944). I myself greatly enjoyed working with Hindemith's music on several occasions. So, too, did Jacques d'Amboise in this ballet, arranged to the *Sinfonietta in E*. The work is a dance occasion, based on the music itself, without story.

SITUATION

> *Choreography by Hans van Manen. Decor and costumes by Jean-Paul Vroom. Lighting by Oliver Wood. First presented by the Netherlands Dance Theatre at the Circustheater, Scheveningen, Holland, April 20, 1970. First presented in the United States by the same ensemble at the Brooklyn Academy of Music, New York, April 1, 1972.*

Situation is a series of dances to a series of sounds, all set in a specific place, a room lined with graph paper, measuring 27 × 20 × 14 feet and with a digital clock on the wall, telling the precise time. This room contains its own story as the dancers come and go through one door to varied sounds: hunting, shooting, machine gun fire, a water tap, a bath filling, a jet engine, walking in gravel, rain on the street, and mosquitoes. The dancers are anonymous, stretching like gymnasts, coupling, responding to the sounds in different ways, responding too to brief periods of silence. Certain sounds appear to turn certain dancers on, others turn them off. There is rejection, satisfaction, unfulfillment, amusement, as the dance reflects the sounds in ways that appear individual to the performers.

SLAUGHTER ON TENTH AVENUE

> *Dramatic ballet within a musical revue. Music by Richard Rodgers. Choreography by George Balanchine. Scenery by Jo Mielziner. Costumes by Irene Sharaff. First presented by Dwight Deere Wiman in the musical revue On Your Toes (Richard Rodgers-George Abbott-Lorenz Hart) at the Imperial Theatre, New York, April 11, 1936, with Ray Bolger, Tamara Geva, and George Church as the principal dancers.*

The ballet *Slaughter on Tenth Avenue* was not a separate dance number in the great musical comedy *On Your Toes*, but a ballet that was part of the story. This story, a take-off on Russian ballet, had for its central theme a question very appropriate for its time: how could an American upstart hope to make good in a famous Russian ballet company?

Junior (Ray Bolger) was the American. Almost overnight he found himself a member of this famous Russian company when he successfully substituted for a dancer who had fallen ill. But young Junior didn't like the ballets the company danced. Sergei Alexandrovitch (Monty Woolley), the company's impresario, preferred ballets in the lush, pseudo-Russian, romantic style.

Junior thought he knew how to remedy this situation. He himself came from a vaudeville family, he knew a lot about music, and he tried to induce the company to accept an idea for a new kind of ballet. The ballerina (Tamara Geva) was all in favor of the idea, but the pompous Russian *premier danseur* (Demetrios Vilan) was jealous of Junior's talent and immediately began to plot against him. Only the enthusiasm of the company's rich patroness permitted Junior to proceed with his plan.

Rehearsals for the new ballet began. It was called *Slaughter on Tenth Avenue* and told a modern story of love and death. Junior himself was to dance the hero, a hoofer who one night visits a low dive on New York's West Side. Here he meets the strip-teaser (Tamara Geva), dances with her, and the two fall in love. But the girl is married to the big boss (George Church), who has been watching his wife dance so warmly with one of the customers. He breaks up the dance, fights with the hoofer, and pulls a knife on him. Accidentally he stabs the girl. She dies. The hoofer attacks the big boss and kills him. He dances around the body.

We learn that the ballet will end with the hoofer's suicide. He has killed the murderer, but is himself a murderer. The girl is dead; he has nothing to live for.

The day of the *première* of the new ballet approaches. Already *Slaughter* is popular with the company. But the *premier danseur* is determined that it shall fail and that Junior shall leave the company. To ensure his ends, he hires a group of gangsters, men very similar to the tough guys standing around the bar in the Tenth Avenue joint depicted in the ballet. The *danseur* gives these men tickets for a box near the stage for the opening night of the ballet, instructs them to eliminate Junior, and tells them how they can do it without being caught. At the end of *Slaughter on Tenth Avenue*, Junior is supposed to shoot himself. If they shoot him from the box, the ballet will end as planned, the curtain will fall, and no one will have any idea who committed the crime.

The gangsters agree. On the night of the *première*, they sit in a box in the theatre overlooking the stage. *Slaughter on Tenth Avenue* begins. We watch the action, are moved by the lyrical *pas de deux* danced by the hoofer and the girl, then see her murdered. As she dies in her lover's arms, the ballerina who is playing the girl speaks to Junior. She warns him of the plot against his life, which she overheard just before the rise of the curtain. She tells him that the gangsters will not dare to kill him if at the end of the ballet he keeps on dancing: he must change the ending and not shoot himself! The ballerina has called the police; they are sure to arrive in a matter of minutes.

When the big boss has been dispatched, Junior begins his dance of despair around the dead man's body. Then he improvises, dancing so artfully a frantic dance of death that the audience is unaware of any change. He moves faster and faster, incredibly spinning with ever greater energy, when his last strength seems to be spent. As he almost collapses on the stage from exhaustion, the police arrive. They arrest the frightened gangsters and the *premier danseur* amid tremendous applause for the new ballet. *Slaughter on Tenth Avenue* is a hit. Junior is the dancer of the hour. His success assured, the upstart hoofer marries the American girl he has loved all along and lives happily ever after.

NOTES *On Your Toes* was the first musical I choreographed in the United States. Working with Lorenz Hart, Richard Rodgers, and George Abbott on this show made my job a pleasure from the start. The team of Rodgers and Hart represented for me, as it did for so many Americans, superb entertainment in the musical theatre. These men devised over the years a seemingly endless series of revues that were melodically and lyrically filled with great wit, touching humor, and eminent theatricality. After *On Your Toes,* it was my privilege to work with them on three other revues. *On Your Toes* was also my first association with the fine artist and comedian Ray Bolger, whose dancing throughout the show, and in *Slaughter,* will scarcely be forgotten by those who saw it.

THE SLEEPING BEAUTY

Classic ballet in three acts, with prologue. Music by Peter Ilyich Tchaikovsky. Choreography by Marius Petipa. Book by Marius Petipa and Ivan Vsevolojsky, after tales by Charles Perrault. Scenery and costumes by Ivan Vsevolojsky. First presented at the Maryinsky Theatre, St. Petersburg, Russia, January 15, 1890, with Carlotta Brianza as the Princess Aurora, Paul Gerdt as the Prince, Marie Petipa as the Lilac Fairy, Enrico Cecchetti as Carabosse, Varvara Nikitina as the Enchanted Princess, and Enrico Cecchetti as the Bluebird. First presented in Western Europe by Diaghilev's Ballets Russes at the Alhambra Theatre, London, November 2, 1921. Staged by Nicholas Sergeyev after the choreography of Marius Petipa. Additional choreography by Bronislava Nijinska. Orchestration of Prelude to Act Three and the Princess Aurora's variation in Act Three by Igor Stravinsky. Scenery and costumes by Léon Bakst. The cast included Olga Spessivtzeva as the Princess Aurora, Pierre Vladimiroff as the Prince, Lydia Lopokova as the Lilac Fairy, Carlotta Brianza as Carabosse, Felia Dubrovska, Lydia Sokolova, Bronislava Nijinska, Lubov Egorova, and Vera Nemtchinova as the Fairies, Ludmilla Shollar as the White Cat, Lydia Lopokova as the Enchanted Princess, and Stanislas Idzikowski as the Bluebird. Revived by the Sadler's Wells Ballet at the Sadler's Wells Theatre, London, February 2, 1939, in a new production staged by Nicholas Sergeyev after choreography by Marius Petipa. Scenery and costumes by Nadia Benois. The cast included Margot Fonteyn as the Princess Aurora, Robert Helpmann as the Prince, June Brae as the Lilac Fairy, and Mary Honer and Harold Turner as the Bluebirds. Revived by the Sadler's Wells Ballet in a new production under the supervision of Nicholas Sergeyev at the Royal Opera House, Covent Garden, February 20, 1946. Additional choreography by Frederick Ashton and Ninette de Valois. Scenery and costumes by Oliver Messel. Margot Fonteyn as the Princess Aurora, Robert Helpmann as the Prince, Beryl Grey as the Lilac Fairy, and Pamela May and Alexis Rassine as the Blue-

birds headed the cast. First presented in the United States by the Sadler's Wells Ballet at the Metropolitan Opera House, New York, October 9, 1949, with Margot Fonteyn and Robert Helpmann, Beryl Grey, Moira Shearer, and Alexis Rassine. Catherine Littlefield, Director of the Philadelphia Ballet, produced a complete version of The Sleeping Beauty *with her own choreography at the Academy of Music, Philadelphia, February 12, 1937. This version was later produced at the Lewisohn Stadium, New York, July 29 and 30, 1937.*

The crashing, commanding chords of the brief overture to *The Sleeping Beauty* herald the special magic of the fairy tale the ballet relates, a fairy tale that is rich and formal in presentation, but warm and intimate in effect. Tchaikovsky and Petipa have so fashioned Perrault's story of the sleeping princess (*"La Belle au Bois Dormant,"* from *Mother Goose*) for the theater that notions of reality are suspended in favor of belief in characters who can live forever, in a curse of black magic that can put a forest to sleep for a hundred years, and in a beneficent fairy whose magic can rescue all goodness from evil. The time is unimportant, as is the place. The nameless mythical kingdom of the mythical King Florestan XXIV becomes the scene of our imagination.

The intensity of the music demands the attention, focusing it, as it were, on the splendor of the opening scene. The overture to *The Sleeping Beauty* also contains in miniature the story it introduces. Concealed within the opening regal chords is a theme that represents the fairy Carabosse, the evil fairy who will cast a spell upon the ballet's heroine and her family. This music is quickly interrupted by the melodious harp, which introduces a soft, slow, magical, compassionate theme—the melody of the Lilac Fairy, whose beauty and goodness will triumph over the evil fairy's challenge.

Now the music changes to a march tempo, quietly at first, then more assertively. The melody swells. The curtain rises.

PROLOGUE: THE CHRISTENING The hall of King Florestan's palace is high-ceilinged. Great arches of stone cross the back of the stage; through them can be discerned the foliage of the garden. Drapery of resplendent color and ornament warms the spaciousness of the scene. On the right, on a small platform, stands the canopied cradle of the Princess Aurora, guarded by two nurses on each side. Two heralds stand at the back. Almost immediately the king's master of ceremonies, Cattalabutte, enters in elaborate full dress. With great flourish, he busies himself seeing that all is ready for the ceremony. Satisfied, he comes forward, gives a page his stick of office, and scans the list of guests who have been invited to attend the christening of the princess.

Twelve ladies in waiting enter the chamber. They circle the stage and ceremoniously ask Cattalabutte if they may see the child. He consents and leads them over to the cradle, where they hover over the princess. Cattalabutte directs a page to notify the king that all the preparations have been made and nervously unrolls the guest list again to check his memory. The ladies retire from the cradle and stand to one side. A fanfare sounds in the distance; it grows louder; three pages enter. To the blaring of trumpets, the king and queen approach. They pause for a moment under the silk canopy that is held high above them by Negroes dressed in gold and survey the scene. Then their attendants drop their trains. The queen goes to the cradle. She kisses the princess and greets the ladies in waiting, who bow to her. She joins the king, who stands in conference with Cattalabutte. After a brief consultation with their servant, the two monarchs mount the steps to their thrones.

An arpeggio on the harp announces the arrival of the fairy godmothers of the princess. The royal fairies are preceded by their pages, who enter two by two and bow to their sovereigns. Five of the fairies enter in a group: the Fairy of the Crystal Fountain, the Fairy of the Enchanted Garden, the Fairy of the Woodland Glades, the Fairy of the Songbirds, and the Fairy of the Golden Vine. Eight maids of honor attend them. Last of all comes the Fairy of the Lilac, accompanied by six cavaliers, one for each of the fairies. The cavaliers carry, on plush cushions, the gifts the fairies have chosen for their godchild. The Lilac Fairy leads the group forward. The fairies bow low to the king and queen, who welcome them cordially, and arrange themselves about the royal cradle to bless the princess. They bow again to the king and queen and leave the scene.

The maids of honor come forward in two lines and, to the syncopated rhythm of a new melody, they dance in linear patterns. They are joined by the cavaliers, who leap boldly in the air. The fairies return, and all dance together briefly. The queen thanks the Lilac Fairy for the dance and asks the group to continue. The Lilac Fairy bows.

A new tender theme is heard, accompanied by runs on the harp. The fairies and their partners arrange themselves in five moving circles, the Lilac Fairy in the center. Two of the girls in the back are lifted to their partners' shoulders and turned around and around so that they appear to be swimming high in the air. The fairies come forward to the footlights. One by one, the fairies pirouette rapidly and pose in attitude supported by their cavaliers. The maids of honor lie at their feet in respectful obeisance.

The tableau is broken; the music subsides, then regains in volume; in a hushed pause, the royal nurses bring the small princess to the center of the stage. There is a magical rushing run on the harp, and the Lilac Fairy is lifted high above the princess. She blesses the babe with her wand. The *pas de six* is over. The harp plays for a moment, the tempo changes, and the fairies leave the stage while the maids of honor dance a new sprightly measure in unison.

Now each of the fairies returns to perform a variation before the assembled court. These variations are very short; they have no literal significance, and the attributes of the different fairies cannot be read into them; but the different music and different dances that Tchaikovsky and Petipa devised for the six fairies gives each of the variations an individual, distinctive character. First is the Fairy of the Crystal Fountain. She enters and waits for her music to begin. Its movement is slow and leisurely; its melody, calm. The fairy dances forward and moves back and forth across the stage on her points, her body in graceful repose. As her feet mark the retarded rhythm of her music, her head and arms depict the quiet sweetness of the melody. She kneels to the king and queen as her variation ends and leaves the stage.

The Fairy of the Enchanted Garden emerges to dance with quick steps to a brighter tempo—music which carries her into swift pirouettes that accelerate as she moves across the stage. For the Fairy of the Woodland Glades, the music is characterized by a soft, tempered pizzicato. This fairy's skill in quiet, slow movement is revealed in the daring figure that highlights her dance: she dances forward on one foot, her other foot extended before her. With subdued brilliance her extended foot moves back, and the girl stands poised for a breathless moment in arabesque. This figure is repeated as she continues to move forward. Then her dance becomes luminous and light, with rapid dancing on point. She ends her variation standing on point, with open arms, one leg raised pertly before her.

In a flashing yellow costume, the Fairy of the Songbirds dances now to a hurried, tinkling melody, her arms moving ecstatically in simulated flight, her bright head turning to the shimmering elevation of the rhythm. She is followed by the Fairy of the Golden Vine, whose dance is characterized by the curt, staccato movement of her head and the quick pointing of the index fingers of both her hands—the so-called "Finger Variation." The tempo of the music increases sharply, and the brilliant fairy whirls to a quick, sudden stop.

The Lilac Fairy comes forward. She stands toward the back of the stage. The orchestra begins a sumptuously melodic waltz, and the Lilac Fairy accompanies its flowing line with extended, open movements in which her raised point traces small circles in the air. Then she turns in arabesque; she pauses briefly each time her body is seen in profile. In the rapid complexity of its movement and in the fullness of the magnificent waltz, the variation of the Lilac Fairy sums up in splendid grandeur the dances of all the other fairies.

Now the cavaliers dance. The maids of honor join them with light, precise movements. The fairies reassemble at the front of the stage. Their cavaliers hold them in attitude. The fairies' gifts are presented to the king and queen. The queen leaves the throne and delightedly examines the presents. There is a deep, rumbling sound, like an earthquake, off stage. Some of the courtiers imagine it to be only thunder, but the king is apprehensive. The queen trembles for the safety of her child, and the master of ceremonies cowers. A page rushes in and gestures helplessly to the king, pointing off to the left. The king understands suddenly and rushes over to Cattalabutte and demands to see the invitation list. He scans it rapidly, then dashes the scroll to the floor in a gigantic rage. Cattalabutte's fate is averted momentarily by the frightening appearance of two great rats, who emerge from the left and dance a few insidious steps. They run back out. Before the court has recovered, they return with other rats, pulling along behind them an enormous black coach. Standing majestically in the coach is the fairy Carabosse, the hunchbacked godmother of the Princess Aurora, whom the forgetful Cattalabutte has neglected to invite to the christening. She grasps at the air in her fury; her black chariot circles the stage, sweeping all the courtiers aside.

Assisted by her four rodent attendants, Carabosse steps down. The music gives a low warning. Her face is a hideous blue-white mask covered with moles and magical, shining spangles. Her long black dress is tattered and dusty, yet she wears it as if it were ermine. Carabosse hobbles forward on her stick and inquires fiercely of the king, by gesture, "Why was I forgotten? Do you realize what this will mean to the fate of your child?" Already, the king is afraid. He points to Cattalabutte as the real culprit. Carabosse approaches the cowardly master of ceremonies, who kneels at her feet. He throws up his hands, begging for mercy and to protect himself, but Carabosse reaches out her talonlike fingers and tears off his wig, which she throws at the hungry rats. Now, deprived of all his dignity, the courtier attempts to escape.

Carabosse raises her stick and, with a quick thrust in the small of his back, sends him flying. She caresses the rats, who form a small square about her as she dances blithely. She gestures to the royal couple, pointing to the cradle: "Your daughter will grow up . . . She will grow up to be a beautiful princess . . . the most beautiful princess of them all; and then"—Carabosse brings down her stick loudly; the music thunders—"and then . . . she will die! . . . She will prick her finger, no one will prevent it, and she will be a beautiful dead princess." The wicked fairy cackles with glee as the king tries to comfort the distraught queen. He motions Carabosse imperiously away, but the evil fairy persists in laughing at his discomfort. She whips her great black cape through the air to the sound of the harp.

The Lilac Fairy steps out. Carabosse tries to approach the cradle to repeat her curse. The Lilac Fairy holds up her wand in quiet defiance; Carabosse stumbles back. All the other fairies gather around her to guard the cradle. She threatens them with her stick, but the good fairies stand placidly impervious. The hideous, servile rats surround the grotesque Carabosse, and she dances a final, frantic jig, at the end of which she holds up her hand in triumph. She climbs back into her carriage; as she stands under its high roof of black plumes, shaking her fists at the whole court, the obedient rats draw the black chariot off. The thunder subsides.

The queen weeps in the king's arms. He cannot comfort her. The Lilac Fairy comes to them. The lovely melody that identifies this good fairy fills the hall. She gestures toward the cradle and gives them this message in panto-mime: "Your daughter, the princess, will grow up to be beautiful, and it is true that she will prick her finger and seem to die . . . but in reality she will only go to sleep . . . she will sleep for a hundred years, and all the court with her . . . but one day a prince, as handsome as she is beautiful, will come to the princess . . . she will wake at his kiss, and all will live happily ever after."

The king and queen bow to the Lilac Fairy and thank her. The release from the evil curse of Carabosse causes the court to be joyful. All the fairies bow to the king and queen, and then the entire assembly turns toward the cradle of the Princess Aurora. The queen stands over her daughter; the ladies in waiting and the maids of honor kneel in homage, and the fairies stand in attitudes of infinite protectiveness. The curtain falls.

ACT ONE: THE SPELL   The scene is the garden of the palace. A colonnade of huge columns, topped by ancient statues, sweeps in a curve about a high foun-tain toward the right to support a great arch of stone over the back of the gar-den. Thrones for the king and queen are arranged at the right. On the left, a flight of wide stone steps leads up toward the palace. Peasants idle in the distance. Ladies in waiting and their cavaliers walk about the garden, marveling at its beauty and anticipating the day's festival. For today is the Princess Aurora's sixteenth birthday, and the king has decreed a celebration in her honor. The king has also invited the court and kingdom to entertain four foreign visitors: princes from England, India, Italy, and Spain, who have come long distances to meet the young princess and pay court to her.

Three old hags in black, their dark hoods concealing their faces, stoop together over spindles. As they sew, they keep looking about cautiously. Cattalabutte enters. He has aged somewhat in the sixteen years that have passed, but still flourishes his cape and stick at every opportunity. The old women dance away from him. Cattalabutte regards them suspiciously. They try to escape, but the master of ceremonies catches them. He takes the spindles from them forcibly and stands over them threateningly. The women cower at his feet as Cattalabutte reminds them that for sixteen years, ever since the curse of the wicked fairy Carabosse, the king has ordered that no spindles be brought within a mile of the Princess Aurora. He is interrupted by the arrival of the king and queen, who are followed by the four princes. The old women scurry into a corner.

The king greets Cattalabutte and wonders what his courtier holds concealed in the hand behind his back. Reluctantly Cattalabutte holds out the dread spindles. The king is shocked and furious. Cattalabutte points to the weird women; the king commands them to come forward. He tells them that they must hang for this offense; how otherwise can he protect his daughter from the spell of Carabosse? The women kneel at his feet and plead for forgiveness. The king is adamant. To a sudden crescendo of surging, pulsating music, the queen steps forward and asks the king to relent. After all, this is Aurora's birthday and the women are truly sorry. The king smiles and consents.

The king and queen mount their thrones, carrying fresh garlands. A group of peasant girls enters. They bow deeply to their lord. The courtiers gather on the steps, and the four princes stand to one side as the girls commence to dance to a flowing waltz. The girls weave in and out under the garlands and arrange themselves in circles that travel around the stage in opposite directions. Cattalabutte thanks them when the waltz is over, and they bow to the monarchs.

Four musicians enter, carrying golden instruments, followed by eight girls—friends of the princess. The four foreign princes stand ready to greet the guest of honor. The music is expectant. The four princes look toward the back of the garden and peer down the colonnade, hoping for a glimpse of the princess. Softly the music hesitates. In the distance, under the arch, we see a beautiful girl in a pink dress embellished with silver. She poses for an instant and disappears like an apparition. Then, brilliantly, to a burst of music, she is on stage, dancing joyfully with the sweet, innocent exuberance of youth. The four princes approach her. The princess goes to her mother, who embraces her warmly, then to the king, who kisses her on the forehead. The king then introduces her to the foreign princes, who bow low to her. She responds gently. The harp plays a rushing cadenza; all the other instruments are silent, waiting; there is a brief hush, a momentary interval of preparation like the soprano's measured intake of breath before a great aria commences. The "Rose Adagio" begins.

The four princes move to the front of the stage in a line. One by one, the princes support the Princess Aurora as she dances softly and openly her preparatory steps. Then she steps back; standing on point in attitude, she greets the first prince. Holding her right hand, he turns her in attitude, as she maintains the graceful pose. When she has come full circle, the prince releases her hand; both hands are raised to form a crown above her head for a moment of balance; then the second cavalier steps forward to hold her right hand. This design is repeated. Finally, as the last prince releases her, the princess extends her body in arabesque and holds this position with breath-taking equilibrium.

One of her suitors now supports Aurora, who modestly displays her dancing skill without conveying the least impression that she is unlike any other young girl who is beautiful and happens to be dancing. Sweetly holding her hands to her cheek, the princess leans forward. She is lifted high in the air. When she is released, she dances alone in a small circle, her arms invoking the melody of the music, her strong points tracing its rhythms.

Each of the enamored princes now presents Aurora with a freshly picked rose. The theme is played softly by the oboe. One prince supports her as the others come forward, one by one, with their gifts. The princess pirouettes swiftly as she accepts each of the flowers. Then, charmingly, she leaves her suitors and presents their flowers to the queen. She moves to the back of the stage and dances forward. Armed with fresh roses, the princes kneel at her feet. As she pirouettes past them, the princes hold out their flowers; the princess pauses in her turning to receive each rose. She holds the flower to her breast for a moment, then tosses them in the air as her dance continues.

The music approaches its fullest, final expression. One of the princes holds her hand as the princess stands again on point in attitude. He releases her, and she sustains her pose as if it were effortless. Then, moving only her arm, she takes the hand of the second prince, to prepare briefly for a second, longer balance. Her modest confidence in balance increases as the adagio comes to a conclusion. When the fourth prince releases her, she stands in what seems perpetually perfect balance until the final chord breaks the enchantment. She runs off into the garden.

The eight friends of the Princess Aurora dance to a tinkling, blithe melody. Soon the princess returns. The four princes beseech her to dance again. She turns to her mother, who encourages her with a smile, and the princess begins a *pas seul*. After posing in attitude and arabesque, she goes to the corner of the garden. She dances forward on point in a diagonal line with slow precision. Step by step, she bends her right knee and brings her right leg up so that it touches gently the back of her supporting leg. The diagonal completed, she dances backward toward the corner in a series of pirouettes, each of which ends in secure, perfect position. The princess circles the garden, with brilliant, accelerating spins, and leaves the stage.

When friends commence to dance, the princess comes back. She dances toward the front with high, broad leaps in which she kicks her front foot forward—a movement that gives her dance a new urgency. She circles the stage again, this time with open, free turns rapidly executed. The tempo of the music builds with her speed, with her joy in dancing.

On the right, in the corner, half concealed by the crowd, an old woman in black emerges. She watches the happy princess, and when Aurora circles near her, holds out a present to the princess. Aurora, barely stopping, takes it and dances on, delighted with the strange, new object. The gift is a spindle! The king rises in terror and warns the court. Everyone attempts to stop Aurora's dance and take the spindle from her. But the innocent, impetuous girl is so charmed by the spindle that she cannot cease to play with it. Suddenly, she pricks her finger. Instantly, she falls to the ground.

The king and queen rush to her. The angry monarch orders the court to find the criminal who presented the princess with the fatal spindle. The princess herself has no idea of what has happened. She stirs, looks into her father's disturbed face, and shakes her head slowly, as if to say, "Don't worry, nothing is wrong." Similarly she comforts her distraught mother. To prove that everything is all right, the anxious girl rises and begins to dance again. She moves rapidly, the music accelerates ominously, and there is a clap of thunder. The princess falls into her father's arms. The cymbals clash in evil triumph, and the old woman in black steps out. She throws aside her cape: she is the fairy Carabosse, come back to court to fulfill her prophecy. She cackles with delight. The princess seems to die. Armed courtiers chase the evil fairy as she runs into the garden.

A trumpet sounds, then the harp, and the melody of the Lilac Fairy is heard. She enters with her wand and comforts the king and queen, telling them that the princess, as she foretold, is not really dead, she is merely asleep, and this is the beginning of the spell that will last a hundred years. The king and queen thank the Lilac Fairy and bow humbly. Courtiers take up the princess and carry her slowly up the steps to the palace. The Lilac Fairy ascends the stairs; the last members of the court disappear. She holds out her wand, casting a spell over the kingdom.

The stage grows dark; the garden fades in the distance. From the ground, enormous shrubs, great branches of foliage rise magically and seem to entwine the garden and the palace, smothering them in sleep. In a small point of light, the Lilac Fairy can be seen dancing softly, waving her magic wand, as the palace and its people, obedient to her command, go to sleep for a hundred years.

ACT TWO: THE VISION   A brief orchestral introduction features the sound of hunting horns, and when the curtain rises on a wooded glen, we are prepared for the entry of the royal hunting party. The scene is the forest of King Florestan XXIV, a part of the forest remote from the sleeping palace; the time, one hundred years later. The setting sun glows in the distance over rocky hills that enclose a still stream. As the hunting party comes upon the scene, it is apparent that the style of dress has changed considerably. Duchesses and dukes, marchionesses and marquesse stride about the wood in their colorful riding habits. Gallison, tutor to Prince Florimund, the leader of the hunt, totters onto the stage exhausted. Prince Florimund follows. Dressed in red riding habit, with high red boots and a feathered hat, the prince bows to his guests. A countess approaches him and makes a suggestion. The prince responds lazily and motions her away gently. The persistent countess does not acknowledge the rebuff, however. She has in mind a game of blindman's buff and persuades the tutor to bind his eyes. The old man obliges her and chases after the royal couples, who egg him on by whipping their riding crops at his feet. He stumbles around, becomes dizzy, and takes the hand of what he imagines to be a beautiful lady. He is somewhat staggered as he takes the handkerchief from his eyes and finds himself embracing a peer.

The game has not amused the guests sufficiently and they turn to other entertainment. Reluctantly the prince yields to the countess' persuasion and takes her as his partner in a stately mazurka. Peasants enter the wood at the conclusion of the dance and perform a farandole, a round dance in which the boys and girls join hands and curve about the stage in a continuous serpentine line. Every member of the hunting party is diverted by the farandole except the prince, who is moody and preoccupied. The hunting horns sound again. Attendants bring in spears for the hunt, and the lords and ladies prepare to leave. But the prince has suddenly changed his mind and urges his guests to leave without him. He will remain in the forest for a little while and rejoin them later. The countess is visibly upset at her inability to attract the prince away; she attempts to change his mind; the prince dismisses her.

Now alone in the glen, the prince walks about. Night falls; the setting sun becomes the new moon. He stares out over the lake, hoping that the beautiful scene will settle his gloom. He turns away dejectedly and walks forward. Just as he turns his back, the theme of the Lilac Fairy is heard and a magical boat floats onto the lake from the right. Its gossamer sail hangs from a silver mast; motioning the boat forward is the Lilac Fairy, who stands with upraised wand in the great sea shell that forms the boat's hull. The boat stops at her command, and the fairy steps down to earth. Still preoccupied with his own thoughts, the prince does not see her. As he moves back toward the lake, he is astonished by her presence. He bows deeply.

The Lilac Fairy then begins to instruct the prince in the cause of his woe. In a palace not far from this forest, she tells him, sleeps a beautiful princess, a princess so lovely that his mind must have envisaged her all his life. This princess has been asleep for a hundred years, yet she is only sixteen. She will sleep forever unless she is kissed by a prince who loves her.

The prince is enchanted, but somewhat skeptical, and impatiently asks the Lilac Fairy to let him see the princess. The fairy consents to show him a vision of the Princess Aurora. She points her wand to the left, and concealed within a dark tree trunk we see a misty vision of the princess. The specter disappears as quickly as it came. The prince demands to see more of her; already he is enamored of Aurora. The Lilac Fairy now allows the vision of the princess to enter in person.

The princess comes in on the right. Still the beautiful young girl of the first act, her movements are now soft and romantic. A haunting melody begins, dominated by the cellos, lending the scene a dark, mysterious atmosphere. The prince lifts Aurora high off the ground and, when he lets her down, attempts to embrace her. Fairies who have followed the princess pull him away from her, and he watches as she dances alone. The fairies form a circular tableau in the center of the scene. The princess moves about this circle, momentarily disappearing from the prince's sight. He pursues her softly, patiently, yet never catches up to her. Finally he holds her for a brief moment in his arms. The vision relaxes against him for an instant and then leaves him, like a phantom. He beseeches the Lilac Fairy to call her back again.

The sixteen nymphs dance for a short interval, and suddenly the princess returns to their midst. The flowing music becomes strongly rhythmical. Standing in the center of the stage, she dances quickly, with staccatolike urgency, a brilliant variation that excites the prince's love for her. He holds out his arms and she vanishes.

The nymphs fill the scene again with their dancing, and the princess makes a final, spinning, illusory appearance. The prince asks the Lilac Fairy, "Where has she gone? Where can I find her again?" The Lilac Fairy calms his curiosity and tells him that to find the princess, they must sail across the lake to her father's palace, where the princess lies asleep. She motions for him to follow, and the curtain falls as the Lilac Fairy's magical boat disappears in the midst of the lake.

ACT THREE, SCENE ONE: THE AWAKENING   The orchestra plays a long overture, the composition that was designed originally to accompany the journey of the Lilac Fairy and the prince toward the palace, a slowly paced interlude during which the fairy's magic barge passed slowly across the lake, surrounded by a panorama of dense forest and splendid vistas of the enchanted palace.

When the curtain rises, the Lilac Fairy and the prince have already disembarked. The fairy leads the prince across the stage from the right. He follows several paces behind her, looking about him cautiously, both amazed and delighted at the sleeping forest. Only shadows can be distinguished in the background. The two walk off at the left and reappear almost immediately behind a gauze curtain. Light emerges from behind; the palace can be seen, rising high on the summit in the distance. On the ground, two guards, frozen in an attitude of perpetual slumber, sleep away their watch. The prince stares at them, unbelieving. The Lilac Fairy leads him off; the light is extinguished, only to come up again in a moment in a high-vaulted chamber—the boudoir of the Princess Aurora. The Lilac Fairy enters first, holding her wand before her. She enters through a maze of great columns entangled with cobwebs, beckoning to the prince to follow. In the half-darkness, on the left, a silken bed canopied with royal drapes dominates the apartment. Guards stand in a line, motionless, sleeping against their upright spears.

The prince enters, marveling at the oppression of the sleeping rooms and the splendor they still contain. He glances incredulously at the sleeping guards. The Lilac Fairy motions him forward to the bed. In the dim light, he sees the sleeping princess. He hesitates, not wishing to disturb her sleeping beauty. The Lilac Fairy waves her wand, and he steps forward toward the bed. Curled in an attitude of peaceful contentment, the princess lies in deep slumber, her head on an ancient, dusty pillow. The prince bends down toward her face; the Lilac Fairy gestures with her wand; he kisses her softly. The music mounts to a vivid crescendo. The princess stirs, wakens, and rises slowly as the prince gathers her in his arms.

The light flashes out, and miraculously the giant spiders who hover over the chamber rise and vanish; the cobwebs are disentangled from the great pillars and gradually fall away. The light comes up slowly, royal pages stand against the high columns, and we see before us the great hall of King Florestan's palace.

ACT THREE, SCENE TWO: THE WEDDING   The lofty columns of stone support high-vaulting arches. In the distance, great, sweeping staircases climb up to the farther reaches of the castle. The thrones of the king and queen stand at the right.

With pomp and ceremony, as if he had not been disturbed by more than a night's sleep, the courtier Cattalabutte enters with all his old-time flourish. He struts about the hall as if he himself were responsible for the festivities that are about to follow.

The king and his queen enter regally. Cattalabutte bows to them and escorts them to the dais. Courtiers and ladies in waiting with their escorts dance in and promenade about the hall to the virile rhythms of a polonaise. Six other la-dies enter. As the dance theme is repeated quietly, the special guests who have been invited to attend the wedding of Princess Aurora and Prince Florimund dance in to pay their respects to the parents of the bride.

These royal guests are perennial fairy tale characters. First comes the White Cat, held high on a pillow which her escorts carry on their shoulders. She paws the air plaintively and washes her face. Behind her comes Puss in Boots, who watches her possessively while waving his hat in greeting. Bluebeard and his wife, Goldilocks and her prince, Beauty and the Beast, and Florestan, the crown prince of the kingdom, and his two sisters follow behind. Last of all come the enchanted princess and the bluebird. Now, led by the Lilac Fairy, all six of the Princess Aurora's fairy godmothers enter in all their glory.

All the courtiers and guests arrange themselves in a great circle about the hall. Prince Florestan, Aurora's brother, and their two sisters step out and stand at the back of the stage toward the right. A lovely, lilting waltz begins; to its enchanting melody, the three dance a *pas de trois*. When the waltz ends, each of the two girls dances a short variation to music that is light and spar-kling in its tinkling sound. Prince Florestan rejoins them, and all three leap off into the wings.

The next *divertissement* features the White Cat and Puss in Boots. This oboe mimes their mewing as Puss in Boots tries to ensnare the winsome cat in a love trap. The White Cat pretends to resist Puss's caresses, but actually she is delighted. Finally Puss can contain himself no longer and puts an end to the flirtation by carrying his ladylove off.

The Enchanted Princess enters with the Bluebird. Both flutter their arms in light, airy motions of flight and commence a *pas de deux*, perhaps the most dazzling dance duet of the entire ballet. The Bluebird, in his variation, seems to be suspended in soaring flight.

Another *divertissement* enacts the tale of Little Red Ridinghood. Four pages bring small trees onto the stage. Red Ridinghood walks lightly through the wood, treading as softly as possible, glancing behind her at every turn. The wolf enters with a bold leap and conceals himself behind one of the trees. The girl passes; he steps out in front of her. Red Ridinghood tries to pretend that he is just another passer-by, like herself, and, holding her basket close, proceeds on her way. The wolf is fooled only for a moment: quickly he throws her over his shoulder and runs off.

Now the moment for which all the court has been waiting finally arrives. Princess Aurora and Prince Florimund enter. A spotlight brightens the brilliant white the bride wears for her wedding day, and all the lords and ladies bow. The royal couple come forward and begin to dance. Their *pas de deux* is gracious and formal. The Princess Aurora reveals, in her mastery of movement and balance, a maturity and perfection for which the "Rose Adagio" was but a youthful rehearsal. Still charming, the youthful princess is now about to be married, and her radiant poise reflects the lesson her love has taught. Prince Florimund supports his bride gallantly, lifting her effortlessly, holding her confidently—by each of his gestures and motions drawing the court's attention to her loveliness. As the *pas de deux* concludes, its tender music ascends to a pitch of everlasting joy. The princess turns with incredible speed on point and dives toward the floor. The prince catches her falling figure and holds her in the daring pose.

A final *divertissement* is offered by the Three Ivans, who perform a virile, stomping Russian dance for the bride and groom. The court is now at the height of good humor, and when the Princess Aurora returns to dance briefly alone, everyone is suddenly saddened by the fact that soon she will go away with her prince. But everyone watches closely this last dance of their princess; the entire assembly is infected by her happiness. Now the whole court—all the fairies, all the nobles, all the fairy tale figures—joins the bride and groom in a spirited mazurka, at the end of which the guests form a circle about the prince and princess who, standing in close embrace, become, in reality, a part of that fairy tale world that brought them together. Everyone kneels to them.

NOTES The success of *The Sleeping Beauty* described here—as presented by the Royal Ballet (then the Sadler's Wells Ballet) in 1946, in London, and three years later in the United States—has led to many other productions. All of these, including new productions by the Royal Ballet itself, retain the main outlines of the story and the principal dances, while adding variations of character, new dances and ensembles to accompany changes in scenery and costume. Notable productions are those of the Leningrad Kirov Ballet (filmed in 1965, with Alla Sizova and Yuri Soloviev), the National Ballet of Washington (staged by Ben Stevenson), and the National Ballet of Canada (staged by Rudolf Nureyev). The latter, with Veronica Tennant as the Princess Aurora and, as guest artist, Rudolf Nureyev as Prince Florimund, was presented on film by Public Broadcasting Service television in the United States at Christmastime 1972 in color. Rudolf Nureyev first staged the ballet independently for La Scala, Milan, September 17, 1970, with scenery and costumes by Nicholas Georgiadis. Margot Fonteyn and Nureyev danced the première.

Nureyev has said of *The Sleeping Beauty* (in an interview in *Dance and Dancers*, January 1972): "It is really a kind of *Parsifal* of ballet and very important to the whole ballet world. It's very long and very lush, and there is nothing you can really cut. Since I had been brought up on the Kirov version, my production was naturally inspired by that."

In writing of Nureyev's *Sleeping Beauty* soon after its New York première in 1973, Andrew Porter in *The New Yorker* reviewed much of the ballet's history: "In ballet history, the usual order is reversed; the Romantic works come first, then the Classical. And the Petipa-Tchaikovsky *Sleeping Beauty*, first performed, in St. Petersburg, in 1890, is the grandest, fullest, and finest achievement of Classical ballet—its 'definitive statement' and an enduring inspiration to later choreographers. Balanchine, Ashton, and Kenneth MacMillan all proclaim their debt to the inventions of Petipa. Brought from Leningrad to London by Nicholas Sergeyev, *The Sleeping Beauty* became, in 1939, the foundation of the Royal Ballet's work, and the dancers, directors, ballet masters, and teachers who have gone out from Covent Garden to play leading roles in ballet across six continents have all been brought up on *Sleeping Beauty* as ballet's Bible. Meanwhile, in Leningrad itself, *The Sleeping Beauty* remains the work that shows Maryinsky-Kirov dancing at its purest and most poetic. The Kirov company brought its *Sleeping Beauty* to London twelve years ago, and left a new mark on all subsequent Western productions. The influence was continued, in a highly personalized variant, by the participation of the ex-Kirov dancer Rudolf Nureyev in the Royal Ballet performances and then by his own stagings of the work—at La Scala, in 1969, and now for the National Ballet of Canada. With a *Sleeping Beauty* 'produced, staged, and with additional choreography by Rudolf Nureyev after Marius Petipa,' the Canadian company made its Metropolitan début last week. It offered an exceedingly grand presentation of the piece—from a scenic point of view the grandest, in fact, that I have ever seen.

"When Auguste Bournonville, that great Romantic choreographer (whose *La Sylphide* is another work in the Canadian repertory), visited Petersburg in 1874, he was distressed by what he saw: 'Much as I wanted to, I could not discover action, dramatic interest, logical continuity, something that would even remotely remind one of common sense. And if, on occasion, I did succeed in finding a trace of something like it (as, for example, in Petipa's *Don Quixote*), the impression was immediately obscured by an endless number of monotonous bravura appearances.' Ivan Alexandrovich Vsevolozhsky, appointed Director of the Imperial Theatres in 1881, changed all that. He instituted production councils in which scenarist, choreographer, composer, and designer got together to plan a new work. Of *The Sleeping Beauty* he was both scenarist and costume designer; Tchaikovsky, 'in large letters,' dedicated the published score to him. Composer and choreographer worked closely together. Petipa told Tchaikovsky exactly how many measures he wanted for each episode, and specified the tempo, the style, even the scoring. Princess Aurora's first variation should be accompanied by violins and cellos pizzicato, and harps; at

Carabosse's unmasking, at the end of Act I, 'a chromatic scale must sound in the whole orchestra'; the Sapphire of Act III, being of pentahedral cut, required an accompaniment in 5/4 time. When, during rehearsals, the Panorama music of Act II came to an end before the great panorama of painted canvas had rolled its full course, Tchaikovsky composed extra music, whose length was determined, literally, by the yard. The three collaborators played each his different role in giving unity to the elaborate *féerie*. Vsevolozhsky had his conception of a glittering dance pageant mounting to its climax in an apotheosispaean to imperial splendor (a paean in the precise sense, since the ending would show Apollo costumed as Louis XIV). Petipa had his sharp-cut scheme for a balanced and well-varied sequence of dances. And Tchaikovsky? He always delighted in the evocation of past centuries. Petipa's blueprint checked his tendency to sprawly form. And he poured out his heart. It is Tchaikovsky's music that gives character to the heroine and expresses the 'inner theme' which raises *The Sleeping Beauty* above the level of a pretty divertissement.

"Most of the fairy tales that adults go to the theater to see again and again— *Swan Lake, Cinderella, Hansel and Gretel,* the *Ring*—symbolically enshrine truths about human experience and human behavior to make their pleasures more than incidental. *Swan Lake,* for example, is a drama involving conflict and character; it gives scope for dramatic expression, for acting, and for diverse striking interpretations. By comparison with Prince Siegfried in *Swan Lake,* Prince Florimund of *The Sleeping Beauty* is a cipher. What does he do to deserve his princess? The briar thicket surrounding his bride is no dangerous Magic Fire through which only the dauntless can pass. And similarly, by comparison with the brave, pathetic Odette and the formidable temptress Odile, Princess Aurora is a passive heroine played upon by circumstance. Can we find a moral in *The Sleeping Beauty* beyond that guest lists should be kept up-to-date lest awkwardness result? Perrault, who wrote the fairy tale on which the ballet is based, suggested, 'What girl would not forgo her marriage vows, at least for a while, to gain a husband who is handsome, rich, courteous, and kind?' Not enough! In a preface to the Penguin edition of Perrault, Geoffrey Brereton remarks that it is 'tempting to adopt the nature-myth interpretation and see the tale as an allegory of the long winter sleep of the earth'— but adds that 'the allegory, if it is one, is obscure.' Tchaikovsky's interpretation was simpler. His *Sleeping Beauty* is a struggle between good and evil, between forces of light and forces of darkness, represented by the benevolent Lilac Fairy and the wicked fairy Carabosse. The prelude, a straightforward exposition of the music associated with the two characters, suggests it; the consistent employment of melodies related to or derived from these themes—the Lilac Fairy's transformation of the Carabosse music at the close of Act I, the Carabosse figuration that propels Aurora's dance with the spindle, the opposition of the two themes in the symphonic entr'acte that precedes the Awakening—makes it clear. These two forces shape Aurora's destiny, and although she initiates nothing, with just a little stretching of the imagination we can accept the declaration of the Russian composer and critic Boris Asafiev that the heroine's three adagios (the Rose Adagio, in E flat; the Vision Scene appearance, in F; the Grand Pas de Deux, in C) tell 'the story of a whole life—the growth and development of a playful and carefree child into a young woman who learns, through tribulations, to know great love.' It is in this sense that Margot Fonteyn, since 1939 our leading Aurora, dances the role.

"That question 'Can we find a moral?' prompts others. Is it right to look for one? Does the 'meaning' of *The Sleeping Beauty* not lie simply in its patterns of movement, as does that of, say, *Ballet Imperial*, Balanchine's homage to Petipa and Tchaikovsky? While spectacle, pure dance, expressive dance, narrative, and symbolism must mix in any presentation of the work, what importance should be given to any single ingredient? Different productions have provided different answers. The Kirov's has modest décor; the dances shine as rich, perfectly cut jewels in a quiet, rather dowdy setting; this Leningrad *Beauty* is not a drama but a long, lyrical poem in varied metres, spun on a thread of radiant narrative. Kenneth MacMillan's presentation, at the German Opera, in Berlin, in 1967, was very grand indeed to look at (the epochs were moved forward, so that Aurora fell asleep in the reign of Catherine the Great and woke a century later, under Alexander II) and also rather dramatic—yet the main emphasis was again not on the story but on the dances, both Petipa's and those that MacMillan added, in brilliant emulation. The famous old Covent Garden version, which did more than twenty years' hard service (and in 1949 introduced the company to New York), balanced all the ingredients listed above, but toward the end it fell apart; though the central Petipa episodes were lovingly preserved, around them was a ragged patchwork. The 1968 replacement was softly romantic, lavishly sentimental in appearance, and did not last long; I have not seen its successor, which opened at Covent Garden in March.

"Nureyev's production for the National Ballet of Canada is different again. The décor, by Nicholas Georgiadis, is even more sumptuous than Barry Kay's in Berlin, though it does not sparkle so brightly. Mr. Kay produced a jewelled effect, of diamonds, rubies, sapphires, with the softer gleam of pearl and opal in the Vision Scene; Mr. Georgiadis prefers an impression of old gold, with touches of rich colors that are muted as if by a layer of fine dust; in the final scene the dominant tone becomes rust red. David Hersey's subtly elaborate lighting subdues the colors still further and blurs distinctions between them; a prevailing amber glow neutralizes all shades in the Vision Scene except when follow spots fall on the principals, or the attendant fairies enter pools of white light stage-front. Blackness at the back strikes an unsuitably sombre note at the christening party of the Prologue; Aurora's wedding, I think, also calls for a more splendid general blaze. All the same, the lighting is carefully and imaginatively wrought. There are some excellent stage effects: a streamer of red ribbon flies across the stage, to shape itself as Carabosse and her retinue; a boat for Florimund and the Lilac Fairy glides magically through the obstacles on the way to the palace. The tableau of sleeping courtiers through which the prince, marvelling, picks his way is a triumph for designer, producer, and lighter at once. Mr. Georgiadis's architecture, substantial and imposing, leaves plenty of space for the dance. His multitudinous costumes are beautiful both in detail and in massed effect. Only the cut of the tutus, which are large, floppy, and thus line-obscuring, is unhappy.

"Nureyev's handling of the piece is extremely elaborate, from the first moment of the fairies' entrée; they come on four at a time, *bourréeing* hand-in-hand, each group with an attendant cavalier, who then lifts the leader while she draws her companions through the mazes of a most un-Petipalike procession. The second fairy variation is danced in duplicate, which is unusual, but in the score the variation does bear the names of two characters (Coulante, Farine). Nureyev's main innovation in the Prologue is to divide the role of the Lilac Fairy into two: a 'Principal Fairy,' who does the dancing, and a Lilac Fairy 'proper,' who turns up at the party, last guest to arrive, only after Carabosse has spoken her curse. Crinolined and heavily draped, an ambulant tea cozy, this fairy can do little more than glide about and wave her wand. Carabosse is played by a woman, as she was by Natalia Dudinskaya in Leningrad a decade or so ago, and she is played by Celia Franca in terms of offended dignity rather than evil malice. Her retinue roughs up the good fairies in a rather infelicitous sequence. Amid all this complication, and with the roles of good and evil genies reduced, the point of the Prologue is not clearly made. The fact that the fairies are endowing young Aurora with the gifts characterized in their variations is unstated, and a newcomer might watch the scene without even becoming aware that a royal infant is the focus of the festivities. The knitting bee, at the start of Act I, becomes another production number, involving slatterns, cat's-paws, halberdiers, hangmen, and a good deal of fussy activity. At the close of the act, the four minor princes, lunging at Carabosse, run one another through. But Petipa's lovely inventions for Aurora are respected, even if eight minstrel girls figure too prominently in parts of the Rose Adagio. Veronica Tennant, Aurora at both performances I saw, places the choreography precisely, apart from a tendency to push forcefully into arabesque. She does not convey much sense of a developing character, and her dancing lacks, above all, legato—that feeling for a flowing line which links one image to the next. It is stop and start again—sequences chopped into short phrases. And this is a general company fault, observable in most of the solo dancing. The musical director, George Crum, has it, too; Tchaikovsky's long melodies do not flow smoothly enough. The anonymous orchestra is proficient but a bit short on strings. Some of Mr. Crum's rhythms are sludgy and undramatic.

"When, in Act II, Prince Florimund arrives, in the person of Rudolf Nureyev (who dances fourteen of the sixteen New York performances), he gives a splendid demonstration of that phrasing command which, so to speak, keeps the line going through the rests. In Petipa's original the Prince was not a large dancing role (the brilliant male technician of the Petersburg company, Enrico Cecchetti, created not the Prince but the Bluebird—and also Carabosse); Nureyev has enlarged it. He has given himself three variations in Act II, the second of them done to Panorama music shifted to an earlier point in the act. Aurora's second solo has been rewritten, without the alternating *relevés*, and not improved. The voyage to the palace and the Prince's entry are, as I said, strikingly achieved. After the Awakening, the climax of the story, there is a letdown. It is mainly Petipa's fault; here, surely, there should be a *pas de deux* for the Princess 'whose radiant beauty' (in Perrault's words) 'seemed to glow with a kind of heavenly light' and the Prince 'who hardly knew how to express his joy and gratitude'—but, instead, the curtain drops after a few bars. In the old Covent Garden version the difficulty was solved by moving straight into the wedding celebrations, and for the 1968 production Ashton composed a tender new *pas de deux* to the music of the entr'acte. In the Canadian version, on the opening night, Miss Tennant and Nureyev made things worse by expressing no great interest in one another. Reactions in this production were often inadequate. Earlier in Act II, the Prince showed little surprise when the Lilac Fairy joined him but behaved as if fairy apparitions were an everyday occurrence. Act III in the Canadian *Beauty* opens not brilliantly but quietly, with the Sarabande, originally the penultimate dance, brought forward. Then things follow much their usual course. The *pas de quatre* of Jewels becomes a *pas de cinq*, with the Diamonds a twin set. (The male Diamond is allotted Sapphire's 5/4 solo variation.) Bluebirds are placed before Cats; Red Ridinghood, Hop-o'-My-Thumb, and Cinderella are omitted; so, unfortunately, is the apotheosis. Again, the plot point—that all the characters of fairyland have assembled to pay homage to the royal couple—is not potently made, but again there is a display of dense dance patterns around the solos, with much rich 'doubling at the octave' in Nureyev's favored manner.

"The National Ballet of Canada was conceived when the Sadler's Wells/Royal Ballet, after its New York triumphs in 1949, went on to appear in Toronto. The official début was late in 1951; the company comes of age with a *Sleeping Beauty* that shows it need yield nothing in scale of presentation to the London company."*

March 15, 1973, the Royal Ballet produced a new version of *The Sleeping Beauty*. Designed by Peter Farmer, with lighting by William Bundy, the ballet used the choreography of Marius Petipa with new and additional dances by Kenneth MacMillan. Antoinette Sibley was the *Princess Aurora*, Anthony Dowell the *Prince*. The fairy variations were danced by Jennifer Penney, Laura Connor, Alfreda Thorogood, Anita Young, Lesley Collier, and Deanne Bergsma (the *Lilac Fairy*). Lesley Collier and Michael Coleman were the *Bluebirds*. Clement Crisp reviewed it in *The Financial Times:* " 'A magical fantasy'—thus I. A. Vsevolozhsky, director of the Imperial Theatres and guiding spirit in the creation of *The Sleeping Beauty* as librettist and designer of the costumes, wrote to Tchaikovsky when he commissioned the score. *Beauty* is, of course, several things: the supreme achievement of Petipa's genius; the pinnacle of nineteenth-century ballet; a *ballet féerie* designed to delight a court audience and pay discreetly flattering homage to the Tsar, whose servants the artists of the Imperial Ballet were. For us it is the signature work of the Royal Ballet—symbol of the company's maturity in the 1946 staging, testimony to the international standing of the troupe at the triumphant New York opening in 1949.

* From *A Musical Season* (Viking Press); © 1973 Andrew Porter. Originally in *The New Yorker*.

"The 1946 staging was decorated by Oliver Messel, and after the austerities of the war it looked supremely opulent. Five years ago a new production, with designs by Henry Bardon and Lila de Nobili—*à la manière de Doré*—was a brave attempt at rethinking the piece; but it lacked airiness, space in which Petipa's inventions could breathe; and hence the new production by Kenneth MacMillan with designs by Peter Farmer, given at a gala in the presence of Her Majesty the Queen last night to pay tribute to the American Friends of Covent Garden whose generosity has paid for this much-needed revision.

"The result is entirely worthwhile. This new staging is Vsevolozhsky's 'magical fantasy,' with steps restored, some choreography renewed, other sections embellished. The *Beauty* has been reawakened, and the whole staging is a reassertion of MacMillan's love and understanding of the classic tradition of which he is a product. To detail the various innovations must wait until later viewings of the production; suffice it to say that the spirit of this great ballet is honored throughout. MacMillan has done his homework—*Beauty* is a well-documented ballet—and both the spirit of the piece and its choreographic structure have been honorably displayed.

"It is the special merit of Peter Farmer's settings that they give ample room for the dances. Each act of the ballet is conceived in one color: the Prologue is almost entirely blue—the most difficult shade to bring off on stage—and in amid the soaring arches of King Florestan's palace, which suggest a properly magical setting for a fairy tale, the arrival of the fairy godmothers had been staged with extraordinary skill as they enter down mysterious flights of stairs hidden from our eyes.

"For Act One we are in a garden setting which, at first viewing, seems too ingratiatingly pretty, but here—as throughout the evening—I was conscious of the care taken that nothing should obscure the impact of the dances. In the Prologue, the Fairy variations glittered diamond-sharp against the indigo darkness of the palace; with Aurora's appearance we could see the majesty of Petipa's inventions plain, and Antoinette Sibley was in superb form as the young princess, and later as the vision, and ultimately and most brilliantly as the bride.

"Carabosse—Alexander Grant, tremendous here as throughout the evening—is placed on stage under the guise of a courtier, and the spell is cast, and the Lilac Fairy intervenes, with a real feeling for the magical element that sustains the whole action of the piece. In this scene, as at every point during the action, there is a concern for dramatic credibility; MacMillan has reworked small incidents that have become dully traditional, and the action is carried forward with a nice appreciation for period style.

"The first two acts are set in a suitably fantastic and improbable realm of fairy enchantment; but with the hunting scene we enter a world which, as Vsevolozhsky intended, has some historical reality. The whole development of the staging moves from the imaginary, dream-like setting of Aurora's youth into the clarity and formal elegance of the age of Louis XIV in which she must awake from Carabosse's enchantment.

"The Prince Florimund is Anthony Dowell, princely in style and technique; his journey to Aurora's palace—with its use of panorama as demanded by

Tchaikovsky's music—is true theatrical magic and the celebrations of the final act are grand and beautiful. Further comment must wait until the *Beauty* enters the repertory next week: until then a welcome for the production, and for the excellence of the company's performance."

For a contemporary Soviet Russian appraisal of Marius Petipa's achievement in *The Sleeping Beauty,* an essay by Vera Krasovskaya in *Dance Perspectives,* No. 49, is of interest. Yuri Slonimsky's monograph, *Marius Petipa,* translated by Anatole Chujoy in *Dance Index* VI, Nos. 5 and 6 (1947), remains the classic account of that master's work, by the renowned Soviet critic and historian. Also of interest is *Russian Ballet Master: the Memoirs of Marius Petipa,* edited by Lillian Moore and translated by Helen Whittaker (New York, Macmillan, 1958).

Now the wheel has come full circle. The Sadler's Wells Ballet production of *The Sleeping Beauty,* designed by Oliver Messel, which introduced the ballet to the modern audience, has been mounted anew by American Ballet Theatre, which staged it at the Metropolitan Opera House, New York, June 15, 1976, with Natalia Makarova and Mikhail Baryshnikov. The production was staged by Mary Skeaping, after Petipa; the lighting was by Nananne Porcher.

Margot Fonteyn's performance in the original Messel production by the Sadler's Wells Ballet in New York in 1949 has been recalled by the critic Dale Harris in *Ballet Review* (Vol. 4, No. 6): "The ultimate proof of Fonteyn's skill was to make her last-act variation into the climax of the entire evening, to transform into the apex of Aurora's good fortune a simple dance designed to provide a lyrical contrast with the *grand adage* that precedes it and the strong male solo and boisterous coda that succeed it. In 1949 there was no male solo and the coda was used for the Three Ivans. Fonteyn's triumph was compounded of all her virtues: the slow opening section showed off her nobly proportioned body, its perfect placement, the pliancy of her back, the clarity and continuity of her line from fingertips to feet, the ballerina head and face which gave focus to the body's expressiveness by directing the audience's attention where she wanted it to be. In the sequence to the perky violin solo, as she flicked her wrists while raising her arms she would draw the rhythm taut by raising her eyes a fraction later than her arms. The same kind of rubato informed her phrasing of the *petits battements frappés* to the pizzicati, so that she seemed to be toying with the music, teasing it out, flirting with it. Yet in the final section her fast, sure *piqué* turns were thrilling precisely because they accorded so exactly with the music's strong, driving rhythm. Fonteyn's musicality was awesome."[*]

Clive Barnes in a long appraisal of American Ballet Theatre's revival of the ballet entitled "A Promise Fulfilled" (the New York *Times,* June 27, 1976) discussed the virtues of the Oliver Messel production and its meaning for the company's dancers and the contemporary audience.

The critic Tobi Tobias wrote an interesting historical overview of *The Sleep-*

[*] Reprinted by permission of *Ballet Review,* Marcel Dekker, publisher.

ing Beauty entitled "Inheritance" for the first issue of American Ballet Theatre's magazine *On Point,* Summer 1976.

SMALL PARADES

Music by Edgard Varèse. Choreography by Glen Tetley. Decor and costumes by Nadine Baylis. Lighting by John B. Read. First presented by the Netherlands Dance Theatre in March 1972. First presented in the United States by the same ensemble at the Brooklyn Academy of Music, New York, March 30, 1972.

A dance ballet to contemporary music in a chaste, modern setting, *Small Parades* is performed to five famous pieces by Varèse: *Intégrales, Density 21.5, Octandre, Hyperprism,* and *Ionisation.* Arranged for ten dancers, the ballet is divided into five parts, like the music, and performed without interruption.

Writing after its U.S. premiere, Clive Barnes said in the New York *Times* that *Small Parades* "is a ballet of space and emotion. Its vocabulary is a perfect amalgam of classic ballet and modern dance, and its structure has a natural strength . . . Tetley uses classic dance here almost as a commentary on his modern-dance experience. These Dutch dancers are the perfect expression of this revealing choreographic ambiguity."

SOLITAIRE

Music by Malcolm Arnold. Choreography by Kenneth MacMillan. Scenery and costumes by Lawrence Shafer. First presented by the Sadler's Wells Theatre Ballet, June 7, 1956, with Margaret Hill, Sara Neil, and Donald Britton. First presented in the United States by the Royal Ballet at the Metropolitan Opera House, New York, September 17, 1957, with scenery and costumes by Desmond Healy.

Solitaire is a playful *divertissement* arranged to the *English Dances* of Malcolm Arnold. Its choreographer calls the ballet "a kind of game for one" and the ballet follows the efforts of an attractive girl to be included in a group of other young people. Time and again she tries to join in their games but is always rebuffed. In the end, she is as alone as she was at the beginning. While this sounds somewhat sad, it is not, because both the music and the dances have a gaiety and warmth that suggest inner as well as conscious security. The girl is lovely, she dances superbly. It is perhaps the people she wants to be with who are missing something!

SOME TIMES

Music by Claus Ogerman. Choreography by Dennis Nahat. Scenery and costumes by Rouben Ter-Arutunian. Lighting by Nananne Porcher. First presented by American Ballet Theatre at the New York State Theatre, Lincoln Center, New York, July 14, 1972, with Mimi Paul, Martine van Hamel, Naomi Sorkin, Ian Horvath, and Dennis Nahat and ensemble.

A ballet about young people in these times, this ballet, without a narrative, plots the interaction of the sexes in a series of dances. A lone girl moves through a social scene as if she were alone. Two boys and a girl fantasize together. The scene, an abstract one, might be any contemporary place in which young persons might be alone, and be themselves.

SONATINE

Music by Maurice Ravel. Choreography by George Balanchine. Lighting by Ronald Bates. First presented by the New York City Ballet at the Hommage à Ravel at the New York State Theatre, Lincoln Center, May 14, 1975, with Violette Verdy and Jean-Pierre Bonnefous. Pianist: Madeleine Malraux.

This little dance ballet opened our Ravel Festival at the New York City Ballet in 1975. The year 1975 was the one hundredth anniversary of Ravel's birth. I have always loved his music, from the time I made a bit of a waltz from his *Valses Nobles et Sentimentales* in Russia, and so we thought it would be a good idea to celebrate this wonderful composer's life and work by arranging new dances to as many scores as we could. We did seventeen ballets, sixteen of them new. Some were very long, like *L'Enfant et les Sortilèges*, with lots of costumes and a big production. Others, like *Sonatine*, were only a few minutes long, simply using Ravel's music and making what we could of it.

The pianist and the dancers are on stage together when the curtain goes up on the ballet. The pianist begins to play; the girl and the boy stand and listen. They like what they hear, apparently, for they begin to move to it, following its line, and gradually becoming imbued with its spirit.

THE SONG OF THE EARTH

Music by Gustav Mahler. Choreography by Kenneth MacMillan. First presented by the Stuttgart Ballet Company, November 7, 1965. First presented in the United States by the Royal Ballet at the new Metropolitan Opera House, April 25, 1967, with Anthony Dowell, Donald MacLeary, Georgina Parkinson, Jennifer Penney, and Ann Jenner in leading roles.

* See also SHADOW OF THE WIND.

Mahler regarded his *Das Lied von der Erde* as a "symphony in songs." The work is set for tenor, alto, and orchestra. Mahler found the text for his songs in a volume of translations of the Chinese poet Li-Tai-Po (702–763) and others. The poems speak of earthly woe, loneliness, youth, beauty, drunkenness and the spring, and farewell, not, in other words, celebrating nature so much as expressing a philosophy of a lifetime. To the last poem, the composer added these lines:

> The lovely earth, all, everywhere,
> Revives in spring and blooms anew,
> All, everywhere and ever, ever,
> Shines the blue horizon,
> Ever . . . ever . . .

The choreographer has said that his ballet is about Death. "This theme comes out very strongly. But I can't say that the man who moves among the dancers like Death actually is Death. That would be too specific. The Germans call him *der Ewige*, the one who is always there, and it is difficult to find an English equivalent. The direct translation would be The Eternal, but probably the best description is in the last line of the last poem, 'Forever . . . forever . . .'

"The Death figure is not at all evil. In fact, he is . . . just there, always hanging about. He wears a colorless mask without any marks on it, and it makes him look like the others, only just that much different. Basically the theme of the ballet is quite simple: a man and a woman; Death takes the man; they both return to her and at the end of the ballet—in the last poem—we find that in Death there is the promise of renewal."

While Kenneth MacMillan has said that people expecting a line by line translation in stage action of the text of the songs are bound to be disappointed, he has tried, as with *Images of Love*, to distill what is spoken, "and to find imagery for the ideas behind the words. My interest was to create movements to describe the essence of the poems."

Since the songs are sung in the theatre in German, a translation of them by Alfred H. Meyer is given here:

THE DRINKING SONG OF EARTHLY WOE

Wine in the golden goblet is beckoning,
But drink not yet, first I will sing you a song!
The Song of Sorrow, let its mockery laugh itself into your soul.

When sorrow approaches, the soul's gardens lie desolate,
Joy and song wither and die.
Dark is life, is death.

Lord of this house!
Thy cellar holds the fullness of golden wine!
Here, this lute I call mine own!

To play upon the lute, to empty glasses,
These are things that fit each other.
At the proper time a goblet full of wine
Is worth more than all the kingdoms of this earth!
Dark is life, is death!

The firmament in its eternal blue, and the earth,
These will long endure, will blossom in springtime.
But thou, O man, what is the span of thy life?
Not a hundred years art thou permitted to enjoy
The idle vanities of this earth!

Look there below! In the moonlight upon the graves
There crouches a wild, ghostly figure—
An ape it is! Hark how his howling
Shrills out into the sweet airs of this our life!

Bring on the wine! The time has come, my comrades!
Drain your golden goblets to the dregs!
Dark is life, is death!

THE LONELY ONE IN AUTUMN

The mists of autumn build their blue wall over the sea;
With hoarfrost covered, stands the grass;
It seems as if an artist had strewn the dust of jade over delicate blossoms.
The flowers' fragrance has spent itself;

A cold wind bows them to earth.
Soon the withered, golden leaves
Of lotus flowers will be scattered upon the waters.
My heart is weary. My little lamp
Has gone out, a-crackling, minding me of need for sleep,
I come to you, blest resting-place!
Yea, give me rest; for I need quickening!

I weep and weep in all my solitude.
Autumn in my heart too long is lasting.
O Sun of Love, never again wilt thou shine,
Gently to dry my bitter tears?

OF YOUTH

Midway in the little pool
Stands a pavilion of green
And of white porcelain.

Like the back of a tiger
The bridge of jade arches
Across to the pavilion.

In the little house friends are seated,
Beautifully gowned, drinking, gossiping;
Some are writing verses.

Their silken sleeves glide
Backwards, their silken caps
Hang from the back of their necks.

On the smooth surface of the quiet pool
All is mirrored
Wondrously.

All stands upon its head
In the pavilion of green
And of white porcelain.

Like a half-moon stands the bridge,
Reversed in its bow. Friends,
Beautifully gowned, are drinking, gossiping.

OF BEAUTY

Youthful maidens are plucking flowers,
Plucking lotus flowers at the edge of the shore.
Between bushes and leaves are they sitting.
Gathering blossoms in their laps and calling
To each other in jest.
The golden sun plays about their forms,
Reflected in the quiet water.
The sun mirrors their slender limbs,
Their sweet eyes,
And a zephyr with gentlest caress raises the fabric
Of their sleeves, wafts the magic
Of their perfume through the air,
O see, beautiful youths at play
On fiery horses, over there at the edge of the shore,
Glistening from afar like rays of the sun;
Between the green branches of the willows
Fresh youth is making its way!
The steed of one whinnies for joy
And shies and rushes past.
Over flowers, grasses, gallop his hoofs,
Whose stormy stamping crushes the fallen blossoms.

Heigh! How his mane flies in the breeze,
How his nostrils dilate!

The golden sun plays about the forms,
Reflecting them in the quiet water.
And the loveliest of the maidens
Sends him long glances of yearning.
Her haughty bearing is no more than feigned.
In the sparkle of her wide eyes,
In the darkening of the eager glance,
Ascends the plaint of the passion of her heart.

THE DRUNKEN ONE IN SPRINGTIME

If life is no more than a dream,
Why bother?
I'll drink, till drink no more I can,
The whole, live-long day!

And when no longer I can drink,
When throat and soul are full,
I'll stagger on till to my door,—
And sleep, and sleep, and sleep.

What hear I, awakening? List!
A bird sings in a tree.
I ask him whether Spring has come,
I feel as in a dream.

The birdling twitters, Yes! the Spring
Overnight has come!
In contemplation deep I brood,
While birdling sings and laughs!

Anew I fill my goblet
And drain it to the dregs
And sing until the moon shines bright
In the dark'ning firmament!

And when no longer I can sing
Again to sleep I'll go.
For what matters Spring to me?
Drunk only let me be!

FAREWELL

The sun is sinking 'neath the hills.
Evening descends into the vales
With its cool, quiet shadows.
Behold! As a bark of silver
The moon rises into the blue heaven.
I feel the motion of a gentle wind
Behind the dark pines.

The brook sings its music through the dark.
The flowers grow pale in the twilight.
The earth breathes the quiet of rest and sleep.
All longing goes a-dreaming.
Weary humanity is homeward bound,
To seek anew in sleep
Forgotten fortune, youth.
Birds are perched upon their branches.
The world falls into sleep.
The cool wind is in the shadow of my pines.

I stand here and await my friend, for a last farewell.
I long, O friend, at thy side
To drink in the beauty of this evening.
Where are you? You leave me long in solitude!
I wander to and fro with my lute
On paths thick with soft grass.
O Beauty! O World, drunk with love eternal—life!

He climbed from his horse and gave his friend a farewell cup; asked him
Whither he was going, and why it needs must be.
He spoke, his voice choking: O, my friend, Fate in this world has not
   been kind to me!
Whither am I bound? I go, I wander into the mountains.
I seek rest for my lonely heart.
I am wand'ring toward my native place, my home.

I shall no longer seek the far horizon.
My heart is still and waits for its deliverance.
The lovely earth, all, everywhere,
Revives in spring and blooms anew,
All, everywhere and ever, ever,
Shines the blue horizon,
Ever . . . ever . . .

The English music and dance critic Andrew Porter has written:

"MacMillan has shaped his response to the score in pure movement. No decor. No costumes. No picturesque lighting. And no 'acting.'

"The music of *The Drinking Song of Earthly Woe* leaps up and the boys leap on in a bounding, unforced surge of invention, patterning the energy and the soaring, plunging emotional contours of the movement. The slow movement, *The Lonely One in Autumn,* is quietly and simply danced by four girls, sometimes partnered, sometimes not ('O Sun of Love, will you never shine again, gently to dry my bitter tears?'). There follow three scherzos. *Of Youth* tells verbally of a cultivated social scene, a pavilion of green and white porcelain where friends sit, chatter, write verses. MacMillan finds playful, exquisitely articulated invention—and when the tenor sings of the reflections in the little pool ('everything standing on its head') the soloist is momentarily inverted!

"In *Of Beauty* the choreographer keeps more specifically to the poet's narrative: the girls plucking flowers by the stream, the boys crashing in on their prancing horses; the love-glance that unites one couple. In *The Drunkard in Spring,* set for four boys, MacMillan has treated drunkenness with great delicacy. It could so easily be vulgar, but his handling is as poetic, as lyrical, as Li-Tai-Po's and Mahler's. There is a wonderful moment when a question is asked: no conventional mime-signal, but a new unforced image that seems to sing.

"Throughout, MacMillan works with extraordinary economy. Only twenty dancers are involved, and the second half of the finale, the *Farewell,* the longest movement, is set only for three: the ballerina, her human partner, and *der Ewige,* the eternal one. A half-mask sets him apart from the others, even while he joins in their dances.

"Whither am I bound? I go, I wander into the mountains.
I seek rest for my lonely heart.
I am wandering toward my native place, my home.

I shall never roam in foreign lands.
My heart is at rest and waits its hour!

"And then Mahler adds the words already quoted. Solos, *pas de deux, pas de trois* succeed one another. Human parting, eternal beauty. It is all so simple, so clear, so poetic."

SONG OF THE NIGHTINGALE

Dramatic ballet in two scenes. Music by Igor Stravinsky. Choreography by Leonide Massine. Scenery and costumes by Henri Matisse. First presented by Diaghilev's Ballets Russes, February 2, 1920, Paris. Revived by Diaghilev's Ballets Russes, 1925, with choreography by George Balanchine and with Alicia Markova in the principal role.

This work, based on the story of "The Nightingale" by Hans Christian Andersen, is both an opera and a ballet; it has also been arranged by the composer as a symphonic poem. First performed as an opera, the score was revised to exclude voices for ballet performance. The opera consisted of three acts. In the ballet the first act was omitted, but it is necessary to mention its contents here.

The scene of Act One is the home of the nightingale, a wood in China, near the palace of the emperor. A fisherman glides his boat across a lake. He sings to himself. As his boat goes into the distance, we hear the magical song of the nightingale. At the emperor's order, the imperial chamberlain and his followers come to the wood to hear the nightingale. As they seek its voice, they mistake other sounds for the song of the bird. They are led to the nightingale by a humble scullery maid. The courtiers are disappointed in the bird's ordinary appearance, but delighted at its song. The nightingale accepts their invitation to sing at court.

SCENE ONE: THE IMPERIAL PALACE   When preparations have been made for his arrival, the Emperor of China enters his court. The nightingale is brought before him. The bird waits until the emperor signals her to begin her song, then commences.

The emperor is so enchanted with the song that he tells the bird she may have anything she wants. The bird replies that she has moved the emperor to tears and that is all the favor she requires.

Now the noble ladies, noting the high favor in which the lowly nightingale is held by their emperor, try to imitate her song. They fail miserably.

A gift arrives from the Emperor of Japan: a mechanical nightingale, beautifully wrought in gold and set with gems. The song of the toy bird delights the emperor and his court, and they forget the presence of the real nightingale. When the emperor tires of the toy and turns to ask the bird to sing again, she has disappeared. The angry monarch thereupon banishes the bird from his kingdom and makes the toy bird principal songster at his court.

SCENE TWO: THE EMPEROR'S BEDCHAMBER   The mechanical nightingale stands by the emperor's bedside. The emperor is dying. Death stands ready to welcome the monarch, and courtiers prematurely prepare the way for his successor. Spirits taunt the emperor with a list of his good deeds and wrongdoings. He cannot bear their chatter and calls for music. He begins to expire.

The song of the nightingale is heard. The return of this beautiful music delights the emperor, and Death is so struck by the wonderful song of the nightingale that he asks the bird to continue to sing.

The bird consents if Death will permit the emperor to live. Death makes this bargain and vanishes as the nightingale again takes up her song.

The emperor recovers completely and again offers to do any favor the bird wishes. The nightingale replies that his tears are her best reward and that she will sing to him every night until the rise of the sun.

Officials of the court, come to continue the deathwatch, enter the bedchamber. They are astonished to find the emperor standing in all his majesty, ready to receive them.

NOTES *Le Rossignol* (*The Nightingale*) was originally composed as an opera in three acts, which Serge Diaghilev presented for the first time at the Paris Opéra, May 26, 1914, under the direction of Pierre Monteux. Alexandre Benois designed the scenery and costumes. This work was first presented in the United States at the Metropolitan Opera House, New York, on March 6, 1926, with Marion Talley in the principal role.

Stravinsky revised his score for symphonic performances, eliminating the first act of the original. He was persuaded by Diaghilev that this new arrangement of his music might be suitable for ballet, and, now called *Le Chant du Rossignol,* the work was presented, with the choreography by Leonide Massine.

A new ballet to this music was my first assignment for Diaghilev's Ballets Russes, soon after I joined the company. I chose for the leading role in the ballet the young artist Alicia Markova, who had just joined Diaghilev's company, when she was only fourteen years old. We saw Markova dance in London, in 1924, at the studio of Serafima Asafieva, where she was a brilliant student. Diaghilev engaged her—the youngest dancer ever to belong to his company—immediately after seeing her dance.

Music by Igor Stravinsky. Choreography by John Taras. Scenery and costumes by Rouben Ter-Arutunian. First presented at the New York City Ballet's Stravinsky Festival, June 22, 1972, at the New York State Theatre, Lincoln Center, with Gelsey Kirkland as the Nightingale, *Elise Flagg as the* Mechanical Nightingale, *Francisco Moncion as the* Emperor, *Penny Dudleston as* Death, *and Peter Naumann as the* Fisherman.

When we were planning our celebration of Stravinsky's ninetieth birthday at the New York City Ballet, one of the composer's works that came immediately to mind was the *Song of the Nightingale,* which had been missing for too long a time from the ballet theatre. The ballet master John Taras undertook the choreography, which retells the lovely story in a most effective way. Writing after the premiere in the *Daily News,* the critic Sam Norkin said:

"John Taras' version of this fairy tale ballet with lavish, colorful decor by Rouben Ter-Arutunian was seen for the first time last night. This is the tale of the Chinese emperor who banishes his live nightingale in favor of a mechanical one, to his regret. Compassionately, the real bird returns in time to save the emperor from the throes of death. The intriguing character solos were beautifully designed and executed. The corps flourished long ribbons and there was a courtiers' pageant. This elegant new ballet belongs in the repertory."

SONGS OF A WAYFARER'

Music by Gustav Mahler. Choreography by Maurice Béjart. First presented by the Ballet of the Twentieth Century at the Forest National Arena, Brussels, March 11, 1971, with Rudolf Nureyev and Paolo Bortoluzzi. First pre-

sented in the United States by Rudolf Nureyev and Friends at the Uris
Theatre, New York, March 1, 1977, with Nureyev and Johnny Eliasen.

It has been said that Mahler's songs are the way to his symphonic works. The
Lieder eines fahrenden Gesellen (Songs of a Wayfarer) indeed leads themat-
ically to sections of the First and Fourth Symphonies, but it is in the beautiful
simplicity of the songs, the words here by Mahler himself, written after an
unhappy love affair, that we begin to catch the complexities the composer was
later to develop. The songs in this case, sung by a man accompanied by orchestra, tell the story of a young man who cannot forget the loss of a girl who
marries another. This theme is another variation on Schubert's *Die Schöne
Müllerin.* At first, the man is sick with grief and despair. Later, turning to nature, he is partially revived but in a wild impetuous third song the dagger that
stabs his breast returns and he cannot escape the girl's dominion over him. The
final song begins with the poet saying that eyes of blue are sweet but fill me
with fear and I must say goodbye to all I hold dear. He continues to wander,
lonely at night, finding rest under a linden tree, finally, where pain is forgotten.

It is important to know what the words are about, for although this ballet
does not reproduce the suggested action of the poem, its subject is the hero's
state of mind. The other dancer who moves with him is his alter ego, representing his states and shifts of mind. They are the only two performers, and
the emotions the hero lives through in his loss constitute the choreographic
fabric.

After the premiere of *Songs of a Wayfarer* in Brussels, the critic John Percival wrote to *Dance and Dancers* magazine that the character Nureyev por-
trays "exists pure and undiluted by any element of story telling, diversion or
contrast—just fifteen minutes of sheer theatrical impact which holds the huge
audience spellbound."

LA SONNAMBULA (*see* NIGHT SHADOW)

LA SOURCE

*Music by Leo Delibes. Choreography by George Balanchine. Costumes by
Karinska. Lighting by Ronald Bates. First presented by the New York City
Ballet at the New York State Theatre, Lincoln Center, November 23,
1968, with Violette Verdy and John Prinz in principal roles.*

My admiration for Delibes as a composer of music for ballet is no secret, I believe; with Tchaikovsky, who knew his music well, of course, and Stravinsky,
he is for me one of the three great musicians of the dance. Some years ago, in
1950, to music from his superb ballet score *Sylvia,* I arranged a *pas de deux*
that was danced by Maria Tallchief and André Eglevsky, and is still danced
by others, with some success. This was later expanded into a *divertissement*

for the New York City Ballet. That, however, was not enough and I kept wanting to use more of Delibes's music. The result is *La Source*, which uses music
from that work and from *Naila*, too. *La Source* puts together an earlier *pas de
deux* of that title with elements from the *Sylvia Pas de Deux and Divertissement*.

The ballet is in effect an extended *pas de deux*, with a soloist and a *corps de
ballet* of eight girls. The curtain rises on an empty stage—only a blue background—soon after the music starts. A boy carries on a girl and their dance begins. After an adagio, each does a variation. The soloist and girls dance now to
wonderfully familiar music by Delibes. In the midst of the ensemble, the couple return and the stage is left to them. The boy dances a second variation, as
does the girl. The ensemble takes the stage again briefly, before the girl and
boy return for a final flourish of dancing.

NOTES   Writing in *Dance and Dancers*, Patricia Barnes wrote of an early
performance: "The two dancers, Violette Verdy and John Prinz, dance the
work wonderfully well . . . The choreography and music for Prinz's second
solo are strongly rhythmic, and the dancing given to him is pure virtuosity—as
an example, a passage of whirling turns in *arabesque* which Prinz manages
with admirable dexterity. This gives way to a precise pizzicato solo for Verdy
ending in a *manège* of turns . . . Verdy gives the ballet just the right radiance,
and Prinz in his first created leading role confirmed that he is one of the most
interesting young dancers in America, or indeed, anywhere."

SOUVENIRS

*Music by Samuel Barber. Choreography by Todd Bolender. Scenery and
costumes by Rouben Ter-Arutunian. Lighting by Jean Rosenthal. First pre-
sented by the New York City Ballet at the City Center, New York, Novem-
ber 15, 1955, with Edith Brozak, Ann Crowell, Carolyn George* (Three
Young Girls), *Arthur Mitchell* (Attendant), *Roberta Meier and Richard
Thomas* (Husband and Wife), *Todd Bolender* (A Man About Town), *Roy
Tobias* (Another Man About Town), *Jillana and Jonathan Watts* (A Lady
and Her Escort), *Wilma Curley and Robert Barnett* (Bride and Groom),
Irene Larsson (The Woman), *John Mandia* (The Man), *Jane Mason* (A
Maid), *Herbert Bliss* (Man in Grey), *Patricia Savoia, Dido Sayers, Ronald
Colton, Gene Gavin, Walter Georgov* (Hotel Guests), *and Eugene Tanner*
(An Attendant).

The designer of *Souvenirs*, Rouben Ter-Arutunian, accurately sets the stage in
a recollection published in *Dance Perspectives:* "The costumes were taken
from the era of silent films and based on a set of fashion plates Todd Bolender
had found . . . The ballet was a spoof of a certain aura of pre-World War I,
and the set was more a series of prop pieces than a decor as such. There was
the prop of the elevator; a few palms, suggesting the court of a European-type
spa; a round banquette, found often in the vestibules of these hotels. Later

there was a set of doors; a couch with a tiger, and a beaded curtain; then, at the end, a pole with banners and a virile lifeguard. There was a minimum of decor. The emphasis was on the costumes, which brought out the satire."

The time is 1914, the scene the Palm Springs Hotel. In six swift episodes the ballet shows us some of the guests and what they are up to: how they make their entrance to the hotel and try to get acquainted; how a bride and groom can get mixed up in a corridor with a Man About Town and his Lady; how girls at dances pine for partners and how one who is pretty can dance with four men at the same time; how a wife can make a new conquest over an argument with her husband; how a siren entices a Man About Town into her boudoir and feigns to protect herself with a gun; how, on the beach the next afternoon, a lifeguard is the center of attention.

The music for *Souvenirs,* originally composed as a suite for two pianos, uses old dance forms that were popular in the days before World War I. The work was orchestrated by the composer for the New York City Ballet.

SPARTACUS

Ballet in four acts. Music by Aram Khachaturian. Choreography by Yuri Grigorovich. Scenery and costumes by Simon Virsaladze. First presented in this version by the Bolshoi Ballet at the Bolshoi Theatre, Moscow, April 9, 1968, with Vladimir Vasiliev, Yekaterina Maximova, Maris Liepa, and Nina Timofeyeva in principal roles.

Not the first Soviet ballet to this story, this one by Grigorovich appears to have attracted the most acclaim. A synopsis of the action, based on classical sources such as Plutarch, relating the fate of the Roman slave Spartacus, follows:

ACT ONE, SCENE ONE: SUBJUGATION The Roman legions terrify their captive empire. The army leader is Crassus, cruel, ruthless, and coldly flamboyant. After campaigns in Thrace, where the land has been pillaged and burnt, he brings back Thracian captives to Rome to sell as slaves. Among them are Spartacus and his wife, Phrygia. Spartacus expresses his love of freedom and his refusal to be reconciled to his new state of slavery.

ACT ONE, SCENE TWO: THE SLAVE MARKET The captives are left at the wall of the capital. Men and women are separated so that each will get a better price for the slave dealer from the Roman patricians. Phrygia is parted from Spartacus. Phrygia is desperate in her grief. Her beloved Spartacus has been reduced to slavery, and she herself is subject not only to Rome but the Roman master who has purchased her, and taken her from her husband forever.

ACT ONE, SCENE THREE: ORGY Phrygia has been bought by Crassus, and taken to Crassus's villa in Rome. Aegina, Crassus's concubine, mocks Phrygia's unhappiness and fears. For her, wine, gold, lust, power, and murder are the only facts of pleasure. Crassus is holding an orgiastic party for his friends. As the climax to this, two masked gladiators are brought in. They are to fight blindfolded until one of them is killed. They fight with blind and deathly intensity until one is slain. The victor takes off his mask. It is Spartacus.

Spartacus looks down at his unwitting victim with a terrified compassion. He has been forced to murder a fellow man, a slave like himself. What has he done? What more will he be forced to do?

ACT ONE, SCENE FOUR: THE GLADIATORS' BARRACKS Spartacus, returned to the Gladiators' Barracks, is full of remorse. He calls upon the gladiators to break their chains and escape from their shameful captivity. With superhuman efforts they do this, and overcoming their guards flee to freedom.

ACT TWO, SCENE ONE: THE APPIAN WAY It is night. The gladiators, escaping in glory, meet shepherds resting by the wayside. Inflamed with the spirit of revolt they call the shepherds to join them, and Spartacus's band is joined by many brave men. It is now an army, dedicated to remove the yoke of Rome. Spartacus is proclaimed its leader.

Alone, Spartacus muses on his forced acceptance of power. He is determined to lead his slave army to victory and to free thousands of Rome's victims. But he realizes that he first must find Phrygia and release her from Crassus.

ACT TWO, SCENE TWO: CRASSUS'S VILLA Spartacus discovers Phrygia in Crassus's villa to the south of Rome, and they are joyfully reunited. Meanwhile Crassus is giving a feast for the Roman patricians at which Aegina is also present.

Aegina contemplates Crassus and herself. She not only wants power over Crassus, but wishes to dominate the entire world. He tries to achieve it with power and cruelty, and she with cunning and duplicity. But they share the same ambitions—power, glory, and riches. Both need to acquire all and relinquish nothing.

ACT TWO, SCENE THREE: CRASSUS'S DEFEAT The patricians pander to Crassus and praise his power and victories. But the praise is cut short by the terrifying news that the villa is all but encircled by the advancing army of Spartacus. Crassus, Aegina, and the patricians depart in defeat, leaving Spartacus in possession of the villa.

Spartacus ponders on his victory. The Roman legions' success rests solely on the weapons of the legionnaires and the submission of the conquered. The Roman leaders themselves are cowards.

ACT TWO, SCENE FOUR: THE CONTEMPTUOUS GENEROSITY OF SPARTACUS Crassus has been captured and is brought before Spartacus, whom he recognizes as his former gladiator. The rebel soldiers want to execute the Roman general out of hand, but Spartacus asserts his authority and permits Crassus to save his life with the same kind of trial the tyrant imposed upon gladiators. But this time the singlehanded combat will not be blindfolded. The rebels are warriors, not murderers. Crassus fights Spartacus but is no match for him. At point of death Crassus pleads for mercy. With a gesture of contempt the rebel leader lets him go.

ACT THREE, SCENE ONE: CONSPIRACY The dishonored Crassus swears revenge, and Aegina fans his hatred. He calls his soldiers once more into the field, and Aegina sees them off to battle. Left alone, Aegina is full of hatred for Spartacus, fearing she might lose Crassus. She vows vengeance.

ACT THREE, SCENE TWO: THE ENCAMPMENT OF SPARTACUS Aegina steals into Spartacus's camp by night. Phrygia's fears are not helped by Spartacus's attempts to console her. Spartacus is told by a messenger that the Roman legions are advancing on him. He now puts forward his plan of battle, and the weaker among his captains are frightened by the daring of his tactics. Spartacus now calls upon all of them to take an oath of loyalty.

Spartacus, left to his thoughts, notes that the rebel forces will be defeated if there is dissension among their leaders. For all this death in battle is preferable.

ACT THREE, SCENE THREE: TREASON The faithful captains of Spartacus await his signal to start the combat and follow him at once. Those of weaker mettle might have followed their example, but Aegina appears out of the darkness bringing wine and whores. They succumb to temptation and fall easily to the advancing vanguard of Crassus's army. Crassus himself rewards Aegina for her help.

Crassus now knows that his revenge will not be complete until Spartacus has been killed, for he cannot forgive the humiliating stain to his honor he suffered as the captive of a slave. He will overtake the remainder of Spartacus's army and annihilate it.

ACT THREE, SCENE FOUR: THE FINAL BATTLE Spartacus's troops are encircled and his army is fast dwindling in the face of vastly superior forces. Spartacus is still fearless and begins to counterattack the legionnaires. Cunningly the Romans ambush him, triumphantly raising him on their spears as he dies a hero's death. Phrygia comes on to the battlefield to find his dead body. She is heartbroken.

NOTES The first Soviet ballet Spartacus had choreography by Leonid Yacobson, music by Khachaturian, book by Nikolai Volkov, décor by Valentina Khodasevich, and was first presented at the Kirov State Theatre in Leningrad, December 27, 1956, with Makarov and Zubkovskaya in the principal roles of Spartacus and Phrygia. Another treatment of the same story was made by Igor Moiseyev, with designs by Alexander Konstinovsky, and given at the Bolshoi Theatre, Moscow, March 11, 1958. This version, presented in the United States at the Metropolitan Opera House, New York, September 12, 1962, by the Bolshoi Ballet, featured Dmitri Begak and Maya Plisetskaya in the main roles.

Writing in the British magazine Dance and Dancers about her impressions of the Grigorovich *Spartacus,* Patricia Barnes said: "Grigorovich's choreography and conception are brilliant. This is an immensely moving work, filled with imaginative theatrical strokes and performed with blazing intensity by Mikhail Lavrovsky, who at this performance dominated the ballet. The dances are fairly clearly divided between the coldly neo-classic steps given to Crassus and his armies and the more plastique work, expressive and eloquent, for Spartacus and his followers.

"Particularly successful has been the way Grigorovich has used his male dancers. Never have I seen an ensemble used with such sweep and grandeur, and rarely has a dance work on such an ambitious scale succeeded so well in putting across its ideas and dramatic theme with such a minimum of mimetic fuss.

"The opening is startlingly effective. Crassus is seen standing in the center of the stage, arm raised, the lower half of his body surrounded by a wall of shields. Seconds later it is seen as the soldiers of his army spill forward filling the vast stage in a profusion of silver uniforms, shields and swords.

"The tragic ending is in its way as admirable as the ballet's opening. The black-clad grieving figure of Phrygia is lifted high by the followers of Spartacus and the body of her husband is handed up to her, together with his battle shield. She lays the shield on his chest and, eyes cast down, sorrowfully contemplates the dead Spartacus. It is a beautifully conceived scene and brings the curtain down on a work of truly heroic dimensions.

"Mikhail Lavrovsky's Spartacus is a wonder to behold. It is a superbly thought-out role and Lavrovsky has explored every dramatic nuance of it. From our first view of him as a slave in bondage, through his moments of resolution as he vows to free the slaves in captivity, until his final battle, he never departs from a characterization that is deeply felt and powerfully projected.

"A particularly superb episode is a gladiator fight. Two men, blindfolded, are brought in for the entertainment of Crassus's court, and fight for their lives. One kills the other—he takes off his helmet, and it is Spartacus, grieving over the fellow slave he has been forced to kill. As he stands there his face reflects the bitter anguish of his heart and with it we see the beginnings of his revolt, the first stirrings of his determination to free himself and his fellow-slaves from his ruthless captors.

"Almost as impressive was the sweetly passionate portrayal of Phrygia by Natalia Bessmertnova. Her dancing, so extraordinarily individual, had the elegiac beauty of a poem and her dark eyes and pale face caught at the heart.

"In a role that was created by Maris Liepa (and one could see how brilliant he must have been), young Mikhail Gabovich was extraordinarily good. If he looked on the young side, he could hardly be blamed, being under twenty, and he nevertheless gave a portrayal of genuine power. He presented Crassus as a warrior both arrogant and heartless, and his dancing was lithely elegant.

"The last of the four principal roles, Aegina, is the least interesting, being rather more of a stereotype. It was performed on this occasion by Svetlana Adyrkhaeva, who danced with a sveltely voluptuous allure.

"Finally, the dancing of the company, for which no praise could be too high. The men in particular outdid themselves in convincing one that the stage was filled with hundreds. Their attack and technical mastery was constantly outstanding."

Clive Barnes in the magazine of the Friends of Covent Garden, *About the House,* said that the Grigorovich *Spartacus* was "undoubtedly the most successful Soviet ballet since *Romeo and Juliet.*" The Grigorovich *Spartacus* was performed by the Bolshoi Ballet in London for the first time July 17, 1969.

LE SPECTRE DE LA ROSE

Ballet in one act. Music by Carl Maria von Weber. Choreography by Michel Fokine. Book by J. L. Vaudoyer. Scenery and costumes by Léon Bakst. First presented by Diaghilev's Ballets Russes at the Théâtre de Monte Carlo, Monte Carlo, April 19, 1911, with Vaslav Nijinsky and Tamara Karsavina. First presented in the United States by Diaghilev's Ballets Russes at the Metropolitan Opera House, New York, April 3, 1916, with Alexander Gavrilov and Lydia Lopokova.

This is a ballet danced by two people, a romantic *pas de deux.* The ballet has a simple story, but the story is so slight that we must refer to the actual dancing for an impression of the ballet. Its first performances convinced audiences that it was possible for two dancers, alone on a stage, to create a story and at the same time to create a mood in which that story could become real, like a lyric poem.

Le Spectre de la Rose is based on a poem, a poem by the nineteenth-century French poet and novelist and great critic of the ballet Théophile Gautier. Just as Gautier adapted the work of another poet, Heinrich Heine, to produce the romantic classic *Giselle,* so his own creative work gave to another age the inspiration for another romantic ballet. In Gautier's poem a rose addresses the girl who wore it to a ball. The rose is grateful for having danced with her all evening, grateful even for death on her breast, and tells the maiden that his ghost will continue to dance, at her bedside, all night long, to express his love.

The ballet *Le Spectre de la Rose* has a real setting but, as in *Giselle,* it is a dream that comes to life within this setting that creates its romanticism. The music is Carl Maria von Weber's *Invitation to the Dance,* as orchestrated by Hector Berlioz.

The curtain rises on a young girl's boudoir. The room is formal, high, and cool, with immense windows that look on to a garden. There is a bed on the right and on the left a small dressing table. The colors are blue and white, and as we look at the walls and the furniture and see the moon through the French windows, we imagine that the girl who lives here is demure and innocent. The room is uncluttered, plain in spite of its elegance; it makes you interested in the life it contains. The young girl enters. She is dressed formally, in a long white gown. She takes off the cape she wears about her shoulders, unties her bonnet, and we notice that she holds in her hand a red rose. She refuses to relinquish it as she moves about the room, turning slowly, dancing with an invisible partner, remembering the excitement of her first ball. She has come back from the dance to her familiar surroundings and finds the room a little old-fashioned; it has not changed as she imagines she has changed. She is in love. She presses her lover's rose against her cheek and sits down in a white chair near one of the windows. Half-asleep from fatigue, she still wishes to relive her first encounter with romance. But sleep soon overtakes her. Her hand falls from her face, and the red rose slips from her fingers to the floor.

There is almost no sound for a moment, and then suddenly, buoyantly, the orchestra plays at full volume a quick, intoxicating waltz. As this rush of sound fills the room, through the open window the spirit of the rose leaps in a high, smooth trajectory to stand poised behind the girl's chair. He dances alone as the girl sleeps, moving about the room effortlessly, seeming to touch the floor almost against his will, dancing with the lightness of the rose petals that adorn his body.

He touches the girl, and now—awake in her dream—she dances with him. When the two dance together to the soaring waltz, the young girl moves with the grace of the spirit she has invoked; as they glide and leap about the room, their dance is absolutely continuous, never-ending, unbroken in its flow of movement into movement; the only thing that can stop it is the music. The girl is inspired by her partner as naturally as she held the rose to her cheek and—with his strong, but tender, aid—she becomes not simply a beautiful young girl in love with love, but a part of the romantic night.

The dream cannot last. The waltz melody fades. The girl goes to her chair and sits as before, her arm limp at her side, pointing to the rose on the floor. The spirit of the rose hovers gently over her head in farewell and in a continuous movement rushes toward the window. He disappears into the oncoming dawn at the high point of a leap that seems never-ending.

The light of the sun disturbs the girl. She moves in her sleep, then wakens lazily, rubbing her eyes, not yet aware of where she is. She is still thinking of the spirit of the rose and looks for her mysterious partner. He is not there! She sees she is alone in her own room and that she must have been dreaming. Then she sees the rose on the floor at her feet. She picks it up gently and holds it against her breast, content that the dream is still with her.

Mikhail Baryshnikov first danced Le Spectre de la Rose at a performance during the first Hamburg Ballet Festival, dedicated to the memory of Nijinsky, June 22, 1975. Lynn Seymour was the girl. She had been advised on her role by Margot Fonteyn, who had known the recollections of Tamara Karsavina. Baryshnikov learned his role from André Eglevsky, the great premier danseur who had learned it from Fokine himself. John Percival reported to Dance and Dancers that he had never seen Baryshnikov "dance better in anything, and I have never seen this role so well done. It was a very demanding version of the choreography that he performed, but he danced at full strength throughout . . . His immensely powerful leaps were done with such soft strength, and he evoked perfectly the mixture of sensuousness and romance which is the ballet's essence." In 1976, Baryshnikov danced the role for the first time in the United States with American Ballet Theatre in a production with costumes by Stanley Simmons. Marianna Tcherkassky was the girl.

Nancy Goldner wrote in *Dance News* after the 1976 revival by American Ballet Theatre: "For once a legendary ballet made immediate sense. In a flash the story became important and full of implication. One could really see and feel the specter as an essence of nature and the sleeping beauty's shy, cautious, and finally rapturous acknowledgment of the rose as a story about maturation. As the dreamer, Tcherkassky was perfect . . . the perfect straight lady to Baryshnikov's more exotic role. He was a marvel of strength and clarity, but the fantastic aspect of his specter was that he reincarnates a historical style without looking mannered . . . The gentle but insistent way he insinuated himself into the girl's mind was a masterful fusion of contradictory impulses. Similarly, his approach to the steps was robust while his body was curling, introspective. Even in the big soaring jumps were his eyes and head lowered, somehow hidden. He was utterly manly, yet utterly a personification of spirit. One could recognize in this *Spectre* the Fokine who made the male solo in *Les Sylphides.*"

On December 6, 1976, the American Ballet Theatre production was seen on WNET television in the program "In Performance at Wolf Trap."

In an account of his training for *Le Spectre de la Rose*, the dancer Mikhail Baryshnikov has recalled (in the book *Baryshnikov at Work*) that the ballet requires a very special style. He characterizes it as "a kind of broken, soft harmony. It calls for the dancer to dance in a less stretched-out way, almost a little 'off.'"

SQUARE DANCE

Music by Arcangelo Corelli and Antonio Vivaldi. Choreography by George Balanchine. Lighting by Nananne Porcher. Square Dance Caller: Elisha C. Keeler. First presented by the New York City Ballet at the City Center, New York, November 21, 1957, with Patricia Wilde and Nicholas Magallanes in the leading roles.

Ballet and other forms of dance of course can be traced back to folk dance. I have always liked watching American folk dances, especially in my trips to the West, and it occurred to me that it would be possible to combine these two different types of dance, the folk and the classic, in one work. To show how close the two really are, we chose old music also based on ancient dances and a new setting, put the musicians on the stage on a platform like a bandstand, and invited the famous square dance caller Elisha C. Keeler to call out the dances. The dances he called out seem to be folk dances, but of course all the steps were purely classic. The spirit and nerve required for superb square dancing are close to what we always want in ballet performances, which is one way perhaps of explaining why so many American dancers are so gifted. The American style of classic dancing, its supple sharpness and richness of metrical invention, its superb preparation for risks, and its high spirits were some of the things I was trying to show in this ballet.

The music, all for strings, consists of Corelli's *Saraband*, *Gigg*, and *Badiniere* from the *Suite for Strings*, and Vivaldi's *Concerti Grossi*, Op. 3 and Op. 10, and the *Violin Concertos*, Op. 3 and Op. 12, *Concerto for Violin and Strings in E major*, Op. 3, No. 12 (first movement), and *Concerto in B minor*, Op. 3, No. 10. Much of this eighteenth-century music was of course derived from old folk dance forms and rhythms that were later refined for the courts of Europe.

In 1976 we decided to revive *Square Dance* at the New York City Ballet, but with some changes, doing it without the caller and with the orchestra in the pit. I also put in a new dance for the boy. Kay Mazzo and Bart Cook danced the first performance of this revival, May 20, 1976, at the New York State Theatre. The following day, Anna Kisselgoff in the New York *Times* noted that while in the first version, you would have heard a call by Mr. Keeler and the music would repeat with the dancers performing the step, now the lead dancer calls the tune by dancing to it and the others follow him. "He is the caller, but uses movement instead of words."

SQUARES

Music by Zoltan Szilassy. Choreography by Hans van Manen. Decor and costumes by Bonies. First presented by the Netherlands Dance Theatre at the Théâtre de la Ville, Paris, June 24, 1969. First presented in the United States by the same ensemble at the Brooklyn Academy of Music, New York, March 30, 1972.

Squares is a way of looking at dance in a setting that frames the action. The setting, on a raised platform, invariably a variation on the square, varies: it is an enclosure, an upright outline, or a frame of light, fluorescent or ultraviolet. It hems the ten dancers in, liberates them, or sets them off.

STARS AND STRIPES

Ballet in five campaigns. Music by John Philip Sousa, adapted and orchestrated by Hershy Kay. Choreography by George Balanchine. Scenery and lighting by David Hays. Costumes by Karinska. First presented by the New York City Ballet at the City Center, New York, January 17, 1958, with Allegra Kent, Robert Barnett, Diana Adams, and Melissa Hayden and Jacques d'Amboise in the leading roles.

Ever since I came to the United States I have liked watching parades and listening to Sousa's marches. For many years in the back of my mind was the hope that one day I might find an opportunity to do a ballet using his music. The problem was always the arrangement of the music for dancing and it was not until I had heard Hershy Kay's arrangement of Gottschalk's music for *Cakewalk* that I thought I had found a solution. I talked about the possibility with the composer, who was just as enthusiastic as I was about Sousa. We went over all the pieces we might use and planned their arrangement together. Kay's score was just what I wanted.

We dedicated the ballet to the memory of Fiorello H. La Guardia, the late mayor of New York City who had epitomized America to so many of us for so many years.

The ballet is a kind of balletic parade, led by four "regiments." The five campaigns or movements feature each regiment in turn and at the end they all combine. In the first movement, to Sousa's *Corcoran Cadets* a majorette leads twelve girls. Another girl leads the second campaign in the *Rifle Regiment* march. *Thunder and Gladiator* march is danced by a regiment of boys, and the fourth, to the *Liberty Bell* and *El Capitan* marches, is a *pas de deux*. All regiments participate in the fifth campaign, the *Stars and Stripes* finale.

Karinska created brilliant costumes for this ballet and it seemed to me that David Hays's setting, and the final display of the American flag he arranged, were ideal.

THE STEADFAST TIN SOLDIER

Music by Georges Bizet. Choreography by George Balanchine. Setting and lighting by David Mitchell. Lighting by Ronald Bates. First presented by the New York City Ballet at the Saratoga Performing Arts Center, Saratoga, New York, in July 1975, with Patricia McBride and Peter Schaufuss. Conducted by Robert Irving.

Hans Christian Andersen's stories are endlessly interesting. I am always coming back to them—sometimes for ballets. This particular story, which I first arranged in *Jeux d'Enfants* in 1955, tells of a toy soldier who goes through an endless series of trials and difficulties for the sake of a doll who does not pay any attention to him. At the end, both toys fall into a fire. What happens in the ballet is a little different, but I hope clear. The doll is an automaton ballerina, a bit like the toy made by Dr. Coppélius but with more soul. She is so enchanted with herself that she just keeps on rejoicing in her steps and gestures. She adores herself and ignores entirely the soldier, who presents her with his heart. Still, she ignores him. Her dancing so overheats her that she opens the window for relief. A draft rushes into the room and sends her up the chimney. The tin soldier mourns her and rejoins his platoon. All he has left is his paper heart.

THE STILL POINT

Music by Claude Debussy. Choreography by Todd Bolender. First presented by the Dance Drama Company, 1954, with Emily Frankel and Mark Ryder. First presented in New York, April 10, 1955, at the YMHA. Presented by the New York City Ballet, March 14, 1956, with Melissa Hayden and Jacques d'Amboise in leading roles. Presented by the City Center Joffrey

*Ballet, September 24, 1970, with Pamela Johnson and Dennis Wayne. Light-
ing by Jennifer Tipton. Assistant to Mr. Bolender: John Mandia.*

The Still Point, which takes its title from T. S. Eliot's poem *Four Quartets,*
is a dance drama arranged to music by Debussy—the first three movements of
the *String Quartet,* Opus 10, transcribed for orchestra by Frank Black. The
drama is about a young girl who, lonely at first and rejected, finds love. She
endures jealousy, embarrassment, and torment as her girl friends rejoice in
young love. Rejected by them, she rejects herself and suffers. She so wants a
young man of her own that she dreams, too, and simply waits, fearing a little a
real encounter. Finally, a boy comes, watches her as she dreams, then touches
her shoulder. She reacts at first as if she had been stung and appears to resist
him. Realizing that he has found an extraordinarily sensitive girl, the boy is
gentle with her. She watches him dance, then they dance together, becoming
closer, too, in thought, as they touch. They find in each other, at the end, the
dreams they have had.

NOTES   Writing in *Dance Magazine* of *The Still Point,* the critic Doris Hering said that "Mr. Bolender has uncanny insight into the feelings of young
women. His girl in *Mother Goose Suite,* his debutante in *Souvenirs,* and the
tortured protagonist of *The Still Point* are all sisters under the skin—poignant
sisters seeking fulfillment in romantic love. Of them all, the girl in *The Still
Point* is the most touching because she is delineated with the most depth and
at the same time with the most simplicity. In fact, simplicity is the prime vir-
tue of this little ballet. Mr. Bolender has had the courage and the care to let
the dancing speak out honestly without any mimetic overlay. And in Melissa
Hayden and Jacques d'Amboise in the leading roles; and Irene Larsson, Roy
Tobias, Jillana and John Mandia in secondary roles, he found responsive instruments. As the lonely girl, Melissa Hayden wove endless nuance and pathos
into her portrayal, and yet the danced outlines were contained and beautifully
clear. As her friend, Jacques d'Amboise communicated the steady masculinity
that we have associated heretofore only with Igor Youskevitch."

STIMMUNG

*Music by Karlheinz Stockhausen. Choreography by Maurice Béjart. First
presented by the Ballet of the Twentieth Century at Brussels University,
Brussels, Belgium, 1972. First presented in the United States at Carnegie
Hall, New York, by the same ensemble, February 14, 1974.*

This ballet is a full-evening concert occasion based on the ambience of sound,
a ballet that requires the attention of an evening's entertainment, without in-
termission. It was inspired by a piece of music, the title of which, *Stimmung,*
carries a number of interesting meanings. Perhaps the best of these meanings,
and the clearest for the dance involved here, is what might be called voiced
atmosphere, or ambience. It is important to realize what the composer meant

in thinking of the piece that accompanies the ballet and what the choreographer contemplated in the course of his composition to this music. Béjart describes his intention, plus the action:

"The ballet *Stimmung* is born from music and through music, and has no other purpose than to prolong in space, by tangible forms, the vibration which comes from the voice, the inner self, the absolute center of man—and which strives to touch this absolute vibration (which some call divinity).

"The ballet is ritual—'magic names'—and magic gestures. Doesn't every gesture which completely absorbs our being, and which is performed with complete concentration, have some impact on the total life of the cosmos? 'I raise my little finger,' said a Zen master, 'and the course of the stars is disturbed.'

"In *Stimmung* the gestures of life become gestures of dance as the dancers interpret and join daily life, inspired by the different intonations of the accompanying voices creating the diverse 'ambience' which succeed each other in the course of the day.

"As in life, from time to time man passes from sadness to joy; eroticism becomes prayer; joy transfigures the ritual; abstraction becomes lyricism; dance—mathematical equation; humor appears under each attitude and (visible or invisible) directs this ceremony which pretends to be serious without taking itself seriously.

"Ten dancers create the subject matter and its multiple combinations, such as the image of the 'Tekraktys' of Pythagoras, the triangle that contains the first ten numbers which are the basis of all mathematical combinations. The eleventh dancer in turn will incarnate himself in this interrogation until, when the cycle is completed, only the breath (which is the beginning and the end of everything) continues to exist.

"No improvisation is permitted, but each dancer finds himself or herself confronted by a series of possibilities which can be resolved differently each performance. The steps, which are 'regulated,' can be combined and repeated by each performer in a different way a number of times, which depends only on the imagination, the schemes, and the mutations which the act itself undergoes each performance according to the singers' inspiration."

The inspiration of the singers is, of course, largely dependent on what the composer has written. He has said that the work was built upon a series of "magic names" assembled for him by an American anthropologist, the names of some thirty deities from varied religions and cultures: Vishnu, Uranus, Uwoluwo, Rhea, Venus, et al. These names are invoked in the sung text. Stockhausen has recalled that the title of the piece, *Stimmung*, originally meant "harmony of pure intervals . . . In addition, and far from the least important, the German word 'Stimmung' corresponds to the notion of fluidity, of frame of mind (for example, one speaks of 'gute Stimmung'—good ambience—or of 'schlechte Stimmung'—bad ambience). It evokes the harmonious resonance of man and his environment. Finally the word 'Stimmung' includes 'Stimme,' meaning voice!"

The work is sung by six singers, who enter simultaneously with the dancers at the start of the piece. Seated about a lamp on a raised platform at the back of the stage, they sing meditatively, their voices amplified so that the softest nuances are heard. Each singer has a command of nine models and eleven magic names that he can, after a "scheme of form" and according to the context, introduce freely. "The others," writes the composer, "can react to these models and magic names with some 'transformations,' 'digressions variées,' 'oscillations,' 'unisson.' Nothing is directed.

"Surely *Stimmung* is meditative music. Time is abolished. One listens to the inside of the sound, to the inside of the harmonic spectrum, to the inside of a vocal INSIDE, with the most subtle undulations. It is scarcely explosive. All the senses are awakened and calm. In the sensuous beauty shines the beauty of the eternal."

THE STONE FLOWER

> *Ballet in three acts. Music by Sergei Prokofiev. Libretto by Mira Prokovieva, based on a story by Pavel Bashov. Choreography by Yuri Grigorovitch. Scenery and costumes by Simon Virsaladze. First presented by the Bolshoi Ballet at the Bolshoi Theatre, Moscow, February 12, 1954. Revised and presented by the Bolshoi Ballet at the Kirov State Theatre of Opera and Ballet, Leningrad, July 6, 1958. First presented in the United States by the Bolshoi Ballet at the Metropolitan Opera House, New York, May 4, 1959, with Vladimir Vasiliev, Marina Kondratieva, Maya Plisetskaya, and Vladimir Levashev in the principal roles.*

The Stone Flower, Prokofiev's last ballet, writes the choreographer Yuri Grigorovitch, "tells of the fate of the stone carver Danila who wishes to see the full power of stone and to show its beauty to the people. The creative urge which possesses Danila and the desire to create more perfect art is the leitmotif of the ballet."

ACT ONE   Danila, a young craftsman, desires to create a malachite vase that will be as simple and beautiful as a flower. He is not satisfied with one vase he has made; the secrets of the malachite seem to elude him. His mind is full of these problems as he meets his beloved Katerina and goes with her to their betrothal party. There Severyan, a bailiff, attempts to purchase the vase Danila has made, but the artist refuses to sell. In the course of the ensuing argument, Severyan becomes fascinated by Katerina and tries to embrace her. Danila and their friends defend the girl and force the bailiff to leave. There is a lyrical scene between the lovers and Katerina departs.

Danila smashes the vase and begins work on a new piece of malachite. The spirit of the malachite appears and with a touch of her hand shapes the stone, but as she disappears the stone resumes its original form. Danila pursues the spirit, who sometimes appears as a fairy, sometimes as a lizard, finally revealing herself to be the Mistress of the Copper Mountain. There she leads Danila to her underground realm where she is surrounded by maidens who are the spirits of the various precious stones. Danila is dazzled as he watches the blossoming of these fairy stone flowers.

ACT TWO   Katerina, missing Danila, dances pensively alone. Severyan attempts to seduce her, but she defends herself with a sickle and he is forced to leave. Danila, meanwhile, is learning the secret of the malachite as he works away in the palace of the Mistress of the Copper Mountain, who is enthralled by him. Katerina searches for Danila at the village fair. There again she is compelled to defend herself against Severyan, who tries to carry her off. The Mistress of the Copper Mountain now enters, transfixes Severyan, places him under a spell, and leads him to his death.

ACT THREE   Still searching for her beloved, Katerina comes into the forest. As she rests there beside a fire, a fair maiden emerges from the flames and leads her to the Copper Mountain. In the palace, Danila has realized his dream. He has created a stone flower. As the spirits of the stones dance in crystalline patterns, the mistress of the palace again tries to tempt him. But Danila's thoughts are only of Katerina. He realizes that he must leave the palace. Angered at his rebuff, the Mistress of the Copper Mountain decides that Danila will be turned into a statue and kept at the palace.

When the fire maiden brings Katerina, there is an emotional *pas de trois* between the boy and the two girls who love him. Danila in the end chooses Katerina and the fearlessness of their love obliges the Mistress of the Copper Mountain to release Danila from her spell. The young lovers return to their village, to share with them the joy of their love and the secret of creating beauty from stone. The Mistress of the Copper Mountain appears to bid them goodby, and vanishes.

NOTES   Describing the ballet, the choreographer has written:

"The foundation for the musical and choreographic structure of the ballet is the combination of the real-life scenes and fantastic dreams. The dance language is fundamentally based on folk choreography. The scene of the party, with the ceremonial features, is constructed in the form of a Ural dance rhapsody.

"Fantastic scenes utilize the classical dance. The movements of the classical dance characterizing the world of the Mistress of the Copper Mountain have a sharp, clean-cut style, emphasizing the nature of formation of stones and crystals. In the dances of the stones there should be reflected the sparkling, shining play of reflected beams. Dances of the main characters Katerina and Danila are also classic, the courage of the human heart showing broadly in the ballet. These dances are quite different from the dances of the stones, since we are dealing with a human quality. The dances of Katerina and Danila have elements of folk dancing and features of Russian painting technique.

"The classic dance also serves as a foundation for the character of the Mistress of the Copper Mountain. This fantastic creature personifies the splendor and beauty of nature. She has two faces; the face of powerful and strong secret force and the face of human justice, full of feminine charm. The author, Bazhov, makes her appear both as a lizard and as the spirit of malachite. This contradictive character determines the means for creating the character for the

ballet. Her dances tend to be classic in style for the stone dances and must
have very flexible elements for the sliding lizard so vividly créated by Bazhov.

"A special role in the ballet is played by Severyan, the bailiff. He is a ruthless, soulless person—the only negative person in the story. Naturally the style
varies from the style which outlines the other characters. Severyan, as with
other characters of the ballet, must be expressed with full dance and plastic
language which the choreographer must create."

SUMMERSPACE

*Music by Morton Feldman. Choreography by Merce Cunningham. Scenery
and costumes by Robert Rauschenberg. Lighting by Nicholas Cernovich.
First presented by Merce Cunningham and his Dance Company at the
American Dance Festival, Connecticut College, New London, Connecticut,
August 17, 1958, with Merce Cunningham, Carolyn Brown, Viola Farber,
Cynthia Stone, Marilyn Wood, and Remy Charlip. First presented by the
New York City Ballet at the New York State Theatre, April 19, 1966, with
Anthony Blum, Kay Mazzo, Patricia Neary, Sara Leland, Deni Lamont, and
Carol Sumner. Lighting by Ronald Bates.*

Summerspace, which Merce Cunningham has subtitled "a lyric dance," is the
second work by this distinguished modern dancer for the New York City Ballet
(the first being *The Seasons,* created for Ballet Society in 1947). The music, a
commissioned score, is composed in Morton Feldman's graph system. The
background by Robert Rauschenberg is a pointillist skyscape and this idea is
continued in the costumes. The choreographer revised his original work for the
ballet idiom. There are six dancers—four girls and two boys.

Writing about his original production in *Dance Magazine,* Merce Cunningham recalled that the principal momentum behind the piece "was a concern for steps that carry one through space, and not only into it. Like the passage of birds, stopping for moments on the ground and then going on, or
automobiles more relentlessly throbbing along turnpikes and under and over
cloverleafs. This led to the idea of using kinds of movement that would be
continuous, and could carry the dancer into the playing area, and out of it."

The resultant space-play is a continuum of movement that appears to swim
in an intense haze of summer heat. The stage space here is a field, in fact,
rather than the usual proscenium-enclosed space with a center of interest, and
as the choreographer explains, since all points are of equal usage, "one does
not lead to any particular other. The eye is not guided but allowed to jump
throughout the space. The corners, in a conventional theatre stage, are nuggets
that can sparkle. The momentum, too, is different. In a general way, the
Balanchine dancers proceed in a vertical accent. 'He usually likes the accent
down.' The force of *Summerspace* is horizontal. The stillnesses are dealt with
as that, and not as positions in preparation." (From an interview with Merce
Cunningham in *Ballet Review,* Vol. 1, No. 4.)

SWAN LAKE

*Dramatic ballet in four acts. Music by Peter Ilyich Tchaikovsky. Book by
V. P. Begitchev and Vasily Geltzer. First presented, with choreography by
Julius Reisinger, at the Bolshoi Theatre, Moscow, March 4, 1877, with
Pauline Karpakova in the leading role. This incomplete and unsuccessful
production was superseded by a new choreographic version by Lev Ivanov
and Marius Petipa, which was presented for the first time in a complete,
four-act production at the Maryinsky Theatre, St. Petersburg, February 8,
1895, with Pierina Legnani in the double role of Odette-Odile. Act Two of
this version was presented for the first time at the Maryinsky Theatre, St.
Petersburg, February 29, 1894, with Legnani as Odette. Scenery by Botcharov and Levogt. First presented in western Europe in complete form in
Prague, Czechoslovakia, June 27, 1907, with choreography by Achille
Viscusi. First presented in the United States at the Metropolitan Opera
House, New York, December 20, 1911, with Catherine Geltzer as Odette-
Odile, Mikhail Mordkin as Prince Siegfried, and Alexandre Volinine as
Benno. This production was staged by Mordkin after the Petipa-Ivanov
choreography. Scenery by James Fox. First presented in England in complete form by the Sadler's Wells Ballet at the Sadler's Wells Theatre, London, November 29, 1934, with the Petipa-Ivanov choreography reproduced
by Nicholas Sergeyev; Alicia Markova as Odette-Odile, Robert Helpmann
as Prince Siegfried. Scenery and costumes by Hugh Stevenson. Presented
complete by the San Francisco Ballet, in a version staged by William Christensen, 1940. The revised Sadler's Wells production, with scenery and costumes by Leslie Hurry, was first presented in the United States October 20,
1949, with Margot Fonteyn and Robert Helpmann. Presented complete with
the original choreography of Lev Ivanov staged by David Blair, by the At-
lanta Civic Ballet, August 24, 1965. Presented complete with Ivanov's choreography staged by David Blair by American Ballet Theatre at the Civic
Opera House, Chicago, February 16, 1967. Scenery by Oliver Smith. Costumes by Freddy Wittop. Lighting by Jean Rosenthal. Presented in varied
versions by many companies.*

Musically, and as a dance drama, *Swan Lake* is undoubtedly the most popular
of all classical ballets. It is possible to see at least a major portion of the complete *Swan Lake*—the famous second act—danced by almost every ballet company in the world. And the ballet is a favorite of ballerinas as well as audiences. All leading dancers want to dance *Swan Lake* at least once in their
careers, and all audiences want to see them dance it. To succeed in *Swan Lake*
is to become overnight a ballerina. Petipa and Ivanov are to the dancer what
Shakespeare is to the actor: if you can succeed in their choreography parts,
there is a suggestion that you can succeed at anything.

Why is it that *Swan Lake* has been so consistently popular with both audiences and dancers for so long a time? What about its chief rivals in the classi-

cal repertory—*Giselle, The Sleeping Beauty,* and *Coppélia*—why are they not as popular? If we set aside practical considerations (unlike *Swan Lake,* these other ballets cannot successfully be shortened into one-act versions; the part does not provide the spirit of the whole), we find the answer in *Swan Lake's* romantic and tragic story and the music that accompanies its unfolding.

The heroines of these other classics all have some relation to the real world—they are peasant girls or princesses. Strange things may happen to them, but they live within determined conventions. The heroine of *Swan Lake* has another story. She is a princess of the night; she is all magic, a creature of the imagination.

On one level, her story is a girl-meets-boy story: girl meets boy, girl loses boy, girl gets boy, and then both are lost. What prevents this from being silly is the character of the girl. She is Queen of the Swans, a beautiful bird, except for the brief time—between midnight and dawn—when the mysterious sorcerer, Von Rotbart, allows her to become a beautiful woman. In the world of sky and water she is at home, but in the real world, where romance is possible, she seems to be irretrievably lost. The great love she comes to have for a worldly prince is doomed at its start; she has no control over her destiny.

The Swan Queen is the opposite of the Firebird, the bird triumphant; she is immediately pathetic, a creature whose initial fear and consuming love interest us immediately. The dignity and courage and authority she possesses as Queen of the Swans become, in the ballet, the dignity of the woman in love. Humanly speaking, even in this magical world she inhabits, she is never unreal or absurd to us, because we see that love does not shatter her dignity; rather, it ennobles her beauty and explains her universal appeal.

ACT ONE: THE GARDEN OF PRINCE SIEGFRIED'S CASTLE   Before the curtain rises, an overture warns us of the impending tragedy of the story. After the woodwinds have introduced the principal romantic theme, and the strings have taken it up, there is a faltering: a soft, gradually building questioning by the strings. And the answer comes in boldly asserted warnings by the crashing of cymbals and resounding trumpet calls. But soon, over these crescendos, the romantic theme returns at full, conquering volume. It quietens, and the curtain rises.

This is Prince Siegfried's twenty-first birthday, and the young prince is celebrating the occasion in the garden of his ancestral palace. Young people from the surrounding estates have come to pay tribute to him. Benno, friend to the prince, is talking to a group of twelve young men. Wolfgang, the prince's old tutor, comes in merrily and is almost immediately attracted to the bottles of wine that stand on a table at the right. The atmosphere is one of anticipation, and as the trumpets blare the climax of a spirited march, the host enters. The handsome prince is not haughty; neither is he familiar. He is delighted to see his friends, thanks them as they congratulate him, claps his old tutor on the back affectionately, and prepares to enjoy the festivities that have been arranged in his honor.

First there is a *pas de trois,* danced by two girls and a boy. (Since the Diaghilev company's second-act version of 1911, this *pas de trois* has often been performed as a *divertissement* in Act Two. Sometimes it is danced by Benno and two cygnets, sometimes by a first huntsman and two swan princesses, as in the production by the Sadler's Wells Theatre Ballet. Where the *pas de trois* is not interpolated in Act Two, the music for the variation of the *danseur* is almost invariably used for a variation by Benno.) For the dance of the two girls and a boy, the music is lightly melodic and flowing. Now each dances alone: the first girl performs to blithe, tripping music that increases in speed; the boy, to strongly accented rhythms that mark the precision of his *entrechats* and turns in the air; and the second girl, to a light, almost joking theme. Climactic music accompanies the final display of virtuosity that all three perform.

While most of the assembled guests have been watching the dance, the old tutor has been privately celebrating the prince's coming of age by drinking as much wine as possible. Just as everyone begins to enjoy the party, the conviviality is disturbed by the entrance of the princess mother and her four ladies in waiting. Siegfried goes to his mother and escorts her into the garden. She observes his friends with considerable disdain; there is an effort to hide the wine bottles, and poor old Wolfgang finds himself in obvious disfavor. The princess mother indicates to her son that his coming of age is hardly the occasion for levity. He responds to this opinion dutifully, but with apparent resistance. Siegfried is further disturbed when his mother points out to him that he must soon choose a wife. Her suggestion is in the nature of a command, and Siegfried turns stubbornly away. Tomorrow night, his mother reminds him, his birthday will be celebrated formally at a court ball, and there, from among the loveliest ladies of the land, he must select his future wife. Siegfried sees that argument is impossible; as he kisses his mother's hand and leads her out of the garden, he seems to bend to her will.

Wolfgang gestures his pleasure at the departure of the dominating princess mother. He attempts to restore the spirit of the happy occasion by claiming that, old as he is, he can dance better than any of the younger men. Everyone laughs at him, but Wolfgang is not to be outdone. He approaches one of the village maidens, who giggles as he takes her by the hand and begins to dance. The melody to which he partners her is subdued and charmingly sentimental, sweetly echoing the joys of youth. Soon Wolfgang is having such a good time that he tries to surpass himself by whirling his partner around and around. In the process he becomes dizzy and falls to the ground, taking his partner with him.

Now Prince Siegfried is convinced that the only thing to do is to enjoy himself to the utmost: tomorrow, after all, is another day. The prince signals that the celebration should continue. Wine is poured for all the guests, and village couples dance a vigorous polka that completely restores to the gathering its natural spirit of gaiety. Still Siegfried broods; the celebration has failed to dispel his apprehension in regard to the morrow.

Night begins to fall. Benno knows that Siegfried must be distracted for the remainder of the evening. He hears the sound of fluttering wings overhead, looks up, and sees in the sky beautiful wild swans in full flight. Against the sound of harp and strings, the oboe sounds softly the theme of these enchanted birds. Benno suggests that the prince form a hunting party and go in search of the swans. Siegfried consents; crossbows are brought, and flaming torches are provided to light the way through the woods. The village girls circle the stage and exit. Wolfgang alone is unwilling to accompany the hunting party. As the full orchestra takes up the mysterious and doomful theme that heralded the swans, Wolfgang tells Siegfried that he is too old, that he will remain in the garden. The young men bid him good-by and rush off into the night. The curtain falls as the old tutor stands alone in the center of the empty garden, his bottle his only friend.

ACT TWO: A LAKESIDE   While the curtain is lowered, the music continues to develop the theme of strange foreboding. Then all is quiet for a moment. As the music resumes, the curtain rises on a forest scene; a great lake, its shining surface undisturbed by the wind, shimmers in the moonlight. The music begins again. The hunting party enters, led by Benno. All carry crossbows. The men look above them through the trees, searching for the swans; they are astonished to see that the swans have settled on the lake and, within a few feet of them, are placidly gliding by. Leading the group of swans is a beautiful white bird, apparently their queen. The diamonds in her crown reflect spangles of light over the dark water.

A flourish from the orchestra heralds the arrival of the prince. The hunting party bows to him. Benno hastens to point out to Siegfried that the swans can be seen close by. The prince directs the men to hasten along the lakeside ahead of the swans; he is about to follow them off, when he sees something in the distance that gives him pause. He stops, close by the lakeside, then retreats hurriedly across the glade to conceal himself. He has seen something so strange and extraordinary that he must observe it closely in secret.

No sooner has Siegfried hidden himself than the most beautiful woman he has ever seen enters the quiet glade. He cannot believe his eyes, for the girl appears to be both swan and woman. Her lovely face is enclosed by swan feathers, which cling closely against her hair. Her pure white dress is embellished with soft, downy swan feathers, and on her head rests the crown of the Queen of the Swans. The young woman thinks she is alone. She poses in arabesque, then remains almost motionless, softly bending her cheek down against her shoulder in a gesture reminiscent of a swan smoothing its feathers. The music informs us of the pathos of this gesture, and Siegfried is so enchanted by the magical creature that he enters the glade. He moves quietly, lest he disturb her.

The girl is terrified, her whole body trembles, her arms press against her breast in an attitude of almost helpless self-protection; she backs away from the prince, moving frantically on points that drive desperately against the ground. Her arms seek the air for freedom, for escape. The prince, already in love, begs her not to fly away. The girl looks at him and gestures that she is afraid. Siegfried wonders why. She points to his crossbow and draws her arm back as if to let fly an arrow, then holds her arm over her face, cowering with fear. The prince indicates that he will never shoot her; he will protect her. The girl bows to him in gratitude.

The prince now asks her who she is, why she is here? The girl's hands enclose the crown on her head: she is Odette, Queen of the Swans. The prince salutes her and says that he will honor her, but how is it that she is the Swan Queen? The Swan Queen asks for his patience and points to the lake. The lake, she indicates, was made by her mother's tears. Her mother wept because an evil sorcerer, Von Rotbart, made her daughter into the Swan Queen. And swan she must always be, except between midnight and dawn, unless a man should love her, marry her, and never love another. Then she will be saved and be a swan no longer.

Siegfried holds his hands to his heart and says that he loves her, that he will marry her and never love another. He swears his faithfulness. Now angry at the fate of his love, he demands to know where this Von Rotbart hides himself. Just at this point, the magician appears at the lakeside. His owl-like face is a hideous mask; he reaches out his claws, beckoning Odette to return to him. [In one-act versions of *Swan Lake,* this lengthy mime passage is often shortened and the music is used to accompany a dance in which the prince, his bow set aside, follows the dancing Swan Queen, lifts her as they circle the stage, embraces her, and supports her gently in poses until she breaks away from him at the entrance of Von Rotbart.] Von Rotbart points menacingly at Siegfried. Odette moves between them, begging Von Rotbart for mercy. Trumpets sound in blaring, warning crescendo. The prince seizes his bow, kneels, and aims it at the magician. Odette beseeches him to stop and runs diagonally across the stage toward Siegfried. She touches his stretched bow and stands over it and her lover in extended arabesque. Von Rotbart disappears. Siegfried rises and embraces Odette. The music quietens. The prince puts his arm about the girl, and they go toward the forest.

The prince tells the girl that she must come the next evening to the court ball. He has just come of age and must marry and at the ball he will choose her as his bride. Odette replies that she cannot come to the ball until she is married—until Von Rotbart no longer has power over her—otherwise the magician will expose her and their romance will perish. She knows, she tells Siegfried, that Von Rotbart will stop at nothing to keep her in his power, that he will contrive artfully to make Siegfried break his promise to her, and that should he do so, should be be faithless, Von Rotbart will cause her own death. Siegfried again swears his faithfulness.

When the lovers have left the glade, Odette's charges, all the swans who, like herself, assume human form only between the hours of midnight and dawn, dance in from the lakeside. They form a single serpentine line that moves toward the front, then face the audience in a triangular grouping.

Soon Benno, the prince's friend, comes upon the dancing swans. They encircle him, rushing past him with their fluttering arms. Benno, unaware of the mystery of these creatures, thinks only of the hunt. The swans cower in fear and rush together in a close group by the lakeside. Benno hails the rest of the hunting party. The huntsmen marvel at his discovery and aim their crossbows at the swans. Suddenly the music crashes warningly; Siegfried runs in and behind him comes Odette. The Swan Queen stands before the group of trembling swans and stretches out her arms to protect them; the huntsmen must kill her first. As Odette begs the men for mercy, Siegfried orders them to lower their bows and to respect the magical birds. When the huntsmen have learned that, like Odette, the swans are really unfortunate girls in the hands of an evil magician, they remove their caps and bow in apology to the maidens.

Siegfried and Odette again vanish into the forest, the huntsmen leave the scene, and the swan maidens come forward in three columns to dance. They dance to a charming waltz; their ensemble is dominated by two swan maidens who emerge from the group to dance in unison between lines formed by their friends. When the dance is over, the swans gather together in picturesque groupings to form a final tableau.

Now the swan maidens gather at either side of the stage. Siegfried enters with Benno. The harp sounds a series of arpeggios. The prince searches for Odette among the swans. He does not find her. The huntsmen return and stand among the swan maidens. Siegfried stands with his friend in the center of the glade. At the back, behind them, Odette enters softly. She touches Benno's shoulder, poses for a brief second in arabesque, then comes forward. It is as if she had not seen the prince. The harp is plucked gently. Odette rises on point, then sinks slowly to the ground. She rests on her left knee, her right leg stretched before her. She bends down low, her arms reach forward like enclosing wings, and to the quiet rhythm of the music her body stirs expectantly. Siegfried comes forward, reaches down to her hands, and raises her. The solo violin begins quietly the wistfully romantic theme of the adagio. Odette pirouettes with slow, romantic adroitness in his arms. Now her love supports her as she bends low in a deep arabesque. Each of the huntsmen, observing the beauty of this love duet, now stands between two swan maidens, his arms about their waists.

Odette moves to Benno, and the prince admires her loveliness as his friend holds her in arabesque. The beautiful Swan Queen returns to her lover, moves in supported attitude, then rests for a moment against his breast. She moves now slightly away, rises on point, takes Siegfried's hand, and then—raising her right leg straight before her—removes her hand from his; for a fraction of a second, as she lifts both arms up, the idyllic nature of this dance is luminously clear: the relation of Odette and Siegfried is one of complete sweetness and absolute trust. Odette falls back, and Benno catches her gently in his arms as her right leg closes against her left. Benno lifts her up, she returns to the prince, nestles against his shoulder as he embraces her softly, and the movement is repeated a second time. Siegfried puts his arms about Odette at its conclusion and leads her toward the lakeside. The swan maidens turn in arabesque, to the gently hopping rhythm of the woodwinds, and cross the stage before the lovers. As the solo violin resumes, Odette and the prince run forward quietly between the swan maidens. Siegfried lifts Odette high in his arms to the violin's music; he lifts her again, and then she pirouettes in his arms. He continues to lift her effortlessly to the demand of the theme; she turns to his encircling arms, then moves away on point with a gesture of obeisance and love.

Now a number of the swan maidens are arranged in a diagonal line across the stage. The huntsmen, standing in back, lift some of the girls to their shoulders. The prince moves back. Odette goes to him, and Siegfried opens his arms to her. She turns away then and, hopping softly, moves in arabesque down the line formed by her charges. Siegfried follows her adoringly and, taking her about the waist, lifts her at arm's length high above his head. He lifts her again, releases her, and, as she reaches the end of the diagonal, lifts her to carry her to the right side of the stage. The violin repeats the theme of the first lifts of the adagio, and this time, to the melody, Odette executes supported arabesques followed swiftly by pirouettes that she terminates with an open pointing of her leg to the left. These movements are repeated with the music.

The swan maidens are now grouped on the left. After the final pirouette, Siegfried stands close behind Odette. She leans back softly against him and balances. The prince opens his arms as Odette opens hers and gently he moves her arms close to her body, as if he were quieting her frightened wings. Siegfried moves slightly from side to side, gently rocking his love. Odette rushes away, seemingly compelled to resist the embrace, and balances in arabesque, both arms encircling her head. From behind, the prince takes her arms, moves them back close to her body, and Odette leans back against him, now confessing the power of her love for him.

The adagio nears its end. Siegfried turns the Swan Queen slowly as she stands on point, her right foot trembling in *petits battements*. She turns a final series of slow pirouettes in his arms and then is held by the prince; both arms over her head, her left leg extended to the side. Siegfried holds her thus, then releases her; she balances for an instant and then, holding her pose, falls to the side; at the last breathless moment she is caught in the arms of her lover's friend. The adagio is over. The two lovers and Benno leave the stage.

Four cygnets appear and dance with bright, youthful precision a *pas de quatre* that is accompanied by lightly bouncing music of great charm. This is followed by a dance for two swan princesses. Here the music is openly joyous, uninhibited in its bounding, youthful expression of happiness in newfound love.

Just as this dance ends, we notice that dawn is approaching. Odette returns and dances a variation that is at first modestly lyrical; her arms stretch back and her neck arches backward as she balances in arabesques, and we feel that to this beautiful woman such a pose is the most beautiful and natural thing in the world. The music increases in momentum, and the variation finishes with a dazzling diagonal of rapid pirouettes across the stage.

The swan maidens are alerted by the coming light and prepare to return to the lake. Odette, in their midst, comes forward and—from the front of the stage toward the back—executes to the driving rhythm of the rapid music a series of quick, desperate movements that reflect her fear at her departure from her lover. Siegfried beseeches her to stay, but she cannot. Benno kneels before her. Now impelled to become again the Swan Queen, she rushes toward Benno and stands in full flight on his extended knee. Siegfried reaches out for her, lifts her down gently. The swan maidens have responded already to the return of the mysterious music that presaged the first appearance of the magical creatures: Odette and Siegfried are alone. Von Rotbart appears by the lakeside, beckoning Odette to come to him. She is helpless and must obey. She holds out her arms yearningly toward Siegfried, but her feet carry her back toward the lake. Her body trembles with helplessness, and she glides farther and farther away from him, to disappear in the new dawn. Siegfried reaches out toward her, unable to console himself by her promise to return.

The huntsmen enter the glade. Benno comforts the prince, and then, at the sound of wings overhead, all look up to see the swans in full flight, led by their queen. The curtain falls.

ACT THREE: THE GREAT HALL OF PRINCE SIEGFRIED'S CASTLE   The time is the following evening. The ball that the princess mother has arranged in honor of her son is about to take place. After a long and regal musical introduction, the curtain rises on the hall of the palace. There is a roll of drums, and a march begins. Here in the great hall, the royal thrones are placed on a dais to the right; on the left, with a short flight of steps leading down to the ball-room, is the formal entrance. Across the back, stretching into the distance, is a long, curved colonnade.

A flourish of music marks the entrance of two royal pages. The prince and his mother enter the room. The assembled guests bow to them as they proceed to the dais. The princess mother turns to speak to her son. Siegfried looks out over the ballroom with a blank stare; he is thinking of his meeting with Odette and his vow to be faithful to her. His mother, jealous of his preoccupation, addresses him somewhat in the manner of Gertrude upbraiding Hamlet: "Are you ill? You must pay attention to our guests; they are beginning to remark your strange behavior." The prince throws off his thoughts and assures his mother that he will not fail in his obligations.

Ambassadors from foreign lands, attired in colorful native costume, have come to pay tribute to the prince on his coming of age. A trumpet sounds a flourish, and a herald announces the arrival of six beautiful girls invited by the princess mother as prospective brides for her son. The girls are attired identically in stunning evening dresses and each carries a large feathered fan. The princess mother nods to them, and they begin to dance before the prince to the strains of a courtly waltz.

Siegfried pretends to watch them, but actually he thinks only of the lakeside glade and his meeting with Odette. His mother taps him on the arm and warns him that he must dance with his guests. The prince descends from the dais and dances briefly with each of the would-be brides. He dances automatically, with no interest, holding the girls casually about the waist and scarcely looking at his partners. The girls are dismayed at his indifference, but cannot display their displeasure too markedly lest their hostess be disappointed in them. Siegfried returns to the dais and again sinks into melancholy.

The princess mother rises and approaches the prospective brides. She thanks them for the lovely waltz and congratulates them on their beauty. Now she turns to the prince, asking him to confirm her opinion. Siegfried gestures that the girls are very pretty, indeed, but he does not wish to marry any of them. He loves another. He bows coldly to the girls. As his mother upbraids him, the music is interrupted suddenly.

Again the trumpet sounds a flourish. All the guests turn to watch the door. A herald hastens to inform the princess mother that a strange couple has arrived.

He does not know who they are, but avows that the woman is a creature of rare beauty. Siegfried looks expectantly toward the door. His mother orders that the guests be admitted. There is a crash of cymbals, the room darkens mysteriously, and the music hurries warningly into a repetition of the theme that marked the fate of the Swan Queen.

The light returns, and a tall bearded knight enters with his daughter. As the knight introduces himself and his daughter, Odile, to the princess mother, Siegfried—excited almost beyond control—stares at the beautiful girl. Although dressed in somber black, she is the image of his beloved Odette. [Although not originally designed for the same dancer, Odile for many years has been danced by the same ballerina who performs the role of Odette; Odette-Odile has become the most famous dual role in ballet.] Odile returns his stare with a steady glance of cold, but passionate, interest. In the distance, framed by an arch of the colonnade, Odette is seen holding out her hands to Siegfried. The prince is so enchanted by the girl he supposes to be the Swan Queen that he does not notice Odette's warning. The vision of the Swan Queen fades. Siegfried takes Odile by the hand. Now he foresees that the ball will be a happy occasion after all! He escorts Odile into the palace garden. Odile's father watches their departure with interest. Unknown to the prince, he is in reality not a knight at all, but Von Rotbart, the evil magician, who has transformed himself and his conniving daughter in order that Siegfried will be deceived and break his promise to Odette never to love another. Convinced that his trickery will doom Odette and Siegfried, Von Rotbart turns to the princess mother with a gracious smile. She is charmed by his flattery and—hopeful that her son will marry a lady of rank, as Odile appears to be—invites Von Rotbart to sit beside her on the dais.

Now the guests from foreign lands, who have come to honor the prince on his birthday, come forward to dance. First, two Spanish couples dance a quick and supple *divertissement* to the sound of music reminiscent of the melodies and rhythm of Spain. Next five Hungarian couples line up and, to the slow, anticipating measures of the music, commence a *czardas* that gathers in speed to end in a whirling finish. A vigorous Polish mazurka danced by eight couples concludes this series of *divertissements*. Von Rotbart indicates his appreciation of this entertainment to the princess mother and then suggests that his daughter, Odile, is the most beautiful dancer at the ball. Just as the princess mother is about to wonder where her son has taken Odile, Prince Siegfried appears with the stunning girl. Von Rotbart leaves the dais and tells Odile that the time has come for her to dance before the princess mother and Prince Siegfried. The orchestra sounds a rhythmic flourish, and the *pas de deux* between Odile and the prince begins. [When it is performed as a separate *divertissement*, this dance is known as the "Black Swan," or "Magic Swan," *pas de deux*. As a *divertissement*, the *pas de deux* necessarily lacks the dramatic impact it possesses as a part of the complete *Swan Lake*.]

This dance dramatically displays the cunning of Odile and the infatuation of the prince. In opposition to the adagio of Act Two, it has another kind of grace: it is full of pride and arrogance, rather than tenderness; it has the cold, dazzling light of a bright diamond. As Odile goes to Siegfried, Von Rotbart stands on the right, watching with guile and satisfaction. The prince welcomes his new love with joy: now his mother and the whole court will see how wonderful she is. Odile pirouettes across the ballroom floor, then turns rapidly in Siegfried's arms. Von Rotbart calls to her, and she goes obediently to her father, standing in arabesque with her hand on his shoulder. Von Rotbart whispers in her ear. Odile looks back at the prince and nods. She has grown confident with the success of her disguise and, when she returns to the prince, is determined to display her power over him with even more breath-taking skill. Siegfried supports her adoringly as she bends low in arabesque, but then Odile lets go his hand to stand alone, poised, balanced, splendidly self-sufficient. She goes back to Von Rotbart, and this time the impetuous prince follows her. After receiving more instructions from her father, she rejoins her lover, who supports her with glowing pride in bold and confident movements. For a moment the two are separated. They promenade across the ballroom floor, Odile walking with masterful authority and steely confidence, and meet in the center of the stage to resume the dance. Suddenly Odette again appears in the distant colonnade. Von Rotbart immediately notes her presence and signals to Odile, who steps between Siegfried and the vision. Odette extends her clasped hands to Siegfried, despairing of her fate if he abandons her. The enchanted Siegfried has no idea that she is there; the cunning Odile smiles at him—a cold, even smile in which he can discern nothing but warmth for his passion. The vision of Odette persists, and Odile becomes angry at this interference. She runs to Siegfried and places her hands over his eyes. Siegfried is so infatuated that he regards this gesture as flirtatious and fails to see that Odette, all hopes gone, has vanished, weeping, in the distance.

The *pas de deux* continues. Odile, now the winning seductress, carries her conceit still farther, and the innocent prince is utterly in her hands. The dance ends as the prince kneels before Odile and the proud, evil girl stands over him in high, conquering arabesque. With the final note of the music, she gives a curt, triumphant toss of her head.

The prince now dances a variation expressive of his great joy in rediscovering the girl he supposes to be Odette. Odile follows with a quick final dance designed to whip Siegfried's passion still further, and she succeeds in this brilliantly. Her variation contains a dazzling circling of the stage with small, swift turns, a series of quick, close movements performed in a straight line from the front of the stage to the back, and finally a series of thirty-two *fouettés*. These relentless, whipping turns sum up her power over the prince and, with disdainful joy, seem to lash at his passion. Helplessly bewitched, he rejoins his enchantress for a brief final dance.

Siegfried then approaches Von Rotbart and asks for Odile's hand in marriage. Von Rotbart immediately consents. Siegfried announces his decision to his mother, and Odile bows before the princess mother. Von Rotbart, still unsatisfied, addresses the prince further: he asks Siegfried to swear an oath of fidelity of Odile, asks him to promise that he will never love another. Siegfried's love for Odile is so great that he is offended by this request, and then, too, he knows that he has heard those words before. Why should they be asked again, he wonders. He looks at Odile, and his fate hangs in the balance.

The music hesitates. He takes the oath. At that moment there is a crash of thunder. The ballroom darkens. The theme of the abandoned Odette screams above the orchestra. Quick flashes of light show the frightened courtiers fleeing the ballroom, the distraught princess mother, and Von Rotbart and Odile standing before the prince in a final triumph of self-revelation. Their hideous, cruel laughter Siegfried cannot bear, and he turns to see in the distance the pathetic figure of Odette, reaching out to him helplessly, her body racked with sobs. He falls to the floor in an agony of guilt.

ACT FOUR: THE LAKESIDE   The swan maidens have gathered by the side of the lake. They are sad and wistful at the fate of their queen. Their grief is reflected in the still tableaux they form with a group of small black swans who have joined them and in the dance the little swans do with their elders to soft, tender music. They yearn for the return of Odette. When she appears, weeping, they try to comfort her, but she tells them they do wrong to give her false hope. "I have been betrayed and I must die: the magician has won."

The music cries out with her grief, and she runs toward the lake. Two swan princesses intercept her and urge her to wait. They remind her that Siegfried is only human, that he could not have known the power of sorcery and thus could have had no suspicion of Von Rotbart's design. "You must wait," they advise her, "and hear the prince." "No," she gestures, "I have lost him and could not bear it."

Some of the swans hear Siegfried in the distance, calling for Odette, and tell her that he approaches. The Swan Queen orders a group of little swans to stand before her so that the prince will not discover her. Siegfried rushes into the clearing and frantically searches for Odette among the swans. Desperate, he asks the swans if they have seen her; he is about to abandon hope when the swans that surround Odette bend down and he sees her standing among them. He runs to her and takes her in his arms, asking for her forgiveness, swearing his infinite love. They go into the forest, and the swan maidens continue their dancing. When the lovers return, Odette has forgiven her lover, but she tells him—with tears streaming down her smiling face—it is no use, for what is her forgiveness alongside her death, which now must surely follow. "Von Rotbart is relentless. My life was forfeit if I should be betrayed. Only in death am I released from his power."

Now Odette dances to music that is tenderly beautiful. She moves softly in a long diagonal enclosed by the swans and, at the moment of her imminent death, expresses her undying love for the prince. Von Rotbart, enraged at Odette's delay, hovers over the scene disguised as a monstrous owl. He vows vengeance on her and all the swans. The swan maidens tremble as Siegfried defies Von Rotbart, who is momentarily overpowered by the strength of the prince's love for Odette.

The lovers embrace as Von Rotbart disappears. Odette then reminds the prince that only in death will she be released from Von Rotbart, only in death will she be free to love him forever. Her gestures are dramatic and sure as she tells him this, and suddenly she rushes across the stage in a swift diagonal to the shore's edge and throws herself into the lake as the music reaches a surging climax. Siegfried is motionless for a moment and stands helpless among the grieving swan maidens. Then, knowing that life without Odette will be nothing, he declares that he will follow her. He runs down the same diagonal that Odette took to the lakeside and drowns himself.

Siegfried's sacrifice of his love that Odette might not be destroyed by the evil magician has caused Von Rotbart's downfall. Again the malevolent owl-like creature appears, but only briefly. He lingers among the distraught swan maidens only long enough to see that love has triumphed in the end. He dies.

The stage darkens. The music softens. The swan maidens form two diagonal lines at the right, and as the light of day gradually rises in a soft glow, we see their figures bent low to the ground in grief at the loss of their queen and in gratitude for their own liberation from the evil sorcerer. Then, on the waters of the lake, a gleaming jeweled bark glides into view, its ornaments brilliant in the morning sun. Odette and Siegfried, clasped in each other's arms, move in the magical bark to a new and perpetually happy life. The swan maidens raise their heads, and their arms move softly, like ripples on the water, in quiet farewell to their queen.

NOTES   March 4, 1952, was the seventy-fifth anniversary of the first performance of *Swan Lake*. In observance of this occasion, Anatole Chujoy wrote the following authoritative article in the April 1952 issue of the informative and popular publication, *Dance News:* "Troubled less than it is in our days, a civilized world would have rested from its labors on March 4 to celebrate an important occasion in the history of ballet and music, the diamond jubilee of *Swan Lake,* the greatest romantic-classic ballet of all times.

"*Swan Lake,* as it were, stands at the highest point of the curve which represents the history of the source of all ballet as we know it today—the romantic-classic era which began with *Giselle* in 1841 and ended with *Les Sylphides* in 1909—the greatest period the classic dance has ever known. *Swan Lake* is often accepted as a strictly classic ballet; actually it is much more a romantic ballet. In conception, content, structure and emotion it is much closer to *Giselle,* for example, than to *The Sleeping Beauty.* In fact, it owes some of its choreographic invention to *Giselle.*

"*Swan Lake,* which has been variously called the greatest ballet of all times and an old war horse, was first presented on March 4, 1877, at the Moscow Imperial Bolshoi Theatre.

"Two years earlier, in the spring of 1875, the Director of the Bolshoi Theatre, V. P. Begitchev, commissioned Tchaikovsky to compose a score for a ballet then called *The Lake of the Swan,* based on a libretto written by the director himself, who was also a playwright of sorts, in collaboration with Vasily Geltzer (the future father of Catherine Geltzer, subsequently the famous prima ballerina of the Moscow Theatre [and the first to dance the complete *Swan Lake* in the United States]).

"Tchaikovsky hoped to create in *Swan Lake* a score that the Bolshoi Theatre would accept with the same regard as orchestras accepted his symphonic works. This hope was not realized. The choreographer assigned to the ballet was Julius Reisinger, a hack ballet master who possessed neither the talent nor the taste to choreograph a work to the music of a major composer.

"The ballerina, Pauline Karpakova, was a run-of-the-mill dancer past her bloom, who insisted upon interpolating sure-fire 'numbers' from other ballets in her repertoire to replace some of Tchaikovsky's music which she could not appreciate, understand or even count. The première of the ballet was to be a testimonial gala in her honor and she was not going to take any chances.

"When the première of *Swan Lake* took place it was a disappointment to everybody, especially to its composer. Herman Laroche, a well-known music critic, composer and friend of Tchaikovsky, wrote about the première as follows:

" 'If during the creation of the ballet he [Tchaikovsky] had pictured fairy-tale splendor and brilliance he must have felt a bitter disappointment when he saw the work of the ballet master on the stage. I must say that I had never seen a poorer presentation on the stage of the Bolshoi Theatre.

" 'The costumes, decor, and machines did not hide in the least the emptiness of the dances. Not a single balletomane got out of it even five minutes of pleasure. The greater, however, was the joy of the melomane. From the very first measures of the introduction one felt the hand of a true master; a few pages later we knew already that the master was in excellent humor, that he was fully at the height of his genius.'

"It cannot be said that *Swan Lake* was a total failure. It had a moderate success with the spectators and it remained on the stage until 1883 during which time it was given thirty-three performances.

"According to another contemporary of Tchaikovsky, N. Kashkin:

" 'It [*Swan Lake*] was kept in the repertoire until the scenery was worn to shreds. The music also suffered a great deal. The substitution of the original numbers with others was practiced to an even greater extent, and toward the end almost a third of the music of *Swan Lake* had been substituted with that from other ballets, usually from the most mediocre ones.'

"When the scenery finally gave out the directorate of the Bolshoi Theatre took *Swan Lake* off the repertoire, and the ballet was not revived until January 1901, when Alexander Gorsky, a talented choreographer not sufficiently appreciated by his contemporaries and almost entirely neglected by historians, staged a new version of it.

"The version of *Swan Lake* which came down to our generation dates back to the St. Petersburg production choreographed by Lev Ivanov and Marius Petipa and first presented at the Maryinsky Theatre on January 17, 1895, more than a year after the death of Tchaikovsky.

"The production of *Swan Lake* at the Maryinsky came about in a rather unorthodox manner. The initiative for it stemmed from Ivanov, not from Petipa, as is generally supposed.

"After Tchaikovsky died of cholera on November 6, 1893, there was a general upsurge of interest in his work. His operas were being revived by Imperial and private opera houses, his orchestral compositions, even those which earlier had not been successful, were being played by symphonic organizations all over Russia.

"On March 1, 1894, an evening honoring the memory of Tchaikovsky was given at the Maryinsky Theatre. The program included several excerpts from the composer's operas and what is now called Act II of *Swan Lake*, independently staged for the occasion by Lev Ivanov, Marius Petipa's assistant who carried the unpretentious title of second ballet master and *regisseur*, the same Ivanov who had staged in 1892 Tchaikovsky's *The Nutcracker*.

"The role of Odette, the Swan Queen, was taken by Pierina Legnani, the great Italian ballerina, who had made her debut at the Maryinsky the year before in the ballet *Cinderella*, in which she introduced to St. Petersburg ballet-omanes her famous thirty-two *fouettés*. The short ballet caught the imagination of the audience.

"Petipa saw the performance and decided to profit by its success. He ordered a repetition of the performance at a gala evening and on that occasion placed his name alongside Ivanov's (and ahead of it) as choreographer. The second performance had an even greater success and Petipa decided to revive the whole ballet.

"Richard Drigo, the composer of the ballets *Talisman, The Magic Flute* and others, who was then conductor of the Maryinsky, was commissioned by Petipa to clean up the Moscow score. Drigo, on the whole, did a conscientious job, but found it necessary for some reason to eliminate several numbers from the ballet and substitute for them a few of Tchaikovsky's short 'salon pieces,' among them *Op. 72 Nos. 11, 12,* and *15,* as well as one number in Act III by an anonymous composer (Drigo himself, perhaps).

"Outside Russia there has often been speculation about what choreographer staged which part of the ballet. Indeed on several occasions the entire ballet, through sheer negligence, has been credited to Petipa, which is not only historically incorrect but also a great injustice to Ivanov. It has been established beyond any doubt that Petipa staged Act I (called Act I, Scene 1 in the original St. Petersburg version) and most of Act III (called Act II in the original version). Ivanov staged Act II, which constitutes the familiar one-act version (called Act I, Scene 2 in the original version), and Act IV (called Act III in the original version).

"Unlike the Moscow opening, eighteen years before, the St. Petersburg première on January 17, 1895, was a huge success. The occasion was also a testimonial gala for Pierina Legnani, who danced the double role of *Odette-Odile* and could not restrain herself from injecting her thirty-two *fouettés* from *Cinderella,* this time as the coda of her *pas de deux* in the ballroom scene (Act III).

"The two acts of *Swan Lake* which Lev Ivanov was permitted to stage were a great achievement for the choreographer and the culmination of his long but frustrated career at the Maryinsky, too little of which is known to the outside world.

"In staging the two acts Ivanov went contrary to the basic artistic direction in ballet during the second half of the nineteenth century, which aimed to demonstrate the technical proficiency of the dancer and the spectacular solution of complicated technological choreographic problems. Ivanov built Acts II and IV on musical principles, thus breaking a strong and generally accepted tradition. An excellent example of this is the adagio in Act II.

"In Petipa's ballets the adagio usually unfolds against the background of a picturesque backdrop or an immobile group of dancers who do not take part in the action. Ivanov's composition of the adagio in Act II is a duet with an active ensemble which accentuates and participates in the dance of the two principals. It is motivated entirely by the construction of the music, which was inspired, according to memoirs of Tchaikovsky's friends, by the vocal duet in his opera *Ondine*, the score for which he had destroyed before the opera was ever produced.

"This may sound less than revolutionary now, but in 1894 it was quite a step forward, so much so, in fact, that no choreographer dared to take a similar step until Michel Fokine, at the very height of his avant-garde Fronde'ism, utilized Ivanov's idea in *Les Sylphides* in 1909. Fokine also made use of some of Ivanov's choreography in *The Dying Swan* which he staged for Anna Pavlova in 1905.

"But Ivanov did more than just violate the canonical principles of the construction of the adagio by subordinating it to the problems of the musical themes. His two acts of *Swan Lake* very effectively dethroned the ballerina as the alpha and omega and, one might say, the *raison d'être* of the ballet. For some forty years Petipa constructed his ballets *ad majoram ballerinae gloriam*. The ballerina was all that mattered and everyone and everything else was on the third plane. Not so in *Swan Lake*. Here Ivanov treated the ballerina only as one of the protagonists. Here she either participates in the dances together with other dancers or alternates with them, or, if she performs a solo passage, the other dancers echo or accompany her. But no one leaves the stage for her variation, no one freezes into the painted backdrop.

"The adagio in Act II is a remarkable example of Ivanov's choreography, a testimonial to his choreographic and musical genius, but it is not the only example. One has but to think of the witty and compositionally perfect *pas de quatre* of the cygnets, the man's variation, and especially the entire last act to realize the great talent of Ivanov that was never allowed to achieve full bloom because of Petipa's dictatorial position in the Imperial Theatre.

"An appreciation of Lev Ivanov in English and an analysis of his work on *Swan Lake* and *The Nutcracker* is still to be done, and this writer hopes to do it before very long. It can be said here, however, that Ivanov's two acts of *Swan Lake* have been an inspiration to many contemporary choreographers whose origin was in prerevolutionary Russia. If one man can be considered the precursor of modern ballet, especially in the musical approach to choreography, that man was Lev Ivanov.

"Since its St. Petersburg première *Swan Lake* has never left the stage. The greatest ballerinas of prerevolutionary Russia, among them Mathilde Khessinska, Olga Preobrajenska, Anna Pavlova, Tamara Karsavina, and Olga Spessivtzeva, have vied for the privilege of dancing it.

"The current production of *Swan Lake* in Russia is based on the Ivanov-Petipa version, revived by Agrippina Vaganova in 1935. It is being given both in Moscow and Leningrad and is unquestionably the most popular ballet of the repertoire of both state theatres. It is also the ballet always presented on gala occasions and it is safe to say that every American and Western European diplomat and dignitary visiting Moscow has seen it.

"In Western Europe the full-length *Swan Lake* is only being given by the two British companies, the Sadler's Wells Ballet and the International Ballet. Both productions are based on the St. Petersburg version and both were staged by Nicholas Sergeyev, a former *regisseur* of the Maryinsky Theatre.

"The familiar one-act version of *Swan Lake* dates back to the Diaghilev Ballets Russes, which presented the ballet first in two acts [November 30, 1911, at the Royal Opera House, Covent Garden, London, with Mathilde Kchessinska, *prima ballerina assoluta* of the Imperial Theatre and Vaslav Nijinsky. Mischa Elman played the solo violin passages for these performances] and later in one act (ca. 1925). With the exception of the small French groups, nearly all professional contemporary ballet companies in America and Western Europe have a one-act version in their repertoire, based more or less on the Ivanov choreography."

Swan Lake is always changing. That is as it should be. Tradition in performance is, unlike teaching, discontinuous, as my friend Lincoln Kirstein has said. It is always interrupted, depends on shifts of directorships, changes of parts, whims of choreographers, dancers, designers, musicians, and the public. Only recently has a way been found to make permanent a record of a performance and I imagine that in the future it will be possible to know about a number of "definitive" *Swan Lakes*. But I also suspect that artists will want always to change it, to remake it for themselves. That is what many of us have done, and I hope will keep on doing.

My own version of Act Two, for example, first presented by the New York City Ballet November 20, 1951, retained then only the central *adagio* and the *pas de quatre*. But I have made many changes in the ballet since and we have new scenery and costumes, too, by Rouben Ter-Arutunian.

In England, the Royal Ballet, which has revised its production a number of times, has arrived at a useful compromise by retaining its older, Sergeyev version of the original in the repertory of its national touring company and presenting newer versions at Covent Garden and on international tours. This keeps the old well intact and at the same time makes possible innovation. One of the major revisions in the Royal Ballet's production was December 12, 1963, when Robert Helpmann staged a production with scenery and costumes by Carl Toms that had new dances by Frederick Ashton and restagings of other dances by Rudolf Nureyev and Maria Fay. Margot Fonteyn and David Blair danced the principal roles.

The Bolshoi Ballet and the Kirov Ballet productions of the complete *Swan Lake* have become familiar. Other productions of interest include a version by Vladimir Bourmeister for the Moscow Stanislavsky Ballet (1953), Rudolf Nureyev's staging for the Vienna State Opera (1964), with Margot Fonteyn and himself, and Erik Bruhn's production for the National Ballet of Canada (1967).

Bruhn's production was fortunately filmed for television in Canada. Produced and directed by Norman Campbell, with scenery and costumes by Desmond Healy, this National Ballet of Canada presentation featured Lois Smith, Erik Bruhn, and Celia Franca. In an hour and a quarter, Bruhn compressed for the television audience the entire ballet, employing new choreography and new arrangements, too, of the score. This version was presented in the United States by the Public Broadcasting Service, July 17, 1972, over Channel 13, New York.

On June 27, 1972, Natalia Makarova of American Ballet Theatre danced *Swan Lake* with the Royal Ballet in London. Clement Crisp wrote in London's *Financial Times:* "Odette and Odile are both magical beings, the one enchanted, the other an enchantress; the particular distinction of Natalia Makarova's interpretation was marvelously to convey this quality of magic.

"Her entrance as Odette is quite extraordinary; the Swan Queen is terrified, a fraught creature at Siegfried's appearance, trembling in his arms. Like Melisande when Golaud finds her, she is lost, a prey to unfathomable terrors, and throughout this first encounter we are made aware how heavily Von Rotbart's spell lies upon her. Infinitely pathetic, she seems not of this world and the menace of the enchanter's presence never seems to desert her during the whole of the act. The result is a profoundly moving characterization, expressed through dancing of exquisite perfection.

"With the Kirov, Makarova's Odette was a marvel; now it seems even more amazing. The great sound-act duet pours out in an unbroken cantilena, long-breathed, phrased with the inevitability of genius. The pure, classic schooling, the lightness that imbues her every movement, make the dancing float on the music—albeit Makarova demands slow tempi and is not, I would hazard, the most musical of dancers. But an *assoluta* is to be allowed her own way with the score, and the means amply justify the end when it results in an interpretation at once classically controlled, in the Kirov manner, and totally communicative of the Swan Queen's tragedy.

"In her Kirov performances, Makarova's Odile was something below the standard of her Odette; this is now no longer true. She plays the third act with prodigious brilliance; the choreographic variants she offers are acceptable since the enchantress in the ballroom shines with a hectic glitter that is totally compelling. No prince could resist this malign beauty, and Donald MacLeary's fine Siegfried is no exception. He is obsessed with her, and very properly so; Makarova's shining presence is hypnotically attractive—witness the fact that after prolonged stage calls following her variation, the truth of her impersonation seemed to carry right through them: we were not cheering a ballerina but Von Rotbart's creation.

"If the fourth act seemed slightly flat, I would blame the production rather than the interpreter; it is unfamiliar to Makarova, and not particularly effective anyway. What shone through the relative dullness of the staging here was the beauty of her style, with its delicacy and impeccable placing, the expressive force of her poses, and such small but thrilling things as a *pas de bourrée* which seems to meet the ground with a feathery lightness. I imagine that some viewers will consider Makarova 'cold' as Odette; her performance is still absolutely true to the canons of the Kirov style in which the very statement of the choreography must contain the essence of the role without any external 'acting' —and I find it entirely satisfying. My only hope is that her interpretation be preserved on film—it is essential for future generations to be able to study it, and to marvel at its magnificence."

There have been a number of films made of *Swan Lake,* or parts thereof (the Royal Ballet's Act Two, with Margot Fonteyn, for example). David Vaughan in *Ballet Review,* Vol. 4, No. 1, wrote at length of the Kirov Ballet's film.

When the first edition of this book of ballet stories first appeared, in 1954, there was only one complete four-act version of *Swan Lake* before the public in the West—the Royal Ballet's, described above. Since then, many other four-act productions have materialized, and in the United States it has been possible to see different versions by the National Ballet, American Ballet Theatre, in a notable staging by David Blair, the Bolshoi Ballet, the Kirov Ballet, the National Ballet of Canada, and the Stuttgart Ballet, among others. The one by John Cranko for the Stuttgart Ballet prompted these remarks by the choreographer: "I am always surprised by productions of *Swan Lake* that claim to have used all the music. Such a production would last about as long as *Die Meistersinger.* While opera lovers can take this length, balletomanes tend to enjoy shorter fare. Something must go and I have, therefore, cut the well-known waltzes and *pas de trois* from Act One and put in their place the equally beautiful but seldom performed *pas de six.* This gives Siegfried the opportunity to dance and also to develop the character. The Black Swan *Pas de Deux* remains in the place Tchaikovsky intended, and in the fourth act the Drigo *pas de deux,* which always seemed too slight for the situation, has been replaced by the beautiful *Elegy for Strings.* I have tried to base my own work on the classic/romantic style of Petipa, working freely and in my own manner, but not losing sight of the great man's direction. Consequently most of the second act has been retained in its usual form. For the opening of the fourth act and the famous elegiac entry of the swans I have 'borrowed' from various Soviet productions. However, all the musical repetitions have been cut and the drama has been strengthened accordingly so that the prince emerges as a living person who experiences a tragic ordeal, rather than being a human crane who simply lifts the ballerina. The national dances have been woven into an overall dramatic arrangement instead of being pointless *divertissements.* What of the ending? There have been many 'happy endings,' where the lovers are reunited after death in 'fairyland,' but I believe that Tchaikovsky intended to write a tragic ballet. Consider the situation: Siegfried proves unworthy, he breaks his vow and unconsciously confuses outward appearances with inner reality, . . . he is a tragic hero and must be vanquished. The tone of the music, especially in the fourth act, is tragic. In the imperial theatre the Tsar (surrounded by so many tragedies) made it an unwritten rule that everything must close happily. But Odette and Siegfried are not the sort of lovers who can 'live happily ever after.' "

Reviewing Margot Fonteyn's *Autobiography* in the New York *Times* (May 15, 1976), the critic Anna Kisselgoff recalled that the ballerina, on May 3, 1972, offered "at the age of 53 an unforgettable *Swan Lake* with Rudolf in

New York that surpassed the effort of any younger ballerina that season. The idea of a technique drenched in emotionalism (for this was the secret of that night's success) is not usually associated with the most regal of the Royal Ballet's ballerinas.

"Yet that is a notion about herself that she accepts fully. Writing of the early years of the Nureyev-Fonteyn partnership, she describes the contrast between the two dancers this way: 'It was paradoxical that the young boy everyone thought so wild and spontaneous in his dancing cared desperately about technique, whereas I, the cool English ballerina, was so much more interested in the emotional aspects of the performance.'"

LA SYLPHIDE

Ballet in two acts. Music by Jean Schneitzhoeffer. Choreography by Philippe Taglioni. Book by Adolphe Nourrit. Scenery by Pierre Ciceri. Costumes by Eugène Lami. First presented at the Théâtre de l'Académie Royale de Musique, Paris, March 12, 1832, with Marie Taglioni as La Sylphide and Mazilier as James. Marie Taglioni danced the title role when the ballet was introduced to London (1832), St. Petersburg (1837), and Milan (1841). A version of La Sylphide was presented in the United States for the first time on April 15, 1835, with Mademoiselle Céleste in the leading role. It was subsequently danced in the United States by the same ballerina: by Augusta Maywood (1838); Amélie Galster (1839), sister-in-law of Marie Taglioni; and by Fanny Elssler (1840). In 1836 Sylphiden was presented by the Royal Danish Ballet in a version by Auguste Bournonville with music by Herman Løvenskjold. Lucile Grahn danced the Sylphide in the first performance of this version, which has been in the active repertory of the Royal Danish Ballet ever since. Taglioni's La Sylphide was revived in 1946 by the Ballets des Champs-Élysées, Paris, with choreography by Victor Gsovsky, scenery by Serebriakov, and costumes by Christian Bérard. Nina Vyroubova and Roland Petit danced the principal roles. The Royal Danish Ballet danced the ballet in the United States for the first time at the Metropolitan Opera House, New York, September 16, 1956. Harald Lander staged La Sylphide for American Ballet Theatre in San Antonio, Texas, November 11, 1964, with Toni Lander and Royes Fernandez. Music arranged and composed by Edgar Cosma after Løvenskjold. On May 20, 1967, Carla Fracci and Erik Bruhn danced in this production at the New York State Theatre. Erik Bruhn staged it for the National Ballet of Canada in Toronto, December 31, 1964, with Lois Smith and himself in the leading roles. These were later taken by Lynn Seymour and Rudolf Nureyev.

Once a curiosity but now popular in repertories in the United States, Canada, England, and the continent, *La Sylphide* deserves continuing attention. Ballet history was changed completely by the work. Marie Taglioni who danced it and the men who created the role for her made a revolution in the art of dancing that we still witness whenever we go to the ballet and see a world of story

—of sylphs, ondine, swan queens, and firebirds—that is both real and fantasy, settings that are both ethereal and natural, costumes of flowing white, satin toe shoes, and dancers who rise on *pointe* and are lifted magically into the air by their partners. The era of the romantic ballet begun by this ballet is still much with us.

ACT ONE   The story of *La Sylphide* is a romance of old Scotland. The scene is the living room of a Scottish farmhouse. The time is 1830. The room is large and high. On the left a fire blazes in a great fireplace; a huge stone mantel rises from it to the rafters. The mantel is hung with trophies of the hunt—colorful stuffed birds, powder horns, and flintlocks. A staircase runs up the back of the room to the upper story, and a bright plaid decorates the banister. Near the first landing of the stairs is a high, peaked window through whose diamond-shaped translucent glass we can discern the break of day.

This is the wedding day of James Reuben, the young Scots peasant who lives in this house with his mother. The bridegroom sleeps restlessly in a high wing chair drawn close to the fire. He is dressed for his wedding: kilts, cap with high feather. His dark head stirs against the back of the chair; he is dreaming. His dream is with us in the room, and we understand his restlessness. For kneeling on the floor at his feet, her long white dress against the bridegroom's bright tartan, is the diaphanous, winged sylphide, who glances with quiet happiness about the room and seems with her penetrating gaze to look into the eyes of her dreaming lover.

Gurn, another young peasant, rests in a corner against the fireplace. In his deep sleep, Gurn is not disturbed by the realization of his friend's dream; he himself dreams of Effie, James's bride-to-be, and the love he will lose this day.

The sylphide rises effortlessly and circles about the chair. She looks down upon the sleeping James with wistful longing, moving around the room with a lightness and grace that make her wings more than a part of her costume. James turns his head as she dances about him; he is still asleep, but in his dream he watches every gesture she makes. Creature that she is from another world, the sylphide now seems a part of this room. Her smile is the considered smile of possession; she is both beautiful and serious, and her face tells us that her love is great enough to endure beyond James's dream. Should James respond to her love, we feel that this dream might become permanent.

James stirs in his sleep. He wakens suddenly and beholds the sylphide before him. He reaches out for her desperately. Frightened now by reality, the sylphide eludes his grasp. She rushes toward the fireplace. She disappears like the smoke from the dying embers. James moves his hand to his forehead in disbelief at the apparition: was she really there, after all? He becomes frantic and unable to understand the mystery and decides to question Gurn. He shakes his friend awake rudely. Did he see the beautiful vision? How long have we slept? Gurn is a little embarrassed at his own dream and is about to tell James yes, he saw the beautiful girl, but he sees that his friend is not talking about Effie, the bride, but about someone quite different. He wonders at his friend.

James is angry at Gurn for allowing himself to sleep so soundly. He is still trying to piece together the fragments of his dream when he hears his mother approach. She comes in from another room with Effie. Reminded by his bride's presence that he has scarcely thought of her, James is embarrassed. Gurn greets the bride first. The beautiful young lass smiles at him. Gurn can hardly control himself, he is so moved by her loveliness; meekly he presents her with a rare bird he killed yesterday while hunting. Effie accepts the gift, but turns to her fiancé. Why, she wonders, is he preoccupied? Has he no greeting for her? James shakes off his dream and kisses her fondly. They embrace. Effie cannot see James's face as he stares over her shoulder into the fireplace. His mother and Gurn watch him curiously.

Again James kisses his bride. Amused by his own formality, he kisses her hand and tells her that this is the day he has long awaited. Effie sees that he is sincere and his old self again. She is therefore a little annoyed when Gurn steps in, takes her hand and tries to kiss it too. She shakes her finger at him, and James, seeing that he has a rival in his friend, jokes with him about it. Gurn, however, is in no mood for jokes and walks away to nurture his private dream.

James's mother embraces her son and Effie. The lovers kneel before her; she blesses them and hopes for their eternal happiness. Effie and James look into each other's eyes; in her sight, he has forgotten his dream.

Now the music brightens and becomes festive with the arrival of Effie's bridesmaids. The young peasant girls, dressed in brilliant plaids, surround the lovers and wish them well. Gurn approaches. The girls giggle at his discomfiture: after all, he might choose one of them instead of Effie, who is already spoken for. The unhappy Gurn pleads with them to intercede for him; can't anything be done, he wonders, before it is too late? The girls put him off and bring out the wedding gifts they have for Effie: bunches of freshly picked flowers, decorative cloths, and simple jewelry. The bride is delighted with the presents, tries on the jewelry, and drapes the new material over her shoulder.

She and her friends do not notice James as he walks away from them and stares into the fire. Gurn watches him suspiciously. What can be wrong with his friend? James turns his head to look at the precise spot where he last saw the sylphide. He catches his breath and jumps back, startled. Someone is there! He reaches out his arms hopefully, and out of the dark corner steps not his sylphide, but a frightening figure: Old Madge, the village sorceress. The girls are pleased and run over to her. Old Madge stumbles forward, bent low over her crude walking stick. Her ragged clothes are filthy; her stringy gray hair hangs loose about her white, ghostly face. She cackles hideously and walks straight over to James and looks up into his face. His fear turns to anger. He orders her away. Madge cowers pathetically, and the girls are shocked at James's behavior.

The bridegroom stalks away. The girls persuade Madge to tell their fortunes. Effie is the first to hold out her hand. She asks the sorceress if her marriage will be a happy one? Effie does not really have any doubts; it is, after all, the conventional question. Old Madge nods her head and grins, "Yes, you will be happy in marriage." Emboldened by this answer, Effie asks another question: does James love her? James looks over at the group. The witch says,

"No," smiling the same toothless smile as she shakes her head. James will tolerate this no longer. Old Madge cackles ominously. He picks up a broom and drives the hag from the room.

Effie, reassured by James's indignation, tells him that she never doubted his love and that Old Madge is a proverbial liar. James believes her and is comforted. As long as Effie is with him and he can look into her eyes, he, too, has no doubt.

His mother comes to take Effie away. It is time for her to dress for the wedding. Mother Reuben laughs at her son when he doesn't want to let Effie go. She takes the girl by the hand and leads her and her bridesmaids up the stairs. Effie glances back at James, who smiles at her reassuringly.

But now, alone in the room, James has his doubts. He cannot get his dream out of his mind, though rationally he knows it is nonsense. Effie is his real love and so she will remain. But will the dream recur? What would he do if it did? Could such a vision really exist? As he asks himself these tormenting questions, he feels a draft. He turns around, and there—standing in the window—is the sylphide! She is leaning against the window frame; her hands are clasped before her; her expression is one of sweet sadness; and her eyes look down, refusing to meet James's glance. James goes to the window and asks her why she is so sad. Before she vanished so mysteriously, the sylphide was blithe and happy; what can be troubling so beautiful a girl? The sylphide replies that she loves someone who does not love her. James turns as if to move away, but the sylphide continues. He must know, she says, that she loves him. She is the one who brought him the beautiful dream; she is the one who will always watch over him and keep him from harm. Gurn, who has been sulking in a dark corner near the fireplace, emerges from the shadows to watch closely.

James reminds the sylphide that he is to be married this very day. The sylphide knows. Tears fall upon her cheeks. She murmurs that there can be no more beauty in her life: she must die. She starts to leave. James can suppress his secret no longer. He kneels before her and tells her that since she disappeared from his sight he has not been able to forget her for a single moment; he has tried, for he owed it to his love for his fiancée, but he could not: he has loved her as she loves him.

The sylphide dances about the room. James is enraptured to see his dream become real and to find the creature even more graceful in life. She moves toward the window, beckoning James to follow her. He does not move. She whispers softly into his ear. The unhappy bridegroom looks toward the stairs and hangs back. The sylphide watches him and sees the source of his anxiety. Lightly, without seeming to have the least idea of what it is, she takes up the plaid Effie has left behind on the chair, puts it around her shoulders, and poses demurely with downcast eyes as the bride. James can resist her no longer. When the sylphide kneels at his feet, he draws her to him and kisses her.

Gurn is now convinced of his friend's faithlessness and dashes up the stairs to Effie. James and the sylphide are frightened. Excited voices approach. Quickly the sylphide cuddles up in a corner of the huge chair. James throws the plaid over her just as Gurn and Effie, in her bridal gown, rush down the stairs. Her friends follow. Gurn accuses James of having kissed another woman in this room. But where is she? James asks him; he laughs and swears he has been quite alone. Effie and Gurn see no one, but Gurn notes the plaid that covers the chair. James trembles. Gurn pulls the plaid away, and underneath is . . . nothing! The sylphide was vanished! James is as surprised as his friend, but immediately reassures Effie, who now berates Gurn for allowing his jealousy to govern his sense of truth. The girls ridicule Gurn mercilessly, and he slinks out of the room.

James's mother enters with the wedding guests—her friends as well as the friends of the happy couple. Refreshments are served, toasts are made, the bagpipes tune up, and soon everyone is either dancing or talking volubly. Everyone, that is, except James. As all the other young men of the village surround the bride, James stands apart, reminded anew of the sylphide. Effie breaks away from her admirers and reminds the bridegroom that he has not asked her to dance. James is shocked at his forgetfulness, and the two begin to dance. The other guests stand back and watch them. The couple dance together happily until the formal pattern of the peasant dance forces them to separate for a moment. At this point the sylphide returns. She is seen only by James, and the other guests are astonished—when James rejoins Effie—to see him turn his head away from his bride. The *pas de deux* becomes a *pas de trois*: every movement of Effie's is imitated and elevated by the sprightly sylphide. The guests join Effie and James in a general dance, while the sylphide runs hither and yon, now visible, now concealed by the turning couples.

James tries not to lose sight of her and whirls Effie around and around as he frantically pursues the sylphide. Effie is so happy she doesn't notice his anxiety. The sylphide continually eludes him, and James can no longer see her. The dance stops, and some of the guests surround James and inquire about his strange behavior.

They are put off, however, by the beginning of the wedding ceremony. The guests stand in formal groups about the fireplace, where James and Effie stand with his mother. The ritual begins. The couple start to exchange wedding rings. James take off his own ring and holds it at Effie's finger tip. He moves to slip it on her finger, when the sylphide darts out from nowhere and takes the ring from his hand. The guests gasp at the sudden disappearance of the ring. James turns away from his bride. The sylphide whispers to him that she will die if he marries anyone else. James is so appalled at this possibility that he now sees his course: he must prevent such a tragedy. The sylphide beckons to him and stands there in the room by the window before his wedding guests; the bridegroom vanishes.

Effie dissolves in tears. No one can understand how or why James has abandoned her thus. Gurn rushes in and announces that he has just seen the bridegroom running across the moor with another woman. Effie will not believe it. Gurn tries to comfort her, assuring her that she can be certain of his love. Mother Reuben and all the guests gather about the troubled bride. Effie sits down in the chair by the fire. The plaid is placed around her shoulders, her wedding veil is removed. Gurn kneels beside her.

ACT TWO   Eerie music suggestive of an unnatural world marks the beginning of this second scene, which will unravel the mystery of the magical
sylphide and confront the romantic James with his destiny. When the curtain
rises, it is still night. On the left, a small fire throws grotesque shadows against
the walls of a small, dark cave. The surrounding forest is impenetrably black.
The witch, Old Madge, emerges from the cave and stands over the fire. Hovering over the flames, she invokes her demons, beseeching them to obey her commands. With her crooked walking stick, she draws a magic circle about the
fire, then hurries into the shadows of the cavern. She returns with her sisters in
witchcraft: hunchbacked, cackling hags who gather about the circle. The hideous women hang a huge black caldron over the fire and dance around and
around it. Suddenly Old Madge orders silence and, walking up to stand over
the caldron, she points her finger downward in unquestioning command. The
other witches are silenced by this gesture and wait expectantly for some result.
Old Madge orders them to dance again; as they circle the fire, smoke and
steam and blue flame arise from the caldron, illuminating the forest for a few
flashing moments. The conflagration in the caldron simmers down, and the old
women crowd around to see what remains inside. With an imperious sweep of
her arm, Old Madge tells them to stand back. The sun is about to rise, and
they must hasten their work. Madge takes her stick and pokes it into the
caldron; when she pulls it out, we see on the end of the stick, like a banner, a
lovely shimmering scarf. The old women grab at it, but Madge holds it to her
breast; only she is aware of the power of this beautiful scarf. She orders her
sisters away, and all the witches disappear into the cave.

In the distance, the sun rises brightly over the fields of heather and we see a
clearing in a thickly wooded glade. The green trees hang down over the scene,
almost obscuring the witches' cave. Dew covers the ground as the morning
mist settles on the earth.

On the right, James enters the forest. No longer dressed like a typical Scots
peasant, James wears a costume befitting the bridegroom of his sylphide:
white tights and a plaid vest. He carries a bird nest in his hand. Carefully he
examines the colorful eggs and replaces them. He looks about the forest for his
love, but she is not to be found. As he begins to approach the cave, he discovers the sylphide standing by his side. He is astonished at the suddenness of
her appearance and asks her where she has been hiding. The lovely girl smiles
back at him so beautifully that James leaves off his questioning. As if to show
him how she appeared so swiftly and silently, she dances about the forest like
a magical sprite; the tips of her toes seem to require only the air to support
them in flight. James is bewitched anew by her charm and becomes apprehensive when the sylph darts in and out behind the trees. He holds out the
bird's nest and tells her he has brought her a gift. The sylph shrinks back; and
we see suddenly that she is not frightened because James has probably harmed
the eggs in the nest, but because the living birds who fly about the forest are
moved by a power quite different from the mysterious force that makes her a
sylphide as well as a woman. The sylphide is afraid of the nest. Scrupulously
she takes it between her hands and runs to place it high on an overhanging

branch. James smiles warmly at what he believes to be her tenderness; lightly
the sylphide moves her finger tips over her diaphanous white gown.

James draws her to his side. The sylphide places her head on his shoulder
for a moment, and James moves to take her face in his hands. Before he can
do so, the sylphide has danced away toward the back. James observes her as
she calls forth a band of sylphs, who pay homage to her and to him. The
sylphs surround the happy lovers, and James would dance with his bride; but
every time he turns to take her in his arms, she is mysteriously gone and before him stands another sylphide. This happens repeatedly, and James becomes frantic in his search. Then, just as if nothing had happened, the sylphide
is at his side again, looking up into his eyes. James is satisfied, but again the
vision disappears: all the sylphs seem to fly away in the blazing light of the
sun.

Alone, James considers that he has made a mistake. Yesterday, in his mother's
house, the sylphide was always appearing and vanishing mysteriously, but that
he could understand—for there he alone shared her secret; but here in the forest with her, with no one to see, why should she wish to escape *him?* She had
sworn that she loved him and would love him eternally, and yet she would be
loved only from afar. Was his love an illusion, he wondered?

On the left, close to where he last saw his beloved, the branches rustle.
James is startled to see Old Madge come out of her cave. In his present state
of mind, he greets her like an old friend. He remembers his rudeness of yesterday and hastens to apologize. Old Madge tells him not to mind, she understands the momentary follies of youth—but why is he here in the forest? What
has happened?

James tells her briefly that he has run away with his true love, the most
beautiful girl in the world. Why then does he look so dejected, Madge
inquires? "Because," James tells her, "the sylphide is never with me: I search
for her, and she is not to be found; I reach out to touch her beside me, and she
eludes my embrace."

Madge offers to help him with her occult powers. James, willing to try any
device to still the sylphide's flight, beseeches the witch to ease his state of
mind and secure his permanent happiness. Old Madge holds out the bright
magic scarf and offers it to James. She instructs him to place this scarf about
the sylphide's shoulders, and then the sylphide will never fly again: her light,
transparent wings will fall to the ground and flutter no more; she will be his,
on earth.

James is delighted with this magic and kneels before the witch in gratitude.
Old Madge's eyes gleam with triumph as she looks down upon him. Then she
hurries away into the dark cavern as she sees the sylphide approaching. James
runs to his bride and embraces her. She responds warmly to his affection and
seems to be charmed by the gift he offers her. James places the scarf about her
shoulders. As the cloth touches her flesh, the sylphide clutches at her heart in a
spasm of agonizing pain. Her wings fall to the ground. She stumbles forward.
James, struck dumb by this outcome, tries to hold her in his arms and comfort
her. The dying sylphide looks at him in horror and pushes him away. Slowly
her body relaxes, and she lies dead before him, like a leaf fallen from a tree.

As James kneels beside her, weeping, the mirthful cackle of Old Madge ricochets against the dark walls of her hidden cavern. The sylphide's winged sisters emerge from the trees above. They do not comfort the despairing hero, but take the sylphide tenderly in their arms. As they lift her from the ground, they themselves are lifted up; the branches of the trees overhead move back, and high into the clear sky the winged creatures carry their dead queen.

James is inconsolable in his grief. The softness of the music that has carried his ideal love away forever is interrupted by the shrill, open sound of joyous bagpipes, reminding him of his home and the happiness he might have found there. Across the forest, in the distance, we see a wedding procession moving over the moor. Gurn and Effie, arm in arm, lead the happy party, and the curtain falls as the faraway church bells sound their welcome.

NOTES The National Ballet of Washington presented *La Sylphide* in the version by Elsa Marianne von Rosen in 1969. When Margot Fonteyn, dancing this ballet for the first time, appeared in this production October 3, 1969, the critic Clive Barnes wrote: "After seeing Dame Margot it seemed only remarkable that she had never danced the role before. It suited her perfectly, for she brings to these Romantic ballets a most exquisite sense of period style.

"The ballet is a kind of Victorian nosegay—sweet, sentimental and yet completely acceptable upon its own period terms. . . . Dame Margot fitted into its ardors with effortless grace. . . . she conveys the mystic character of the sylph with a seductive mixture of femininity and charm. It recalls her beguiling performance in Ashton's *Ondine*, all thoughtless wiles and innocent raptures."

When American Ballet Theatre staged a new production of *La Sylphide* in New York, July 8, 1971, the staging was by the Danish dancer, choreographer, and producer Erik Bruhn. Clive Barnes commented in the New York *Times* the next day: "By far the best aspect of the production is Mr. Bruhn's staging. This is far more authentic than the first production of *La Sylphide* he created for the National Ballet of Canada some years ago. Indeed, it follows the original fairly carefully and with considerable sensibility.

"The only major addition is a brief new solo for Effie, which is reasonable enough. As is common nowadays, the hero, James, dances the second male solo in this act, and his rival, Gurn, dances the first. Mr. Bruhn takes further than any other production the current trend to romanticize Gurn and to remove him from the original comic tradition, and I can see no harm in this, even though it eliminates some of the traditional pantomime.

"There were other details of the production I was less happy about. I would like to have seen more stage machinery used—this is part of that particular period. I regret the omission of some of the smaller touches that are usually introduced—such as the Sylphide, on persuading James to run away from home, bringing him his cap. There were even details of choreography missing—including James's quite celebrated turn-and-a-half, where he ends a sequence with his back to the audience facing his ballerina.

"These are quibbles, but perhaps the kind of details that give authenticity to the authentic. But at last Ballet Theatre has found a good and valid version of this very important classic, and it will fit well into the company's repertory.

"At this first performance, the Sylphide was danced by Carla Fracci, with Ted Kivitt as her swain, James. Miss Fracci, with her fugitive smile wreathing the corners of her mouth, her tarlatan skirt frothing, and her shy yet captivating manner, is the epitome of the Romantic ideal, when, poetically, women often meant to be more myth than reality. And her dancing had the right febrile grace.

"The Sylphide herself is all spirit—an image rather than a character, an unattainable sex symbol for an age that in polite literary terms had no explicit sex but merely its lost promise. James, the Highland lad, who, rather foolishly, throws away everything to follow her into the heather, has more of the dimensions of reality, and Mr. Kivitt acted with a simple forcefulness.

"Probably the most rewarding character in *La Sylphide* is that of Madge the Witch, who ruins James and insures all ends unhappily. This is now played by Dennis Nahat, who is wearing one of the two or three most interestingly twisted noses I have ever encountered, and glowers with genuine power. It is a good idea to have this role played by a man—it often is in Denmark—and Mr. Nahat, with his unfailing sense of style, is already good and will soon be even better."

Erik Bruhn performed the role of Madge in New York, in August 1974, in the production of *La Sylphide* he had staged for the National Ballet of Canada. Writing in *Dance Perspectives* about his famous roles in the essay "Beyond Technique," Erik Bruhn recalled the first time he appeared as James in *La Sylphide:* "It was a pretty difficult assignment—to do James at the age of 23. I would consider any age between 18 and 24 as the right age for James on the stage. Of course we are all that age at one time or another. But to play him that way is possible only if you can achieve and sustain an idea about how you see him. To play yourself or to play your own age is not enough; to play young when you are young is very hard. When you are mature you can look on youth from a certain distance and this makes you objective. But when you are terribly involved with what is happening to you at this age it is difficult to re-create this. Some people would say that when you look back it isn't the truth you are seeing anymore, it is what you think the truth is. Yes, the role is also what you think it is. It is what you bring to it—your thoughts, your mind. You give life to the role by bringing to it what is true for you at that moment.

"For me, James is the youngest in the gallery of Romantic ballet heroes. He is an idealist, a poet. In the end when he tries to grasp his ideal and tries to make her a real woman, he dies. Without this dream, this illusion, he can no longer exist. All he wants to catch is a dream which exists only in his head and which nobody else can see. He is a true escapist. Nobody can actually get hold of James. His mother, his fiancée—none of the real people understand him. But when he is alone with his dream he is quite himself; he is a total being. When the dream is gone, he must die with it. He believes only in this dream and it is sad that he could never grasp reality. James dies without knowing that he is licked, which becomes a very beautiful thing.

"Unlike James, Albrecht in *Giselle* is on the point of entering maturity. He realizes that he has done something terrible and that he must suffer. If he can survive his night of remorse he will come out the better for it. He pays the price as James never did. Therefore he can live."

For an interesting analysis of the difference between the Bournonville style and the classic style taught in Russia, as well as for a penetrating account of *La Sylphide*, readers are referred to the book *Baryshnikov at Work*, where the dancer describes with Charles Engell France characteristics of performances he has known.

LES SYLPHIDES

Classic ballet in one act. Music by Frédéric Chopin. Choreography by Michel Fokine. Scenery and costumes by Alexandre Benois. First presented by Diaghilev's Ballets Russes at the Théâtre de Châtelet, Paris, June 2, 1909, with Anna Pavlova, Tamara Karsavina, Maria Baldina, and Vaslav Nijinsky as the principal dancers. Fokine's first arrangement of this ballet was presented on March 21, 1908, in St. Petersburg, under the title Chopiniana. The dancers were members of the Imperial Ballet; Pavlova and Oboukoff danced a classical pas de deux to the "Waltz," which was the only part of the original production without a realistic setting or suggestion of plot. The second production, given by Fokine's students, April 6, 1908, was wholly classical; like the first "Waltz," it had no plot, and the musical structure was altered. Preobrajenska, Pavlova, Karsavina, Nijinsky, and Bekeffy were the principal dancers. This second version was costumed in the long white ballet dress made popular by Marie Taglioni in La Sylphide. The title of this famous ballet of Taglioni's was Diaghilev's inspiration for the new name he applied to Chopiniana when it was first presented in Western Europe in substantially the same form as its second production. First presented in the United States in its authorized version by Diaghilev's Ballets Russes at the Century Theatre, New York, January 20, 1916, with a cast that included Lydia Lopokova, Lubov Tchernicheva, Xenia Maclezova, and Adolph Bolm. An unauthorized version, not credited to the choreographer and not supervised by him, was presented in the United States by Gertrude Hoffman's Saison des Ballets Russes on June 14, 1911, at the Winter Garden, New York, with Maria Baldina, Lydia Lopokova, and Alexandre Volinine as the principal dancers.

No one knows exactly when the first *ballet blanc*, or white ballet, was first performed. It is probable that this kind of ballet, which involved a new conception of dance based on ethereal atmosphere, soft music, and diaphanous white costumes, was first performed before *La Sylphide;* but it was *La Sylphide*, and the dancing of its ballerina, Marie Taglioni, that made the *ballet blanc* famous. *Les Sylphides*, its twentieth-century namesake, has carried this fame into our time more than any other ballet.

For the *ballet blanc* did not remain popular. Théophile Gautier, who first used the phrase, was complaining in 1844 that since *La Sylphide* the Paris stage was so dominated by white gauze, by tulle and tarlatan, that the "shades became mists of snow in transparent skirts" and "white almost the only color in use."

And so the misty white ballets gradually passed out of fashion. The ballets that replaced them for half a century were more concerned with dancing than with mood—more devoted to elaborate, regal stage spectacle, and the development within this frame of the classic dance, than to simple stories of fantasy and ethereal romance.

Les Sylphides restored the *ballet blanc*, now embellished with the developed classic dance; but it did so without a story. Here, instead of characters with definite personalities and a narrative, we have simply dancers in long white dresses and a *danseur* in white-and-black velvet, whose movements to music invoke the romantic imagination to a story of its own. It is the music, and the care with which the classic dance embodies it, that tells us the story of these magical creatures who dance in the light of the moon.

The overture, *Prelude, Opus 28, No. 7*, to the ballet is quiet and contemplative. The curtain rises on a secluded wood near an ancient ruin, where lovely girls in white are grouped about the scene in a still, charming tableau. The light is bluish white, soft, and misty. As the *Nocturne, Opus 32, No. 2*, commences, some of the girls begin to dance to the light, airy melody. They are joined by the principal dancers, who stand in a cluster at the rear.

Now a girl dances a variation to a gentle but joyous waltz, music suggestive of beautiful and controlled happiness.

The next dance, like the *Mazurka, Opus 33, No. 3*, that accompanies it, is not as soft; it is bolder, more open and free, but still restrained in its exuberance as the ballerina bounds diagonally across the stage in *grand jetés*, over and over again.

A variation to another mazurka, *Opus 67, No. 3*, is danced by the *danseur* after the girls have formed a decorative tableau about the stage.

When the overture is repeated, the sylphs form picturesque groups, the girls kneeling about central figures. The *danseuse* who now enters comes softly, pauses, and seems to listen to a distant call. She moves among the groups adroitly and sweetly, but completely removed from them in her rapt attention to what she might hear.

The *Waltz, Opus 64, No. 2*, commences, and the *danseur* lifts the ballerina across the stage from the wings. She appears to be so light that it must require no effort to hold her. She is released, and the *pas de deux* begins. Throughout this dance, as the music increases in momentum, the girl responds with unhesitating swiftness and flight to the inspiration of the music and the night: she abandons herself to the air.

The stage is empty for a moment, there is no music; then, to the final buoyant *Waltz, Opus 18, No. 1*, the dancers return, move diagonally across the stage, mingle, brush past each other, and fill the stage with movement like the swift fluttering of butterfly wings. The principal dancers join them for short solos; and at the final chords, there is a swift, silent rush and all are standing still, in the same tableau in which we first saw them.

NOTES *Les Sylphides* is associated with many famous dancers. Fokine staged his work for the Royal Danish Ballet on October 21, 1925 (in a revised version), for René Blum's Ballet Russe de Monte Carlo in 1936, and for Ballet Theatre in 1940.

In the first Diaghilev production in Paris, the first solo, Waltz, was danced by Karsavina; the second, Mazurka, by Anna Pavlova; the third, Mazurka, by Nijinsky; the Prelude, by Maria Baldina; the *pas de deux*, Waltz, by Pavlova and Nijinsky; and the final Waltz, by all the soloists and the *corps de ballet*. Vaslav Nijinsky danced Les Sylphides in the United States on April 14, 1916, at the Metropolitan Opera House.

The music for Fokine's first arrangement of the ballet that was later to become Les Sylphides was orchestrated by Glazunov. Music for the second version was orchestrated by Keller and Glazunov. Music for the Diaghilev production was orchestrated by Stravinsky (his first Diaghilev commission), Tcherepnine, Glazunov, and Liadov. Later orchestrations include those of Vittorio Rieti and Lucien Caillet.

On January 13, 1972, *Chopiniana*, the work on which Les Sylphides was based, was presented for the first time outside Russia:

> *Music by Frédéric Chopin. Staged by Alexandra Danilova after Michel Fokine. Pianist: Gordon Boelzner. First presented by the New York City Ballet at the New York State Theatre, Lincoln Center, with Kay Mazzo, Peter Martins, Karin von Aroldingen, and Susan Hendl in the principal roles.*

The title *Chopiniana* derives from a suite of four piano pieces by Chopin, orchestrated by Alexander Glazunov (*Opus 46*, 1894). Fokine, planning these for a charity performance ballet, asked the composer to add the *C Sharp Minor Waltz* (for Anna Pavlova and Mikhail Oboukoff, Nijinsky's teacher). This first *Chopiniana* was danced March 21, 1908, comprising five scenes: a Polonaise in Polish court dress; an evocation of Chopin and his Muse who repels nightmares of dead monks in his Mayorquin monastery; a Mazurka for a peasant wedding; the Waltz; and, as finale, a Tarantella based on Fokine's memory of a Capri festival.

A second (this current) *Chopiniana* introduced April 16, 1908, used different piano pieces orchestrated by Maurice Keller, retaining Glazunov's Waltz but eliminating all character dancing and mime for a visualized abstraction. Set in three days, Fokine described: "Some of the *corps de ballet* groups accompanying the dancing of the soloists were staged by me, just before curtain time." Diaghilev produced it in his initial Paris ballet season, June 2, 1909, under his own title as Les Sylphides, with Pavlova, Karsavina, and Nijinsky, in a long blond wig which the designer Alexandre Benois said "seemed a trifle comic when I saw it on stage . . . his slightly caricatured appearance made the artist look like a figure from some old beaded reticule or painted lampshade." Some critics frowned on piano music in arrangements made then (and later) by Keller, Liadov, Rieti, Malcolm Sargent, Sokolov, Stravinsky, Taneef, Tcherepnine, etc. Scenery was by Benois; later by A. Socrate, Leon Zak, etc. In 1932, for René Blum's Ballets du Théâtre de Monte

Carlo under Balanchine's artistic direction, a Corot landscape was used. Fokine restaged his work for the Royal Danes in 1925 as *Chopiniana*, by which it was familiar in Russia before and since. In 1936, for Les Ballet Russes de Monte Carlo, he altered music and steps for the male solo. Other changes have crept in over sixty years, some due to individual dancers of which Fokine complained; others to the memories of rehearsalists after his death in 1942.

Costumes and scenery suggested the "romantic" (classic) lyricism of the 1830s. However much long skirts evoked Taglioni, Fokine's choreography surpassed any *tableaux vivants* inspired by static popular lithographs of the period. This was the first ballet as a whole (with precedents from Ivanov and Gorsky) in which movement itself projected from important music was a prime factor rather than a propulsive accompaniment. Fokine's fluent pattern held no pretext for virtuosity or pageantry. Layers of sentiment or sentimentality have tended to dull the force, logic, and ingenuity of this academic masterpiece. The original was planned for large opera house stages; later, scenic frames shrunk spatial possibilities due to the need for touring smaller theaters, while musical tempi increasingly decelerated. The present recension is not offered as a pious museum restoration but as a testimony of approximate efficiency in a context of its contemporary choreographic vitality.

Reviewing *Chopiniana* in *Dance News,* the critic Nancy Goldner wrote: "The decision to strip *Les Sylphides* of its scenery, costumes, orchestration, and by implication its sense of period, even genre—as the City Ballet has done with *Chopiniana*—will strike some as cantankerous and perverse; to others, like myself, a stroke of genius. While watching American Ballet Theatre's production during the last few seasons, I have been continually discovering that there is sturdy, tightly constructed, and subtle but unmistakable climax-building choreography underneath all the aspects that bring historicity to the ballet but have little to do with choreographic fact. One went to see *Les Sylphides* for great performances.

"Now we can more clearly see *Chopiniana* for great choreography as well. On the most obvious level, we can see what choreography is in the legs, since the girls wear short white tunics. It is easier to see that Fokine has been brilliantly economical. Alexandra Danilova's staging has also brought out the choreography's precision and deliberateness. The ensemble looks more vivid, more important. The placement of dancers now looks more linear, lending to the pretty formations a welcome touch of austerity. With this production, one also becomes more aware of lovely repetitions and the fact that *Chopiniana* is, in one aspect, a study on entrances and exits. The ballet is as beautiful as ever, but it is not of a genre. The City Ballet production, in other words, does not preclude style, just stylization. In its de-interpretation, it restores and preserves. This is useful."

NOTES *Ballet Review* (Vol. 4, No. 5) published in 1973 an interview with the ballerina and teacher Alexandra Danilova that is of special interest in view of her part in the staging of the New York City Ballet revival of *Chopiniana:*

BALLET REVIEW "How did you think the New York City Ballet's *Chopiniana* turned out?

ALEXANDRA DANILOVA "Well, I think the first performance was beautiful, and I think the angle that we took is very interesting, and it was very clever of Mr. B. to suggest all these things, because *Chopiniana* is usually done with long skirts, blue flowers—

BR "But this was really radical.

AD "But it is not, if you think that from the beginning it was done with the piano. Chopin never orchestrated. And in Paris people said it was illogical to orchestrate Chopin when he wrote strictly for piano.

BR "Was it the Glazunov orchestration?

AD "Yes, it was Glazunov, then it was Stravinsky, then it was Dorati. So Mr. Balanchine wanted to go right back as like it was done, and now we have the ballet done with the piano, so this time they say why is it not with orchestra?

BR "The principal criticism has been that the ballet was done for a particular reason with the costumes that it had, that when Fokine made the ballet the whole mood and the whole aura of the piece had a lot to do with the production and that these elements were very important to it.

AD "I think a little bit different. I don't know what they wore originally because it was done for annual school performance, and they probably, like we have, just had that white wardrobe tutu past the knee. But then when Diaghilev bought *Sylphides* from Fokine he asked I think Benois to do the costumes, and Benois did the costumes which we wear for forty or fifty years, let's say. And then the time come when the costumes are not necessary, like the scenery is not necessary. So it is a good angle to put just in tunic to see all the beauty of the movement.

BR "I, personally, thought it was very beautiful.

AD "But it is always—you can't please everybody. Don't forget that all our geniuses go twenty-five years ahead of the audience. The beginning, people spit when Stravinsky *Petrouchka* and *Firebird* was played. And now it's the classic. It took twenty-five years for public to catch up, and they love *Petrouchka*. They have such a habit of having *Sylphides* done the way Diaghilev did, but why not to show another angle? I know some people wrote me a letter that they just can't go and see old *Sylphides;* they think it's too heavy.

BR "I thought it was both interesting and beautiful, but many people thought a part of what the ballet meant to them was gone.

AD "Well it's too bad if they take so personally, but a lot of times you come to the rehearsal and admire the ballet before it's done with the costumes, and sometimes costumes ruin the ballet. But this was absolutely pure like crystal. There was pure art of Chopin and pure choreography of Fokine."

SYLVIA

Ballet in three acts and four scenes. Music by Léo Delibes. Choreography by Louis Mérante. Book by Jules Barbier and the Baron de Reinach. Scenery by Chéret, Rubé, and Chaperon. Costumes by Lacoste. First presented at the Théâtre de l'Opéra, Paris, June 14, 1876, with Rita Sangalli as Sylvia and Louis Mérante as Amyntas. *Revived at the Paris Opéra, by Léo Staats, December 19, 1919, with Carlotta Zambelli; by Serge Lifar, February 12, 1941, with Lycette Darsonval; by Albert Aveline, 1946. First presented in Russia at the Maryinsky Theatre, St. Petersburg, December 15, 1901, with Olga Preobrajenska in the title role. First presented in England in a one-act version, produced by C. Wilhelm, at the Empire Theatre, London, May 18, 1911, with Lydia Kyasht as* Sylvia.

Until recently, *Sylvia,* or *The Nymph of Diana,* was more familiar to the English-speaking world for its music than for its dancing. Its original choreography survives only at the Paris Opéra, where the production has long been one of the glories of France. To the rest of the world, selections from the ballet's score, selections such as the often-played *Valse Lente* and *Pizzicato Polka,* have been the principal reminders of the ballet's existence. These selections, as a matter of fact, are so familiar to us that we sometimes forget that they are part of a score for a three-act ballet and that this particular score was extraordinary for its time, as it remains for ours. The American critic Carl Van Vechten reminded us some years ago that before Delibes composed his ballets, "music for dancing, for the most part, consisted of tinkle-tinkle melodies with marked rhythm." Before *Sylvia* and *Coppélia,* Delibes' first great ballets, ballet music was universally subservient to the dancer: it had no drama to it and merely accompanied the steps of a dance with embellishing sound. Delibes changed all that, fusing drama with lyric melody, to become the father of modern ballet music, the inspiration of Tchaikovsky in his own ballet scores, and the precursor of Igor Stravinsky.

The story of Delibes' ballet *Sylvia* is a return to mythology. Sylvia, nymph of Diana, chaste goddess of the hunt, is loved by a mortal, Amyntas, the shepherd. The gods contrive against the romance until, with godlike privilege, they change their minds and the nymph and the mortal are united forever.

ACT ONE: A SACRED GROVE   The orchestra plays an Olympian prelude before the curtain rises. In this regal-sounding music—with its majestic trumpet calls suggestive of a royal hunt and its alternate light, open, joyous melody—we have a brief musical picture of the ballet's story.

The curtain rises on a grove sacred to the goddess Diana. Dominating the scene is a statue of Eros, the child god of love, armed with his bow and arrows. It is night. Magical creatures of the wood, fauns and dryads, cavort about by the light of the moon. The fauns flirt playfully with the dryads and finally succeed in ensnaring the creatures with garlands of flowers. But the sylvan lovers soon pause in their flirtations. A stranger is approaching! They conceal themselves to watch in secret.

Amyntas, the shepherd, enters the grove. He thought he had heard singing and dancing and looks about suspiciously. He sees nothing and cannot understand. Some nights ago he looked into this place and saw dancing a lovely nymph, the most beautiful girl he had ever beheld. Perhaps he was dreaming, but no—there is a soft horn call and soft, rustling, tripping music, as if a mysterious, unfelt wind had disturbed all the leaves of the forest.

Amyntas hides and observes the scene as his beautiful nymph, Sylvia, comes into the wood with her followers. They dance in honor of the chase, the pursuit of their patron goddess. Their innocent joy in the hunt seems to be curiously out of place as they dance before the statue of Eros, who would surely think them unnatural creatures to be so satisfied. Soon the girls tire and rest.

Now it happens they are observed by another. Orion, giant hunter of the forest, loves Sylvia in secret and wishes to abduct her. He is disturbed when some of the nymphs find the shepherd's crook and cloak lying on the ground and is immediately jealous. Sylvia orders her nymphs to seek out the intruder in the sacred grove, and Amyntas is brought before her. Enraged that a man has cast his eyes upon her and intent above all on preserving her purity, Sylvia determines that he must die. She draws her bow, though the young man is obviously in love with her. The love that he feels, Sylvia decides, he himself is not responsible for: it is some mischief of Eros. She therefore aims her bow at the statue.

Amyntas, shocked at this offense to the god who has inspired his love for her, runs across the wood and stands before the statue of Eros to protect it. But Sylvia has drawn her bow: her arrow sinks into the shepherd's breast, and he falls to the ground. Now the statue comes to life and Eros retaliates by aiming his arrow at Sylvia's heart. The girl collapses, clutching at her heart. Her nymphs gather about her, fearing that she is dead, but Sylvia holds out the arrow of Eros and says that she has not been hurt, it is nothing. She departs from the forest as day begins to dawn.

Villagers enter the forest and pay tribute to Eros. They do not notice the body of Amyntas. As soon as they depart, Orion enters in search of Sylvia. When he discovers the dead shepherd, he rejoices that he now has no rival and makes a new plan: he will capture Sylvia with a golden chain. Orion is observed by a straggling peasant, who remains on the scene in hiding to see what will happen.

Sylvia returns to the forest. Orion hides. The girl, remorseful at the death of the shepherd, hovers over his body. We wonder at her change of heart and then recall that she brushed off Eros' arrow too lightly. Orion takes advantage of her lack of vigilance, throws the chain of gold about her, lifts the struggling nymph into his arms, and runs toward the inner darkness of the forest.

A peasant who has seen all this is unable to help Sylvia. He runs to tell the other peasants that Amyntas is dead. His friends try to revive Amyntas, but the shepherd does not stir. An old magician comes forward and presses a rose to the shepherd's lips, and he returns to life. When he discovers, however, that Sylvia has disappeared, he wishes himself dead again. The sorcerer comforts him and tells him that perhaps Sylvia loves him; perhaps the arrow of Eros really touched her heart. Amyntas is then told of Sylvia's capture by the hunter Orion. He instantly prepares to save her; before departing, he bows to the statue of Eros. The statue again comes to life: Eros points the way to Orion's hiding place, and Amyntas sets out to rescue his beloved.

ACT TWO: THE CAVE OF ORION   Orion watches as his captive wakens. As soon as she opens her eyes and sees her abductor, Sylvia attempts to escape from him. But the weapons of the hunt have been taken from her, and she has no defense. She is impervious to his declarations of love, and the repulsed Orion grows angry. Sylvia placates him with wine, which the hunter has never tasted before. His servants willingly prepare it at their master's suggestion.

At first the wine merely increases Orion's passion, and the nymph dances before him to encourage him to drink more. He does so, but—tiring of the dance—seizes Sylvia in his arms. She easily eludes him, and the intoxicated giant falls to the ground.

Still she cannot escape. Orion has blocked the entrance to the cave with a huge boulder. The girl prays to Eros. The god appears to her, takes her by the hand, and leads her into the forest. There he turns around and, with an impatient godlike gesture, causes Orion, his grotto, and his servants to vanish into the earth.

The sound of a hunting horn causes her to rush to the nymphs she has abandoned, but Eros reminds her of Amyntas, who more than anyone grieves over her disappearance.

ACT THREE, SCENE ONE: A WOODED LANDSCAPE ON THE SEACOAST   Amyntas is still unaware of Sylvia's rescue; he enters lonely and dejected soon after the curtain rises on a celebration in honor of the god Bacchus. The sea stretches into the distance behind the trees; at the left is the sacred temple of Diana. Bacchantes dance and present grapes to the god of wine.

A ship is seen approaching the shore. A pirate captains this ship and as it reaches shore, he interrupts the festival and attempts to interest the natives in the purchase of slave girls. In reality, this pirate is Eros, who wishes to return Sylvia to Amyntas. Eros urges the veiled slave girls to surround the shepherd, but the moody Amyntas takes interest in only one of the girls, who seems to him strangely familiar. The girl dances before the youth to a pizzicato melody. He is completely delighted with her and when she removes her veil, he is overcome with happiness. He clasps Sylvia in his arms.

Orion bursts in on the scene. Eros has not been able to suppress the hunter, and Sylvia, knowing the giant's power, rushes into the temple of her patron goddess. Amyntas prepares to engage Orion in combat, but Orion runs past him to force the doors of the temple.

ACT THREE, SCENE TWO: THE TEMPLE OF DIANA   A distant roar that grows louder and louder reminds us of the anger of the gods. Lightning flashes. Within her temple, Diana, her bow drawn tight, stands over Sylvia, who kneels before her protectress. Orion dashes toward Sylvia. Diana releases her bow, and the evil hunter is pierced through the heart.

The angry goddess, who divines the real reason for Sylvia's fears, asks her how it has happened that she is in love. Sylvia confesses that Eros wounded her with one of his darts. Upon this declaration, Eros removes his disguise. Diana threatens him, but the god of love reminds her that once upon a time even she was grateful for his gift of love: the one time Diana was moved by his power and kissed the sleeping Endymion by the light of the moon.

The embarrassed goddess, confronted by her one fault, forgives Sylvia for breaking her vow never to love. She rises to her high seat in her temple with Eros. All her handmaidens bow low to the god and goddess, and the village peasants stand amazed as Amyntas and Sylvia—having received the blessing of Olympus—are transfigured by their love.

NOTES Frederick Ashton revived *Sylvia* in London, September 3, 1952, with scenery and costumes by Robin and Christopher Ironside. Margot Fonteyn, Michael Somes, John Hart, and Alexander Grant danced the principal roles as they also did September 29, 1953, when the Sadler's Wells Ballet brought it to New York.

SYMPHONIC VARIATIONS

Classic ballet in one act. Music by César Franck. Choreography by Frederick Ashton. Scenery and costumes by Sophie Fedorovitch. First presented by the Sadler's Wells Ballet at the Royal Opera House, Covent Garden, London, April 24, 1946, with Margot Fenteyn and Michael Somes, Pamela May and Brian Shaw, and Moira Shearer and Henry Danton. First presented in the United States by the Sadler's Wells Ballet at the Metropolitan Opera House, New York, October 12, 1949, with the same cast but with John Hart replacing Henry Danton.

This classic dance ballet is arranged to Franck's *Symphonic Variations* for piano and orchestra. There is no story, only a mood created by the setting and costumes, the music, and the dancers' response to it.

When the curtain rises, six dancers are on stage. Three girls stand forward in a line parallel to the front of the stage. In the back, turned away from us, are three boys. The backdrop is of abstract design: curved and slanting black lines on a light green cloth.

The orchestra begins. The dancers do not move: they stand quietly in youthful meditation on the music. Directly the piano begins, the girls commence to dance. As if activated only by the instrument, they pause as the orchestra takes up the theme. A variation on the theme is stated, and one of the boys comes forward. He takes turns dancing with the three girls, then remains still as they dance about him. Now he holds the girls, one by one, as they whirl in his arms.

The girls rest as the two other boys join the leading male soloist in a line similar to that which was formed at the beginning by the three girls. The three dance—the two boys on the outside miming in motion the part of the orchestra, while the soloist, in the center, takes the part of the piano. The boys dance now to the girls, who respond to their statement of a theme. Two of the girls dance alone, then with one of the boys. They retire; another boy takes the center of the stage and dances a variation.

The principal ballerina now comes forward and, while the boys in the background dance quietly, she moves with sweet splendor to the music of the piano. The male soloist joins her, and they dance a *pas de deux*.

After this romantic sequence, all six dancers move together. Now they are not so much separate individuals responding to the music, as one group animated by the same theme. The boys and girls divide, come together in couples, and make swift, open patterns about the stage while the music rushes toward its conclusion. Their swift ebullience is broken at the end, as the dancers resume the meditative poses with which the ballet began.

NOTES   Ashton has said of his ballet and the time it was composed, just after World War II, in *Frederick Ashton and His Ballets*: "My mother died in 1939, just before the war. So I was independent at last, although it didn't do me any good. Almost as soon as the war started I had to go into the R.A.F. Everyone was being called up—all the dancers and everyone I knew in the theatre—and I wanted, I suppose, to share their agony. I must say, I thought it was the end of everything. It was a period of enormous frustration to me because I felt I hadn't said nearly enough to be ready to die on it.

"The importance of the war was that it gave me a period to think and read a good deal and also, because I was rather unhappy, I went in for mysticism. I read St. Theresa of Avila and St. John of the Cross and lots of books about mystics and mysticism. After all, one was told that it was the end of the world.

"During the war, the tendency in all the ballets seemed to become much too literary and dramatic. During the last part of the war, I was stationed at the Air Ministry as an Intelligence officer and I saw everything that was going on, although at this stage I couldn't do any work myself. It was very frustrating, and originally I think that *Symphonic Variations* was very much overchoreographed. I remember doing a tremendous amount of eliminating, especially in the finale; I pared and pared and pared until I got the kind of purity I wanted. You see, when I started I was going to do something very complicated, with lots of people and a sort of seasonal theme. But then I thought one day that six dancers would be enough. When one begins to do things one is apt to overcharge everything, and if things get too intense, one blurs the vision of the audience. By simplifying, you make it easier for an audience to take in your intentions.

"With *Symphonic Variations* I had to do a lot of experimenting to find the sort of movement that I wanted. That was what took the time, but once I had achieved it the rest went fairly well. I was able to ride on the music quite a bit because I knew it very well and I'd listened to it during the war. I'd always hoped I would get round to using it one day."

Margot Fonteyn has also written of the time of the creation of this ballet: "When *Symphonic Variations* was almost finished, Michael Somes had to have an operation on the cartilage in his knee. The first night of *Symphonic* was postponed for something like two months while Michael had his operation and got back into training.

"When we started to rehearse it all again Fred took out a lot of things and simplified and purified the choreography. Instead of having his usual deadline for the dress rehearsal and the first performance, he had time to reassess the choreography. I think that's one reason why it turned out to be one of his masterpieces. I remember a lot of discussion and all sorts of different ideas and versions and several different endings, and Sophie Fedorovitch at the rehearsals and coming in each day to say what she thought. A lot went into revising *Symphonic*. It's probably the only ballet he's ever had the opportunity to revise before the first night."

The critic and dancer David Vaughan, writing in *Ballet Review,* has said of this ballet: "The postponed première of Ashton's *Symphonic Variations* was for him a kind of manifesto similar to *Apollo*—a clearing away of literary and scenic paraphernalia, just six dancers on an open stage, given an illusion of even greater spaciousness by Fedorovitch's airy decor. If Ashton had shown at various times in his earlier career the influence of Nijinski and Massine, to say nothing of Pavlova and Duncan, there were moments in *Symphonic Variations* that inevitably, maybe coincidentally, suggested Balanchine's masterpiece, especially in the passages of supported adagio involving three women and one man. But more important was the final distillation of Ashton's own classicism: it marked the beginning of his exploration of various motifs that became trademarks of his *pas de deux* at that time—the skimming lifts with *batterie* or *pas de bourrée* just off the floor, the scissor-like movements, the *arabesques élançées.* Notable also was the courage to be simple, to leave out anything extraneous to the piece's lyric utterance: there is never any sense of strain after the ingeniously original lift or step, indeed, some of the most eloquent passages are the transitions when the dancers join hands in a simple run.

"*Symphonic Variations* was, then, a kind of summation, and a consummation, of Ashton's career up to that point, made possible, no doubt, by the kind of fallow period he had been obliged to go through during his war service, however frustrating that must have been at the time. From there he could move on to the inevitable next step in the development of British ballet—or at any rate of the Wells, as it acquired official recognition as the national ballet in the form of the royal charter—the creation of full-length ballets that could stand alongside the classics of the repertory, *Giselle, Swan Lake, Sleeping Beauty,* and the rest."

David Vaughan's biography *Frederick Ashton and His Ballets* examines in detail the making of this ballet and its subsequent history in performance.

The British writer James Monahan, whose admiration for this ballet is well known, has again described it in his book *The Nature of Ballet* (London, 1976).

SYMPHONIE CONCERTANTE

Classic ballet in three movements. Music by Wolfgang Amadeus Mozart. Choreography by George Balanchine. Scenery and costumes by James Stewart Morcom. Lighting by Jean Rosenthal. First presented by Ballet Society at the City Center, New York, November 12, 1947, with Maria Tallchief, Tanaquil LeClercq, and Todd Bolender in the principal roles.

Set to Mozart's *Sinfonia Concertante in E flat major for Violin and Viola* (K. 364), this ballet follows closely the design of the music. It has no story. Its gold backdrop represents the formal classical frame into which both music and dancing fit. The three parts correspond to the three movements of the score. There are two ballerinas, corresponding to the solo instruments, a *danseur,* a group of six secondary soloists, and a *corps de ballet* of sixteen dancers.

FIRST MOVEMENT: ALLEGRO MAESTOSO   The curtain rises and the stage is empty. The music begins, allegro maestoso. After the opening chords, eight dancers emerge from either side of the stage, dancing to the light, quick rhythm of the music. They arrange themselves in a pattern that encloses the front part of the stage. The six soloists enter and dance in a close line. Now they move to the back and dance forward in rapid, crossing diagonals.

The introductory passage is over. Quietly the solo instruments are heard. All the dancers move to the sides of the stage, and slowly the ballerinas enter at the back. They meet in the center of the stage and dance together. Then, as the violin alone is heard against the orchestra, one of the ballerinas dances briefly alone. The other ballerina succeeds her as the viola returns with the same melody. The two dancers follow the turns of the solo instruments throughout the ballet, dancing together and alternately. They do not represent the instruments in any literal sense; their dances are simply accompanied by the instruments. The ballerinas leave the stage when the violin and viola are silent, returning when the instruments are heard again. Three girls enter with each of the ballerinas in turn and support them in brief, extended poses, after which the two dance together.

The opening section of the first movement is now repeated. The *corps de ballet* kneels, and the two ballerinas enter as they did at the beginning. The violin, which took priority over the viola, now takes a secondary position. The ballerinas dance closely together, almost touching, as the two instruments intertwine the melody. One of the ballerinas supports the other as the violin plays in the background against the dominant viola. Then both pirouette off while the *corps de ballet* accompanies the final orchestral bars. All kneel on the last chord.

SECOND MOVEMENT: ANDANTE   The six soloists remain on stage as the *corps* exits. The second movement begins, and the girls dance forward slowly. They separate and retire as the two ballerinas enter with the *danseur,* who supports each of the girls in turn to the music. When the principal theme of the movement is stated by the orchestra, the six soloists cross the stage with measured pace. The *danseur* leads the ballerinas to the back, the soloists dance, then the ballerinas move forward again to dance to the intricate alternation of violin and viola. The movement ends as softly as it began. As the three principals exit, the six soloists enclose them in a moving semicircle.

THIRD MOVEMENT: PRESTO   To the high-spirited, joyous finale, the two ballerinas and their partner take turns in dancing alone and in the brief duets and trios. The *corps de ballet* forms a moving background to their movements.

Each of the principals circles the stage brilliantly. The dancing becomes brisk with the clipped, delightful cheerfulness of the music. The girls flick their wrists elegantly as the movement draws to its conclusion, then dance together with the principals, who kneel before the group as the ballet ends.

NOTES   This ballet is a good example of how dancing might aid appreciation of the music. Mozart's *Sinfonia Concertante* is long and difficult; to the inexperienced listener it might be boring; perhaps only the musician likes it immediately. The ballet, on the other hand, fills the time measured by the music with movement and seems to shorten the length of the music. What seemed dull at a first *hearing*, is not so dull when the ballet is first *seen*.

It is interesting that although Mozart wrote no music for ballet, of all composers his music is most adaptable for ballet, of all composers his music is the most danceable. Children who hear Mozart's music without knowing what it is, instinctively wish to dance to it. They appreciate its true quality better than their elders, who are often too impressed by Mozart's greatness to listen to his work with unaffected ears.

SYMPHONIE POUR UN HOMME SEUL (Symphony for a Man Alone)

Score by Pierre Schaeffer and Pierre Henry. Choreography by Maurice Béjart. First presented by the Ballets de l'Étoile in 1955 with Michèle Seigneuret and Maurice Béjart in the principal roles. First presented in the United States by the Ballet of the Twentieth Century at the City Center, New York, November 30, 1971, with Suzanne Farrell and Jorge Donn in principal roles.

One of the ballets that established the international fame of European choreographer Maurice Béjart and his subsequent ballet company, the Ballet of the Twentieth Century, *Symphony for a Man Alone* was the first dance work to use an electronic score, a popular complement to dance from that time forward. The signature of the ballet has been given by the choreographer himself. Béjart writes:

"How reply to the clamor of the crowd? . . . with violins? With oboes? And what orchestra can boast of rendering that other cry which man in his solitude is powerless to utter? Let us leave the sound of the violoncello, too easy for present-day man, his daily epic and collective anguish. Footsteps, voices and familiar sounds will suffice. Footsteps press upon him, voices go through him, who make love and war, the whistle of bombs or the tune of song . . . May the modern dancer, without costume or decor, be without drum or trumpet. To the rhythm of his own heart, if he is sincere, dance will be the more true."

The choreographer's response to the demands of his audience produces in this case the situation of a man, alone, entrapped, as in a prison, among strands of rope hanging from above. The man is haunted throughout the ballet by a girl, an illusive figure with whom he cannot establish any kind of permanent relationship. He tries, but the girl always at the crucial moment vanishes or escapes his grasp. At the end, he seems to despair. Man, alone, no matter what the quality of the music to accompany his solitude, seeks another.

SYMPHONY IN C

Classic ballet in four movements. Music by Georges Bizet. Choreography by George Balanchine. First presented under the title Le Palais de Cristal *by the Paris Opéra Ballet at the Opéra, July 28, 1947, with Lycette Darsonval, Tamara Toumanova, Micheline Bardin, Madeleine Lafon, Alexandre Kaliujny, Roger Ritz, Michel Renault, and Max Bozzoni as principals. Scenery and costumes by Léonor Fini. First presented in the United States by Ballet Society at the City Center, New York, March 22, 1948, with Maria Tallchief, Tanaquil LeClercq, Beatrice Tompkins, Elise Reiman, Nicholas Magallanes, Francisco Moncion, Herbert Bliss, and Lew Christensen in the principal roles.*

Symphony in C is not based on a story, but on the music to which it is danced. Bizet's symphony is in four movements; each of these movements develops different themes, different melodies. Correspondingly, in the ballet, there is a different dance scheme and development for each of these four movements. Each movement has its own characteristic ballerina, *premier danseur,* and *corps de ballet.* Toward the end of the ballet, when the different groups have danced their special parts of the symphony, all the groups combine with their ballerinas for a kind of dance summing up of all that has gone before. There is no scenery, only a blue background; the dancers are dressed in classical ballet costumes.

FIRST MOVEMENT: ALLEGRO VIVO   The curtain rises before the music begins. Two small groups of girls begin to dance with the opening chord. As the orchestra plays the first theme and repeats it, the two groups dance in opposition, first dancing all together, then alternately following the movements of two leaders.

The ballerina appears as the second theme is announced by the oboe and strings. She dances forward in crisp, open movements to the rhythm of the melody, turning gracefully as she poses and balancing for a moment as she waits for the theme to begin anew. Her dance now becomes brisk and flourishing. She pirouettes swiftly as the two soloists join her, balances again briefly, and leaves the stage.

After the orchestra has given an intimation of the first theme and horns have played a short transition, two boys enter to support the soloists. The ballerina returns with her partner. She dances around the stage, retires to the rear, and, as the first theme of the movement returns, leads the ensemble. On the last clipped chord she stands supported in a quick, graceful pose.

SECOND MOVEMENT: ADAGIO   The *corps de ballet* moves slowly to the introductory passage. A second ballerina enters with her partner as the soft central theme of the movement is sounded by the oboe. She is lifted low off the floor and moves as if in slow motion, then is lifted high, her legs describing sweeping arcs in the air. Her partner supports her in long, slow lifts and held poses while the *corps de ballet* gathers about her. As the movement ends, the ballerina falls back in her partner's arms.

THIRD MOVEMENT: ALLEGRO VIVACE Here the music is spirited and lively. Six girls, in a third *corps de ballet,* dance forward; two couples join them to leap across the stage; and, finally, a third ballerina and her partner enter to circle the stage in broad leaps. They dance together briefly, turning rapidly in the air together, and rush off into the wings. Soon they return, repeat their dance, and lead the *corps de ballet* to the bright, ebullient music. At one point the boy lifts the ballerina off the floor and drops her, pushing her forward, so that she seems to bounce to the music. The entire group joins in the final measures, the *corps de ballet* kneeling as the ballerina is held in a graceful pose at the last chord.

FOURTH MOVEMENT: ALLEGRO VIVACE In the final movement, the principals of the first three movements join with a fourth ballerina and her partner in an exhilarating display of virtuosity that becomes at times a contest. The fourth ballerina and her accompanying group dance first. They are followed by the ballerina of the first movement and her *corps de ballet.* The ballerina of the Adagio movement appears next, then the ballerina of the third movement.

The thirty-two girls who have made up the four *corps de ballet* now line the stage at the sides and across the back. All four ballerinas dance in their midst, each executing the same brilliant steps. Their partners enter for their turn, while secondary soloists dance behind them. At the close, all forty-eight dancers—soloists and *corps de ballet*—join the principals in a brilliant finale. As the last chord of the music sounds, the ballerinas turn quickly and fall back over their partners' arms as the secondary soloists are lifted high behind them in a climactic tableau.

NOTES *Symphony in C* was originally mounted for the Paris Opéra during my visit there as guest choreographer in 1947. For the Opéra, I staged revivals of three ballets: *Apollo, Le Baiser de la Fée,* and *Serenade,* and although the two latter ballets had never been seen in Paris before, at the end of my engagement I wished to stage a new work especially for the principal dancers of the Opéra.

It seemed fitting to select for this new work music by a French composer. I accordingly chose the little-known *Symphony in C Major* written by the French master Bizet when he was only seventeen years old. Composition of the ballet was completed in about two weeks.

The ballet was staged for Ballet Society in New York the following spring. When this company became the New York City Ballet seven months later, *Symphony in C* was the concluding ballet on the first program. The ballet has been a part of the permanent repertory of the New York City Ballet ever since.

In 1973, the New York City Ballet made a series of films for television in Berlin. Writing about the film of *Symphony in C* the critic Robert Greskovic said in *The Soho Weekly News*: "Though this and the 15-or-so other films of Balanchine's ballets were made for TV, this projected print made a dazzling image. Unlike the Tharp tape, the filming here plays no camera tricks. With the exception of some close-ups for the *adagio pas de deux* of the second movement, the camera maintains its eye as a transfixed spectator from an imaginary vantage point about the twentieth row center of a visionary theater. The familiar white tutus of the female dancers and (alas, equally familiar) black sequined leotards, tights and white sweat socks of the male dancers are neutrally and delicately set off by a consistently cool, pale olive background. The cast is Karin von Aroldingen, Jean-Pierre Bonnefous—first movement; Allegra Kent, Conrad Ludlow—second movement; Sara Leland, John Clifford— third movement; and Marnee Morris, Victor Castelli—fourth movement. The full-stage picture is always clear and yields the full force of this work by the company at its very best. With the brisk flow that Robert Irving's magic-wand baton makes of this symphony, Bizet via Balanchine strikes a focus/blend of perfection throughout. The careful camera make-up gives everyone in the cast a theatrical patina that glows and radiates a screen persona to the perform- ance. (Especially glamorous here is von Aroldingen . . .) The angle of vision hovers slightly above the floor space, defining a steady rake to the dancing plane that opens at you like the palm of a hand extended in formal presen- tation. The depth of field grows physical as the choreographic/symphonic lines occupy more and more space with diagonal and flanking formations. The paths that the solo dances describe become lines of force that draw their length in after-images of energy. As the fourth movement shifts into the repeats of the finale, the space further deepens as it fills with the *corps de ballet* and soloists from the preceding three movements. That horse-shoe formation of ballerinas has never looked so precise and pure as legs and arms rapidly angle and arc in unison and frame the principals' and soloists' coda sections like a rainbow of warm white light."

SYMPHONY IN E FLAT

Music by Igor Stravinsky. Choreography by John Clifford. First presented at the New York City Ballet's Stravinsky Festival, June 20, 1972, at the New York State Theatre, Lincoln Center, with Gelsey Kirkland, Peter Mar- tins, and ensemble.

Stravinsky's first symphony, dedicated to "my dear teacher N. A. Rimsky- Korsakov," was first performed in 1907. The young dancer and choreographer John Clifford, who had done his first ballet to Stravinsky's *Symphony in C* for us, and other fine ballets since, was a natural to undertake the choreography for this work's presentation at the New York City Ballet's Stravinsky Festival. There are four movements—*Allegro moderato, Scherzo allegretto, Largo,* and

Finale, Allegro molto. The dancing is the choreographer's story of the music; what he sees happening in it.

Reviewing the ballet the next day in the *Daily News*, Sam Norkin wrote of *Symphony in E Flat:* "Intricate maneuvers and groupings are complemented by the expert pas de deux and solo sections for Gelsey Kirkland and Peter Martins. Tiny Gelsey is a fine lyric dancer who can turn into a pocket dynamo or fly away without warning. She is an exciting thing to observe."

SYMPHONY IN THREE MOVEMENTS

Music by Igor Stravinsky. Choreography by George Balanchine. First presented by the New York City Ballet at the Stravinsky Festival, 1972, at the New York State Theatre, Lincoln Center, June 18, 1972, with Helgi Tomasson, Sara Leland, and Edward Villella in principal roles. Lighting by Ronald Bates. Conducted by Robert Craft.

I remember Stravinsky's talking to me about this music during World War II, when I visited him in Hollywood. It is a magnificent, major work, and I had wanted for many years to make a ballet to the music. The appropriate opportunity came in 1972, when we were preparing the Stravinsky Festival at the New York City Ballet.

The score is a short one for a symphony—about twenty-one minutes—and is in three movements. Stravinsky has written that "the formal substance of the symphony exploits contrasts of several kinds, one of them being the contrast between the principal instrumental protagonists, harp and piano. Each instrument has a large obbligato role in a movement to itself, and only at the turning-point fugue . . . do the two play together and unaccompanied."

"Composers combine notes," Stravinsky said. Choreographers combine movements and the ones I arranged for this music follow no story line or narrative. They try to catch the music and do not, I hope, lean on it, using it instead for support and time frame. If I were to try to relate that a boy and sixteen girls begin the ballet, that would not be very interesting, or that a girl in purple dances with eight others to music for clarinet, piano, and strings soon follows. What is really interesting is the complexity and variety of the music, from the propulsive drive and thrust of the vigorous opening (which also closes the ballet) to the developed use, almost like a concerto, of the piano in the first movement, the harp in the second and the two together in the finale.

The central movement, Andante, is a *pas de deux.* One writer has called this a "strangely quiet, sensuous, meditative interlude with a pronounced Eastern tinge." I had not thought of that but paraphrasing Stravinsky, how and in what form the things of this world are impressed upon my dance is not for me to say.

After the ballet was in our repertory, I heard that the first movement of the symphony was actually composed as a possible accompaniment for a film about China and that the second movement was also composed (but not used) for a film project—the apparition-of-the-Virgin scene for the film of Werfel's *Song of Bernadette.*

TALES OF HOFFMANN

Ballet in prologue, three acts, and an epilogue. Music by Jacques Offenbach, arranged and orchestrated by John Lanchbery. Choreography by Peter Darrell. Design by Alistair Livingstone. Lighting by John B. Read. Scenario by Peter Darrell from stories by E. T. A. Hoffmann. First presented by Scottish Theatre Ballet at the Kings Theatre, Edinburgh, Scotland, April 6, 1972, with Peter Cazalet as Hoffmann. First presented in the United States by American Ballet Theatre at the New York State Theatre, Lincoln Center, New York, July 12, 1973, with sets and costumes by Peter Docherty and with Cynthia Gregory and Jonas Kage in the principal roles.

Those who are familiar with Offenbach's opera of this title, or with the popular film, will know all about E. T. A. Hoffmann, the German teller of tales whose stories have already made ballet history in *Coppélia* and *The Nutcracker.*

PROLOGUE: A TAVERN OUTSIDE AN OPERA HOUSE   Hoffmann is drinking with friends while awaiting the arrival of La Stella, his latest love, who is appearing at the opera. He is asked to explain the meaning of three souvenirs on his table but at first refuses. La Stella arrives and gives her maid a note for Hoffmann which, unseen by him, is intercepted by Counsellor Lindorf. Hoffmann, now a little drunk, agrees to tell the stories behind the three souvenirs and the tales proper begin:

ACT ONE (THE FIRST TALE): THE CONSERVATORY IN SPALANZANI'S HOUSE Spalanzani, an inventor, has invited some friends to see his latest invention, the lifelike mechanical doll, Olympia. Hoffmann as a very young man observes Olympia from afar and tries to meet her. Spalanzani announces that Olympia will dance for his guests, but first insists that Hoffmann put on a pair of magic spectacles. Hoffmann immediately falls in love with Olympia and asks her to marry him. Spalanzani, delighted with the success of his deception, agrees at once. Hoffmann, whirling Olympia about in a dance, loses the magic pair of glasses. The doll thereupon falls apart and poor Hoffmann realizes he has been tricked.

ACT TWO (THE SECOND TALE): THE MUSIC ROOM OF ANTONIA'S HOME   Ten years have passed. Hoffmann, in love with Antonia, is taking music lessons from her father. Behind her father's back, Antonia flirts with Hoffmann while dancing to his playing. When they are discovered, the father warns Antonia that too much exertion will be fatal to her. Doctor Miracle suddenly appears. He promises to cure Antonia and hypnotizes her into believing that she is a great ballerina. Hoffmann returns and Antonia, enthralled by her vision, implores him to play so that she may dance again. Urged on by Doctor Miracle, Hoffmann reluctantly does so until, overcome, Antonia dies in his arms.

ACT THREE (THE THIRD TALE): DAPERTUTTO'S SALON   Now an older and more serious man, Hoffmann has turned to religion for comfort from his earlier disappointments. He finds himself in the salon of Dapertutto, who tries to lure him again to the enjoyment of sensual pleasures but without success until the arrival of Giulietta, a lovely courtesan. Encouraged by Dapertutto, Giulietta so seduces Hoffmann that he even renounces his faith. Then he realizes, when his reflection disappears in a mirror, that he has lost his immortal soul. In his anguish he prays that he may be forgiven and, as his reflection reappears, Giulietta and Dapertutto are drawn into the mirror and vanish.

EPILOGUE: THE TAVERN   Hoffmann, his stories told, is offered more drink by the sinister Counsellor Lindorf. La Stella emerges from the opera house looking for Hoffmann and finds him in a drunken sleep, her note crushed on the ground. Sad and disappointed, she is led away by Lindorf. Hoffmann, roused from his stupor, realizes that yet again he has been duped by the evil presence that has pursued him throughout his life.

THE TAMING OF THE SHREW

Ballet in two acts after Shakespeare. Music by Kurt-Heinz Stolze after Domenico Scarlatti. Choreography and production by John Cranko. Scenery and costumes by Elizabeth Dalton. Lighting by Gilbert V. Hemsley, Jr. First presented by the Stuttgart Ballet at the Wurttembergische Staatstheater, Stuttgart, Germany, March 16, 1969, with Marcia Haydée and Richard Cragun in the principal roles. First presented in the United States by the same ensemble at the Metropolitan Opera House, New York, June 12, 1969.

The Taming of the Shrew turns out to be just as amusing to see in dance form as it is in the spoken theater. The action of the ballet follows closely that of the play:

ACT ONE, SCENE ONE: OUTSIDE THE HOUSE OF BAPTISTA, A WEALTHY NOBLEMAN   Hortensio, a fop, Lucentio, a student, and Gremio, an elderly roué, serenade the beautiful Bianca, one of the nobleman's daughters. Their love songs are rudely interrupted by her sister, Katherine, who thinks herself just as beautiful. In addition, Baptista explains to the suitors that Kate, as the elder of the two, must be married first. Neighbors, awakened by the serenade and the rumpus, chase the thwarted lovers away.

ACT ONE, SCENE TWO: A TAVERN   Here Petruchio, a gentleman of more generosity than means, is robbed of his last penny by two ladies of the streets. The suitors suggest that he, therefore, might be interested in the charms and fortune of Katherine. He readily agrees.

ACT ONE, SCENE THREE: INSIDE BAPTISTA'S HOUSE Bianca muses over her preferences among her three suitors. She is interrupted by a jealous outburst from Kate, a rowdy tomboy of a girl, who calls her a scheming flirt. This dispute is further interrupted by the arrival of Petruchio, who is accompanied by Bianca's suitors in disguise. Petruchio is none too favorably received by Kate. Alone with Bianca, the suitors throw off their disguises and continue their wooing in the form of singing, dancing, and music lessons. Bianca soon recognizes Lucentio as the most desirable.

Kate reacts violently against Petruchio's protestations of passion, thinking that they are a false mockery, but something in his manner convinces her, nevertheless, to accept his offer and they agree to get married.

ACT ONE, SCENE FOUR: A STREET Here neighbors on their way to Kate's wedding treat the whole matter as a huge joke. The three suitors, now in high hopes that Bianca will soon be released to marry one of them, join them.

ACT ONE, SCENE FIVE: INSIDE BAPTISTA'S HOUSE The guests have arrived. Kate in her bridal array is all expectant and waiting, but the bridegroom appears to have forgotten the day. When he does appear, in fantastic garb, Petruchio behaves very badly, ill-treating the priest and carrying off Kate before the wedding festivities have started.

ACT TWO, SCENE ONE: PETRUCHIO'S HOUSE Kate is a fiery-tempered girl and Act Two shows what Petruchio aims to do about it. In the first scene he finds fault with the food and the girl has to go without her supper.

ACT TWO, SCENE TWO: A CARNIVAL Meanwhile, in a scene at the carnival, two of Bianca's suitors, Gremio and Hortensio, encounter a masked and cloaked stranger. Both of them believing her to be Bianca are only too eager to take their marriage vows. Too late they discover that they have been duped and married to ladies of the street, who have been suitably briefed, bribed, and disguised by Lucentio.

ACT TWO, SCENE THREE: PETRUCHIO'S HOUSE When Petruchio finds fault with the new clothes that he has ordered for Kate, her weary resistance finally crumbles and she capitulates, only to find that her master is a kinder, wittier husband than she thought possible.

ACT TWO, SCENE FOUR: ENROUTE TO BIANCA'S WEDDING Petruchio indulges in more whims, fancies, and tricks, but Kate has learned her lesson and joins in the fun.

ACT TWO, SCENE FIVE: BAPTISTA'S HOUSE At Bianca's wedding the action is all tied up. Gremio and Hortensio have found out that the joys of marriage are a mixed blessing, and even Lucentio has reason to fear that Bianca is not the angel that she appeared to be. Kate, on the other hand, and to everyone's astonishment, turns out to be the truest, most obedient, most loving of wives.

Which goes to show that women are not always what they appear to be or, in other words, never judge a book by its cover.

TARANTELLA

Music by Louis Moreau Gottschalk, reconstructed and orchestrated by Hershy Kay. Choreography by George Balanchine. Costumes by Karinska. First presented by the New York City Ballet at the New York State Theatre, January 7, 1964, with Patricia McBride and Edward Villella.

This *pas de deux* is one of a long series of short ballets I have made for the gifts of specific dancers. The music is for solo piano and orchestra, based on the *Grande Tarantelle* of the New Orleans pianist-composer Louis Gottschalk who dazzled Europe and the United States with his recitals a hundred years ago. This work, which I asked Hershy Kay to orchestrate for us, is thought to be the first work for piano and orchestra ever composed by an American. It is a dazzling display piece, full of speed and high spirits. So, I hope, is the dance, which is "Neopolitan" if you like and "*demi-caractère*." The costumes are inspired by Italy, anyhow, and there are tambourines.

TCHAIKOVSKY CONCERTO NO. 2 (*see* BALLET IMPERIAL)

TCHAIKOVSKY PAS DE DEUX

Music by Peter Ilyich Tchaikovsky. Choreography by George Balanchine. Costumes by Karinska. First presented by the New York City Ballet at the City Center, New York, March 29, 1960, with Violette Verdy and Conrad Ludlow.

When Tchaikovsky composed his ballet *Swan Lake*, some of the music did not fit in with the plans of Petipa, his choreographer, and was discarded. When I learned that this music had recently been discovered in the Bolshoi Theatre archives, I was naturally interested to see what it was like. Upon receiving the score through the Tchaikovsky Foundation, I decided at once that the pieces would form an accompaniment to a *pas de deux* for two of our leading dancers. As such, it is of course a display piece, based on the music and the maximum gifts of virtuoso performers. Once, after a successful first performance of a similar display *pas de deux*, one of our dancers said that she did not know if she would be able to do the piece again. Of course she did it again, and again and again, and better! What had seemed at the beginning a stretching of her capacities became easy second nature and she went on to new achievements. Violette Verdy and Edward Villella have appeared frequently in this *pas de deux*, which is also in the repertory of the Royal Ballet and other companies.

TCHAIKOVSKY SUITE NO. 2

Music by Peter Ilyich Tchaikovsky. Choreography by Jacques d'Amboise. Production designed by John Braden. Lighting by Ronald Bates. First presented by the New York City Ballet at the New York State Theatre, Lincoln Center, January 9, 1969, with Marnee Morris, John Prinz, Allegra Kent, Francisco Moncion, Linda Merrill, and John Clifford as principals. Conducted by Robert Irving.

The first of a series of Tchaikovsky suites in the New York City Ballet, this dance ballet is performed to music from the composer's *Suite No. 2* for orchestra. In keeping with Tchaikovsky's music, which is fascinating in its Russian references, the ballet makes gestures to Russian, Georgian, and Ukrainian folklore or costumes, but the dances may be said to take place in any time and place. If you do not know this music of Tchaikovsky's, and it is no doubt the least famous of the four suites for orchestra, I with pleasure recommend that you become acquainted with it.

Reviewing the ballet for the New York *Times*, the critic Clive Barnes wrote: "Mr. d'Amboise, a strong dancer himself, of course, creates gratefully for dancers. Here in the first movement he has precisely caught in the delightfully skittish quality of Marnee Morris, the special lilt of laughter in her dancing, and contrasted this with the pouncing, very virile quality of John Prinz. Both dancers responded happily.

"The deep-set mystery of Allegra Kent and the somber power of Francisco Moncion have inspired the softer-toned second movement. Miss Kent showed just the right misty poetry, while Mr. Moncion, filled with a kind of animal nobility, made her an ideal partner.

"For the third movement the ballet reverts to the lighter-hearted tone of the beginning, and here Linda Merrill (in her first major created assignment) and John Clifford fly around blithely and impressively."

TCHAIKOVSKY SUITE NO. 3

Music by Peter Ilyich Tchaikovsky. Choreography by George Balanchine. Scenery and costumes by Nicolas Benois. Lighting by Ronald Bates. First presented by the New York City Ballet at the Saratoga Performing Arts Center, Saratoga, New York, July 23, 1970, with Karin von Aroldingen and Anthony Blum, Kay Mazzo and Conrad Ludlow, Marnee Morris and John Clifford, Gelsey Kirkland and Edward Villella in the principal roles.

In 1947, for American Ballet Theatre, I did a ballet called *Theme and Variations* that used the last two movements of Tchaikovsky's *Suite No. 3 in G*

Minor. The first three movements of this *Suite* I have always liked, too, and so I decided in 1970 to make dances for them. Putting all the dances together, plus *Theme and Variations*, we had a new work, *Tchaikovsky Suite No. 3*. It is interesting that when this *Suite*, not envisioned as a dance score, was first performed in St. Petersburg (1885), it was an enormous success, while his ballet score to *Swan Lake* (1877) was considered "too symphonic" and his music for *The Sleeping Beauty* (1890) was judged simply "very nice" by the Tsar.

1. The curtain rises on the *Élégie* after the orchestra has established a pensive, romantic mood. We are in an empty, dark space, behind a scrim, perhaps a ballroom. Ghosts are possible. A boy kneels left. Seven girls appear to him. He seems to seek another and then before we are aware of it he is dancing with one of the girls. She, like him, barefoot, dances with him in ecstatic abandonment. Both sense that this will not last long, that he is bound to lose her. She rests her head on his shoulder and acknowledges this. And soon she is one of seven girls again. She is the last to leave him as he kneels before her in the abandoned room.

2. *Valse Mélancolique:* A *pas de deux* for another couple, again with a mysterious atmosphere, behind the scrim. Nothing is permanent. She disappears, returns, goes again.

3. The *Scherzo* is danced by a girl and boy and eight supporting girls. Here the vitality of the score supports a flowing animation in the *pas de deux* and there is an impression of endless speed. Here in a brighter light, we make out chandeliers in the distance. As the music ends, the scrim rises and brilliant lighting illuminates a grand ballroom.

4. *Tema con Variazioni* begins in this space. See *Theme and Variations*, page 636.

TEXAS FOURTH

Music: traditional songs by Harvey Schmidt arranged by David Baker and orchestrated by Elizabeth Myers. Choreography by Agnes de Mille. Scenery by Oliver Smith. Costumes by A. Christina Gianini. Lighting by Nananne Porcher. First presented by the Agnes de Mille Heritage Dance Theatre at the North Carolina School of the Arts, 1973. First presented by American Ballet Theatre at the New York State Theatre, Lincoln Center, July 8, 1976, with Dennis Nahat, William Carter, Rebecca Wright, Eric Nesbitt, George de la Pena, Buddy Balough, and Ruth Mayer in principal roles.

A bicentennial celebration of memory and recollection, *Texas Fourth* reminds us what the Fourth of July was like in Texas back in 1936. It begins with four couples square-dancing on the plains while a fiddler calls the tune. A boy does a buck and wing. Next, we are in the midst of a razzmatazz Fourth in a small town. A vigorous batonist leads a troupe of drum majorettes and there is a girl who likes a boy. Everyone seems to be having a rousing, noisy great time when there is a time-stop. The girl sees the ghost of her mother and has a vision, too, of the people of *her* time, dancing and behaving in a quite different, decorous, polite, and genteel way. Texas was different then. But so is the girl, now! We are our ancestors but ourselves, too. Blessed by her mother, she rejoins the boy and the future begins.

After the first performance of *Texas Fourth* by American Ballet Theatre, Agnes de Mille was given the Handel Medallion, New York City's highest award for artistic achievement. She remarked in her acceptance speech that *Texas Fourth* is about "all those lovely, old-fashioned virtues." The action of the ballet takes place in Baird, Texas, her husband's birthplace, and the piece is dedicated to the memory of his grandmother, Roma Foy.

THEATRE

Music by Richard Strauss. Choreography by Eliot Feld. Costumes by Frank Thompson. Lighting by Jennifer Tipton. First presented by the American Ballet Company at the Brooklyn Academy of Music, New York, January 6, 1971, with Eliot Feld, Elizabeth Lee, and Edward Verso in the principal roles.

Theatre is a tragic *commedia dell'arte* ballet. Here we see the classical figures Pierrot, Columbine, and Harlequin in a new combination. The character of the ballet is prefigured by a note in the program quoting John Keats:

I asked to see what brings the hollow brain
Behind environed; what high tragedy
In the dark secret chambers of her skull
Was acting.

The score is the *Burlesque for Piano and Orchestra* of Richard Strauss.

The central figure in *Theatre* is Pierrot, whom we first see sitting making up backstage. Naked to the waist, he stares out at us, as if we were his mirror, examining his face. His countenance is a pasty mask and it is difficult to imagine its being amused at anything. A curtain comes down, lights come up, and suddenly we are on stage, with Columbine and Harlequin and other dancers. The two lovers dance together; alongside their convivial happiness Pierrot is rejected, tearful. Harlequin dances in a kind of triumph and Pierrot joins in to play ball with them. Here, too, he fails. Pulcinella doesn't help matters by introducing a bag of money into the situation. Nothing will cure Pierrot's misery. As he dances alone now his deep despair seems almost overwhelming. As if to crush and release him simultaneously a shower of colored balls falls on Pierrot from above. Now the dancers return and the sad figure of Pierrot leaves the scene.

Writing of *Theatre* in *Dance and Dancers* magazine, Patricia Barnes said that "Feld is quite exceptional in the role of Pierrot, deeply poignant yet never sentimental. It is a performance I shall treasure. As Harlequin, Edward Verso has just the right air of cool mischief. His dancing, quickly precise, helped to create a character, and Elizabeth Lee was equally successful with her sleekly feminine Columbine.

"Among the major assets of the ballet were the incredibly beautiful costumes by Frank Thompson, which must be among the most successful created for an American company in recent years. In their color, cut and conception they were ravishing. While placed within the world of *commedia dell'arte*, they were nevertheless freshly and brilliantly realized and once again Jennifer Tipton's lighting helped enormously. Throughout the season Christopher Keene produced playing from the orchestra of a consistent high standard. He is a young conductor of immense talent, and has been of enormous help to this company."

THEME AND VARIATIONS

Classic ballet. Music by Peter Ilyich Tchaikovsky. Choreography by George Balanchine. Scenery and costumes by Woodman Thompson. First presented by Ballet Theatre at the City Center, New York, November 26, 1947, with Alicia Alonso and Igor Youskevitch in the leading roles.

In addition to his ballet scores, Tchaikovsky composed a great deal of music ideal for dancing. This was perhaps natural for a man who had discovered in ballet a genuine inspiration. Between the time of his first ballet, *Swan Lake* (1877), and his second, *The Sleeping Beauty* (1890), Tchaikovsky wrote four orchestral suites. They were not composed for dancing, yet to listen to them is to think immediately of dancing. They remind us that it is a pity that the composer was not, during this period, a favorite of his contemporary choreographers.

In 1933 I arranged the ballet *Mozartiana* to the fourth of these orchestral suites. *Theme and Variations* is arranged to the final movement of the *Suite No. 3, in G.* This is a dance ballet; like *Ballet Imperial*, it evokes that great period in classical dancing when Russian ballet flourished with the aid of Tchaikovsky's music.

When the curtain rises, we see that the setting is formal: the scene is a great ballroom with huge, towering pillars decorated with vines, luxurious red draperies, and crystal chandeliers containing thousands of candles. A formal garden can be seen in the background. There is a *corps de ballet* of twelve girls arranged in two groups about the ballerina and the *premier danseur*. The girls are dressed in muted colors; the ballerina is in white with a coronol of white flowers. The *premier danseur* wears a blue costume and a blue beret embellished with a white plume.

The music begins, and the ballerina points her toe, dancing softly as the violins play the principal theme. Her steps are simple and graceful, like the melody, and with her feet she seems to point to the quiet charm of the music. Her partner similarly introduces the music and leaves the stage with the ballerina. The twelve girls move forward lightly. They dance a brief ensemble as the theme is repeated on insistent plucked strings to the accompaniment of flutes and clarinets.

Now the tempo increases. The ballerina returns and, surrounded by the *corps de ballet,* begins to display her virtuosity, whirling quickly and brightly in *fouettés* to a restatement of the theme which the strings treat like a *perpetuum mobile.*

The woodwinds announce the theme in a slower tempo; the *corps de ballet* of twelve girls divides into three close groups and describe shifting, flowing lines on the stage. The music becomes assertive again in the fourth variation. The full orchestra plays the theme with a flourish, and the *premier danseur* performs a graceful, yet animated, dance.

When the soloist has left the stage, the orchestra snaps the *corps de ballet* into movement with a sudden chord and plays a fast fugue to which the girls dance their first brilliant ensemble. Just as suddenly, the variation ends. The *premier danseur* now dances alone, describing diagonals across the stage with long, bold leaps. The music is staccato, the strings whirring in tarantella fashion to strong, persistent chords.

The seventh variation is a subdued and noble treatment of the theme. Four girls gather softly, hold hands, and move slowly on point. The ballerina enters. The girls cluster about her in a close semicircle. The English horn varies the theme, and the girls support the ballerina as she executes beautiful adagio movements.

The music trippingly accelerates. The ballerina separates herself from the *corps* and dances vigorously and joyously to the demanding rhythm, her pose changing with quick elegance to the beat of the music, her *pointes* stabbing at the floor in response to the sharp attack of the orchestra. She turns rapidly across the stage and pauses.

The *premier danseur* joins her. A solo violin sounds the melody, and a *pas de deux* begins. Its beginning is softly playful; but as a new variation sweeps the orchestra into a piercing, flowing melody, the dancing is noble and tender. To this theme of open joy and romance the ballerina, supported by her partner, executes slowly and perfectly movements—simple, yet also difficult—that display her full beauty.

When the two principals leave the stage, a drum roll sounds, followed by a bright fanfare on the horns. Eight boys enter with a flourish. The *corps de ballet* joins them, with the two principal dancers, as the orchestra announces with blaring pomp a regal polonaise. There are swift variations by the two principals—the ballerina accompanied by the girls; the *premier danseur,* by the boys—and rapid regroupings and shiftings of partners in the ensemble as the final variation increases in liveliness. The two principals, hand in hand, lead the dancers about the ballroom in a sweeping circle. There is vigorous dancing to the final crashes of music, and then, at the last chord, a tableau in which the ballerina is lifted high to her partner's shoulder while all her court salutes her.

THE THREE-CORNERED HAT

Dramatic ballet in one act. Music by Manuel de Falla. Choreography by Leonide Massine. Book by Gregorio Martínez Sierra. Scenery and costumes by Pablo Picasso. First presented by Diaghilev's Ballets Russes at the Al-

hambra Theatre, London, July 22, 1919, with Leonide Massine as the Miller, Tamara Karsavina as the Miller's Wife, Leon Woizikowski as the Corregidor, and Stanislas Idzikowski as the Dandy. First presented in the United States by the Ballet Russe de Monte Carlo at the St. James Theatre, New York, March 9, 1934, with Leon Woizikowski as the Miller and Tamara Toumanova as the Miller's Wife.

The Three-Cornered Hat tells a love story of Spain with humor and warmth. The scene is a small Spanish village. The Spanish tone of the ballet is established immediately by the music, by cries of "Olé! Olé! Olé! Olé!" from behind the curtain, and by the sound of rhythmic castanets, dancing feet, and hand clapping.

The curtain rises on the village scene. The village miller stands before his house, whistling to a black bird who sits in a cage. The bird will not sing as he wishes it to. The miller's wife comes out of the house and teases her husband. He chases her and they embrace.

The couple go to the well to draw water. While the miller is busy at the well, a dandy passes by and blows kisses to his wife, who responds flirtatiously. The miller looks up and sees this exchange and chases the dandy off. He is not angry with his wife. He is delighted that other men find her as beautiful as he does. They are very much in love.

Now the governor of the province, the corregidor, enters with an escort. A doddering old fool, he looks absurd in his finery among the simple folk of the village. He wears a three-cornered hat, symbol of his class and position.

Almost immediately the corregidor eyes the miller's wife and decides that she must be his. The miller's wife is polite to him, but no more. He passes on. Noting that his wife is getting all the attention, the miller decides he'd better give another girl some favor. He playfully flirts with one of the lovely girls of the village. Now that both husband and wife have cause to be jealous, they are amused at each other and embrace.

The miller goes into the house. His wife, remaining outside, dances a brilliant fandango. The corregidor has come back and secretly watches her. Soon he approaches her and tries to make advances. The woman eludes him cleverly and flees. The old man, however, pursues her.

The miller has watched this scene from inside the house and runs out to help his wife. The corregidor can run no more and falls to the ground, exhausted. The miller and his wife pick him up, dust him off, and try to act as if it were all an accident, but the corregidor, furious with them, suggests that this is only the beginning of what they may expect of him. The husband and wife dance together.

Evening falls. The village folk come to the miller's house to join in a festival with the happy couple. The miller gives them wine and then dances alone a farruca, which everyone applauds. The villagers hear the approach of marching soldiers. The escorts of the corregidor enter. The men arrest the miller and take him off. Abandoned by her friends, the miller's wife is alone.

But not for long. The corregidor is back again, seeking her favor now with real determination. The miller's wife throws him to the ground as he clumsily holds her. He rises with difficulty and pursues her to the village bridge, which crosses a running stream. On the bridge, the corregidor again attempts to embrace the girl. In the process of pushing him away, the miller's wife pushes him off the bridge into the stream. She laughs at him, but helps the corregidor out of the water. But the old fool takes up the chase again. The miller's wife takes a gun from the house and, threatening the corregidor with buckshot, flees over the bridge away from the village.

The corregidor stands in front of the miller's house, alone, his clothes still dripping from the dunking he got in the stream. He takes off his outer garments and his three-cornered hat, lays them out to dry, and goes into the house to sleep.

Dawn comes. The miller has escaped the corregidor's henchmen and returns home. In front of his house he sees the corregidor's clothes and the three-cornered hat! Then he observes the corregidor himself, walking around in one of his own nightshirts! The miller decides there's only one thing to do. He will pursue the corregidor's wife, who is also young and beautiful! On the walls of his house he draws a caricature of the corregidor and leaves.

Now the poor corregidor is attacked by his own soldiers, who don't recognize him in the miller's nightshirt. He curses them, and the village folk come to see what the trouble is. The miller and his wife, who have found each other outside the town, come in. Their friends are told what the corregidor has tried to do, and in anger all the people rise up against the governor and his cohorts. The intruders are routed, and all dance triumphantly, led by the miller and his wife. A dummy representing the defeated corregidor is thrown higher and higher into the air by the crowd.

NOTES   Although Leon Woizikowski first danced the miller at the American première of *The Three-Cornered Hat*, Leonide Massine later danced the role in the United States. The ballet was revived by Massine for Ballet Theatre in 1943 and for the Sadler's Wells Ballet in 1947.

Tania Massine, the choreographer's daughter, assisted by Yurek Lazowski, staged a revival of *The Three-Cornered Hat* for the City Center Joffrey Ballet in New York, September 25, 1969. Luis Fuente was the *Miller*, Barbara Remington the *Miller's wife*, Basil Thompson the *Corregidor*, Rebecca Wright the *Corregidor's wife*, and Frank Bays the *Dandy*. The original Picasso designs were reconstructed by William Pitkin.

THREE ESSAYS

Music by Charles Ives. Choreography by Lar Lubovitch. First presented by American Ballet Theatre at the City Center, New York, January 15, 1974, with Warren Conover, Christine Sarry, Clark Tippet, and Ian Horvath in leading roles.

Like an earlier work by the dancer-choreographer Lar Lubovitch for the same ensemble (see *Scherzo for Massah Jack*), this ballet is a period piece based on its score. The American master Charles Ives was, of course, remarkable in his many gifts, among them a memorable capacity to recollect the past, which is what the ballet here also aims to do. The composer's notations for the three parts of the music are embodied by the choreographer: "Elegy to Our Forefathers"; "The Rockstrewn Hills Join in the People's Outdoor Meeting"; "From Hanover Square North at the End of a Tragic Day (1915)."

What we see portrayed in dance terms is a commentary on these themes of the composer, and an ironic one, relating to World War I, and all that conflict meant, or seemed to mean, to Americans, together with its consequences.

Commenting in *Cue* magazine, the critic Robert Jacobson wrote: "Lubovitch's piece is marked by turbulence . . . and commands respect . . . His images are often memorable and he leaves you thinking."

THREE VIRGINS AND A DEVIL

> *Music by Ottorino Respighi. Scenario by Ramon Reed. Choreography by Agnes de Mille. Scenery and costumes by Motley. Setting designed by Arne Lundborg. First presented by Ballet Theatre at the Majestic Theatre, New York, February 11, 1941, with Agnes de Mille as the* Priggish One, *Lucia Chase as the* Greedy One, *Annabelle Lyon as the* Lustful One, *Eugene Loring as a* Devil, *and Jerome Robbins as a* Youth.

The critic Robert J. Pierce has called this ballet a burlesque in the form of a medieval morality play. Arranged to Respighi's *Ancient Dances and Airs for the Lute,* this *danse caractère* personifies three typical but differing young women and shows what happens to them under devilish circumstances.

After a short overture the curtain rises on a medieval landscape, a monastery gate at the right, with door shut; a grotto at the left, leading to a cave. Three girls come in. Their leader, a priggish lass, is trying to drag her friends to church. She displays maximum piety in this undertaking, trying to persuade the Greedy One, who is decked out in finery, to put her belongings in the alms box. Not to be overlooked, the Lustful One, a child of nature with a garland of flowers, sees the directions things are taking and decides to renounce her wreath. When a prancing Youth enters to find all the virgins swaying in prayer, he is clearly astonished at such unanimous piety. He cannot persuade any of the girls to join him.

Now a hermit enters, asking the Greedy One for money. The beggar is a peculiar sort of fellow, almost spastic in his movements as he seems to try to hide one of his feet under his cloak. The foot keeps trembling and bothering him. When he can bear it no longer, he throws off the cloak and reveals himself as a Devil, tail, horns, cloven foot, and all.

The virgins, in their uniform piety, are appalled, but when he brings out a sort of cello and starts to play, they all dance lustily to his tune. They get so carried away by their revels that when the Youth returns, again beckoning to the Lustful One, she jumps obligingly onto his back, whereupon he carries her swiftly into the grotto—a gate, of course, to hell.

The Devil tempts next the Greedy One, who responds to his offer of a bright jewel and follows her sister to the other world. The Priggish One, of course, is harder to tempt and the Devil has his own time of it getting from her the proper response. She mothers him and strikes terror into him by trying to get him into the monastery. Unable to bear such tactics any longer, he begins to chase her like a man possessed. In terror she flees, running from him in a wider and wider circle, but pursuing him, too, determined to have yet another convert. The widening circle of the chase leads to the grotto entrance, where the Devil stands aside and permits the lady to dash down to hell with her own momentum.

NOTES   Agnes de Mille first produced a ballet to this theme in London, in 1934, at the Palace Theatre, in the musical comedy *Why Not Tonight?* Greta Nissen, Elizabeth Schooling, and M. Braithwaite were the Girls and Stanislas Idzikowski the Devil. The music was by Walford Hyden.

American Ballet Theatre revived *Three Virgins and a Devil* at the New York State Theatre, Lincoln Center, New York, July 25, 1973, with Sallie Wilson (now called the Fanatical One), Ruth Mayer, and Christine Sarry as the Virgins, Dennis Nahat as a Devil, and Daniel Levans as a Youth. The conductor was Akira Endo and the lighting was by Nananne Porcher.

TIL EULENSPIEGEL

Ballet by Jean Babilée. Music by Richard Strauss. Choreography by Jean Babilée. Scenery and costumes by Tom Keogh. First presented by Les Ballets des Champs-Élysées, November 9, 1949, at the Théâtre des Champs-Élysées, Paris, with Jean Babilée in the title role. First presented in the United States by Ballet Theatre at the Metropolitan Opera House, New York, September 25, 1951, with a cast headed by Jean Babilée and Ruth Ann Koesun. Costumes by Helene Pons.

Richard Strauss's score *Til Eulenspiegel's Merry Pranks* was not composed to be danced, but the fact that the music has a plot and relates incidents in the life of one of the most popular figures in European folklore has made it naturally attractive to choreographers. Til Eulenspiegel is the perennial prankster who never seems to get his comeuppance. Although he may hurt people when he tricks them, he really has no harmful intentions; he is a maker of fun motivated by his own innocent pleasure and not by cunning. Such a man sooner or later runs into trouble with the law, for much as we may admire his artfulness and daring, the law will be more impressed with the number of his misdemeanors.

This ballet shows us the roguery of Til—his inability to conform to convention and his contempt for the law. Here his pranks are so good-humored that even the law is inclined to forgive him.

The curtain rises as the music begins. The scene is an improvised impression of an ancient market place. Against a mottled gray background, five colorful booths are arranged in a semicircle. The light is dim; spotlights shine down on the brightly colored awnings over the booths. A girl enters. She is small, has long blond hair, and wears a flowing dress. She dances across the market place to the soft opening bars of the music and disappears.

Two by two, a group of ragamuffin merchants march out to stand behind their booths and wait for customers. As soon as they are all stationed at their jobs, they look in unison from right to left. A quiet, impudent theme is heard in the orchestra, and the men sense that something is going on behind their backs. They are right. Til Eulenspiegel dances in. His face is chalk-white beneath his orange hair, but this does not disguise his expression of impudence. His dance is spontaneously graceful and grotesque at the same time; we imagine already that anything he does will be funny.

As he runs about the market place, Til almost collides with a young girl. Immediately he begins to make up to her. He kneels before her, begging for a mere glance. The girl, dressed in formal medieval costume, will have none of his impertinence and repulses him. This only encourages Til, who encircles her in a tumbling dance that infuriates the girl. When he sees that she does not like him, Til makes fun of her behind her back. The merchants are delighted. The girl orders him away. The exuberant Til complies and jumps up backward to sit on one of the booths. There he watches the girl with what seems to be an innocent eye. But the cymbals crash, the music bursts into a loud ruckus. At a sudden signal from Til, all the merchants jump out from behind their booths. They grab the girl and toss her in the air. She crawls off, disheveled, on all fours—no longer a charming young lady: Til's magic has turned her into a witch.

Til and the merchants go back to their booths. A courtly theme is heard, and a gentleman enters with his lady. Til is very amused at their formal ways and laughs at the flowing feather in the gentleman's cap. They try not to notice him, but Til forces himself between them and tries to engage the lady's attention. He jumps up and down in his excitement to please her. He pleads with her to notice him and to send her escort away so that they may dance together alone. The lady, however, is shocked by this behavior. Unfortunately her escort cannot assist her, for just as he flirts with the lady, Til is also trying to humiliate the gentleman. He runs out and returns quickly, dressed in a hat filled with variously colored long-flowing feathers. When he bows to the lady, these absurd feathers reach to the floor. She now thinks him ridiculous as well as rude and will never respond to his advances. Til must have his good-humored revenge. He throws down his hat with a flourish at the lady's feet and challenges her lover to a duel. The lady is aghast as the two men assume dueling stances before her. The merchants applaud the combat. The two duelists rush each other, turn each other upside down in a cartwheel of movement, and roll over and over together, their bodies joined in a tumbling hoop. The gentleman has clearly had enough by this time and, seizing his lady by the hand, dashes off.

No sooner have they departed than a group of ragged hunchbacks come into the market place, begging for alms. The lights dim, Til runs out, and the merchants hide behind their booths. Now Til is back again, but dressed in a long black cape and a high-peaked hat. He, too, is a hunchback all of a sudden; he joins the pilgrimage of the stricken men. The men accept him as their equal in misery and marvel when by a quick miracle he is cured: the hump on his back has vanished! They congratulate him on his cure and, to ensure a cure for themselves, do what Til anticipated: they give him all their money and walk out of the square, certain that this tribute to one of their former fellows will hasten their own recovery. The wealthy Til rids himself of cap and cloak and counts his fortune.

His girl, Nell, the blonde who appeared at the beginning of the ballet, comes into the square. In the soft light, she and Til dance together. Now completely happy, he swings her around and around in the air. A distant trumpet call is heard; Til cups his hand to his ear for a moment to listen, but then continues with the dance. He and Nell rush off into the night together.

The trumpet theme grows in the orchestra. Til runs back in and circles the stage in leaps timed to its open, joyous melody. The merchants jump out from behind their booths, tear down the awnings, and—using the awning poles for lances—surround him in a mock military drill. Til, in the center, jumps up and down in glee. The merchants form a parade and rush around the stage. At the theme's fullest crescendo, Til leaps onto their backs and rides high above them in triumph.

But the theme is cut short sharply. There is a menacing drum roll, the theme of the gallows, and ominous, plodding music changes Til's ebullience into fear. Six soldiers dash in and rush him. Til runs for one of the booths, but the soldiers jump up after him. Til escapes between their legs and hides underneath. Til's impudent theme, sounded by the clarinet, laughs at the loud, heavy theme of the law. The soldiers gang up on him again; again he escapes and the music ridicules them. Finally they grab him and hold him securely after a long tussle.

One of the soldiers runs off. He returns with a judge and a hangman. Til's legs run in the air as he is held motionless; he wraps his legs around one of the soldiers in his fright. The judge flourishes a scroll and begins to read the indictment against Til for all his crimes. The criminal is led forward, his head bowed. A soldier kneels down to form the chopping block, and Til is placed across it. The hangman aims the ax. The sonorous theme of authority is sounded firmly; Til's merry theme reaches a high shriek of terror and disintegrates as it descends the scale. There is a moment of silence. Still the ax is posed above Til, but the executioner does not move. Nell enters on the right. The judge, the executioner, the soldiers—all turn to look at her. They pardon Til because of the reality of his love for her and imagine that with Nell he will lead a less prankish life. His head still on the block, Til anxiously feels the back of his neck. He looks up carefully. When he sees that they don't intend to execute him, after all, he rushes over to Nell and kneels to her in gratitude. He touches her hands then, and they dance briefly.

Now that everything is back to normal, now that he still has his neck and his Nell, Til reverts instantly to his old ways: he runs over, assaults the judge, and berates him for treating him like a common criminal! Before the judge can retaliate, Til has run off after Nell.

Babilée's *Til Eulenspiegel* was the second ballet based on Richard Strauss's famous score. The first was by Vaslav Nijinsky, whose last ballet it was. Nijinsky's *Til* was presented for the first time by Diaghilev's Ballets Russes at the Manhattan Opera House, New York, October 23, 1916. The scenery and costumes were by Robert Edmond Jones. Carl Van Vechten wrote of this performance:

"*Til Eulenspiegel* is the only new ballet the Russians have produced in America. In selecting this work and in his arrangement of the action Nijinsky was moved, no doubt, by consideration for the limitations of the company as it existed. The scenery and costumes by Robert E. Jones, New York, were decidedly diverting—the best work this talented young man has done, I think. Over a deep, spreading background of ultramarine, the crazy turrets of medieval castles leaned dizzily to and fro. The costumes were exaggerations of the exaggerated fashions of the Middle Ages. Mr. Jones added feet of stature to the already elongated peaked headdresses of the period. The trains of the velvet robes, which might have extended three yards, were allowed to trail the full depth of the Manhattan Opera House stage. The colors were oranges, reds, greens, and blues, those indeed of Bakst's *Scheherazade*, but so differently disposed that they made an entirely dissimilar impression. The effect reminded one spectator of a Spanish omelet.

"In arranging the scenario, Nijinsky followed in almost every detail Wilhelm Klatte's description of the meaning of the music, which is printed in programme books whenever the tone-poem is performed, without Strauss' authority, but sometimes with his sanction. Nijinsky was quite justified in altering the end of the work, which hangs the rogue-hero, into another practical joke. His version of this episode fits the music and, in the original *Til Eulenspiegel*, Til is not hanged, but dies in bed. The keynote of Nijinsky's interpretation was gaiety. He is as utterly picaresque as the work itself; he reincarnated the spirit of Gil Blas; indeed, a new quality crept into stage expression through this characterization. Margaret Wycherly, one of the most active admirers of the dancer, told me after the first performance that she felt that he had for the first time leaped into the hearts of the great American public, whose appreciation of his subtler art as expressed in *Narcisse, Petrouchka*, and even *Scheherazade*, had been more moderate. There were those who protested that this was not the Til of the German legends, but any actor who attempts to give form to a folk or historical character, or even a character derived from fiction is forced to run counter to many an observer's preconceived ideas."

TILT

Music by Igor Stravinsky. Choreography by Hans van Manen. Decor and costumes by Jean-Paul Vroom. First presented by the Netherlands Dance Theatre, January 21, 1972, at the Circustheater, Scheveningen, Holland. First presented in the United States by the same ensemble at the Brooklyn Academy of Music, New York, April 7, 1972.

The choreographer, Hans van Manen, has described his own ballet: "Stravinsky's *Concerto in D for String Orchestra* [the same score Jerome Robbins used in 1951 for his ballet *The Cage*] is played in its entirety twice—the choreography being almost exactly the same for both versions. However, with the repeat of the music, as opposed to the first time it is played, the choreography for the six dancers is redistributed as follows:

—the first variation for six dancers is divided into three *pas de deux*
—the *pas de deux* is danced simultaneously by three couples
—the male variation is performed by three girls.

In the section that follows the sexes are transposed—the girls dance the parts of the men and the men those of the girls.

"The next three *pas de deux* remain unchanged but are danced by different couples. The finale is repeated in mirror-image with a change in each of the two *pas de deux*. Movement alone has no meaning for me in itself; it takes its significance only from the context in which it is placed."

TIME PAST SUMMER

Music by Peter Ilyich Tchaikovsky. Choreography by Benjamin Harkarvy. First presented by the Pennsylvania Ballet at the Academy of Music, Philadelphia, February 14, 1974, with Alba Calzada, Joanne Danto, and Lawrence Rhodes in leading roles.

Eleven Tchaikovsky songs accompany this ballet, which looks back to the Russia of Chekhov and some of the characters in his memorable plays and stories. Writing in the *Dancing Times* the critic George Dorris said: "People at a Chekhovian garden party listen to two singers and think over their lives . . . An effective, moving ballet."

LE TOMBEAU DE COUPERIN

Music by Maurice Ravel. Choreography by George Balanchine. Lighting by Ronald Bates. First presented by the New York City Ballet at the Hommage à Ravel at the New York State Theatre, Lincoln Center, May 29, 1975. Conducted by Robert Irving.

Ravel said that, in style, *Le Tombeau* is not so much a homage to the great French composer François Couperin as a tribute to eighteenth-century French music in general. The music, orchestrated from an original piano suite dedicated to friends of Ravel who had died in World War I, is in six parts: *Prélude, Fugue, Forlane, Rigaudon, Menuet,* and *Toccata*. The ballet that I arranged to this music doesn't say anything beyond the combination of these particular dancers moving to Ravel's lovely score, his memorial to Couperin.

These particular dancers are sixteen in number, eight couples divided into two quadrilles. They are mid-twentieth-century dancers moving to the work of a man who, in 1919, wrote tributes to a composer who flourished at the court of Louis XIV.

The American composer Norman Lloyd has written in the Golden Encyclopedia of Music that Couperin "is one of the greatest composers of the Baroque period, and one of the subtlest and most musicianly minds France has produced." I wholeheartedly agree; one of the pleasures this particular piece gave me as we made so many ballets so swiftly for our homage to Ravel in 1975 was my recollection of this master's work.

TRACES

Music by Gustav Mahler. Choreography by John Cranko. Scenery and costumes by Jürgen Rose. First presented by the Stuttgart Ballet at the Württemberg State Theatre, Stuttgart, Germany, April 7, 1973. First presented in the United States by the Stuttgart Ballet at the Metropolitan Opera House, New York, May 30, 1973, with Marcia Haydée, Heinz Clauss, and Richard Cragun in the principal roles. Conducted by Stewart Kershaw.

Traces is a dramatic ballet about the past, as recalled in the present. The score is the *Adagio* from Mahler's *Tenth Symphony*. To its music a woman, released from obviously terrible captivity (a concentration camp?), adjusts to her new freedom while the past pulls at her memory.

The scene is an empty ballroom, with a sofa and chair. The woman enters. Her lover greets her, patient, understanding, warm. As they look together toward the back of the room, a group of dancers emerges. In the midst of their dance the woman sees a vision of a man in her past. He, a victim of persecution, head shaven, thin, in ragged clothes, draws her sympathy. In his spell her world seems to change completely. In the darkness the dead appear to waken. They rise slowly and crawl toward us. The man in her past stands out among them, leaping and springing in a kind of frantic agony. The woman joins him and comforts him when he collapses. Alternately drawn toward him and away from him, dreading yet cherishing the memory, the woman flings herself against the man. Now he leaves. She goes mad with grief. In the mass of prisoners he falls. They step over him—another victim, as they themselves shall likely be. The woman seeks refuge in her new lover's arms. She looks back at the prisoners, who turn suddenly and drop the rags from their backs to reveal numbers. They crouch down again and the ballroom dancers move among them. The woman dances with her new lover but is not to be comforted by his gentleness. Moving rigidly as in a trance, she walks slowly with him toward the back, toward a glowing circle of fire that might be the sun.

TRIAD

Music by Serge Prokofiev. Choreography by Kenneth MacMillan. Setting and costumes by Peter Unsworth. First presented by the Royal Ballet at

*the Royal Opera House, Covent Garden, London, January 19, 1972, with
Antoinette Sibley, Anthony Dowell, and Wayne Eagling. First presented
in the United States by the Royal Ballet at the Metropolitan Opera House,
New York, in 1972.*

The three principal dancers in *Triad* are a girl, a boy, and his brother. The two
boys are devoted but from the start there is a problem. One of them is upset
and cries. A girl comes to them and dances. One brother tries to shield the
other from the effects of this dance of the girl's but the girl will not permit it.
Now one of the boys dances for the girl, then she again for *him*. After a dance
for all three, the girl tries to persuade one to come away with her. She goes
but he stays. The two boys dance, one continuing to try to shield the other.
But not for long. When three male "companions" enter, the stronger brother
throws the weaker to them, only to rescue him at the last minute. After a passionate *pas de deux* between the stronger boy and the girl, the younger
brother despairs. He leaves but returns, tries to separate them, fails, again despairs.

NOTES   Writing in *Saturday Review* about *Triad,* the critic Walter Terry
said that while the ballet "may seem to some to have homosexual overtones, I
felt it to be rooted in something like the deep mystique of twins who are both
dual and one. MacMillan captures this feeling tastefully but, what is more,
imaginatively. The contours of his movements are generally balletic, but the
dynamism is that of modern dance; that is, indeed, a striking integration of the
elegance and dignity of classicism with the passionate, almost visceral, expres-
sivity of free dance.

"In the cast I saw, Dowell and Wayne Eagling were most appealing as the
brothers whose bond goes deeper than physicality, and Miss Sibley, as the girl,
touched the heart with a portrayal involving need, desire, rejection. A most rewarding, adult ballet, rich in striking designs as well as in dramatic intensity."

TRINITY

*Music by Alan Raph and Lee Holdridge. Choreography by Gerald Arpino.
Lighting by Jennifer Tipton. Conductor: Walter Hagen. Rock Group: Virgin Wool. Organ: Hub Miller. Boys Choir: St. Luke's Chapel. First presented
by the City Center Joffrey Ballet, October 9, 1969, with Christian Holder,
Gary Chryst, Rebecca Wright, Dermot Burke, Donna Cowen, Starr Danias,
and James Dunne in principal roles.*

Named for its three parts, *Sunday, Summerland,* and *Saturday, Trinity* is a
homage to youth, joyful and aspiring. It uses for music themes reminiscent of
Gregorian chant and Baroque styles translated into rock, employing sections of
the regular orchestra, a boy's choir, and a rock group, "Virgin Wool." There are
two conductors, one for the orchestra and chorus, one who leads the rock
group from the organ.

Thirteen dancers participate in *Sunday*, which is heralded by a brass chorale before the curtain rises. The dancers enter gradually until finally all are present to respond to the throb of the rock organ. This is a group dance, exuberant, demanding in its rhythm and pulse, persistent, rejoicing in companionship and celebratory of youth. There are a number of solos and small ensembles as the mixture of rock and Baroque mounts in intensity. At the end, all lie in a circle on the floor as lead boy leaves.

In the part called *Summerland*, the pulse of the score slows down. The dancers rise from the circle and in varied ensembles suggest the sweetness of young love. Couple after couple now take the stage, one of them dancing a protracted adagio of affection. The accent here is on high spirits, too, shown in the many remarkable lifts in which the boys reach the girls up to the skies. All six couples rejoin as chimes sound twice and the boys carry the girls off.

Saturday, standing for the ancient Sabbath, begins as two boys enter the darkened scene carrying candles. The entire group follows, each bearing a lighted candle. They leave then and a boy comes forward to perform a dance to the hymn/rock beat, a version of the *Ite, missa est* that concludes the Latin Mass. He is joined by other male soloists and we have an impression that there is nothing on earth like lifting your arms and responding to the swell of the mighty organ that dominates the music here. The score intensifies in cracking crescendos of sound. All of the dancers then re-enter, each putting a candle on stage. The music gradually diminishes and the lights diminish, too, so that all we see on stage is the presentation of the candles.

NOTES Speaking of his ballet to Anna Kisselgoff of the New York *Times*, the choreographer of *Trinity*, Gerald Arpino, said, "I think I'm in tune with my time. . . . This is my Aquarius ballet. I wanted the classic idiom with its escape from gravity—for the highest reach man can assume. I don't want to sound corny, but this is a ballet about man seeking his inner self. When the kids leave the candles on the floor, it's not meant to suggest just the literal peace marches. In the end, each individual must express himself. All he can leave is the light of himself."

The critic Andrew Porter reviewed *Trinity* at the time of the City Center Joffrey Ballet's London debut in May, 1971: "Gerald Arpino's *Trinity* made a whizzing start. For here the company seemed to be the 20th century's answer to the Bolshoi Ballet: which is to say nothing prissy, and nothing pretentious, but tremendous vigour and soaring virtuosity; flashing, exhilarating achievement rather than refined niceties; punch rather than polish. But—unlike the Bolshoi—an imagery both on stage and from the players that belongs to the present day: thoroughly demotic images supercharged into a buoyant art.

"The score, for the company's own group The Virgin Wool, choirboys, electric organ and orchestra, strikes into plain chant and Palestrina, and turns them into rock—not self-consciously but exuberantly. The dancing strikes into classicism at times, and breaks it into modern movement. The whole is heady and joyful, a celebration of a youth that can effortlessly encompass and transform the past."

John T. Elson in *Time* magazine wrote that *Trinity* "represents a throbbing fusion of classic dance with the sound of now. It perfectly epitomizes the jaunty style and passionate, youthful temperament of the New York City Center's Joffrey Ballet."

Patricia Barnes, in *Dance and Dancers*, wrote: "*Trinity* is_a hard ballet to describe for its vitality, sincerity and passion, its dynamic coloring, both choreographic and musical, must be seen. Nor can words alone convey the personality and power of dancers such as Gary Chryst, Christian Holder and Dermot Burke; these three did a great deal to make *Trinity* the success it was. However, the whole cast had a splendid exuberance that made the ballet a pleasure to watch."

In the *Village Voice*, writing of the work of choreographer Gerald Arpino, Deborah Jowitt said: "His new ballet, *Trinity*, never lets go of you, never stops pounding and hurling fast, smart-alecky movement at you. He ignores—or perhaps uses—several basic dichotomies with magnificent ease. The Joffrey dancers are young and phenomenal. The best of them may grow in artistry or sensitivity, but they will probably never be more indomitable. Although they are young, they already have a discipline that very few people their age possess. I think it is the combination of discipline and vigor that excites Arpino. The three-part *Trinity* is set to some very good rock music (written by Alan Raph and Lee Holdridge and played by Virgin Wool), and the whole dance seems a taut by-play between the freedom inherent in rock and the control necessary for ballet. The dancers progress from the flung *développés* of Broadway to perfectly centered pirouettes rendered dangerous and exciting by fast, off-balance head circles or contrary arm gestures. This gives the movement an odd duality; ballet with a loose, whizzing quality in one part of the body only.

"Rock is heavy, ballet light. In *Trinity*, the dancers skid and wiggle on top of the beat; they punch it, but rarely drop onto it. Another interesting paradox. The movement is, for the most part, fast and very intricate—except for a slow ritual with votive candles in the last section and a softer second movement that features those stunning one-arm lifts that drove the crowd wild."

THE TRIUMPH OF DEATH

Dance drama in ten scenes after Eugène Ionesco by Flemming Flindt. Music by Thomas Koppel. Scenery and costumes by Poul Arnt Thomsen. Lighting by Jorgen Mydtskov. Music recorded by The Savage Rose. First presented by the Royal Danish Ballet at the Royal Theatre, Copenhagen, Denmark, February 19, 1972. First presented by the same ensemble at the Metropolitan Opera House, New York, May 27, 1976.

A harsh and direct statement of the ills of this and other times, set to a score by a Danish rock group, this ballet sets out to deliver a message against all the destructive forces in the modern world, from pollution to political tyranny and human corruption. In a universal protest designed to force audiences to open their eyes, Flindt shows a materialistic society destroyed by corruptive influences.

TROIS VALSES ROMANTIQUES

Music by Emmanuel Chabrier. Choreography by George Balanchine. Costumes by Karinska. First presented by the New York City Ballet at the New York State Theatre, April 6, 1967, with Melissa Hayden and Arthur Mitchell, Gloria Govrin and Frank Ohman, and Marnee Morris and Kent Stowell in the principal roles.

This is the third ballet I have done to music of Chabrier, a favorite composer of mine. I first heard music by this marvelous Frenchman soon after I left Russia and joined Diaghilev's Ballets Russes. In Paris I heard a concert of his music and liked it right away. I thought then that doing a ballet to Chabrier's music would be a pleasure and when the first opportunity presented itself some years later, I arranged *Cotillon*. The third of the *Trois Valses Romantiques* was included in that score. Then there was *Bourrée Fantasque*.

The ballet has no subject beyond the music and what it stands for to me. The first waltz is marked *Très vite et impétueusement*, the second *Mouvement modéré de valse* and the third *Animé*. The dances I arranged to these lovely pieces are simply expressive of the music as I see it, dances for a boy and a girl with two supporting couples, and a *corps de ballet* of six couples. The dances are about love and romance and what might happen.

TWICE

Music by Herbie Mann, Steve Miller Band, James Brown, and Santana. Choreography by Hans van Manen. Film visualization by Jean-Paul Vroom. Assistant film direction by Richard Brink. Costumes by Joop Stovkis. First presented by the Netherlands Dance Theatre at the Sadler's Wells Theatre, London, November 2, 1970. First presented in the United States by the same ensemble, April 2, 1972, at the Brooklyn Academy of Music.

Like *Mutations*, the signature work of the Netherlands Dance Theatre in the early 1970s, *Twice* relies on both live dances and dance on film. Hans van Manen was responsible for the cine-choreography of *Mutations*, a technique he elaborates here. The title, originally *Sock It to Me*, applies to repeats in movement and to the mirroring of live movement in film.

Twice consists of four parts. The first, *Double*, to Herbie Mann's "Memphis Underground," is performed by an ensemble on stage whose movements are seen, too, on a movie screen high above the scene. The camera closes in on certain individuals and focuses the general attention on particular gestures and movement. In the second part, *Superimpositions*, a masked couple dance to the Steve Miller Band playing "Song for Our Ancestors." A flowing dance, the *pas de deux* yields to an ensemble, where other masked dancers pick up choreographic themes we have just seen.

Anna Pavlova in *La Fille Mal Gardée*. Dance Collection, N.Y.P.L. at Lincoln Center, Astor, Lenox and Tilden Foundations.

Tamara Karsavina and Vaslav Nijinsky in *Le Spectre de la Rose*. Dance Collection, N.Y.P.L.

Tanaquil LeClercq and Francisco Moncion in *Afternoon of a Faun*. Photo by Fred'k Melton.

Cynthia Gregory and Ivan Nagy in *Giselle*. Photo by Louis Péres.

Fernando Bujones in *Le Corsaire*. Photo by Martha Swope.

Mikhail Baryshnikov in Pushkin's class at the Kirov school, Leningrad, 1968. Photo by Patricia Barnes.

Lynn Seymour in *Homage to Isadora*. Photo by Beverley Gallegos.

Maria Tallchief in *Firebird*. Photo by George Platt Lynes.

Suzanne Farrell and Jacques d'Amboise in *Apollo*. Photo by Martha Swope.

Suzanne Farrell and Arthur Mitchell in *Agon*. Photo by Martha Swope.

Lydia Abarca and Derek Williams in *Agon*. Photo by Anthony Crickmay.

Lawrence Rhodes in *At Midnight*. Photo by Martha Swope.

Marcia Haydée and Richard Cragun in *Daphnis and Chloë*. Photo by Beverley Gallegos.

Paul Russell in *Le Corsaire*. Photo by Martha Swope.

Violette Verdy in *Liebeslieder Walzer*. Photo by Martha Swope.

Edward Villella in *Brahms-Schoenberg Quartet*. Photo by Martha Swope.

Margot Fonteyn in *Homage to the Queen*. Photo by Houston Rogers.

Theme, the third part, is a solo for a boy to James Brown singing "Sex Machine." The dance begins slowly, builds to a frantic finish, and the scene blacks out. The finale, *Twice*, to music by Santana ("Savor"), gives the stage again to all twelve dancers, whose movements assume a brilliant staccato to the rhythm of strobe light.

THE TWO PIGEONS

An Allegory in two acts, based on the Fable by La Fontaine by Henry Regnier and Louis Mérante. Music by André Messager. Choreography by Louis Mérante. First presented at the Opéra, Paris, October 18, 1886. Presented by the Royal Ballet in a new version with choreography by Frederick Ashton at the Royal Opera House, Covent Garden, London, February 14, 1961. Scenery and costumes by Jacques Dupont. The principal roles were danced by Lynn Seymour, Christopher Gable, Elizabeth Anderson, and Johaar Mosaval. First presented in the United States by the Royal Ballet at the Metropolitan Opera House, New York, April 24, 1963, with Lynn Seymour, Alexander Grant, Georgina Parkinson, and Johaar Mosaval in the principal roles.

The historian and critic Ivor Guest has noted that the discovery at the Royal Opera House of the score used for a 1906 presentation in London of *The Two Pigeons* prompted Frederick Ashton to stage a new version of the ballet. For this he discarded the scenario of the old ballet in favor of an allegorical treatment of the fable of his own devising. The story the ballet depicts is based on the poem *Les Deux Pigeons* by La Fontaine. While the two birds love each other, one tires of home and longs to roam abroad. When his love protests the pigeon replies that she is not to worry; after all, he will be gone only three days and just think of the adventures he will be able to tell! After his trip is over, the pigeon gratefully returns to his true love and they live happily ever after.

The choreographer has situated the action in Paris, where a young painter and his love live in an attractive garret. The painter is restless, however, and when a band of gypsies happens by, he is so enchanted by their free spirit— and also so interested in one of the girls—that he goes off. As his girl looks sadly after him from the balcony of the garret, a pigeon flies across the stage.

In the gypsy encampment, the boy learns that the transient life is not all moonlight and roses. He also learns that his affection for the gypsy lady has aroused the jealousy of her lover. There is much fiery gypsy dancing and appropriate displays of passion. The boy sees the gypsies have been kind to him only as a trick, but before he can escape they have tied him up and given him a rough time.

Meanwhile, back at the studio, his faithful love still sits on the balcony, awaiting his return. When she sees him her arms touchingly imitate the happy flapping of pigeon wings. They are reunited, dance ecstatically, and then rest by a chair, where first one pigeon comes to rest, and then another.

TZADDIK

*Music by Aaron Copland. Choreography by Eliot Feld. "For My Grand-
mother Bessie." Setting and costumes by Boris Aronson. Lighting by Jennifer Tipton. First presented in 1974 by the Eliot Feld Ballet at the Newman
Theater, New York, with Eliot Feld in the leading role.*

There is a saying, Eliot Feld, the dancer and choreographer, reminds us: "A
Jew without learning is incomplete." His ballet is a dramatic dance about an
old rabbi and two students. The music is a trio, too: Copland's *Vitebsk.*

The students are two young men. Devoted to the master and anxious to do
what he wishes, what they do is never enough for him. They are younger, after
all, and represent the possibly dangerous and innovatively new. Amid the displayed exhortation it is easy to imagine the learned man's acquiring such
knowledge of the young men that they are forever in his power, for their own
good and the love of God. In the end, at his command, the sacred scrolls are
unraveled. The students and their master are wound up in them, wholly committed to the sacred text.

Writing about *Tzaddik* in *Dance and Dancers* magazine, the English critic
John Percival said: "This is an unusual theme for dancing, but it works, thanks
to the striking imagery Feld has discovered for its expression. The movement
is often hectic, small in scale and agitated. The impression is not of calm academic learning but an intense desire to convey beliefs deeply held . . . The
performance by Feld as the teacher is intense and impassioned."

TZIGANE

*Music by Maurice Ravel. Choreography by George Balanchine. Costumes
by Joe Eula. Lighting by Ronald Bates. Solo violin: Lamar Alsop. Conducted by Robert Irving. First presented by the New York City Ballet at the
Hommage à Ravel at the New York State Theatre, Lincoln Center, May
29, 1975, with Suzanne Farrell and Peter Martins as principals.*

The tziganes were Hungarian Gypsies who lived near Vienna. Haydn and
Schubert, who summered nearby, both used elements of their music. Liszt,
who was born in their midst, wrote that the tziganes played "as if suddenly
given the power to express their pleasure, they flew to their violins and cymbals and began playing in a fury of excitement."

Ravel's music, for violin and piano originally (1924), was composed for the
Hungarian violin virtuoso Yelly d'Aranyi. It was later orchestrated.

The ballet we made for our Hommage à Ravel to this exciting music tried to
catch its atmosphere and dynamism. The first part is a solo for the ballet's heroine to the accompaniment of a long, pleading solo by the violin. A boy joins

her. He and a small *corps de ballet* of eight dancers then gather for a cumulative dance of joy and exultation to the driving force of the music.

UNDERTOW

Ballet in one act with prologue and epilogue. Choreography by Antony Tudor. Music by William Schuman. Libretto by Antony Tudor, after a suggestion by John van Druten. Scenery and costumes by Raymond Breinin. First presented by Ballet Theatre at the Metropolitan Opera House, New York, April 10, 1945, with a cast headed by Hugh Laing as the Transgressor, *Alicia Alonso as* Ate, *Diana Adams as* Cybele, *Nana Gollner as* Medusa, *Shirley Eckl as* Volupia, *Patricia Barker as* Aganippe, *and Lucia Chase as* Polyhymnia.

Modern ballets are continually enlarging the subject matter of the dance. It might seem strange to us now, but not until 1936—when Antony Tudor produced *Lilac Garden*—did we ever see on the ballet stage people, who looked and acted somewhat like ourselves, in a dramatic ballet. The women in *Lilac Garden* wore long party dresses, not romantic *tutus;* the men were anxious lovers, not mechanical cavaliers. And the characters in the ballet were caught up in a dramatic situation that was dominated by their inner feelings.

Undertow represents another effort to extend the dramatic dance. It attempts to show us why a young man, called the transgressor, commits murder. It shows us where he was born, the people he grew up with, and the people who influenced his life. All the characters in the ballet, except the hero, have names derived from mythology. They are thus not particular personalities, but universal characters recognizable in the life of every man. The time is the present.

PROLOGUE: BIRTH AND INFANCY   The light is dim. We make out Cybele, great mother of gods, in labor. She gives birth to a son, who creeps out from between her limbs and cries. The mother is revolted by the sight of her son and the agony she has suffered. She abandons him and seeks a lover—Pollux, the immortal youth who is born anew each day. Her son instinctively despises his mother and nurtures his grief. Even as a child, the transgressor discovers in the world no love.

THE CITY: ADOLESCENCE AND MANHOOD   The scene is a street in the slums of a huge city. We sense immediately the irony of the splendid statues that dominate the nearby square: great winged horses fly away from a place the inhabitants can never leave. Their life is so miserable that they cannot entertain the notion of accustoming themselves to anything else. A woman, made up hideously, stands pouting, waiting for someone to notice her. She is Volupia, here a bedraggled personification of sensual pleasure.

The transgressor, now a youth, enters with a pretty young girl. Her name is Aganippe and she is innocent inspiration. They appear to be having a good time together until the boy notices the streetwalker. He is fascinated by her and observes her with open curiosity. His girl abandons him. Volupia looks at the boy contemptuously and smartens up for a man who now struts onto the scene. He goes directly to her and follows, as she knowingly leads the way.

A rowdy bunch of boys race into the street. What seems to be playfulness on their part is genuinely mean and cruel. They are aware of nothing else in the world but the nuisance they may cause. The hero observes them. On the surface he has no reaction; underneath we suspect that he despises his life and is compelled to watch these people only because he seeks an explanation of their grossness.

Volupia, her first mission over, comes back looking for another man. An old man makes furtive advances toward her. He is so timid that the woman turns on him and ridicules him. He leaves the scene.

The youth's companion, Aganippe, comes back into the street. She is accompanied by another girl, Nemesis, with whom she is playing a private game. The man who has just recently finished his rendezvous with Volupia is attracted by Aganippe's beauty and innocence. He tries to strike up a conversation with her. The transgressor turns on him in a rage, orders him to leave the girl alone, and chases him off.

Polyhymnia, the muse of sacred music, enters as an overcheerful, pious busybody who is deluded into thinking she can change the lives of the people in this slum with the right word. She is recruiting an audience for a prayer meeting and invites all the passers-by to come. Several people join her: among them, Pollux, still the handsome youth, who is now courting the modest Pudicitia, and Ate, the hideous creature who would lead all men into evil. Ate's body is demure and innocent, her face and gestures grotesquely obscene. She accompanies the religious woman only out of malice and soon leaves.

Ate approaches the transgressor, but he is immune to her invitations and she seeks the company of Aganippe's discouraged admirer. In vivid contrast to this sordid couple, a bride and groom, Hymen and Hera, enter and—in a gay and tender dance—suggest to the young hero the true power of love. The transgressor watches them enviously, then disbelieves in their happiness to conceal his own misery.

Three lewd drunken women cavort about the scene noisily, braying and bawling Polyhymnia's call to prayer. Ate comes back to seek more mischief with the gang of dead-end kids. The transgressor and Aganippe watch her. She runs off with the gang, and the two innocents look at the ground in disgust. When Ate re-enters, this time alone, the youth goes directly to her and accosts her. He puts his hands around her neck and threatens to choke her to death. Aganippe flees. The transgressor proceeds to kill Ate, but stops, frightened, when the girl Nemesis comes in, guiding home one of the besotted women. Ate takes advantage of the youth's hesitation to elude him.

Still another kind of woman comes on the scene to disturb the hero. Medusa, true to her name, seems to be attractive, but her beauty is empowered to turn men to stone. She is so different, and yet so like the streetwalker and Ate, that the transgressor watches her with interest. She tries to take up with Pollux, but this youth has sense enough to repulse her. Medusa looks toward the transgressor: she must have someone. He is about to join her, when Polyhymnia begins to lead a revival meeting in the middle of the street. The youth participates in the meeting, hoping to escape. Medusa perceives this ruse and sends Polyhymnia and her crowd packing.

Now the transgressor is alone with a woman for the first time in his life. He is tense, expectant. The woman appears to control the youth as he responds to her advances. But gradually his true feelings become plain and we see that in reality he has control of the woman. Finally he can no longer conceal the hatred he has felt for women all his life. He becomes violent, and Medusa is afraid. The transgressor laughs. It is too late. He throws her to the ground, embraces her as she at first desired, and in the act, seizes her throat and chokes her viciously to death. The full orchestra is unleashed in a thundering, violent crescendo. The scene blacks out.

EPILOGUE: GUILT The hero is alone on the scene. In the back, the misty panorama of the city and the winged horses of the square gradually rise into the sky, as if the very scene of the crime would flee from the criminal. The transgressor moves as if recovering from a hideous nightmare, the dream that has been his life. Yet in remembering the end of the dream, he sees that he has destroyed his life. He wonders what else he could have done, what other ending such a dream could have had. He finds no answer. But perhaps no one knows what he has done! Perhaps he can escape!

Curious people come into the street to watch him. He ignores them. Surely, in every way, he is better than they. Then Aganippe comes in, playing with a balloon. She stops and stares at him. The transgressor recalls their early friendship, smiles at her, and walks toward her. But the girl knows. She points at him, and everyone watches as her forgotten balloon rises in the sky. His guilt reaffirmed by the one person in the world he respects, the hero walks away to meet his end.

UNFINISHED SYMPHONY

Music by Franz Schubert. Choreography by Peter Van Dyk. Costumes by Kalinowski. Lighting by Nananne Porcher. First presented in Paris, 1958. First presented in the United States by American Ballet Theatre at the New York State Theatre, July 1971, with Cynthia Gregory and Michael Denard.

A dance ballet to Schubert's great *Unfinished Symphony*, the choreographer has created here a dance for two persons. They are lovers but there is a sense of experience and apparent detached civilization in their approach to each other. There is no radical discontent but there is a continuing sense of potential drama about their relationship.

Writing in *Cue* magazine, the critic Greer Johnson wrote of the ballet: ". . . This is a full-bodied if serenely understated hymn to two mature lovers so responsive to one another that touch and gesture are transformed into literally metaphysical poetry. The work is quiet; it enfolds you; it flows and caresses to make its unhurried, knowingly sensual point."

Deborah Jowitt, writing of *Unfinished Symphony* in the *Village Voice*, found the ballet "a curiously hypnotic duet performed by Cynthia Gregory and Michael Denard. They're both in blue-gray, and the lighting creates a blue ambience, and they move quite slowly with a smooth, barely inflected dynamic. Everything they do looks thoughtful and deliberate; even the more abandoned poses are carefully charted. They might even be sleepwalkers. Once they look sharply at each other and then at one corner of the stage, and the contrast is startling. . . . The calm heroism of some of the poses at times suggests a dream battle in which they are both engaged—sometimes as colleagues, sometimes as antagonists. Both Gregory and Denard sustain the gliding, weightless choreography beautifully, and the Schubert music provides the plangent tension that keeps the somnambulism from being soporific."

UNION JACK

> *Music by Hershy Kay, adapted from traditional British music. Choreography by George Balanchine. Scenery and costumes by Rouben Ter-Arutunian. Lighting by Ronald Bates. Conducted by Robert Irving. First presented by the New York City Ballet at the New York State Theatre, Lincoln Center, New York, May 12, 1976, with Jacques d'Amboise, Helgi Tomasson, Sara Leland, Peter Martins, Kay Mazzo, Karin von Aroldingen, Suzanne Farrell, Patricia McBride, and Jean-Pierre Bonnefous as principals.*

It is no secret that I love England. Ever since I first went there, in the 1920s, soon after I left Russia and joined Diaghilev's great Ballets Russes, I liked London best of all the cities we visited. After Diaghilev died and I wanted to find the best place to make ballets, England was where I should have liked to remain. The immigration laws did not then permit such a step and when later Lincoln Kirstein came to see me and made it possible for me to come to America, I seized the independent alternative. I was lucky. Ever since, however, I have gone back to Britain whenever I could, and recall with affection the New York City Ballet's visits to London and Edinburgh and other cities. *Scotch Symphony* grew out of one of these visits and I shall never forget the long engagement the New York City Ballet had at Covent Garden in 1950. It was the longest period up to that time that we had had to dance on any one stage, and when we came back to the City Center the autumn of that year, everyone knew, I believe, that there was no stopping the objectives Lincoln Kirstein and I had set out to accomplish. So it is not only that I love Britain; we owe it a lot. When it was a question of what we as a ballet company should do to celebrate the American bicentennial, for me as for Lincoln Kirstein it was no question: we should celebrate as we could the English and what they have given us. We were helped in this ambition by many friends, from the composer Hershy Kay, our magnificent dancers, and the designer Rouben Ter-Arutunian, to our supporters, like Jacques d'Amboise's wonderful friends, the Leslie R. Samuelses. Making the ballet, for this time and place, was a pleasure.

As Lincoln Kirstein recalls, Americans and others in London at 11 A.M. precisely every morning may observe at Buckingham Palace the changing of the guard, a ritual of care that has its equivalent in Scotland and throughout the United Kingdom. It is a question of order and protection, perhaps only a symbol in these days of potential higher threats no guards could control, but for many of us it is the ultimate civilized gesture, as it has always been. My ballet is meant as a tribute to all that represents.

Our ballet is a three-part salute that acknowledges those ritual aspects of Britain as alive today in military ceremony and theatrical vitality as they have been for the past two centuries. It utilizes folk, military, naval, and music-hall themes for action as well as music. The music is composed by Hershy Kay on themes and variations drawn from the following sources, which by name and association give the best idea of associated action:

Part I: *Scottish Guards*. A procession of dancers to the music of "Keel Row," "Ye Banks and Braes o'Doon," "Caledonian Hunt's Delight," "A Hundred Pipers," "Dance wi' My Daddy," Regimental Tattoos: "Amazing Grace."

Part II: *Costermonger pas de deux* (Pearly King and Queen), a dance for the hero and heroine of the annual Cockney celebration for those born within the sound of the bells of St. Mary le Bow in the City of London, accompanied by: music-hall songs of London, 1890–1914, and "The Sunshine of Your Smile," "The Night the Floor Fell In," "Our Lodger's Such a Nice Young Man," "Following in Father's Footsteps," and "A Tavern in the Town."

Part III: *Horn Pipe*, with music based on "Rule, Britannia."

LES VAINQUEURS

Ceremony in five tableaux based on an idea of Richard Wagner's. Choreography by Maurice Béjart. Decor and costumes by Yahnele Toumelin. Lighting by Serge Apruzzese. First presented by the Ballet of the Twentieth Century, December 10, 1969, at the Théâtre de la Monnaie, Brussels. First presented in the United States by the same ensemble at the Brooklyn Academy of Music, New York, January 30, 1971.

Few persons are aware of the importance of Buddhism in the life and work of Richard Wagner. The choreographer of this ballet about love and renunciation, Maurice Béjart, has said: "It is curious to observe the little importance that biographers of Richard Wagner place both on his discovery of Buddhism and the influence that Buddhism had on his life and work beginning in 1855. Yet it is only in full awareness of this development that his two greatest works *Tristan* and *Parsifal* can be musically and intellectually understood. The theory of the leitmotif carried to its logical conclusion reflects the psychological concept of the states of consciousness of Buddhism and their constant mutations.

"It is interesting to note, too, that many scholars have found great similarities between the Celtic cosmogony and myths and the Indo-Tibetan Buddhist. And the two works of Richard Wagner, *Tristan* and *Parsifal*, in which Buddhist influence is strongly present, are in fact based on Celtic lore.

"'*Parsifal* is a Buddhist scion transplanted to a Christian soil and climate, or, even more exactly, an attempt to correlate and fuse Buddhism and Christianity, but then the word "attempt" does not sit well on Wagner, so let us say, rather, an aim fairly well accomplished, for the duality of the religious sources does not bother the spectator and has not much concerned the critics.' (G. Leprince: *The Presence of Wagner*)

"If *Les Vainqueurs* has not been published, the reason could very well be *Tristan*. It is hard to bring forth two great works at one time: one will always end up swallowing the other: the night of *Tristan* has darkened the light of *Les Vainqueurs*. And if no sketch has been found of a subject on which he worked for so long a time, it is simply that the passion of Isolde absorbed the musical material of the love of Ananda for the pure Savitri.

"What is the meaning of this 'ceremony'? The dance is a rite. A ballet which descends to the roots of its origins is always a ceremony. Every work of art has multiple meanings. This is more so the case in a dance work where the idea transcends the word and the limits of the word, for dance belongs wholly and integrally to the world of form. Consequently what the public discovers in it is a reflection of its own thought.

"If people see nothing but a magic universe of shapes and colors, they are pretty nearly right. Whether they read into it a wondrous fairy tale, a romantic and exotic love story, the psychoanalytic version of the Tristan myth, or the initiation voyage toward illumination, will depend upon their own bent of mind. Some, to be sure, will see the work as a sacrilege, others, I hope, as an act of love, a love which for Wagner transcends human love, as 'it is the road which leads to elimination of the individuality, abjuration of the urge to live, achievement of the peace of Nirvana.' It is this cosmic love that makes Isolde declare at the end of the work:

In the mass of waves
of this sea of delights
in the thunder, the clamor and the din
waves of perfume
breathing into ALL
by the breath of the world,
to sink, to drown, to lose consciousness,
joy supreme."

Béjart uses as a signature for the ballet verses from the Buddhist Mantra:

"Thou, the Victor, the Delivered, Deliver!
Arrived upon the other shore.
Cause the other there also to arrive."

The music of the ballet, as so often in the work of this choreographer, alternates in contrast, the one here between Wagner's score from *Tristan und Isolde* and Indo-Tibetan ragas.

A dramatic Buddha figure at the beginning of the ballet turns into a Tristan figure. He finds his love, there is a voyage, reminiscent of the action of the opera. The action then shifts to the contemporary, and there is a dance celebration by performers in jeans. Everything appears to be timeless.

Maurice Béjart has spoken of the libretto inspired by the life of Buddha that Wagner was writing at the same time he was working on *Tristan*. To a reporter for *The New Yorker*, Béjart said: "The libretto—which is also called *Les Vainqueurs*—exists, but nobody has ever discovered a note of the music. So I made a theory from my own experience as a choreographer. If you work on two ideas simultaneously and produce just one of them, the dominant work absorbs the ideas you prepared for the other one. I think that some of the music Wagner wrote for *Les Vainqueurs* ended up in *Tristan*, so I combined the two works. The final words of Isolde, when she says, 'I sought to dissolve myself in the ocean of life,' are very like a well-known Buddhist prayer."

VALENTINE

Music by Jacob Druckman. Choreography by Gerald Arpino. Lighting by Jennifer Tipton. Contrabass: Alvin Brehm. First presented by the City Center Joffrey Ballet at the City Center, New York, March 10, 1971, with Rebecca Wright and Christian Holder.

Valentine is a dance for a girl and a boy accompanied by a double bass. The composer Jacob Druckman has said of the music for *Valentine:* "The work is one of the most difficult ever written for the contrabass and demands that the player attack the instrument with bow, tympany stick, both hands alternating percussive tapping on the body of the instrument with pizzicato harmonics, while the voice sustains tones, sings counterpoints, and punctuates accents. All of this necessitates the player's assaulting the instrument with an almost de Sade-like concentration (hence the title)."

That is the way of the dance, too, for the dancers are dressed and behave like competing boxers in the ring. They shadowbox, spar, stand off, get together, and react to the ferocity of the score.

LA VALSE

Ballet in two parts. Music by Maurice Ravel. Choreography by George Balanchine. Costumes by Karinska. Lighting by Jean Rosenthal. First presented by the New York City Ballet at the City Center, New York, February 20, 1951, with Tanaquil LeClercq, Nicholas Magallanes, and Francisco Moncion in the principal roles.

Ravel called his composition *La Valse* a "choreographic poem." It was composed to be danced, "a sort of apotheosis of the Viennese waltz . . . the mad whirl of some fantastic and fateful carrousel." The ballet follows in outline the theatrical scheme Ravel imagined for his music: "At first the scene is dimmed by a kind of swirling mist, through which one discerns, vaguely and inter mittently, the waltzing couples. Little by little the vapors disperse, the illumination grows brighter, revealing an immense ballroom filled with dancers . . ." Prior to this scene, the ballet makes use of another composition of Ravel's, *Valses Nobles et Sentimentales,* a group of eight short waltzes that introduces the ballroom scene and its principal dancers.

PART ONE: VALSES NOBLES ET SENTIMENTALES   The first waltz serves as the overture. Percussion instruments underline the liveliness of the animated waltz rhythm. The curtain rises, and the second waltz begins.

Three girls stand before a blue net curtain in formal dress. They hold their white-gloved hands in a light, mannered pose. The music is soft and beguiling. The girls bow low and begin to dance, at first somewhat wistfully, then coyly, but always their movements are as formal as their long white gloves, which seem to accent every one of their gestures. Underneath their slate-colored costumes their full skirts are brilliant red, and as they separate and move more freely, the whirling dresses color their dance. Far behind the blue net curtain, in the obscure distance, hangs a cluster of dimly lighted chandeliers. The girls exit modestly, their white-gloved arms before their faces.

A handsome couple, holding hands, dance out gaily to the tinkling tune of the third waltz. Their lighthearted duet is marked by quick, sprightly steps. They dance together closely and separate only as they exit at opposite sides of the stage.

The next waltz is more open in its melody, and to its rapid rhythms another couple dance boldly and freely. They run past each other in high, joyful leaps. The fifth waltz begins with subdued, romantic contrast. The girl who dances it moves gracefully and deliberately. Her partner kisses her hand and kneels. The music becomes blithe, and the ballerina dances before the boy with close, lighthearted steps. The boy marvels at her beauty and reaches out to claim her. This girl dances alone to the sixth waltz, after which her partner rejoins her.

As this couple exit toward the right, they are met by two girls. The couple pause, then the ballerina leaves the stage and a third girl takes her place. These are the same three girls who danced the first waltz. The seventh waltz begins. They claim the boy, covering him with their arms. One girl breaks away to dance, then another. The boy joins them, lifts them high as the music races its tempestuous theme. The four stand together, and one of the girls falls back in the boy's arms. He kneels as the girls run off. The music hesitates in its momentum, and the girls and boys of the earlier waltzes rush in and out, over and about him. He rises, turns swiftly, and the three girls confront him. He dances with them again as the waltz theme returns, then leaps off into the wings.

The stage is empty as the sinuous, final waltz commences. A girl in white emerges. She steps forward, opening her arms slowly; her body recoils slightly as she moves forward. She walks over to the right; her arms mime the flow of the expectant music. A boy enters at the back. They do not see each other. They exchange positions, then each bends backward and recognizes the other. They approach, touch hands warily, and with formal, sophisticated movements of her arms, the ballerina gives her partner her hand. They separate, pass, and come together back-to-back in the center of the stage, where they turn together, their arms entwined. Now they separate again and repeat their introduction. The boy lifts the ballerina slowly; her white dress flows with the final measures of the waltz. He lifts her off into the wings.

PART TWO: LA VALSE   The lights dim, the blue net curtain is raised, the distant chandeliers brighten, the music to *La Valse* begins. The music throbs low and mysteriously; light catch-phrases from a waltz hover over a deep, foreboding background of sound. A spotlight picks up a boy, who runs onto the stage in search of a girl he cannot find. He looks for her helplessly in the dark ballroom. Another boy enters with his dancing partner. They appear to be lost. Suddenly, on the opposite side of the stage, the spotlight shines on three girls, whose white-gloved arms are held up before their faces like masks. The boy chooses one of the girls and starts to dance with her, but the girl falls back strangely in his arms as they move in a circle. They exit. Another couple moves across the scene hurriedly, and three girls and three boys run on and off seeking their partners. All the dancers seem to be waiting for the waltz to emerge through the weird music that holds it in abeyance. The waltz rhythm pulsates; a sparkling rush of sound from the harp heralds its full waltz melody. The ballroom brightens; eight couples fill the stage.

They dance joyously in a large circle; the color of the girls' skirts contrasts vividly with the black walls of the room. As the couples swirl past, we see that the chandeliers are hung with crepe. The black cloth hangs low into the room. The couples change partners in the center of the circle and continue their tempestuous dance. A loud fanfare in rapid waltz rhythm announces the arrival of two new groups of dancers, who cross the stage diagonally as the others stand back. Two couples dance before the group, then the boys gather in the center of the circle, where they choose partners. Now there are two girls for each boy.

The ballerina of the fifth waltz enters with her partner, and the fierce, pounding waltz abates to a soft, mellifluous volume and tempo as they dance softly. The boy exits; the ballerina dances with a group of girls as the couples stand and watch. The cymbals clash, the momentum increases, and the ballerina in white enters. She leaps toward the front, all the dancers gathering on each side of the stage to form wide, opening doors of movement to heighten the speed of her dazzling entry. The dancers move toward the center of the room, where one of the girls is lifted high above them all; the group circles about her. In back, the black crepe swirls as the dancers pass.

The ballerina in white dances happily with her partner; the waltz is quiet again. The couples stand aside and converse and do not notice them. Their dance is slow at first; the ballerina's movements are retarded and she seeks to move more freely as the waltz attempts to resume its previous intensity. But the music hesitates overlong; it unwinds with a snap of sound like a spring that has been wound up too tightly. Disintegrating patterns of waltz melody and tempo struggle helplessly against the orchestra. The once brilliant theme sounds with the pathetic intensity of a hurdy-gurdy. The girl turns with despairing speed to her partner's arms. A staccato trumpet heralds a pause; the weird, warning first bars of *La Valse* cause all to stand aside. They all look toward the back.

A figure in black emerges beneath the funereal chandeliers. His head is bowed as he walks forward slowly. About his neck hangs a heavy black medal on a black chain. The girls kneel before him; their partners turn their faces away. The ballerina in white turns away in terror. The black specter is followed by a page, who holds in his arms a mirror and a black gown. The music whirls frantically in anticipation.

The girl in white staggers toward the man unwillingly, as if hypnotized by his presence; she goes to him recognizing her own fears of his fatal attraction. He presents her with a splendid necklace and holds the mirror before her. He waits anxiously for her reaction. The girl turns away in horror: the mirror is cracked black glass. Her horror turns to fascination as the waltz attempts to penetrate the mystery of sound and sight. It races suddenly to a desperate loud statement, falters away again. The man offers the girl a pair of long black gloves. He holds them open, and she slides her arms into them as the music sounds a booming, relentless crescendo. Presented now with a black gown, the girl slips into it delightedly and covers her white costume. The stranger rewards her finally with a black bouquet. He kisses her hand, takes her about the waist, and begins to turn her about the room.

The crescendo has now receded, and the waltz attempts again to come to life. The girl is moved faster and faster by her partner as the waltz resumes its momentum. She throws down her bouquet and begins to fall limp in his arms. He turns her faster; she cannot break away. The waltz reaches the peak of driving, irrevocable rhythm; crashes of its beauty tear the air. The girl falls back, then rises to the close embrace of the grotesque black figure. She dies. The specter disappears. Her lover drags her off.

The couples return to their dancing, now rushing about the cold, dark ballroom in frantic pursuit of the pleasure the music will no longer allow them. The exhausted waltz is now heard only in a climactic struggle of instruments. The boy enters in the back, carrying the dead girl in his arms. The boys lift her away from him to their shoulders. Her head falls back, her arms hang loose. Her lover attempts to embrace her, but she is lifted high above him. All of the dancers close in. The girl's body is turned around and around. About the circling center, the group races in a fateful, fantastic carrousel.

Elena Bivona, in an essay on Patricia McBride in *Ballet Review* (Vol. 3, No. 3), wrote of a performance of *La Valse:* "From a ballet of delicate suggestion she has extracted religious horrors without leaving a smudge on the delicate framework. In one performance, her first waltz had marvelously slow-sharp inflections of arm and hand; the gestures clawed and sank at the same time, brittlely artificial and softly demanding. As Bruhn can in *Giselle's* last act, she interfused tension with luxuriance to make a dream-ridden girl innocent of her own evil but evil nonetheless. And against the articulate arms she countered a tense neck, the tight muscles keeping her head alert, watching without object, waiting half-aware. Another performance made the same waltz the world of a woman a thousand years old in corruption, her movements still and stretching, her vitality at a controlled scream-pitch ready to devour new adventures, and there are obviously none left but the destruction she finally conjures up, to her astonishment, fear, and joy. On this night, the girl was no innocent; she was the hostess, her white dress an obscenity of wit, her physical youth a Dorian Gray monstrosity, her corruption radiating as if it were beauty, and she is so fascinating she must feed on the fascination she draws to herself. Vampira. A monster—or two monsters, three, a slightly different one each time to find out who this death-lover in her, in Balanchine, in us, is.

"She met Death once with a hypnotized, terrified blankness, tight neck muscles hardened to a vise for her staring face, and her body a Bunraku doll's manipulated by a puppet master: fluent in her upper body, simple and a little jerky from the waist down. She could abandon that possibility another night to make her softness an all-knowing perverted eroticism, her presence so strong Death himself makes no impact until the moment, when he seizes her for their first dance, that his strength overpowers hers; and that, perhaps only because she and Death are a single identity and the recognition itself is what claims her, is what lets loose the chaos of the ballet's finale. *La Valse* that night became a circle of evil seeking its own face for which Death holding his mirror was the perfect metaphor."°

VARIATIONS

Music by Igor Stravinsky. Choreography by George Balanchine. Lighting by Ronald Bates. First presented by the New York City Ballet at the New York State Theatre, March 31, 1966, with Karin von Aroldingen, Karen Batizi, Diane Bradshaw, Marjorie Breler, Elaine Comsudi, Rosemary Dunleavy, Susan Hendl, Ruth Ann King, Jennifer Nairn-Smith, Delia Peters, Donna Sackett, Lynne Stetson, Robert Maiorano, Paul Meija, Frank Ohman, John Prinz, David Richardson, Michael Steele, and Suzanne Farrell.

Stravinsky composed his *Variations for Orchestra* dedicated to the memory of Aldous Huxley in 1963–64. Soon afterwards I was able to see the score. I decided that as soon as possible I would like to do a ballet to the music. What kind of ballet it was to be, however, was not then clear. Stravinsky's work is concise, lasting only four minutes, forty-five seconds, which is not in the theatre a sufficient time to develop and hold the attention, not to mention the ears, of the audience. Stravinsky's music also demands to be heard not just once, but many times. I accordingly decided to have the music played three times for a set of three dances.

The curtain rises and twelve girls are seen on the stage. There is no setting. Stravinsky's piece was composed, he tells us, on a pitch series, a succession of twelve notes that came to his mind as a melody and was then seen as material for variations. As the music begins, the girls face the audience in two groups of six. There is a variation for twelve violins in the orchestra which is taken up in a different way by mixed strings, and later by twelve woodwinds. The dancers

° Reprinted by permission of *Ballet Review*, Marcel Dekker, publisher.

reflect these changes in the orchestra in different groupings and separations, each of the twelve dancing a little differently from the others. As the first part ends, the original two groups of six have become three groups of four. Stravinsky has said in a program note: "The halves . . . are unities as well as fragments, and are therefore divisible in turn, and invertible, reversible, mirror-invertible, mirror reversible."

The second playing of the music is danced by six boys, who stand at the beginning in two rows of three. They dance in various combinations, one of them at a certain point being singled out by the other five.

For the third playing, a girl dances on stage quickly. In yet another version of the same subject, she reflects the conciseness of Stravinsky's score.

VARIATIONS FOR FOUR

Music by Marguerite Keogh. Idea and choreography by Anton Dolin. Costumes by Tom Lingwood. First presented by Festival Ballet at Royal Festival Hall, London, September 1957. First presented in the United States by American Ballet Theatre at the Metropolitan Opera House, New York, September 25, 1958.

Many ballet-goers are familiar with Anton Dolin's re-creation of the great nineteenth-century ballet *Pas de Quatre,* in which the four leading ballerinas of the day appeared together for a single performance of display and polite competition. Dolin, renowned as a *danseur* since his debut with Diaghilev's Ballets Russes, conceived the idea of staging a similar showpiece for four outstanding male soloists. The result is a popular work both here and abroad, where it has been performed by gifted *premiers danseurs*.

The bright music that raises the curtain heralds a festive occasion. The four dancers enter to a stately theme, pose and dance together briefly, then separate to perform independently their special skills in a series of variations. These vary in tempo and energy, building to a brilliant display of speed and virtuosity for all four. There is also a sustained *adagio* for one of the soloists, to remind us of the *danseur's* romantic role. All four participate in a rapid, flourishing finale.

NOTES   After its revival by American Ballet Theatre at the New York State Theatre, July 12, 1972, Clive Barnes wrote in the New York *Times:*

"Let me confess to a prejudice. I love Anton Dolin's *Variations for Four.* In classic ballet women have so much of it their own way. For years the male dancer has stood politely, sometimes sufferingly, behind his ballerina, flexing his muscles and practicing his humility. Dolin was one of the first great male dancers of the century—with Serge Lifar he was one of Diaghilev's last two premier danseurs, and he played a principal role in the development of both British and American ballet—and this pas de quatre is almost a charter of Men's Liberation in ballet. There are just four men dancing; brilliantly, competitively and with no apologies.

"Since the work was first created for London's Festival Ballet, a company Dolin himself formed, it has been in the repertory of many leading companies, including American Ballet Theatre. But on Wednesday night at the New York State Theatre the ballet had its first revival with the company since its original American production in 1958. It was exultantly danced.

"In some ways, rather like the Royal Danish Ballet, the male dancers of Ballet Theatre are more interesting than the women. Undeniably Ballet Theatre has gathered together a most unusual collection of men, and this *Variations for Four* can show some of them off in style. At the first performance it was danced by an immaculate Ted Kivitt, a forceful John Prinz, a gutsy Alexander Filipov and, in the final solo, Ballet Theatre's newest star, the Italian Paolo Bortoluzzi. Mr. Bortoluzzi needs to be careful of his fine Italian hands—he is at times too flamboyant for New York taste—but he is a magnificent dancer with a special pulse and arrogance of his own. He is like an Italian racing car—extravagant, different but powerful."

VARIATIONS POUR UNE PORTE ET UN SOUPIR

Sonority by Pierre Henry. Choreography by George Balanchine. Scenery and costumes by Rouben Ter-Arutunian. Lighting by Ronald Bates. First presented by the New York City Ballet at the New York State Theatre, Lincoln Center, January 17, 1974, with Karin von Aroldingen and John Clifford.

Variations for a Door and a Sigh has an interesting score, or sonority, as the French composer Pierre Henry calls it. I first heard work by the composer when I visited him some years ago in Paris, at the suggestion of Nicolas Nabokov, and decided then that I would like to do a ballet to this piece one day. Henry was the first "traditionally oriented" composer to interest himself in electro-acoustical techniques. This particular piece makes maximum use of the whole gamut of sounds that can be associated with sighs and the opening and closing of doors. I picked out fourteen of the twenty-five variations Henry wrote for the original concert version, and arranged to them a *pas de deux*, a duet for the female door and the male sigh. The ballet begins with a sigh.

It is dark and silent as the curtain rises. A spotlight reveals a male figure all in white responding to the sound of sighs. We hear then the sound of a creaking door and the woman is revealed, also in white, but with a black silken skirt attached to her waist that stretches like a wide train across the whole stage. In its center, like the central support for a tent that has yet to rise, she dances to the door sounds. Her limbs open and close, creaking and slamming, about an invisible hinge. She approaches the man and then he dances again. They continue to alternate dances as a relationship becomes more intense. Her enveloping skirt is agitated and rises and falls in waves of blackness that engulf the stage. She is all cool control, he white heat. He achieves an ultimate sigh as her inundating black skirt enfolds him. He disappears in its folds; she, too, bows beneath it.

A number of persons have called *Variations* "the male liberation ballet." I prefer to think of it as an every-man-for-himself ballet. Maybe it shows, in a way, man's weakness—how he strives to get involved but, once there, doesn't know how to get out.

In 1965, in Brussels, Maurice Béjart arranged his own cycle of Pierre Henry's variations for seven dancers in homage to the visual talent of the artist Arman: "Seven dancers enter the stage to create a ballet in which choreography has no place." The dancers improvised their movement according to suggestions from the sonorous structure; each time sequence was propelled by the dancers themselves.

In 1972, in Glasgow for the Scottish Theatre Ballet, Peter Darrell staged his ballet *Variations for a Door and a Sigh*. A program note stated that the work "explores the realms of sexual behavior and the conflicts of personal commitment." Peter Darrell also alluded to a quotation from Tolstoy as the starting point for his ballet: "Man survives earthquakes, epidemics, terrible illnesses and every kind of spiritual suffering, but always the most poignant tragedy was, is and ever will be the tragedy of the bedroom."

VESTRIS

Music by Genaidi Banschikov. Choreography by Leonid Jacobson. First presented at the International Ballet Competition, Moscow, June 1969, with Mikhail Baryshnikov. First presented in the United States by American Ballet Theatre at the Kennedy Center of the Performing Arts, Washington, May 20, 1975, with Baryshnikov. Costume by Marcos Paredes. Conductor: David Gilbert.

One of the greatest dancers of all time, Auguste Vestris appeared to be the natural subject for a ballet in which a young dancer might show, in a very short time, the complete range and versatility of his gifts, in dance and mime. The Soviet choreographer Leonid Jacobson accordingly responded to the young dancer Mikhail Baryshnikov and made for him a seven-minute display piece that sums up a forgotten but illustrious dancer in a forgotten time.

Vestris was born in Paris in 1760 and died there eighty-two years later. Famed for his elevation, pirouettes, and *batterie,* Vestris's performances enthralled Europe for many years, from his debut at age twelve until his retirement at fifty-six. Parliament recessed to watch him and his father, another virtuoso, in 1781. Vestris danced the first performances of great ballets by Noverre and later taught pupils who were to govern ballet in Europe: Didelot, Perrot, Auguste Bournonville, and Marie Taglioni. There are many lithographs and prints of Vestris in performance of many roles, all of which were studied by Jacobson and Baryshnikov as the ballet was being made.

The action is divided into seven brief sections and the basic idea is not to re-create Vestris historically so much as to give a notion of his time as another dancer displays a similar range of versatility. The seven parts are: "An Old

Man Dancing a Minuet," "The Coquette Dance," "The Preacher-Prophet," "Classical Dance Variations," "Prayer," "Laughter," and "Dying Man."

In formal ballet dress fashioned after the eighteenth century, with white wig, white jacket and tights, the star dancer acts his age, relives youth and shows what he is made of.

Vestris was performed at Wolf Trap, near Washington, in 1976, filmed for television, and broadcast first by WNET, New York, on December 6, 1976.

Reviewing the ballet in the New York *Times,* the critic Clive Barnes said "the dance itself is a perfect joy—a cameo impression of a dancer, of a style, of a period and of a man. Within its brief compass it manages to convey a whole sheaf of dramatic and choreographic messages."

In the book *Baryshnikov at Work,* the dancer recalls the genesis of the ballet, which has been recorded there in marvelous pictures by Martha Swope.

VIOLIN CONCERTO

Music by Igor Stravinsky. Choreography by George Balanchine. First presented by the New York City Ballet at the Stravinsky Festival, at the New York State Theatre, Lincoln Center, June 18, 1972, with Karin von Aroldingen, Kay Mazzo, Peter Martins, and Jean-Pierre Bonnefous in the leading roles. Lighting by Ronald Bates. Conducted by Robert Irving. Violin soloist: Joseph Silverstein.

Stravinsky has written (see NOTES below) that he did not like the standard violin concertos. I myself have always preferred Stravinsky's. Some years ago, when the Original Ballet Russe happily gave me the opportunity, I made a ballet to this violin concerto of his. It was called *Balustrade,* largely after splendid scenery by the great artist Pavel Tchelitchew, who painted a décor that was dominated by a white balustrade in perspective in the background. *Balustrade* was first danced at the Fifty-first Street Theatre, New York, January 22, 1941, with Tamara Toumanova, Roman Jasinski, and Paul Petroff in the leading roles. I do not remember this ballet; but not, alas! What I did then was for *then,* and what I wanted to do to this same music for our Stravinsky Festival at the New York City Ballet represented more than thirty years' difference. The dancers were different and I liked the music even more.

The score is in four movements, the middle part being a center or core of two "Arias" enclosed by introductory Toccata and a final Capriccio.

And so is the ballet in four movements, the center being arranged as two *pas de deux* for different couples to accompany the Arias. The introductory Toccata introduces the principal dancers with a small *corps de ballet.* All four of the soloists participate in the Capriccio finale. The best guide to the character of these dances is a number of hearings of the music.

NOTES   In the book *Dialogues and a Diary,* Stravinsky recalled that "The *Violin Concerto* was not inspired by or modeled on any example. I do not like the standard violin concertos—not Mozart's, Beethoven's, Mendelssohn's or

Brahms's. To my mind, the only masterpiece in the field is Schoenberg's, and that was written several years after mine. The titles of my movements, Toccata, Aria, Capriccio, suggest Bach, however, and so to some extent, does the musical substance. My favorite Bach solo concerto is the one for two violins, as the duet with a violin from the orchestra in the last movement of my concerto must show. But the *Violin Concerto* contains other duet combinations, too, and the texture of the music is more often chamber music in style than orchestral. I did not write a cadenza for the reason that I was not interested in violin virtuosity. Virtuosity for its own sake plays little part in my concerto, and the technical difficulties of the piece are, I think, relatively tame.

"The ballet *Balustrade* (1940) by George Balanchine and Pavel Tchelitchew, and with the music of my *Violin Concerto,* was one of the most satisfactory visualizations of any of my theatre works. Balanchine worked out the choreography as we played my recording together and I could actually watch him imagine gesture, movement, combination, composition. The result was a dance dialogue in perfect co-ordination with the dialogues of the music. The dancers were few in number, and the whole second Aria was performed—and beautifully performed—as a solo piece, by Toumanova. *Balustrade* was produced by Sol Hurok, that master judge of the *vox populi* (I imagine *Balustrade* must have been one of his few misjudgments in that sense). The set was a very simple white balustrade across the back of the dark stage."

Reviewing *Violin Concerto* in *The Nation,* Nancy Goldner wrote of the dance to the second Aria: "The duet for Kay Mazzo and Peter Martins is amazingly complex and dense, as is most of the ballet. It churns and seems to be a continuous process of knotting and unknotting. In their first phase, she faces him for a second, grabs his waist and slides to the floor, resting on her front haunch while her back leg is tensely stretched. He looks to the right. She looks to the left, her arm partly covering her face. There is discord here, which builds and builds as their sculptured and quickly changing poses become more multi-dimensional. Too, their relationship with the music becomes increasingly independent, until they finally seem to be in total counterpoint, though never in disharmony. Perhaps that is one reason why Mazzo's simple big movement to the one resounding chord in the score is such a shock. Another reason is that nothing is simple between this couple. But as soon as she has made that simple declaration the duet turns convoluted again. She collapses her knees inward and rotates away from Martins, who is grasping her ankles. The choreography is so innovative, intense and rich that detailed analysis of it, and clues as to why it seems to be a profound embodiment of inner turbulence, must await further performances. But first let me describe one luscious detail in it. Martins rolls Mazzo from one foot to another. In this little air voyage, she starts out with one foot pointed and the other flexed. With great deliberation and yet speed, she simultaneously points the flexed foot and flexes the pointed one. We can almost see each dot along the arced paths her feet trace. As the trip ends, she lands on one foot and whips her flexed foot along the floor into a point. This is an exclamation point to a juicy five-second game. Many choreographers have played with flexed feet in classical ballet, but Balanchine's version is now the definitive one."

VIVA VIVALDI!

Music by Antonio Vivaldi. Choreography by Gerald Arpino. First presented by the Robert Joffrey Ballet at the Delacorte Theatre, Central Park, New York, September 10, 1965, with Robert Blankshine, Jon Cristofori, Edwina Dingman, Luis Fuente, Ian Horvath, Margo Sappington, and Trinette Singleton in leading roles.

This lively dance ballet with a Spanish flavor is set to music by Vivaldi (*Violin Concerto in D major, P. 151,* arranged for guitar and orchestra). A display piece for fine dancers, who perform both allegro and adagio roles, there is no story, only the tempo and melody of the score and the expression of the dance accompaniment.

VOLUNTARIES

Music by Francis Poulenc. Choreography by Glen Tetley. Designed by Rouben Ter-Arutunian. Lighting by John B. Read, executed by Gilbert V. Hemsley, Jr. First presented by the Stuttgart Ballet at the Württemberg State Theatre, Stuttgart, December 22, 1973, with Marcia Haydée and Richard Cragun in the leading roles. First presented in the United States by the same ensemble at the Metropolitan Opera House, Lincoln Center, New York, June 4, 1975, with the same principals.

Created in memory of John Cranko, the Stuttgart Ballet's founder, *Voluntaries* is a dance tribute and valedictory by Glen Tetley. It was Tetley's first work for the company, of which he was appointed director in the winter of 1974 after Cranko's sudden death in the summer of 1973.

The choreographer's program note for the ballet tells us that, by musical definition, voluntaries are free-ranging organ or trumpet improvisations that are often played before, during, or after religious services. The Latin root of the word also connotes desire or flight. The choreographer says that the ballet is conceived as "a linked series of voluntaries." The music is Poulenc's *Concerto for Organ, Strings, and Percussion;* the soloists in New York were Calvin Hampton, organist, and Howard Van Hyning, timpanist.

The stage action is both a tribute and a dance celebration, a ritual of remembrance and rededication that looks forward rather than back. A stranger to the occasion would know only of the dance event itself and not of its sentimental pretext.

Voluntaries is danced before a painted backdrop of concentrated color and design that suggests liveliness, a kind of microscopic slide depicting continuity and no interruption. The stage action shows Cranko's principal dancers in combinations and permutations of movement that remember. They also look forward to the future!

Writing of the New York premiere, the critic Clive Barnes said in the New York *Times* that *Voluntaries* "is an outstanding amalgam of classic ballet and modern dance and, probably, Mr. Tetley's more purely beautiful and sinuous work to date . . . At the end the cheers for the company and Mr. Tetley engulfed the opera house."

WALK TO THE PARADISE GARDEN

Music by Frederick Delius. Choreography by Frederick Ashton. Setting by William Chappell. First presented by the Royal Ballet at the Royal Opera House, Covent Garden, November 15, 1972, with Merle Park, David Wall, and Derek Rencher.

Frederick Ashton has called this brief ballet a *Liebestod*—or love-death. The music is from Delius' great lyric opera, *A Village Romeo and Juliet,* and it serves as the prelude to the final scene of that work, where the two lovers kill themselves. Similarly, in the ballet, the lovers, after ultimate expressions of joy in each other, discover no other course but suicide to perpetuate the depth of their passion. They meet white-robed Death, submit, and rejoice again.

Writing in *The Times* of London after the premiere, the critic John Percival said that this was "the first big part Ashton has created for Merle Park, and he reveals in her a lyricism and natural warmth her usual bravura roles have hidden. She and David Wall play a pair of lovers, entirely absorbed in each other . . . What they have to do includes some fantastically difficult things. Not only the familiar Bolshoi . . . tricks, like spinning the girl horizontally through the air and catching her again, but even a moment when she is held upside down high above his head. Yet Ashton sets these virtuoso tricks so smoothly into the dance, and they are so effortlessly done by this couple, that you hardly notice the difficulty, rather the rapture they express. Yet there is about the dance a sense of stolen time, an undertone of feeling that the moment cannot last, and at the end this manifests itself chillingly in the form of a stern angel all in stark white (Derek Rencher), who draws the lovers to him, parts them and allows them to be joined again only in death. Ashton has caught the mood of the Delius music perfectly, although seeing deeper into it than his audience perhaps expected. A handsome setting by William Chappell completes a small but perfectly-formed work."

In his authoritative biography of Frederick Ashton, David Vaughan describes the process of the ballet's creation in detail. He also remarks: "This dance was the most important role that Ashton ever choreographed for Merle Park, and as with so many other dancers he brought out reserves of passion that had been hidden until then."

WALPURGIS NIGHT

Music by Charles Gounod. Choreography by Leonid Lavrovsky. First presented by the Bolshoi Ballet at the Filial Theatre, Moscow, 1941. First presented in the United States by the Bolshoi Ballet at the Metropolitan Opera House, New York, April 23, 1959.

The Walpurgis Night scene in Gounod's opera *Faust* occurs at the beginning of the last act. Here Mephistopheles brings Faust to witness the revels that traditionally take place on the eve of May Day at Brocken, highest point of the Hartz Mountains. There Mephistopheles summons the shades of famous courtesans. The ballet freely depicts the height of the revels.

WATERMILL

Music by Teiji Ito. Choreography by Jerome Robbins. Costumes by Patricia Zipprodt. Lighting by Ronald Bates. Décor by Jerome Robbins in association with David Reppa. First presented by the New York City Ballet at the New York State Theatre, Lincoln Center, February 3, 1972, with Edward Villella, Penny Dudleston, Hermes Conde, Jean-Pierre Frohlich, Bart Cook, Tracy Bennett, Victor Castelli, Deni Lamont, Colleen Neary, and Robert Maiorano in the principal roles. Musicians: Dan Erkkila, Genji Ito, Teiji Ito, Kansuke Kawase, Mara Purl, and Terry White.

The score of *Watermill*, by the contemporary composer Teiji Ito, is radically different from the music we customarily hear in the ballet theater: it is quiet, full of pauses (what the composer calls "silent sounds") and stems mainly from the religious ceremonial and theatrical music of the Orient. It employs numerous percussion and wind instruments, including the Shakuhachi, a bamboo flute used in Japan in the thirteenth century. This flute was played mainly by Zen Buddhist priests whose compositions for the instrument still survive. These musical-religious works are usually contemplative evocations of nature and the seasons. So also is this ballet—a contemplation on a man's life as seen through the passage of the four seasons. However influenced by the music and theater of the East, the ballet—its world, people and events—are not to be taken as Oriental.

Writing of *Watermill*, Jacqueline Maskey in *High Fidelity/Musical America* aptly described the theme: a ritual of remembering.

"The man recalls: himself as a youth, light and graceful, boneless as a leaping fish; the ritual games that test and harden him; the perfections of love in which his partner seems woman, earth, moon-goddess; then the devils, irrational phantoms that tear and torment. Peasant figures—sowing, reaping, winnowing, gleaning—thread through his recollections. He recognizes, in a ceremony with grain stalks, nature and his oneness with it and, in a bent figure, the inevitability of old age. As he gazes, boys release curious and buoyant paper shapes which rise into nothingness as must his own dust, and the curtain falls.

"*Watermill* is a particular view of human existence, expressed in terms of the inexorable cycle of the seasons. Man matures and declines; the moon waxes and wanes; the earth is fruitful, then fallow; snow follows sun."

The six musicians, all in Japanese costume, enter and sit on the right of the stage. A framed scrim faces us. As the music begins with a plaintive sound, we discern behind it gradually three high mysterious shapes that we can't quite make out—they are not trees, for wasp-waisted, they spread out at the base, too; they are not giants or windmills. They stand in a field filled with mist under a crescent moon. As the mist lifts a bit, we see that they are high sheaves of grain, the stalks gathered in tightly at the middle. There is a fence in the distance, and before we know it, we see there is a man there, too, standing in the field in a long black cloak, his face hidden, a part of the natural landscape, too. What we have gradually seen here and made out patiently in the mist is characteristic of the voyage of recollection and discovery that now begins for this man and for us.

Slowly, slowly, looking up for a moment at the sky, the man comes toward us. He kneels, rises, leaving his cloak on the ground. He takes off his shoes then, and his shirt and trousers. Standing now almost naked, he stretches out his arms as figures bearing multicolored lanterns approach him. They come up to him closely, their lanterns poised at the end of long wands, as if to illumine his body fully, then go away. To a chanted song that rises from the music, the man begins to dance. But not for long. He sits down and youths enter with kites, an umbrella, etc.

A boy runs as men in the background till the fields. The man notices the boy, reaches out his hand to him, but the boy sees another man in the distance and goes to him. Five boys trot across the field, five more, too, these carrying sticks. The man walks among them. They do warlike gymnastics, as if preparing for battle. But the man runs off. He returns as the youths stop and remain motionless.

A woman enters in a long green dress and turban. In the background, a group of young persons arrange a picnic on the grass behind one of the sheaves of grain. The woman puts down a rug on the grass. There is a longer period of waiting. She lets fall her outer garment and her long hair, which she combs slowly. The man watches her some distance away. We have the impression that he is both with her and is remembering her, their contact is so close. She lies down to sleep; so does he. Darkness falls. A boy—the man in his youth?—enters and goes to the woman. He pulls her body to his and she stretches around him; to the light of the moon they embrace closely. They roll and undulate together on the blanket and stop. The picnickers in the back rise and go; the moon keeps on descending.

The man awakens and lifts his arm. The boy on the blanket raises his arm simultaneously. The girl, too, hails the descending moon. The man and the boy rise together; the man goes to the girl as the boy backs out. The man takes the girl's hand, then lies with his head in her lap as, on the right, the boy of the first scene sleeps. The girl gets up, takes her rug, and leaves as the man and boy sleep.

There is a menacing atmosphere. A bearded creature enters; two black figures follow. The man wakes up the boy, and to howls it seems of dogs and the beat of percussion, there is an attack of some sort. The man watches; the boy runs off. The man stretches out now as if dead. Figures enter with baskets to gather pebbles. Leaves flutter down in the autumn air. The man glances up, then sits bowed over, head on knees. Rose petals fall. Peasants enter, take shafts of wheat and let them balance and fall within their fingers. The moon rises and is seen in eclipse. The man kneels and watches the peasants as ever so slowly they wave the stalks of wheat in the still air, then return them to the shaft. One girl remains and gives the man two wheat stalks. He holds them aloft, balancing them carefully; they seem to be balanced extensions of his arms. Snow falls gently. The man dances as it were with the stalks of wheat; they quiver in the evening air. The man kneels within a cross they have made of the stalks. A girl and boy come in with more wheat stalks as the snow thickens. The man moves, holding the stalks; they seem extensions of his arms and tremble at his every movement. Snow falls. He dances as it were with the stalks of quivering wheat, crossing them and kneeling as they cross. A girl and a boy enter with wheat tassles. They soon leave and the man rises as the boy returns; the girl does, too. The man lays down the cross of wheat and the boy who died. The snow has stopped. The man is alone. He takes up his cloak and leaves as an aged figure with a stick comes in. So, also, do men who carry on their shoulders heavy burdens. They cross the stage, slowly, at the back. Suddenly their burdens begin to lift off their shoulders and rise into the air. The curtain falls.

NOTES   Nancy Goldner reviewed *Watermill* for *Dance News:* "Jerome Robbins's *Watermill* is one of the most perfect productions I have seen. It is beautiful, by all means—but it is more than that. It is exquisite. The details are the thing, although the work deals with large themes. The ballet is a meditation on nature. There is a meditator. His world is populated by seeders, tillers, harvesters, and phenomena of nature—the moon, wind, snow, stalks of wheat. Even the music, written by Teiji Ito and played by him and friends on the side of the stage, is as natural sounding as it is sounds of music. But it is always the details. Some boys wave small kites; each bobs at a different altitude. They also carry lanterns at different heights. This sensitivity to slight variation is exciting and moving. Four of the lanterns are large, in primary colors. Two of them are tiny and white. They look so fragile next to the larger ones. In addition to going through its phases, the moon ascends and descends. It seems to move when you're not looking. Its changing aspects are always something of a surprise. The wind which causes the wheat bundles to rustle is slight; it becomes a presence, like the moon. When fall comes, the leaves float onto the stage one by one. Even the snow seems to have been sprinkled over the land by a Haiku poet-god, so gentle is the fall and isolated the flakes. The list could go on. . . .

"The Orientalisms are not only in the music, props, and use of props. The entire spirit of *Watermill* is Orientally meditative. It unfolds slowly. With the exception of the dance of the spring/youth figure and the running sequence, which in itself is a rare-faction of the action—the boys and protagonist do a trot-like stylization of a run—the dancers move slowly, very slowly. Time becomes thick, sliceable. Edward Villella, the meditator-dreamer, has a quality here that suggests great power beneath the stillness. It is this suggestion of action that makes him so compelling, and maddening. Like the wind and moon, he becomes a presence. Unlike the moon, he does not mark the passing of time but seems to be a second of time stretched into forever. You either settle into his state of consciousness, or go insane. Maybe you can settle on a compromise by coughing and fidgeting. But you can't go to sleep. Robbins gets at some part of you.

"There are some obscure sections. Some actions are not definable by line and verse, but they do make emotional sense. Some things make such sense that they become permanent images in the mind. One such moment was the sound of wind before the nightmare. It struck to the core. It was one of the great moments in the theater. Oddly enough, though, the nightmare itself hit sideways. For me, the totality of the piece was not equal to some of the parts. Not because the parts were unconnected to each other and to the larger theme; on the contrary, never have I seen a dance so perfectly interrelated. But because the ballet is not so much about nature, time, life cycles, and whatnot as it is 'about' a particular state of consciousness. And now I must confess that I was one of those who were going insane. The moments when I was thoroughly engrossed were the moments when I was most detached from the proceedings, when my attention was drawn away from the slow-moving dancers and from time. Only my aesthetic sense was engaged and heightened. Robbins wanted the whole being to be there. Those who find dwelling on a stalk of wheat exhilarating will find *Watermill* a masterpiece to end all masterpieces. I can only admire Robbins' essay."

Writing in *Dance and Dancers* magazine, Patricia Barnes said: "Every so often—but not that often—a ballet turns up which instantly convinces one of its place in dance history. It becomes a landmark. Such a one is Jerome Robbins's *Watermill*, a creation of such imagination, depth and profundity that no one seeing it can remain untouched in some way by it. The first night audience greeted it with a mixture of cheers and boos; some were clearly baffled by its newness and just sat looking stunned and perplexed. But it is not just that it is new and different: innovation alone does not make great art. *Watermill* is, in addition, a work of extraordinary beauty: a poetic and deeply felt work that seems to have been torn from the very soul of its creator. It has even been suggested that the ballet is part autobiographical, and certainly the title is the same as the island where Robbins has his country home.

"In 1964 Robbins studied the Noh technique, and clearly what he learned has been stirring in his mind ever since. *Watermill* incorporates much that can be traced to Noh—the deliberation, refinement and simplicity of movement, the stripping away of excessive gesture—but despite the influence of the music and theater of the East, this ballet's world, people and events, according to a program note, are universal and not to be construed as Oriental.

"Another influence on this particular world appears to be Robert Wilson, the fascinating and provocative young director who has forged a whole new theater style, and who recently performed in Paris with enormous success. But the creative genius of *Watermill* is Robbins alone. How incredible this choreographer is, never sitting back on the laurels of past successes, never choosing the easy way, but constantly challenged by new vistas and new ideas, a choreographer who can equally touch the heart and stimulate the intellect."

A WEDDING BOUQUET

Comic ballet in one act. Music by Lord Berners. Choreography by Frederick Ashton. Words by Gertrude Stein. Scenery and costumes by Lord Berners. First presented by the Vic-Wells Ballet at the Sadler's Wells Theatre, London, April 27, 1937, with Mary Honer as the Bride, *Robert Helpmann as the* Bridegroom, *Margot Fonteyn as* Julia, *June Brae as* Josephine, *Julia Farron as* Pépé, *and Ninette de Valois as* Webster. *First presented in the United States by the Sadler's Wells Ballet at the Metropolitan Opera House, New York, October 25, 1949, with Margaret Dale as the* Bride, *Robert Helpmann as the* Bridegroom, *Moira Shearer as* Julia, *June Brae as* Josephine, *Pauline Clayden as* Pépé, *and Palma Nye as* Webster.

When *A Wedding Bouquet* was first presented, one critic called it a *ballet bouffe*. That is exactly what it is: a comic work that achieves some of its funniest farce by exposing the absurdity of great dignity and seriousness. Its subject, a wedding in a provincial French town near the turn of the century, presents a set of conventions that must not be upset; and at the cost of many laughs, all the conventions are observed. They are observed in the determined, apparently senseless fashion with which people in René Clair movies observe their conventions: everything seems to combine against them, but in the end everything is all right. It is possible to watch *A Wedding Bouquet* and see it as a continental comic equivalent to the Edwardian pathos of such a ballet as *Lilac Garden*. Gertrude Stein's commentary on the action is spoken during the ballet by an observing orator.

The curtain rises on the garden of a farmhouse near Bellay. There is a long table set out for the wedding feast, and the ballet begins as people scurry about preparing the refreshments. Webster, the maid, is certain that things will not be ready by the time the bride and groom arrive. On the right, sitting apart from the scene, is the orator. He pours himself a glass of champagne.

As the guests begin to arrive, the orator speaks over the music to tell us about some of them. In addition to the peasant girls and boys and the usual gate crashers, there are Josephine ("She may be wearing a gown newly washed and pressed") and her two friends, Paul ("Pleasant, vivacious, and quarrelsome") and John ("An elder brother who regrets the illness of his father"). There is the aggressive young lady Violet ("Violet, oh will you ask him to marry you?"), who eagerly pursues a young man named Ernest ("May be the victim of himself"). Ernest eagerly repulses Violet's advances.

Now Julia enters. The orator tells us that she "Is known as forlorn," and
forlorn she certainly is. She can hardly walk, she is so dejected. Apparently the
trouble is that the fickle bridegroom of the day has abandoned her. Tagging
along behind Julia is her dog, a Mexican terrier called Pépé ("Little dogs
resemble little girls"). Julia directs all her affections to Pépé, and Pépé
switches her tail like a little girl honored with a lollipop. One of the men tries
to cheer Julia up, but Pépé protects her mistress. It appears that Josephine is
terribly sorry for Julia. She tries to comfort her like a true friend, and Julia
sulks with lunatic pleasure.

The bridal party approaches. First, the bride ("Charming! Charming!
Charming!"). The bridesmaids dance together under her bridal veil. The
bridegroom is clearly harassed. ("They all speak as if they expected him not to
be charming.") As if the silly wedding weren't enough, he must now deal with
the guests ("They incline to oblige only when they stare") and with Julia. The
sight of this demented past indiscretion of his makes the bridegroom despair.
Patiently he poses with the bridal party for a photograph of the wedding
group. Then he tries to act as if nothing had happened.

Julia won't let him. She hangs on him like a cat. She won't give him up! The
guests titter and chatter among themselves, guessing at the bridegroom's situation. Pépé tries to distract the bride, who begins to be suspicious. The
bridegroom tries to push Julia off, and she throws herself at his feet. The bride
despairs.

Now Josephine, too, is crying in her beer. She is so upset, because Julia is
upset, that she drinks far too much. She starts to make the inevitable scene
and is asked to leave. The groom, alone with Julia and all the other girls he's
been intimate with, dances a bright tango. When he observes all these demanding women, he is lighthearted: marriage has set him free at last! Apparently his new bride sees how lucky she is.

Night begins to fall and the guests start to leave ("Thank you. Thank
you."). The bridegroom goes to his bride, and the unhappy Julia is left alone.
She still has Pépé, however. The dog tries to comfort her as Julia stupidly
stares off into space.

WEEWIS

*Original commissioned score by Stanley Walden. Rock group: Virgin Wool.
Choreography by Margo Sappington. Lighting by Jennifer Tipton. First
presented by the Joffrey City Center Ballet at the City Center, New York,
October 28, 1971, with Gary Chryst, James Dunne, Rebecca Wright, Christian Holder, Susan Magno, and Tony Catanzaro.*

The name of this ballet is a small mystery: it is the name of the choreographer's cat. *Weewis* is a dance ballet, a series of duets, performed to the
music of a rock group. Writing of the ballet in *Time*, the critic John T. Elson
said that the three couples "appear to exemplify the varying moods of love
(definitely profane)." The first dance is for two boys. The second is for a girl

and boy and shows the sinuous variations possible in sophisticated lovemaking. The third dance is a fierce apache number for another girl and boy.

WESTERN SYMPHONY

Ballet in three movements. Music by Hershy Kay. Choreography by George Balanchine. Scenery by John Boyt. Costumes by Karinska. First presented by the New York City Ballet at the New York City Center, September 7, 1954, with Diana Adams, Herbert Bliss, Janet Reed, Nicholas Magallanes, Patricia Wilde, Tanaquil LeClercq, Jacques d'Amboise, and others.

My idea in this ballet was to make a formal work that would derive its flavor from the informal American West, a ballet that would move within the framework of the classic school but in a new atmosphere. Earlier ballets on American folk themes (*Billy the Kid, Rodeo,* et al.) have been based on cowboy lore, but these have been story ballets. I wanted to do a ballet without a story in an unmistakably native American idiom. To accomplish that, I needed a new score and turned to the young composer Hershy Kay.

Western Symphony was a close collaboration between us. I was neither interested in local atmosphere nor narrative pantomime and told Kay that I wanted to try a symphonic American dance work which, by the impetus of indigenous melodies, would help me to use the universal language of the classic ballet in a fresh way. He liked the idea and wrote a symphony to order, a work in four movements, based on themes like "Red River Valley," "Old Taylor," "The Gal I Left Behind Me," "Rye Whiskey," "Golden Slippers," and others. To these movements I arranged a series of dance ensembles that I hope have some of the sentiment and candor of the time and places where those tunes were first sung.

I have crossed the United States by car some dozen times, have camped in the open air in New Mexico and Wyoming, in Montana and South Dakota. The vast sweep of the land, the impression of the Rockies and the plains, and the vision of the men who crossed the mountains and worked the plains, on foot and on horseback, cannot fail to move any newcomer, particularly one who has fresh memories of Europe, most of which is closely settled and where there have been few empty natural spaces for thousands of years.

Western Symphony was originally presented in practice clothes without a set. This was regrettable but we had no money at that time and had to wait for the following season for the designs of John Boyt and Karinska to materialize. The original four movements of the ballet have since been cut to three, omitting the third movement. In 1956, in Paris, during our third European tour, the United States Information Agency made a color film of the ballet with all its four movements.

THE WHIMS OF CUPID AND THE BALLET MASTER

*Music by Jens Lolle. Choreography by Vincenzo Galeotti. First presented
by the Royal Danish Ballet at the Royal Theatre, Copenhagen, October 31,
1786. First presented in the United States by the Royal Danish Ballet at
the Metropolitan Opera House, New York, September 22, 1956. Scenery
and costumes by Ove Christian Pedersen.*

This is said to be the oldest ballet in the repertory. It has survived for almost
two centuries at the Royal Theatre in Copenhagen and has never been omitted
for such a length of time as to prevent several of the previous cast from assist-
ing the new production, thus carrying on the original choreography by Galeotti
in the proper spirit. Galeotti, who came to Denmark from Italy as early as
1775, is the first choreographer of importance to the Danish ballet.

The story is a comedy about lovers from many countries who come to pay
tribute to the god Cupid. They dance before him the characteristic styles of
their lands and then he plays a trick, blindfolding the couples. The curious
matchmaking that results leads to hilarity and what the original program
called a finale of "great confusion."

WHO CARES?

*Music by George Gershwin, orchestrated by Hershy Kay. Choreography by
George Balanchine. Costumes by Karinska. Lighting by Ronald Bates. Pianist: Gordon Boelzner. First presented by the New York City Ballet at the
New York State Theatre, Lincoln Center, February 5, 1970, with Karin
von Aroldingen, Patricia McBride, Marnee Morris, and Jacques d'Amboise
as the principal dancers.*

This ballet is a set of dances to some songs by George Gershwin that I have always liked very much. "Who Cares?" goes back to 1931 and *Of Thee I Sing.*
In Europe in the late 1920s and 1930s, we all knew Gershwin's music and
loved it; it is beautiful, very American, too. Before I came to America I saw
the Gershwin musical *Funny Face* in London and admired it. I did some work
in musical comedies in London after that and continued to make dances for
them after I came to New York. I don't think I would have done that if it had
not been for George Gershwin's music. There are popular songs and popular
songs; Gershwin's are special.

I was lucky enough to know Gershwin, who asked me to Hollywood to do
dances for the movie *Goldwyn Follies.* Gershwin gave me a book of his songs,
arranged in the way he used to do them in concerts. One day at the piano I
played one through and thought to myself, Beautiful, I'll make a *pas de deux.*
Then I played another, it was just as beautiful and I thought, A variation! And
then another and another and there was no end to how beautiful they were.

And so we had a new ballet. No story, just the songs. Here they are, with the dancers who first danced them: "Strike Up the Band" (1927), Ladies and Gentlemen; "Sweet and Low Down" (1925), Ensemble; "Somebody Loves Me" (1924), Deborah Flomine, Susan Hendl, Linda Merrill, Susan Pilarre, Bettijane Sills; "Bidin' My Time" (1930), Deni Lamont, Robert Maiorano, Frank Ohman, Richard Rapp, Earle Sieveling; "'S Wonderful" (1927), Susan Pilarre and Richard Rapp; "That Certain Feeling" (1925), Deborah Flomine and Deni Lamont, Bettijane Sills, and Earl Sieveling; "Do Do Do" (1926), Susan Hendl and Frank Ohman; "Lady Be Good" (1924), Linda Merrill and Robert Maiorano; "The Man I Love" (1924), Patricia McBride and Jacques d'Amboise; "I'll Build a Stairway to Paradise" (1922), Karin von Aroldingen; "Embraceable You" (1930), Marnee Morris and Jacques d'Amboise; "Fascinatin' Rhythm" (1924), Patricia McBride; "Who Cares?" (1931), Karin von Aroldingen and Jacques d'Amboise; "My One and Only" (1927), Marnee Morris; "Liza" (1929), Jacques d'Amboise; "Clap Yo' Hands" (1926), Karin von Aroldingen, Patricia McBride, Marnee Morris, Jacques d'Amboise; "I Got Rhythm" (1930), Entire Cast.

NOTES   The first performance of *Who Cares?* had only an orchestral beginning ("Strike Up the Band") because the composer Hershy Kay, who was arranging the songs for us, was busy with a musical. Gordon Boelzner, the pianist, played all the other songs except for "Clap Yo' Hands," where we played a recording of Gershwin doing the piece himself. We still do.

We did not have much scenery for the ballet at the beginning. This was provided later by Jo Mielziner, November 21, 1970, who gave us a scrim with two layers of silhouetted skylines of New York in a kind of fan shape for the backdrop and, for the sides of the stage, skyscraper cliffs.

When *Who Cares?* was first done, Lincoln Kirstein wrote an extensive note for our program: "*Who Cares?* is both the name of a new ballet in the classical idiom by George Balanchine and an old song George and Ira Gershwin wrote in 1931 for *Of Thee I Sing*. The dictionary says *classic* means standard, leading, belonging to the highest rank of authority. Once it applied mainly to masterpieces from Greco-Roman antiquity; now we have boxing and horse racing classics, classic cocktail dresses and classic cocktails. Among classic American composers we number Stephen Foster, John Philip Sousa and George Gershwin (1898–1937). First heard fifty years ago, the best of the Gershwin songs maintain their classic freshness, as of an eternal martini—dry, frank, refreshing, tailor-made with an invisible kick from its slightest hint of citron. Nostalgia has not syruped their sentiment nor robbed them of immediate piquancy. We associate them with time past, but when well sung or played, or preferably both at once, they not only revive but transcend their epoch. Lovely in themselves they are by way of becoming art songs, which that beautiful singer Eva Gauthier long ago realized when she first sang them in concert well after they had become familiar hits. The Gershwins wrote hit songs which were art songs. Most art songs pretend to be love songs; the Gershwin genre seem to be about playmates more than lovers. It was not by accident the best dance team of the time, Fred and Adele Astaire, were brother and sister.

"To the musician George Gershwin, perhaps their most important element was their potential as piano pieces. He played energetically, long and magically at private parties and in public. His semi-improvisational style was taken seriously even by 'serious' critics. Gilbert Seldes, our first popularizer of what we now call pop art (in painting as well as theater), indeed complained that *The Rhapsody in Blue* was a masterpiece marred by Liszt-like extended cadenzas; certainly Gershwin was a hypnotic virtuoso as well as a knowing and generous analyst of the jazz style of which he was a master. This he traced to the individual ragtimers at the turn of the century whose collective ingenuities in piano playing built up a tradition which he inherited, and which he used with a new articulate sophistication, flexibility and brilliance.

"But there is another serious aspect of the Gershwin songs which marks their sturdy structure—words supporting the tunes, mainly by his brother Ira. The wit, tact, invention, metaphor and metric of Ira's rhymes meant that you not only left the theater whistling melodies, but singing words. His phrasing was simple enough, his phrases sharp enough to impose themselves at one hearing; once heard, they were almost infectiously memorable. Love & dove, June & moon, true & you long comprised the pidgin English of Tin Pan Alley. Ira Gershwin not only transubstantiated such base metal; with condescension or parody he created a new prosody, a new means for lyric writing which incorporated the season's slang, references to local events, echoes of the vernacular rhythms of ordinary speech in a frame of casual thrown-away elegance which was never false, insistent or self-conscious. He seemed to have stumbled on what was right, fitting, appropriate, surprising and charming, as if such had been coins tossed in his path. But such coinage is art, not accident, and Ira incidentally was a poet and a master of mnemonics. He was also a satirist; there had always been comic ballads, but it is odd to find in 'Strike Up the Band' (1927), an ostensibly patriotic hit tune, its almost Brechtian tang. . . . Ira Gershwin's lyric style involved his skill in manipulating repetition, shift of breath, perfect punctuation, instinct for vulgarism in a mosaic of unusual context, plus a laconic polish. His vocabulary was small; both Noel Coward and Cole Porter were more literary; Lorenz Hart's smashing pastiches depended on a wide reading. These three derived from Gilbert and Sullivan, a more operatic or light-operatic tradition. Ira was in the line of minstrelsy—the minstrel show and the ancient descent from troubador soloists. All the songs sang 'I love you,' but Ira's hummed it with a unique American, or rather Manhattan (cocktail), simplicity and savor. Lyrics are to be sung, not enunciated like patter songs, or launched—like arias. In love songs, intense emotion is usually in inverse proportion to the heartbreak clarity of words. George Gershwin's tunes were not impassioned but playful. Their pretext was not profound feelings, but sportive sex, flirtatious games, gallantry in a tennis tournament: love, set, match. George Gershwin took forms and archetypes as he received them and composed something unheard before out of formulae. He did not so much write parodies of Negro spirituals, barroom ballads or cowboy songs; he appropriated familiar atmospheres and by his mastery whipped them into the strict form of the hit song, as someone might break a green colt into a pacer. He alternated tenderness with ironic narcissism, or contrasted a smashing climax with the most delicate expression of loss or confusion. And Ira's lyrics were indeed—lyric: personal, enthusiastic, eminently singable. The Gershwins were showmen; they gloried in hits, show stoppers, grand finales with everybody shouting in the aisles, but their brashest choirs never obscured the fragility of certain solos when George almost seemed to be singing to himself. Idiosyncratic serenades, at once self-deprecatory and wistful, they were as elegant, athletic and lonely as he was in life, which no one knew better than his brother.

"This faintly confessional residue of George Gershwin is a touching legacy. In 1930, for *Girl Crazy*, he and Ira wrote a deliberately paced number for a chorus of dubious cowboys, dude ranch gigolos leaning on the fence of a Reno divorce ranch. The wrangler of 1930 had already become a drugstore cowboy on his way to becoming a midnight cowboy; but forty years ago he was more the dandy than the hustler. And in Ira's deft quotation of the titles of four popular songs in his introduction, we have his compliments to colleagues in the song writing industry, a delicious in-joke of the era, as well as a not unjustified boast of the Gershwin superiority, as aristocrats of American lyricism, masters of music to the American electorate. The Gershwins' beautiful manners and high style, their instant melange of insouciance and shrewd innocence, their just estimation of the imaginative elasticity of an elite audience which they had developed, have left a body of words and music which lives, unblurred by vulgar rhetoric or machine-made sentiment. To combine an intensely personal attitude with a flagrantly popular language is a feat which few popular artists manage, and it is appropriate that Balanchine has used the songs not as facile recapitulation of a lost epoch, but simply as songs, or melodies for classic, undeformed, traditional academic dances, which in their equivalence of phrasing, dynamics and emotion, find their brotherly parallel."

Soon after the first performances, Arlene Croce, editor of *Ballet Review*, wrote about the ballet in the *Dancing Times*: "The title of Balanchine's Gershwin ballet, *Who Cares?*, has a double significance. It means, Who Cares what we call it ('as long as I care for you and you care for me'), and it suggests that the piece is an elegant throwaway. That's how it looks, too—like nothing much. The curtain goes up while the orchestra is playing 'Strike Up the Band' and we see a double exposure of Manhattan skylines projected in a pinkish haze on the backcloth. An excellent idea, but it stops there. The rest of the stage looks bleak. The girls wear their very well-cut Karinska tutus, this time in turquoise and lemon-yellow. The skirts have pleats and look 1920s and mini-mod at the same time. So do the boys' black bellbottom slacks. Like the title and the skyline, everything has a double impact, with one effect or style superimposed on another—Now on Then, ballet dancing on show tunes. The two planes of meaning are so shuffled that we're never completely in one world or the other, we're in both at once. Or rather, we're in four worlds since *Who Cares?* scrambles two elements, classical dancing and show dancing, and two eras, the Twenties and the Seventies, with equal paronomasiac facility. And since the Twenties was itself a period of classical revival, the play of references can grow almost infinitely complex. When Balanchine has five boys do double air turns (one boy at a time) in 'Bidin' My Time,' we're pleased with ourselves for thinking of the boys' variation in *Raymonda*, Act Three (the metrical swing of

the music is pretty much the same), and even more pleased when we remember the masculine ensemble that made the song famous in *Girl Crazy.*
That's simple enough. But when toward the end of the ballet his four stars fly
across the stage to 'Clap Yo' Hands' in what is unmistakably a series of quotations from *Apollo,* we catch an unframeable glimpse of the multiple precedents
Who Cares? is made of. It's then that we see, for just the flash of the moment
that he gives us to see it, how comradely the links are between the Gershwin
of *Lady Be Good!, Tip Toes, Oh, Kay!* and *Funny Face,* and the syncopated
Stravinsky of *Apollon Musagete.* We notice that the dancers in the ballet wear
necktie-belts in homage not only to Astaire but to the Chanel who in 1928
knotted men's striped cravats around the waists of Apollo's muses. But the al-
lusion to 1928 isn't endstopped; it reverberates with *Apollo's* own recapit-
ulations of the Nineties and Marius Petipa—high noon at the Maryinsky—and
so we are borne back ceaselessly into the past. To the question 'What is classicism?' Balanchine responds with a blithe shrug and a popular song. Classicism is the Hall of Fame viewed as a hall of mirrors. The Fun House. . . .

"The ballet suddenly . . . finds its own life—when the boys and girls start
dancing out in pairs to ''S Wonderful,' 'That Certain Feeling,' 'Do Do Do,' and
'Lady Be Good'; the dance invention tumbles forth, so does the applause, and
we realize that what we're going to see is not a clever foreigner's half-infat-
uated, half-skeptical view of a popular American art form, we're going to see
the art form itself, re-energized. But this spectacle we see isn't like a musical
comedy, it's more like a lieder recital with a few social mannerisms mostly in
the pleasant, sappy, ingenue style of Old Broadway. Just when you think that
maybe the dancers do represent a musical comedy chorus full of stock types
(with Linda Merrill as the company's inevitable redhead), they vanish and another ballet, or musical, or recital begins.

"The second half of *Who Cares?* has an *Apollo*-type cast—one boy (Jacques
d'Amboise) and three girls (Patricia McBride, Marnee Morris, and Karin von
Aroldingen). Each girl dances once with the boy and once by herself and then
the boy dances alone. They are all four together in the Apollonian coda. The
music is the same parade of Gershwin hits that has been going on since the beginning, only now, with the lights blue and the stars out, we listen more intently. If this is a musical comedy world, it's the most beautiful one ever imagined. In 'Fascinatin' Rhythm,' Patricia McBride holds a high extension in
second and then in two or three lightning shifts of weight refocuses the whole
silhouette while keeping on top of the original pose. It's so charming to see in
relation to that unexpected stutter in the music which unexpectedly recurs,
that it hits the audience like a joke, but that's fascinating rhythm, and that's
Who Cares? Classical syntax, jazz punctuation. I couldn't begin to say what
d'Amboise's solo to 'Liza' is composed of, though—it suggests soft-shoe virtuoso
tap and classical lift and amplitude all at once, and d'Amboise, whose style in
classical ballet has characteristically a casual, crooning softness played against
sudden monkey-like accelerandos and sharp bursts of detail, dances it in total
splendor. Everywhere the tight choreography sustains an almost unbelievable
musical interest.

"As if it weren't enough for Balanchine to give us dances of extreme tension and wit and elegance, he also gives us back the songs unadorned by their usual stagey associations. 'Stairway to Paradise' isn't a big production number; it's one girl (von Aroldingen) covering ground in powerful colt-like jumps and turns. And in the duets, the emotion is more serious (the sense of receding hopes, for example, in 'The Man I Love') for not being acted out. It isn't emotion that dominates the stage so much as a musical faith that the choreography keeps, and that's what convinces us that the songs are good for more than getting drunk at the St. Regis by—that they have theatrical momentousness and contemporary savor. Gershwin in 1970, in the age of Burt Bacharach, has no trouble sounding classical, and that is how Balanchine hears him.

"I am also persuaded that Balanchine hears Gershwin the way Gershwin composed, i.e. pianistically, and this brings up the subject of orchestration and Hershy Kay. Kay had been set the task of orchestrating sixteen of the seventeen songs that Balanchine uses in *Who Cares?* (one number, 'Clap Yo' Hands,' is a recording made by Gershwin himself at the piano), but because of commitments to the Broadway show *Coco*, Kay has so far orchestrated only the opening ('Strike Up the Band') and closing ('I Got Rhythm') songs. The remaining fourteen songs were played for the three performances of *Who Cares?* that were given this season, with his customary sensitivity and attack, by Gordon Boelzner, from Gershwin's own concert arrangements. These piano arrangements were unvaryingly simple: verse followed by chorus followed (sometimes twice) by chorus repeat. But they are also beautiful examples of Gershwin's highly developed keyboard technique. Gershwin's pianism was comparable in its own time to Gottschalk's, and I hope Kay's further orchestrations of Gershwin are as good as the ones he did for the Gottschalk ballet *Cakewalk,* by far his best orchestration for the ballet theater. To my disappointed ear, his 'Strike Up the Band' and 'I Got Rhythm' were in the vulgarized idiom of his 'Stars and Stripes'-hotcha added to heat; and while the musical format of *Who Cares?* precludes his 'symphonizing' in the style of *Western Symphony,* orchestral thickening could destroy the bone-dry delicacy, the tonal transparency of this music and should be avoided like temptation. The more so as Balanchine has taken such evident delight in choreographing the countermelodies, cross-rhythms and abrupt syncopations out of which Gershwin built his compositions—it isn't all razz-ma-tazz—and not since the heyday of Fred Astaire have such felicities been observed.

"Fred and Ginger, Fred and Adele, George and Ira, George and Igor . . . it's easy to be seduced by the nostalgia of it all, but the remarkable thing about *Who Cares?* is how infrequently it appeals to that nostalgia. It certainly makes no appeal on the basis of period glamor or period Camp. The multiple images, the visual punning, the sense of a classical perspective—all of that sweeps by with a strength of evocation more powerful than any individual moment of recognition. It's mysterious, the mythological intensity built up by a ballet that doesn't seem to have a thought in its airy head. No single cultural myth seems to be at the core of it. Manhattan in the Golden Twenties, penthouse parties, where composers of brilliance entertained at the baby grand until dawn, are lovely to think about but aren't the subject of *Who Cares?* any more than a rainbow on a wet afternoon is. To put it as simply as I can, this wonderful ballet enriches our fantasy life immeasurably, as works of art are meant to do. It's tonic, medicinal, too. Its fresh unclouded feeling seems to strike with special directness at the city's depressed spirits. Just before the première (on February 5), Balanchine received New York City's biggest award for cultural achievement, the Handel medallion, on the stage of the State Theatre. He made a number of jokes in the disreputable manner of his hero on such occasions, Bob Hope, had what they call in show business a 'good roll,' and then rang up the curtain on a Gershwin march. The Higher Seriousness didn't have a chance, but who cares?—the ballet was a beaut."

The critic Robert Sealy has also written at length of his impressions of the first performances of *Who Cares?* (in *Ballet Review,* Vol. 3, No. 3).

"*Who Cares?* is a brilliant high wire act: a classical ballet to Gershwin show tunes. It must have been difficult to get it all set, balanced and in focus, to keep it from becoming what it most definitely is *not:* nostalgia, show biz, Broadway, dear old Busby or anything, for that matter, to do with the past. It is to be danced at the moment, in the now of things. What it's really about is the inherent joy of being a man or a woman with a healthy body and the ability to *dance, dance, dance.* As usual, Balanchine has walked the wire over the falls.

"Like all strong, self-assured artists, Balanchine makes his intention clear right at the beginning; he puts his hands on your head and *makes* you see it his way. The principals do not appear in the *Raymonda* part. To emphasize that *Who Cares?* is a classical ballet, eight songs ('Strike Up the Band,' 'Sweet and Low Down,' 'Somebody Loves Me,' 'Bidin' My Time,' ''S Wonderful,' 'That Certain Feeling,' 'Do Do Do,' 'Lady Be Good') have been made into a suite of classical dances, by turns dainty, humorous, robust and romantic, and given to the ensemble. Many people squirm in their seats (as they would through the prologue to *The Sleeping Beauty* or the first act of *Swan Lake*) waiting for the stars; they object to this 'Eat your greens before dessert' attitude—but I think the greens are delicious. 'Somebody Loves Me,' the second number after the 'icebreaker,' is rather daring in that it is a *very* long pas de cinq. Four little girls who might be on the field hockey scrub team, led by Captain Bettijane Sills, twirl and kick over and over, so sweetly, so demurely, the sort of thing the swan girls do while waiting for Odette. It is very appealing, but it makes the audience rather cross. This is exactly the sort of thing in NYCB repertory where proper setting and lighting would help (a hockey field in Riverside Park just before spring dusk, for example). As it is, it must flounder about by itself and get crushed by the big kids. In the first 'act,' 'Bidin' My Time' is the crucial support of the piece, the stem of the flower: heavily masculine quotes from *Raymonda* danced by five men. Unfortunately, the boys are too willowy and not up to it. What is wanted is the easy coordination of a basketball team warming up, easily, almost languidly, the tension is ahead. The last four songs are one long dance with a fresh use of strutaways and rapid turns, especially in the breathless pas de quatre, 'That Certain Feeling.'

"A Gershwin *Apollon Musagéte*—behind the Metropolitan Museum certainly. This memorable quartet dances to eight songs: 'The Man I Love' (Apollo, Terpsichore); 'I'll Build a Stairway to Paradise' (Calliope); 'Embraceable You' (Apollo, Polyhymnia); 'Fascinating Rhythm' (Terpsichore); 'Who Cares?' (Apollo, Calliope); 'My One and Only' (Polyhymnia); 'Liza' (Apollo) and 'Clap Yo' Hands' (the fingers-to-chin, muscled roundabout, Apollo-and-the-muses-at-play part, before the call to Mount Olympus). I am afraid I must call it an affair of sentiment, retire before it and pass out. Never in a theater have I wanted so much to jump the moat and join in. It is pure, unmitigated, uncut joy, an open, palpitating, vulnerable heart on the sleeve. Patricia McBride as Terpsichore clears the high Petipa hurdles of 'Fascinating Rhythm' with room to spare; Jacques d'Amboise (who else?) as Apollo does the big solo leaps in yellow shoes and has a finish of arms-raised ecstasy; and the two of them in 'The Man I Love,' angular, cat-wary, in and out of each other's arms, alternately aloof and impassioned, alert to the rising and falling sounds from the piano, have the memory-burning dance of a lifetime. It is finally Gershwin's music itself, with its slight pretentiousness, its striving after The Better Things (this uniquely New York thing that makes 'Rhapsody in Blue' and *Porgy and Bess* rise above derivation, surpass eclecticism and become great light music) that jells the ballet, preserves Balanchine's fast-stepping, high-breasted, cheeky, slightly put-on attitudes and keeps the whole thing from becoming a dance cavalcade of evergreens."*

WILLIAM TELL VARIATIONS

Music by Gioacchino Rossini. Choreography by Auguste Bournonville. Staged by Hans Brenaa. Lighting by Thomas Skelton. First presented in the United States by the City Center Joffrey Ballet at City Center, New York, March 23, 1969, with Charthel Arthur and Luis Fuente as principals.

This dance ballet by the great Danish ballet master has an interesting history. There are several versions of it, one claiming that the ballet originated in another form as a *divertissement* in the first production of Rossini's *William Tell* at the Paris Opéra, August 3, 1829, another that it derives from Bournonville's *Tyrolerne*, an idyllic one-act ballet with music by J. F. Frohlich first performed March 3, 1835. *Tyrolerne*, according to Clive Barnes, who knows the Danish ballet and its history extremely well, also had music by Rossini; it is his theory that Bournonville later expanded the Rossini score with music from *William Tell*. The ballerina Marie Taglioni danced a famed *Tyrolienne* at the first performance of Rossini's opera but the choreography for her dance was by Aumer, not Bournonville.

In any case, Bournonville's ballet is a treasure of the Danish tradition and was taught to Hans Brenaa, who staged the work, when he was a young student at the Royal Danish Ballet School.

It is a dance ballet for a girl and a boy and two supporting couples, an entertainment for the eye and ear to glorious music by Rossini.

* Reprinted by permission of *Ballet Review,* Marcel Dekker, publisher.

THE WIND IN THE MOUNTAINS

A Country Calendar. Music by Laurence Rosenthal. Choreography by Agnes de Mille. Costumes by Stanley Simmons. Lighting by Jean Rosenthal. First presented by the American Ballet Theatre at the New York State Theatre, March 17, 1965, with Joseph Carow, Karen Krych, Gayle Young, Judith Lerner, and William Glassman in the principal roles.

To a score based largely on early American songs and folk tunes, this dance narrative traces the progress of the seasons in the country—"Traveling Weather," "Wind," "Ice," "Rain," "Natural Catastrophe," "All Clear," "Apotheosis." It begins with a cowboy shouting out to the mountains and the world, "Hello, there," and his words echo back from the hills. A pathfinder enters, then a young couple in love dance with their friends. A lady in red tries to lure the boy away, he follows her and his girl laments. Another suitor tries to cheer her up but she falls on the ice and is undone. Then in the rain she is alone and sad when she sees her lover. A man prays and the rain stops. A train is heard in the distance and in comes a stranger, a Wild West traveling salesman who delights the whole town. The ladies fall at his feet, except the girl, who remains faithful to the memory of the boy. The boy comes back. A square dance is called and around and around in a big circle to a hymnal tune the friends and neighbors go.

WITCH BOY

Music by Leonard Salzedo. Libretto and choreography by Jack Carter. Scenery and costumes by Norman McDowell. First presented by the Ballet der Lage Landen, Amsterdam, May 24, 1956, with Norman McDowell in the title role. First presented in the United States by the National Ballet at the Lisner Auditorium, Washington, D.C., March 29, 1971, with Gerard Sibbritt in the title role.

Based on the American folk ballad of Barbara Allan and set in the Smoky Mountains about the turn of the century, *Witch Boy* is the work of British choreographer and dancer Jack Carter. Carter has said that the theme of the ballet "is that very nice, ordinary people can, by force of circumstances, be turned into a mob." *Witch Boy's* story, of frontier days, tells of the unwelcome advances a Preacher makes to Barbara Allan, who flees to the mountains to escape him. There on the mountainside, she meets the Witch Boy, a possessed, handsome youth, child of the Conjureman. They fall in love.

Bringing the Witch Boy back to her home town, Barbara Allan finds that things are not so simple. Though the two join in the dancing they find there, her friends and relatives clearly think the Witch Boy an odd choice for her to make, particularly when the Preacher loves her. In addition to his quaint

mountain garb, the Witch Boy behaves in a manic way that visibly makes all
the townsfolk nervous. The Preacher, seizing the chance to put down the competition, craftily suggests to his parishioners that the boy is guilty of witchcraft. Their response is instantaneous and violent: they beat the boy and lynch
him. As he hangs from a tree, the Conjureman returns, mourns, and by the
magic he possesses, a new Witch Boy appears, born afresh to haunt the community and future Barbara Allans.

NOTES   *Witch Boy* was an important vehicle for the English *premier danseur* John Gilpin, whose dramatic interpretation was much applauded. He first
danced the part in the London Festival Ballet's production of November 27,
1957, with Anita Landa as Barbara Allan.

Talking with critic Jean Battey Lewis of the Washington *Post* at the time of
Witch Boy's American premier, in 1971, Jack Carter spoke of the power of
classical ballet: "Putting on a ballet in sneakers and jeans doesn't make it original. And I don't think you need bare feet and dirty soles to show emotion. I
think classical ballet technique is so strong it can absorb new discoveries in
movement. I'm interested in movement to say something. Antony Tudor
started me off. In *Lilac Garden* you can see people think through movement.
I'm interested in people and the human relationship."

Reviewing the National Ballet's production, Clive Barnes wrote in the New
York *Times* that *Witch Boy* "is a sensationally theatrical ballet, with a couple
of parthenogenetic births, a hell-fire preacher and a lynch party. It is a very
strong dramatic work with a wonderful part for the Witch Boy. Gerard
Sibbritt danced with great dramatic strength, providing the role with febrile
agony, and that animalistically evil quality, ill-defined but menacing, that the
Witch Boy must possess." The part of the Preacher has been notably danced in
England by Anton Dolin and by Frederic Franklin in the United States. Lydia
Diaz-Cruz danced Barbara Allan in the National Ballet's production.

A selection
of Balanchine's Essays

How to Enjoy Ballet

It is strange that many people think ballet is a difficult thing to enjoy. Ballet isn't any harder to enjoy than a novel, a play, or a poem—it's as simple to like as a baseball game.

Yet imagine a person who goes to a baseball game for the first time. He hasn't played the game, he doesn't know the rules, and he gets confused trying to watch everything at once. He feels out of place and annoyed because he isn't sure why everyone else is so excited.

If he had played baseball himself, he wouldn't have this problem. But he doesn't have to play to enjoy. Once he knows what it's all about, once he understands why the players run and slide and leap and catch as they do, he begins to appreciate the game. He becomes familiar with its elements, he enjoys it. The same thing is true of ballet.

Dancing is very popular here in America. Most of us learn to dance when we are young. And I don't mean ballet dancing. We hear music just about everywhere we go; we have a response to its rhythm and melody and want to express this response in a natural way, so we begin to dance. Ballet dancing is an entirely different thing from ballroom dancing, the dancing most familiar to us, though that, too, requires skill. Ballet also began in the ballroom, in the courts of Italy and France, but over the years it has been elevated to the stage and has become an art. This art is based on something natural to us, response to music, but it expresses this response in a specific, formalized way. Over the past four hundred years, dancers and ballet masters have built up a grammar of movement, a synthesis of what is anatomically possible and pleasing. This is the basic vocabulary of the dancer and the people who make ballets. They have to learn it like a language, from the elementary forms and words. The choreographer chooses certain elements he wants from ballet's extensive vocabulary, makes some new ones, and arranges all these in a new pattern to a meter he derives from music. But we don't have to understand this language in detail to enjoy ballet, any more than we have to know about the pigments of the painter or the complex meters of the poet.

Ballet takes our natural impulse to move, to make signs, to make ourselves as attractive and graceful as possible, and turns it into something new, something entirely different. Perhaps what we see the first time we go to the ballet we don't like at all. Dancers in strange costumes do nothing but move to a piece of music we're unfamiliar with; people who represent characters in an ancient Greek myth, for example, dance a story we don't remember much about; or characters in a modern story-ballet behave quite differently from the people next door. We come away saying that ballet's unnatural.

This is exactly true: ballet is unnatural, it has nothing to do with our daily lives in an immediate sense. What ballet does is to take movements we're all familiar with—running and jumping, turning and balancing, lifting and holding

—and mold attitudes that underlie these actions into a spectacle that entertains. The melodies we hear in music are very different from the natural noises we hear in the everyday world: the slamming of doors, running brooks, the sound of wind in the trees. Melody is artificial, it is made by man. Ballet is artificial in this same sense: its roots are in everyday life, but it is created by artists. What ballet takes from life it transforms.

Broadway at Times Square, for example, is certainly a kind of spectacle, but it doesn't always entertain. It depends on how good we are at seeing. A talented choreographer can see superbly: he can watch this same scene and, by showing us special patterns of movement and behavior, entertain us with a character ballet, make us laugh or make us sad. He makes order out of what seems to us crowded and chaotic, makes what is fleeting and transitory permanently interesting.

The choreographer can do this in a number of ways: in ballets with stories, in ballets that aim to create a certain mood, or simply in dance ballets, where the music provides the plot the dancers move to. I think it's important to understand these distinctions.

Story ballets are entirely different from the stories we read in books: or they should be. In a story depicted on the ballet stage, we *see* what happens, it can't be explained. The plot is simple, the characters easily identifiable, and what happens to them is luminously clear.

What I've called "mood" ballets don't necessarily tell any kind of story; usually, as in *La Valse,* they are ballets in which an outside force, like destiny, seems to control the movement of the dancers.

In dance ballets there is no story, no outside force, only the music. The choreographer works with the music he has chosen much as the poet works with his meters. Most ballets, indeed, are like dramatic or lyric poems: they are created in relation to music and sometimes set within a fable or story. In ballet, the clumsy becomes graceful, the hesitant, inarticulate thought is expressed in direct, eloquent gesture, and nothing appears impossible; love can triumph over everything. In many great ballets, love does.

If you say that all this is fantasy, all imagination, you are right. Some people try to persuade us that poetry and painting and music and dancing are like what we see and do every day. In order to convince us that art is interesting, they tell us that the rumble of drums and the loud crash of cymbals in a piece of music represents Fate, for example, or that a certain portrait painter has depicted a girl's coloring just as it was in real life.

These people, well intentioned as they often are, actually put a stumbling block in our path. They make art easy in the wrong way. If we're told a great deal about a moment of history represented in a painting, for instance, and learn the background of the historical event, our appreciation is severely limited. Our appreciation is intellectual, based on something besides the picture. We could much more profitably spend our time just *looking* at the picture.

Some works of art can be appreciated intellectually, but not many good ones. To enjoy the good ones, we must have an openness of mind in addition to information or their beauty will forever escape us. First of all, we must suspend our prejudices.

As adults, we are well informed about certain things and we have definite ideas on many subjects. But in a sense we are all prejudiced. The older most of us get, the more we have to unlearn in order to learn something new. For instance, many of us were introduced in school to only certain types of music, only certain forms of poetry, and only particular schools of painting. As a result we have a tendency to resist anything new, as well as innovations in something we have become fond of. Children don't have this problem. You can play a Bach suite or a Mozart serenade to a child, and she may very well dance to it. It doesn't occur to her that these composers are old and "classical" or dull and cold or different from what she hears over the radio. She realizes instinctively that the exciting thing about all the arts is that they don't confirm what we already know, so much as they inform us of something new. They contain, in words, in music, in movement, new visions of the world.

Just as a child has her ears open, she keeps her eyes open if you take her to the ballet. Don't be afraid that she will be bored—with no trouble at all she'll become part of the magical world ballet is portraying and she'll not resist its impact. She is not afraid of being afraid (she even enjoys it a little when a wicked fairy appears), she is capable of being moved by love, by the attitudes people have toward one another on the stage. She will sense instantly that a boy partnering a girl well is gentle, respectful, eager for the girl to be as beautiful as possible and that a boy who is a bit of a show-off is not right in his part. She is apt to know, in short, much more than we do.

In order to place ourselves in her position and learn what she knows instinctively, we must go to the ballet with an open mind. If we go often, if we learn gradually that we can't see everything on the stage at once, if we learn to identify dancers and see different dancers in the same part, we'll establish a familiarity with the art and begin to enjoy it. There's no sense in being like the man who says he doesn't know anything about dancing, but he knows what he likes. By saying this, he cheats himself, protects his prejudices from exposure, nurses his own stubbornness. He's not only unwilling to learn anything, he would be embarrassed to learn anything.

Where ballet is concerned, learning by doing is impossible for most of us. We can learn, however, by seeing and by listening; we can learn nothing if we don't go see the ballet, and our appreciation of it will be severely limited if we do not have an awareness of the music that is played there. For ballet is not dancing alone: it is a composite of music and dancing. The relation of dancing to music is not a literal one. It is not a matter of plotless interpretation, a note-by-note, bar-by-bar rhythmic picture of music. On the contrary, it is a complement to the music, something added that is in the mood and spirit of the music as a choreographer sees it. We all have certain emotions when we hear a piece of music. So does a choreographer. He expresses and orders his emotions by placing people on the stage in a particular fashion and arranging their movements so that they have a certain quality: they may be sad, for example, though there isn't always a story to give them a reason for this. The music is sometimes the story. If the choreographer has chosen his music well, we will appreciate the complement the dance makes to its sound: the music will be, as it were, the floor on which the dancer moves. It will not be an excuse for the imposition of literary ideas foreign to music.

But frequently a too sensitive awareness of music can be a disadvantage to the inexperienced balletgoer. Some music lovers are very stubborn, they know what they like, they hold certain things sacred and won't even entertain the notion that they might enrich their musical experience. Their ears are open to only a few pieces, or they think dance "violates" the pieces they love. It may be difficult in such cases to expect a music lover to keep both ears *and* eyes open. I know an intelligent young lady, for example, who walked out on a performance of *The Sleeping Beauty* because she didn't like Tchaikovsky; and a young man who said he loved Bach so much that he could not watch *Concerto Barocco*. Both these people missed a chance, I think, to see in ballet things that might have changed their minds. Love of music can be so intense with some of us that it is acutely private and we resent any intrusion on that privacy.

Ballet in many cases can show us how to appreciate music. The structure of a symphony, how a piece of music is put together, may be something we have no interest in now, but continual attendance at the ballet will cause us to think differently. Dancing is always pointing to music, showing it, making it visually interesting. If our eyes are entertained, we begin to listen in a new way.

Reading about the ballet can be of help to the balletgoer. The numerous story-ballets with complicated plots are not always intelligible when we see them the first time, and it is advisable to know what happens. After our appreciation has matured somewhat, we will find other books—histories and criticism —interesting. Some two or three books of criticism on dancing, such as Noverre's *Letters* and Gautier's ballet reviews, are among the finest works of art appreciation.

But until we have *seen,* no amount of reading will help us. There is no short cut to seeing. *What* you see is not important. Good ballet can be seen frequently throughout the United States. Ballet companies may not visit your community with any regularity, but many of the large cities have their own permanent ballet organizations. Nor does it matter which you see. You cannot tell who is or who is not a good dancer if you don't know anything about the subject, and it is absurd to let anyone tell you. He may very well be wrong, and you'll miss a great deal, perhaps never go back to the ballet because you thought he was right. Much antagonism toward ballet is often created by someone who tells us that so-and-so is the world's greatest dancer in such-and-such a ballet. The inexperienced balletgoer sees the ballerina, doesn't like her, and never goes again.

Certain people don't like "cold" dancers. They use this word as if it meant something bad, something negative. The strange thing is that this quality of "coldness," which some regard negatively, often achieves positive results. I think you will find that people who say they prefer "hot," fiery dancers tend to create their own image of what they want to see, instead of watching the stage and seeing that the dance has its own quality—which might be cool and clear as crystal or, like a diamond seen in different lights, first cold, then hot.

What is it, then, that we should appreciate about a dancer? What things should we watch for the first time we go?

You will often hear people talk about the technical accuracies of dancers. They will say, "It's not important how many *fouettés* a girl can do, it's important that her supporting foot remain in place" and "Male dancers must always point their toes while doing *entrechats*." These things are quite true, there are many other such things, many finer points of technique, and we learn them as we watch, but all these criticisms are only part of a general appearance and manner that we must watch for first.

We should be ready, too, to enjoy the artist who perhaps has not yet achieved great success. We may discover later on that we saw the first of many dances that made her eventually a ballerina. That will be exciting. However, the good dancer will not in performance remind us of this kind of success. Watching her dancing over the years, we will see and appreciate the movement, the victory she appears to achieve in executing effortlessly a particular step or gesture at a specific time in a specific place. Her dancing will refract and amplify and make spacious, as music does, the emotion a particular dance intends. She is not someone we are in love with, or someone we should like to love, though some of her dancing reminds us of the happiness, the understanding, the playfulness and tenderness love has.

Only the professional dancer can analyze a performance and tell us that a certain dancer missed something. Dancers are not automatons. Every performance is different. Dancers must adjust themselves at almost every performance to a new pair of shoes, just as the tennis champion adjusts his hand to a new racket and the violinist adjusts to a new bow. Moreover, the condition of the stage floor is crucial to all dancers. No dancer dances well on a stage with a bad floor. If you have been to ballet performances where famous ballerinas seemed to be holding something back, where all the members of the *corps de ballet* danced hesitantly, refusing to commit themselves wholly to the dance, it was probably because they were risking their professional lives on the floor they were dancing on. The ideal stage for dancing is unfinished pine, smoothed over: it is not glossy linoleum or highly polished hardwood or the shiny plastic distances we see in the movies, or wood laid over cement or linoleum. When the nineteenth-century French critic Gautier remarked that an Italian dancer's feet were "like two steel arrows rebounding from a marble pavement," he was able to make the simile because she was dancing on a wooden stage. The dancer feels most secure when she knows that her ballet slippers are in real contact with the floor when she wants them to be; when she can feel the friction of the floor as she turns in pirouettes; when she can descend from a jump without fear of sliding.

Some stages, too, are precariously raked, or pitched: the back of the stage is higher than the front. The designers of such stages had more consideration for the audience's ability to see than for the perfection of the performance that entertains the audience. The degree of rake differs from stage to stage in old theatres, and it is naturally extremely hard for dancers to adjust their balance to them. These are not excuses; they are the conditions under which every dancer works, and no dancer should be punished for them. In one recital a pianist plays millions of notes; if you aren't a pianist yourself, you won't know the ones he missed. The great pianist Anton Rubinstein once said that if he'd been paid a penny for every note he missed, he'd be a very rich man.

Ballet is now so advanced in the United States that very seldom do we see incompetence on the stage. Bad dancers appear less and less. Our dancers are professionals. Like professional ball players, they must possess a technique. Usually their technique is so great that however tired they are (and tired they often are, with eight performances a week), their exhaustion is invisible to the audience. Only the professional can see it.

The audience must watch technique as part of a performance, not as a separate thing. The stage illusion and the atmosphere created by the dancing are destroyed if you sit in your seat and count turns or stop-watch changes of position. We take it for granted that flowers are beautiful; we don't have to take them apart to see this. We take them as they are. The taking apart is the job of the botanist, just as the technical analysis of a performance is the job of the professional dancer.

Great technical ability is only part of being a great dancer. At first we might find ourselves applauding a feat that seems astonishing, and six months later, when we've seen dozens of dancers do the same thing with an equal amount of facility, we might applaud less. We have to see to know better. We have to compare. But what we will all like at the beginning and what will make us want to go again soon is a dancer who interests us in an extremely simple way: we will remember afterward what her dance looked like. We will remember the girl, but only because of the dance she showed us. No doubt she was attractive, but she didn't play on that and make us think of it. No doubt she did some steps that seemed incredibly hard, but she didn't stress this, she didn't try to hit us between the eyes with her skill as if to say, "Look! *This* is good." Instead, the big moments of the dance came with the same lack of effort and stress as the small ones. She will quietly and effortlessly seem to conquer the stage space in which she moves to the time of the music.

Where the dancing of dramatic roles is concerned, we must beware of standard images. Some people think that the heroine in *Swan Lake* must always be very slender, short, have black hair parted in the middle, and dance like a bird, with lyrical feeling. Actually, what they mean by lyricism is often lethargy. I have seen dozens of Swan Queens. Some of them looked like birds, others did not, and all gave fine performances. Great ballets were not devised for one type of dancer. Sometimes I hear people say, "But so-and-so wasn't like Pavlova." They forget that if Pavlova and other great dancers of the more distant past were here today, they would not be so sentimental. They were professionals. They would appreciate the greater technical difficulties of modern classical choreography and admire our dancers with an affectionate, professional understanding. If they were dancing today, they know, they would be trying to do the same things our 'dancers do.

Seeing great classical ballets of the past is like seeing great plays: we are so familiar with *Hamlet* and *Romeo and Juliet*, know the lines so well that we think we can say them with more understanding than any actor. We may see these plays many times and come away disappointed, but one day we experi-

ence an extraordinary thing. We hear an actor say the words that are so familiar to us, and suddenly they are no longer private quotations to us. The play
becomes new and moving. The same thing happens at the ballet.

Like all the arts, ballet is many things to many people. It is high-brow and
something to make fun of to some people because they are afraid to understand it. Others have no wish to understand it and go to the ballet merely to
show off their clothes, to see their friends or to make new ones. Still others
seek the fashionable and go to the theatre because a particular dance or
dancer has been praised extravagantly. Finally, there are those who enjoy the
ballet with no pretension at all. They are able to do this because they understand what ballet is as a particular form of entertainment, because they are not
frightened by other people telling them that ballet is "important" and
"significant." Ballet is important and significant, but first of all it is a pleasure.

When we first start going to the ballet, it is no more significant or important
than most of the other things we enjoy watching. It may become significant
later, after we have enjoyed it and been entertained by it, after it has become
important to us in a personal way. But at first we should simply watch it, as
we watch our friends swimming or ice-skating, or playing baseball or tennis.

Music, we all know, is an aural perception: reading notes is not sufficient,
we must hear them. Ballet is a visual art, like painting or architecture. But
unlike painting or architecture, ballet is a visual spectacle that moves: it is not
static. We can always see famous paintings by going to museums or famous
buildings. Ballet, by comparison, is transitory. We no sooner take in a particular movement in a ballet than it has become another movement. The movements accumulate rapidly, and if we don't watch carefully, we are lost. We
must train ourselves to see.

I think we must do this for the same reason and in the same way that we
train ourselves to enjoy any of the other arts. To read a book—and we all have
experience with this—is not necessarily to understand it. Similarly, to listen is
not always to *hear*, and to look not always to *see*. Often, when we want to say
that we understand something, we say that we "see" it. Ballet, with applica-
tion and attention, can be seen and not merely watched.

We go to the theatre to see ballet and watch dancers—people like ourselves,
with bodies and heads and arms and legs, running and jumping and lifting to
a piece of music. We ask ourselves, why should they do this? The answer is
that ballet displays the most beautiful movement of which the human body is
capable. The human body, of course, has its limitations. We can bend it and
stretch it and lift it, but only to a certain degree. We can, however, decrease
the body's limitations with practice. After we have learned to walk, we can
run; after we have lifted light objects, we are able to lift heavy ones. The
dancer's concern is to fulfill the maximum of what the body can do in a beautiful way.

But the skill of dancers is useless unless it is displayed in a certain form. No
one would enjoy watching a group of dancers jump about the stage aimlessly,
no matter how well they jumped. Ballet asks the body to move in time. Ballet
uses music to indicate time.

Not only in its movement and transitory nature, then, is ballet different from other visual arts. It is two things at once: a composition, a unification of music and dancing. We must hear and see at the same time. This process is something like reading a poem or watching a movie. A poem says something to us, but it speaks in a certain rhythm, a certain time scheme, a certain music. In a movie, the continuous pictures the camera shows us are controlled in sequence and length by what the script specifies. Music is ballet's timekeeper.

To show dancers moving with ideal strength and grace requires beautiful people. Few dancers are beautiful when they begin to study, but when they dance well, they become beautiful. Beautiful dancers are easily associated with ideal characters in stories, with kings and queens and princesses, with love, victory over evil, and death. Many ballets have stories with such heroes and heroines. But sometimes there is no literal story at all in ballet, no narrative. Just as people in real life make different gestures and stand in different positions when they are in different moods, so do dancers in a ballet. A *pas de deux*, for example, is simply a dance for two people, a man and a woman; and even when it is performed on a bare stage with no surrounding story, a *pas de deux* is always a kind of romance. The man is tender and admiring as he lifts the woman and supports her in order to display her beauty, while she, in her reliance on his strength and assurance, admires him in return. This quality in the *pas de deux* may not be apparent to the newcomer to ballet, but the more often this kind of dance is seen, the clearer become its romance and tenderness.

Program music is very easy for most of us to understand. When a composer tells us that his symphony is about a thunderstorm, we immediately have something to compare it with. Some ballets are like program music. These ballets require program notes to tell us what the ballet is really about. Some things, of course, are impossible to represent clearly on stage without the spoken word, but the central idea of every dramatic ballet is clear the first time we see it.

Many ballets are like symphonies that only have identifying numbers. A *pas de deux* or a dance ballet may have to be seen a number of times before we begin to enjoy it. Then passages we were able to like at the beginning become connected with other passages we appreciate later; we soon retain in our minds all the different passages and detect their connections.

Here are a few final suggestions which I hope will enhance your enjoyment of this great art. All ballets are accompanied by music, but because it is hard to listen to music and watch dancers at the same time, play the music over before you go to the ballet or listen to it on records. This is particularly important, naturally, in ballets that do not have conventional stories, where the ballet is based on the music.

Many ballets have plots. There are stories taken from fairy tales (*The Sleeping Beauty*), from ancient myths (*Orpheus*), from the Bible (*Prodigal Son*), from poems (*Illuminations*), and from stories devised especially for particular ballets. Not all of these stories are simple, and brief program notes are often insufficient. As I have said, ideally the best stories for ballets are those that can be *shown*, stories that require no elucidation at all in the written word. But stories inevitably have their complications. These complications were cleared up in the old ballets by pantomime. People could understand this when these ballets were created, for they were familiar with the mime vocabulary, but today, when that vocabulary has gone out of fashion, miming on the stage is often obscure to us and we aren't sure what is happening. Read the stories through, then, and in the theatre you will not be looking down constantly at an incomplete program note. You will be watching the stage.

Many people who go to the ballet, and not only newcomers, feel there is something suspect about ballets without stories—about dance ballets pure and simple. They think there is a hidden meaning they don't grasp. The real point is that they are trying to appreciate ballet intellectually. They expect ballet always to be like the theatre or literature or the movies, which, quite naturally, it is not. Ballet is like nothing so much as dancing. To appreciate it you have to watch it, not think about it. If you only think about it, you'll probably miss the next step and miss something you might have liked very much.

Don't hesitate to go to see ballet companies that you don't think are first-class. Only by seeing *all* the companies can you compare, analyze, and discover what you prefer.

Another thing I'd like to mention is this. Many of us are interested in reading ballet criticism in newspapers and magazines. This criticism can be informative and revealing but I think it is important for us, if we read critics, to read *all* of them, and then go to the ballet and see for ourselves. You will often find that critics radically disagree. How can you discover which one is right unless you see the ballet in question? It also happens very often that dance critics change their minds. Dance critics, like music critics, review the same pieces year after year; what they disliked one year they sometimes like another. If you have read a particular dance critic or music critic over the years, you will discover this to be true.

And, finally, no one can enjoy the ballet if he decides he will go only a certain number of times. If you go only occasionally, once or twice every few years, say, you will never be fully entertained. You must go as many times as possible, as often as you read a novel, as often as you go to the movies or the theatre, as often as you look at paintings or listen to a concert or an opera. We come to enjoy all of these arts through persistent exposure to what each has to teach us about the pleasures that life contains. If we neglect the ballet, we are depriving ourselves of one of the greatest of these pleasures. Naturally, we can live without art: we can eat and sleep and live by our senses alone. But throughout history man has never been satisfied with the necessities of life. He has sought entertainment and enlightenment through art and has become a happier being.

A Brief History of the Ballet

Our word *ballet* comes from the Italian *ballare*, to dance, and it is to the courts of Italy at the height of the Renaissance that we trace the beginning of ballet as we know it today. Dancing as primitive ritual—as a form of hero worship and worship of gods, as glorification of the dead, as a means of celebrating the seasons and the elements—is fundamental in history. Dancing as a popular skill embodied in folk dances is familiar in every country. Dancing as a skill, as a refined human discipline, was developed in religious rites of Mediterranean countries and in the ancient Orient, where chosen persons were taught godlike gestures and movement in order to emulate and celebrate for the populace the drama of their common deities. In the choral dance of Greece, dancing as an art designed for entertainment grew out of the native ritualistic dance. Now the trained performer of a common ritual became the dedicated dancer who aimed to give pleasure to a nondancing audience.

Greek drama began with group or choral dances interrupted and embellished with storytelling. As the chorus of dancers began to sing and to participate in the action of the stories devised by poets, pantomime and meaningful movement evolved. The masks worn by the Greek chorus were a feature of the theatrical dance till late in the eighteenth century. The poet Aeschylus, whose plays were performed by two principal actors and a chorus, rehearsed his choruses in the postures, movements, and gestures proper to the dramatic situation. With his successors, Sophocles and Euripides, the importance of the chorus was proportionately reduced with introduction of a larger cast of characters, but a basic vocabulary of theatrically effective mimicry, attitude, and movement had been established.

What the Greeks achieved was extended by the Romans, who exploited the comic possibilities of mime and dance. The Romans combined the two with acrobatics and circus routines and used them to illustrate popular fables. Tumblers, jesters, and buffoons so humanized dancing that the ritualistic base of Greek tragedy was wholly forgotten.

The comic art of the Romans was reborn in sixteenth-century Italy by traveling players who embodied the *commedia dell'arte:* skilled popular comedians who improvised variations on stock characters—Pulcinella, Punch, Columbine, Pierrot, Harlequin, and others—in stock plots. The gestures, costumes, and characterization of these actors became comic archetypes for all of Europe, influencing many others—the dancers of Paris, the plays of Molière, the carnival puppet shows (*Punch and Judy, Petrouchka*) of the Western world.

While these troupes entertained the provinces of Italy and southern France, the capitals of the Renaissance saw splendid revivals of Roman opulence in the form of pageants and staged celebrations. The rulers of these capitals used every happy event—engagements, marriages, visits of notable persons, military victories—as an excuse for spectacular entertainment in poetry, painting, dance, song, and theatrical mechanics. Appropriate myths inherited from Rome were adapted for the particular occasion, depicted by artists, and danced by the masked members of the court. Interludes of dancing were performed at pageants between recitations and songs, between courses at banquets, and to accompany with appropriate representation the serving of rare dishes at great feasts.

Like the popular art of the *commedia dell'arte,* court dances also had special forms. The folk dances that the courts had sophisticated were further refined into precise floor patterns, simple set steps that required set preparations, and endings performed with elegant bows and flourishes. Popular court dances of this time were called *balletti* (diminutive of *ballo;* hence *ballet*); they were similar to the English morris dance. Castiglione, master of Renaissance manners, wrote in *The Courtier:*

"There are certain other exercises that can be practiced in public and in private, like dancing; and in this I think the Courtier ought to have care, for when dancing in the presence of many and in a place full of people, it seems to me that he should preserve a certain dignity, albeit tempered with a lithe and airy grace of movement; and although he may feel himself to be very nimble and a master of time and measure, let him not attempt those agilities of foot and double steps which we find very becoming in our friend Barletti, but which perhaps would be little suited to a gentleman. Yet in a room privately, as we are now, I think he may try both, and may dance morris-dances and brawls; but not in public unless he be masked, when it is not displeasing even though he be recognized by all." Within the aristocracy of the court a new aristocracy developed—the aristocracy of the best dancer.

Catherine de Médicis introduced the new Italian pageantry to France. Under her influence, Italian musicians and dancing masters came to Paris and staged for the court spectacles consisting of vocal and instrumental music, spoken dialogue, pantomime, dancing, and mechanical effects. The combination of these elements produced the *ballet de cour,* or court ballet, the European model for costly entertainment. With the assistance of their ladies, gentlemen of the court performed *masques*—allegorical plays with poetry and dancing—and *mummings*—colorful dances performed by masked figures among dancers at court balls.

Toward the end of the sixteenth century, Catherine de Médicis, with the assistance of an Italian musician turned dancing master, produced at her court an entertainment that superseded in extravagance and purpose all those previously seen in Europe. This work was called the *Ballet Comique de la Reine.* It employed all the familiar elements of the *ballet de cour* and Italian opera—music, singing, dancing, royal processions, declamation of verse, elaborate scenery and mechanical effects—but for the first time these elements were fused in a dramatic whole that made sense to the spectators: the disparate parts were not mere diversions at a court function, they represented a conscious design to entertain an audience with a unity of comedy, dance, music, and spectacle. The performance cost 3,600,000 francs, lasted for five hours, and was witnessed by some ten thousand people. Its success assured the future of dancing as a necessary part of regal entertainment. It was, in effect, the first ballet as we recognize the term today—a combination of music, dancing, plot, and design.

Seven years later there appeared in France a book that provided the first foundation for the establishment of dancing as a profession. Arbeau's *Orché-sographie* (*The Writing of Dancing*) illustrated and gave directions for executing the popular court dances of the time. Arbeau also indicated the principles for the five basic positions of the feet that were to become the foundation of the classic dance. In an effort to teach the dances that had become so popular, it was necessary to arrive at principles upon which all teaching could be based: the limitations of the human body, how and in what directions it could move, and the fundamental steps that best prepared it for movement.

The popular dances of the continent had meanwhile become the courtly habit in England, where Queen Elizabeth appointed a gentleman to the post of Lord Chancellor because "he wore green bows on his shoes and danced the *pavane* to perfection." The poets Ben Jonson, Milton, and Campion, and the great designer Inigo Jones developed masques in imitation of the *ballet de cour*. The masques featured dancing by members of the court, but the real contribution England made to the development of ballet was in the antimasque, a pure dance that preceded the performance of the masque proper, danced by professionals. Ben Jonson thus addressed Queen Elizabeth in 1609:

"And because Her Majesty (best knowing that a principal part of life in these spectacles lay in their variety) had commanded me to think on some dance, or show, that might precede hers, and have the place of a foil, or false masque: It was careful to decline, not only from others, but mine own steps in that kind, since the last year, I had an *antimasque* of boys; and therefore now devised that twelve women, in the habit of hags or witches, sustaining the persons of Ignorance, Suspicion, Credulity, etc., the opposites to good Fame, should fill that part, not as a masque, but a spectacle of strangeness, producing multiplicity of gesture."

In France, dancing flourished at the court of Louis XIV, himself an accomplished dancer. In 1661 Louis XIV founded the first dancing academy in the world, an institution for the instruction of dancing that has continued down to the present day at the Paris Opéra. Under the direction of Beauchamp, the king's dancing master, and the Italian musician and dancer Jean Baptiste Lully, students were taught professionally, to perform on a stage. The great dramatists Molière and Corneille collaborated with Lully in the production of comedy and tragedy ballets that secured the admiration of court and public. The excellence of stage performance gradually superseded the court dances; the larger, freer movements possible in the theatre replaced the confined gestures of the ballroom. Louis Pécourt became the first *premier danseur*, the first dancer to excel in performances in a theatre. Soon women appeared as professional dancers for the first time.

Beauchamp specified the Five Positions of the classic dance, positions of the feet that became the prerequisite for a dancer's training at the French Academy and the instinctive basis for all performance. The positions are still the basis of ballet today. These positions are absolute in their anatomical authority: the ease with which they are taught to young students, the ease and security they allow the dancer on stage, and, most important of all, the variety of movement made possible by their use. They are as essential to ballet as fundamental techniques of sound structure are to architecture. The Five Positions, with their embodiment of the turned-out leg, distinguished ballet from all other forms of theatrical dance. Ballet dancing had now become a profession, one that could be taught and learned and mastered.

Now that there was fundamental agreement on the basis of the classic dance, there were quarrels about innovations of technique. While Lully in his years at the French Academy had devised dances that were complex in pattern and floor design, he had not considered dancing off the floor, dancing that aimed at elevation, at flight. His successor, Rameau, thought differently and encouraged his dancers to turn in the air and perform steps high off the floor. In Lully's time, when dancing was moved from the ballroom to the stage, it was quite natural for ballet to imitate the technique of dancing in a ballroom—where performers and spectators stood on the same level—but Rameau realized that on a raised stage the dancers were seen from an entirely different perspective by the spectators, that the dancers' feet were clearly visible for the first time, and, accordingly, that the dance must make an adjustment of technique to hold its audience. The conservative adherents of Lully, those who advocated a "horizontal" dance, contested the theories of the new, rebel "verticalists" of Rameau.

This contest between the Lullists and the Rameauists contained the basic argument that runs throughout the history of ballet down to the present: the argument between "tradition" and innovation, between strict classicism and expressiveness, between pure dance and "literary" ballets, between ballet and modern dance. This argument was embodied in two popular dancers of the time: Marie Camargo and Marie Sallé. Camargo, champion of the new *danse verticale*, was a brilliant technician, praised for her airiness and strength. She was the first *danseuse* to perform the *entrechat-quatre*, to execute high *cabrioles* and jumps. To display her skill, Camargo shortened the conventional cumbersome ballet dress so that her agile steps might be seen. A great innovator, Camargo was also a traditionalist, interested in technique rather than the human and dramatic elements of the dance.

Camargo's rival, Marie Sallé, "muse of gracious, modest gesture," exemplified in her refined and gracious dancing a spiritual rather than technical elevation. Here the accent was on nobility of posture and deportment and on characterization of a particular part for dramatic effect. Sallé did not dance simply for the sake of dancing. Her most famous role, that of the statue beloved by Pygmalion, she devised for herself. Called a *ballet-pantomime* in opposition to the rigid and formal opera-ballets of the Paris Opéra, Sallé's dancing in this work was faithful to the Greek style of its story. Effecting another innovation in costume, Sallé let her hair down and over her corset and petticoat wore only a muslin dress "draped about her in the manner of a Greek statue."

Rameau's ballets at the Paris Opéra accommodated both the new technique and dramatic expression within the frame of the opera-ballet, a series of danced *entrées* connected by a threadlike plot. The *entrées* depicted dances in various countries—Turkey, Peru, Persia, America—which allowed for spectacle as well as for occasional dramatic interest in stories imposed upon the natives. With their great geographical variety and concern for imitation of native dances throughout the world, Rameau's ballets brought down to earth the mythological characters with which the dance had been preoccupied since the Renaissance.

Another dancer wanted ballet to go still further. After Rameau's death, ballet at the Paris Opéra degenerated to the point where each of its elements—dancing, music, story, and spectacle—seemed to exist for its own sake. The dancers' technical proficiency was displayed, with marked contempt for music, in ridiculous dramas. Jean Georges Noverre, a student of Louis Dupré, a great admirer of Marie Sallé and of the English actor David Garrick, wanted to unify the elements of ballet into a dramatic whole. He wrote, in ballet's first critical text, *Letters on the Dance and Ballets,* that poetry, painting, and dancing should be a "faithful likeness of beautiful nature," that dancing should be united with pantomime to ensure dramatic expression, and that such expression must be related directly to music. Working with such musicians as Christoph Willibald Gluck, whose reforms in opera were closely allied to Noverre's in ballet; with such dancers as Gaetan Vestris, first great classical dancer in Europe; with Marie Allard and Madeleine Guimard, superb mimes as well as dancers; and with the patronage of such notable persons as Marie Antoinette—Noverre successfully initiated reforms in ballets that were seen and applauded all over Europe. His ballets were danced in London, Vienna, Paris, Milan, and St. Petersburg. All of Europe delighted in the new *ballet d'action*—works in which dancers reflected in their movement and gesture the dramatic intention of plot and music. Among Noverre's students were Vincenzo Galeotti, who became ballet master at the Royal Theatre, Copenhagen; Charles Didelot, the Frenchman who became "the father of Russian ballet" at the Imperial Theatre in St. Petersburg; and Jean Dauberval, who, in *La Fille Mal Gardée,* created what was perhaps the first comic ballet.

One of Dauberval's pupils, Salvatore Vigano, extended Noverre's reforms in spectacular ballets produced in his native Italy. At La Scala, Milan, Vigano mounted works that unified music, dancing, and mime as Noverre had never been able to do. Mime, Vigano regarded as the expression of the "movement of the soul: it is the language of all peoples, of all ages and times. It depicts better than words extremes of joy and sorrow . . . It is not sufficient for me to please the eyes. I wish to involve the heart." Indeed, he regarded mime with such importance that the composer Rossini remarked to Stendhal, the choreographer's great admirer, that Vigano's ballets had too much pantomime and not enough dancing. Vigano's idea was the *choreodrame,* ballets in which Noverre's principle of dramatically expressive embodiment was seen in every dancer on stage, in the *corps de ballet* as well as in the performances of principal dancers. Within particular settings and plots, Vigano worked tirelessly to arrange dances appropriate to drama and score. Under his direction, La Scala became the greatest ballet theatre in all of Europe.

This pre-eminence of Italian ballet was sustained by the dancer, choreographer, and teacher Carlo Blasis, student of Dauberval, who wrote—in his *Elementary Treatise upon the Theory and Practice of the Art of Dancing* (1820) and in the *Code of Terpsichore* (1829)—the first lexicons of the classic dance. Here the basic theories of all the great dancers and choreographers who preceded Blasis were tacitly assumed in general instructions to pupils and ballet masters and were embodied in detailed, illustrated instruction on practice: the proper execution of positions, poses, movements, and steps of elevation—all the resources known to the classic dancer. Blasis' work has been the foundation of all instruction in the classic dance ever since. The classic disciplines he insisted upon in his teaching at La Scala were precursors of the instruction that later dominated the Russian Imperial School at St. Petersburg and ballet everywhere.

Vincenzo Galeotti produced in 1786 in Copenhagen a ballet still in the current repertory, *The Whims of Cupid and the Ballet Master*. His most distinguished student, August Bournonville, who studied also in Paris under Vestris, advanced Galeotti's commitment to dramatic expression in ballet. Audiences at performances of the Royal Danish Ballet today recognize the importance of pantomime and drama that Bournonville introduced in the more than fifty ballets he choreographed for that company. They recognize, too, a vigorous dance style that Bournonville established and taught to Christian Johansson, the Swedish dancer who became in St. Petersburg the most celebrated *premier danseur* of his time. From 1860 until his death in 1903, Johansson taught in St. Petersburg all of the great dancers of the Russian ballet.

Founded in 1735 to teach court cadets the fashionable dances of Europe, the Russian Imperial School, adjunct of the Imperial Theatre, was directed by a series of French and Italian ballet masters, who produced in St. Petersburg the work of European choreographers and invited to the Russian capital foreign dancers to star in these works. The Frenchman Charles Didelot was the first to establish the Russian school and theatre on a firm base. Didelot, student of Noverre, Dauberval, and the *premier danseur* Auguste Vestris, was appointed ballet master at St. Petersburg in 1816. He established at the Imperial School a consistent foundation of classical instruction and mounted such excellent ballets at the Imperial Theatre that the poet Pushkin was moved to say that in Didelot's ballets there was more poetry than in all the French literature of that time. After Didelot's death (1837) the Russian Theatre continued to flourish, but principally as an opulent setting not for Russian, but for the finest ballets and dancers of Western Europe.

In Western Europe of the 1830s, the supremacy of Italian dance technique combined with the Romanticism that dominated the other arts of the time to produce a new kind of ballet. Romanticism in ballet, as in the other arts, was a rebellion against classical subject matter, classical technique, and classical attitudes. The Romantic ballet extended the classical dance technique with daring innovations: girls danced on their toes for the first time, and new steps of elevation were devised to display voluptuous real-life heroines who by theatrical magic became idealized, unattainable creatures of wood and glade. Heroines of ballets were no longer characters from classical mythology: wronged peasant girls and sylphs displaced the Medeas, the Junos, the Aphrodites. Audiences rejoiced in the theatrical display of the beauty of the broken heart. Paris, again, and London were the ballet capitals of the world.

Marie Taglioni, creator of the wistful *La Sylphide*, became the first famous dancer Europe had ever known. The ballet *Giselle*, inspired by the Romantic poet Gautier, superseded Taglioni's vehicle in excellence of plot and dance, and enthralled audiences from St. Petersburg to Boston. Taglioni's contemporaries—Carlotta Grisi, the first dancer of *Giselle;* the Danish ballerina Lucile Grahn; the lively Fanny Cerrito—appeared in a score of ballets on romantic themes, while the great Fanny Elssler, Taglioni's archrival, was so secure in her reputation that she could abandon the opera houses of Europe for two years and dance on tour throughout the United States. Elssler's phenomenal success in America in 1840–42 was typified by the reception tendered her by President Van Buren and his Cabinet at Washington and by the banquet given by members of Congress in her honor at the Capitol. In 1845 Jules Perrot, the Romantic ballet's finest choreographer and the one male dancer who managed to hold his own in this age of romanticism, staged in London a special dance for Taglioni and three of her rivals—Grisi, Cerrito, and Grahn. The success of this *Pas de Quatre* obliged *The Times* to call the ballet "the greatest Terpsichorean exhibition that ever was known in Europe."

While the triumphs of these first great ballet stars increased the popularity of the art, the art itself began to suffer. Interest in all performances was centered on the stars and what they danced; people cared less and less about the music they danced to, the plots they acted, or the productions that displayed them. Taglioni or Elssler, alone, was enough. Prospective dancers and choreographers therefore saw little profit in remaining in Paris and London. In Russia, they knew, the Tsar's court required spectacular entertainment. And it could support it by the most bountiful treasury in Europe.

In the year Taglioni retired (1847), a young Frenchman, Marius Petipa, was engaged as a dancer at the Russian Imperial Theatre. Petipa was successful as a dancer in St. Petersburg; there he watched the work of the French ballet masters Jules Perrot and Arthur Saint-Léon as they entertained a new avid audience of aristocratic balletomanes. Then suddenly there was an opportunity to create a ballet of his own. In 1860 he had restaged the Perrot-Coralli *Giselle*, the romantic ballet that seemed certain to remain a permanent fixture in the Russian repertory. But ballet by this time required a new impetus, which Petipa discovered in a reawakened classicism. He devised for his ballet a mass dance on a tremendous scale, with spectacular stage effects. Beginning in 1862, with his first great success, a four-act dance extravaganza set in the desert, with pyramids and colossal palaces of ancient Egypt, Petipa succeeded Jules Perrot as ballet master to the Imperial Theatre. His influence was to dominate the Russian ballet almost up to the time of his death fifty years later. His supremacy survived the reigns of four Tsars, who delighted in the entertainment he provided their courts and in the universal model of excellence he caused the Russian ballet to become. Petipa created fifty-seven full-length, evening-long ballets, devised countless shorter *divertissements*, restaged seventeen ballets by other choreographers, and mounted ballets in thirty-four operas during his years at the Imperial Theatre.

St. Petersburg was now the ballet capital of the world. The French ballet master Petipa welcomed to Russia dancers and teachers from Italy, France, Germany, and Scandinavia; with their assistance he made the Imperial Ballet School the greatest in the world. Petipa's school provided the standard for the dancer's training, as his theatre was the exemplar for the dancer's performance. Foreign dancers who came to Russia for guest engagements introduced diverse technical elements from all of Europe: brilliant classicists, who had been trained in Italy under the disciplines founded by Blasis, contributed to the growth of a new style. This style was not so much Russian as polygenous. It was historic in its all-inclusiveness, in its gigantic assimilation of classic dance techniques as they were practiced in all of Europe. It produced, toward the end of the nineteenth century, great Russian dancers, who danced in such ballets as *Swan Lake* and *The Nutcracker,* works by the Russian choreographer Lev Ivanov, who produced them under Petipa's direction, and Peter Ilyich Tchaikovsky. Tchaikovsky was commissioned by Petipa to write the score for the ballet that turned out to be the masterpiece of both men. *The Sleeping Beauty,* Russian ballet music, as well as Russian ballet and Russian dancers, was the accepted standard throughout the Western World.

Petipa died in 1910. Some years before his death, the classical ballet he had perfected had passed its zenith; it began to disintegrate as its elements became disassociated. A young dancer and choreographer, Michel Fokine, who in 1905 created for the ballerina Anna Pavlova the short lyric dance *The Dying Swan,* rebelled against the omnipotence of "tradition." Like Sallé, Noverre, and Vigano before him, Fokine aimed at unification of dancing, music, and design. He asserted that dancing was interpretative, expressive. "The ballet must no longer be made up of *numbers, entries,* and so on. It must show artistic unity of conception . . . Ballet must have complete unity of expression, a unity which is made up of harmonious blending of the three elements—music, painting, and plastic art." Fokine's suggested reforms were rejected by his superiors at the Imperial Theatre. They were championed by a man who understood music, painting, and dancing: Serge Diaghilev.

Diaghilev wished to take the Russian ballet to Paris. In 1907 he had presented Russian music to Western Europe for the first time, and he now wished Europeans to admire what he knew to be the finest dancing in the world. He chose Fokine as choreographer to a company to be known as Diaghilev's Ballets Russes. Anna Pavlova, Tamara Karsavina, and Vaslav Nijinsky secured leave from the Imperial Theatre to be his principal dancers. His designers, his musicians, were the finest in Russia.

On May 18, 1909, Diaghilev's Ballets Russes opened their first season in Paris. In the new ballets of Fokine, ballets like *Prince Igor* and *Les Sylphides,* and in the quality of the dancing, the music, and theatrical design, the season was an unprecedented success. This pattern of success continued the next year, with the Stravinsky-Fokine *Firebird,* and the next, with the Stravinsky-Fokine *Petrouchka,* and the next, with the Debussy-Nijinsky *The Afternoon of a Faun* and the Fokine-Weber *Le Spectre de la Rose,* and so on, season after season, year after year, for twenty years of dance entertainment based on an inviolable rule of uniform excellence in choreography, music, decor, and performance.

Paris was again the world capital of dance. Diaghilev's Ballets Russes provided a center of artistic endeavor such as Europe had not known since the Medici courts of the Renaissance. And Diaghilev, like the Renaissance princes, not only perpetuated established talent, he discovered, encouraged, and developed talent. He numbered among his principal female dancers Pavlova, Karsavina, Lopokova, Spessivtzeva, Dubrovska, Nemtchinova, Sokolova, Tchernicheva, Egorova, Nijinska, Danilova, and Markova; among the men, Nijinsky, Fokine, Vladimiroff, Bolm, Mordkin, Novikoff, Volinine, Cecchetti, Massine, Woicikowski, Idzikowski, Dolin, and Lifar. Among his composers were Stravinsky, Debussy, Ravel, Richard Strauss, Fauré, Satie, Respighi, De Falla, Prokofiev, Poulenc, Auric, Milhaud, Dukelsky, Rieti, Lambert, Berners, Sauguet, and Nabokov. His designers were such painters as Benois, Roerich, Bakst, Soudeikine, Doboujinsky, Larionov, Picasso, Derain, Matisse, Braque, Gris, Utrillo, Miró, Tchelitchew, Di Chirico and Rouault. His choreographers were Fokine, Nijinsky, Massine, Nijinska, and myself.

Since the disbandment of Diaghilev's company following his death in 1929, his dancers and choreographers have influenced ballet throughout the world. Serge Lifar has been for many years ballet master at the Paris Opéra, which, with the Royal Danish Ballet at Copenhagen, continues the oldest traditions of teaching and performance in the free world. Ninette de Valois, a soloist with the Diaghilev company, founded a ballet company and an associated school in London which became in time the Royal Ballet, the national company of Great Britain. Massine and I were the first choreographers of the Ballet Russe de Monte Carlo, founded in Europe in 1932. In America, I founded with Lincoln Kirstein the American Ballet, precursor of the present New York City Ballet. The American Ballet's complementary group, Kirstein's Ballet Caravan, produced, in addition to classical works, ballets based on native American material—*Filling Station, Billy the Kid, Yankee Clipper*, etc.—with choreography by such American dancers as Lew Christensen, Eugene Loring, and William Dollar and with music by American composers. The New York City Ballet, with its associated school, the School of American Ballet, represents the result of many years of work toward the achievement of excellence in classical performance.

The Ballet Theatre, now the American Ballet Theatre, founded by Lucia Chase and Richard Pleasant, grew out of the New York ballet school of Mikhail Mordkin. Fokine, who had staged many of his own works for many ballet companies, supervised productions of his ballets by the Ballet Theatre and created his last ballet for this company in 1941. The English choreographer Antony Tudor, who—like Frederick Ashton, principal choreographer to the Sadler's Wells Ballet—had been a student in London of Marie Rambert, joined the Ballet Theatre at its inception. This company has produced many works by native American choreographers.

Many other companies have appeared since. The City Center Joffrey Ballet in New York, the Pennsylvania Ballet in Philadelphia, the Boston Ballet, the Dance Theatre of Harlem, the Eliot Feld Ballet are representative of the tremendous growth in the number and talent of our dance ensembles. In Canada, the National Ballet of Canada and the Royal Winnipeg Ballet have concurrently set high standards for performance. Companies from England, Denmark, Germany, Russia, France, Holland, Belgium, Australia, and other countries that visit North America regularly bring us new repertories. It is possible to compare.

Our schools for the teaching of ballet have established new criteria for excellence. You cannot really have a ballet company without a school to train the talent you require. Dancers from all over the world come to work at our schools when they visit us, just as we go to theirs. Ballet is a truly international art; everyone understands.

Nancy Hanks, chairman of the National Endowment for the Arts, acknowledged in 1976 that dance is "the fastest growing art in the nation." In New York it used to be that the summer was the doldrums and no ballet companies would appear. Now, it is almost impossible to find enough theatres for the companies who wish to perform here in the summer. The dance season is now a year-round affair that never stops.

Writing in the New York *Times* about ballet's soaring popularity, the critic Anna Kisselgoff noted: "In 1965, the report of the Rockefeller Panel on the Arts placed dance attendance in the United States at one million. For 1975, it was fifteen million, according to the Association of American Dance Companies . . . These are not fanciful figures. One has only to compute the number of seats and performances among the array of dance companies scheduled in New York between April and September 1976 to realize that close to one and a half million people will attend dance performances in this city in just the next four months."

With more persons watching dance performances regularly, knowledge of and concern for ballet have grown, too. Many companies, like the New York City Ballet, have wonderful subscribers—interested persons who have come to know what we represent, wish to keep up with it and to see more, regularly. Their support, needless to say, is vital to us. And I do not mean in terms of financial support, valuable as that is; I mean in terms of interest and response. They simply *know* more than those who come only occasionally and they are a most rewarding and perceptive audience. The more companies fortunate enough to have that kind of support, the better for all of dance. Ballet has come a long way from its beginnings at the court of Catherine de Médicis in the sixteenth century.

How I Became a Dancer and Choreographer

A dancer's history usually begins at the age of eight or nine. I myself began to study dancing, in Russia, when I was nine. In my case, this was almost accidental. My father was a musician, a composer, and we were naturally a musical family. My brother played the piano, my sister played the violin, and from the time I was five years old, I, too, studied the piano. There was no idea that I should be a musician; I only studied music because my parents felt I should be missing something important in life if I knew nothing about it.

Many men in my mother's family had been in the army, and for a while it was thought that I would become one of the Tsar's cadets. But one day my mother happened to be visiting the Imperial Ballet School in St. Petersburg. She had always loved dancing, and when one of the governors of the school suggested that she try to enter me, she agreed. After all, I could always go into the army if I didn't turn out to be good.

That was in 1914. In August of that year the Imperial School held its regular auditions for new pupils in St. Petersburg. These were auditions for the eight-year course in ballet, drama, and music. The final choice of which art the student would permanently pursue was made after he had learned something about each one. But these were not auditions in any real sense; we had never danced before, and there was very little they could tell. First, a doctor examined us briefly. He felt our muscles, listened to our hearts and our breathing, and sent us to the large auditioning room of the school. There were about a hundred and fifty boys seeking admittance and more than two hundred girls. In small groups, the boys and girls separately, we went in before the judges, who were seated at a table down at the end of the auditioning room. Karsavina was there, I remember. Even then I knew what a great ballerina Karsavina was and I was a little afraid. I thought I looked awkward.

The judges asked us to walk and observed our posture, our carriage. We knew absolutely no dancing and could not have executed a step if we'd been asked. The judges picked a few boys out of each group that came before them. I was picked out, but from the judges' manner I couldn't tell if this was because I was good or bad. We were told to go to another room, and after a long wait we were asked to come back. The judges watched us again, then divided the group, sending some of us to one side of the room. Again we waited. We had no idea who had been chosen or who had been eliminated. At the end of the day, they announced the names of those who had been selected as new students. I was one of seven or eight boys.

Until I actually entered the school, I didn't know whether to be pleased or not. Once in the Imperial School itself, I was decidedly displeased. I didn't like it. I was homesick, and the army seemed to me a much better idea than ballet.

The first year, we were all on trial at the school. Only if we passed that first year successfully would we be admitted as permanent students. I didn't care. All of us lived at the school, in Theatre Street, in St. Petersburg. We could go home only at Easter, Christmas, and during the summer; our parents could not visit us. The discipline was very strict: we all got up at the same time, washed at the same time (always in cold water, except on Friday before dinner), ate on a strict schedule, went to the same classes, and were sent to bed promptly at nine o'clock. We wore blue uniforms, with silver lyres on the stiff collar and on the cap.

And I did not like it. My fellow students knew this because I sulked so much. They didn't help matters by calling me "Rat" all the time. When I thought I couldn't stand it any more, I ran away. I knew my parents would be very angry, so I went to the home of an aunt who lived in St. Petersburg. She was understanding, but also she was firm with me. She took me back.

Still I hated the school. I was certain I had no aptitude for dancing and was wasting my time and the Tsar's money. The only people who thought differently then were Olga Preobrajenska, the great *prima ballerina* at the Maryinsky Theatre, who was very kind to me, and my favorite teacher, S. M. Andreanov, who instructed me in classic technique.

Every day at the Imperial School we had the same schedule: ballet class, lessons in character dancing, classes in Russian literature, French, arithmetic, music (we all had to play some instrument), and religion. We also took fencing lessons. This was a curriculum similar to that of any fine European school, except for the ballet classes. I liked the classes in religion and music best, but still, even though I was admitted as a permanent student after the first year, I thought I was in the wrong place. I remembered that there were other departments at the Imperial School—drama and music—and thought that I might be better off there.

Then everything changed. What happened was very simple. In the first year at the school, we went only to classes; we were not associated with the Imperial Theatre, the Maryinsky, in any way. The second year, as was customary, we became a part of the theatre, dancing in large groups with the *corps de ballet*. I first danced on the stage of the Maryinsky in the garland dance in *The Sleeping Beauty:* the waltz in the first act. I also appeared as a cupid on one of the carriages in the final act. The Maryinsky was a beautiful theatre, all blue and gold, and as children we were very excited about dancing on its stage, where almost any magical effect could be made: real waves, scores of swimming swans, fire, and great cascading fountains banked in tiers. We learned very early what it was to be a part of a theatre; the theatre became a home to us, a natural place to be.

The garland dance in *The Sleeping Beauty* was performed by scores of people in the regular *corps de ballet* of the Maryinsky, and we children were naturally unimportant, but that evening nevertheless changed my whole life. At that moment I saw that others had been right about what was good for me. I saw then what ballet was in terms of a theatre.

The Maryinsky production of *The Sleeping Beauty* was wonderfully elaborate, a real spectacle, the kind of thing Hollywood tries to achieve in its huge productions. Only here there was more magic. The Tsar's treasury could afford it! There were about two hundred and fifty dancers in the company; all were professionals. The first act of *The Sleeping Beauty* was marvelous in scenic effect: a huge garden with cascading fountains. When the wicked fairy Carabosse appeared in the prologue, her great coach was drawn by a dozen mice. Later, when she appeared in disguise and tricked the princess into pricking her finger, her appearance changed completely. She turned to the king and queen and said that the princess would die, and then, miraculously, her disguise disappeared into the floor and they saw before them the wicked fairy they had forgotten to invite to their daughter's christening. It was fantastic— there she was, a bent old lady, harmless, and the next moment her disguise had fallen through the floor and she was black and shiny, the wicked fairy. Fire came up all over the stage and everyone despaired. Of course, the Lilac Fairy then intervened and predicted that the princess would wake up in a hundred years. Then the whole palace went to sleep. From the stage floor, great trees and shrubbery arose and climbed higher and higher, vines entwined about the colonnades of the garden, so that the whole palace was overgrown and it was quiet, asleep.

Later, when the Lilac Fairy took the prince to the palace, there was a wonderful panorama scene, not an interval with music, as this part of the ballet is performed nowadays. The music was played slowly, as it should be, and the Lilac Fairy guided her boat across the stage. The scenery moved from left to right so that the boat really seemed to be moving over a lake in an enchanted forest. Then, in the finale, where the Princess Aurora is married, there was a spectacular apotheosis: the stage was deep and high, and from high up in the back down to the center of the stage there was a great flight of steps. On either side of the steps there was a flight of fountains, which spilled over, one into the other, so that there was a continuous waterfall. All the fairies were grouped on the stairs with their cavaliers, and they and all the court bowed in tribute to the princess. It was beautiful.

And so I began to like dancing very much. I started to work very hard. I wanted to dance more on the stage, and to do that I knew I had to be good, very good. I was only ten, but I was experiencing with ballet the same kind of lesson I had learned with music.

When I first took piano lessons, I hated them, too. For two years the only thing that would make me practice was the thought of being sent to bed without my supper. Then, when I was seven, I learned a part of a Beethoven sonata. I didn't play it well at first, but well enough to hear how lovely it sounded. I loved it and wanted to play it well, so then it would sound even more beautiful. And now I was learning the same thing about dancing: it took work, but when you saw what the work could produce, you wanted to work very badly.

Ballet performances at the Maryinsky in St. Petersburg were given only twice a week, on Wednesdays and Saturdays. The rest of the week, the theatre was devoted to opera. All of us looked forward to the ballet evenings, when the official court carriages would come to the school and take us to the theatre for our appearances. Only when we were brought back to the school, at midnight, did we have our supper. We were so excited about going on stage at the theatre that, young as we were, we were not hungry until it was all over.

As a child, I danced in all the ballets in the Maryinsky repertory that required a large male *corps de ballet:* in the first real Russian ballet, *The Humpbacked Horse;* in the Petipa classics *Paquita* and *Don Quixote;* in *The Nutcracker,* where I began as one of the toy soldiers and gradually danced bigger parts—the king of mice, the nutcracker prince, and dance parts in the *grand divertissement.*

In 1954 I finally arranged our own production of *The Nutcracker.* At the Maryinsky, the first act of this ballet was not merely a small family party with a miniature Christmas tree. There was an enormous Christmas tree with hundreds of presents under it. When the children had been sent to bed and little Clara tiptoed downstairs to rescue the nutcracker, her favorite gift, the stage picture changed completely. At the stroke of midnight, the toys under the tree came to life. The chief toy soldier became a general, challenging intruders. Mice invaded the room, and there on stage a great pitched battle between the soldiers and the rats took place. They fired muskets and shot off cannon balls of candy. Clara tried to help the soldiers, but only when her beloved nutcracker was transformed into a brave, handsome prince was the battle won. This kind of thing we do not see nowadays in revivals of *The Nutcracker.* People think of *The Nutcracker* as a "suite" rather than a ballet. First it was a ballet.

In the Maryinsky *Swan Lake,* too, there were marvelous stage effects. At the beginning of Act Two there was not just one swan swimming across the lake, as we see so often today: there were two dozen swans, gliding across what appeared to be real, rippling waves. Actually, each swan was secured to a long stick, which members of the Tsar's Finnish regiment maneuvered underneath the stage between the rippling canvas waves. Later, when the twenty-four swan maidens appeared on stage, the audience didn't have to guess who they were: they had already seen them.

In another Maryinsky production, Mazilier's famous ballet *Le Corsaire,* there was a real shipwreck. A gigantic ship was tossed high on the waves and completely demolished. The Tsar's Finnish regiment worked again here, moving large sheets of canvas so that they undulated like storm waves. After the ballet was over, the soldiers formed ranks and drilled out of the theatre with impeccable military style, as if their regiment had just won honors at a parade.

I've gone into some detail here about the Maryinsky production for two reasons: first, to give some idea of the natural excitement these ballets had for all of us at the Imperial Ballet School; and second, because I find that people in general are very curious about what they call "Russian ballet." There used to be a time, until very recently, in fact, when people thought that *Russian* ballet was all there was. That was wrong, of course. Only because the Tsar's treasury could afford it, only because the courts of the Tsar in the nineteenth century required opulent entertainment, and because schools had been provided to train people to provide it, did it happen that in Russia there was a great period in ballet. The Tsar's wealth created great theatres, schools were started to supply these theatres with dancers, and from all over Europe—the

Frenchmen Didelot, Perrot, and Petipa; the Italian Cecchetti; the Swede Johansson—ballet masters and teachers, dancers and musicians all came to embellish the Imperial courtly entertainment.

Contrary to the general belief, ballet was not taken very seriously by the Russian public. It was an entertainment almost exclusively for the aristocracy, among whom there were perhaps only a few gentlemen who were not primarily interested in what the ballerinas were doing after the performance. After the first performance of The Sleeping Beauty, Tsar Nicholas I said condescendingly to Tchaikovsky, "Very nice." The Tsar was familiar with every ballet in the repertory of his theatre and yet he had no idea that he had just heard the greatest ballet score the Russian theatre has ever produced. Like the rest of the Russian audience, he had a dilettante attitude toward ballet.

The Russians, as I have said, established ballet schools, and in these institutions the best teachers in Europe made great Russian dancers. All the influences—the French, the Italian, the Scandinavian—all the talent commingled to form in the nineteenth century in Russia the finest dancing academy in all the world.

By the time I first saw ballet at the Maryinsky Theatre, both Pavlova and Nijinsky had left Russia, never to return. But there were still in St. Petersburg many great dancers. Principal among these were Tamara Karsavina, our ballerina, and Pierre Vladimiroff, who had succeeded Nijinsky as premier danseur. We idolized these dancers and strove to perfect ourselves.

I worked very hard at the school, appeared in my first character role, a Spanish dance in Fokine's Jota Aragonese, in January 1916, and acted also on the stage of the Alexandrinsky, the Tsar's dramatic theatre. At the ballet school we were trained in acting, too, and mime, where we learned the importance of stage gesture. We learned how different stage appearance was from ordinary life, how to work within theatrical disciplines to create illusion. One of my teachers, Paul Gerdt, appeared as a young man in Fokine's Pavillon d'Armide with two of his students, Pavlova and Nijinsky. Gerdt was then sixty-three years old, but from his stage presence he appeared as young as his students.

At the Alexandrinsky Theatre, I acted the part of the young student in Andreyev's Professor Storitsyn, among other roles, and at the Mikhailovsky, the Imperial Theatre for opéra-comique, I danced and acted in A Midsummer Night's Dream to Mendelssohn's music and danced one of the Furies in the Meyerhold-Fokine Orpheus. Like all other students at the school, I was almost oblivious to what was going on in the world outside. Few of us knew there was a war.

When Tsar Nicholas II abdicated in March 1917, the Imperial Ballet School was closed down. I lived at my aunt's in St. Petersburg, waiting for the school to open again. I worked as a bank messenger, as a saddler's apprentice, and at nights played the piano for silent movies in neighborhood theatres. During the October Bolshevik Revolution later that same year, Lenin selected the balcony of the prima ballerina assoluta of the Imperial Theatre, Mathilda Kschessinska, from which to address the people. I remember hearing him that night. I had gone, with a group of my fellow students from the school, to see what was attracting the huge crowd. All of us thought the man on the balcony must be a lunatic. Then we were young; we did not understand the Revolution.

The Bolsheviks did not wish to reopen the Imperial Theatres: the theatres were, after all, aristocratic and "bourgeois" institutions. But Lunacharsky, the new Bolshevik Minister of Education, was a balletomane. He persuaded the Bolsheviks to use the Tsar's old theatres for party meetings and for speeches to the public. Party members and the public were compelled to attend. In 1918 Lunacharsky further persuaded the Bolsheviks to allow the old Imperial Ballet Company and students of the school to perform *divertissements* in the old Maryinsky after these official functions were over. And so we danced again, this time in a "state" theatre, though it was the same Maryinsky, and the school was reopened. There was no heat, either in the theatre or at the school, and food and clothing were very scarce. On stage, in flimsy costumes, we could see our breath almost freeze; in the audience, people wore fur coats. At the school, we burned the polished parquet floors to keep warm and made trousers out of the draperies. The Tsar's carriages, which had previously driven us to the theatre, were not available, and we had to walk to and from our performances.

We worked hard at taking up our studies again. A new course in Marxian history at the school seemed a small sacrifice for the resumption of training for our chosen profession. We were not paid, we were undernourished and ill-clothed, but still we studied and danced. When Lunacharsky came to take us to see Griffith's movie *Intolerance* in 1920, we still wore the remnants of our Imperial uniforms.

In 1921 I was graduated from what had become the Academy of Opera and Ballet (now the Kirov Academy of Opera and Ballet). I had been a government charge since I was ten years old, and the Bolsheviks, like the Tsar before them, expected all graduates of state schools to remain in state theatres until they were pensioned. As an honor graduate, I secured good roles in the theatre's repertory.

This same year, 1921, I entered the Conservatory of Music in St. Petersburg. The famous composer Glazunov was then director of the conservatory. My interest in music had not diminished during the years I had spent learning the theatrical arts; rather, it had greatly increased. I had played the piano regularly at the school and on vacations, and it now seemed to me time to learn even more about music. For three years at the Conservatory of Music I studied theory, composition, and piano while I continued to dance in the state ballet company at the old Maryinsky. I wanted to be a fine pianist as well as a good dancer.

Meanwhile I had become interested in choreography. I do not know how to explain this interest. I had learned to dance, to move, I loved music, and suddenly I wanted to move people to music, to arrange dances. In 1920 I had arranged my first ballet, a short ballet in the Fokine style, to the music from Rubinstein's *La Nuit*, which was danced by my fellow students at the school. The boys and girls who were in my ballet liked it very much, though its quality of movement was new to them. Our teachers did not like it at all. I saw immediately that I should never be able to convince the management of the state theatre to become interested in my work. I would have to present it myself.

This I did, in St. Petersburg, in 1923, in a program called "Evenings of the Young Ballet," which I organized with Vladimir Dimitriev, who has remained in Russia as a designer. In this program I was responsible for all the choreography. I tried to show the evolution of ballet in Russia from Petipa's classicism through Fokine's reforms to my own ideas of movement. The dancers were members of the state company who had been graduated with me. We had a hard time finding a place to put on this program, which was finally presented in the amphitheatre formerly occupied by the Tsar's State Duma (Parliament).

The "Evenings of the Young Ballet" were popular with the dancers who performed them and with the young people in the audience, but they were not liked by the directorate of the state theatre. The director informed my dancers that they could not appear in my ballets and continue as members of the state company. We were therefore compelled to stop our performances, and I was obliged to arrange dances elsewhere.

At the Mikhailovsky Theatre I arranged the dances for Ernst Toller's *Broken-Brow*, devised pantomime ballets to the Milhaud-Cocteau *Le Boeuf sur le toit* and to Alexander Blok's poem *The Twelve*, and began work on a ballet set to Stravinsky's *Pulcinella*, which had already been staged in Western Europe by Diaghilev's Ballets Russes. I also arranged a dance scene for a production of Bernard Shaw's *Caesar and Cleopatra* at the Mikhailovsky. (This was the opening scene, which I depicted as a cabaret. Later, when I knew English and could read Shaw in his own language, I saw what nonsense this was!)

All this time, I was still dancing at the old Maryinsky as a member of the state company. The modern ballets of the Diaghilev repertory were becoming a part of the traditional Russian repertory. These ballets excited me enormously: I loved their music and choreography and marveled at the imagination of a man like Serge Diaghilev, whose Russian company in France could produce so many masterpieces so consistently. Needless to say, no equivalent creativeness existed in the theatre at St. Petersburg.

In 1924 I thought it would be a good idea to take a small group of Russian dancers to Western Europe. We had some difficulty with the Soviet authorities, but in those days it was actually possible to leave Russia and the authorities thought the tour might well have propagandistic value. They consented, provided that we went to Europe on our summer vacation from the state theatre. We were called the "Soviet State Dancers." There were actually very few dancers—Alexandra Danilova, Tamara Geva, Nicholas Efimov, and myself. I was then twenty, the oldest of all. I arranged a number of ballets, among them pieces to the "Oriental Dance" from Mussorgsky's *Khovantchina* and a waltz of Kreisler's. We learned these dances perfectly and in June 1924 sailed from St. Petersburg (it had become Leningrad) on a German boat. We were bound for Berlin, where we had secured our first engagement.

In Berlin we danced with some success, then went on to perform in German watering places and at Mannheim. Then we accepted an invitation to dance at the Empire Theatre in London. From London we went to Paris. There we were fortunate enough to secure an audition with Serge Diaghilev, the genius impresario who had brought the Russian ballet to Europe fifteen years before and had caused the ballet capital of the world to shift from St.

Petersburg back to Paris. Diaghilev had seen one of our performances; he liked our dancing and our dances. He invited us to join his Ballets Russes.

When I became ballet master to Diaghilev's Ballets Russes, I was twenty-one years old. I was humble in this position in the most famous ballet company in the world and sought to learn everything possible from Diaghilev, the man who had fostered Fokine and Nijinsky and commissioned from Igor Stravinsky that great composer's first ballet scores, *Firebird* and *Petrouchka*. I had just arrived in Europe and, though I had learned European languages at the ballet school in St. Petersburg and knew the culture of Europe in general, I had much to learn.

Several years ago Anatole Chujoy's *Dance News* published an article of mine on Diaghilev to commemorate the twentieth anniversary of his death. What I said then seems just as true to me now:

"Perhaps it is only today, almost twenty-five years after his death, that all contemporary choreographers begin to realize the true proportions of the enormous artistic debt we all owe to Serge Diaghilev. If we analyze the work we have done since his death in 1929, we see that we are still following in his footsteps, still adhering to the principles laid down by him during the twenty years he guided the fortunes of his unique Ballets Russes. Were he alive today, Diaghilev would probably find a new direction in his beloved art form, a new approach to the creation and presentation of ballet. He was always twenty-five years ahead of his time.

"Diaghilev had the capacity to see not only the potentialities inherent in an artist, be he choreographer, composer, designer or dancer, he also knew what work, what style, what period, suited that artist best. Great though it was, his genius for discovery would not have been so overwhelming had he not had that innate and cultivated taste which alone distinguishes true artistic quality from a sense for novelty and craftsmanship.

"If I were to describe Diaghilev simply, I should say that he was a man of high culture. It so happened that he was a great ballet impresario, a patron of the arts, but he could just as easily have been a statesman, an ambassador: he could have held any post that required knowledge, intelligence, culture, taste. He was at home in world literature, music, painting and sculpture. He spoke three languages with the fluency and in the idiom of the native. Never a professional musician, he could read a musical score as one reads a book.

"Stravinsky has described Diaghilev's intimate musical knowledge in his *Autobiography* and Nicolas Nabokov, who also composed his first ballet for the Ballets Russes, has written of Diaghilev's great understanding of music in his book *Old Friends and New Music*. Never a choreographer or a dancer, Diaghilev knew what was exactly right and what was wrong about a particular ballet or in any portion of it. Never a painter, he possessed an unerring and intimate knowledge of art.

"These qualities made Diaghilev a creator, a real producer. He was not just the director or manager of a ballet company who guessed what the public would accept and what it would reject. He did not follow the public; the public followed him. He did not really care very much whether people agreed with him or not. What mattered to him was the work done by the best and most suitable choreographer, musician, designer and dancers. If they succeeded, their work was a success. Diaghilev so inspired the artists who worked under his direction that it is' not too much to say that any ballet created for his company bore his personal stamp as well as that of the composer, painter and choreographer.

"Strangely enough, he did not interfere with work in progress. Before work began, he discussed projected ballets with their creators in great detail. We argued and recognized each other's points. Diaghilev had great respect for artistic integrity. By the time actual work began on ballets, every phase of their production represented a collaboration between artists and their producer.

"Even if we discount for the moment the fact that companies the world over are still using ballets created for the Diaghilev company (*Petrouchka, Les Sylphides,* etc.) and that much of what else there is in ballet today stems from the Diaghilev roots, we cannot escape the fact that it was Diaghilev who invented the formula of presenting three short ballets in one evening and thus made possible the presentation of ballet not only by big resident companies in the few opera houses of European capitals, but also by touring companies in big and small cities and towns in America and Europe.

"If it can be said at all that one man took ballet from the thin aristocratic stratum of society and gave it to the people at large, Diaghilev was the man who did it. To Diaghilev's additional credit, one is reminded that he never attempted to lower the artistic standard of ballet to the level of those who had no prior knowledge, taste or appreciation of the art form. On the contrary, by constant and painstaking work to present ballet of the highest calibre to the people to whom ballet was new, he succeeded in elevating the people to the appreciation of ballet, in developing their taste and increasing their enjoyment.

"Personally, I owe to Diaghilev my growth and development during the second period of my artistic life. The first part of it I owe to the Russian Imperial Theatre where I was brought up, to its strict discipline, to its classicism, the basis of all ballet, to its two-hundred-year-old tradition which instilled in me a love for ballet and a respect for its history and artistic principles.

"The second period of my artistic life began in the Diaghilev company, where I learned to recognize what was great and valid in art, where I acquired the ability and strength to analyze a work of art on its true merits and where, finally, I learned to be on my own, to do what my artistic sense prompted me to do—in short, to be an artist. All this I owe to Diaghilev without any reservation."

For Diaghilev's company, beginning in 1925, I rehearsed the repertory and danced with the company in addition to creating ten new ballets. I don't think there's any question that *Apollo* (1928) was the most important of these, certainly the most important for me personally, for I regard this ballet as the crucial turning point in my artistic life. In the first ballets I choreographed for Diaghilev I had been successful, I think, but for the wrong reasons. *Pastorale,* for instance, which I arranged to music by Georges Auric in 1925, contained diverse types of movement—at least ten different types—whereas only one type was sufficient for the piece: the others should have been set aside and the one proper type developed. Stravinsky's score for *Apollo* taught me that a ballet, like his music, must have a restraint and discipline. Stravinsky's music had a wonderful clarity and unity of tone, and I saw that gestures, the basic material of the choreographer, have family relations, like different shades in painting and different tones in music. Some are incompatible with others: one must work within a given frame, consciously, and not dissipate the effect of a ballet with inspirations foreign to the tone or mood one understands it must possess. *Apollo* depicted Stravinsky's music visibly.

Prodigal Son and *Le Bal* (with Danilova, Nikitina, Dolin, and Lifar) were my last ballets for Diaghilev. A few months after the first performance of *Le Bal*, Diaghilev died in Venice. His company disbanded: there then came to an end the most important and entertaining twenty years of creativity in music and painting and dancing that Europe had seen since the Renaissance.

After some months had passed, I accepted an engagement as ballet master at the Royal Theatre, Copenhagen, with the Royal Danish Ballet, which, with the Paris Opéra, has the oldest continuous tradition of instruction and performance in the world. After this, I worked in London on my first musical comedy and in France helped to organize the Ballet Russe de Monte Carlo and staged for them their first new ballets: *La Concurrence, Cotillon,* and *Le Bourgeois Gentilhomme.*

My own company, Les Ballets 1933, was formed soon after this. This company performed in Paris and in London. It was during performances of Les Ballets 1933 that the painter Pavel Tchelitchew introduced me to the young American Lincoln Kirstein, who with Edward M. M. Warburg invited me to come to the United States to found the ballet school he knew was necessary if the classic dance was ever to flourish in America. We opened the School of American Ballet in New York on January 2, 1934, in studios that had been used in years past by Isadora Duncan. The school has become, over the years, the largest institution for the training of professional dancers outside the European state schools. Students from this school have danced in every American ballet company and in many companies in Europe. More specifically, they have been the basis for the founding of ballet companies that Lincoln Kirstein and I have directed. These companies have evolved and matured in the New York City Ballet. Morton Baum, Chairman of the Executive Committee of the New York City Center of Music and Drama, and the directors of that corporation invited Kirstein and me to found in 1948 this permanent, resident ballet company at the New York City Center. It is not for me to comment on the New York City Ballet: this would be like a father telling you about his own children. I can only invite you to come and see it, as I urge you again to see all ballet companies in New York and on tour throughout America.

Writing about ballet is difficult for me, even talking about ballet is difficult for me; if I were naturally a writer or a lecturer, and expressed myself well in writing and speaking, I should not be a choreographer. But I have tried to make clear a number of things in this book that will be of help to the audience and to the potential dancer. This book, however, as I have said elsewhere, is no substitute for the ballet you can see on the stage. Only by seeing ballet repeatedly in the theatre can you understand why it has entertained audiences for three hundred years and how it has given some of us happiness because we have been able to provide some of that pleasure.

Notes and Comments on Dancers, Dancing and Choreography

QUESTION   What country produces the finest classical dancers?

ANSWER   Classical dancing isn't a nationalistic question, and for a very simple reason: it isn't nationalistic dancing. Native character or folklore has nothing to do with it. The ability to "turn out" properly, for example, has nothing to do with the country from which a dancer comes. Americans have a great deal of ability because their bodies are strong and also because they are a very musical people. Maybe it's because we hear music, all kinds of it, everywhere here. Children respond to this rhythmical music. They clap, dance, and develop rhythmical sense almost by nature. This sense of rhythm needs schooling, very good schooling; but with such a background in your students, you can develop very great dancers. In France there are also lots of strong, well-built dancers who are musical, and certainly the same is true of England, Italy, and other countries. In other words, people of all nationalities make wonderful classical dancers. The problem really narrows down to where the best schools are. Where you have the best teachers, you have the best dancers, no matter what their nationality.

QUESTION   Is there such a thing as purely American ballet?

ANSWER   In answer to this question and the two that follow, I'd like to paraphrase the comment that I made on these subjects in Serge Lido's *Ballet 2*, some years ago.

From the time ballet began, it has been influenced by *all* the countries where it developed, from Italy, to France, to Scandinavia, and it has adapted itself to the physical abilities of the different countries. The historical development of the art has been traced in another part of this book. I hope I have successfully shown that the classic dance is a fully developed art form, which has now become universal. It has a body of classified and organized techniques which will remain as the basis of the vocabulary of classical dance until such time as ballet is replaced by some other form of theatrical entertainment.

I think that if there is such a thing as purely American ballet, it is reflected not in style but in subject matter. For example, a ballet about cowboys might be called American, as a ballet about Sherlock Holmes might be called English, or the cancan might be called French. The latter case, however, is a question of national rather than classical dance.

QUESTION   Are there different styles of classical dancing for each country?

ANSWER   As for style of dancing for different countries, there are naturally some small differences in execution, but they are mainly differences of personality. For example, there may be ten different interpretations of *Swan Lake* or *Giselle* in England, France, Denmark, Italy, and the United States—all equally valid. Some people, whose taste is inclined toward the obvious, have come to expect certain stylistic clichés from dancers—as, for example, that the dancer should be warm and passionate—but a dancer does not necessarily have to be warm or passionate. Some people are readily inclined to look for the obvious on stage. There are two types of personalities, for example, which seem to be universally pleasing to audiences: one is the vampire, almost like a female Mephistopheles; the other personality is like the lyrical or the poetic one, often almost lethargic. Yet some very good dancers that I have seen in my life were beautifully cold, like birds with no warmth at all. Others were like Oriental queens; others, again, were like pure crystal. The technique of classical dance necessarily creates a certain uniformity in dancers, which has little or nothing to do with nationality, but which is certainly modified by the personality of the dancer. I am, of course, talking about dancers with talent. Talent is God-given: it is not given by a nation or a passport. A dancer must certainly have this gift, but the gift can manifest itself in forms as various as the universe. One cannot say that sunshine is better than shade, or that a glass of cold water is worse than a flaming chimney.

There are many so-called connoisseurs who try to dictate a certain style of ballet dancing, and they talk about a tradition that they never knew. Fortunately, this does not endanger the progress or development of ballet, because the real public—the people who sit in galleries, at a small admission price which most of them can ill afford—can distinguish good dancing from an inferior imitation of a style which was interesting a hundred years ago. Every performance demonstrates that this is the true ballet public, without prejudice or fake balletomanism.

I was brought up in St. Petersburg. The style of dancing there was very strict and precise. At the same time, in Moscow, six hundred kilometers away, the style of dancing was close to that of a circus performance. The Muscovites accused us in St. Petersburg of being cold, and we accused them of bad taste. History shows that the dancers and choreographers who later influenced ballet as a whole came mainly from St. Petersburg.

QUESTION   What is the future of ballet in America?

ANSWER   The future of ballet in America, as well as in the other countries, depends on the rise of new choreographers capable of furthering its development. A school of dancing is not enough. A school naturally perpetuates the technique, but it cannot lead to a new style in the ballet; nor can a new style of ballet be invented. Progress in any art is a slow and complex process, and therefore it cannot be generated by one person only. Many people are necessarily involved. In the field of ballet, it is not only the personality of the dancer and the art of the choreographer which achieve or create a style—one should not forget the composers. Delibes and Tchaikovsky are, I believe, as responsible for what is now traditionally known as classic ballet as its choreographers and dancers.

Any good company needs a professional choreographer, just as any good restaurant needs a good chef. If a ballet company does not develop successfully, the blame must be laid at the feet of its choreographer. If he was given all possibilities of choosing the best dancers, and if he was given the liberty to do what he wanted, he should not have failed in his task of achieving adequate results.

QUESTION How does a choreographer originate his ballets?

ANSWER This is a question I can only answer by telling you how I go about creating a new ballet, because, of course, different choreographers have different ways of proceeding with their work. When I am about to produce a ballet, I begin in one of two ways: either I begin with the idea and then look for suitable music, or I hear a certain piece of music which inspires me with an idea.

This idea need not be explicitly dramatic, as in a narrative ballet such as *Prodigal Son* or *Orpheus;* it need not have a written libretto. On the contrary, the idea might consist only in a *location,* a place, where I might wish dancing to take place, the particular people I want to dance there, and a special mood. *La Valse,* for instance, doesn't have a plot, but it is dramatic in its casting, its dancing, and the mood which action and music evoke.

If I begin with an idea, I much prefer to have the music specially written for me and to be in constant touch with the composer while he is writing it. I try to tell him exactly what I want, and together we conceive the general mood and we time some of the dance sequences. I have found that most ballet composers like to have a definite timing for a ballet: they like to know when such-and-such occurs and how long it will last, whether a sequence is a dance sequence or a *pas d'action,* and so forth. Like novelists, they are interested in structure first. In this way, they can start to compose at any point in the ballet and not begin at the beginning. Working on the story ballets *Prodigal Son* and *Orpheus* was a collaboration between the composers, Prokofiev and Stravinsky, and myself.

If I begin with the music, I familiarize myself with the score thoroughly and try to understand what the composer had in mind musically when writing it. When he wrote his *Concerto in D minor for Two Violins,* Bach had no idea of composing music for a ballet; but in listening to this music, it is possible to conceive of movement that harmonizes with the score. Actually, it seems to me that the music of Bach and Mozart is always very close to dancing. It would be wrong to say that all music should be danced, but I think the greatest music is never far from dancing. I agree with the poet who said that music rots when it is too far removed from the dance, just as poetry rots when it departs too far from music.

To familiarize myself thoroughly with a piece of music, I study the score and listen to it. If a piano transcription of the score exists, I play the piece over and over on the piano; if it does not exist, I make a transcription myself. Often I spend much more time learning a score than I do working out a ballet. The Mozart score for *Caracole,* for instance, I had in mind for three years, whereas setting the steps took only seven days.

There is always music that I wish to arrange dances to. Sometimes I make the ballets right away, if this is possible. One night, some years ago, the composer Alexei Haieff played me some pieces of his on the piano. I liked the music, but I didn't think of producing a ballet. Several days later, when this music kept running through my head, I wanted very badly to make dances to it. The result was *Divertimento*. If I were a poet, I'd probably have written a poem about what this music sounded like and looked like; but I am a choreographer, a dancer, and only in dancing do I express myself naturally. In other cases, I have known the music for many years and have kept it for the right moment. This was the case with *Symphonie Concertante*, music which has always seemed to me Mozart at his most beautiful; it was also true of *Symphony in C, Bourrée Fantasque*, and many other ballets.

Before beginning rehearsals, then, I have an idea of what the general scheme of a ballet will be. I never arrange any of the dances or movements until I actually rehearse the dancers. I discuss scenery and costumes with the designer, so that they will be in accord with the idea. I discuss the lighting, and I discuss the music with the composer and the conductor, but I don't discuss the ballet with my dancers unless we are doing a story ballet.

If the ballet has no story, there is no need to discuss their parts with the dancers in any detail; these parts the dancers work out by themselves, in individual practice. But in the case of a story ballet, I tell them what characters they are playing and what their relation is to the other characters.

Other choreographers, naturally, work differently. In working on story ballets, some choreographers spend lots of time talking to the dancers, explaining the story to them: the time the story took place, the history of that era, and so forth.

I have no fixed procedure. I don't come to rehearsals with any idea so definite and fixed that it can't be changed on the spot. I never write anything down. Often I try a step, or a series of movements, on a particular dancer and then I change it to something else. I indicate the steps first, and then the dancers repeat after me. It is very simple to mount a ballet using dancers you have worked with: they understand your smallest gesture and know what you want almost instinctively.

Sometimes I arrange the end of a ballet first; sometimes I commence in the middle. Rehearsal time is limited, and I can't always indulge in the extravagance of following the order of the music. If I have plenty of time, I work with each dancer until he or she is absolutely perfect; but the natural thing is for the dancers to want to practice the steps alone and perfect themselves. This they automatically do when there is little time, as in the case of *Prodigal Son*, which was produced in ten days in 1929, and with *Firebird*, which was produced in a week in 1949.

It has been my experience that dancers drop naturally into their parts; they gradually come to live them. Every detail is given: I show them every precise movement and the smallest mimed gesture and action.

QUESTION   Is it proper for the old classical ballets to be revived and revised by present-day choreographers?

ANSWER   Yes, I don't see why not, if the choreographers have respect for the original music and for the intention of the work as it has come down to us. This is a question that many people ask very seriously, as if it meant the life or death of ballet. They talk about tradition as a matter of remembering old steps accurately and reproducing them on the modern stage. The trouble is that no one can possibly remember all the steps of the ballets he saw years ago. A consistent form of accurate, intelligible dance notation has only recently been perfected—in 1940.

What, then, do these people mean when they talk of preserving the classics in their original state? They mean, very simply, nothing at all. They don't know, nor does anyone else, exactly what those ballets were like. They just take the word of so-and-so that the old ballets, in fact, looked like such-and-such. But this is just one man's impression, and surely a faulty one: our memories are not as accurate as the movie camera.

We can naturally accept this man's word in part if the revivals he produces entertain us, but there is no use in deceiving ourselves into thinking that now, in the middle of the twentieth century, we are watching dancing and acting precisely as they were done in the nineteenth century. Those ballets—and their music—were changed radically and materially by dancers, conductors, ballet masters, and choreographers within the lifetime of their original creators.

It doesn't make sense to ask for the original, in short, if you have no idea of what the original was. People who always talk about tradition in a narrow, limited sense remind me of the story of the young Russian tenor who was to sing a leading part in a revival of an opera. During rehearsals, he was instructed to interrupt the dramatic action of one of his scenes and almost conceal himself at the back of the stage before he began to sing a difficult aria. The young tenor thought this was senseless and complained about it. But he was told that Mr. X, who had been very famous in this role, used always to interrupt the action in this manner and that he, too, must do so. The singer did as he was told, though he thought it was very foolish indeed. Some time later he asked the famous old tenor why he had changed the action of the opera. The old tenor was surprised and amused; he said, "Well, confidentially, I found that aria very difficult and I always needed to spit before I started to sing it, so I walked upstage a little and no one saw me."

QUESTION   Can anyone be taught to be a choreographer?

ANSWER   No. To be a choreographer, it is first of all necessary to be a dancer, a good one. This was true of choreographers in the past, as it is today; all our distinguished choreographers have been dancers of real quality. To become a good dancer, you must study at a ballet school for some years. Then you join a ballet company. This ballet company will dance good and important things, old ones and new ones, and there you will associate with conductors, musicians, and designers—as well as dancers. They advise you and you begin to learn. It's not, in other words, a matter of just learning how to dance and then starting to choreograph. You have to go through a period of preparation. If I told fifty well-trained dancers to move, to dance, to entertain me, they would not know what to do.

You must go through tradition, absorb it, and become in a way a reincarnation of all the artistic periods that have come before you. For instance, you must be able to know and feel how people acted and moved in Molière's plays, what sense of humor those people had, what their stage looked like. If you are going to do an Italian ballet set in a certain period, you try to go to Italy and become a part of that world. Then you put everything together—your dancing technique, your preparation in tradition, your knowledge of music, your ability—and something happens. A ballet is born.

Sometimes nothing happens. Then, I'm afraid, nothing can be done. There is no school where you can learn to be a choreographer. People can be advised about technique, they can be told to do this or that differently, but you cannot advise a person to be talented. He is born talented. It is a strange thing: your life is made somewhere, you are pushed in a certain direction, and you move that way.

There's no school that can teach choreography, just as there is no school where you can learn to be a novelist or a poet. Schools can give you technique, but from that point on you are on your own. At ballet school you can learn to dance, just as you can learn to write correct English and poetic meters in other schools, but that is only the beginning. Nothing really helps but the person himself, what inclination he has, what talent. We ought to remember the story of the famous English novelist who wanted to bring his son up to be a novelist, too. He worked with the boy, made him notice details in the way people acted, tried to teach him all the things he had learned with so much difficulty. He was deadly earnest about all this. His son turned out to be not a novelist, but a sheep farmer in Australia.

A choreographer must also be a teacher. I learned this myself when I did my first ballet, a composition in the Fokine style. I was fifteen years old and I taught this little ballet to eight boys in my class at the Imperial Ballet School in St. Petersburg. They were very good dancers. To make them stretch and extend themselves the way I wanted, I had to show them how to execute movements altogether new to them.

Choreographic movement is used to produce visual sensations. It is quite different from the practical movement of everyday life, when we walk, lift things, stand up, and sit down. Movement in choreography is an end in itself: its only purpose is to create the impression of intensity and beauty. No one intends to produce beautiful movements when rolling barrels or handling trains or elevators. But in all these everyday movements there are important visual dynamics if you look for them. Choreographic movements are the basic movements that underlie all gesture and action, and the choreographer must train himself to discover them. It's only natural that these basic movements will seem at first affected and artificial to the body that is accustomed only to the practical movements of everyday

life. The object of the dancer's technical training is to enable him to perform—with perfect ease—choreographic movements, movements not limited by considerations of practical, daily life.

People in love all over the world have a certain attitude of sweetness
and tenderness in the way they look and talk and touch. A choreographer
notices this and finds movements to portray not the romance of A and B,
but romance in general. A choreographer must see things that other people don't notice, to cultivate his visual sense. He must understand the
stage space in a particular setting and how to fill that space with interesting movement; and to do this well, he must know music—know how to
play it, preferably, and how to read it. For ballet is all a matter of space
and time—the space on the stage, the time of the music to which the
dancer moves.

The structure of a ballet must be tight, compact, like the structure of a
building; good ballets move in measured space and time, like the planets.

The choreographer frees his mind from the limitations of practical time
in much the same way that the dancer has freed his body. He turns not
away from life, but to its source. He uses his technical proficiency to express in movement his essential knowledge. Talent, inspiration, and personality are not sources which come to an artist in a flash and go away;
they are the accumulated results of all he has felt, thought, seen, and
done—the stories he heard as a child, the art he has enjoyed, his education, and his everyday life—and are always with him, capable of being
reached by his technical ability and transformed into dynamic designs of
the utmost intensity.

If movement is the main means, possibly the only way, of presenting
the art of dancing in its fullest significance, it is easy to understand the
importance of connecting movements to each other with subtle care, yet
at the same time emphasizing, by contrast, their continuity. For example,
very brief and small movements to a fast or slow tempo—in every angle
or degree of angle—are developed in relation to subsequent broad, large
movements in the identical tempo, and increased from their use by one
dancer to their use by many dancers. A kaleidoscope of such movements
lives within the choreographer's brain, not yet, of course, set to any
tempo. They are as yet only abstract memories of form. Of these, silence,
placidity, and immobility are perhaps the most powerful forces. They are
as impressive, even more so, as rage, delirium or ecstasy. When the body
remains transfixed and immobile, every part of it should be invisibly tense,
and even in relaxation there should be an inner muscular control.

The steps which a dancer has learned (and after he has studied about
ten years with good teachers, he should have an impressive vocabulary of
movements) are, when separate, devoid of meaning; but they acquire
value when they are co-ordinated in time and space, as parts of the continual, rhythmic flow of the whole.

The student choreographer should at first work out simple technical exercises: for example, fitting eight bars of movement to eight bars of
music. Many different interpretations may be given to music; there is no

single meaning behind it which the listener must discover, and the chore-ographic student can fit any number of combinations of movements to the same eight bars of music. On the other hand, he can fit the same combi-nation of movements to several different pieces of music. Or he can fit bars of movement to silence, which has a tempo of its own. But if he uses music, he must be sure to fit the movements to it completely.

There is a lot of talk about counterpoint in dancing. It is generally believed that counterpoint is based on contrasts. Actually, counterpoint is an accompaniment to a main theme which it serves to enhance, but from whose unity it must not detract. The only kind of counterpoint that I can see in dancing is the movements of arms, head, and feet which are con-trapuntal to the static—or vertical—position of the body. For instance, in the *croisé* position the body is vertical—but one arm is raised, the other horizontal; one foot points forward, while the other supports the body; and the head is inclined toward one of the shoulders. All this is an accom-paniment to the main theme, which is the vertical position of the body. In dancing one should not strive to achieve counterpoint by contrasting the movements of two dancers or two groups of dancers on the stage. This re-sults not in counterpoint, but in disunity. (There is no need to apply mu-sical terms to the dance; but if it is done, their meaning must be clearly understood.)

The eye can focus perfectly only on objects which are in the center of its field of vision. Those objects which are not head-on are seen clearly only because the observer knows and imagines what they are, while he focuses on the center object. If some new or different form is placed in the secondary part of a composition, the eye instinctively changes its focus and convinces itself of the identity of each individual form. And as vision is the channel through which the art of choreography reaches its audience, this inevitably results in confusion and a loss of attention to the main theme. But the eye can follow the movements of a large group of dancers if these form a harmonious pattern within its central field of vi-sion.

It is impossible for choreographers to work very satisfactorily unless they are associated with a ballet company. You can compose music with-out an orchestra, but you cannot create a ballet without working directly with dancers.

In ballet companies, too, you learn many other things. When I was new in the Diaghilev company, I didn't know anything about Italian painting. I had just left Russia. Diaghilev took me to see pictures all over Italy. At first I was bored, but soon I became very interested: I saw that these pic-tures had a relation to other traditions I had absorbed, and I began to love them.

Choreography, finally, becomes a profession. In making ballets, you cannot sit and wait for the Muse. Union time hardly allows it, anyhow. You must be able to be inventive at any time. You can't be like the cook who can cook only two dishes: you must be able to cook them all.

INDEX